BUDDHISM AND SOCIETY

BUDDHISM

A Great Tradition

AND SOCIETY

and Its Burmese Vicissitudes

MELFORD E. SPIRO

HARPER PAPERBACKS
Harper & Row, Publishers
New York, Evanston, San Francisco, London

- Buddhism ~~and~~ Burma
- Sociology, Buddhist -- Burma

Quotations from *Dialogues of the Buddha* and from *The Questions of King Milinda* are used by permission of the Pali Text Society; quotations from *Buddhist Monks and Monasteries of India* are used by permission of George Allen & Unwin, Ltd.; quotations from *An Introduction to the Study of Theravada Buddhism in Burma* are used by permission of Calcutta University Press.

 For information address Harper & Row, Publishers, Inc., 49 East 33rd Street, New York, N.Y. 10016. Published simultaneously in Canada by Fitzhenry & Whiteside Limited, Toronto.

This book was originally published in hardcover by Harper & Row, Publishers, Inc. in 1970.

First HARPER PAPERBACK edition published 1972.

STANDARD BOOK NUMBER: 06-139475-0

For Mike and J.P.

Contents

Preface

Acknowledgments

This is the second of a projected three-volume study of Burma. The first volume, *Burmese Supernaturalism*, was concerned with Burmese folk religion. The third volume will be devoted to personality and social structure. Although it is my hope that the entire study will constitute an original contribution to Burmese studies as such, my concern in these volumes is not so much with Burma per se, as to use Burmese data to explore in depth certain theoretical relationships among society, culture, and personality.

My interest in Buddhism, the subject of the present volume, was first aroused almost twenty years ago while studying an Israeli kibbutz (Spiro 1955, 1958). Impressed with the otherworldliness (in Max Weber's sense of "otherworldly") inherent in the ideology of that socialist community, I became interested in exploring otherworldliness in a society where this orientation was inspired by a religious rather than a secular ideology. Buddhism immediately suggested itself as an object for exploration. It was not until 1958, however, that a fellowship at the Center for Advanced Study in the Behavioral Sciences provided the leisure to learn about Buddhism and about Southeast Asia. While holding that fellowship I was able, in the summer of 1959, to visit Ceylon and Burma for preliminary investigations preparatory to a systematic field study. The latter was not undertaken until 1961, when with the support of the National Science Foundation I began fourteen months of anthropological field work in Burma. A fellowship at the Social Science Research Institute of the University of Hawaii, as part of its project in Culture and Mental Health (supported by the National Institute of Mental Health) provided the leisure, in 1967-68, to begin work on this book, and a grant from the National Institute of Child Health and Human Development for the continuation of my studies in Southeast Asia enabled me to complete it.

I wish to acknowledge my indebtedness to all the above agencies for their generous support. In addition, for their many personal kindnesses I wish to express my gratitude to Dr. Ralph Tyler and the members of his staff at the Center for Advanced Study in the Behavioral Sciences, and to Dr. William Lebra and Dr. Thomas Maretzki (codirectors of the Culture and Mental Health project) and the members of their staff at the Social Science Research Institute. I wish also to thank Mrs. Freda Hellinger and Mrs. Peggy Friedmann for their forbearance while typing and retyping the many drafts of the manuscript, and Miss Kae Knight for seeing it through the press.

Although field work in Burma was completed in 1962, publication delay is due in part to other responsibilities, and in part to the closing of Burma's doors to foreign scholars. When I first went to Burma in 1961, it was with the expectation that I would be returning periodically to fill in the gaps in the data and to check their interpretations. Unhappily, this proved to be impossible because, since seizing political power in 1962, the present military government has permitted no foreign scholarship in Burma. Hence, although I have been able to work with members of the Burmese community in Thailand, there are serious limitations in the study of "culture at a distance," and I have delayed publication with the hope that the government would change its policy. There being no indication that its policy would be changed, I decided to publish this book, despite its gaps, and its inevitable errors both in fact and in interpretation. It is only fair to call to the attention of the reader the likelihood of such errors. No doubt there are other errors as well, but their sources must be sought elsewhere.

If it is true that one is part of all that one has met, then this book is the joint product of scores of persons whose ideas I have borrowed, used, and exploited, and which I now believe to be my own. Still, there are three explicitly identifiable intellectual influences: A. I. Hallowell, who taught me how to trace the relationships between culture and personality; Max Weber, whose sociology of religion opened new and exciting vistas in the study of religion; and Sigmund Freud, whose genius made it possible to perceive (and perhaps resolve) some of the intellectual challenges encountered in this study.

More immediately, I am indebted to my wife, Audrey Spiro, for ideas shared in and out of the field; to Konrad and Sarah Bekker, hosts and companions in Burma, Thailand, and Switzerland (where, more often than not, we talked about Burma); and to Professor F. K. Lehman, who generously read the entire manuscript, and corrected many of its errors. Those that remain are a reflection on my obstinacy rather than his knowledge. The transcription of Burmese words is also borrowed from Lehman's system.

Finally, I wish to thank my many friends in Burma, but especially my assistants U Ba Thaw and U Aung Thein, and my Burmese *hsaya,* U Ko Ko, of Mandalay University. To the people of Yeigyi, for permitting me to record their Buddhist beliefs and observe their Buddhist behavior, while seldom becoming impatient with my persistent questioning, my sentiments are best expressed by the Burmese proverb: *Amei kywei kyaun/Apyei hpaya: laung:*—The questioner is like a cowherd/His answerer is like an Embryo Buddha.

A Note on the Spelling, Pronunciation and Use of Foreign Terms and Texts

Unavoidably in a book on Burmese Buddhism, Pali (the sacred language of Buddhism) and Sanskrit, as well as Burmese, concepts are bound to play a prominent role. Although there is some slight danger in rendering these concepts in English, the other alternative—to inundate the reader with terms he does not know and which he could not, except with the greatest difficulty, memorize—seems to me even less desirable. In any event, having myself suffered through many anthropological monographs with their proliferation of exotic terms, I had already decided never to impose a similar burden on my readers. Wherever possible, therefore, foreign terms in this book are relegated to parentheses, while the concepts they express are rendered by their closest English equivalents, or approximations. In those few cases in which no suitable approximations are available, Sanskrit rather than the Pali or Burmese terms are used, on the assumption that the former are best known to the Western reader. Indeed, some of them have become part of our own lexicon. Hence nirvana is used rather than the Pali *nibbāna* or the Burmese *neikban;* and karma is used rather than the Pali *kamma* or the Burmese *kan.* When a Pali term is rendered in Burmese, the parenthetic "Burmese" may designate either the Burmese equivalent, the Burmese-Pali equivalent, or the Burmese pronunciation, of the Pali term.

The absence of a standard system for the transcription of spoken Burmese continues to present a problem for those who write on Burma. The system employed here, and described in the Appendix, is based on the recent work of Maran La Raw and F. K. Lehman. The Romanization of Pali terms is taken from the *Pali-English Dictionary* of the Pali Text Society.

For those readers interested in exploring the Buddhist texts quoted or cited, it should be indicated that I have used two translation series: one, the *Sacred Books of the Buddhists* (SBB), the other, the *Sacred Books of the East* (SBE). The former series translates the title of the book as well as the text, while the latter transliterates the title. Thus, when (as sometimes happens) chapters of the same book are quoted from both series, an unwary reader might believe they are from separate books, when in fact they are the same. For example, the *Sutta-Nipàta* and *Woven Cadences* are the same book, the former being in the SBE, the latter in the SBB series.

Since the references cited are scattered equally throughout the text and footnotes of this volume, the use of *ibid.* has been broadened to refer, not just to the previous footnote, but to the last source cited whether in footnote or text.

Author's Note for Torchbook Edition

Except for one or two minor changes, the Torchbook edition is identical with the original hardback. Thanks to Dr. Richard Gombrich, a number of typographical errors have been corrected in this edition.

I

PROLOGUE

CHAPTER 1

Theravāda Buddhism: An Anthropological Problem

Introduction

Even ignoring the plethora of popular books on Buddhism, the scholarly works alone comprise a small library.[1] Few of these works, however, treat Buddhism from what might be termed an anthropological point of view. This is not to say that historical and exegetical studies of Buddhist Scripture, philosophic analyses of Buddhist doctrines, or descriptions of the historical career of Buddhism are of no interest to the social scientist. On the contrary, such studies are—or at least ought to be—important grist for the anthropological mill; anthropologists who ignore them are ill-prepared to confront the problems which Buddhism poses for the comparative study of religion. Nevertheless, although relevant for an anthropological treatment of Buddhism, these studies do not in themselves constitute such a treatment. Indeed, so far as Buddhist scholarship is concerned, one might say that the anthropologist takes off where the textual and historical scholar ends, for the anthropologist is not concerned with religious texts per se, but with the interaction between the doctrines found in these texts and conceptions found in the heads of religious devotees, and consequently, with the relation between these religious conceptions and the general ordering of social and cultural life.

Although textual, i.e., normative, Buddhist doctrine poses a serious challenge to most of our generalizations about religion, and ultimately to our very notions about human nature itself, modern anthropologists (and other social scientists) who study the beliefs and rituals of practicing Bud-

[1]The best systematic guide to Buddhist scholarship is the excellent annotated bibliography of Gard (1965).

dhists, have with some few exceptions ignored the normative sources from which they derive;[2] and since frequently the former bear little resemblance to the latter, the challenge posed by normative Buddhism has seldom been confronted.[3]

This is a pity, for Buddhism after all is not the creation of contemporary Buddhists, but a religion with deep historical roots. Although anthropological studies of nonliterate societies have converted a methodological necessity (the ignoring of history) into a theoretical virtue (the theory of functionalism), to ignore the historical, i.e., normative, roots of contemporary Buddhist belief is to convert this theoretical virtue into a methodological absurdity. Hence the present study, though anthropological in nature, not only does not ignore doctrinal Buddhism, but is especially concerned with the relationship between the beliefs of Buddhist actors and the doctrines of Buddhist texts. Certain of these textual doctrines have become the beliefs (or misbeliefs) of the religious actors; others, even some of the more central doctrines, have been ignored and even rejected by them; still others have been assimilated to nonnormative and even antinormative beliefs, thereby giving them legitimacy. I submit that unless one understands the motivational and cognitive bases for these three types of interaction between religious actors and normative religious doctrines, one cannot understand the role of religious ideas in human affairs.

The present study, then, is an attempt to fill the gap between textual scholarship, which underscores the uniqueness of Buddhism, and anthropological field investigations which place it within the normal cross-cultural range of religious variability. Each of these alternative emphases, although true to some extent, can be misleading when pursued in isolation from the other. Thus to hold, on the one hand, that religion consists in a set of textual doctrines, in which few people in fact believe (and in which few, probably, ever did believe), is to hold a strange notion of "religion," in contrast to theology or philosophy. In the case at hand, it would result in denying that

[2]Indeed, some social scientists deliberately ignore canonical Buddhism as a self-conscious methodological stance. (Cf. Tambiah 1968:43.) At the other extreme are scientists who, like Max Weber (1958), assume that normative Buddhist doctrine is more or less identical with the beliefs of practicing Buddhists, and then proceed to relate this doctrine to their social behavior and institutions.

[3]Sometimes, on the contrary, problems are raised when none exist. Thus, numerous students of Burma have professed to see an incompatibility between Buddhism and the Burmese propitiation of spirits *(nat)* on the ground that Buddhism rejects spirit propitiation. Had such critics been acquainted with canonical Buddhism they would have known that canonical Buddhism not only recognizes the existence of numerous forms of spirits, demons, ghosts, and so on, but that it sanctions their propitiation. Hence, this alleged incompatibility could only arise if the Burmese believed—which they don't—that spirit-propitiation is a means to salvation.

Similarly (to cite a personal experience) before I became acquainted with canonical Buddhism, I encountered many forms of Buddhist magic in Burma which (based on my reading of Western rationalistic interpretations of Buddhism) I assumed to be Burmese innovations, when in fact they were found in and sanctioned by Scripture.

millions of Burmese, Cambodians, Laotians, Sinhalese, and Thai, are *Theravāda* Buddhists, despite the fact that this religious system is practiced nowhere else, and never was practiced anywhere else, in the world. To hold, on the other hand, that normative religious doctrine is irrelevant for an understanding of the beliefs of religious actors is to evade one of the most important theoretical problems in the anthropological study of religion (and more especially of the higher religions), viz., the relationship between the real and ideal, the actual and doctrinal, the existential and normative, dimensions of belief systems.

In one sense the above set of discrepancies may be seen as posing a traditional anthropological problem in culture change—that is, to what extent and under what conditions does (religious) change occur over (historical) time? In another sense, however, but with equal cogency, the problem may be phrased as one in cultural conservatism: How and why do the great revolutionary religions, like Buddhism, revert ultimately to the religious status quo ante? The latter, of course, is a much more interesting problem; and since the Buddhist revolution was perhaps the most novel in religious history, the answers to this problem have important implications for our understanding of human nature and of the parameters of human emotional and cognitive plasticity.

This emphasis on the interaction between a normative tradition and the social actors who have acquired—or at least have been exposed to—that tradition is, of course, far from innovative. Fourteen years ago, Robert Redfield (1956: ch. 3) introduced the notion of the "great tradition" into the comparative study of civilizations, a notion which he contrasted with that of the "little tradition"—the refraction of the great tradition through a village lens. Although I do not fully accept the great-tradition–little-tradition dichotomy, I am not only in agreement with the notion of the great tradition but have borrowed the term for the subtitle of this book. In this case the interaction, specifically, is between the great tradition of *Theravāda* Buddhism and the people of Burma—hence its "*Burmese* vicissitudes."

If I seem unduly to stress beliefs and ideas, it is not because this study is not concerned with religious behavior, but because, in the last analysis, even religious behavior is dependent on religious ideas: the performance of a rite or ceremony depends on certain conceptions of how and why they work, how much power they have or can harness, under what conditions they are relevant, and so on. A large part of this study, therefore, is concerned with religious doctrine and religious ideas, both as dependent variables (why do people hold them?) and independent variables (what are the consequences of holding them?).

I should emphasize, however, that this concern with ideas is far removed from the current anthropological interest in the theories of Claude Lévi-Strauss, and is even further removed from those current interests that are variously called by such terms as ethnoscience, ethnosemantics, etc. I do not subscribe to the notion that people are primarily interested in cultural ideas because (as Lévi-Strauss once said about totemic ideas) they are "good to think"; and in the case of religious ideas I reject this notion out of hand. I also reject the thesis that seems to dominate much of the current interest in cognitive anthropology that cultural (including religious) systems are primarily classification systems. Of course people must classify and order their natural and social worlds if they are to find their way through them, and of course religion is one of the cultural systems which serves this function. But this, surely, is not the primary function either of cultural ideas or of the subset—religious ideas—with which we are concerned in this volume.

In my view, which informed this entire research project, religious ideas are not so much used to think about, or classify with, as to live by. That is, they are used to provide hopes, to satisfy wishes, to resolve conflict, to cope with tragedy, to rationalize failure, to find meaning in suffering. In short, religious ideas deal with the very guts of life, not with its bland surface. This instrumental conception of ideas (a conception which is derived from Dewey, Freud, and Weber) is abundantly supported, I believe, by the vicissitudes of the Buddhist ideas examined in the following chapters.

The Problem: The Uniqueness of Buddhism

Normative Buddhism, as is well known, is currently expressed in two major forms: *Mahāyāna* and *Theravāda.* Itself divided into various denominations—or, as they are usually termed, sects—the former is found, for the most part, in northern and eastern Asia. With its numerous saints and saviors, its masses for the dead, its elaborate and ornate rituals, *Mahāyāna* Buddhism—the Buddhism of the Greater Vehicle—is related to *Theravāda* Buddhism—the Buddhism of the Elders—much as Catholicism is related to Protestantism.[4] Lacking saints and saviors, and possessing a few simple rituals, the latter form of Buddhism is found primarily in Southeast Asia, most notably in Burma, Cambodia, Ceylon, Laos, and Thailand. It is with *Theravāda* Buddhism, in both its normative and its more recent historical expressions, and on both the lay and the monastic levels, that we shall be concerned.

It should be emphasized at the outset that by "normative *Theravāda* Buddhism" I mean the doctrines contained in the *Theravāda* canon, which

[4]Designating itself as the Greater Vehicle—because through it everyone can eventually attain nirvana, especially by the assistance of those saints *(Bodhisattvas)* who, before attaining salvation, remain in the world to help save others—the *Mahāyāna* school designates the *Theravāda* school as Hinayāna Buddhism—the Lesser Vehicle—because it offers nirvana only to those few who can attain it through their own efforts. Rejecting this pejorative term, the latter school designates itself by the term *Theravāda*—the school which represents the teachings of the Elders (of Buddhism).

may or may not correspond with the teachings of the historical Buddha. Even if Buddhist historical scholarship were unequivocally successful in distinguishing the teachings of the Buddha Himself from those which represent later additions and emendations to Buddhism, this "quest for the historical Buddha" is irrelevant to the aims of our inquiry because the distinction itself is foreign to believing Buddhists. For them, *all* the words which the canon attributes to the Buddha are, indeed, His words. For them, all the doctrines contained in the canon represent the teachings of the Buddha. Hence, when I refer to nonnormative beliefs and practices, I do not mean those which diverge from "what the Buddha taught," but those which diverge from canonical doctrine.

Normative *Theravāda* Buddhism comprises a complex of doctrines and attitudes which, in their totality, render it unique in the religious annals of mankind. Indeed, its uniqueness has led a number of religious scholars to question whether it can legitimately be designated a religion at all. Without prejudging this issue (I shall return to it in later chapters), we may at least agree that normative *Theravāda* Buddhism—which for simplicity I shall henceforth designate merely as "Buddhism"—is sufficiently unique to pose an array of problems for the social scientist. Before exploring some of them, however, we must briefly examine in what ways this religion is truly unique.

In his discussion of the Buddhist creed, J. H. Bateson (1911) summarizes the teachings of Buddhism in the following five concepts: materialism, atheism, pessimism, nihilism, and egoism. To this conceptual set, I would add one more concept, viz., world-renunciation, the attitudinal and behavioral consequence of subscribing to the above set. Even a brief discussion of these doctrines will indicate how unusual they are when taken as the defining doctrines of a *religious* tradition.

Materialism. Contrary to almost every other religion, one of the foundation stones of Buddhism is the doctrine of nonsoul. Man is an aggregate of five material factors and processes which, at death, disintegrate without residue. The belief that behind these material processes there exists some spiritual or incorporeal essence—a soul—which guides and directs behavior and which survives the dissolution of the physical body, is a Buddhist heresy. The building block of the world, and of man, is the atom. Man, like the rest of the world, consists of atoms in motion.

Atheism. Buddhism is a religion without a God. Just as the body has no soul which guides and directs its action, so the universe has no Creator who brought it into being, who guides its course, or who presides over the destiny of man. More important, there is no Being—no savior God—to whom man can turn for salvation. Each man, as it were, must save himself. Durkheim (1954:29-32), it will be recalled, was so impressed with the Buddhist example that he argued that the belief in God could not be used as a defining characteristic of "religion." Other scholars, themselves the products of the eighteenth-century Enlightenment and of nineteenth-century rationalism, found the precursor of these latter movements in Buddhism. Believing that it denied souls and God(s), and that it adjured reliance on mysterious forces and supernatural powers, Buddhism was viewed by many of its Western interpreters as an essentially ethical religion, akin to modern Humanism or ethical culture.

Nihilism. The doctrine of no-soul is intimately associated with a second building stone—the doctrine of impermanence. According to Buddhism everything in the universe, including the universe itself, is impermanent. There can be no supreme reality because anything that is "real"—anything that exists—is in a perpetual flux, in a constant state of creation and dissolution, of coming into and passing out of existence. But Buddhism makes an even more radical claim—and this is a second meaning of Buddhist nihilism: even if there were some permanent reality, perhaps some condition of immortality, it is not a condition to which man ought aspire. Rather than aspiring to an eternal existence, the Buddhist (in theory) aspires to the extinction of existence (at least, as we ordinarily understand "existence"). Like all Indian religions, the aim of Buddhism is to bring the otherwise endless cycle of rebirth to an end. Stevenson's characterization of the orientation of all Indian religions applies, *pari passu,* to Buddhism.

> The desire of India is to be freed from the cycle of rebirths, and the dread of India is reincarnation. The rest that most of the spiritual seek through their faith is a state of profound and deathlike trance, in which all their powers shall have ceased to move or live, and from which they shall never again be awakened to undergo rebirth in this toilsome and troubled world.
>
> If, therefore, we would try reverently and sympathetically to grasp the inner meaning of an Indian faith, we must put aside all thought of the perfectly developed personality which is our ideal, and of the joy and zest that come from progress made and powers exercised, and, turning our thoughts backwards, face for a while another goal, in which death, not life, is the prize, cessation not development the ideal. [Stevenson 1915:1]

Notice, then, the Buddhist inversion of the typical attitude to life and death. For the Westerner, for example, death, which is inevitable, is the ultimate tragedy; and all three Western religions hold out the hope of averting this tragedy by offering eternal life (in the next world). For Buddhism, it is the continuation of life across an almost endless cycle of rebirths which is inevitable, and it is this possibility which is the ultimate tragedy. The extinction of life, which others might lament as man's automatic and inevitable fate, is viewed by Buddhism as neither inevitable nor lamentable. On the contrary, for Buddhism, it is not the extinction but the persistence of life that is automatic and—but for the practice of Buddhist discipline—inevitable. It is only through incredible effort, requiring a staggering amount of cosmological time, that the Buddhist can achieve that state which the Westerner achieves effortlessly, however much he tries to avoid it.

Pessimism. Buddhist nihilism is reasoned, not capricious. Just as Calvinism teaches that there is no conceivable act of even the most righteous man which is not sinful (in the sight of God), so Buddhism teaches that there is no conceivable act of even the happiest man which is not painful (when analyzed in the crucible of Buddhist meditaton). Associated with the doctrines of no-soul and impermanence, the doctrine of suffering forms the third of the famous Buddhist trinity. From the lowest hell to the highest heaven suffering is an inescapable and essential attribute of life. Since so long as there is life there is suffering, the only reasonable goal to aspire to, according to Buddhism, is the extinction of life as we ordinarily understand it.

Renunciation. Religions not only take different attitudes to the world, but these attitudes vary systematically with their basic doctrines, and especially with their doctrines of salvation. Thus, religion may accept the world, viewing it as not incompatible with its soteriological goal; it may be indifferent to the world, viewing it as irrelevant to that goal; it may reject the world, viewing the latter as the major obstacle to attainment of that goal. The last attitude, the rejection of the world, may lead, as Weber has shown, to such diverse responses as innerworldly asceticism, mysticism, and otherworldly asceticism. (Weber 1946:323-58.) Buddhism is a religion, par excellence, of otherworldly asceticism. Viewing attachment to the world as the cause of suffering, and hence as an irreducible obstacle to salvation, Buddhism insists that suffering can only be escaped through detachment from and renunciation of the world. By renouncing the world, the Buddhist aspires to detachment from persons, from material possessions, and even from himself (his sensations, his desires, his self).

Here, then, is a religion which challenges some of our fundamental notions about religion and about man. It denies the existence of God and souls; it views all human experience as caught up in suffering; it denigrates the world, valuing rather detachment from it and stressing the extinction of all worldly desires; as its ultimate goal, it offers the hope of the cessation of life (i.e., of rebirth); finally, it teaches that man must achieve salvation, unaided, without any supernatural assistance. These doctrines, moreover, do not constitute the philosophy of a solitary thinker, nor are they even the teachings of an austere philosophic school. They are, on the contrary, the message of a world religion, the official religion, moreover, of most of the societies of South and Southeast Asia.

It is this latter fact that poses the intellectual challenge to the anthropologist. For, although anthropology is profoundly aware of the great diversity and wide variability in human culture (including religion), the Buddhist doctrines and attitudes summarized above are so far outside the normal range of cross-cultural expectations as to constitute a profound exception to most of our generalizations about society, religion, and culture. Thus *Theravāda* Buddhism is atheistic, where the devotees of other religions turn to supernatural assistance in their quest for salvation. *Theravāda* Buddhism rejects the belief in a soul, where other religionists believe in one soul at the very least. *Theravāda* Buddhism teaches that all experience entails suffering, where most people agree that many experiences afford pleasure and even true happiness. *Theravāda* Buddhism insists that the extinction of desire is a requisite for salvation, where most people believe that the satisfaction of desire is one of the marks of salvation. *Theravāda* Buddhism demands emotional detachment and the renunciation of the world, where most people seek attachment to friends and loved ones, power and position, self and possessions.

But these doctrines and attitudes of Buddhism not only constitute exceptions to what we know about society, religion, and culture; their alleged internalization as the personal beliefs and attitudes of millions of people—most of them simple peasants at that—challenges most of our conceptions of human behavior and human nature. Thus, before embarking on this study, I expected (on the basis of anthropological and psychoanalytic theory) that everywhere people would believe in supernatural helpers; that everywhere people would seek to maximize rather than extinguish physical pleasure; that nowhere, except in a clinical population of depressives, would people believe that life is suffering; and that everywhere the attachment to self, and of persons and objects associated with the self, would be the normal and necessary mode of human psychological functioning.

For me, then, *Theravāda* Buddhism seemed to present the anthropologist with at once a stunning problem and some remarkable opportunities—the chance to uncover those social and cultural conditions that lead to the acquisition of beliefs and attitudes which constitute dramatic exceptions to our empirical knowledge and our theoretical expectations concerning human nature and religion (thereby leading to their amendment), and the opportunity to discover the consequences—more especially the cultural and social consequences—attendant upon their acquisition.

Unfortunately, these opportunities were never realized because the problem turned out to be a pseudo problem. In the first place, some of the doctrines adumbrated above are not normative Buddhist doctrines; the secondary sources from which I had derived my knowledge of Buddhism had—through both under- and overemphasis—often distorted some of the important normative doctrines. More significant, my research in Burma, and concurrent research by anthropologists in other societies of Southeast Asia, revealed that although *Theravāda* Buddhism is indeed the normative religion in these societies, many of its doctrines are only rarely internalized by the members of these societies, because they are either ignored or rejected by the faithful. In short, unlike the conclusions which might have been deduced from textual Buddhism or books on Buddhism, anthropological studies of living Buddhism have shown that Buddhists differ very little from people in general. The study of the beliefs and behavior of Buddhists (in contrast to the normative doctrines, actual or alleged, of canonical Buddhism) serves to confirm rather than challenge our empirical generalization and theoretical expectations concerning human nature and human behavior. It should be noted, incidentally, that the very fact that Buddhists do not subscribe to all the doctrines of normative Buddhism is itself an indication of how similar they are to other people—Christians or Jews, for example, who reject many normative doctrines of Christianity or Judaism while still claiming to be "Christians" or "Jews."

But I was studying Buddhism, not Christianity or Judaism; and having discovered in my Burmese research that the doctrines of normative Buddhism only rarely constitute the Buddhism of the faithful, I also discovered that the latter have acquired other additional forms of Buddhism which for them are equally, or nearly equally, normative. Although these forms are discussed in detail in the chapters that follow, it is necessary to adumbrate them here so as to point up some of the problems to which this research was addressed.

The Problem Confounded: The Three Systems of *Theravāda* Buddhism

In his perceptive essay on ancient Indian culture, a noted Sanskrit scholar observed that ancient India was characterized by two radically different religious systems, or (as he preferred to call them) "norms of conduct" (Edgerton 1942). One system—the "ordinary norm"—was intended for the religious majority; the other—the "extraordinary norm"—was confined to a much smaller group, those whose primary concern was with salvation. Since, in all Indian religions, salvation refers to release *(mokṣa)* from the continuous round of rebirths, the doctrines comprising this system provided the means for release from the Wheel of Life, while those comprising the former system provided the means for enhancing one's position within the Wheel. Although the goal of the ordinary norm was regarded as religiously inferior to that of the extraordinary norm, both were equally normative, in that both were rooted in the classical literature of the sixth and fifth centuries B.C., and hence represented traditional ideals; and both contained specific rules of conduct which were prescribed for their respective devotees.

Normative Buddhism, a child of ancient Indian culture, was one of a number of Indian religious systems purporting to have discovered the way to Release; and, almost without change, it persists even today as the religion of those Buddhists who aspire to this soteriological goal. From its very inception, however, Buddhism (like Hinduism) realized that Release cannot be the goal of ordinary men, and therefore it, too, developed an ordinary as well as an extraordinary norm. Viewing the cycle of rebirths which constitutes any individual's career as a kind of religious pilgrimage, in which one becomes progressively sensitized to its soteriological message, Buddhism holds that until they reach the end of that pilgrimage, ordinary men need only follow its ordinary norm. Insofar as these worldlings (as they are called) accept the latter, attending to its message and complying with its discipline, they are viewed as having reached, as it were, a halfway house or a way station to normative Buddhism.

To the outside observer, however, the worldling is not so much a halfway Buddhist as another kind—a radically different kind—of Buddhist; the one aspires to Release from the Wheel, the other remains tied to it. Stemming, however, from a common tradition and holding many doctrines in common, both may be called Buddhists, although the one is an adherent of a normative, the other of a nonnormative Buddhist soteriology.

Although fundamentally a salvation religion, even normative Buddhism is not disinterested in man's fate in this world. Hence, in addition to two types of soteriological Buddhism, we may distinguish still a third type of Buddhism, one which is concerned with man's worldly welfare: the curing of illness, protection from demons, the prevention of droughts, and so on. This being so, Buddhism is best viewed as comprising not one, but three separate if interlocking systems: two soteriological systems (one normative and one nonnormative) and one nonsoteriological system. Since the latter is primarily concerned with protection from danger, I shall call it *apotropaic* Buddhism. The two soteriological systems may be called *nibbanic* and *kammatic* Buddhism, respectively. Since its major concern is with release from the Wheel, or nirvana *(nibbāna)*, nibbanic Buddhism is an appropriate term for normative soteriological Buddhism. Nonnormative soteriological Buddhism, concerned with improving one's position on the Wheel by improving one's karma *(kamma)*, is appropriately termed kammatic Buddhism.[5]

Having delineated three distinctive Buddhist systems, I do not wish to suggest that living Buddhism presents itself as packaged into three neat bundles of belief and practice. On the contrary, when first encountered, living Buddhism appears as a bewildering hodgepodge of beliefs and practices, some canonical and some noncanonical, which it is difficult to distinguish from those comprising the non-Buddhist religious systems found in all Buddhist societies (Spiro 1967:ch. 14), let alone from each other. Nevertheless, within this hodgepodge one can discern systems and even subsystems.

In one sense, of course, these systems are analytic constructs abstracted by the investigator, but in another they reflect and designate the "native category system." Thus, although the Burmese, for example, may not be aware of all the distinguishing features of the three systems alluded to above, they are certainly aware of, and can distinguish, their major features.

[5]These latter two systems have been previously distinguished by King in an illuminating discussion (1964:161-75).

Further, although they don't use these terms, they know precisely how nibbanic differs from kammatic Buddhism, in both aim and technique. If they follow the latter system, it is not from ignorance of the former, nor from a confusion of the two; it is, rather, because they have knowingly chosen the one and rejected the other. Moreover, they usually justify their choice by recourse to a perfectly valid normative explanation, i.e., that they are not yet spiritually qualified to practice nibbanic Buddhism.

But to say that there are three systems of Buddhism in Burma (or in Thailand or Ceylon) does not mean that there are three kinds of Buddhists in these societies; rather, all three systems are found in varying degrees in all Buddhists. Still, as I have already observed, most Buddhists (being "worldlings") have little to do with nibbanic Buddhism, though they are aware of and genuinely believe that they ought to aspire to it; and even that small band of pious monks who are genuinely devoted to that system hold doctrines and attitudes appropriate to the other two.

The anthropologist learns two difficult lessons—one bearing on human nature, the other on religion—from this defection from otherworldliness, detachment, asceticism, nihilism, and other doctrines of nibbanic Buddhism adumbrated in the foregoing section. Confronted with the dramatic variability inherent in the cross-cultural record, we anthropologists have frequently proposed that there are almost no limits to human plasticity; human nature, we have argued, is a product of culture, and culture can mold human nature in almost any shape or form it chooses. Human nature no doubt, *is* a product of culture, at least to some extent, but our experience with Buddhism announces clearly and loudly that there are limits to its plasticity, beyond which culture is impotent to mold it. Indeed, on the basis of the Buddhist data, I would argue that these limits are dramatically narrower than we have traditionally conceded them to be. After approximately a thousand years of Buddhism, the Burmese and the Cambodians, the Sinhalese and the Thai, appear to me to exhibit (more or less) the same human nature as, say, the Americans or the British, the Germans or the Russians. Attachment, not detachment; persistence, not annihilation; drive-satisfaction, not drive extinction—these and many other attributes allegedly restricted to "Western" man are as pronounced in the former group as in the latter.

Related to anthropology's rather extravagant claims concerning the plasticity of human nature has been its equally extravagant claims concerning the variability of human culture. For almost any cultural norm, value, or practice to be found in one society, its opposite—so we have claimed—can be found in another. This claim may perhaps be supported in other cultural domains, but the Buddhist data teach us that, in the religious domain at least, variability is again restricted to rather narrow limits. Thouless came to this conclusion thirty years ago. "It is sometimes suggested," he wrote in a little-known work (1940:5),

> that the original message of all religious leaders is at bottom the same. The truer view is, I think, that different religious leaders have taught very different messages; it is in what men do to those messages in the process of forming religious institutions that there is essential similarity. One religious leader teaches that God is the Father of all men, and that their salvation comes from doing the will of God; another teaches that no god can save man from his own weakness, but that it is by his own mental effort that man's salvation must come. From these conflicting and irreconcilable messages, men have created religious institutions which are in many ways remarkably alike.

Despite the dramatic differences in the teachings of religious founders, religions are "remarkably alike"—so Thouless argues—because of the tendency, which he calls "conventionalization," for all religions

> . . . to lose more or less what is characteristically different about the teachings of their founders and to become, therefore, more like the religious systems from which their founders reacted and more like other religious systems in general. . . . This process tends to make all religious systems become much more alike than were the original teachings of their founders. [*Ibid.*:35]

There is little question but that this has taken place in the case of Buddhism. As it is lived and practiced, Buddhism has not only reverted to many of the Indian beliefs against which its founder rebelled, but in so doing, it has recreated most of the other attributes usually associated with religion. Souls and gods, rituals and festivals, heavens and hells—these and many more have all been reincorporated into Buddhism as we know it. If religion is viewed, as I view it, as a symbolic expression of a restricted set of needs, fantasies, wishes, conflicts, aspirations, and so on which are deeply rooted in a universal human nature, we need hardly be surprised that Buddhism has come to reveal most of the defining characteristics of religion in general. This is not to say, of course, that Buddhism, even as we now know it, is not "different." It would be absurd to claim otherwise. But, as I have already indicated, since nowhere is Buddhism an exclusive religion, since wherever found, it is associated with at least one other (primitive or high), their combined attributes render the religion(s) of Buddhist societies very similar to the religion(s) of other societies.

It would seem, then, that man has certain universal needs which will not for long be frustrated, and that ideas and doctrines—like some of the ideas and doctrines of normative Buddhism—which frustrate or violate these needs will eventually be modified or replaced. This at least is what has happened to *Theravāda* Buddhism in every society in which it has put down roots. Having discovered this in the society where I was conducting field work, I found a new array of problems commanding my attention. Before turning to them, however, it will be well to describe the social and cultural contexts in which this work was conducted.

Field Work: The Burmese Setting

If religion is to be studied as a living system rather than exclusively as a body of canonical doctrines, it must be studied in its historical and cultural contexts. Hence, although when I first embarked on this study I was interested in *Theravāda* Buddhism in its generic expression (and not specifically in Thai, or Burmese, or Sinhalese Buddhism), it was in Burma that I conducted my field work. Moreover, within that country my research was focused on one village in Upper Burma, which I have called "Yeigyi."

I chose to study Buddhism within a village setting, not because I was interested either in village Burma or in village Buddhism per se, but because —in Southeast Asia at least—the village is at once the maximal manageable sociocultural unit within which religion can be studied, and the minimal sociocultural context within which its basic cultural—though not social—patterns are known, if not always found. That Southeast Asia happens to be 85 per cent rural, and that village Buddhism therefore happens to be the most typical living expression of *Theravāda* Buddhism, lends credence to the generalizations I often draw (below) from my own limited data, but this —it must be admitted—is a fortunate happenstance of an essentially methodological decision rather than the basis for it.

To repeat, then, the village of Yeigyi was the locale of this study rather than its subject; but since I could not know initially how typical its Buddhism was, it was necessary to obtain comparative data from other contexts, which differ from the Yeigyi on four dimensions—spatial, ecological, cultural, and temporal. Hence, in addition to the *intensive* data collected during the nine months in which I lived and worked in Yeigyi, another three months were devoted to collecting *extensive* data from a range of villages in Upper Burma. Moreover, throughout this entire period I made biweekly excursions to Mandalay, the former capital of Burma, where I was able to collect material on urban Buddhism. Since, however, Mandalay is a traditional city, an additional two months were spent in Rangoon, the modern capital, collecting data from westernized government officials and Buddhist intellectuals especially. In addition, all available documentary and firsthand accounts of Burmese Buddhism were consulted for both historical and regional comparisons. Finally, my own firsthand but superficial observations in Thailand and Ceylon—for three months and one month, respectively—were supplemented by firsthand descriptions of Buddhism in those and other *Theravāda* countries of Southeast Asia.

To the extent, then, permitted by the limitations of these data, it was possible to make a four-way comparison of Buddhist belief and practice: rural-rural, rural-urban, Burmese–non-Burmese, contemporary-historical. Although these comparisons yielded some interesting differences, most of which are noted below in the appropriate chapters, they are differences primarily in detail rather than in fundamental patterns. In general, Buddhism in Rangoon differs little from Buddhism in Yeigyi, and neither is very different from the Buddhism of traditional Burma. In short, with some few exceptions, the Buddhism practiced in Yeigyi seems to be a typical expression of Buddhism anywhere in Burma.

But I would go further. On the basis of the Burmese–non-Burmese comparisons, I believe it is fair to say that wherever it is found, *Theravāda* Buddhism is remarkably similar to the Buddhism I observed in Burma. Hence, although there is no denying that this is a study of *Theravāda* Buddhism primarily in Burmese garb, the justification for entitling this book "*Theravāda* Buddhism" is that its Burmese garb differs from its Thai or Sinhalese garb in only minor ways. The differences are variations on a common set of themes. Indeed, rather than its [Buddhism's] "*Burmese* vicissitudes," the subtitle of the book might just as well have referred to its "*historical* vicissitudes."

I have stressed this ecumenical character of Buddhism, not only to argue for the generalizability of my findings, but to underscore the thesis that the weakness of nibbanic Buddhism is a characteristic not of Burmese Buddhism in particular, but of *Theravāda* Buddhism in general. Indeed, if anything, Buddhism, on the peasant level at least, appears to be stronger in Burma than in Ceylon, and much stronger than in Thailand (let alone Laos and Cambodia, where it seems to be the weakest).

We may now return to the village of Yeigyi and briefly describe this sociocultural context in which most of the Buddhist data to be explored below are embedded. (With some minor changes, the following paragraphs are taken from Spiro 1967:9-12.) With a population of approximately five hundred people, Yeigyi is situated on a central irrigation canal, irrigation being indispensable for the wet rice cultivation which is the dominant economic activity of the entire region. The village comprises 119 houses, each of which is typically inhabited by a nuclear family. Although a few families, mostly basket makers and loggers (who emigrated from a district about forty miles northwest of Mandalay), are relatively recent arrivals in the village, most of its inhabitants were born and raised in Yeigyi or in one of its neighboring villages.

Surrounded on three sides by paddy fields—blue with water during the transplanting season and golden in the growing season—and by the foothills of the purplish Shan Mountains on the fourth, and protected from the cruel tropical sun by clumps of shade trees, the village offers a most attractive approach. Like most villages in Upper Burma, however, Yeigyi is reached only after traveling for four or five miles on a dirt road, which in this case connects with the highway leading to Mandalay.

Although the oxcart is the main means of transportation (a few wealthy inhabitants own bicycles), a bus stop about four miles from the village makes Mandalay easily accessible. The city's main bazaar is used by the villagers for important shopping, its famous pagodas beckon to them on Buddhist holydays and pagoda festivals, and its moneylenders and rice merchants are important mainstays of their agricultural economy. This, then, is not an isolated village, remote from outside contacts or influence. On the other hand, although the British conquered Upper Burma in 1885 and administered it (except for the brief interlude of the Japanese occupation) until Burmese independence in 1948, Yeigyi and its environs show much less British cultural influence than villages in Lower Burma. As far back as the early nineteenth century, the Mandalay region was, and continues to be, the heartland of traditional Burmese culture.

From very early times Yeigyi and its neighboring villages were caught up in the economic and cultural orbits of the various royal courts of Burma, and especially of the last court at Mandalay. Prior to the British conquest of Upper Burma, Yeigyi performed services of various kinds for the court, and after the conquest it was affected by the insurgency and unrest that attended the exile of Burma's last king, King Thibaw. Despite their minimal contact with the British Raj during the fifty-year period before the Japanese occupation, the villagers certainly felt the British political presence, and in retrospect at least respected and appreciated it.

World War II ushered in a long period of tension and unrest, which continues to the present. The Japanese occupation, harsh and brutal, was experienced directly by the village, as were the series of insurrections against the central government which, following the achievement of independence, sprang up in many parts of Burma. The area around Yeigyi witnessed numerous battles between government and insurgent troops, and as late as 1959 Yeigyi itself was occupied and reoccupied by at least two of the insurgent groups. Indeed, a small number of men, and a few women as well, joined one or another of these groups for short periods. The most recent upheaval to impinge on the village was the coup of 1962, which replaced the civilian with the present military government. Since that government has practiced a strict exclusionary policy, scholars have been unable to work in Burma since 1962. Hence my description does not take account of changes that may have taken place since that time.

Despite all these changes and upheavals, there were few differences between the basic social and cultural patterns which I encountered in Yeigyi in 1961-62 and those described in early—indeed, the earliest—published reports on Burmese life. Paddy cultivation continues to be the basic economic and subsistence activity. The nuclear family household, related through bilateral kin ties to other households both within and outside the village, remains the basic social unit. The village continues to be governed by a village headman—who, however, is now an elected rather than a hereditary official—and a council of village elders. It is to them, rather than to government courts or magistrates, that most intravillage disputes are brought. Buddhism continues to be the single most important cultural force in the village, and certainly its most important basis for social integration, as we shall see below. Side by side with Buddhism, there exists today, as in the past, an important and vital spirit religion, as well as a belief in and practice of witchcraft, sorcery, astrology, and other occult phenomena (cf. Spiro 1968). Technologically, too, the village has undergone few changes. It has no radios, no tractors, no electricity; all tasks are performed by either manpower or ox power. Farming and sex, gossip and intrigue, worship and celebration, Buddhist holydays and spirit festivals—these have been and continue to be the major axes along which the sociocultural matrix of life in Yeigyi, and in Burma in general, can be ordered.

Field Work: The Buddhist Setting

To study Buddhism in Burma is to study it in a society in which, as I have already indicated, it occupies a preeminent position. Buddhism originated in India[6] in the sixth century B.C., but there is no clear evidence for its presence in Burma until the fifth century A.D. (Coedès 1968:17), when it was centered in the ancient capital of the Pyus. Among the ethnic Burmese, early Buddhism was Mahayanist in character until, in the eleventh century, *Theravāda* Buddhism became the official religion at the ancient capital of Pagan. Although frequently weakened in its early history by a falling away from monastic purity, and sometimes requiring infusions of orthodoxy from Ceylon, *Theravāda* Buddhism soon struck wide and deep roots in Burma, where historically it has played a dominant social and cultural role.

But its importance in modern Burma is no less pronounced than in Burma's historical past. Thus in Burma both the Fifth and Sixth Buddhist Councils were convened (in 1871 and 1954, respectively), and it was in nineteenth-century Burma that the Buddhist meditation technique, which has since been adopted by most of the *Theravāda* world, originated. Demoted by the British from its position as the state religion, Buddhism nevertheless persisted in full strength throughout the colonial period, and in the post-Independence period, it has continued to be a predominant force in Burmese society, on both cultural and individual levels.

With respect to the cultural level, it would be only a slight exaggeration to say that most aspects of Burmese culture have been influenced at least to some extent by Buddhism. Pali loan words occupy a conspicuous place in the Burmese lexicon, particularly its lexicon of psychological, philosophic, scientific, and ethical terms. Burmese literature is predominantly Buddhist in both content and influence. The *Jātaka*, for example, which recount

[6]In one of those ironies of history, Indians are the most reviled people in Burma, despite the fact that Buddhism originated in India and that its Indian founder is tendered homage worthy of a God. (In addition, the most famous historical *nat* spirits of Burma, the Taungbyon Brothers, were also Indian.) The parallel, in Christendom, to the role of Jesus in Christianity and the historical attitudes held toward the Jews is striking.

the lives of the Buddha Gautama prior to his becoming a Buddha, are not only well known in themselves, but some have become the basis for Burmese folk tales, while others not only form an important core of Burmese dramatic literature, but their performance constitutes the standard repertory of the Burmese classical theater.[7] Burmese art, of course, would be unthinkable without Buddhism; almost all Burmese sculpture and painting is inspired by, and represents, Buddhist themes and motifs. Similarly, Burmese architecture, to the extent that it is interesting, dramatic, or unique, is Buddhist architecture (pagodas, monasteries, etc.). One could go on and on. Traditional Burmese conceptions of man and society, of grammar and monarchy, of geography and cosmology—these and many more have all been taken from Buddhism. Deprived of Buddhism, the culture of Burma —like the culture of Europe deprived of Christianity—would have been drastically impoverished.

Religion, of course, can be significant on the cultural level and yet have little weight in people's personal lives. This is not the case in Burma, where the importance of Buddhism in the lives of the people is revealed in a number of ways: in the extraordinary percentage of the average family income devoted to Buddhism, in the high percentage of males who enter the Buddhist order (and the great reverence in which they are held), in the large amounts of time and energy expended toward Buddhist ends, in the importance of Buddhist piety as a crucial dimension in political success, and many other things. Since these are all discussed at length in later chapters, I should like here to mention three other matters which, though not explored below, are equally significant, if more subtle.

In the first place, it is essential to emphasize the importance of Buddhism as a fundamental ingredient of Burmese identity. For the Burmese villager, at least, to be a Burman is to be a Buddhist. Burmese who are not Buddhists are viewed, for the most part, as non-Burmese. Thus, during the national debates surrounding the establishment of Buddhism as the state religion (in 1961) Burmese peasants argued that Buddhism was not just any religion, but the *Burmese* religion; without Buddhism there could be no Burma. Burmese who are not Buddhists, they argued, had no right to object to the establishment of Buddhism since, fundamentally, non-Buddhists are really not Burmese.

Burmese who are not Buddhist are viewed as marginal in almost every sense. Even when they occupy important positions or play prominent roles in Burmese society they are viewed by others as somehow not quite belonging, and they in turn (at least those that I know) view themselves in the same manner. Almost without exception they suffer from an identity problem.

[7]Professor Gordon Luce, the doyen of Burmese historical and cultural studies, claims that "it would scarcely be an exaggeration to say that they [the *Jātaka*] have formed the basis of half our art and literature." (Luce 1956:302)

To be sure, the marginal position of most non-Buddhists in Burma is contaminated by their ethnic marginality. Ethnically most non-Buddhists, it will be recalled, are also non-Burmese. The Hindus and Muslims are Indian, and the animists and most of the Christians are members of one of the tribal groups (Kachins, Chins, Karens, etc.).[8] But the same marginality characterizes that handful of non-Buddhists—usually Christians—who *are* ethnic Burmese. In one village, for example, the elders informed me that "all Burmese" believed in a two-party political system (a claim, incidentally, which is not true). When I objected, saying that their own Township Officer did not share this belief, there was an almost spontaneous response: "He's not Burmese, he's Christian." That this Township Officer was not only ethnically Burmese but an official of the Burmese government—the highest official a typical peasant is likely to meet—and an intense Burmese nationalist, was all irrelevant. For these elders, as for the Burmese in general, Buddhism is the salient attribute of a Burman; being Christian, the Township Officer was not completely Burmese.

On his part, the Township Officer was acutely aware of, and highly sensitive to, his marginality. He would take great pains to self-consciously make decisions which could not be regarded as stemming from his Christian values. Another Burmese Christian, one of the most prominent and influential men in Burma, told me that he felt he was never quite trusted, despite serving as confidant and adviser to cabinet ministers and army generals.

Constituting an essential—perhaps the essential—ingredient of the Burmese definition of their own identity, it is little wonder that Buddhism was deeply implicated in the rise of the Burmese nationalist and independence movements. No doubt there is much truth in the contention of historians (cf. Cady 1958:190) that it was used as a political weapon in the independence struggle. Stated in this manner, however, it is a misleading—because an oversimplified—contention. If Buddhism was used as a political weapon by the Burmese, it was not from Machiavellian motives, but because Buddhism was and is both the symbol and the essential ingredient of their national identity.

A second measure of the importance of Buddhism in the lives of the Burmese is its normative role in Burmese society. On the village level, at least, it is the measure of all things: against Buddhism all values, ideas, and behavior are ultimately to be judged. To be concrete and specific, Scripture is constantly appealed to in order to justify one's own or to criticize another's behavior. This is not to say that villagers are Buddhist scholars; except for a few *sutta*, which they learn as students in the monastery school,[9] most villagers are acquainted primarily with the *Jātaka*. Still, the *Jātaka* alone

[8] At the time of the 1931 Census, the Christian population, mostly Baptist, numbered 331,000. In 1953, authoritative but unofficial estimates put the combined Hindu-Muslim population at 800,000. (Tinker 1959: 184,188)

[9] Most of these *sutta* are used, as we shall see below, as protective incantations *(paritta)*.

are constantly appealed to as a court of last resort whenever a moral is to be drawn, a point to be made, a position defended.

Let me cite only a few examples from the many scores recorded in the course of this study. Factionalism? It is bad, and unity is good, because the Embryo Buddha, in the form of a pigeon, united the other pigeons who had been caught in a net, and they were thereby able to escape. Is it necessary to have a Buddhist initiation ceremony to attain nirvana? Not at all. A hunter, who had atoned for the sin of killing a deer, was admitted to the Buddhist Order by a Buddha himself because of that act of atonement. Is youth an impediment to political leadership? On the contary. The Embryo Buddha pointed out that the last chicken to be hatched is the strongest because, as an egg, it has the longest period of maternal care. Is there a limit on the sacrifices one should make for others? No. One should be willing to sacrifice as much as the Embryo Buddha who, as king, removed both his eyes and gave them to a blind man so that he might be able to see.

It need merely be added, before passing on, that it is not only the simple peasant who uses Scripture as a self-evident cultural and moral arbiter; the prime minister may use it with equal frequency, and greater consequence. Thus, for example, in defending the government policy of killing insurgents, executing criminals, granting licenses for the slaughter of cattle and for distilling liquor, Prime Minister U Nu admitted that the "Buddha would not like these, and personally I would never be able to do it." Still, sometimes it is necessary, he argued, to perform undesirable acts to achieve some higher end, and "there are many instances in the Jātaka Tales to support this." (*The* [Rangoon] *Nation*, May 24, 1961) He then recounted, among others, the tale of the Embryo Buddha who, as a crab, killed a crow and a snake to prevent them from taking out the eyes of a Brahmin.[10]

A third measure of the importance of Buddhism in the life of the average Burman—at least on the village level—is its continuous fascination for him as an object of interest, a fascination that approaches obsessive dimensions. For the anthropologist interested in studying Buddhism, this concern is, of course, a great windfall. Villagers are not only willing to submit to long interview schedules devoted to Buddhist belief and practice, but—even more important—Buddhism is frequently the main topic of conversation when friends meet to pass the time together. For me, these discussions were a primary source of data concerning village Buddhism, as well as a measure of the Burmese concern with Buddhism and everything related to it.

Almost nightly I listened to discussions of the meaning of karma, nir-

[10]The moral which U Nu drew from these selected tales was that political action cannot always be judged by religious criteria, because sometimes antireligious acts have to be performed by governments because of worldly considerations. Of course, at other times U Nu justified his own political actions by reference to religious criteria, and in those cases he easily found a *Jātaka* to support that position as well.

vana, merit, monks, the Buddha, and so on, because, regardless of what else might be mentioned, the conversation would almost inevitably touch on some Buddhist concept. Sometimes these talks seemed interminable. Once, having sat up until one o'clock in the morning listening to a group of men engaged in a heated Buddhist discussion (women participate only rarely in such discourse), I encountered the same men in the same place at nine o'clock the next morning: they had gathered again to continue the debate. On another day, when I accompanied a group of villagers to a district meeting in another village, Buddhism was the exclusive subject of conversation from the time of our arrival at seven o'clock until the meeting began at eleven, and was resumed for another hour after the meeting ended.

Most of this talk, to be sure, is neither profound nor original, nor does it always stem from genuine conviction. Many of the central Buddhist doctrines, including those that are debated and argued with great passion, are often neither deeply believed nor acted upon. Indeed, much of this talk, from a communication point of view, is merely "noise." Although meditation, for example, is a frequent topic of discussion, and nearly everyone agrees that only through meditation can nirvana be achieved, almost no one ever meditates—because, they claim, they do not have the time. They certainly have plenty of time, however, to talk about it; indeed, if the time spent talking about meditation were devoted to meditating, there would be a great deal of meditation in Burma.

Nevertheless, although the "noise" factor in Buddhist discussions is important for the light it sheds on Burmese character, it does not weaken the claim concerning the importance of Buddhism in Burma. Even "noise" is in a Buddhist key! A key, it should be added, which is sounded over and over again. The same concepts may be discussed and dissected repeatedly with seldom a new idea being added to the small repertory of ideas from which the discussions take their departure. Indeed, I was more than once astounded to hear a man analyze a Buddhist doctrine for a companion, which the latter had outlined to him only the night before and in almost the same words; the companion listening with immense interest, as if hearing these ideas for the first time. This becomes less surprising when it is realized that Buddhist doctrines are not only of great interest to the Burmese—so that they can listen to repetition of the same ideas many times without boredom—but that to know and be able to explain and explicate them is a mark of great prestige. In any event, this is yet another indication of the paramount importance of Buddhism in village Burma.

Field Work: The Research Problems and the Data

Having briefly delineated the social contexts and the religious setting in which this research was conducted, it remains to describe the nature of our data. As might be expected, they are highly variegated. Based on participant observation, many of the data concerning lay Buddhism consist of ceremonies practiced, holydays celebrated, and discussions overheard—and, of course, of responses given to the hundreds of questions which the anthropologist asks as rituals unfold and conversations develop. For the anthropologist, these day-to-day observations of religion as it is practiced and talked about are his primary sources. They not only provide him with a picture of religion as it is lived, but are indispensable for suggesting additional beliefs to be studied, problems which must be resolved, questions for which answers must be found, paradoxes whose dimensions must be explored. To elicit information relevant to these matters three procedures were adopted.

First, an *extensive* Buddhist interview schedule was administered in almost every household in Yeigyi, and to selected informants in other villages. This schedule was designed to collect information concerning the beliefs and practices of Buddhist adults, to discover to what extent they were aware of formal Buddhist doctrines, and to evoke their attitudes toward them. Typically, these interviews were conducted in two separate sessions, different members of the household coming in and going out, as they liked, in the course of the interview sessions. This procedure provided a general profile of village Buddhism showing both the range and distribution of Buddhist beliefs and attitudes found in the village.

Since culturally constituted belief systems must be acquired anew in each generation, and since their component beliefs are acquired at different points in the life cycle, it was also important to study Buddhist beliefs developmentally. This dimension was investigated by means of a less extensive interview schedule administered to twenty randomly selected school children of both sexes, ranging from seven to twelve years of age.

Like all religions, but probably more than most, Buddhism poses a large number and great variety of philosophical and logical problems. To explore these in depth, an *intensive* interview schedule, extending over two to three sessions, was administered to a small panel of fifteen village men. Far from constituting a representative group, these men—mostly in their thirties through fifties—were selected precisely because of their extensive Buddhist knowledge, their Buddhist piety, and their special interest in Buddhist philosophy and metaphysics. All had studied in the monastery school, all had spent some time (as novices) in the yellow robe, and two had been ordained as monks. Referred to in the text as the "blue-ribbon sample," these men are the most knowledgeable and sophisticated Buddhists in the village. If they are ignorant of certain normative concepts, if they misinterpret others, or reject them, it is safe to conclude that this falling away from normative Buddhism is even more characteristic of the average lay Buddhist.

The study of lay Buddhism, however, was only one facet of our inquiry. Since Buddhist monks, presumably, are the most knowledgeable Buddhists, and since they are the formal spokesmen for normative Buddhism, I wanted to compare *their* Buddhist beliefs with those of the laymen. Moreover, since the monk, in the eyes of Buddhism, is the quintessential Buddhist, it was important to study both Buddhist monasticism and the Buddhist monk, per se.

For the study of monastic Buddhism, a number of procedures were employed. First, on and off for almost a year, in periods ranging from a few hours to a few days, I observed the unfolding scene in the three monasteries in Yeigyi. Second, informal interviews were conducted with perhaps fifty monks in monasteries scattered throughout villages in Upper Burma, in Mandalay, and in Rangoon. Third, a smaller group of twenty-one monks, all from Upper Burma, were selected for intensive study. Although I believe that these were a representative group of village monks, I cannot be sure that this is so. To these monks was administered the same intensive Buddhist interview schedule as had been administered to the blue-ribbon lay panel; they also underwent a battery of psychological tests, including the TAT and the Rorschach; and information was obtained concerning their premonastic backgrounds and their possible reasons for entering the Order. Fourth, interviews were conducted in Mandalay and in Rangoon with the leaders of the three associations of "political monks." Finally, interviews were conducted with the officials of the Ministry of Religion in Mandalay.

These, then, are the data described and analyzed in the chapters that follow. In some cases the confrontation with the data raised the problems discussed in these chapters; in others, the data were collected in order to cope with the problems which had initially motivated the field work. Having discovered rather early in the research that many of the original questions I had hoped to investigate were pseudo problems—living Buddhism, as I have indicated, being very different from canonical Buddhism—I turned my attention to other questions. Although all are attended to in great detail in the succeeding chapters, they may be briefly outlined here.

One set of problems, already alluded to, was posed by the initial finding that canonical and living Buddhism often do not coincide. First, given that many normative doctrines are rejected by the faithful, why is it that only some doctrines are rejected, while others are accepted? Second, how do the faithful resolve the tension between their normative and their actual religion? Third, why do doctrines which, though lip service is paid them, are really rejected continue to be transmitted, generation after generation?

In addition to this set of questions, which relates to the discrepancy between normative and living Buddhism, I was concerned with a second set, relating exclusively to the latter religion: i.e., to all three systems of Buddhism delineated earlier. In this connection I was especially interested in two doctrinal problems. First, what conditions account for the internalization of these doctrines—or, if you will, why do the Burmese believe in them? Second, what social and cultural consequences flow from their belief? To put it in more technical terms, I was interested in discovering the causes of belief, on the one hand, and its functions and dysfunctions, on the other.

A final set of problems relates to Buddhist monks and monasticism. First, with respect to the monks themselves, I wanted to know how they differ from lay Buddhists in background, experience, personality, and so on. In short, what accounts for monastic recruitment? Second, I was concerned to uncover the functions (if any) served by monasticism, both for the monks and for laymen. Third, I wished to discover why a worldly society, such as Burma, tenders such extraordinary reverence to those (the monks) who live, or at least are expected to live, by the otherworldly norms of Buddhist monasticism.

In the most general terms, one might say that, given these research problems, this book is addressed to two sets of questions. It attempts to explain Burmese Buddhism, both lay and monastic, taken as the dependent variable, by means of certain features of Burmese society and personality; and it attempts to discover the effects that Buddhism, taken as the independent variable, has had on Burmese culture and society. The first question is explored, in separate sections, in almost every chapter; the latter is dealt with only, but exclusively, in the last two chapters.

Although this, then, is a problem-oriented monggraph, it also contains detailed accounts of Buddhist belief and behavior which may sometimes seem only tangentially relevant to these matters. This raises the perennial anthropological question of how much detail ought to be included in an analytically conceived study. Although I cannot speak for my colleagues, my own decisions are governed by two considerations. First, I believe that anthropologists have a responsibility to set the ethnographic record straight (to the extent that we are able), so that area specialists can fill in the gaps in their descriptive knowledge of an area, while theoretical and comparative scholars may have access to the detailed information necessary for comparative and theoretical research, and our readers and critics have sufficient information to evaluate independently our interpretations and conclusions. With respect to this set of responsibilities, I believe it is better to err on the side of too much rather than too little detail.

The second consideration that governs my decision about the amount of descriptive detail to be included in a study of this type is methodological. For myself, I have never been able to read through a purely descriptive monograph because, unrelated to a theoretical problem, I find the facts meaningless, not to mention boring. But if, for the particular to have meaning, it is necessary to see the general *in* the particular, it is equally necessary, if the general is not to evaporate into empty and vacuous abstractions, to see the general *by means of* the particular. Still, those readers who have no interest in Burma or in Buddhism, *per se,* might wish to skip Chapters 9, 10, and 11, which are almost exclusively descriptive.

Some Problems in Interpretation

Viewed as a cultural system, religion cannot be relegated to a privileged position *vis à vis* all other cultural systems; the same explanatory theories and tools of analysis that apply to them *mutatis mutandis* apply to it. For some, conditioned to homiletic interpretations of doctrine and ritual, this scientific approach to the study of religion is often upsetting. Since religion is concerned with the "spiritual" and the "sacred" dimensions of existence, the normal opposition to the so-called reductionism of scientific explanation is understandably intensified when it (religion) is the subject of explanation. That this opposition is understandable does not, however, render it valid; in both cases, the criticism tends to be misplaced.

The fact that scientific biology discovers the ultimate origin of life in the primordial slime does not mean that man *is* slime. By the same token, to attribute part of the roots of a work of art to some neurotic conflict in the artist does not mean that a painting *is* a neurosis. The same logic holds in the case of religion. Interpreting belief in some religious doctrine by reference to some structurally induced experience, or explaining the performance of a religious ritual as the resolution of a childhood conflict is not to say that the doctrine *is* an element of social structure or that the ritual actor *is* a child. It is to say, however, that religious phenomena, like the above-mentioned biological or artistic phenomena, are to be explained by reference to variables which, phylogenetically and/or ontogenetically, are prior to the phenomenon to be explained.

With the Psalmist one can agree that man is little lower than the angels, without denying that to explain how he arrived at that exalted position we must turn to the mundane concepts of evolution and microbiology. With the poet we can celebrate the beauty and fragrance of a flower and yet recognize that in order to explain these qualities we must look to such uninspiring variables as soil and fertilizer. In religion too there is a division of labor between homiletics and science, between uplift and edification on the one hand, and dissection and analysis on the other. Both are necessary. And it is only when these very different jobs and their rather distinctive cultural products are confused—as when the root of a plant is confused with its flower—that there is trouble.

In order to avoid such trouble I wish to state at the outset that this is a scientific treatise, not a homiletic tract. As such its interpretations are intentionally and explicitly "reductionistic." It attempts to understand a religious system by looking for the nonreligious variables which, according to the theory that informs the entire volume, may have brought it into being, and which may perhaps account for its persistence and change. Thus, its interpretations are "reductionistic" not in the sense of reducing *religion*, but rather in reducing its *explanation*, to structural, psychological, and other antecedent variables.

I mention this not only to indicate my own position—my bias, if you will—concerning the epistemological status of religion in the science of culture, but also to indicate the equal status of Buddhism in my approach to the comparative study of religion. Since this volume is devoted to an analysis of Buddhism—rather than, say, Christianity or Judaism—I wish to emphasize that its explanations of Buddhism are not intended as uniquely applicable to that religion—nor, for that matter, to religion in general. Rather, they reflect my theoretical position concerning the explanation of any religion—or of any other cultural system. I stress this point because some (mostly humanistic) reviewers of my *Burmese Supernaturalism* objected to its putative lack of sympathy for the Burmese and its perception of their beliefs as "superstitions" when, in fact, both claims are false. Precisely the same theory employed for the explanation of Burmese animism would have been used to explain American Protestantism, German Catholicism, or Polish Judaism had I been writing about those religions. (And in none of these cases do the explanations imply disparagement of religion, any more than an explanation of a flower by reference to its roots implies disparagement of the flower, or of its fragrance and beauty.)

If this sounds like an *apologia pro libro suo*, it is intended not so much to disarm my humanistic critics as to apologize to my Burmese (and other Buddhist) readers for any unintentional anger I may cause them. They may nevertheless take sharp issue, as indeed I would expect them to, with some of my secularist interpretations of phenomena which for them are sacred. Still, I hope these comments will convince them that in doing so I mean no disrespect to them or to Buddhism. I was drawn to Burma and to Buddhism because of my great admiration for the latter and respect for the former, and my admiration and respect, have alike increased with time and direct acquaintance. Lest, however, some misunderstanding remains, I should like to make my position even more explicit.

When I interpret the Burmese belief in a particular Buddhist doctrine as having the function, say, of resolving some intrapsychic conflict, it is not because I believe that the conflict is uniquely Burmese or that Buddhist doctrine alone is used in this manner. Rather, it is because I view all people as having such conflicts, and elements of all religions as being used in this manner, that I believe this view to be valid for the Burmese and Buddhism as well. Similarly, when I view Buddhist monasticism as a means for satisfying unconscious needs developed in childhood, it is not because I believe that only the Buddhist clergy have such needs or that the Buddhist monastery is especially a means for institutionalized regression. Rather, it is because I believe that all human beings have unconscious needs, and that all religions—indeed, all cultural and social systems—contain cognitive patterns and social roles which, *inter alia*, are used for their sublimation. On a different level, when I view Burmese Buddhism as a compromise between the requirements of normative Buddhism and the demands of Burmese personality, it is because I view all the great religions as products of the same conflicting forces.

If, then, these interpretations may be taken by some to mean that Buddhism and the Burmese are especially characterized by these attributes and relationships, it is because other studies of religion, indifferent or opposed to the view of society and culture underlying this volume, ignore many of the psychological variables and processes which are attended to here. It is necessary, therefore, to make this view explicit. For me society and culture are not only the producers (as many social scientists would have it), but they are also the products, of human cognitive orientations and motivational dispositions. Which is to say that they are the products of psychobiological organisms with desires and beliefs, drives and emotions, aspirations and tensions; of creatures of flesh and blood who laugh and cry, suffer and enjoy, who have dreams and frustrations, ideals and fears; of human beings with aspirations and anxieties, depressions and elations, conflicts and goals. Viewed in this manner, social and cultural systems represent (among other things) complex historical attempts to deal with these sets of cognitive and affective needs. Complex, not only because of the frequent incompatibility among the components of these sets, but because their incompatibility is, to a very significant extent, created by the social and cultural systems designed to deal with them. Complex, therefore, because the very systems which render many of these needs and cognitions forbidden and shameful, provide them with (disguised) means for expression and satisfaction.

Inevitably, of course, there is a relationship between theory and explanation in scientific research. The theory guides the data collection in that it determines which facts, among the infinite welter, are to be considered as evidential—i.e., are to be collected as data; and their explanation, in turn, is derived from the same theory by which they were selected. Since, then, the theory delineated above guided my field research in Burma, it is understandable that the explanations found in this volume have reference to antecedent structural and psychological variables, interpreted especially in terms of personal drives and cultural goals, of personal conflict and the cultural resolution of conflict.

With this description of research methods and intellectual style, we may turn at last to the study itself, beginning with Buddhist ideology. After outlining nibbanic Buddhism, I shall proceed to a more detailed account of the other ideological systems which have spun off from it.

II

BUDDHISM
AS AN IDEOLOGICAL SYSTEM

CHAPTER 2

Nibbanic Buddhism: A Religion of Radical Salvation

To attempt to summarize the main doctrines of normative Buddhism in one brief chapter is not only presumptuous, but since Buddhism is a luxuriant forest, it is almost impossible to identify all the main paths by which it might be traversed. Since different scholars would map the terrain rather differently, the following sketch will no doubt evoke some dissent concerning many of its details. Still, based as it is on the important sources (primary and secondary) of *Theravāda* Buddhism, as well as discussions with numerous scholarly monks in Burma, the major outlines will probably be acceptable to most scholars. It should be added that if certain doctrines have been unduly emphasized and others unduly slighted, it is usually because our theoretical interest in the contrapuntal relationship between textual and Burmese Buddhism demands this kind of shading.

The Founder: The Buddha

Buddhism is the Path to Deliverance taught by a Buddha, i.e., a Supremely Enlightened one. In every world cycle *(kappa)* there are many Buddhas, each of whom teaches the identical Path. The last Buddha, the twenty-seventh in the series of twenty-eight in this world cycle, was born as Siddartha Gautama, an Indian prince of the sixth century B.C. Having discovered the means by which Deliverance is achieved, he—like all Supreme Buddhas—delayed his own Deliverance till he could share his gnosis *(bodhi)* with his disciples. He taught his message for forty years before he died and attained complete salvation *(parinibbāna).* Neither God nor Savior, this man Gautama is yet the towering—indeed, the only—figure in Buddhist history and Buddhist thought. As Hall (1903:127) has observed,

> The Buddha stands alone. Of Maya his mother, of Yathodaya his wife, of Rahoula his son, of his great disciple Thariputra, of his dearest disciple and brother Ananda, you see nothing. There are no saints in Buddhism at all, only the great teacher, he who saw the light. Surely this is a curious thing, that from the time of the prince to now, two thousand four hundred years, no one has arisen to be worthy of mention or record beside him. There is only one man holy to Buddhism—Gautama the Buddha.

It is not surprising, then, that in Burmese, as in English, it is by His title that His religion is named: in Burmese, Buddhism is referred to alternatively as *Boukta ba-tha* (the worship of the Buddha) or *Boukta Tha-thana* (the doctrine of the Buddha).

Nevertheless, and despite the fact that it was He who discovered the Path to Liberation, the Buddha is conceived in normative *Theravāda* tradition not as God, but as a human being. To be sure, the Mahayanist trinitarian conception of the Buddha—a human being, a Spiritual Principle, and a Glorified Body—elevates Him, in His aspect of Glorified Body, to the status of Godhood in some, at least, of the *Mahāyāna* sects (cf. Conze 1953:34 ff). But this conception has no place in the *Theravāda* tradition. In the *Theravāda* texts, as Suzuki has observed, sermons are

> delivered by the Buddha as a rule in such a natural and plain language as to make the reader feel the presence of the teacher, fatherly-hearted and philosophically serene; while in the latter [*Mahāyāna*] generally we have a mysterious, transcendent figure, more celestial, and even demoniac, and this mystical central character performing some supernatural feats. . . . [Suzuki 1963:242]

In the *Theravāda* tradition, the Buddha is not a god either in the Hindu-Buddhist or in the Judaeo-Christian sense of the term. He is superior to all the gods in the Hindu-Buddhist sense of "god" *(deva)*—a supernatural being who, although possessing great power and enjoying great bliss, is nevertheless still subject to the universal law of rebirth—for He had achieved Liberation, whereas they, like all beings in the Wheel of Rebirth, must follow in His path if they are to achieve that goal. Nor is He a god in the Judaeo-Christian sense, for the Buddha is neither a Savior—in *Theravāda* Buddhism, as we shall see, man must save himself—nor is He alive. Like everything else in the Wheel of Existence *(saṃsāra)* the Buddha too was subject to the law of impermanence; like all sentient creatures, He, too, had to die. Consoling His disciple, Ānanda, who is grieving for His impending death, the Buddha remonstrates with him:

> How, then, Ânanda, can this [that I should not die] be possible—whereas anything whatever born, brought into being, and organized, contains within itself the inherent necessity of dissolution—how, then, can this be possible, that such a being should not be dissolved? No such condition can exist. [*Mahâ Parinibbâna Suttanta* v, 13-14, in *Dialogues of the Buddha,* Pt. II, p. 159]

Like Christ, then, the Buddha too died, but unlike Christ He was not resurrected. To be sure, He entered nirvana upon His death, but whatever the normative conception of nirvana might be—and, as we shall see, the meaning of this concept is disputed—it is a state to which "life," as that term is ordinarily understood, does not apply. For all practical purposes the Buddha is not alive, and one who is not alive cannot save.[1]

Although a human being, the Buddha was far from an ordinary mortal. He not only attained nirvana—an extraordinary achievement in itself—but (something which is even more unusual) achieved Buddhahood.[2] The rarity of this achievement may be gauged by the fact that in our world epoch only three other persons have succeeded in achieving that state. To measure it differently, it required four hundred million aeons of rebirths for Gautama to achieve those Ten Perfections *(pāramitās)* which are requisite for Buddhahood. These are qualities which in an imperfect form are found among many, if not most, men; only in Buddhas, however, do they reach perfection.[3] They include generosity *(dāna)*, even to the point of self-sacrifice, morality *(sila)*, renunciation *(nekkhamma)*, wisdom *(paññā)*, energy *(viriya)*, forbearance *(khanti)*, truthfulness *(sacca)*, resoluteness *(adhitthāna)*, loving-kindness *(mettā)*, and equanimity *(upekkhā)*.[4] In addition to these Ten Perfections requisite to Buddhahood, a Buddha possesses Nine Virtues *(guṇas)* as a result of attaining Buddhahood. He is a saint, supremely enlightened, proficient in knowledge and conduct, one who fares well (to ultimate Deliverance), world-knower, peerless driver of men to be tamed, teacher of gods and of men, enlightened, the Blessed One.[5]

[1]The question of the "existence" of a Buddha after His death is one which the Buddha Gautama refused to answer. Whether He exists, or does not exist, or both exists and does not exist, is, according to the Buddha, irrelevant to the salvation quest; therefore the answer to the question ". . . is not revealed by the Exalted One." (*Pāsādika Suttanta*, 30-31, in *Dialogues of the Buddha*, Part III, pp. 128-29.) Although agreeing that He is not a Savior, only some Burmese agree, as we shall see, that He is not alive.

[2]Hence, He is addressed neither by His proper name (Siddhartha) nor by His family name (Gautama), although the latter, when attached to "Buddha," may be used in reference, as when the Burmese speak of *Boukta Gautama*, the Buddha Gautama, thereby distinguishing Him from the three previous Buddhas of our world epoch. Typically, however, He is referred to as the Lord Buddha (*Boukta hpaya:* in Burmese), and is addressed as Lord *(Hpaya:)*. "Lord" is used not in the sense of god, but in the sense of royalty. Thus, in traditional Burma, kings were addressed as *hpaya:*—as were on occasion British officers in the colonial period. Since *hpaya:* is also the term for pagoda, as well as for monk, it would seem that its underlying meaning involves "sacred," "power," and so on.

[3]It is of interest to compare these Theravadist *pāramitās* with those found in *Mahāyāna* Buddhism. Cf. Suzuki 1963: 321-22, and Basham 1954: 276.

[4]This list of perfections is exceedingly important, both morally and ritually, in contemporary Burma. In sermons and in speeches, monks and politicians exhort their listeners to emulate any or all of these perfections and praise historical figures for having exemplified them, at least to some degree. These are the qualities, so audiences are reminded, which in their nonperfected form are requisites both for Buddhist life and for civil society.

[5]For an authoritative analysis of each of these Virtues, see Buddhaghosa's *Visuddhi-magga*, VII *(The Path of Purity)*.

These Virtues (Burmese, *goung:do)* are recited in Burma when saying the rosary, and (as

If, although an extraordinary being, the Buddha is neither God nor Savior, what function if any does he carry out in the lives of men? The answer, in the words of the *Dhammapada* (xx, 276), is that He is like a signpost which shows the Way (to salvation). This too is the interpretation of the towering Buddhaghosa (5th century) in his authoritative albeit post-canonical manual, the *Visuddhi-magga (The Path of Purity)*. The Pali canon, of course, is not all of one piece, and Buddhaghosa's opponents no doubt could have compiled a manual expressing a different interpretation of the canonical point of view.[6] Still, Buddhaghosa's interpretation certainly seems to represent the dominant scriptural view. The Buddha, as the following representative scriptural passages indicate, is the Way, not the Savior.

> Live as islands unto yourselves, bretheren, as refuges unto yourselves, take none other as your refuge, live with the Norm [*Dhamma*] as your island, with the Norm as your refuge, take none other as your refuge. [*Cakkavatti Sīhanāda Suttanta*, 27, in *Dialogues of the Buddha*, Pt. III, p. 74]

> Therefore, O Ānanda, be ye lamps unto yourselves. Be ye a refuge to yourselves. Betake yourselves to no external refuge. Hold fast to the Truth as a lamp. Hold fast as a refuge to the Truth. Look not for refuge to anyone besides yourselves. [*Mahâ Parinibbâna Suttanta, II, 26, in Dialogues of the Buddha*, Pt. II, p. 108]

---

will be noted in Chapter 10) their utterance in situations of danger possesses powerful magical efficacy.

[6]Early Buddhism, it must be remembered, represented only one of two types of rebellion against the prevailing (Vedic) sacrificial religion of ancient India. One type emphasized *bhakti*, or devotion to a god; the other emphasized *magga*, or the Way (to Deliverance). As Dutt (1962:180) has put it:

> Bhakti is a *sine qua non* in all religions that are "religions of grace". Religions of this type are soteriological: they postulate a Saviour. To him it is left to grant the fruits of a man's work and endeavour—to bestow on the devotee the ultimate salvation. The Saviour must be propitiated, not by holy living alone, but by refuge *(Śaraṇa)* being sought in him, by adoration *(Vandanā)*, prayer and supplication *(Stava* and *Stuti)* and by ritual worship *(Pūjā)*.
>
> Over against these "religions of grace", there are faiths and creeds in which a Saviour has no place. The salvation, the goal of religious life, . . . [is] not a gift but an attainment to be reached by steadily progressing stage-to-stage along a Way *(Magga)*.

Although the latter type is preponderant in *Theravāda* Buddhism, both types find expression in the texts, as the appearance of both *saddhā* (Sanskrit, *śraddhā*) and *bhatti* (Sanskrit, *bhakti*) testifies. The former term implies

> a firm faith and conviction that the Way of Dhamma (the *Magga*) must lead one assuredly to the goal of *Nibbāna* [Nirvana]. The term *Bhakti* is of rare occurrence in it and has nowhere the implications and nuances that belong to its use in Mahayanist as well as in non-Buddhist scripture. Yet the two trends in the "psychology of religion" that are typified by *Śraddhā* and *Bhakti* appear side by side even in *Theravāda* Buddhism. Along with the idea of volitional self-effort appears also the idea of a Saviour who has to be propitiated and in whom refuge *(Śaraṇa)* is sought. [*Ibid.*:181]

Hinder not yourselves, Ānanda, by honouring the remains of the Tathāgata [Buddha]. Be zealous, I beseech you, Ānanda, in your own behalf! Devote yourselves to your own good! Be earnest, be zealous, be intent on your own good! [*Ibid.: v, 10, in Dialogues of the Buddha,* Pt. II, p. 154]

Behold now, bretheren, I exhort you, saying:—"Decay is inherent in all component things! Work out your salvation with diligence!" [*Ibid.:* vi, 7, in *Dialogues of the Buddha,* Pt. II, p. 173]

The above verses reflect not only the dominant conception of the Buddha found in the *Theravāda* canon, but the attitude of the typical Burman as well. On this dimension the Burmese conception is, for the most part, normative. The following anecdote expresses this normative conception very well.

When Bishop Titcomb, the first Anglican Bishop of Rangoon, went out to Burma in 1877 he was anxious to obtain knowledge at first hand as to the fundamental tenets of Buddhism. Seeing a yellow-robed "religious" performing his devotions at the great golden pagoda he asked him, through an interpreter, to whom he was praying, and what he was praying for. The reply promptly given was, "I am praying to nobody, and for nothing." [Nisbet 1901: Vol. 2, 89]

But one need not rely on old anecdotes. A contemporary village monk expressed the same view: "Since the Buddha is dead, only His *Dhamma* (Teaching) is left. The *Dhamma* is our god." Similarly, the following quotation from a Burmese layman is typical (albeit a more sophisticated expression) of the lay attitudes found in a Burmese village. When I asked him, as I asked the other villagers, whether one could achieve nirvana by praying to the Buddha, he replied:

If one's deeds are good and if one has a good mind the consequences will be good. There is no agent that can help; you can rely only on yourself [by acquiring merit] to fulfill your wish. Mind is crucial. Even the Buddha cannot take you to nirvana or send you to hell. There is mind and there are acts—there is no other agent. Mind is the most important. Everything is the result of mind. You can rely on yourself. No one can help you, either for good or for evil. You can only help yourself. All the myriads of Buddhas, with all their compassion, cannot save you from misery. You can only save yourself.

To sum up, then, the preponderant view concerning the Buddha in normative Buddhism (a view which is shared by almost all Burmese) is that, having attained nirvana, He is no longer alive, in any sense at least in which He can serve as a Savior. He shows the Way to, but is not the agent of, salvation. This being so, Buddhism as a salvation religion is not so much concerned with the Buddha as with His Way, i.e., His message of salvation. To this message we must now turn.

The Promise: Deliverance from Suffering

The Premise: Life Is Suffering

All salvation religions share a common message: "Follow this path so that you may obtain deliverance." They differ in (among other things) what they promise deliverance *from.* Buddhism promises deliverance from suffering. Suffering, for Buddhism, is one of the three inevitable attributes of sentient existence which, though distinct from its other two attributes—impermanence and egolessness—is related to them.

According to Buddhism, *everything* is impermanent *(anicca).* Creation and dissolution are constant and universal processes, extending from the microscopic level, where the constituent atoms of existence are in a permanent state of flux, arising and passing away, to the macroscopic level—empires rise and decay, the entire universe comes into being and passes out of existence.

What is true of existence in general is also true of sentient existence. Hinduism, Buddhism's parent religion, postulates permanence at both the cosmic and personal levels. At the cosmic level, Brahman, the ground of existence, underlies the constant flux of appearance; at the personal level the soul, or *ātman,* is the unchanging reality underlying the changing body. The soul not only remains changeless, but in some ultimate sense is identical with Brahman. When the body dies, the soul survives, finding a new abode in a newly formed body. In opposition to Hinduism, Buddhism, however, not only denies the existence of a permanent ground of being underlying the universal cosmic flux, but also denies the existence of a soul, ego, or self. Hence, opposing the doctrine of *ātman,* Buddhism teaches the doctrine of *anattā,* the doctrine of nonself. For Buddhism the impermanent body is not survived by a permanent self or soul—because there is no self or soul to survive. According to Buddhism a person consists of five components or "heaps" *(khandhās),* viz., matter, feeling, perceptions, impulses, and consciousness. These heaps, and these alone, comprise a human being; and like everything else in the universe they are in constant flux. The belief that over and above these heaps there is some unchanging or permanent entity comprising a self or an ego is an illusion, which must be destroyed if one is to achieve Liberation.[7]

Of the three attributes of being, that of nonself is the least understood and least accepted among the Burmese. To be sure, there are some exceptions to this generalization, as the following quotation from a member of my blue-ribbon sample indicates.

[7]The classical explication of the *anattā* doctrine is found in *The Questions of King Milinda,* II, 1, 1.

> When you meditate you know that there is no body, that it merely consists of numerous cells, constantly coming into being and disintegrating . . . Through meditation one achieves wisdom, and through wisdom one knows that the constituents of being are wind, water, fire, and air. And only then can one be freed of desire. If nothing is permanent, then you too are impermanent, you are nothing. And if you know that you are nothing, you then realize that the other too is nothing, that both of you are null. Hence, like an *arahant* [saint] you have no desire for anything, no desire for property, or for sexual intercourse. . . . The statement, "this is my paper, this is my pencil," is nonsense, because there is no paper, there is no pencil; there is no me; there is nothing. Take a cup of tea: a cup consists of elements, the tea consists of elements. It only looks like a cup, or like tea. So, too, there are no creatures; there are only combinations of elements.

Statements of this kind, however, are rare. On the doctrinal level, most Burmese confuse the nonself doctrine with the doctrine of impermanence —this at least was the tendency of the respondents in my sample. But on the existential level they tend to repudiate the belief in such a notion. We shall examine their attitudes in the next chapter.

Sentient existence is characterized not only by impermanence and the absence of self, but by suffering *(dukkha),* and from the perspective of Buddhist religion (in contrast to Buddhist philosophy) this is its most important characteristic. That life entails suffering is an obvious and, when stated in that form, trivial observation: everyone has experienced the frustration of ambition, the death of a loved one, the pains of illness. But the truth of suffering, the first of Buddhism's Four Noble Truths, is saved from triviality by its radical claim that life not only entails suffering, but *is* suffering. This claim is related to and follows from the other two attributes of existence. If everything is impermanent, suffering is the inevitable consequence of all experience, both pleasurable and nonpleasurable, since it then results equally from attainment of one's desires or from their frustration. Consider: everything being impermanent, one achieves a desired object only to lose it—which leads to suffering; or one worries about the possibility of losing it—which also leads to suffering. Moreover, if the self, too, is no more permanent than anything else—if it, too, is in a constant flux—one is never content with what one has. Having attained the object of desire, one immediately longs to satisfy yet another desire which, whether attained or unattained, is the cause of still more suffering. In the words of the Buddha, as found in the famous *Dhammacakkappavattana Sutta*

> Birth is attended with pain, decay is painful, disease is painful, death is painful. Union with the unpleasant is painful, painful is separation from the pleasant; and any craving that is unsatisfied, that too is painful. In brief, the five aggregates [*khandhā*] which spring from attachment are painful. [Tr. in *Buddhist Suttas,* p. 148.]

Although this radical claim of normative Buddhism is held, as we shall see in the next chapter, by only a minority of Burmese laymen, it is the central formal belief of a large percentage of Burmese monks. As they put it, not only are some forms of suffering unavoidable, but everything one does is caught up in suffering. Eating is suffering, and not eating is suffering; sleeping is suffering, and not sleeping is suffering; standing is suffering, and sitting is also suffering. To be sure, they admit, most people view some of these (and many other) activities as pleasurable, but this illusory belief is easily dispelled through the practice of Buddhist meditation. Moreover, even granting that certain experiences are truly pleasurable, this pleasure cannot compensate for the four inevitable and universal conditions of suffering postulated by Buddhism: birth,[8] illness, old age, and death. These, no living creature, regardless of his abode or station, can avoid.

Suffering, to conclude, is inescapable. So long as there is life there is desire (*taṇhā;* literally, thirst), and so long as there is desire there will be suffering. For desire leads to craving for what one does not have and to clinging to what one does have, and both conditions produce that constant state of restlessness and discontent which is suffering. This, at least, is the message of the second of Buddhism's Four Noble Truths. As the *Dhammacakkappavattana Sutta* expresses it:

> Verily, it [the cause of suffering] is that thirst (or craving), causing the renewal of existence, accompanied by sensual delight, seeking satisfaction now here, now there—that is to say, the craving for the gratification of the passions, or the craving for a (future) life, or the craving for success (in the present life). [*Ibid.*]

The Aim: Release from Rebirth

The Noble Truth of Suffering is not merely one of the doctrines of Buddhism; it is its central doctrine. Unlike some salvation religions (Christianity, for example), in which sin is the primary concern, the primary concern of Buddhism is not with sin, but with suffering. This is not (as some people claim) because sin does not exist for Buddhism. Lying, stealing, killing, and so on—all these and many more are Buddhist sins; in the Buddhist lexicon they are acts of demerit *(akusala).* The difference is that, although Buddhism recognizes the existence of sin, unlike Christianity it does not see it as inevitable. All human beings have the capacity to become saints *(arahant),* and thus sinless. For Buddhism, it is not sin but suffering

[8]Curiously, it is not so much birth (which the Buddha Himself mentions) as gestation—"being in the mother's womb"—that some Burmese stress. Nirvana, said one monk, means that "you will never have to enter a womb again." What does this intrauterine suffering consist of? Various informants suggest the following: remaining for nine months in the same position; suffering from hot or cold food eaten by the mother; the awkward fetal position; suffering from the mother's movements—if she bends over, the fetus is in pain—and so on.

that is inevitable. Just as Christianity teaches that any being, however pure, remains in the sight of God a miserable sinner, so Buddhism teaches that any being (even a god), however blissful, cannot escape suffering.

If—unlike some salvation religions, such as Judaism—Buddhism pronounces life to be suffering; nevertheless—unlike other salvation religions, such as Hinduism—it attaches no spiritual value to suffering. On the contrary, for Buddhism suffering is an evil; it is something to be avoided rather than accepted, let alone (as in certain forms of ascetic Hinduism and Christianity) pursued. For Buddhism it is as self-evident that man *should* avoid suffering as it is that he might *wish* to avoid suffering. This being so, the soteriological message of Buddhism is inescapable. Just as for Christianity, in which sin is an inevitable element of existence, salvation consists in salvation *from sin*, so for Buddhism—in which suffering is the inevitable element of existence—salvation consists in salvation *from suffering*. The message of the Buddha is "suffering and release from suffering."

Now, if salvation consists in deliverance from suffering, the means to its achievement would seem to be obvious. For, if suffering is caused by desire, deliverance should be achieved either by the elimination of desire or by the cessation of life. Let us examine each in turn.

That suffering can be eliminated by the elimination of desire is, indeed, the third of the Four Noble Truths. To eliminate suffering one must extinguish desire; that is, one must achieve an attitude of detachment *(upekkhā)* to all things, neither craving that which one does not have, nor clinging to that which one does have. As the Buddha puts it:

> Now this, O Bhikkhus [monks] is the noble truth concerning the destruction of suffering.
>
> Verily, it is the destruction, in which no passion remains, of this very thirst; the laying aside of, the being free from, the harboring no longer of this thirst. [*Ibid.*: 149]

This is the message, not only of scriptural Buddhism but of its contemporary monastic spokesmen in Burma. "The point of Buddhist discipline," said one monk, "is the extinction of the fire, the fire of craving." Or, as another monk put it, "Most persons are slaves of desire; therefore, they have no peace; they continue to suffer. Desire and contentment are in constant struggle; they are mutual enemies. Whatever the act, it is the result of desire. People are slaves to things. To achieve peace, one must extinguish desire." In answer to my query, still another monk said that he had seen his family only three times in fifteen years; he has cultivated an attitude of detachment toward them. "If I were to visit them and find that they are rich, I would want to enjoy their wealth. If they were poor, I would be saddened. Therefore, it is best to remain detached both physically and emotionally." This attitude is exemplified in the behaviour of an ancient monk described by Eliot (1921:160).

> A monk was meditating under a tree when his former wife came and laid his child before him, saying: "Here, monk, is your little son, nourish me and nourish him." The monk took no notice and sent her away. The Buddha, seeing this, said "He feels no pleasure when she comes, no sorrow when she goes: him I call a true Brahman released from passion."[9]

Genuine detachment (hence the avoidance of suffering) is achieved by the realization of the truth of nonself. Aging is suffering, illness is suffering, death is suffering, because—but only because—they are (falsely) viewed as *my* illness, *my* aging, *my* death, and so on. But if there is no self—if, that is, the above phenomena are not related to an *I*, a *me*, a *mine*, they can entail no suffering; they are, instead, affectively neutral bodily changes. In short, suffering is engendered by the delusion of selfhood. By overcoming this delusion, by realizing that everything is empty *(suññatā)* of self or of anything belonging to self, one destroys clinging and craving and hence suffering.

From this discussion it might seem that the third Noble Truth is the message of a naturalistic psychology, viz., since suffering is caused by the frustration of desire, the cessation of suffering can be achieved by the extinction of desire. And this is certainly the claim of those, both in the East and in the West, who would convince Western intellectuals that the message of Buddhism is primarily a psychological message, one, moreover, which is cast in a modern naturalistic idiom. But this claim is at best a half truth; for when Buddhism asserts that suffering can be eliminated only by the extinction of desire, it is making primarily an ontological (rather than a merely psychological) assertion.

If the message of the third Noble Truth were primarily psychological, then if release from suffering were not achieved during one's lifetime (by the extinction of desire), it would certainly be achieved by death; and since everyone dies, everyone would automatically and inevitably achieve salvation. It would seem, then, that having accepted the truth of suffering, the

[9]This attitude is remarkably reminiscent of Jesus' attitude to his family. Thus,

> He that loveth father or mother more than me, is not worthy of me; and he that loveth son or daughter more than me, is not worthy of me. [*Matthew* 10:37]

Similarly, when He was informed that His mother and brothers wished to speak with Him, He answered:

> Who is my mother? and who are my brethren?
> And he stretched forth his hand toward his disciples, and said, Behold my mother and my brethren!
> For whosoever shall do the will of my Father which is in heaven, the same is my brother, and sister, and mother. [*Matthew* 12:46-50—see also *Mark* 3:31-35.]

problem for the Buddhist who has failed to extinguish his desires is to decide whether he should hasten his deliverance by suicide or defer it until his natural death. This conclusion would be inescapable if death were in fact the end of one's existence. But Buddhism, like its parent religion, Hinduism, denies this (for many of us) seemingly obvious fact. For Buddhism, death is not the cessation of existence; it is merely the cessation of one among many lives, past and future, which constitute one's total existence. Although it marks the end of this life, death is also the beginning of a new life; and, since every form of life is suffering, death does not signal deliverance from suffering, but rather its rebirth. Thus to obtain release from suffering it is necessary not only to overcome suffering in this life, but to be delivered from the entire Wheel of Existence.

The Wheel of Existence, or the realm of rebirth *(saṃsāra),* comprises thirty-one separate abodes *(loka)* or planes of existence. Twenty-seven of these constitute the "fortunate" planes. These include the twenty-six abodes of the gods *(deva)*[10] and the human abode. The four remaining planes of existence are known as the "states of woe." Proceeding from the least to the most unpleasant, these include the planes of animals, demons, ghosts, and hell. (The tortures found in the eight Buddhist hells are reminiscent of the Christian hell, except for their being—since everything according to Buddhism is impermanent—of temporary duration.)[11] Depending on one's karma (see below), rebirth may occur in any of these thirty-one abodes, and any individual will probably have been reborn in all of them as he wanders, over countless aeons of time, from rebirth to rebirth. In short, rebirth for Buddhism is as ineluctable a fact of existence as birth; indeed, if there were no rebirth, how could there be birth?

Although a religious doctrine,[12] rebirth is not so much an article of faith in Buddhism as an obvious fact of nature; for Burmese Buddhists, for exam-

[10]Proceeding from the most blissful, there are four abodes of *brahma deva,* entirely spiritual, or formless *(arūpa)* beings; sixteen abodes of yet another group of the same *deva,* who maintain a tenuous corporality or form *(rūpa);* and six planes of *sammā deva,* corporeal *deva* who enjoy countless sensuous delights.

[11]For an extended discussion of these thirty-one abodes, cf. Bigandet 1912: Vol. 2, pp. 217-27; La Vallée Poussin 1911; Sangermano 1893: chs. 2-4; Waddell 1911.

[12]From a religious point of view rebirth is the pivotal Buddhist doctrine for, as we have already observed, without rebirth Deliverance would be achieved inevitably and automatically by the simple act of death. In a sense, therefore, rebirth is one of the few dogmas in this singularly undogmatic religion. Indeed, if Burma can be taken as representative of contemporary *Theravāda* societies, it may be said that Buddhist ecclesiastical authority not only views the doctrine of rebirth as a central dogma, but places the same importance on the ancillary belief that human rebirth can occur in any of the thirty-one realms of existence. Thus, a few years ago a Burmese monk, Shin Okkahta, published a highly controversial book, *Lu-Thei Lu-Hpyit,* in which he argued that the rebirth of a human being cannot occur in any realm lower than the human; having already attained the latter status, one might be reborn in a higher realm, but not in any of the four lower realms. After labeling this book as a "menace against the Buddhist religion" and a "sacrilegious attack on Buddhism," the executive committee of the All-Burma Abbots' Association voted to excommunicate Shin Okkahta. (C.f. *The* [Rangoon] *Nation,* May 2, 1963.)

ple, the evidence for rebirth is incontestable. Evidence aside, however, this doctrine is crucial for Buddhism, for it is only within the framework of rebirth that the Four Noble Truths of Buddhism assume their full soteriological significance. Although rebirth may take place in all thirty-one planes of existence, in none of them, including the most blissful of the heavens, can one escape from suffering, for *saṃsāra,* the realm of rebirth, is everywhere the realm of suffering. This is the real message of the first of the Four Noble Truths, and the reason that Buddhism has been characterized as a "pessimistic" religion. Since, therefore, every form of life in all thirty-one planes of existence is suffering, deliverance from suffering can only be achieved by release from the Wheel of Existence, i.e., from the countless rounds of rebirths.

But if rebirth is an ineluctable fact of nature, if birth follows death as predictably as death follows birth, how is it ever possible to obtain release from suffering? This is the basic question with which the Buddha is concerned, and this is the question answered by the second and third of the Four Noble Truths. Since all phenomena are subject to the law of cause and effect, it is possible to bring an end to the cycle of rebirth—hence to the persistence of suffering—by uprooting its cause. What, then, is its cause? The cause of rebirth is desire, or *taṇhā;* rebirth is caused by clinging to one's present existence and craving for a future one. The cycle of rebirth can be brought to an end by destroying the desire for all existence.

The Buddhist message then, as I have said, is not simply a psychological message, i.e., that desire is the cause of suffering because unsatisfied desire produces frustration. It does contain such a message to be sure; but more importantly, it is an eschatological message. Desire is the cause of suffering because desire is the cause of rebirth; and the extinction of desire leads to deliverance from suffering because it signals release from the Wheel of Rebirth.

Although, given its premise, the logic of this message is unexceptionable (for if desire causes rebirth, and rebirth is suffering, it follows that the cessation of rebirth marks the extinction of suffering), its premise demands explication: How *is* rebirth caused by desire? To answer this question we must turn to still another central doctrine of Buddhism, the doctrine of karma.

The Means: Extinction of Karma

Just as the physical universe is governed by the law of action and reaction, so the moral universe is governed by the law of karma *(kamma),* i.e., the law of action and retribution. Every volitional act *(kamma),* if instigated by desire, produces an appropriate consequence, desirable or undesirable, for the actor. There are two types of volitional acts: the morally good *(kusala)* and the morally bad *(akusala).* If action is instigated by desire, either for the act or for its consequence, then, if the act is morally good, it produces merit *(puñña)* for the actor; if morally bad, it produces demerit *(apuñña)* for him. According, then, to the law of karmic retribution, the fruit *(vipāka)* of meritorious action will yield pleasant, the fruit of demeritorious action, unpleasant consequences for the actor. In either case, if these karmic consequences cannot work themselves out within the compass of one life, they must then be worked out in successive lives; and in cases of exceptionally meritorious or demeritorious action, it may require many lives before full recompense is completed (or, as Buddhists say, "before the fruit [of action] is ripened"). In short, so long as action bears fruit there will be rebirth; and since desire is the cause of fruit-bearing action, it is the cause of rebirth. This causal chain, leading from desire to rebirth, can be delineated in the following diagram.

FIG. 1

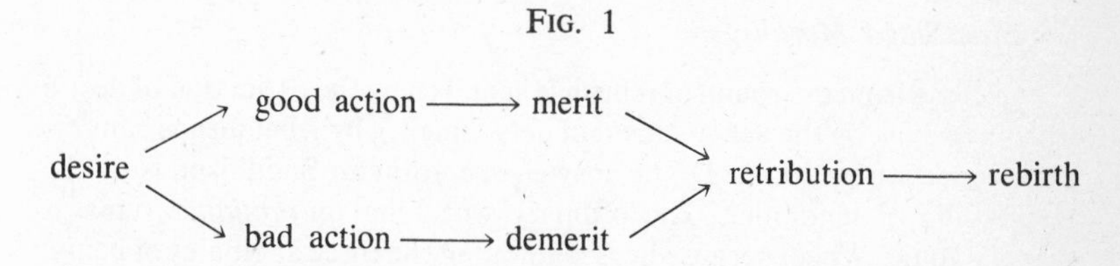

It will be observed that rebirth takes place as long as the law of karma is operative, i.e., as long as volitional action produces karmic formations—those consequences of action (merit and demerit) which require retribution. But not all action produces consequences. The law of karma applies only to those volitional acts which are instigated by desire; they, and they alone, bear fruit in this and future lines. For, according to Buddhism, it is the intent *(cetanā)* behind an act rather than the act itself which bears fruit. As the *Dhammapada* (I, 2) puts it: "All that we are is the result of what we have thought: it is founded on our thoughts, it is made up of our thoughts." An act, although volitional, which is performed without the intention of satisfying desire, produces no karmic consequence. Hence, the only way to destroy the fruits of action—and thereby prevent rebirth—is to destroy its roots, i.e., to extinguish desire. This has two effects. First, although the extinction of desire does not lead to the extinction of all action, it does lead (for reasons which are not clear) to the extinction of morally bad action, and therefore to the cessation of additional demerit. Second, although morally good action is not extinguished, it is performed in a state of emotional detachment *(upekkhā)*, which, since it is not concerned with satisfying desire, produces no merit. Creating neither merit nor demerit, desireless action bears no fruit (i.e., requires no retribution), either in this or in future births. This being so, the causal chain leading from desire to rebirth is broken, as the following diagram shows.

FIG. 2

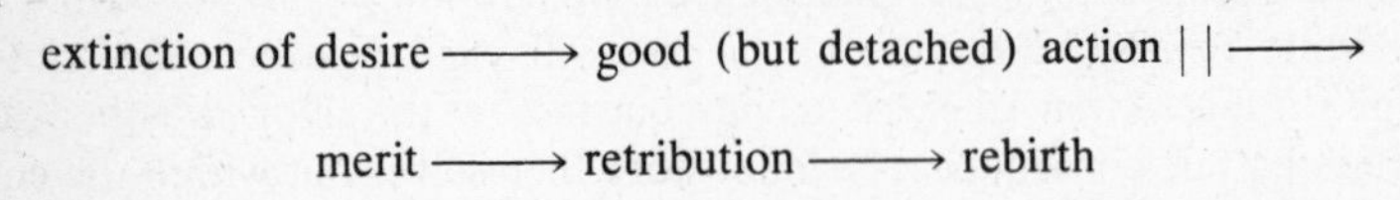

It must be noted, however, that the extinction of desire does not lead to immediate release from the Wheel of Rebirth. There still remain to be worked out the karmic consequences of meritorious and demeritorious action performed in previous lives. This obstacle, however, can be removed (as we shall see below) through Buddhist meditation.

The Technique: The Buddhist Path

The First Stage: Morality

If release from the round of rebirth is achieved by the extinction of desire (or, conversely, by the achievement of detachment), by what means can this latter condition be attained? The answer, according to Buddhism, is by the overcoming of ignorance. The ordinary worldling *(puthujjana)* remains attached to the Wheel because he is ignorant of the three attributes of being. Hence, in order to achieve the condition of detachment, he must come to understand that he has no self to cling to, that all existence is impermanent, and that therefore desire can only lead to suffering. To attain this understanding, the Buddhist must follow the Noble Eightfold Path, the Path which is outlined in the last of the Four Noble Truths.

This Path comprises three stages:[13] morality, meditation, and wisdom. The first stage, the stage of morality *(sīla)*—which at the very least includes observance of the Five Buddhist Precepts (see below)—does not in itself lead to Deliverance. Unless it is practiced with detachment, it has karmic consequences which necessarily lead to rebirth—to be sure a better rebirth, but still rebirth—rather than to release from it. Nevertheless, morality is conducive to Deliverance because it produces that self-discipline *(sikkhā)*, or character training, which is a necessary condition for achieving the next two stages on the Path. Indeed, even for the meditating monks, who in theory have reached the second stage, morality continues to be the essential mark of the earnest Buddhist. As one Burmese monk put it: "To live accord-

[13] As it is stated in the *Dhammacakkappavattana Sutta*, the fourth Noble Truth lists eight characteristics which comprise the Path, without indicating any hierarchy or sequence of stages. It was Buddhaghosa who (in *The Path of Purity*) first ordered these characteristics in three sequential groups. Numbers 3-5 (right speech, right action, and right living) comprise the stage of morality; 6-8 (right effort, right mindfulness, and right concentration) comprise the stage of meditation; and 1 and 2 (right view and right aim) comprise the stage of wisdom. The first two stages, then, are the means, the causes, by which the final stage—the result—is attained.

ing to the precepts, and to obey the Buddha's doctrines—this is the essence of Buddhism. The Buddha does not distinguish among the races. All who observe His doctrines are pure Buddhists." And on this point Burmese laymen are in agreement. When confronted with Micah's question—What does the Lord require of thee?—in Buddhist garb, all but two of the villagers in my sample answered in effect: "Compliance with the precepts."

The Buddhist precepts *(sīla),* which comprise the core of Buddhist morality, include three sets of prohibitions: a minimum set of five, and an expanded set of eight or ten. The Five Precepts, which are incumbent on every Buddhist, include abstention from killing (a prohibition which applies to all creatures, even including insects), stealing, illicit sexual relations, lying, and imbibing any intoxicant conducive to "slothfulness." Popularly, this is taken as complete abstention.[14]

Before continuing, a word must be said about Buddhism's radical attitude toward killing. Like Hinduism, its parent religion, Buddhism interdicts the killing of *all* beings, not merely (as in the case of Judaism or Christianity) human beings. Unlike Hinduism, however, the Buddhist interdiction stems not so much from the Hindu notion of nonviolence *(ahimsā),* but from its own concept of *mettā,* or loving-kindness. *Mettā,* for Buddhism, is the noblest of all sentiments; it is the mark of the truly moral man. From a Buddhist point of view, the taking of any form of life is a denial of *mettā* and is accounted as murder. Thus, it is extremely rare, if not impossible, to find a Burmese Buddhist slaughterer—almost all slaughterers in Burma are Muslims; for the same reason, it is rare to find a Buddhist cattle-raiser —although he himself does not slaughter the animals, it is enough that they are raised for slaughter.[15] Similarly, Burmese hunters, unless they are Christian, are almost nonexistent; and although Burmese fishermen do exist, their occupation is viewed with disdain, and few Buddhists will marry them or their children. In Yeigyi, the houses of the two families of fishermen are set apart from the other houses. (The fishermen themselves offer a traditional explanation for their seemingly anti-Buddhist behavior—they do not kill the fish, they only take them from the water.) The Buddhist attitude toward killing accounts, too, for the difficulty in introducing insecticides into Burma. When DDT was first introduced as part of its antimalarial campaign, the Burmese government employed the same kind of casuistry that is employed by the fishermen: i.e., the government does not kill the mosquitoes, it merely sprays the houses; if, then, the mosquitoes die from contact with DDT, their death is not caused by the government, it is self-caused or accidental. But few Burmans will assist the work of the DDT. If flies, mosquitoes, or other insects alight on a Burman, he brushes them off with

[14]Cf. the *Dhammika Sutta* of the *Sutta-Nipāta,* 18-26, for the scriptural rendition of the precepts.

[15]In Tibet butchers, being viewed as "professional sinners," are the "most despised of all classes." (Waddell 1967:567)

his hand, but never kills them. Similarly, if a poisonous snake is discovered in a courtyard or in a house, it is caught and later released in a safe place; it is not killed.

Normatively, one may not kill even in self-defense; if charged by a wild animal or by a snake, one may not kill the attacker in order to protect oneself. As one informant put it: "Let him kill me, but I must never kill him." The reasoning on which this attitude is based is derived from the theory of karma. "If it is your karma—because of your past evil deeds—that you should be killed, he [the attacker] is merely the agent of your karma." If a poisonous snake attacks and kills someone it is both necessary and just —it is karmic retribution—that he die; conversely, if death by snake bite is not karmically ordained, he will not be attacked, or, if attacked, he will not die.

Despite this emphasis on the nondiscriminatory application of *mettā*, most Burmese do not believe that killing a mosquito is as heinous as killing a man. Most monks, too, concur in this judgment. Thus, although all the monks I interviewed maintain that the prohibition on killing applies to *all* forms of life (from insect to man), most of them agree that taking an insect's life is not as horrendous as taking the life of a man or, for that matter, of some other mammal. On the other hand they all agree that habitual killers of animals—such as hunters, butchers, and fishermen—will unquestionably go to hell.

Beyond the Five Precepts, every Buddhist must periodically—usually on Buddhist Sabbaths and holydays, and if possible during the three-month Lent—observe the Eight Precepts. These include the five already mentioned and an additional four. They are called Eight Precepts because, conventionally, the seventh and eighth are combined and counted as one. In observing them, however, the injunction to abstain from only *illicit* sexual relations is extended to *all* sexual relations. The further abstentions include taking any food after the noon hour, watching or participating in any form of theatrical entertainment, the wearing of perfume and jewelry (or other forms of facial and bodily ornament), and sleeping on a high or ornate bed. The Ten Precepts comprise the above eight (or nine) with the added abstention from the handling of money.

Since this is not a treatise on Buddhist ethics,[16] we shall not be concerned here with the principles underlying Buddhist morality. Nevertheless, it is important to mention, at least, three dimensions of the ethics of nibbanic Buddhism because of their special relevance for Buddhist behavior. The first, to which I have already alluded above, is that of intention (*cetanā;* Burmese, *seidana*). Action, according to Buddhism, is neither good nor bad except insofar as it is willful, intentional, purposive action. To lie

[16]For a discussion of Buddhist ethics, cf. Tachibana 1926; Grimm 1958:311-16; King 1964.

unwittingly or to kill unintentionally is not accounted as evil or sinful.[17] Conversely, the intention to commit an immoral act is accounted as an immoral act; for an immoral act committed in the mind is in itself an act of immorality.

As a form of spiritual discipline, then, Buddhist morality is concerned not so much with abstention from immoral acts as with the extinction of the desires that instigate them. This rather extreme emphasis on intention as an ethical principle is crucial in nibbanic Buddhism, because of course the core of its soteriology is psychological. Hence, Buddhist morality, like Buddhist meditation, is primarily a technique of mind-training. To be sure, moral and immoral behavior have karmic consequences, but compliance with moral norms should not be based on a concern with these consequences; this is to base behavior on impure intentions. To perform a moral deed or an act of kindness from such self-seeking motives is not accounted a virtue. Moral and immoral behavior, of course, have social as well as karmic consequences, but they too (or their avoidance) are not the intended goals of Buddhist morality. For nibbanic Buddhism, morality is primarily a form of spiritual discipline; it is a means to the attainment of a certain psychological state which is the first condition for the achievement of nirvana.

This leads to the second dimension of Buddhist ethics which I wish to mention here. The psychological state whose attainment is the goal of Buddhist morality is one in which all worldly passions, or "mental impurities" *(kilesa)* are destroyed. The relationship between these "impurities" and Buddhist morality is, however, paradoxical. On the one hand, their destruction, viewed as the first stage on the Path to Deliverance, is the goal of moral action; on the other hand, their destruction is the necessary condition for the practice of true moral action. Since paradox is the heart of religious theory, I can only record, without resolving, this paradox. Of the various "impurities," three especially are to be uprooted: greed *(lobha)*, hatred *(dosa)*, and ignorance *(moha)*. It is perhaps no exaggeration to say that in contemporary Burma this triad recurs more frequently, both in sermons and in lay discussions, than any other set of technical Buddhist concepts. War and adultery, insurgency and factionalism, rivalry and corruption—these and many more are attributed to these "impurities" (Burmese, *ki-lei-tha)*.

This brings us to the third dimension of the ethics of nibbanic Buddhism. The mental state which results from the destruction of the above impurities

[17]This emphasis on intentionality can, of course, lead to considerable casuistry in practice. Thus, the Burmese often gloss over a violation of a precept by claiming that the violation was in deed only, but not in intention. When, for example, I reminded U Sa Mya that he had been untruthful when he had told me that he knew nothing about Burmese politics, he said that he had lied only "in the mouth," not "in the mind." This being so, he had really not violated the Buddhist injunction on lying.

is accompanied by an emotional state—the only emotional state ultimately valued by nibbanic Buddhism—that of detachment *(upekkhā)*. Ultimately, the behavior of the true Buddhist (unlike, say, the true Christian) is governed, not by love but by detachment. This is not to say that, from the perspective of Buddhist morality, love is morally bad; on the contrary, it is, as we have seen, the first step on the Path to Morality. Moreover, since love is a morally good emotion, action instigated by love produces merit for the actor. But from the perspective of nibbanic Buddhism a good emotion, such as love, is as dysfunctional as a bad emotion, such as hate; for by producing merit, and therefore retribution, love (no less than hate) leads to rebirth—and therefore to suffering. Only by the destruction of all emotion, i.e., by the attainment of detachment, can the cessation of rebirth and thus the end of suffering be attained.

In short, in assessing the place of love in Buddhist thought, it is important to distinguish between its ethical and its soteriological value. In Buddhist ethics, love is the only valued basis for moral behavior. Indeed, rather than using the global term, love, Buddhism breaks it down into three component concepts. In ascending order of ethical importance, Buddhism distinguishes between loving-kindness *(mettā)*, or a generalized friendliness for all creatures; compassion *(karuṇā)*, or pity felt for those who suffer; empathetic joy *(muditā)*, or pleasure felt for the happiness of others. Only after proceeding through these stages can one finally achieve the stage of emotional detachment, with respect to both one's own fate and the fate of others, which is necessary for salvation. In this state, one's acts continue to be moral, but since they are affectively neutral they bear no fruit.

The Second Stage: Meditation

Based on the foundation of morality, the second stage along the Path is that of meditation *(bhāvanā)*. This stage has two aspects: first, tranquility *(samatha)*, and second, insight *(vipassanā)*. Only through insight can one attain that wisdom *(paññā)* which is necessary for the achievement of nirvana.

Since the mind, according to Buddhism, is in a constant state of flux, it is necessary, as the first stage in the meditational process, to overcome the "impurity" of mental agitation in order to attain a state of calmness and tranquility of mind such that all stimuli, both internal and external, are extruded from consciousness. Only after achieving such a state, by means of tranquility-meditation *(samatha-bhāvanā)*, a state which permits one-pointed concentration, can one proceed to the second stage, that of insight-meditation *(vipassanā-bhāvanā)*. In Burma both types of meditation are referred to as *kammahtan* (Pali, *kammaṭṭhāna*).[18] Let us begin, then, with

[18]Although contemporary Buddhists talk a great deal about meditation, and although much has been written on the subject, it remains a confusing subject. Its basic concepts—even apart from their loose and ambiguous connotations—are used somewhat differently by different

tranquility-meditation (Burmese, *thamata. bawana.*), by which calm or tranquility is attained. It is because the mind, according to Buddhism, is characterized by wandering or restlessness—under normal conditions the mind is never at rest—that such meditation is necessary. The following quotations from Burmese village monks are typical.

> One can't control the mind; it always wanders. The mind moves very fast.

> The mind travels if it is not controlled. Therefore, the monk [when meditating] must control his mind. The mind cannot remain physically in one place; it always travels.

> Even in a meditation center, there are too many stimuli; therefore, the mind always wanders. It is difficult to control the mind. Even when one sleeps, the

---

authors and informants. Thus *kammaṭṭhana*, according to the *Pali-English Dictionary*, refers to the instruments of meditation, not (as Burmese informants use it) to meditation itself. Again, although most authorities agree that *samatha* is to be translated as "calm" or "tranquility" (cf. Nyanaponika 1962; or *Pali-English Dictionary*) *samādhi* (a concept we shall encounter below) is variously glossed as "concentration of mind" (Nyanaponika; *Pali-English Dictionary*) or as "meditation" (German monks interviewed in Mandalay; or *Pali-English Dictionary*). More important than the translation problem are the differences found among authorities concerning the relationship between these two concepts. For some (Nyanaponika) *samādhi* is the condition for *samatha.* U Ko Ko, professor of Pali at Mandalay University, says that, on the contrary, *samatha* is the condition for *samādhi,* as does Conze (1953:100-105), while Anesaki and Takakusu (1911) say that *jhāna* (see below) rather than *samatha* is the condition for *samādhi.* To compound the difficulty, Burmese informants use *samatha* (Burmese, *thamata.*) to refer to a process rather than a goal. For them, *(thamata.)* is the practice of "concentration" which is the means for achieving tranquility. This is also the view of some Burmese scholars (cf. U Hpe Aung 1954). Clearly it is impossible for the anthropologist to adjudicate these and other differences which are found in our sources. In general, when these semantic differences cannot be reconciled, I tend to follow the usage of Nyanaponika and the *Pali-English Dictionary.*

As I have already intimated, this discussion of Buddhist meditation is based on selected primary and secondary sources (see below) as well as on extensive interviews with two Burmese meditation masters (both monks, one in Rangoon and one in Mandalay), two German meditating monks, the professor of Pali at Mandalay University, numerous village monks, and many Burmese laymen.

Although there are numerous discussions of meditation scattered throughout the Pali canon, the primary source is the famous *Mahā Satipaṭṭhāna Suttanta* of the *Digha Nikāya,* which is chapter 22 of *Dialogues of the Buddha,* Pt. II. Of the secondary sources, the most important is Nyanaponika (1962). Lounsbery (1935) is elementary and of limited use. Grimm (1958:316-57) is an excellent, if partisan, discussion.

Since meditation has received greater emphasis in Burma than in other Theravadist countries, much of the Western discussion of *Theravāda* meditation is based on meditation in Burma. For a general theoretical discussion King (1964:ch. 6) is illuminating, as is his description of his personal meditational experience in Burma (*Ibid.:* Appendix). Shattock (1958) and Byles (1965) also provide some rather interesting accounts of their personal experiences in Burmese meditation, as does Huber (1967), who moreover compares his experience in Burmese meditation with his experience in Zen meditation *(zazen)* in Japan. Despite their differences, the similarities between these two types of Buddhist meditation are even more salient. The best account of *zazen*—descriptive, experiential, and analytic—in English is, no doubt, that of Kapleau (1967).

mind is active, because one dreams. It is very difficult to control the mind. . . . The important thing is mind control. One must control the mind lest it wander.

The final quotation is from a meditation master in a Rangoon monastery. (Tin Swe 1965:43)

> Keeping the mind under control is like tethering a wild bull. It is not easy at first. When you first tether a wild bull he will struggle violently with the tether and try to break it off. The animal will keep on struggling like that for quite a while. Then he calms down little by little. Finally the bull will get so used to the tether that even if you release him he will not go away. Like tethering a bull, as you go on meditating you will find it easier and easier to concentrate.

Traditionally, concentration can be achieved by meditating on one (or more) of thirty-eight objects, classified into five classes. First, one can meditate on a series of ten objects *(kasiṇa),* of various form and color, continuing to do so until one can visualize the particular object of one's choice without looking at it, so that finally it becomes exclusively a conceptualized object.

Second, there are ten meditations on the human corpse (known as *asubha* meditation); these are often, but not always, practiced in a cemetery. Prominent among these ten is concentration on the "thirty-two parts of the body"[19] and on the "nine apertures"[20] from which "filthy and repulsive substances" flow unceasingly. (For a detailed description of this type of meditation, cf., Hardy 1850:247-49.)

Third, there are ten thematic subjects, such as the Buddha, the *Dhamma,* the *Saṅgha,* the body (to which we shall return), and so on.

Fourth, the four sublime emotions (loving-kindness, compassion, altruistic joy, and equanimity) are also subjects of meditation.

Fifth, there is meditation on the four formless states—space, consciousness, nothingness, and the state of neither perception nor nonperception.

All of these methods are conducive to tranquility because they lead to the weakening of conceptual thought, and in some cases to attainment of the four *jhāna. Jhāna* (Burmese *zan*) is a type of trance, absorption, or ecstasy—a "special, extramundane experience," as U Thittila puts it (in Morgan (ed.) 1956:109). There are four stages of *jhāna,* each producing a certain type of concentration, which (it is believed) determines which of the Buddhist heavens one will eventually enter. With the attainment of *jhāna,* one also attains five supernormal powers (Pali, *abhiññā;* Burmese, *abinyin*), including clairvoyance, clairaudience, remembrance of one's past and

[19]Hairs of the head, hairs of the body, nails, teeth, skin, muscles, sinews, bones, marrow, kidneys, heart, liver, membranes, lungs, spleen, intestines, mesentery, stomach, excrement, brain, bile, digestive juices, pus, blood, grease, fat, tears, sweat, spittle, snot, fluid of the joints, urine.

[20]Eyes, ears, nostrils, mouth, urethra, anus.

knowledge of one's future rebirths, the power to know the thoughts of others, and the power of levitation.

Interestingly, however, although the attainment of *jhāna* is a possible consequence of tranquility-meditation, it is not, from the point of view of nibbanic Buddhism, to be cathected as an end in itself. The reason is simple. The object of meditation, according to nibbanic Buddhism, is the achievement of nirvana. At best, *jhāna* is a way-station of this goal—as a means for understanding the four Noble Truths—but at worst it may prevent its achievement, because the meditator may prefer to perpetuate his jhanic pleasures rather than proceed to nirvana. From the point of view of nibbanic Buddhism, tranquility-meditation is important only as a means to that concentration and one-pointedness of mind which is conducive to insight-meditation and the attainment of nirvana.[21]

Although tranquility and one-pointedness of mind can be achieved by meditating on any of the thirty-eight objects alluded to above, the favorite Burmese method, following the *sutta* by the same name, is the *satipaṭṭhāna* method, or the practice of mindfulness (Pali, *sati;* Burmese, *thadi*). Essentially this is the method by which one attends to, and is self-consciously aware—in the minutest detail—of one's every act, thought, sensation, and emotion. Thus, when walking, one notes that the left foot is being lifted, that the right foot is descending, is touching, is pressing, is lifting, and so on. In this manner one achieves complete concentration on whatever it is one is doing, to the exclusion of all other stimuli, both external and internal.

As a variant on this method of complete mindfulness is the "mindfulness

[21]Indic scholars will note that this first stage of Buddhist meditation is highly similar to Yogatantra in Hinduism. In both cases there is meditation, for example, on loathsomeness, restraint of the breath, use of *kasiṇa* and other objects, and the inducement of jhanic and similar states. (Cf. La Vallée Poussin 1921.) The interesting aspect of this comparison, however, is not in the similarity but in the dissimilarity of Buddhist and Hindu meditation. Those consequences, such as *jhāna* and supernormal powers, which in Buddhism are to be left behind in order to proceed to nirvana, are the very goals which are sought in Hindu meditation. (Cf. Carstairs 1957:99-101.) Thus the paradox which La Vallée Poussin (1921:194) has shrewdly observed:

> A monk must perform in a Buddhist spirit, i.e., for the sake of *nirvana,* a number of rites and meditations which confer the most precious "mundane" advantages; he must disregard these advantages—which, in India, are the surest mark of holiness—while he perfectly knows that he can enjoy them when he likes.

This paradox which La Vallée Poussin observes in the case of the Buddhist monk is, it will be realized, the dilemma which Weber saw in the case of the Puritan. Although he must work in the world, the Puritan may not enjoy the fruits of his labor; instead, he must use them as a means for glorifying God.

In Burma, as we shall see below, there are at least some Buddhists who view the jhanic and supernormal products of meditation precisely as the Hindus do; for them, it is the supernormal aspects of meditation that are sought. Similarly, for many Buddhist laymen, it is the supernormal products of meditation which they view as holy and for which they venerate monastic meditators who, allegedly, have achieved these supernormal states.

of breathing" *(ānāpāna-sati)* method, in which, in a state of immobility, one attends exclusively to one's breathing, either at the nostrils or at the abdomen. By this minute attention to one's breathing in and breathing out, one not only attains total concentration, but also becomes aware in one's own body of one of the characteristics of existence, viz., impermanence.

This state of total concentration or absorption is known as *samādhi*, a condition marked by the guarding of the senses, self-possession, contentment, and emancipation from the Five Hindrances (lust, malice, sloth, worry, and doubt). As one meditation master observed, "while in *samādhi*, the mind has no companions"; hence, since the emotions of lust, malice, and so on, are aroused only when in the presence of, or thinking about, others, these emotions cannot be aroused while in this state.

Still, this type of meditation does not in itself lead to nirvana, for the above-mentioned emotions which lead to rebirth are only transcended in *samādhi;* they are not extinguished. When one passes out of this state of absorption, they return, and one is again caught up in the karmic forces that make for rebirth. To achieve the permanent extinction of the emotions noted, one must pass from tranquility meditation to insight meditation *(vipassanā-bhāvanā)*.

Vipassanā (Burmese, *wi.pa-tha-na*) is usually translated as insight or intuitive understanding. Specifically, *vipassanā* meditation is that type which leads to insight into the three Buddhist truths concerning existence. By analyzing one's meditational experience—whether it be the experience of total mindfulness or the experience of mindful breathing—under the guise of these truths, one comes to an intuitive awareness of the fact that there is no self—"there is nothing in this experience that can be called *me* or *mine*"—that every experience is impermanent—"existence is a series of fleeting sense impressions"—and that in no experience can one find abiding pleasure—"all is suffering." And this, of course, is the ultimate goal of all Buddhist discipline.

> The aim of the Buddha-way is the destruction of the Thirst [craving] for the world imbuing us. This destruction is achieved [by the cognition] that each possible object to which this Thirst might be directed, in the end effects Suffering, nothing but Suffering. [Grimm 1958:316]

It is by means of this cognition that one reaches the last stage of the Buddhist Path, the stage of *paññā*, or Wisdom. "Wisdom," for Buddhism, refers to a very specific form of knowledge, viz., knowledge by means of which salvation can be achieved; and this knowledge is not intellectual—no amount of intellectual knowledge can lead to Deliverance—but intuitive. That impermanence, nonself, and suffering comprise the characteristics of sentient existence is a truth which every Buddhist child is taught at his mother's knee. But mere intellectual assent to its truth does not in itself produce those emotional and behavioral changes which lead to Deliverance. The latter can be achieved only through personal knowledge, derived from an immediate and direct experience of these three attributes. When such knowledge is truly achieved, when one actually experiences—not merely assenting to—the truths of impermanence, nonself, and suffering, one realizes the futility of the continuation of any form of samsaric existence and loses all desire for it. And only with the extinction of such desire can one achieve salvation. For, since the mental impurities—the bad roots of action—have already been destroyed through the discipline of morality, there are no karmic formations produced by demerit; and, since the good roots of action—the various forms of love—are now characterized by detachment, there can be no karmic formation produced by merit. Hence, in the absence of a sense of self, and with the realization that all experience entails suffering, there is no clinging to or craving for existence;[22] in the absence of these forms of emotional attachment, there is no merit- or demerit-producing action; in the absence of merit or demerit, there are no karmic formations; in the absence of karmic formations, there is no rebirth; and, release from rebirth means deliverance from suffering.[23]

Ultimately, then, Deliverance is achieved only through meditation. As the Buddha says (in the *Mahā-Satipaṭṭhana Sutta*), meditation is

> the one and only path, Bhikkhus leading to the purification of beings, to passing far beyond grief and lamentation, to the dying-out of ill and misery . . . to the realization of Nirvana. . . . [*Dialogues of the Buddha*, Pt. II, p. 327]

[22]Indeed, one Burmese monk—pressing Buddhist ontology to its idealist extreme—announced that insight into the Buddhist characteristics of existence leads to total emotional detachment because of the realization not only that the self does not exist, but also that nothing else can be said to exist; and how can one be attached to nothingness? In short, *vipassanā* meditation, according to him, leads to the realization that the external world (like the self) has no independent existence, that it is merely an illusion. The belief in an external world, he argued, is an artifact of the belief in a self; to enhance its pleasure the self creates the illusion of a world to be enjoyed, when in reality there is nothing but atoms in a void. This, of course, is decidedly a minority view.

This same notion is expressed by a sophisticated Buddhist scholar. If it is true, writes Grimm (1958:325), that the world of the five senses

> is wretched and miserable, it can be taken for granted that it may only be desired in consequence of a tremendous illusion, a grotesque self-delusion, hence in consequence upon the *ignorance* in respect of its real nature. Further, in the same degree as the insight and therewith the knowledge in the real nature of this world arises, all Thirsting for it must extinguish. We recognize *that we do not miss anything, if such objects disappear forever* [original italics].

[23]Although the attainment of detachment *(upekkhā)* precludes the production of new karmic formations, it does not in itself lead to an immediate release from rebirth for there still remain the karmic consequences of past action which require retribution—presumably in future rebirths. Nevertheless, although the law of karma can never be circumvented, *vipassanā* meditation can also provide the technique for dealing with these karmic residues. In the course of meditation, these karmic formations are, as the Buddhists say, "burned up," so that retribution occurs, so to speak, in the very process of meditation.

A Note on Meditation in Burma

Although, as we shall see below, meditation is found only infrequently in Burma, and even less frequently in other Buddhist societies, it is found to some extent. Hence, in addition to the theory of meditation outlined above, it is necessary to describe, if only briefly, its Burmese practitioners, their regimen, and their experience.

Typically, insight-meditation is practiced by monks living in meditation monasteries, usually but not always found in the larger cities;[24] by laymen who seek meditation instruction from them; and by monks living in forest hermitages. Like the monks, laymen who enter the monastery for meditation must continuously observe the Ten Precepts. The following is the typical regimen (for monks and laymen alike) in a meditation monastery. Retiring at 9:00 P.M., the meditators arise at 4:00 A.M. While the monks spend about two hours of the morning on their alms rounds, and as many as three hours a day on study, the laymen devote only some of this time to study, the rest being spent in meditation. For one hour a day, monks and advanced laymen receive a didactic lesson from the head meditation master, usually the abbot. In addition, laymen as well as neophyte monks report their meditation experiences to their personal meditation master; the latter interprets their experiences for them, gives them guidance when they are having difficulties, evaluates their progress, and so on. The remainder of the day, usually about twelve hours, is devoted to private meditation.[25] How many of these hours are actually spent in meditation varies, of course, from one person to another. For some it is no more than one or two hours; others may meditate almost the entire time.

The regimen in the forest hermitage, where an isolated monk lives by himself, is self-imposed. In the two cases I observed personally, one meditated continuously for eight hours. The other divided his meditation into two periods of two and a half hours each: from 11:30 to 2:00 and from 2:30 to 5:00. The remainder of the time, in both cases, was devoted to study.

The careers of meditating monks vary greatly. Some have displayed no interest in meditation until late middle age, while others have begun to meditate in their teens. Thus, to give an example of the former type, the most serious meditator I know, the abbot of a meditation monastery, was fifty when he began his meditation exercises. Before he began to meditate he paid little attention to the classical Buddhist types of suffering—sickness, old age, and death—although, as he put it, he saw people becoming ill,

[24]Thus there is a meditation monastery in a village about twenty miles from Yeigyi. All of its resident as well as itinerant monks devote most of their time to meditation. Sometimes, especially during the Buddhist Lent, they are joined by laymen, who for varying periods of time take meditation instruction from them.

[25]Unlike Zen meditation, for example, which takes place publicly in a meditation hall, the Burmese meditator is physically isolated from his meditating brethren.

getting old, and dying before his eyes. When he began to meditate he discovered impermanence and suffering in every activity he performed, in eating, sitting, walking, and so on. It was only then that he learned "the truth of these Buddhist teachings, not only in the abstract and in general, but concretely, and in their minute forms. By realizing that everything is impermanent, that there is no continuity, even from second to second," he hopes to escape from the Wheel of Rebirth.

I know another monk who, on the contrary, first became interested in meditation at the age of nineteen, and after four years of study under a meditation master spent eight more years meditating in a forest hermitage. He then established his own meditation center in a village monastery.

The careers of lay meditators are equally variegated. Some practice mindfulness for a brief period each day. Others enter the monastery periodically, for a two- or three-week period of intensive meditation.

The experience of meditators is as variegated as their careers. I know of no layman who has attained the state of insight *(vipassanā).* Those few monks who hinted that they had achieved such a state either would not describe it, claiming that to do so would be in violation of their vows, or could not describe it, claiming that it is an ineffable experience. As one put it to me, "It's like sexual intercourse; unless you've had the experience yourself, it cannot be explained. If you want to know what the meditation experience is like, you must meditate yourself." The most that one monk was willing to say was that it is an experience of "coolness, great inner coolness."

Laymen, when describing their attempts at meditation, uniformly describe either an itching sensation—in the nostrils, the eyes, the ears, even the intestines—that accompanies their experience, or the sensation of sharp pains, like the constant pricking of a needle, or the feeling that some organ —the head, for example—is expanding beyond all recognizable proportions. Others report hearing voices while meditating. One says he heard a voice calling, "Wake up! Wake up!" Another says he heard a voice admonishing him to "note" his sensations. (To "note," in Buddhist meditation, is part of the regimen of mindfulness in which, as we have seen, one takes cognizance of and names everything he does: "Now I am lifting my foot; now I am lifting my other foot; now I have an itch on my arm," etc.) The voice went on to say, "Look, you have slept for a long time in the laymen's life. Note from now on what you do." Some tell of having visions—visions of beautiful maidens, of flowing streams, of old men with grey hair and wrinkled faces. In all cases, they claimed either that these visions are rather ecstatic or that they are affectively neutral. I was never told—although it has been reported by others—of frightening or traumatic visions. One meditator reported that his most pleasurable life experiences derived from meditation.

> There is a tingling sensation in every part of the body, much more pleasurable than any sexual experience, including orgasm. In orgasm, the pleasure is restricted to one organ, whereas this meditation pleasure suffuses the entire body; it is felt in all of one's organs.[26]

Having described the Buddhist Path we must now return to the goal—the form of salvation—for whose attainment this Path is the means.

The Goal: Nirvana

Thus far we have characterized Buddhist salvation as meaning deliverance from suffering which, in effect, means release from the Wheel of Rebirth. But Buddhism is not content to articulate this notion in merely negative terms. As in Christianity, in which deliverance from sin means the attainment of heaven, so for Buddhism deliverance from suffering means the attainment of nirvana (*nibbāna*). If anything, however, the meaning of nirvana is even more obscure than the meaning of heaven. That it means release from rebirth and its ills—conception, sickness, old age, and death—is clear, but this is a negative formulation. The question remains whether any positive qualities can be attributed to this Buddhist *summum bonum*.

Logically, it would seem that the question can only be answered in the negative. For if nirvana signals the cessation of rebirth—and hence the destruction of those material factors or "heaps" (*khandhā*) that comprise the body—and if, according to Buddhist doctrine, there is no soul which survives the dissolution of the body, it would logically follow that nirvana can only mean permanent extinction. This logic seems to be supported by the favorite scriptural metaphor for nirvana, the "blowing out" of the flame or fire (of life). That it might, however, mean something other than extinction is implied by the many other metaphors and poetic images that are used to characterize nirvana. Each of the following expressions is variously found in Scripture:

> the harbor of refuge, the cool cave, the island amidst the floods, the place of bliss, emancipation, liberation, safety, the supreme, the transcendental, the uncreated,

[26]The comparison between this introspective report and Alexander's psychoanalytic interpretation of Buddhist meditation is dramatic. He describes the meditational experience as a ". . . feeling of pleasure, a consummate voluptuousness of all organs, tissues, and cells, a pleasure completely freed from genitals, an orgasm diffused throughout the whole body. . . ." (Alexander 1931:134).

One meditator described experiences of a clinical nature. In his second year of meditation, he would experience a huge erection, accompanied by intense sexual desire, whenever he began to meditate. This would last for about a week when, unable to resist his sexual urge, he would return to his home with the intention of having intercourse with his wife. But upon his return, his erection would subside and his urge disappear. When he came back to the meditation center his desire would again become aroused, and again, when he returned to his wife, it would subside. This pattern, he said, continued through the entire second year of his meditation. It has not occurred, however, since that time.

> the tranquil, the home of ease, the calm, the end of suffering, the medicine for all evil, the unshaken, the ambrosia, the immaterial, the imperishable, the abiding, the further shore, the unending, the bliss of effort, the supreme joy, the ineffable. . . ." [Rhys Davids 1908:71-72]

Textual scholars, however, are sharply divided concerning the meaning of these and other characterizations. La Vallée Poussin (1917) is categorical in his insistence that, for Pali Buddhism, nirvana means deliverance from existence, from all existence. Many, if not all, of the early founders of Buddhism, he argues, deemed life in any of its forms to be so miserable that "deliverance—unqualified deliverance—seemed to them a goal for which it is worth while to strive." (1917:376) Still, even he concedes that from a scriptural point of view the matter is not so simple, for, he admits, scriptural passages can be cited to support three alternative positions concerning the meaning of nirvana. Thus (1) it may refer to total annihilation, (2) it may refer to some "inconceivable existence," or (3) it may refer to either, both, or neither. Despite the ambiguity occasioned by these alternatives, La Vallée Poussin argues that Buddhist metaphysics and ontology logically entail the first conception, and that this is the conception conveyed by the bulk of the scriptural passages dealing with this subject.

Suzuki (1963:50-51), just as categorically, states that nirvana does not refer to

> annihilation of consciousness nor a temporal or permanent suppression of mentation, as imagined by some; but it is the annihilation of the notion of ego-substance and of all the desires that arise from this erroneous conception. But this represents the negative side of the doctrine, and its positive side consists in universal love or sympathy (*karuna*) for all beings.

A Burmese Pāli scholar proffered a similar interpretation. When I informed him that a majority of Buddhist monks whom I interviewed believed nirvana to be total extinction, he said that this is a heretical opinion. Nirvana, he insisted, does not refer to total extinction, but to the extinction of suffering. When all impurities are extinguished, there still remains something that can be said to exist. "The purities exist and pleasantness exists." When, however, I asked him what this can possibly mean, since with the destruction of the ego there is nothing to which the purities are attached and no being who can enjoy the pleasantness, he admitted that this was a difficult question.[27]

[27] As the Pali texts became known to European scholars in the mid-nineteenth century, a serious debate ensued among Buddhist experts concerning the textual meaning of "nirvana." That "nirvana" meant extinction was a repugnant idea to many of the protagonists in the debate, and in view of our empirical information concerning the nirvana beliefs of Buddhists, it is interesting to observe that many of them based their views not on an explication of the texts, but on an appeal to human nature. For them it was inconceivable that human beings like

In general, and the above scholar to the contrary notwithstanding, contemporary Burmese Buddhists exhibit the same three points of view concerning the meaning of nirvana (Burmese, *neikban*) that La Vallée Poussin attributes to Scripture. A small group says that short of experiencing nirvana, nothing can be said about it (other than that it entails the absence of suffering). It is, they say, like an unmarried girl who asks her married sister to describe sexual intercourse, and is told that the only way it can be described is to have the experience oneself.

A second group says that although we cannot say what nirvana is, it is not extinction or annihilation. Some members of this group argue that although nirvana means the complete extinction of the physical aspect *(rūpa)* of life, its spiritual aspect or mind *(nāma)* remains. Others insist that although mind, too, is destroyed, there remains a special kind of awareness (known in Burmese as *abinyin seik*) which experiences the joy (Pali, *sukha;* Burmese, *thukha*) of nirvana. When pressed, however, even the latter admit that it is hard to define this joy except in negative terms, i.e., as the absence of suffering. Still others (especially a minority of monks) say that there is a purified spirit (known in Burmese as *thaṇ shin:*) which persists into nirvana, and it is this spirit which exists free from all suffering. Finally, some members of this group express a point of view which is best represented by

---

themselves could adhere to a religion whose soteriological goal was extinction. Consider, for example, the following quotations.

> A great deal has been spoken and written recently about the diversity of races. Whatever this difference may be, it would not destroy the general similitude of our faculties and the unity of the human species. The human genre constitutes one and the same family, in which all members are endowed with the same reason, illumined by the same consciousness, and have the same notions of the just and the unjust, of being and nothingness. I cannot admit that three hundred million people live in the hope of their future annihilation and know no other religion than this. No nation, no human race could be reduced to this horrible condition. Otherwise there would have to be, not varieties of the human species, but several humanities with differing faculties, intelligences, and natures. [Ad. Franck, *Séances et travaux de l'Académie des sciences morales et politiques de l'Institut Impérial de France,* 1862, p. 344. Quoted in Welbon 1967:77.]

Or, again:

> Well, then, if the Buddha truly was a sage, an ardent lover of mankind, a revealer of good law, a committed apostle—and nothing indicates the contrary—does it not injure his memory to attribute to him almost the following: "My dear disciples; fate condemns you all to revolve eternally in the moving circle of transmigrations which you fear. Well, have faith in my word. I shall deliver all of you from it, but it will mean your annihilation. And what is more, you will only obtain this exemption from rebirths on this condition: that you practice religiously all your life the virtues, the penances, the mortifications, and the austerities that I ceaselessly commend to you in my discourses and that I myself practice in preaching to you from example. . . ." Is it not to malign the good sense of the Buddhist peoples—who, if they are not exactly like us, are, after all, our own brothers, . . . is it not to do injury to all humanity to pose this strange proposition as an article of Buddhist faith: For twenty-five centuries the faithful and fervent ascetics are forced to practice the rigorous discipline of their master in order to be rewarded with nothingness! [Obry, Jean Baptiste Francois. *Du Nirvāna bouddhique en response à M. Barthélemy Saint-Hilaire,* 1863. Quoted in Welbon 1967:81-82.]

the argument of a Western-educated monk and former Christian. Although admitting that nirvana means the extinction of individuality, he denied that this means total annihilation. The whole problem, according to him, can be conceived analogically. Consider space, for example, which is one and indivisible. Suppose now you build a house, thereby enclosing a part of space, and individualizing it. Suppose, too, that this enclosed space is, in turn, further subdivided by walls, thus making individual rooms. But now suppose the inside (room) walls are knocked down, and then, finally, the outside (house) walls are knocked down. What has happened to the individualized space? It is no more; it is now part of boundless space. So too, he continued, the individuality of the self is artificial; through enlightenment, the walls that separate it from the totality of Being are broken down and its individuality is destroyed. That is nirvana.

Although both of the above two groups have adherents among the Burmese whom I interviewed, the third group—those who believe that nirvana means total extinction—is the largest. Nirvana, as they put it in Burmese, means *ba-hma. mashi.bu:* ("nothing exists"). Emptiness, nothingness, annihilation—these and other synonyms are used by them to characterize it.[28] This point of view is shared by monks and laymen alike, but monks insist on it even more strongly than laymen. When asked why extinction is an end to be desired, their answers are unanimous. Every and all forms of existence are filled with suffering, from those in the lowest hells to those in the highest heavens; only by the cessation of existence can one escape suffering.

Still, although they believe that nirvana means extinction, some Burmese are unwilling to speak of it in negative terms. Consider, for example, the following summary of a not untypical point of view.

> When I asked him the meaning of *neikban*, he emphasized *ba-hma. mashi.bu:* —there is no mind, there is no soul, there is no body; there is only peace. There is no feeling of any kind; if there is some feeling, then it is not *neikban*. Still, it is not true to say that *neikban* is nothing—there is something. That is, there is peacefulness.

Believing (as they do) that nirvana means extinction, most Burmese do not view it as a desirable goal. The resulting tension has produced considerable modification in this doctrine, as we shall see in the following chapters.[29]

[28]Consistent with their conception of nirvana as extinction, this group, in contrast to some other reports from Burma, denied that in nirvana there is reunion with one's loved ones. Although many said they would like to be united with parents, spouse, or children, not one respondent (even among those who were disinclined to the extinction conception of nirvana) thought that this was possible. Indeed, many said they did not desire it: family attachments, like all attachments, can only lead to suffering.

[29]For a further and more extended discussion of nirvana, in both its scriptural and Burmese meanings, see Slater (1951).

The Personal Ideal: The *Arahant*

Although there is ambiguity concerning the meaning of nirvana, there are clearly delineated stages through which one must pass in order to attain it. The first stage is that of *sotāpanna* (Burmese, *thotaban*), the stage of the "Stream-winner." Emancipated from three of the Ten Fetters that bind one to the Wheel—viz., the illusion of self, doubts concerning Buddhist truths, and belief in the efficacy of ritual as a means to salvation—one who has attained this stage cannot be reborn in any of the subhuman worlds. He will be reborn seven times at most before attaining nirvana.

The second stage is that of *sakadāgāmin* (Burmese, *tha.ga.da-gan*), the stage of the "Once-returner." For him the fetters of physical passions and malice have considerably diminished, but have not yet fallen away. He will be reborn only once again.

In the third stage, that of *anāgāmin* (Burmese, *ana-gan*), all five fetters mentioned above are destroyed. He cannot be reborn in any of the material planes.

The fourth, and final, stage is that of the *arahant* (Burmese, *rahan:-da*). Being delivered from the remaining five fetters,[30] he will immediately attain nirvana.[31] For nibbanic Buddhism arahantship is the ideal for which every Buddhist should strive.

The *arahant* is best described by contrasting him with a Buddha. Although the attainment of nirvana through knowledge of the three attributes of sentient being is the defining characteristic of both a Buddha and the *arahant,* they yet differ in three important attributes. First, a Buddha is one who discovers by himself the Path of Deliverance; the *arahant* follows the Path taught by a Buddha. Second, a Buddha not only attains Enlightenment, but unlike the *arahant* he also attains omniscience, universal knowledge, and omnipotence. Third, the *arahant,* having achieved Deliverance for himself, has no concern for the Deliverance of others. On this score, he is identical with one of the two types of Buddha, the *Pacceka* Buddhas. The latter, although discovering by themselves the way to Enlightenment, do not reveal their discovery to others. These Silent Buddhas are to be distinguished from the *Sammāsam,* or Perfect Buddhas. The latter defer their own Deliverance until they can reveal their discoveries to others so that they, too, can attain nirvana. All the historical Buddhas, including the present Buddha Gautama, are Perfect Buddhas.

[30]The remaining fetters are desire for a future life in the heavens of corporeal gods, desire for a future life in the heavens of incorporeal gods, pride, self-righteousness, and ignorance.

[31]As the Burmese use these terms, those in the first three stages are known as *ari.ya* (noble ones, or saints). They are to be distinguished, on the one hand, from the *puthujjana,* the ordinary wordlings, and on the other from the *rahan:da,* those who are so to speak at the very door of nirvana.

Since Buddhahood is almost as rare in Buddhism as is divinity in monotheistic religions, arahantship rather than Buddhahood is the projected personal ideal in nibbanic Buddhism. To become an *arahant* is the object of all Buddhist practice, the purpose of all Buddhist discipline. Although this ideal has been criticized by Western commentators as callously selfish, no Westerner has attacked it as harshly as have the spokemen of *Mahāyāna* Buddhism. "Religiously considered," writes Suzuki (1963:9), the Silent Buddha "is cold, impassive, egoistic, and lacks love for all mankind." The *arahant* is "inferior" even to him, for he not only shares all the above defects, but in addition "does not possess any intellect that enables him to think independently and to find out by himself the way to final salvation." *(Ibid.)* In both cases, however, the outstanding attribute is "selfishness."

> It was not theirs to think of the common weal of all beings, and, therefore, when they attained their own redemption from earthly sins and passions, their religious discipline was completed, and no further attempt was made by them to extend the bliss of their personal enlightenment to their fellow-creatures. (*Ibid.*: 280) [Hence, their Buddhism] is the most unscrupulous application to our ethico-religious life of the individualistic theory of karma. All things done are done by oneself; all things left undone are left undone by oneself. [*Ibid.*:282]

For *Mahāyāna* Buddhism, the ideal is not the *arahant*, but the *Bodhisattva*, one who defers his entry into nirvana in order to help others in their quest for Deliverance. This is effected by transferring his own merit to others. As Suzuki puts it:

> Whatever rewards he [the *Bodhisattva*] may get for his self-enjoyment as the karma of his virtuous deeds, he would turn them over *(parivarta)* towards the uplifting of the suffering masses. And this self-sacrifice, this unselfish devotion to the welfare of his fellow-beings constitutes the essence of Bodhisattvahood. [*Ibid.*:282]

Having presented the point of view of a partisan, it may now be asked whether these invidious comparisons of the *arahant* and *Bodhisattva* are justified. It should be observed in the first place that, whatever its ethical status, the *arahant* ideal is the logical consequence of the Buddhist teachings concerning merit and karma. Since rebirth is a function of one's karma, one's own actions alone can affect one's future destiny. Everyone, as the Buddha put it, must seek his own salvation (with diligence); no one else—not even the Buddha—can save him. What one is, and what one will become, is a consequence of one's own action. Hence, however great one's compassion for others, and however strong one's desire to help them to attain salvation, there is no way by which this can be done. In the words of the *Dhammapada* (XII, 165-66):

'Tis by the self evil is done, 'tis by the self one comes to grief; 'tis by the self evil is left undone; 'tis by the self a man is purified; the pure, the impure, this is of the self; one man cannot another purify.

Let no man worsen welfare of the self for weal of other man however great! When he weal of the self has come to know, let him pursue intent that very weal.

It should be noted in the second place that, psychologically, the salvation method entailed by the *arahant* ideal is sounder than that permitted by the *Bodhisattva* ideal. The technical problem of merit transfer aside (this will be examined below), nirvana is achieved, as we have seen, not through the mechanical process of acquiring merit, but through the self-transformational consequences of religious discipline. The *Bodhisattva* ideal, which permits salvation to be achieved by a mechanical process—the transfer of merit from Bodhisattva to devotee—demands no personality transformation in the devotee as a condition for Deliverance. Hence, whatever one's moral judgment concerning the *arahant* and *Bodhisattva* ideals, it should not obscure this—the crucial—difference between them. If deliverance from suffering requires intensive psychological transformation, the personal sacrifice of the *Bodhisattva*, however noble, will not help the devotee to achieve this end.

Although the *Bodhisattva* ideal is not found—nor for reasons just suggested, could it be found—in the *Theravāda* tradition, some of the moral, compassionate qualities associated with it are by no means absent from this tradition. Aside from such qualities as love *(mettā)* and compassion *(karuṇā)*, which are stressed by Buddhist morality and in theory are acquired by, and are necessary conditions for becoming, an *arahant*, the towering figure of the *(Sammāsam)* Buddha Gautama is a ubiquitous model for the Buddhist. Although the Buddha, given Theravadist teachings regarding nirvana, cannot directly save others, He attempted to achieve the same end indirectly by sharing His Wisdom with them. When He attained Enlightenment, the Buddha could have entered nirvana immediately. Because, however, of His compassion for mankind, He deferred His Deliverance so that, by revealing His discovery to others, they too might learn how to attain salvation. In sum, although He did not (because He could not) save others, He showed them the Path by means of which they could, if they chose, save themselves.

It is interesting to observe, then, that in Theravadist Burma, where, restricted to a small group, there has been a long tradition of aspiration to Buddhahood, the aspiration is for *Sammāsam*, rather than *Pacceka* (silent) Buddhahood. Most Burmans, to be sure, do not aspire to Buddhahood; the notion staggers the imagination. If the chances of being born even as an ordinary human being are small—in the words of one favorite simile, as the grains of dust on one fingernail compared to all the dust of the earth—

imagine the chances of being born as a Buddha! And imagine what hubris is required to entertain such a fantasy. Still, as I have said, there has been in Burma a long and persistent tradition of aspiration to *(Sammāsam)* Buddhahood. I myself have met a few Burmans who refer to themselves as an Embryo Buddha *(hpaya: laung:)* one who is striving for and hopes to attain Buddhahood, though only of course after numerous rebirths.[32] It should be added, moreover, that although few Burmans are experts in the niceties of Buddhist doctrine, I was nevertheless surprised to find vestigial *Bodhisattva* beliefs among them. Even former monks told me, when I asked why they aspire to Buddhahood, that they not only wish to attain nirvana but want to take others with them. And this, they said, they can only do as Buddhas. But it cannot be denied that, to the extent that the Burmese are concerned with nirvana—as we shall see, a limited extent—most of them aspire to arahantship rather than to Buddhahood. And this means that they are concerned exclusively with their own Deliverance. To characterize this aspiration as "selfish" makes no more sense, however, than to characterize a Christian concerned with his personal salvation as selfish.[33]

The Social Ideal: World Renunciation

Depending on its salvation message, a salvation religion (as Weber has pointed out) can adopt one of four stances with respect to the "world." Viewing it as good, religion may embrace the world as the arena within which the salvation quest can properly take place. Or, as in the case of mystically oriented religions, its stance may be one of indifference; an inward religion views the world as irrelevant to its concerns. Again, religion may attempt to reform the world. Prophetic religion, for example, condemns a sinful sociocultural system and, with its religio-ethical values as its charter, attempts to reconstruct it. Finally, religion may reject the world in all its forms, actual and conceivable; the world, under any guise, is an irreducible obstacle to the quest for salvation. This is the stance of normative Buddhism. Salvation can only be achieved by the extinction of attach-

[32]In the *Jātaka* stories, which recount His various lives prior to His attaining Buddhahood, the future Buddha is referred to as a *Bodhisat,* a term which the Burmese translate as *hpaya: laung:* Embryo Buddha. Neither term, however, has soteriological connotations.

[33]Some observers have argued that this "selfish" religious ideal makes for selfish, egocentric behavior in ordinary social life. I personally doubt that there is a causal relationship between the *arahant* ideal and the alleged egocentricity of the Burmese. Still, there are even some Burmans who, lamenting the "selfishness" of their fellows, attribute this alleged trait to the *arahant* emphasis in *Theravāda* Buddhism. As a prominent intellectual put it, "it is because of the *arahant* ideal that the Burmese are concerned only with themselves; this selfishness is Burma's greatest problem. What is required is for some people to be willing to become *Bodhisattvas* and to work for others." (This, of course, is a misreading of the *Bodhisattva* doctrine, which pertains only to salvation.) When I asked if this were not inconsistent with *Theravāda* teachings, he replied with not a little acerbity, "Not at all. It's quite consistent with the texts; only in Burma they have chosen to ignore them. After all, there are 550 *Jātaka.*" (This, as we have seen, is another misreading.)

ment to the world and all its vanities. Craving for and clinging to the world, in any of its manifestations, must be totally uprooted. This, in turn, requires rejection of and retreat from the world, not only because its temptations render the extinction of attachment all the more difficult, but also because of the additional difficulties of practicing morality, concentration, and wisdom—the threefold means to salvation—within it. The true Buddhist is the world-rejector, the monk *(bhikkhu)* who has renounced the world. In the words of Scripture (in the *Sāmañña-Phala Sutta*):

> Full of hindrances is household life, a path for the dust of passion. Free as the air is the life of him who has renounced all worldly things. How difficult is it for the man who dwells at home to live the higher life in all its fullness, in all its purity, in all its bright perfection! Let me then cut off my hair and beard, let me clothe myself in the orange-coloured robes, and let me go forth from the household life into the homeless state. [*Dialogues of the Buddha,* Pt. I, p. 78]

To be sure, the lure of the world is strong; the attachment to relatives and friends, to sensuous pleasures and physical passions, seems all but binding. But the attachment can—indeed, it must—be broken if, for each attachment, one considers: "This is a tie, in this there is little happiness, little enjoyment, but more of pain, this is a fish-hook" (*Khaggavisānasutta* 3, 27). Then,

> Having torn the ties, having broken the net as a fish in the water, being like a fire not returning to the burnt place, let one wander alone like a rhinoceros. [*Ibid.*:28, in *Sutta-Nipāta,* p. 9]

Notice, however, that for Buddhism renunciation of the world does not mean (as it often means in other religions of renunciation) a life of self-torture or bodily mortification; it means, rather, the rejection of worldly values and the abandonment of normal society for the homeless state. The Noble Eightfold Path, which is the Path of the world-renouncing monk, is the Middle Way between two extremes. Buddhist renunciation rejects, on the one hand, the practice "of those things whose attraction depends upon the passions . . . a low and pagan way, unworthy, unprofitable, and fit only for the worldly-minded." And it rejects, on the other hand, the practice of asceticism "which is painful, unworthy, and unprofitable" (*Dhammacakkappavattana Sutta,* 2; in *Buddhist Suttas,* pp. 146-47).

For nibbanic Buddhism, then, the true Buddhist is the world-renouncing monk. To be sure, even primitive Buddhism recognized two classes of Buddhists: *upāsakas* or lay devotees, who remained in the world, and *bhikkhus,* the wandering mendicants who rejected the world. The former, however, are still far from the Path; their primary religious value consists in the support they render to those who have the spiritual attainments necessary to renounce the world. The latter alone are sons of the Buddha.

It should be obvious, now, why nibbanic Buddhism is properly characterized as a religion of radical salvation, both ideationally and sociologically. Ideationally, its conception of salvation is indeed a radical one, entailing the transcendence of the entire physicotemporal world. Sociologically, its charter for a soteriological community is equally radical: in order to transcend the physicotemporal world, it is necessary to abandon the sociopolitical world. But physical retreat from the world is not sufficient; it is merely a necessary condition for yet another, a psychologically radical act: having abandoned the world, one must sever all ties to it and withdraw all cathexes from it. Salvation can only be achieved by a total and radical rejection of the world in all its aspects. Nibbanic Buddhism expects no more; it demands no less. Max Weber—from whom the expression was borrowed—was correct in characterizing (nibbanic) Buddhism as ". . . the most radical form of salvation striving conceivable" (Weber 1958:206).

CHAPTER 3

Kammatic Buddhism: I. A Religion of Proximate Salvation

The Shift in the Soteriological Goal

The Buddhist ideology described in the last chapter, which, based on its soteriological doctrine of nirvana, I have designated as nibbanic Buddhism, is truly an ideology of radical salvation. It rejects everything within the spatiotemporal world *(saṃsāra)* as a possible goal of salvation—the attainment of salvation (nirvana) means the transcendence of *saṃsāra*—and it demands the renunciation of *lokiya,* the sociocultural world, as the arena within which one can best strive for the attainment of salvation. That this, the normative ideology of *Theravāda* Buddhism, is not in its entirety the operative ideology of Burmese (or any other *Theravāda*) Buddhists is hardly surprising. Since the normative ideology of any of the great world religions is the invention of religious virtuosos, its diffusion (to continue with Weber's felicitous metaphor) to the religiously unmusical masses necessarily entails important transformations in the original message. On the assumption, then, that there is an inevitable discrepancy (at least in the great world religions) between the set of ideas that comprise the normative ideology of a religion, and that which, in fact, constitutes the operative ideology of its religiously unmusical devotees, such a discrepancy would surely be expected in a religion whose normative ideology is as austere as nibbanic Buddhism. Indeed, given the wide gap between the psychological orientation of the original converts to ancient Buddhism and that of its later (including contemporary) practitioners, it is surprising that the discrepancy is not even more marked than it actually is. For if, as seems most probable, early Buddhism appealed primarily to a cultural stratum of urban, world-weary intelligentsia, it could hardly have perdured as the religion of an unsophisticated peasantry without undergoing important changes.

In the process of becoming a popular salvation religion, the soteriological ideology of nibbanic Buddhism has indeed undergone important changes, which relate to both the means and the goal of salvation. Although the description of these changes will occupy most of this and the two following chapters, it will be well to summarize them briefly at the outset.

Typically, instead of renouncing desire (and the world), Buddhists rather aspire to a future worldly existence in which their desires may find satisfaction. Contrary to nibbanic Buddhism, which teaches that frustration is an inevitable characteristic of samsaric existence, they view their suffering as a temporary state, the result of their present position in *saṃsāra.* But there are, and they aspire to achieve, other forms of samsaric existence which yield great pleasure. These range from the earthly existence of a wealthy human being to the heavenly existence of a blissful *deva.* Frustrated in their striving for greater pleasure in their present lives, the Burmese—to particularize this generalized discussion—hope to find it in a future life. Their aim is not to transcend the samsaric world, but to alter their fate (in a future life) within it.

Contrary, then, to the ideology of nibbanic Buddhism, Buddhism for most Buddhists is a means not so much for the extinction of desire as for its satisfaction; not so much for the cessation of rebirth as for a better rebirth; not so much for some kind of absolute Deliverance—whether this be conceived as the extinction of being or, less extremely, of an individualized ego—as for the persistence of the individuated ego in a state of sensate happiness. Hence, even when the soteriological aim is expressed in nibbanic rhetoric—"May I attain nirvana"—the content of the aspiration is samsaric rather than nibbanic. What is desired in kammatic Buddhism is the extinction of samsaric suffering, but not samaric pleasure. This, then, is worldly —even when projected into a remote rebirth, the goal is worldly— rather than otherworldly salvation. The cathectic orientation, in technical Buddhist terms, has shifted from *lokuttara* to *lokiya.* In sum, compared to the radical soteriology of nibbanic Buddhism, kammatic Buddhism, which, for reasons which will become apparent below, is the name I have given to the soteriological ideology of the great majority of contemporary *Theravāda* Buddhists, is best characterized as a religion of proximate salvation.[1]

The Normative Basis for Kammatic Buddhism

When the doctrines that comprise the ideology of kammatic Buddhism are examined in detail (as we shall do presently), it is apparent that the changes

[1]It need not be emphasized, I assume, that "radical" and "proximate" are relative terms. For a Burmese Buddhist, rebirth as a human being, let alone a *deva,* is an extraordinarily unique event, one which requires immense amounts of merit and which only the few can hope to attain. Most rebirths occur in the four "states of woe" (animal, demon, ghost, and hell). According to Buddhism, rebirth as a human is one of the Five Rarities, along with becoming a Buddha, hearing the preaching of a Buddha, becoming a monk, and becoming a righteous man.

that have occurred in nibbanic Buddhism with its diffusion to the religiously unmusical do not consist so much in an incorporation of foreign elements into the normative ideology[2]—although that has occurred to some extent —as in a selective emphasis and reorganization of the original elements. In this selective process some of the doctrines of the normative ideology have been retained, others have been modified, and—although lip service may be paid to them—still others (as we have already seen) have been rejected. In short, although kammatic Buddhism accompanied, and developed in response to, the sociological shift in Buddhism from an elitist to a mass religion, it would be false to view it as a creation *ab nihilo* of the religious masses. On the contrary, nibbanic Buddhism itself contains all the elements from which this new orientation developed and by which it has been legitimized. Given the psychological press for the new orientation, kammatic Buddhism merely transplanted seeds already sown by the contradictions inherent in the very fabric of nibbanic Buddhism. Hence, before examining kammatic Buddhism in detail, and before explaining the psychological grounds for the selective process that gave it birth, it is necessary to uncover those elements in nibbanic Buddhism on which it is based.

From an ontological point of view, Buddhism postulates the existence of two planes which, like parallel lines, never meet. On the one hand there is *saṃsāra*, the worldly *(lokiya)* plane; on the other hand there is nirvana, the otherworldly *(lokuttara)* or transcendental plane. Existence in the worldly plane is determined by the persistence of old and the creation of new karma. Attainment of the otherworldly plane is achieved by the extinction of karma. These two planes, however, are not only ontologically discontinuous, they are also hedonistically dichotomous. The former is the realm of unmitigated suffering; the latter is the realm of the cessation of suffering. Diagrammatically, the two might be depicted as follows.

FIG. 3

nirvana = nonsuffering

---

samsāra = suffering

The Buddhist world view, however, contains still other elements which

[2]This statement would be a misleading half-truth were it taken to imply that the religious belief of the Burmese and other Buddhists were exclusively Buddhist. The contrary is the case: in Burma, as in all other Buddhist societies, Buddhism is not the exclusive religion. In addition to Buddhism, the Burmese believe in and practice another religion, which however is nonsoteriological—i.e., concerned with this existence exclusively. If, as is often the case when a great religion comes into contact with an aboriginal one, these two religions had entered into some kind of syncretistic fusion, Burmese Buddhism—if the term were still appropriate—would look quite different from what it is now. For a description of this nonsoteriological religion and a discussion of its relationship to Buddhism, cf. Spiro 1967.

create serious strains in the structure of this parallelism. Although *saṃsāra* is characterized as the realm of suffering, nevertheless, even according to nibbanic Buddhism, suffering is not uniformly distributed throughout the plane. Extending from the lowest Buddhist hell, whose inhabitants experience tortures of nightmarish quality, and continuing through the highest Buddhist heavens, whose inhabitants, though not exempt from the universal law of suffering, enjoy the most blissful delights, *saṃsāra* is characterized by a continuum of pleasure and suffering. More important for the present problem, this differential distribution of pleasure and pain is a direct retribution for action performed. According to the law of karma, it will be recalled, action performed in conformity with Buddhist morality produces merit whose karmic recompense is a pleasant rebirth; the greater the merit, the more pleasurable the rebirth. Conversely, action which violates the Buddhist precepts produces demerit, whose karmic retribution is an unpleasant rebirth; the greater the demerit, the more painful the rebirth.

It should be apparent, then, that the attempted integration of the doctrine of nirvana with the doctrine of karma has produced an inherent and complex "double bind." Whereas according to the doctrine of nirvana (in which even the blissful life of a *deva* is a detour rather than a way station on the road to salvation), *saṃsāra* and nirvana comprise two distinctive and discontinuous planes of existence, by contrast, according to the doctrine of karma they comprise one hedonistic continuum, ranging from the suffering of hell at the one pole to the nonsuffering of nirvana at the other. And whereas according to the doctrine of karma samsaric pleasure is the just and proper reward for (Buddhist) moral action, according to the doctrine of nirvana this is not only an illusion but a snare, diverting one from the quest for true salvation; hence such pleasure should not be sought, and if achieved, should not be cathected. Hence the antinomies in nibbanic Buddhism: the consequence of moral action is a pleasant rebirth which, on the one hand, it holds out as a reward (while denigrating its pursuit as unworthy of a true Buddhist), but which, on the other hand—since all samsaric existence is painful—it sees as a persistence of suffering (although it is the harvest of action which it itself requires).

Although nibbanic Buddhism, as indicated in the last chapter, attempts to resolve some of these contradictions, the resolution is rejected by the average Burmese Buddhist. Instead, the Burmese and all other *Theravāda* Buddhists have used these contradictions as a lever for the transformation of nibbanic into kammatic Buddhism. In effecting this transformation, they use one of two strategies. The strategy of one group is to remain in *saṃsāra* and aspire to rebirth as wealthy humans or (even better) as *deva*. As far as they are concerned, this is salvation; nirvana can wait. The strategy of the second group is somewhat different. Although continuing to hold nirvana as their goal, they have transformed the meaning of "nirvana" from a state of nonsuffering into that of a heavenly state, similar to the blissful abodes of devahood, only more so. Both approaches will be examined in detail below. Here it is sufficient to state that they lead to the same result: a soteriology based on samsaric-like pleasure, even when it is called "nirvana," and an emphasis on merit and good karma as the primary conditions for attainment of this soteriological goal.

To conclude, then, the Burmese (together with the other Theravadins of Southeast Asia) have been able to affirm their loyalty to orthodox Buddhism, despite their rejection of the otherworldly message of normative doctrine, by exploiting the worldly implications of the normative doctrine of karma for their own soteriological goals. Hence, although the ideology of Burmese Buddhism is kammatic rather than nibbanic in its orientation, it is recognizably a Buddhist ideology.

The Psychological Basis for Kammatic Buddhism

A Conceptual Framework

Underlying the discussion above one may point to a simple psychological process: by reason of a variety of cultural, social, and motivational pressures, religious actors are loath to reject normative religious doctrine outright. Rather than reject a doctrine, their first preference is to modify or reinterpret it in such a way that, although on the one hand it becomes consonant with their own cognitive, perceptual, and motivational structures, on the other hand it is recognizable as normative doctrine. We shall have occasion to see this process at work in the case of still other doctrines of kammatic Buddhism as well. But shifts in religious ideology consist not only in the modification of some normative doctrines, but also in the acceptance of others and the rejection of still others. The selective process underlying this differential acceptance or rejection of a religious (or any other) ideology is determined by the psychological structure of the faithful, and more specifically by their cognitive-perceptual and motivational systems.

In the first place, doctrines are accepted if they are consistent with the religious actors' own conceptions of the world, i.e., with their cognitive and perceptual structures, which for the most part are derived from their personal experience. Like Durkheim (1954), I believe that the significant experiences in this connection are social, so that the perduring cognitive and perceptual structures which determine the acceptance or rejection of religious doctrines are rooted in and reflect social relations. Like Freud (1956), however, I believe that in most cases the experiences that leave the most persistent psychological residues are those had early in life, so that the social relations that most importantly determine these cognitive and perceptual structures are those a child has in his family. In any event, when religious doctrines are consistent with these psychological structures they become mutually reinforcing: the actors' own personal backgrounds provide experiential confirmation for the truth of the religious doctrines, and the latter provide authoritative sanction for the actors' own convictions. This is true, for example, of the Burmese acceptance of the Buddhist doctrines of karma and of impermanence.

It follows, then, that when religious doctrines are inconsistent with the actors' cognitive and perceptual structures, they will be rejected (although, because of various kinds of pressure, they may pay lip service to them). A case in point is the Burmese rejection of the Buddhist doctrine of suffering. Similarly, those doctrines which, although not inconsistent with the psychological structures, nevertheless do not resonate with them, will also be accepted, but will be held without strong (intellectual) conviction or (emotional) cathexis. This is true, for example, of the Burmese acceptance of the Buddhist doctrine of the *arahant.*

The second psychological structure which determines the differential acceptance of a religious ideology is the religious actors' motivational system. Religious doctrines are accepted if they can be used to satisfy various of the needs of the faithful, i.e., if (in one of the meanings of the term as used in the following chapters) they are functional. This proposition derives of course from the Freudian thesis that belief, no less than behavior, is motivated (Freud 1956). It follows, then, that beliefs which frustrate, or are inconsistent with, the actors' needs will be rejected, while those that are neutral with respect to their needs will be accepted, but without conviction or cathexis. The Burmese Buddhist examples alluded to above, in connection with the cognitive and perceptual systems, are also relevant here. This theoretical framework will be used to explain various of the doctrines of kammatic and other forms of Buddhism, as we encounter them in subsequent discussions. Here, we can apply them to the two important doctrines which have already been discussed in the shift from nibbanic Buddhism: nirvana and karma.

A Psychological Explanation

If the psychological theory outlined above is correct, it must follow that contemporary devotees of Buddhism reject nirvana as a sociological goal because they are different in psychological makeup from the founders and the early devotees of *Theravāda* Buddhism. This, indeed, seems to be the case. Early Buddhism, as Weber (1958:225-28) and others have pointed out, was the religion of "well-educated intellectual(s)," recruited predominantly from "great noble families and from rich burghers." In short, Buddhism was the product, ". . . not of the underprivileged but of very positively privileged strata." (*Ibid.*:227) Although Weber adduces a number of reasons for this conclusion, the most important, so far as the ideological transformations that have ensued with the diffusion of Buddhism is concerned, is that summarized in the following quotation. "The kind of salvation which was promised to the mendicant monk certainly was not one of the taste of the socially oppressed strata, which would have rather demanded compensation in the hereafter or this-worldly hopes for the future." (*Ibid.*:228)

This conclusion, I believe, is profoundly true; it both conforms to theoretical expectation and is borne out by what we know of contemporary Buddhist societies, including Burma. So far as theoretical expectation is concerned, the commitment of an entire society (by contrast to a small group of religious virtuosos) to the kind of world-rejecting ideology described in the previous chapter is a consequence, I would assume, of two conditions: disillusionment with worldly satiation, or a feeling of hopelessness concerning the possibility of worldly happiness. Let us examine these conditions *seriatim*.

After tasting the pleasures of the world and finding them wanting, a world-rejecting ideology becomes one viable alternative to what I take to be the modal mammalian orientation to the maximization of worldly pleasure. When a life which is successfully devoted to worldly pleasure is ultimately experienced as frustrating and (perhaps even more important) as meaningless, the renunciation of the social-cultural world can then be entertained as a desirable alternative. If, in experience, the satiation of the desire for worldly pleasures is as unpleasurable as its frustration, the desire itself (rather than the frustration) may then be perceived to be a source of unhappiness. Moreover, the prospect, for such a person, of a never-ending cycle of material rebirths is so dreary to contemplate that an ideology which offered the promise of its extinction would surely enjoy a very good chance of being adopted. For such a person, then, both dimensions of the radical soteriology of nibbanic Buddhism—its means and its goal—would have a strong appeal.

Conversely, it is hard to imagine that one whose worldly desires have not been satisfied would view his consequent unhappiness as due to anything but the frustration of desire. The aim of such a person, surely, would not be the renunciation of the desire for worldly pleasure, but rather its pursuit; for since, as he perceives it, suffering is occasioned by the frustration of desire and not by desire itself, happiness can be achieved by its fulfillment. For him, then, we would expect salvation to consist not in the extinction of desire, but in its satisfaction. For him, too, the renunciation of the sociocultural world—unless he is living on the edge of starvation and despair—would make little sense since, given his values, this would entail even more suffering than he is already experiencing. Finally, the prospect of cutting off all future rebirths—assuming that he believes in rebirth—would not be pleasing for such a person, since it would deprive him of the possibility of achieving the worldly pleasures he desires at some future time. Only if all his future lives were expected to be as painful as his present life would this prospect have a likely chance of being cathected; but since Buddhism holds up the prospect of unlimited worldly pleasure in his future lives, it is more likely that, for him, salvation would consist in the perpetuation of the cycle of rebirth, rather than its extinction. For such a person, then, neither dimension of the radical soteriology of nibbanic Buddhism would have much appeal: instead, salvation would be conceived positively as a state of pleasure, rather than negatively as the absence of suffering.

These theoretical expectations, as we have seen, are borne out (with certain qualifications to be considered later) by the evidence from Burma and other Buddhist societies in Southeast Asia. Thus, (a) while nibbanic Buddhism stresses impermanence as a characteristic of samsaric being, most Burmese reject this notion as it applies to the self. The pursuit of self-persistence in pleasant future rebirths is a central motif in Burmese thought and motivation. Related to this, (b) while nibbanic Buddhism insists on the doctrine of nonself, few Burmese either understand or accept this doctrine. The self is real; its persistence is desirable. (c) While nibbanic Buddhism sees desire as the root of suffering and the extinction of desire as the means to salvation, the Burmese view the frustration of desire as the source of suffering, and its fulfillment as the essence of salvation. (d) While the attainment of nirvana is the *summum bonum* of nibbanic Buddhism, the Burmese prefer the continuation of a samsaric-type existence—even when they call it nirvana—with pleasure, and even bliss, guaranteed by certain kinds of samsaric rebirth.

With this overview of the shift in the goal of *Theravāda* Buddhism, we may now turn to a detailed examination of the changes that have occurred in Buddhist ideology in its shift from a nibbanic to a kammatic soteriology, i.e., from a radical (otherworldly) to a proximate (worldly) salvation.

The Shift in the Conception of *Dukkha*

Nibbanic Buddhism, it will be recalled, is based on the first of the Four Noble Truths. Since, according to this Truth, all worldly existence is characterized by suffering, the single-minded goal of Buddhism is the extinction of samsaric existence in all its forms. Since, moreover, all worldly pleasure must be repaid in the coin of suffering, prudence and wisdom alike dictate an attitude of worldly detachment, a withdrawal of all cathexes, as a means for avoiding suffering. Pratt (1915:33) expresses the consensus of most Western interpreters in his characterization of Buddhism as,

> almost pathologically afraid of sorrow. . . . Turmoil of mind, inner disturbance, disappointment, the weariness of weakness and of old age, the grief that comes from the loss of dear ones and the defeat of ambition: these to it seem very dreadful indeed, so dreadful, in fact, as far to outweigh the joy that comes from health, successful effort, and human love.

Although this may be a proper characterization of normative Buddhism, it rarely characterizes the attitudes of Buddhists—not those, at least, whom

I know. Even the sophisticated villagers of Yeigyi, whom my Burmese assistant dubbed as "the philosophers" and who insist that "everything, even picking up a cup of tea, is suffering," are far from believing in the Buddhist explanation for suffering. If their behavior is an index of their conviction, it may be said of them that, instead of rejecting the world, they are very much of it. They are attached to wives and children; they aspire to better homes and more expensive clothes; they seek the pleasures of food and of sex. When challenged, they resolve this inconsistency by saying that although the Buddhist doctrine of suffering is unassailable, they have not yet reached that state of spiritual perfection which would allow them to act upon it. As worldlings, they are still attached to sex and family, to wealth and luxury. Though realizing that these all cause suffering, yet they cannot give them up because of the pleasure they afford.

If this is the attitude of the "philosophers," it is not surprising to find it even more strongly held by the average Burman. Although the meaning of *dukkha* (Burmese, *doukkha.*) is known to all Burmans—every member of my sample used the term in its technical denotation—few are convinced of its austere truth. That much of life entails suffering they are, of course, acutely aware. *Dukkha (doukkha.)* is probably the most frequently used term in the Burmese lexicon; it is on everyone's lips. One hears it scores of times every day—at work, at school, in the house, on a trip. For the Burmese, as for the rest of mankind, the notion that life involves suffering is not an article of faith; it is a datum of everyday experience. But it is one thing to agree that life *involves* suffering, and another to agree that life—every form of life—*is* suffering. This the Burmese find difficult to believe. To be rich, to enjoy good food, to attend a festival—these, surely, are *thoukkha.* (pleasure), not *dukkha (doukkha.).* If the life of a rich man or of a *deva* entails suffering, then surely (they argue) there are degrees of suffering. The *deva,* surely, suffer less than the rich, and they in turn suffer less than the poor. Or, to put it positively, although all forms of life may entail suffering, some forms involve so much pleasure as to render the suffering insignificant. With very few exceptions, all our interviews indicate that what the average Burman wants most of all is to be reborn as a wealthy human or—what is even more desirable—as a *deva* in one of the material heavens. The latter existence, although not permanent, since Buddhism denies permanence to any form of existence, is greatly to be desired. It is a life of overwhelming bliss: rich food, beautiful clothes, and every other conceivable pleasure, including—perhaps especially—sexual pleasure. As a village monk put it in a sermon, "The pleasures portrayed in American movies are as nothing compared to the pleasures of heaven."[3]

[3]Except for sexuality, the pleasures of the Buddhist heaven are very similar to those of the Christian. In a recently published treatise, already in its third printing, the Italian Jesuit, Luigi Majocco, stresses that in heaven, human pleasures are "heightened beyond conception." Physical deformities are erased; only the "best" wines and foods will be served at "eternal feasts"; music, dance, and sports will be enjoyed; "an infinite" range of "new and delicate

If the bliss of devahood or the pleasures of wealth are too much to be expected, the Burmese are then quite content to aspire to a somewhat better life than the one they enjoy at present. Most Burmese, as I have already remarked, do not believe that all existence is painful, or if it is, that this is caused by desire. Pain, as they see it, is caused by frustration; and, since most of their desires could be satisfied either as rich humans or as *deva*, they are prepared to suffer the few frustrations they entail. When pressed they concede that they are still worldlings, who see things from a worldly or secular *(loki)* perspective, which admittedly is conditioned (and deceived) by appearance. Were they able to see things from a religious *(lokuttara)* point of view—as reality really is—they would recognize the truth of the Buddhist explanation for suffering. In the meantime, given their limited perspective, they want to enjoy their physical pleasures.

This attitude to life explains the frequently observed but only apparent paradox of the Buddhist doctrine of suffering and the Burmese attachment to the world and its pleasures. The Burmese enjoyment of life is not only readily observable, but is reflected in their desire for its long duration. Indeed, thousands of monks and many more laymen invest much time and great wealth to the end of prolonging their lives through an occult practice (described in chapter 6) by which they aspire, not to immortality, since according to Buddhism everything is impermanent and that goal is impossible to attain, but to the prolongation of their lives for anywhere from 2,500 to 60,000 years. The former figure is provided with a (heterodoxical) Buddhist legitimacy: when the future Buddha, Maitreya, appears in 2,500 years, those fortunate to be living at that time can, by worshiping the resurrected Buddha Gautama, attain nirvana.

Rejecting the first Noble Truth, it is not surprising that the Burmese reject the second and third Noble Truths—the doctrines of the cause and extinction of suffering—as well. Following kammatic Buddhism, in which *saṃsāra* is graded from states of great suffering to states of great pleasure, the Burmese believe that suffering is caused, not by desire, but by the frustration of desire. Hence, for them deliverance from suffering does not mean the extinction of desire, but its satisfaction in a pleasant if not blissful rebirth. And the latter goal is achieved, not by the extinction of karma, but —as Buddhism teaches—by an increase in good karma.

When asked for the cause of suffering, almost everyone in my sample mentioned such immediate causes as a rapacious government, the action of evil spirits *(nat)*, lifelong poverty, the failure of crops, and so on. And almost all of them attribute these causes to the underlying cause of "bad karma" *(kan-makaung:bu)*. When asked how suffering can be relieved, the answers

---

fragrances" will be savored; and so on. These are not the fantasies of an evangelical preacher, but the serious pronouncements of the spiritual director of a Jesuit seminary in Turin. (*Newsweek*, July 8, 1968)

were uniform: the creation of "good karma" by such meritorious acts as the saying of beads, practicing the precepts, making offerings to monks, worshiping the Buddha.

The doctrine of suffering may properly be viewed as the fulcrum on which the entire ideological structure of Buddhism rests. Depending on the Buddhist's interpretation of this doctrine, the edifice can be tilted in the direction either of nibbanic or kammatic Buddhism. For observe: from the premise that samsaric existence is suffering, the twin conclusions of nibbanic Buddhism are inescapable, viz., salvation must consist in the transcendence of *saṃsāra*, a goal which can only be achieved by the cessation of the cycle of rebirth, i.e., by the attainment of nirvana. On the other hand, from the premise that samsaric existence can be pleasurable, the twin conclusions of kammatic Buddhism are inescapable: salvation can be achieved within *saṃsāra*, a goal which can be attained by assuring a pleasant rebirth.

With this background, we may now return to explore in greater depth the Burmese attitude toward nirvana.

The Shift in the Conception of Nirvana

Since nirvana is an ambiguous concept in normative Buddhism, and its attainment (whatever it means) means the cessation of samsaric existence, one's attitude toward it is obviously a function of two conditions: his conception of nirvana and his assessment of *saṃsāra*. If, as in nibbanic Buddhism, samsaric existence is conceived to be a state of unmitigated suffering, and if nirvana (whatever else it may mean) is conceived as the extinction of suffering, then logically nirvana becomes a—or the—most desirable goal. If, however, certain forms at least of samsaric existence are conceived (as they are in Burma) to be highly pleasurable, then one's desire for nirvana depends on one's assessment of the relative pleasures of *saṃsāra* and nirvana. Since most Burmese reject the Buddhist doctrine of suffering, there are basically two attitudes toward nirvana (Burmese, *neikban*) in Burma. Those who conceive of it as total extinction reject it as a desirable goal, while those who accept it as a desirable goal have transformed it into a state of great pleasure, a kind of superheaven. Let us explore these two attitudes.

Although Buddh*ism* is frequently cited, by the proponents of cultural relativism, as disproof of the alleged ethnocentric belief that the desire for immortality and the distaste for extinction are universal, this argument finds little support from Buddh*ists*. *Mahāyāna* Buddhism, if it ever had such a concept, has long abandoned the notion of nirvana as a state of total extinction; and *Theravāda* Buddhism, which according to some scholars does indeed conceive of nirvana as extinction, is followed in this belief by very few Buddhists. In Burma, most of those who conceive of nirvana as extinction have no desire to attain it. For them *saṃsāra* is preferable to nirvana, rebirth to the cessation of rebirth.[4]

The Burmese, of course, are not the only *Theravāda* Buddhists for whom a pleasurable rebirth is preferable to nirvana. All our evidence indicates that this preference obtains throughout the *Theravāda* world. The following attitudes, although referring to the Thai, are typical of Buddhists (so far as they have been described) everywhere.

> The ordinary Siamese never troubles himself about Nirwana, he does not even mention it. He believes virtue will be rewarded by going to heaven (Sawan), and he talks of heaven, and not of Nirwana. Buddha, he will tell you, has entered Nirwana, but, for his part, he does not look beyond Sawan. A man of erudition would consider this Sawan to be the heaven (Dewaloka) of Indra, a heaven that is not eternal. The ordinary Siamese does not consider whether or not it be eternal; it is at least a happy state of transmigration of vast duration, of which he does not recognise the drawbacks, and it is quite sufficient for his aspirations. [Alabaster 1871:xxxviii]

It will be noted, too, that this attitude to nirvana is not a product of modernization, westernization, urbanization, what have you; the above quotation refers to the situation in Thailand a hundred years ago. Purser and Saunders (1914:47), on the basis of extensive interviewing of Christian missionaries, reported the same situation in Burma more than fifty years ago. Indeed, as we shall see below, this same attitude was held in ancient Pagan, at the very beginning of Buddhist history in Burma.

[4]Although most Burmese who conceive of nirvana as extinction reject it as a goal, this is not uniformly the case. I did encounter some few Burmese—almost all of them monks—who aspired to the attainment of nirvana precisely because they conceive of it as extinction. Unhappy and world-weary, their one wish is to bring an end to their suffering. Thus, for example, one monk (who lived in a meditation monastery) said he devoted most of his time to meditation so that he might attain nirvana, which he defined as "extinction." When I asked him why he desired extinction, he said: "Everything is *doukkha.;* hence, extinction is much preferable to continued rebirth." Or, to take another example, a layman (who subsequently entered the Order) said he wanted nirvana (defined as "extinction") because "only in *neikban* will there be no suffering." When I asked him if he found none of his bodily activities pleasurable, he said: "No, there is no pleasure, neither in eating, in sex, in sleeping . . ." What, then, I asked him, about other forms of pleasure? Didn't he obtain pleasure from his children (to whom, I knew, he was strongly attached)? To this he said that no doubt he was happy with them, but "ultimately, they too give me *doukkha.*."

What was striking about both of these men—and about the few others for whom extinction was a desirable goal—was their seemingly acute state of depression. Unlike the typical Burman, who at least externally seems outgoing and gay, these men appeared to be markedly withdrawn and, clinically speaking, depressed. That they should have desired extinction over persistence, if persistence meant—as it did for them—the pain associated with deep depression, is hardly surprising.

Theoretically, the world-weary need not be the only type for whom extinction is a welcome or, at least, an acceptable end. There are also those who, having led lives of complete fulfillment, are ready to die (with no expectation of a future life) because, as the Bible says of the patriarch, they are "full of years." (*Genesis* 25:8) Typically, however, this theoretically possible type is empirically empty, whether in Burmans or elsewhere.

Those Burmese who, conceiving of nirvana as extinction, reject it as a goal, are caught up in a serious conflict. All the teachings of Buddhism, as found in the texts and as taught by the monks, describe life as suffering and hold up nirvana as the *summum bonum.* Moreover, all Buddhist prayers conclude with the wish—"that I may attain nirvana." Pious Burmese often repeat the admonition, which they constantly hear from monks (and others), viz., that all religious action should be motivated by the desire to attain nirvana. It is true, they will add, that acts of charity and morality will lead to a better rebirth, on either the human or the *deva* plane, but (they will caution) the consequences of these acts should not be confused with, or become the basis for, their motivation. The only legitimate goal of a Buddhist is nirvana, and the only legitimate motivation for religious action is the hope for its attainment. As one villager put it,

> Even *dāna* is no good if it is motivated by a desire to be reborn into a higher abode. The only motivation for any religious act must be the desire to attain nirvana. Otherwise, it is no good.

Another put it this way:

> Pious people pray only for nirvana; they do not pray to be rich or to go to some other abode. If they pray for these, they are not pious.

Every Burman, then, has learned to use the rhetorical mode of nibbanic Buddhism, and many Burmese have sufficiently internalized its goal to feel guilty about the nonnibbanic motivation for their Buddhist practice.[5] Nevertheless, their nibbanic aspirations are expressions more of traditional rhetoric than of a personal wish. Indeed, it is precisely because so many Burmese have lapsed from the nibbanic ideal that monks and others emphasize that the hope for nirvana is the only legitimate motive for Buddhist action; it is precisely because people want the fruits of merit (in the form of a good rebirth) that they are warned that this is a spurious motive. Spurious or no, the Burmese do not aspire to nirvana, if nirvana means the cessation of existence, and for the more thoughtful among them the conflict between normative expectation and personal desire poses a painful dilemma. This was poignantly expressed by (among others) the Yeigyi headman. In response to my query he said that he prefers nirvana to rebirth as a wealthy man. Since, however, he had previously said that nirvana means total extinction, I asked him why extinction attracted him. He

[5]One does not have to look too hard to find the guilt. After we had both given a contribution for the construction of a pagoda, my village landlord said he hoped that, as a consequence, we would both be wealthy in our next existence. When I said that I aspired not to wealth but to nirvana, he became noticeably upset, due, I believe, to two factors. As a pious Buddhist he should, himself, have expressed the nirvanic aspiration. His discomfort was compounded by the fact that his heterodox wish was implicitly criticized by a non-Buddhist.

laughed, in that special way in which Burmese laugh when they are embarrassed, and said in a low voice that actually he preferred a wealthy rebirth, but that it was not seemly that he should admit to this preference; were he to do so publicly he would be called a *lu-hsou:*, an evil person. He then proceeded, in a troubled tone, to talk about nirvana. It is, he said, "very perplexing. To desire nothingness *(ba-hma. mashi.bu:)* is hard to understand. It is *khette, theik khette* (difficult, very difficult) to accept."[6]

Because, as good Buddhists, the Burmese experience both guilt and embarrassment when they express such heretical views, most of them then go on to say that this desire for a pleasant rebirth does not mean that they will *never* want nirvana. It is only, they say, for the short run that they wish to attain the pleasures of rebirth. Having had them, they then wish to achieve nirvana. They have not rejected nirvana, they merely—like St. Augustine in the matter of celibacy—wish to defer it.

This attitude is remarkably similar to that expressed by their ancestors in Old Pagan, almost ten centuries ago. The following inscription—and there are many like it—records a prayer offered following an act of merit.

> Meantime, before I reach Nirvana by virtue of this great work of merit I have done, may I prosper as a man, and be more royally happy than all other men. Or as a spirit, may I be full of colour, dazzling brightness and victorious beauty, more than any other spirit. More especially I would have a long life, freedom from disease, a lovely complexion, a pleasant voice, and a beautiful figure. I would be the loved and honoured darling of every man and spirit. Gold, silver, rubies, corals, pearls and other lifeless treasure, elephants, horses and other living treasure—may I have lots of them. By virtue of my power and glory I would be triumphant with pomp and retinue, with fame and splendour. Wherever I am born, may I be fulfilled with noble graces, charity, faith, piety, wisdom, etc., and not know one speck of misery; and after I have tasted and enjoyed the happiness of spirits, when the noble law of deliverance called the fruit of Sanctity blossoms, may I at last attain the peaceful bliss of Nirvana. [Ray, 1946:165]

Some Burmese, however, do not even pay lip service to the doctrine of nirvana; they reject it out of hand. Thus a government engineer said, "Nirvana is not for me. Nirvana means the absence of motion; where there is no motion, there is no action. I would be constantly bored." Another informant, a businessman and like the former a resident of Rangoon, put it this way, "In nirvana there is no body, no soul, nothing. Who wants that?"

[6]Rather interesting, in this connection, are the remarks of a simple village monk torn between, on the one hand, his need to conform to the nirvanic ideal, and on the other, his obvious enjoyment of his present life. In the course of a lengthy interview, he admitted that he enjoys his present life as a monk, so that despite its frustrations he would prefer to be reborn as a monk to the attainment of nirvana, which he defined as extinction. But, he went on, he does not know what his lot might be in his future rebirths: he might be reborn as an animal or in some other unpleasant form. Rather than face such contingencies, he prefers nirvana, even though it means extinction.

Since most Burmese, viewing nirvana as extinction, reject it in favor of a worldly goal, rebirth as a wealthy human or as a *deva*, it is important to observe that when they are asked directly, as I asked them on a Buddhist interview schedule, "What do you desire for your next existence?" the overwhelming majority (of the household heads in Yeigyi) respond with "nirvana." (Table 1) Since these elicited responses seem to contradict attitudes expressed in noninterview ("real life") contacts, some discussion of them is necessary. There are, in my judgment, at least two factors which account for the preponderance of the nirvana response in the formal interviews. First, given the normative and rhetorical pressures alluded to above, one would expect "nirvana" to be the majority response. Indeed, given these pressures it is surprising that this response category was not larger; despite these pressures, nirvana was preferred by only 73 per cent of the males and 56 per cent of the females.

The second factor which influenced this finding is that, as we have seen, for many Burmese nirvana is not viewed as extinction but as a blissful state, similar to but even more blissful than the material *deva* heavens. For those who view nirvana as a heavenly superparadise, this interview response is entirely consistent with their soteriological aspirations expressed in noninterview contexts.

That nirvana, for most of the respondents who expressed a desire for it, is indeed viewed as a kind of superparadise is supported by internal evidence from Table 1. Since males and females differ markedly in their responses, we shall examine the responses of each sex separately.

Ignoring nirvana, and examining the other responses under "First Choice" in the Table, it becomes apparent that for the males the attainment of some form of physical pleasure is a theme pervading almost all of them. Thus, rebirth as a wealthy person, as a *weikza*, or as a *deva* together comprise most of the male responses. Except for "*thama. Boukta,*" the remaining responses, too, involve rebirth to physical pleasure (though somewhat diluted in intensity). In short, 90 per cent of the males who did not offer nirvana as their first choice projected a hedonistic goal as their preference for their next existence. If so, then, given the fact that "nirvana" is a stereotypic response (and its meaning, moreover, obscure), it is at least plausible that many who offered "nirvana" as their first choice view it as a kind of superparadise. The plausibility of this interpretation is greatly strengthened when their second choice is examined. As the Table reveals, their second choice overwhelmingly represents a hedonistic goal. Hence, it is reasonable to conclude that the first choice is also conceived in hedonistic terms—only more so.[7] This conclusion is supported, too, by the first choice

[7]It is more than a little surprising, given the veneration of monks and the generally accepted notion that the monastic life is an important means for the attainment of nirvana, that so few indicate a desire to be reborn as monks.

TABLE 1
RESPONSES IN YEIGYI TO THE QUESTION,
"WHAT DO YOU DESIRE FOR YOUR NEXT EXISTENCE?"

First Choice

DESIRE	Male	Female	Total
nirvana	61	43	104
rich	8	6	14
weikza	3	0	3
thama. Buddha *(Boukta)*	2	0	2
cult/trad/craft	2	0	2
male	2	16	18
heaven/*deva*	2	1	3
he has it now	1	0	1
avoid hell	1	0	1
don't know	1	2	3
rich male	0	7	7
ari.ya	0	1	1
monk	0	0	0
rich female	0	0	0
	83	76	159

Second Choice

DESIRE	Male	Female	Total
rich	19	7	26
nirvana	10	4	14
monk	5	2	7
heaven/*deva*	3	2	5
male	2	7	9
rich male	2	4	6
ari.ya	2	0	2
cult/trad/craft	1	0	1
weikza	0	0	0
thama. Buddha *(Boukta)*	0	0	0
he has it now	0	0	0
rich female	0	1	1
don't know	0	1	1
avoid hell	0	0	0
	44	28	72

TABLE 2
SECOND CHOICE FOR NEXT EXISTENCE
OF MALE RESPONDENTS IN YEIGYI
WHOSE FIRST CHOICE IS NIRVANA

DESIRE	*N*
rich	20
work	4
nirvana	3
miscellaneous	3
deva	2
ari.ya	2
	34

of those ten males for whom nirvana was their second choice. Although not shown in the Table, half of them gave some hedonistic goal (wealth, *deva*, *weikza*) as their first choice.

That nirvana, for many Burmese, connotes a kind of superheaven, is even more strongly supported by the female responses. Without exception, all the females (Table 1) who expressed a preference (two said that they did not know what kind of rebirth they desired) and who did not name nirvana as their first choice, named a goal whose primary attribute is hedonic. More important (Table 3), 89 per cent of those whose first choice was nirvana offered, as their second choice, a clearly hedonic goal.[8]

TABLE 3
SECOND CHOICE FOR NEXT EXISTENCE
OF FEMALE RESPONDENTS IN YEIGYI
WHOSE FIRST CHOICE IS NIRVANA

DESIRE	*N*
rich	20
work	4
nirvana	3
miscellaneous	3
deva	2
ari.ya	2
	34

[8]A most significant finding for the females, whose full discussion, however, must be deferred for another context, is the frequency with which the desire to be born as a male is found: next to nirvana, rebirth as a male is the most frequent first choice, and for those for whom nirvana is the first choice, it ties as the most frequent response in the second choice. Indeed, maleness pervades almost all the responses of the female respondents. Where it is not mentioned alone or explicitly, it is mentioned in conjunction with some other attribute, such as "rich-male," and it is implicit in such responses as monk, as well as in many of the "wealth" responses (since wealth in the village is generally associated with males). That Burmese

Even more interesting than these findings is the fact that most of the Burmese who desire nirvana, because they have transformed the hedonistic dichotomy of nibbanic Buddhism into a hedonistic continuum (ranging from the absolute suffering of the lowest hell to the absolute bliss of nirvana), have also, wittingly or unwittingly, destroyed the ontological dichotomy between *saṃsāra* and nirvana. Even when conceived as ontologically discontinuous, *saṃsāra* and nirvana are no longer conceived as constituting two separate planes, but rather as occupying separate positions on the same plane. Diagrammatically, the relationship has shifted from the parallelistic, two-plane ontology of nibbanic Buddhism (Fig. 4) to either a continuous (Fig. 5*a*) or discontinuous (Fig. 5*b*), but in either event a one-plane, ontology.

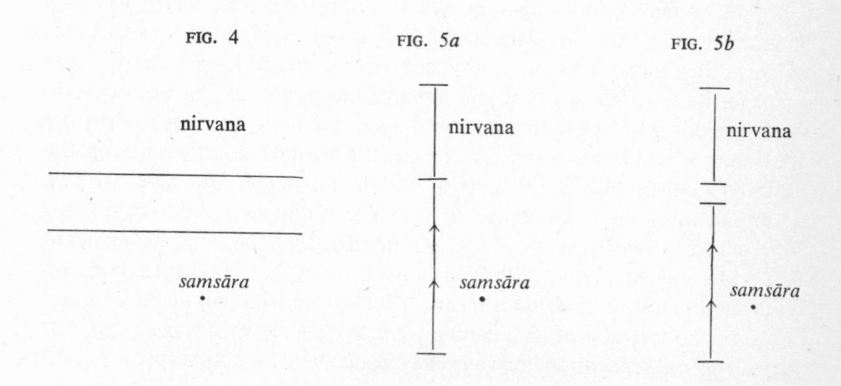

In the parallel planes of nibbanic Buddhism, no road leads from *saṃsāra* to nirvana (Fig. 4). Admission to each plane is governed by a set of different prerequisites and qualifications. If the prerequisite for *saṃsāra* is karma (or, more precisely, karmic merit or demerit), the prerequisite for nirvana is the extinction of karma. And these prerequisites are in turn based on different qualifications: ethically relevant (moral or immoral) action for the former, meditation for the latter.

For kammatic Buddhism, *saṃsāra* and nirvana, even when conceived as ontologically discontinuous, involve different locations on the same plane

women, who are among the most emancipated in the world, should desire to be reborn as males is, though paradoxical, not surprising. Males are conceded by both sexes to be superior to females. It was from a female that I first heard the Burmese expression: "A male dog is superior to a human female." This same woman, perhaps the most emancipated in the village, became visibly hostile when I suggested that she really did not give much personal credence to this proverb. Male superiority is accounted for in a variety of ways. Thus, only a male can be a Buddha, males are "nobler" than females, males have a pleasanter life than females, females have the task of bearing children, and so on.

(Fig. 5*b*). Nirvana is, as it were, the final destination of a road which begins at one end of *saṃsāra* and continues to nirvana as its other end. As one informant put it, the attainment of nirvana is like a train ride. In traveling from Mandalay to Rangoon, for example, the train passes through a number of stations en route. Similarly in traveling to nirvana, one passes through a number of "stations," i.e., a series of abodes, each more pleasurable than its predecessor, until the ultimate pleasure, nirvana, is attained.

That *saṃsāra* and nirvana are conceived by many Burmese to occupy the same plane is inferred not only from their heavenlike conception of nirvana, but from their belief that both require the same prerequisites and qualifications for admission. Unlike nibbanic Buddhism, in which admission to nirvana requires the extinction of merit as well as demerit, Burmese Buddhism insists that nirvana, like *saṃsāra,* is attained by the accumulation of merit. When asked why they are so concerned with merit, the vast majority even of the sophisticated Buddhists in my sample said this was because they wanted to attain nirvana. As they see it, karmic merit is the prerequisite for both *saṃsāra* and nirvana: the greater the karmic demerit, the more distant nirvana; the greater the karmic merit, the closer nirvana.[9]

I cannot leave this discussion of nirvana without commenting on the children's conception of this central Buddhist concept. Our most striking finding in this connection is that in a sample of nineteen children, ranging from seven to twelve years of age, ten insisted that they had never heard of nirvana and three more, although admitting that they had heard of it, said that they did not know what it meant. All of those who had heard of it and had some conception of its meaning were at least eleven years of age. For them, without exception, nirvana was conceived as a superparadise. In nirvana, one has all the joys of heaven in their quintessential form. As one girl put it, "nirvana is the most enjoyable form of life."

The Shift in the Conception of *Anattā*

The doctrine of nonself *(anattā)* is not only a crucial concept in Buddhist ontology, but the recognition of its truth is a fundamental element in nibbanic soteriology, being a prerequisite for the attainment of nirvana. Theoretically, it would seem plausible that the nonself doctrine would be most congenial to those for whom nirvana, viewed as extinction, is a desirable end. If so, it would follow that for those by whom a pleasurable rebirth, and therefore persistence, is desired, the doctrine of nonself would find little psychological resonance. This expectation is supported by the Burmese data.

Burmans, as we shall see, not only reject the concept of nonself, but many of them, including the most knowledgeable Buddhists in Yeigyi, do

[9]On this note it is of interest to observe that none of the respondents believe they had sufficient merit to attain nirvana in their subsequent rebirth.

not even know its meaning. In responding to my query, almost all of them confused the doctrine of nonself with the doctrine of impermanence, as the following (typical) responses indicate: "Nothing is permanent." "There is no permament material entity." "Everything is extinguished." Here is the comment of the most sophisticated Buddhist in the village: "Everything changes from moment to moment. As a human being I do not wish to die, to be blind, to get old, etc., but I must. I have no power to prevent them. This is *anattā.*"

On the assumption that a doctrine might be known and believed despite an apparent ignorance of the meaning of the technical (Pali) term by which it is designated, it might be argued that the inability of the Burmese to define *anattā* does not in itself imply that they believe in the existence of a soul or a self—on the contrary. And there is some evidence to support this argument. Using the Pali-Burmese term as *nan-teiya* (Pali, *nāma*) or the Burmese *wi.nyan* (Pali, *viññāṇa*), to refer alternatively to a person's spirit, consciousness, mind, or soul—for Buddhism distinguishes between the psychological *(nāma)* and the physical *(rūpa)* dimensions of all organisms—the more sophisticated villagers agree that this entity is impermanent; it comes to an end with a person's death. As one informant put it, "We distinguish, in the language of convention, between mind *(wi.nyan)* and body. But in reality there is only the body. Therefore, there is no entity which feels or tastes or thinks; there are only sense organs that have these functions."

Despite this indication for their disbelief in a permanent soul, even these knowledgeable Buddhists, however, share the universally held Burmese belief in the "butterfly spirit" *(leikpya).* Acquired from their pre-Buddhist ancestors, the butterfly spirit is in essence a permanent soul. (Cf. Spiro 1967:33-34, 69-70, 216-17.) Viewed as the essence of life, its permanent departure from the body is the immediate cause of death, and its reembodiment in a new form is the basis for rebirth. Since the *leikpya* of the deceased often desires to remain in its former haunts, and since if it does it can often cause trouble, a mortuary ritual is performed to prevent this from happening. When a corpse is taken to the cemetery, a relative breaks a branch from a tree and brings it to the home of the deceased. Here the butterfly spirit rests for seven days. On the seventh day monks are invited to chant certain scriptural passages which, among their other functions, send the *leikpya* away, never to return. *Leikpyas* of those with good karma are then reborn in pleasant abodes; others are reborn in unpleasant abodes.[10]

The apparent inconsistencies reflected in the foregoing paragraphs,

[10]The Burmese are not the only Buddhists who, contrary to Buddhist doctrine, believe in the existence of a soul. The Shans also explain rebirth by means of a soul belief. (Cf. Milne and Cochrane 1910:110-11.) Some Sinhalese go one step further by postulating the existence, not of one but of two souls—an "animal soul," which is closely connected with the body, and a "spiritual soul," which survives it after death. (Pertold: 1929:321)

which raise serious problems for nibbanic Buddhism, are readily explicable in the context of kammatic Buddhism. For most Burmese concerned with merit and karma, the belief in a permanent ego which survives the death of the body is both a psychological necessity and a moral imperative. The psychological necessity follows from their hope to achieve a better and avoid an unpleasant rebirth. Without the notion of a permanent ego persisting from one rebirth to the next, this hope (so they argue) would be irrelevant, the belief in karma would lose its motivational significance, and behavior would lose its religious (Buddhist) underpinning. Let us see.

In taking over the Hindu doctrine of rebirth, while yet rejecting its doctrine of a perduring self or soul *(ātman)*, Buddhism seems to have created a most serious paradox. Although, according to the rebirth doctrine, every being comes into existence as a result of rebirth, each new birth, according to the nonself doctrine, represents a new formation, having no relationship, material or spiritual, to any previous being. The classic attempt to resolve this paradox is found in *The Questions of King Milinda.* The King, addressing the Venerable Nāgasena, asks:

> What is it, Venerable Sir that will be reborn?
> A psycho-physical combination, O King.
> But how, Venerable Sir? Is it the same psycho-physical combination as this present one?
> No, O King. But the present psycho-physical combination produces karmically wholesome and unwholesome volitional activities, and through such karma a new psycho-physical combination will be reborn. [*The Questions of King Milinda,* 46, II, 1, 6]

But if this is so, if there is no continuity of identity from rebirth to rebirth, why, the Burmese (together with the critics of Buddhism) ask, should anyone be concerned with any existence except the present? To aspire to a happier rebirth (or even nirvana), or to attempt to avoid a painful rebirth seems pointless if, as they put it, "it is not *I* who am reborn, it is not *I* who enjoys the delights of heaven or who suffers the pains of hell." To be sure the being who will enjoy these delights or suffer these pains is produced by my karmic formations, but since that being is not *I*—"it is not my body" as the Burmese say—why should *I* be concerned with acquiring merit from which *he* will benefit? Conversely, if, with my body's death, I die without residue, why should I fear the tortures of hell? Since it is not *my* body but *that* body which is tortured, why should I not enjoy all those forbidden pleasures from which I abstain for fear of karmic retribution? As the Burmese couplet expresses it: *Di kou sa:me/ Hou kou hkan-me.* (*This* body will enjoy/ *That* body will suffer.)

Unlike their indifference to other problematic aspects of Buddhist metaphysics and ontology, the Burmese, as this discussion indicates, are both aware of and very much concerned about this particular paradox, a concern which they share with many early Buddhists (La Vallée Poussin 1917:ch. 2). This is understandable, since the paradox is especially vexatious for kammatic Buddhism. This is not to say that it is not a problem for nibbanic Buddhism as well, but for it the problem is primarily intellectual—a problem for Buddhist ontology—rather than pragmatic or existential as it is for kammatic Buddhism. That is, nibbanic Buddhism, concerned with the extinction of karma and convinced that suffering is the very stuff of *saṃsāra*, is not troubled by the notion that the actor himself is not the recipient of his karmic retribution. For kammatic Buddhism, however, in which karmic retribution is the essence of its soteriology and morality, this paradox strikes at its very foundation.

In general, thoughtful Burmans, monks and laymen alike, have several "Buddhist" solutions for it. One postulates the existence of a substantial essence or soul—the *nan-dei.ya.* (or *nan*) alluded to above—which is not dissolved with the dissolution of the body, but which on the contrary persists from rebirth to rebirth. Hence, though it is *not* my body, it *is* my soul, and therefore it is I who enjoy or suffer the future consequences of my present actions. But then, I queried a monk who proposed this heterodox solution (heterodox because the *nan*—the Buddhist *nāma*—is merely the designation for the psychological processes of organisms, which Buddhism lumps together as "form," and which, like everything else are impermanent), what of the doctrine of nonself? This, he replied, does not refer to the impermanence of the soul, but to that of the body. Then why, I persisted, is there a need for the separate doctrine of nonself, when according to his account it could be subsumed under the doctrine of impermanence? Surely, according to that account it is redundant? To this he strongly demurred. The nonself doctrine refers to the belief that the body is impermanent; impermanence refers to the belief that everything is in flux, in a constant process of creation and dissolution. This process, however, does not apply to the soul *(nan)*, which he insisted persists throughout all rebirths and only comes to an end with the attainment of nirvana.

This solution, however, is clearly not doctrinal. The doctrine of impermanence does mean, to be sure, that everything is impermanent; but the doctrine of nonself refers not to the body but to the self—the self is illusory, and if *ex hypothesi* there is no self, how can this nonexistent entity be reborn?

A second solution which the Burmese offer for this paradox is quite different from the first. Conceding that every rebirth produces a new being, rather than the old being in new garb, it is nevertheless argued that though there is no *identity* between the two—I am not he—there is continuity. The new being is aware of—can recall—his past existence; or more properly, is aware of the being whose karmic formation produces him. As one informant put it, it is like the child who, though not identical with the man, is still continuous with him.

Now, if everyone were aware of past existences, this would not be an unsatisfactory solution to the problem. For then, although realizing that my karmic formations will produce a totally new being, I would nevertheless be concerned about the fate of that being who, though not identical, is yet continuous with me. Unfortunately, however, the number of persons who claim to remember their previous birth is small. For the majority, characterized by amnesia as to their previous births, this is not a satisfactory solution.

A third attempt to deal with this problem invokes the much-used distinction between appearance *(loki)* and reality *(lokuttara)*. From a religious point of view—i.e., from the perspective of truth or reality—there is no permanent soul; but from a worldly point of view, from the perspective of appearance or illusion, such a soul exists. Since we live in the world of appearance, we act on the belief that it is we who will experience our own karmic retribution. This is at best, however, an unsatisfactory—because deceptive—solution and one which few Burmese take comfort or refuge in.

A fourth solution to the paradox, although held by the Yeigyi "philosophers," is blatantly antidoctrinal. For them the soul admittedly does not survive the death of the body, but the *khandhā* (described in chapter 2) do. Hence, it is indeed *my* body (though not my soul) which enjoys or suffers the future consequences of present action. This is antidoctrinal because, according to the doctrine of impermanence, nothing is permanent, least of all the *khandhā*.

Another and final solution was offered by the monks of a monastery in Mandalay. According to their view, the soul *(nāma)* refers to a reified consciousness or understanding which is carried by a disklike element in the blood. (Hence, the blood, too, is called *nāma*.) Although this consciousness does not survive the death of the body, it produces the "spark" which ignites the new fire of life, the new birth. This spark, then, is the basis for one's continuous identity. Thus, one of these monks argued, when a person is reborn in hell, its ruler *(Ma.ra.na. Tha-na Min:)* asks him what sins he has committed to merit such punishment. This must mean, he continued, that the person knows what he is to be is identical with what he has been. This sense of identity, however (so he argued), is a moral identity only. The person is aware of his former good and bad deeds, but unaware of his national, racial, familial, etc., identity. (This, of course, is inconsistent with reported cases of rebirth, alluded to in chapter 2, in which the memory of these latter attributes provides "proof" for the belief in rebirth.)

From this confused, and no doubt confusing, discussion, we may formulate the following conclusions. Most Burmese are unaware of the meaning of *anattā*. Most of those who know about and/or understand the concept are reluctant—indeed find it psychologically impossible—to face up to its consequences. To do so would undermine the very basis of their soteriological aspirations and render meaningless the renunciations entailed by Buddhist morality. Committed to kammatic salvation, they insist—normative

Buddhism notwithstanding—on the existence of an enduring soul which, persisting from rebirth to rebirth, experiences the consequences of karmic retribution. This soul is conceived to be either the pre-Buddhist *leikpya*, or in the case of the more sophisticated, an entity *(nāma)* derived from (but inconsistent with) normative Buddhist metaphysics.

It is of interest to observe that (consistent with our explanation for the selective process underlying ideological change), the Burmese, although rejecting the doctrine of *anattā*, are entirely convinced of the truth of the cognate doctrine of impermanence (Pali, *anicca;* Burmese *aneiksa*). The latter doctrine is not only widely, perhaps universally, known (its meaning is understood without even one exception in my sample), but the term is constantly on the tip of the tongue. A death, the burning of a house, a crumbling pagoda, a decayed monastery, the loss of political office—all these and many more not only evoke the comment *Aneiksa!* from even semiliterate peasants, but constitute ineluctable proof for the truth of this doctrine. Moreover, the more sophisticated among them engage in endless discussions and dissections of its meaning. The following are typical of some of their statements.

> Nothing is permanent. Everything exhibits creation and dissolution. Even the Buddha could not overcome this law. He could live only eighty years. Then he entered nirvana.

> Everything is impermanent; everything consists of atoms. Hence, everything depends on naming. It is through naming that objects are distinguished from each other, and are believed to persist over time.

> Nothing is permanent; everything consists of four elements—fire, wind, earth, and water. When objects dissolve into their elements, fire and wind combine, and water and earth combine. Generally, these four elements are combined [to give the appearance of persistence]. In fact disintegrative forces, known as *a-ka-tha*, are always at work. For example, there are five fingers on the hand; you think that you see them simultaneously. But this is not true. Each one is seen separately, and it is the mind which creates a unified perception.

These, of course, are intellectualized statements which, although sincere, do not express what I take to be the experiential basis for the Burmese conviction of the truth of this doctrine. Their conviction, I believe, rests on their perception of themselves and of others.

One of the singular characteristics of the Burmese is what might be termed the high contingency quotient that characterizes their perception of their own beliefs, sentiments, attitudes, and so on. Almost invariably, the answer to any question concerning a villager's habits, his likes and dislikes, his attitudes toward his work, his headman, or almost anything else, concludes with such common refrains as: "That is the way I feel now, but I can't tell about the future," or "Thus far I have no regrets, but I don't know about the future," or, "That's what I think today, but I can't say that I will think the same tomorrow." This element of contingency is based, the Burmese say, on the (for them) obvious fact that "the mind is fickle" or "the mind is always changing" or "the mind wanders," and so on. In short, for the Burmese it is a fact of experience that any mental state is always liable to change, and one can never be sure that one will think, feel, or believe tomorrow what one thinks, feels, or believes today. This lability in their own emotional and mental states forms, I believe, one of the bases for their generalization that nothing is permanent, a generalization which, deriving from their own experience, provides empirical underpinning for their acceptance of the doctrine of impermanence.

However, there is still another and more important empirical basis for its acceptance. The Burmese view not only their own inner states as evanescent, but look upon interpersonal relationships in the same manner. When studying friendship in the village I was struck by the comment, made over and over again, that there really is no such thing as a friend, because (as with one's inner state) no friendship can be presumed to last. "He is my friend today," the Burmese say, "but he may be my enemy tomorrow." Every friend is a potential enemy, and (though the converse is not so prominent) every enemy is a potential friend. You can never confide too much to a friend because tomorrow, if he becomes your enemy, he will use your confidences against you. The reason one can never be sure that a friendship will last, so the Burmese say, is that "you can never know what is in another person's mind."[11] This perception of the fluidity in interpersonal relationships, grounded in personal experience,[12] is I believe the second empirical basis for the Burmese conviction of the truth of the doctrine of impermanence.

[11]The similarity between the Burmese and the Thai in this respect, including the use of this very expression, is striking. In virtually all their interpersonal relations, writes Piker (1968: 391), Thai villagers

> . . . are wary of the intentions of others, repeatedly cautioning that, 'one can never know what is in the mind of others.' . . . Accordingly, the villager approaches interpersonal involvement with considerable caution and suspicion, and interpersonal relations are characterized by a relative absence of binding, mutual commitment. This pattern of expectation implies a low likelihood that stable relationships—such as enduring cooperative groups, or dyadic friendships—will be invoked as aids in surmounting life's inevitable crisis.

[12]The prototypical experience and, I believe, the fundamental basis for this perception is found in the parent-child relationship. After his initial experience in infancy as an object of continuous expressions of love, affection, and care, the Burmese child rather suddenly and (for him) inexplicably experiences a radical transformation in his relationship with his parents. As described in chapter 5, he is dethroned from his position of centrality, his desire for overt affection and emotional dependency tends to be ignored, and he is (frequently) an object of punishment. This is the paradigmatic experience, I believe, for the Burmese perduring perception of the inherent instability of interpersonal relationships. It is not surprising to discover that this perception both influences their interpersonal relationships and, at the same time, is confirmed by them. (Cf. Spiro 1969.)

Thus far we have explored one dimension of the shift from nibbanic to kammatic Buddhism—that of the soteriological goal involved. Unlike nibbanic Buddhism, whose aim is to transcend *saṃsāra* and attain nirvana, the aim of kammatic Buddhism is the enhancement of one's status within *saṃsāra.* But this shift from nibbanic to kammatic dimension involves, as we shall see, a change in yet another soteriological dimension—that of means. Whereas in nibbanic Buddhism, salvation must ultimately be attained by knowledge, in kammatic Buddhism it is attained by meritorious action. To explore this change, however, we must turn to the next two chapters.

CHAPTER 4

Kammatic Buddhism: II. The Central Concept of Merit

From Salvation Through Knowledge to Salvation Through Works

The Shift in the Conception of Soteriological Action

Although religious sociology has typically argued for the priority of ritual over myth, of behavior over thought, of action over ideas, this argument is based more on dogma than on evidence. Consistent with the dogmas of classical behaviorism (in which mind is epiphenomenon), of orthodox Marxism (in which ideology is superstructure), of vulgar Freudianism (in which ideas are always rationalization)—in short, consistent with an intellectual zeitgeist in which ideas are only responsive to, but are never the guides of, behavior—the determinants of religious behavior have often been sought in anything but in the minds and hearts of religious actors. Whatever the *general* status of the theology-ritual problem, there is little question but that in this *particular* case the shift in the soteriological goal of *Theravāda* Buddhism initiated innovations in, and changes in the conception of, normative Buddhist action. This is hardly surprising; for, if behavior is goal-oriented—and in my opinion religious behavior, contrary to those who view it as primarily expressive, is most frequently goal-oriented—then a change in goals must necessarily entail a change in means and/or a conceptual reinterpretation of traditional means. Both kinds of changes have occurred throughout the Buddhist world, including Burma.

Since, in nibbanic Buddhism, the soteriological goal consists in the cessation of rebirth, and since karma is the cause of rebirth, the aim of soteriological action is the extinction of karma. With the shift in soteriological goal to the persistence and enhancement of rebirth rather than to its cessation, the aim of soteriological action is the improvement rather than the extinction of one's karma. Hence, in nibbanic Buddhism salvation is achieved, not by works (and certainly not by faith), but only by knowledge *(paññā);* and since meditation alone produces the knowledge requisite for salvation, meditation is *the* soteriological act of nibbanic Buddhism. Any other kind of action, even moral action, is subversive of salvation, for morality produces karma, which in turn causes rebirth. Among contemporary *Theravāda* Buddhists, on the other hand, not knowledge but merit is the goal of religious action, for merit alone improves one's karma, and good karma is prerequisite for *their* soteriological aim, viz., a happy rebirth. Hence, since giving *(dāna)* and morality *(sīla)* are the primary means for acquiring merit, they (and not meditation) are viewed as *the* soteriological acts by the latter Buddhists. In short, there has been an important shift in *Theravāda* Buddhism from salvation through knowledge to salvation through works.

In Burma, although the importance of meditation as the royal road to nirvana is known to every schoolboy, and although almost any peasant can (and will) talk almost endlessly about it, the number of genuine meditators, as we have seen, is small despite the fact that there is probably more meditation in Burma than in any other Buddhist country.[1] Moreover, for some meditators, meditation itself (as we shall see below) has been reinterpreted in accordance with kammatic Buddhism, so that its aim is not knowledge but merit.

In Yeigyi, although meditation is universally admitted to be the quintessential act of Buddhism, only five men and no women in the entire village admitted that they ever meditate, and even these self-designated meditators do not practice what would be technically characterized as "meditation." Similarly, in my district sample of village monks, less than one-third admitted to practicing any type of meditation, and only four in my judgment were serious meditators. One of these said he meditated "all the time"; the others meditated anywhere from three to eight hours every day. When asked why they did not meditate, the nonmeditators gave fairly stock answers: their health was not good, they did not have the qualifications *(pārami),* they were too busy.

The Conceptual Centrality of Merit

We have seen that the shift from a nibbanic to a kammatic soteriology has entailed an important change in the conception of soteriological action.

[1]When one considers that Buddhist meditation requires a most subtle attention to physiological and psychological processes which (one may assume) is characteristic of only a small number of sophisticated and specially trained minds, this is hardly surprising. What *is* surprising is that an ordinary peasant, who has had no education beyond one or two years in a monastery school, should attempt to spend any time at all in meditation, or that, whether he practices it or not, he should value meditation as a soteriological technique.

Rather than constituting an irreducible obstacle to salvation, karma is viewed instead as its ultimate determinant. But karma, it will be recalled, is not a *deus ex machina.* It in turn is produced by merit (Burmese, *ku.-thou*) and demerit *(aku.thou).* These are the building blocks of Buddhist belief and practice in Burma; without them the entire edifice of kammatic Buddhism would collapse.[2]

There are, to be sure, some exceptions to this generalization. Those few Burmese who, although conceiving of nirvana as extinction, nevertheless aspire to its attainment, relegate merit to a secondary place. Consistent with nibbanic Buddhism, they disdain merit and the means by which it is acquired. As one sophisticated villager put it:

> Charity and morality [the means for acquiring merit] are reserved for the ignorant. The learned think only about meditation [the means for attaining nirvana]. . . . I do not want merit; I never think about merit. . . . For nirvana, only knowledge is needed, knowledge concerning suffering, impermanence, and non-self. If you know the meaning of these three [acquired through meditation] you attain nirvana.

This attitude, however, is restricted to a tiny minority. Even in my sample of sophisticated Buddhists only two respondents out of fifteen professed such an outlook. The vast majority of these knowledgeable Buddhists not only held the acquisition of merit to be their most important Buddhist activity, but viewed it as the indispensable means to the attainment of nirvana.[3] Hence before explicating the doctrine of karma we must first analyze the notion of merit.

Merit, the Burmese believe, is acquired in three ways—by charity or giving (Burmese *da-na.;* Pali, *dāna*), morality (Burmese, *thi-la;* Pali, *sīla*), and meditation (Burmese, *ba-wa-na;* Pali, *bhāvanā*). Although derived from Scripture,[4] the Burmese conception of this triad is yet dissimilar from its normative conception in nibbanic Buddhism, as described in chapter 2. The differences are instructive. Although, according to nibbanic Buddhism, these three types of action produce merit, it is not merit but wisdom *(paññā)* that is the means to salvation. Since wisdom is acquired through meditation, giving and morality are important only insofar as they produce the moral condition which is a prerequisite for meditation. Although morality and meditation produce merit, nibbanic Buddhism values them not for this reason, but as steps leading to the kind of wisdom necessary to achieve nirvana.

[2]This is true everywhere, of course, in *Theravāda* Asia. For Thailand, cf. Wells (1960: 11-12). For Ceylon, cf. Rahula (1956:254).

[3]A Mandalay monk went so far as to say that since merit is necessary for salvation, knowledge of merit is the defining characteristic of human nature. "A human being *(lu)* is one who knows merit and demerit, their causes, and their effects. . . Everything is created by merit and demerit, and everything is the effect of merit and demerit."

[4]Cf. the *Sagīti Suttanta* of the *Dīgha Nikāya* III, 1, 218, in *Dialogues of the Buddha,* Pt. III, p. 211.

For attainment of the soteriological goal of nibbanic Buddhism, the important, nirvana-producing triad is that of morality-meditation-wisdom. This, it will be recalled, is a capsule summary of Buddhism's Noble Eightfold Path. For nibbanic Buddhism, the members of the triad are viewed as successive rungs on a ladder leading to nirvana, the attainment of a lower rung being a prerequisite for each successive higher rung. In kammatic Buddhism however, with its samsaric soteriology, merit—not wisdom—is the (at least proximate) means to salvation, and it is the merit-producing triad of giving-morality-meditation that occupies the central position in its conception of soteriological action.

Actually there are in Burma at least two alternative conceptions of the relation between the members of this triad and the attainment of salvation; and both in turn differ radically from the nibbanic conception. According to one of these notions, this triad, like the nibbanic triad, is viewed as a ladder leading to salvation. But one climbs it, unlike the nibbanic ladder, in order to enhance one's karma by acquiring merit—not to extinguish it. Moreover, while merit acquired by giving *(da-na. ku.thou)* and morality *(thi-la. ku.thou)* is a means for improving one's future rebirths, meditation alone produces the merit necessary for nirvana. Hence, the first is known as "worldly merit" *(lo:ki ku.thou)* and the latter as "otherworldly merit" *(lo:kouktara ku.thou).* Nevertheless, this triad is conceived as a ladder, for by giving one acquires merit not only for a better rebirth but for the acquisition of those qualifications necessary to the practice of morality. Similarly, the practice of morality produces the merit to be reborn with qualifications necessary for meditation and hence for nirvana. In this conception, then, nirvana is achieved, as in nibbanic Buddhism, through meditation; but unlike nibbanic Buddhism, here meditation is efficacious not because it produces wisdom but because it produces merit. Nirvana, in short, is conceived as the karmic consequence of the merit acquired through meditation.

According to the second conception of this triad, giving, morality, and meditation, rather than representing steps on a ladder leading to nirvana, represent alternative (albeit differentially efficient) paths *(lan:)* for its attainment. These paths are known (in Burmese) as *kan-lan:*, *zan-lan:*, and *nyan-lan:*, respectively. The first path includes the practice of giving and of morality, those activities by which, according to nibbanic Buddhism, good karma *(kan)* is achieved.[5] Although this path is believed to lead to nirvana, it is an inefficient path: one must be reborn countless times before sufficient merit for nirvana can be acquired.

Zan-lan: is one of two meditational paths to salvation. Meditation, it

[5]There is a confusion, as we have already observed, in the Buddhist use of "karma." Technically, karma is volitional action which produces retribution *(vipāka).* Often, however, "karma" is used to refer to the retribution for action; thus, when speaking of good karma or bad karma, the Burmese have reference to the favorable or unfavorable retribution for action. It is in this sense that *kan-lan:* is the path which leads to nirvana by the acquisition of merit.

will be recalled, can issue either in mystical, trancelike states (Pali, *jhānas;* Burmese, *zan),* or in wisdom or insight. The former states, however, are a by-product of meditation, which if achieved may constitute a detour from the nirvanic path. Contrary to this normative view, the Burmese proponents of the *zan* path claim that succession through the four traditionally described trancelike states represents progression along a path leading from *saṃsāra* to nirvana without the necessity for insight *(vipassanā),* for *zan* produces merit necessary for salvation. Still, this path too is inefficient, for these psychic states are so absorbing that, rapt in ecstasy, the meditator may wish to delay interminably his entry into nirvana.

The third path, *nyan-lan:,* is the path of insight-meditation which, as we have already seen, leads to Buddhist wisdom or gnosis (Pali, *paññā;* Burmese, *nyan*). This is the path of nibbanic Buddhism, in which nirvana is achieved by the extinction of desire. For kammatic Buddhism, however, insight-meditation is the means to salvation, not because it produces insight, but because it produces merit. Indeed, meditation is sometimes referred to as *maha-da-na.,* the highest *da-na..* Whereas ordinary *da-na.* produces merit that leads to proximate salvation, *maha-da-na.* (meditation) produces merit that leads to salvation. In short, the normative emphasis on meditation as a means for the achievement of detachment and the extinction of craving has been replaced by a view of it as an almost mechanical means for the production of merit.[6]

[6]Aside from the doctrinal impropriety of this conception of meditation, there are two moral dangers implicit in the attitude. In the first place, those who hold it—and who also claim to practice meditation—tend to be self-righteous, if not arrogant. Since meditation enjoys high esteem in Burma, they tend to view themselves as superior to those who follow the other paths. In their own eyes they are an intellectual elite, while the others (the vast majority) are an inferior breed, rather like country bumpkins. They tend, too, as we shall see below, to hold less than respectful attitudes toward Buddhist monks. After all, they say, the monks are no better than they are, for they too (like the monks) are meditators; and, since meditation is the royal road to nirvana, their chances of obtaining nirvana are as great as the monks'.

This arrogance is accompanied by yet another moral danger, that of political and social immorality. There are two reasons for this. In nibbanic Buddhism it is assumed that meditation is both accompanied by, and—even more important—a consequence of, a spiritual regimen which has its foundation in morality. Without this moral foundation, meditation is not only impossible, but useless. For the small group I am describing, however, morality is not a necessary condition for meditation; rather, morality and meditation are different paths *(lan:)* leading to the same destination. Granted that immorality leads to demerit—yet, they claim, the merit derived from meditation is sufficient to neutralize any such demerit. As one of the village monks, criticizing this group, observed: "They want to be on top of the tree without first planting its roots." Or, to use another of his metaphors, "They have a superstructure without a foundation."

This danger is compounded when, as is often the case, the members of this group are political activists. In its initial conception, meditation was an activity pursued by monks or others who had renounced the world. For those who not only remain in the world but are politically active, the danger in the approach to meditation outlined here is obvious. They can commit any political crime, violate any precept, and yet have no fear for their salvation so long as they meditate. In short, when political activists hold the belief that meditation without morality is the road to salvation, the social consequences are dangerous indeed. Fortunately, this attitude toward meditation in Burma is held by only a tiny group.

It will be noted, then, that whichever of the two conceptions they have of the giving-morality-meditation triad, most Burmese view the acquisition of merit as the key to salvation. Those who seek samsaric rather than nirvanic salvation are, of course, exclusively concerned with merit; this is the expected concern. What is revolutionary (and heterodoxical) in Burmese and other forms of kammatic Buddhism is that the same orientation holds for those seeking nirvanic salvation. If these conceive of the triad as a ladder, their main aim is the acquisition of merit, for, whatever rung they happen to occupy, merit will bring them to the next rung on the way up. If, on the other hand, they conceive of the triad as a set of alternative paths leading to nirvana, they almost inevitably choose the giving-morality path *(kan-lan:)* because, they say, they do not have the qualifications for the other two paths. And although this, they concede, is a very long path to nirvana, still it will take them through a series of highly desirable rebirths. In either case the concept of merit occupies the central position in the structure of their Buddhist ideology.

To summarize, then, the centrality of merit in kammatic Buddhism stems both from doctrinal and motivational shifts from nibbanic Buddhism. For the latter, in which nirvana is the normative goal of Buddhist action, merit occupies a secondary position because, rather than leading to nirvana, the accumulation of merit leads to rebirth. Thus nibbanic Buddhism aims at the extinction of merit. From this position two shifts have occurred in kammatic Buddhism. For some Burmese the soteriological goal has changed from nirvana to a pleasant rebirth in *saṃsāra*—the "motivational" shift. For others, the attainment of nirvana, which remains their soteriological aspiration, is conceived, like any samsaric goal, as recompense for merit-producing action—the "doctrinal" shift. Given either shift, merit becomes salient, for in both cases the soteriological goal is achieved by an enhancement rather than the extinction of karmic formations.

Probably reflecting these motivational and doctrinal shifts, it is important to comment on a terminological shift which, as much as anything else, constitutes an index of the centrality of merit. In nibbanic Buddhism, it will be recalled, there is a distinction between *kusala,* good action, and *puñña,* merit acquired by such action. Throughout the *Theravāda* world, however, one or the other of these semantically distinctive lexemes—*puñña* and *kusala*—has been dropped and its meaning assimilated to that of the retained lexeme. "Merit" and "good," distinctive concepts in nibbanic Buddhism, have been fused into a semantically undifferentiated concept which is rendered by one lexeme alone. Thus, in Ceylon and Thailand, *kusala* has been dropped in favor of *puñña* (Sinhalese, *pin;* Thai, *boon*), while in Burma *puñña* has been dropped in favor of *kusala* (Burmese, *ku.thou*). This important linguistic change is consistent with both the doctrinal and motivational shifts alluded to. Since, according to the doctrinal shift, all action entails karmic retribution, good *(kusala)* action necessarily produces merit *(puñña);* they are undifferentiated. And since, according to the motivational shift, it is desirable that good action should produce merit, it is precisely because of its merit *(puñña)* that an act is deemed good *(kusala).* Again they are undifferentiated. In kammatic Buddhism, in short, what is important about an act, from the actor's point of view, is that it be meritorious, and if it is meritorious it is "good." If it is not meritorious, then at best it is irrelevant, and at worst bad. This being so, "good" and "meritorious" are tautological, and either *puñña* or *kusala* is redundant.

Means for Acquiring Merit: Morality

Morality and Merit

The Burmese agree almost unanimously that the merit obtained from giving and morality leads to a better samsaric existence—morality leads to a long life; giving leads to wealth[7] or to devahood.[8]

There are two ways of acquiring morality-based merit *(thi-la. ku.thou).* One way is to live in accordance with the (five, eight, or ten) Buddhist precepts, the other is to take an oath to comply with them. This oath, administered by a monk on Sabbath and holydays, is an important source of merit, as we shall see below. Here we shall be concerned with the behavioral compliance. He who continuously lives according to the Five Precepts, without ever falling away from virtue, can expect to reap the following consequences promised by the Buddha Himself.

> Fivefold, O householders, says the Buddha, is the gain of the virtuous person through the practice of virtue. In the first place the virtuous person, strong in virtue, acquires great wealth through his industry; in the next place, the good reports of him are spread abroad; thirdly, whatever society he enters—whether of nobles, Brāhmans, heads of houses, or members of the Order—he enters confident and self-possessed; fourthly, he dies without anxiety; and lastly, on the dissolution of the body, after death, he is re-born into some happy state of heaven. This, O householders, is the fivefold gain of the virtuous person. [Quoted in Tachibana 1926:63.]

[7]Recognizing the inconsistency between Buddhist norms and the desire for wealth, sophisticated Buddhists will say that even when offering *dāna*—whose merit leads to wealth—one should aspire not to wealth but to release from *saṃsāra.* Others say that wealth is desirable, not for its own sake, but to provide both the leisure that makes possible the practice of Buddhism, and the opportunity for more *dāna.*

[8]It should be noted that the retribution for worldly merit may occur in this as well as in a future birth. Thus U Mya Gyi, a sophisticated villager, pointed out that having offered little *dāna* when he was young he lost almost all of his inheritance. In his middle age he began to offer *dāna,* with the result that he has begun to recoup his losses. Especially when confronted with a crisis, the Burmese (as we shall see) perform meritorious acts in the hope that the acquired merit will produce immediate karmic consequences.

Interestingly enough, however, the main Burmese motivation for complying with the Buddhist precepts is not so much the expectation of merit as reward for compliance as it is of demerit as punishment for noncompliance. The Burmese have a set of conventional beliefs concerning the possible karmic consequences for the demerit of violating various of the precepts. Thus, for the sin of adultery, the man will be reborn with a small penis, the woman will be reborn as a prostitute. For adultery with a married woman, however, the consequence is hell. For killing a parent, teacher, or monk, one goes to hell for an interminable duration; for killing other persons or creatures, the penalty is hell for a shorter period, or a short human life. In general, despite the absolute prohibition on taking of life, the Burmese view the demerit acquired from killing as falling along the following moral gradient: pious man, impious man, mammal, vertebrate, invertebrate. If one steals, the consequence is pauperhood in one's future rebirth. White lies may have no serious consequence; chronic lying may lead to hell. Intermittent drinking, like the telling of white lies, can be expiated through meritorious acts; chronic drinking, however, will lead to hell.

Although the above beliefs are widely held, the variation in belief is much greater than this catalogue indicates. Thus, for example, some people believe that the violation of any precept leads to hell; others that one does not suffer in hell for the violation of any precept unless violation is chronic; some believe that if a male violates any of the precepts, he will first be reborn as a woman, after which he will be reborn in hell, and so on.

Buddhism and Moral Behavior

Although all five precepts are equally incumbent upon all Buddhists, it is of interest to know in what order of importance they are held by contemporary Buddhists, and hence how they are viewed from the point of view of merit and demerit. This problem was explored in a number of ways. First, I asked a sample of laymen and a sample of monks to rank the precepts in order of their "importance." Surprisingly—or, perhaps, not so—there was almost no agreement within or between these samples. In the monastic sample some monks insisted that all the precepts were of equal importance; others, for various reasons, ranked them in a variety of ways. Interestingly, however, they were about equally split concerning the precept considered to be the most "important." Some assigned this position to the prohibition on killing; others to the prohibition on alcohol. Those who stressed the latter based their reasons not on the intrinsic evil of drinking, but on its consequences: drunkenness leads to loss of control, which in turn leads to the violation of all the other precepts.

It is interesting to observe, however, that a scholarly abbot of a meditation monastery outside of Mandalay disagreed strongly with his colleagues, claiming that the prohibition on lying is the most important precept, and supporting his claim by scriptural arguments. Thus, an Embryo Buddha, he pointed out, never tells a lie; he may violate every other precept—and the Buddha Gautama, in his previous lives, was guilty of such violations—except for the precept prohibiting lying.[9] Moreover, he argued, in all the *Jātaka* stories lying is the only offense whose punishment consists in being swallowed by the earth. In this, he was referring, of course, to the *Cetiya Jātaka* (No. 422 in the Cowell edition), which records the first lie ever told. The king of Ceti decided to make a friend the court Brahmin by claiming that this friend, the younger brother of the previous court Brahmin, was in fact his elder brother, so that he rather than his brother's son should inherit the position. On the day on which he was to tell this lie, a "great multitude" assembled in the king's courtyard to hear the lie, something they had never before heard. The retired Brahmin also appeared before the king and warned him that if he uttered this lie he would lose his four supernatural powers: the guardianship of four *deva*, his ability to fly through the air, his sweet-smelling mouth, and his sweet-smelling body. Nevertheless, he told the lie, and lost his powers.

The Brahmin then beseeched the king to tell the truth, so that his powers might be restored. Instead, he repeated the lie, whereupon he sank to his ankles in the earth. He repeated the lie successively five more times, and each time sank further—to his hips, his navel, his chest—until finally the earth opened, flames from hell leaped up, and he was swallowed up.

But just as a lie is the worst moral offense, so telling the truth, according to the same abbot, is the most important of the moral virtues. An act of truth has tremendous power and can effect crucial changes. Thus, the abbot recalled the tale of a young boy who, after being bitten by a cobra, was taken by his parents to a monk to be cured. The latter said that no medicine could cure the boy, but that he would attempt a cure by an act of truth. He said that in his fifty years in the robes he had been happy

[9]In the *Hārita Jātaka* (No. 431 in the Cowell edition), when the ascetic, Hārita, having had sexual relations with the queen, was asked by the king if he had indeed committed this offense, he thought to himself:

> If I were to say I am not indulging in sin, this king would believe me, but in this world there is no sure ground like speaking the truth. They who forsake the truth, though they sit in the sacred enclosure of the Bo tree, cannot attain Buddhahood.

And the Buddha, who is recounting the story of Hārita (the Buddha Himself in a prior life), adds:

> In certain cases a Bodhisattva may destroy life, take what is not given him, commit adultery, drink strong drink, but he may not tell a lie, attended by deception that violates the reality of things.

only during the first seven years following his ordination, and "if I am telling the truth, let the poison flow out of this child's body." When he uttered these words, the poison flowed from the boy's head to his chest.

Then the father, saying he would tell a truth, said that he did not like to give *dāna,* although he had been doing it all his life. At this, the poison flowed from the boy's chest to his waist.

Then the mother said she would tell a truth. She said that she had not been happy with her husband during their entire married life. At this, the poison flowed completely out of the boy's body.[10]

We shall encounter below another instance of the magical importance of telling the truth in Buddhism. By an "act of truth" many dangers can be averted; one of the most important spells *(paritta)* of apotropaic Buddhism derives its power from such an "act of truth" performed in the past (see pp. 146-147).

Since the monks, then, differed among themselves in the relative importance they attached to the Buddhist precepts, it is little wonder that laymen, too, exhibited similar differences. The laymen did agree, however—almost unanimously—on the most important precepts, and to a lesser extent on the least important. Unlike the monks (who stressed either killing or drinking), laymen assigned the prohibition on adultery to the most important position. Interestingly, too, the sexes were consistently split on what they deemed to be least important. Almost unanimously the males said stealing, while the females said drinking had the least importance.

The laymen's emphasis on adultery is consistent with other findings. To the question: "What acts might you perform that would cause you to be ashamed?" and excluding those which cause shame only if they are witnessed by others, none of the males mentioned violation of any of the precepts; fourteen of the twenty-four responses of the females, however, include violation of precepts, and twelve of the fourteen consist in illicit sexual behavior. More important in this connection are the responses to the question, "What acts might you perform for which others would blame you?" Of the seventy-four responses (some subjects mentioned more than one act), thirty-eight dealt with the violation of precepts, and as Table 4 shows, illicit sexuality and stealing lead the list. (It is of interest to observe in passing that the category with the most frequent responses is that of abusive behavior, a nonprecept category.)

[10]The monk, although unhappy in the robes, remained because of his fear of being criticized for leaving. The husband offered *dāna,* despite his reluctance, because of a hereditary obligation to do so. The wife remained with her husband because she feared she would bring disgrace on her family should she leave him.

TABLE 4
BEHAVIOR DEEMED MOST BLAMEWORTHY BY BURMESE VILLAGERS
(*N* = 42)

Act	*Sex*		
	Male	*Female*	*Total*
Abusive behavior (physical and verbal)	6	11	17
Steal and cheat	6	7	13
Sexual immorality	8	5	13
Drink	5	0	5
Kill	5	0	5
Gamble	4	1	5
Lie	2	0	2
Misc.	10	4	14
	46	28	74

Upon further inquiry, however, it became apparent that for the laymen the social and pragmatic importance of the precepts is not related to their merit-demerit value—nor, therefore, to their motivational importance. (Since I did not explore this question with the monks, I do not know what their opinions concerning this issue might be.) When the laymen were asked to name the acts which conferred the most merit, not one male and only one female mentioned any of the five precepts. (The one female listed abstention from killing.) In short, however the Burmese view the social and pragmatic importance of the precepts, compliance with their injunctions is not in their minds an important way of obtaining merit. Almost unanimously, they stressed various kinds of giving *(dāna)* as the means, par excellence, for obtaining merit. (This finding is consistent with yet another. To the question, "What is the best thing to do?" none of the males, and only six of the females mentioned compliance with any of the precepts.) I shall return to this topic below.

Turning to demerit, however, the reverse is the case; the largest category of responses concerning the most demeritorious act (thirty-five out of forty-two responses) consists of the violation of one or more of the five precepts. (Table 5) Among the five precepts, moreover, the one which evoked the most responses, from males and females alike, was the injunction on killing, and not—as they had indicated when they were asked to rank their "importance"—adultery. For the second and third most frequent responses, there are important sex differences: drinking and illicit sex are tied for second place among the males, whereas stealing occupies second place among the females.

TABLE 5
BEHAVIOR DEEMED MOST DEMERITORIOUS BY BURMESE VILLAGERS
($N = 42$)

ACT	Sex		
	Male	*Female*	*Total*
Kill	4	11	15
Steal	1	7	8
Sexual immorality	3	2	5
Ill-will envy	2	2	4
Lie	1	3	4
Drink	3	0	3
Abusive	0	1	1
Misc.	0	2	2
	14	28	42

Means for Acquiring Merit: Giving

The Primacy of Giving

Giving *(dāna)* is the means, par excellence, for acquiring merit in kammatic Buddhism.[11] When asked to list the ways in which merit can be achieved, the Burmese, almost without exception, mention *dāna* to the exclusion of anything else. That giving is so much more important than morality as a means for acquiring merit requires an explanation. We have already observed that the Burmese concern with morality is more negative than positive. They are much more concerned, that is, with the demerit derived from violation of the precepts than with the merit derived from their observance. Indeed, one of the major motivations of the Burmese is to accumulate sufficient merit by other means—especially by giving—to compensate for the demerit accumulated through violation of the precepts.

There are, I would suggest, several bases for the lesser importance of morality, compared to giving, as a means for acquiring merit.[12] First, since the precepts are formulated negatively—one must refrain from this or that activity—compliance with them is an ambiguous and therefore psychologically unsatisfying method for acquiring merit. More especially, how can one calculate the amount of merit involved—and the Burmese are very much interested in such calculations—in abstention? There are no units by which abstention from a prohibited act can be measured. Hence, when the Burmese wish explicitly and deliberately to acquire morality-based merit, they

[11]The belief in karmic retribution for *dāna* is not, of course, an invention of Buddhism. For a discussion of its roots in pre-Buddhist India, see Mauss 1967:54 ff.

[12]In Thailand, too, giving is ranked higher than morality as a means for acquring merit. (Tambiah 1968:69-70.)

reverse the injunction against killing, and transform it into a positive act. That is, instead of merely complying with the prohibition against killing, they liberate animals who would otherwise be sold for slaughter. This is a positive act; its various dimensions can be counted and measured, and a rough estimate of the merit obtained from this moral act can be assessed in terms of the number and cost of the animals liberated.

Its measurability, then (so difficult to achieve in the case of morality), is one of the reasons for the primacy of giving. *Dāna* can be quantified—how often, how much, at what cost—and the resultant merit calculated. And this is of crucial importance to the Burmese, who are deeply concerned to know what is in store for them in their future existence.

But giving is psychologically more satisfying than morality, as a means of acquiring merit, for yet another reason. In sermons and tales, the soteriological fruits of giving are always explicit and clear, while those of morality are clear only for moral dereliction, not for moral conformity. Discussions of morality, as I have already indicated, constantly stress the karmic punishments attendant upon killing, adultery, lying, and so on; rarely does one hear of the karmic rewards for chastity, honesty, and so on. Discussions of *dāna,* on the other hand, not only tell of the punishments for the tightfisted, but emphasize the rewards for the openhanded; and these rewards are highly resonant with the goals and values of the Burmese. When monks take part in, or are the recipients of, public acts of giving—the offering of robes, the construction of a pagoda, the induction of a postulant, and so on—they almost without exception deliver a homily on the importance of *dāna* and its requital. Physical beauty, long life, great wealth, material pleasures, honor and respect—all of which comprise the core of Burmese aspirations—are only some of the rewards. Giving, of course, is an important virtue, but apparently it is also (as Franklin said about honesty) the best policy to follow in serving one's self-interest.

This observation leads to yet a third reason for the Burmese emphasis on giving as a means for acquiring merit. The emphasis is related, I believe, to the shift from the inwardness of nibbanic to the externalism of kammatic Buddhism. Giving can be—and in Burma often is—a purely mechanical act which neither requires nor entails much inwardness. Similarly, the merit whose acquisition is the motivation for giving can be achieved mechanically and automatically without the prior requirement of psychological or spiritual change. Rahula's characterization of medieval Ceylon is applicable without change to Burma. "It was easier for the ordinary man to do good deeds which were considered meritorious than to develop a good and pure spiritual character. . . . All their religion seems to be limited to external 'meritorious' deeds" (Rahula 1956:254).

The movement away from the "inwardness" of nibbanic Buddhism is best exemplified in the general change in soteriological action from meditation to merit, whether acquired through morality or giving. For in either case the aim of the action has changed from transformation of the self to a transformation in the social and material status of the self. Although an instrumental act, meditation as conceived by nibbanic Buddhism does not aim at changing either the world or one's future status in the world. It aims, rather, at changing the self from a creature of passion—characterized by desire, hate, and delusion—to an enlightened being, wholly liberated from these three "cankers." Action in kammatic Buddhism, on the other hand —i.e., meritorious action—is intended to change one's karma, not one's moral or spiritual character. The desired transformation in material and social status is achieved without any corresponding transformation in the self. This claim may be observed most vividly in the Buddhist initiation ceremony, by which the young boy is inducted into the Buddhist novitiate. This is the most important religious event in the boy's life. It is not merely his initiation or "baptism" into the Buddhist church; it is almost the necessary qualification for his becoming a truly human being. Although he may remain in the monastery for the duration of only one *Wa* (the three-month rainy season—the canonical period in which a monk must remain in retreat, in residence in his monastery), this monastic experience, in theory, lays the foundation for a lifelong spiritual discipline.

Contemporary practice, however, bears little relationship to normative theory. The mechanical acquisition of merit is of far greater importance than the spiritual discipline acquired by the boy. This attitude is shown in two ways. In the first place, the ceremony is often performed at a very early age—as early as two years—before the initiate can learn any spiritual discipline. Moreover, rather than remaining for the duration of one full Lent, the boy often remains for merely a week or two. Very young boys may remain only overnight. Thus, although much merit may be acquired from the mere donning of the yellow robe—or so the Burmese believe—its acquisition is entirely mechanical, neither demanding nor producing any transformation of self.

Since this ceremony initiates the boy into the Buddhist church, its sponsorship is perhaps the most valuable form of *dāna*, yielding great merit. A second measure of the external quality of contemporary Buddhism is afforded, therefore, by the observation that the initiation is Burma's most important Buddhist ceremony—not because of what it can do for the initiate, but primarily because of the merit which, mechanically acquired, accrues to the sponsor. That the transformation of self has been relegated to a secondary goal is shown even more clearly in the cases in which a boy undergoes more than one initiation. An adult without a son may sponsor an initiation for a boy who has already gone through the ceremony, not because the youngster might thereby acquire a firmer basis for Buddhist spiritual discipline, but so that the sponsor may acquire merit.

These examples, illustrate the paradox of a virtue (generosity) coming to exhibit the same properties as the vice it was intended to combat (selfishness). *Dāna*, to be sure, has beneficial consequences for its recipient, but it is motivated primarily by the self-interest of the donor. I have used the initiation ceremony to illustrate this paradox because this ceremony looms so large in Burmese Buddhism, but other examples, both trivial and important, could equally illustrate the paradox. Perhaps one trifling example will suffice. At a monk's funeral soda water was distributed to the many hundreds of participants. Having already consumed many cups of tea, I passed the tray of bottles as it came to me, explaining that I was not thirsty. My companion, a brother of the sponsor of the ceremony, asked if I would not, nevertheless, drink part of a bottle so that his brother might acquire merit. The water was not so much intended to quench the thirst of the participants as to provide merit for their benefactor.

A more interesting and less petty example of the moral paradox in merit striving is afforded by the ritual of merit sharing and transfer described in the next chapter. Although seemingly an unambiguously altruistic act, its motivation is in fact quite ambiguous. In some cases self-interest is the exclusive motivation; in others the motivation is mixed. For those who, while practicing the ritual of merit sharing, nevertheless deny that merit can be shared, self-interest is often the exclusive motivation: by offering to share their merit with others they themselves acquire merit—for, it will be recalled, merit attaches to the intention of an act, not to its objective consequences. For those who believe that merit can be transferred, self-interest is still an important—though not the exclusive—motive since, for the reason suggested below, merit is acquired by both persons. Indeed, even for the person who shares merit, his act (unlike the sharing of money) has the paradoxical consequence of augmenting rather than decreasing the original quantity in his possession. For as the Burmese point out, by performing some type of meritorious act with the intention of sharing the consequent merit, one not only acquires merit from the original act, but in addition from the meritorious intention of sharing. This, then, is truly a system in which to him who giveth, it shall be added unto him.[13]

My point, then, is that inwardness is foreign to an orientation in which giving is superior to morality as a means for acquiring merit. This is not to say that it need be so, and indeed in the theory of nibbanic Buddhism it is not. According to the latter, giving in itself does not produce merit for the donor unless his act is accompanied by a pure intention *(cetanā)*, by which is meant a real concern for the welfare of the recipient regardless of its consequences for the donor. Monks, who frequently preach on *dāna,* often remind their audience that the merit derived from giving depends on this pure intention, i.e., the spiritual quality of the benefactor. For the most part, however, the Burmese have reversed this relationship between donor and

[13]Still, not everyone is willing to share his merit. One old lady who had just completed the restoration of a monastery told me that she would not share her merit with her children because she wanted it all for herself. My Burmese assistant later pointed out to me that this woman's motives were not unambiguous. Frequently, he said, Burmans who do not get along with their parents or their children will not share their merit with them, not only because they dislike them, but also because they do not wish to be together with them in their next rebirth.

recipient. For them the merit deriving from *dāna* is proportional to *the spiritual quality of the recipient* rather than that of the donor. It is for this reason primarily that they insist, as we shall see, upon the piety of their monks. The donor may be a terrible person—wicked people attempt to expiate their sins by offering great amounts of *dāna*—but he receives much merit by giving to pious monks. For the same amount of *dāna* the merit acquired by the crook is no less than that acquired by the saint.

Human behavior, however, is seldom unidimensional either in meaning or in motivation, and to compound the difficulty, its multiple meanings and motivations are often contradictory. This being so, it must now be made clear that in trying to account for the primacy of giving as a means of acquiring merit we cannot overlook the importance of sacrifice as a dominant theme in Burmese (Buddhist) culture. Although it exists in a state of tension with the previous two bases for the primacy of giving, its internalization by the Burmese constitutes a fourth basis for their emphasis on giving. That Burmans, on the one hand, respect power and wealth is obvious to anyone who is even superficially acquainted with Burmese life. That on the other hand they respect sacrifice and renunciation is, however, equally obvious. The incredible veneration which the Burmese tender their monks is based almost exclusively on the sacrificial character of their lives. Giving, although rewarded, partakes of this sacrificial quality. To give to others is to give up something of one's own; the more one gives, the more one gives up. When one examines the amount of income and saving that the Burmese devote to *dāna,* it is readily apparent that it does indeed constitute a form of sacrifice. For in the most elementary meaning of sacrifice, the inordinate amount of wealth that is offered as *dāna* represents an important (in some cases, an extreme) diminution in present comforts and pleasures, and in general in the average Burman's style of living. *Dāna,* on the scale which characterizes Burmese giving, represents genuine deprivation. Even when *dāna* is a mechanical act, it entails self-deprivation; for the Burmese, it is the act of self-deprivation that is most conducive to the acquisition of merit.

When this is kept in mind, one arrives at a somewhat different perspective on the relative position of morality and giving in Burmese Buddhism. Unlike the stringent moral code of the monk, ordinary lay morality does not require great sacrifice, and if sacrifice is—as it is in Burma—the mark of piety, *dāna* becomes a more meaningful indicator of piety than moral conformity. "After all," a village elder observed when discussing this problem with me, "if morality is the criterion, almost everyone is pious—how many people kill, fornicate, etc.?" It was for this reason, he continued, that everyone considered the hated village usurer, the widow Daw Kyi, to be pious. Although most people detested her, they had to concede that the lavish scale on which she offered *dāna* represented considerable renunciation and therefore genuine piety.

For the Burmese the most important symbol of self-sacrifice, and the crucial model for their own emphasis on the primacy of giving, is the Buddha Himself. Various *Jātaka* stories, those tales which recount the past lives of the Buddha, describe the sacrificial behavior of the Buddha in his pre-Gautama incarnations. The most famous of these, at least in Burma, is the *Vessantara Jātaka.* Taught to every schoolboy, alluded to frequently in conversation, recounted repeatedly in sermons, and—even more important —regularly enacted in dramatic form as part of the standard fare of the itinerant Burmese repertory troupes, the story of Prince Vessantara is probably the best known and most loved of all Buddhist stories. Its sacrificial idiom provides the charter for and reinforces the Burmese belief in the religious efficacy of giving. As we shall see below (chapter 13), Vessantara not only renounced his royal title but even gave up his family—first his children, then his wife—to a Brahmin, so that by his sacrifice he might obtain salvation.

Lest this dwelling on sacrifice be misunderstood, its soteriological goal must be underscored. Sacrifice is not a selfless act, an end in itself. It is valuable, rather, as a means to the all-important soteriological end. This is as true of the extreme sacrifice of Vessantara as of the minor sacrifice *(dāna)* of the average Buddhist.

Concerned as they are with their future lives, the Burmese are also—and deeply—concerned with their present lives. It must be stressed, then, that a fifth basis for the accent on *dāna* lies in the honor and prestige that attach to giving in Burmese society. Ordinary giving, of course, goes unnoticed: it is the least that can be expected of a human being. To abstain from feeding monks, or refrain from contributing to the collective purchase of monastic robes, and so on, would be unheard of. Special giving is both noticed and commented upon. People are respected for the amount of money they spend, and their prestige is graded accordingly. And since these amounts are matters of public knowledge, every effort is made to lay out as much as possible on public *dāna.* We shall have more to say about this prestige function of giving in a later chapter.

These, then, are five bases—there are probably more—for the primacy of giving as a means for the acquisition of merit. Sometimes, indeed, it seems as if the Burmese view it as the only means to this end. For, retrospectively at least—i.e., when they attempt to explain what appears to be unusually good or unusually bad karma—*dāna* offered in his past lives is almost always given as an exclusive explanation for a person's fortunate or unfortunate life. X is wealthy because, having offered much *dāna* in his past lives, his karma is good. Y has suffered numerous tragedies because she offered little *dāna,* and therefore her karma is bad.

The Content of Giving

Although *dāna* is glossed as giving, liberality, or munificence (cf. *Pali-English Dictionary*), it must be stressed—as some of these examples have implied—that for the Burmese it is primarily concerned with religious giving. To contribute to the support of a monk, to erect a pagoda, to offer flowers to a Buddha image—these are *dāna.* To contribute to the support of a widow, to build a school, to bring flowers to the sick—these are not, or at best are inferior *dāna;* little if any merit is to be gained from them. Thus, as the Burmese put it, the feeding of a hundred dogs is equivalent in merit to the feeding of one human being; the feeding of a hundred laymen is equivalent to the feeding of one novice; the feeding of a hundred novices is equivalent to that of one ordinary monk; and so on.

That *dāna* consists primarily of religious giving is underscored by the fact that all the acts which comprise the category of "meritorious celebration" *(ahlu),* an act especially productive of merit, are religious. These include the sponsorship of the Buddhist initiation rite, the sponsorship of a monastic ordination, the sponsorship of a monk's funeral, the feeding of monks, and the construction of religious structures, such as monasteries and pagodas.

As in the case of the charitable acts discussed above, these various types of *ahlu* are also graded according to the amount of merit they yield. Thus, the most merit is acquired by building a pagoda, closely followed by the building of a monastery. Sponsorship of an initiation follows closely upon the erection of a religious edifice. Providing for the needs of monks is ranked next, and this too is graded according to the piety or the holiness of the monk: the greater his piety, the greater the merit of his benefactor. Offerings to the Buddha (at an image or a pagoda) are usually taken as less meritorious than offerings to monks.[14] In any event, the fact that few Burmans can afford to build a pagoda or a monastery has had the consequence, of course, of confining the meaning of *dāna* to the latter form of giving, especially of food.[15]

This cannot be stressed enough. When the Burmese think of merit and *dāna,* they typically think of monastic feeding ceremonies. Indeed, the care and planning that go into the feeding of monks probably consume more village time and energy than any other single activity, agricultural labor

[14]The same hierarchy is found in Thailand. (Cf. Tambiah 1968:69)

[15]But Buddhism, as is well know, is very fond of classifications, and *dāna* has not been immune to this propensity. According to one classification, the Burmese distinguish between two types of giving: one consists of offerings to monks—robes, food, medicine, and so on—*(pyizzaya anoukaha dāna),* the other of preaching and spreading the Buddhist doctrine *(Dhamma dāna).* The latter, as the folk saying has it, is the most valuable form of *dāna (thabba danan Dhamma danan zinati),* and being the most valuable, it produces the most merit. Thus, some monks pointed out to me that by answering my questions concerning Buddhism, they were not only helping me in my research, but were acquiring for themselves the highest form of merit.

All of these classifications are given in the combined Burmese-Pali rendering of the Pali terms, for it is from the Burmese that I obtained them.

Since the latter type of *dāna* is interpreted not merely as teaching the doctrine oneself, but as making it possible for others to teach and practice it, the sponsorship of a ceremonial offering may also be interpreted as *Dhamma dāna,* which thereby confers on the sponsor the highest form of merit, *Dhamma* merit.

excepted. They are offered not only their daily meals, but are feasted at almost every important event in the individual and collective life of the Burmese—engagements, marriages, funerals, initiations, holydays, house-warmings, political rallies, exorcisms, departures for a journey, etc.—as well as any other time in which someone feels like adding to his merit. In addition to feeding monks, invited laymen are also fed at many of these ceremonies which also results in *dāna*-produced merit.

As might be expected the Burmese have given much thought to the calibration of merit and *dāna*. Thus, although they distinguish (according to amount) four types of giving—less than one can afford *(hinza dāna)*, as much as one can afford *(mizima dāna)*, more than one can afford *(pinita dāna)*, and finally, sacrificial giving *(prissiga dāna)*—[16] it is generally held that the second type, or giving as much as one can afford, is the proper one to follow. Moreover they define "as much as one can afford" by a simple rule of thumb: one-fourth of one's income. The Burmese say that one-fourth of one's income should be contributed as *dāna*, one-half should be spent on living expenses, and one-fourth should be saved. To contribute more than one-fourth (especially if one is poor) is not only unwise, for this can lead to financial worry and even mental illness (and the Buddha is surely against this), but from the point of view of merit, it is not necessary. Although merit is proportional to the amount of *dāna* offered, this proportion, in principle, is relative to one's income. Thus, although the absolute difference may be enormous, a poor man who offers 25 per cent of his income as *dāna* acquires no less merit than a wealthy man who offers 25 per cent of his.

Although, in principle the above statement is believed to be true, most Burmese act (and believe) as if it were not. There is little doubt that for the average Burman the rich, by virtue of the greater absolute amount of their giving, are believed to acquire much more merit than the poor. This may be inferred from various observations. Regardless of relative income, the Burmese believe that feeding ten monks produces more merit than feeding one; building a monastery for a monk confers more merit than offering him a robe; and so on.[17] This holds for the dead as well as for the living. The merit transferred to the dead from the feeding of ten monks is greater than that which is transferred from the feeding of one; and this difference might be critical in determining the deceased's rebirth. In short, since the rich are

[16]Cutting across the last category is still another graded classification, according to content. One may sacrifice one's property *(dāna prissiga)*, one's child *(poutta prissiga)*, one's wife *(bhariyā prissiga)*, a part of oneself—e.g., limb—*(inga prissiga)*, or one's life *(ziwita prissiga)*. The last type is exemplified only by an Embryo Buddha *(hpaya: laung:)*.

[17]For those Burmese who are excessively concerned about these matters, the relationship between giving and merit raises some intriguing casuistic questions. Thus, if merit varies with the amount of alms offered to monks, and if it also varies with the number of monks to whom one offers alms, does it make any difference, for example, if one offers 100 *kyat* to one monk or 10 *kyat* to ten monks? I have listened to many and lengthy discussions of this and similar issues.

rich because of their past *dāna*, and since they will become even richer in their next existence because of their (and their descendants') present *dāna*, it is the old story of to him who hath shall be given.

The Motivational Salience of Merit

Since merit is the basis of their entire soteriology, it is not surprising that its acquisition is, for the Burmese, a ubiquitous concern. The Yeigyi headman put this concern in normative terms: "Every place is to be viewed as a cemetery," so that, conscious of the imminence of death, one will "always look for an opportunity to acquire merit." And the Burmese act upon this prescription. Every action is viewed from the standpoint of its merit potential; no opportunity for acquiring merit is rejected. The unpleasantness of an act may be redeemed by discovering some merit potential inherent in it. Thus, when the army ordered Yeigyi to repair its road, the men devoted an entire evening to discussing whether they might acquire merit from this most distasteful chore.

Merit is not only of great concern to the Burmese, but the acquisition of merit is, for them, the primary motivation for Buddhist action. This orientation has led critics of Burmese Buddhism to characterize it—not without some justification—as "selfish." Compliance with the moral code of Buddhism, for example, most often stems from a desire to obtain merit, or conversely to avoid demerit, rather than from conscience or a consideration of its social consequences.

That the acquisition of merit is the primary motivational basis for Buddhist practice has been implicit in this entire discussion, most especially in connection with giving. There can be no doubt that the desire for merit is the primary basis for the practice of *dāna*, and their great concern with *dāna* is a true measure of the salience of merit in the Burmese motivational system.

This concern is dramatically exemplified in the lavish support of monks described in chapter 17. If anything, it is demonstrated even more strongly in the extraordinary amount of wealth expended on all forms of giving, described in chapter 19. Finally, it is manifested in their careful merit bookkeeping. Like those Calvinists described by Weber (1930:124) who kept religious account books, many Burmese keep merit account books,[18] which at any time permit them to calculate the current state of their merit bank. Consistent with their view that giving is the most important form of acquiring merit, these are exclusively concerned with *dāna*. To be sure, the

[18] As we shall see in a later chapter, there is an important difference between the Calvinist and Buddhist calculations. The Calvinist recorded his sins, temptations, and progress made in grace because of his concern to know whether he had been elected for salvation. The Buddhist records his meritorious deeds because he is concerned to know to what extent his soteriological efforts are commensurate with his soteriological goal.

poor, whose contributions are relatively small, have no need for such books. Poor or wealthy, whether he recites from memory or from an account book, almost any villager can say to the last penny how much (and for what) he has expended on giving—which is why the anthropologist is able to obtain detailed accounts of the financial aspects of Buddhism. It is as if each unit of *dāna*—however it be calculated—produced a commensurate unit of merit, so that in order to calculate one's store of merit and hence predict one's future existence, it is merely necessary to keep a cumulative account of one's giving. Where merit account books are kept, each case of *dāna* is entered in the following detail: the date, the occasion, the number of persons involved, and the total cost. One villager told me that he examines his merit book frequently because, when contemplating all his merit, he is happy.[19] The practice may not be typical, but the attitude is.

A Note on Children

Given the centrality of the concept of merit in Burmese Buddhism, it is of interest to know how early this concept is learned and at what age its acquisition becomes an important motive for action. It is rather surprising to discover that no child under the age of nine—no child, at least, in my sample of nineteen children—has any conception of the meaning of merit. Indeed, this statement holds for some children as old as eleven, although by that age most children do have some notion of the significance of the concept. Table 6 summarizes the children's conceptions of "merit." This Table requires no further explanation.

TABLE 6
CONCEPTIONS OF "MERIT" HELD BY VILLAGE CHILDREN*

CONCEPTION	*N*
Do not know	6
Will not go to hell	3
A good future existence	3
Become a *deva*	2
Wealth in next existence	2
Attain nirvana	2
Not become an animal	1
	19

*Ages from seven to twelve.

[19]In Ceylon, merit account books are—or at least were—also used magically. A man's merit book was read at his deathbed so that the dying man, gladdened by his many merits, would acquire pure thoughts, which according to folk Buddhism would assure him a good rebirth. (Cf. Rahula 1956:254.)

As these children see it, merit is acquired in a variety of ways, as Table 7, which summarizes their responses, reveals. This, like the previous Table, speaks for itself. It need only be pointed out that the view that monks are the most important instruments for the acquisition of merit is acquired very early.

TABLE 7
CHILDREN'S CONCEPTION OF THE MEANS BY WHICH MERIT IS ACQUIRED (*N* = 19)*

MEANS	*N*
Worship and feed the monks	8
Worship one's elders	6
Observe the Five Precepts	6
Worship the Buddha	5
Help one's elders	4
Help others	2
Gild a pagoda	1
Worship the personal guardian *nat*	1
Refrain from tormenting animals	1
Dig canals and wells	1
Build monasteries and pagodas	1
Express gratitude to teachers	1
Remain patient when offended	1
Maintain good relationships with others	1
Offer charity to nuns and beggars	1
Do not know	1
	41

*Ages from seven to twelve.

CHAPTER 5

Kammatic Buddhism: III. The Key Doctrine of Karma

The Metaphysics of Karma

Since the soteriology of kammatic Buddhism views salvation in samsaric terms, it is concerned, as we have seen, with the enhancement of (good) karma rather than with its extinction. Karma, of course, is intimately related to merit, and in order to understand the concept of karma it is important to grasp its relation to the concept of merit. This relation however is extremely ambiguous, varying according to whether it is explicated in terms of nibbanic or kammatic Buddhism.

According to canonical Buddhism, it will be recalled, "karma" refers to volitional action, of which there are (morally viewed) two types: good *(kusala)* and bad *(akusala)*. Good karma produces merit *(puñña)* for which there is favorable or pleasurable retribution (*vipāka;* literally, fruit) while bad karma produces demerit *(apuñña)* for which there is unfavorable or unpleasant retribution. Hence, "one's life fate is determined by one's karma" is an ellipsis for "one's life fate is the consequence of one's own prior action (karma)." Diagrammatically, this may be represented as follows:

FIG. 6

karma (good/bad) ——→ merit/demerit ——→ retribution (pleasant/unpleasant)

In the normative conception, then, karma is to merit/demerit as cause is to effect.

In Burmese Buddhism karma is conceived not as the cause but as the effect of merit or demerit. Produced by merit/demerit, karma (Burmese, *kan*) is conceived somewhat as a metaphysical force which is responsible for the retribution for one's actions. As the Burmese use these terms, then, good and bad action produce merit and demerit, respectively; they in turn produce good and bad karma; and karma produces the appropriate retribution for the action. Diagrammatically, this conception of the relationship between merit and karma may be represented as follows:

FIG. 7

action (good/bad) ⟶ merit/demerit ⟶ karma (good/bad) ⟶ retribution (pleasant/unpleasant)

Hence, in this Burmese conception, "one's life fate is determined by one's karma" is elliptical for "one's life fate is the consequence of that force (karma) produced by all of one's past action." Thus, when the Burmese say a certain person is ill because of his *kan,* or that he is rich because of his *kan,* or that he failed his examination because of his *kan,* they mean that each of these events (viewed as retribution for his past behavior) is caused by karma, the metaphysical force produced by his past behavior. (Present karma, produced by past behavior is *bwa: kan;* future karma, produced by present behavior, is *nauk bwa: kan*).

The difference between the canonical and Burmese conceptions of karma, then, is in part lexical and in part conceptual. For the former, "karma" is used to refer to any action which entails moral retribution for the actor; for the latter, "karma" refers to that metaphysical force which, as the consequence of such action, is the cause of the retribution. They both agree, however, that one's destiny represents retribution for one's own meritorious and demeritorious actions, and that this retribution is the expression of the law of karma, i.e., the law of moral cause and effect, by which merit is rewarded and demerit is punished.

Still, although the law of karma is the law of moral retribution, the Burmese do not always conceive of it in this way. In some cases the cause-effect relationship is viewed in mechanical rather than in moral (retributional) terms. Thus, for example, a husband and wife, are said to have married each other (rather than thousands of other possible mates) because of their karma. Or a person is said to have been born in Yeigyi rather than in some other village, because of his karma. Or the anthropologist is said to have come to this village because of his (and their) karma. And so on.

Though deprived of its retributional dimension, "karma" in the above examples retains the dimension of causality. Often, however, it loses even this dimension and is used rather as a synonym for luck, fortune, fate, chance. Thus, when a person's misfortune is explained, as it frequently is, by *kan makaung;bu:*—"his karma is bad"—what is meant is that he has had some bad luck. And often, too, when some action is taken, after a series of misfortunes, to "improve one's karma"—moving into a new house, for example—the meaning is not to acquire additional merit but rather to change one's luck. When one is informed a few weeks later that this same person's "karma is good"—*kan kaung:ba-de*—what is meant is that his luck has changed for the good.

Although "karma," then, is often used in Burma in this latter sense, it is more often used in its more technical, causal sense, and more specifically in its retributional sense. Nevertheless, the relations (as the Burmese see them) among karma, merit, and retribution are not unambiguous. Indeed, since any human being performs both meritorious and demeritorious acts, there are at least two logically possible interpretations of their relationship, and both are found in Burma. According to one, accumulated merit produces good karma *(ku.thou kan),* which in turn produces rewarding consequences; and accumulated demerit produces bad karma *(aku.thou kan),* which produces painful consequences. At the risk of tedium it must be observed further that this interpretation, in turn, has two variants. According to one, the above conception of the relations among merit, karma, and retribution may be diagrammed as follows:

FIG. 8

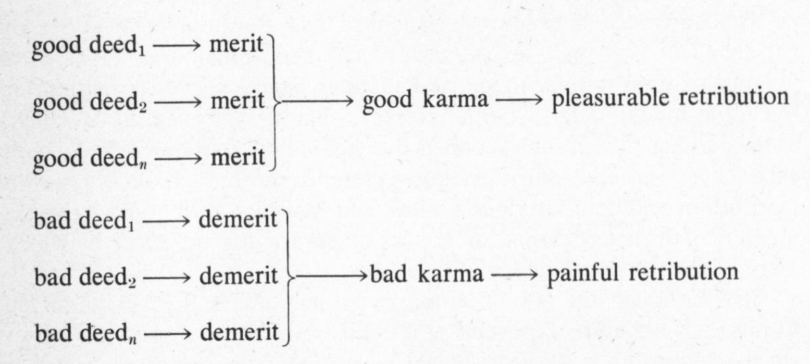

According to this variant of the first conception of karma, good and bad karma represent, respectively, the sum of one's merits and demerits. Although every volitional act has karmic consequences—i.e., creates merit or demerit, it does not produce a separate retribution; retribution (Pali, *vipāka*) is for aggregates of acts rather than for individual ones. Every act contributes its share to a person's store of merit or demerit; these stores comprise one's good and bad karma, respectively; and each type of karma produces an aggregated retribution. Thus, because of his bad karma, a person was reborn as an animal; because of his good karma, he will be reborn as a king, and so on.

According to the second variant, however, it is not the case that each volitional act contributes to an aggregated retribution; rather each act (or more typically, each type of act) produces a separate retribution, which moreover is specific to the type of act(s) performed. This interpretation is shown in the following diagram.

FIG. 9

good deed$_a$ ⟶ merit ⟶ good karma ⟶ pleasurable retribution$_a$
good deed$_b$ ⟶ merit ⟶ good karma ⟶ pleasurable retribution$_b$
good deed$_c$ ⟶ merit ⟶ good karma ⟶ pleasurable retribution$_c$

bad deed$_x$ ⟶ demerit ⟶ bad karma ⟶ painful retribution$_x$
bad deed$_y$ ⟶ demerit ⟶ bad karma ⟶ painful retribution$_y$
bad deed$_z$ ⟶ demerit ⟶ bad karma ⟶ painful retribution$_z$

Here, retribution is *separate* (either for an act or for a type of act) and *specific* (each type of act produces its own type of retribution), rather than aggregated and general. When interpreting retribution in this manner the Burmese use the term *wut* (Pali, *vuṭṭha,* that which arises of itself, i.e., automatically and as a consequence). If each act, or type of act, produces a separate and specific retribution, then, obviously, demerit cannot be neutralized—the retribution is absolutely determined. Thus, the punishments suffered by the selfish monk in the story recounted below represented retribution, specifically, for a given type of demerit. Having deprived his fellow monk of food, he himself was made to suffer various forms of food-deprivation.

Typically, the Burmese are much vaguer about the *wut* for meritorious, than for demeritorious, deeds. Thus, the retribution for giving is rebirth as a wealthy human or a *deva;* that for morality is a long life. *Wut* for demerit is much more specific; the punishment not only fits the crime, but—as the below story shows—tends to exemplify the talion principle. Dacoits who attack others will, in their next existence, be attacked by dacoits. Those who welsh on their debts will be reborn as the servants of their creditors. Those who give no charity in one existence are poor in another existence—i.e., they have no money for charity. This is a recurrent topic of conversation: people are poor because they have not been charitable in their past existence (all fourteen of the poorest villagers in Yeigyi said they were poor because they had not given sufficient *dāna* in their previous rebirths), and they are rich because they have offered charity. Those who cannot control their lust will be reborn as lustful animals. In some cases, such as murder, one act is sufficient to produce the retribution; in other cases, such as charity, it is a pattern of miserliness rather than a specific act that is required.

Almost daily, unusual fortune or misfortune is explained as *wut* for some specific act or type of act performed in a previous life. Similarly, sermons and speeches are filled with allusions to or descriptions of various kinds of *wut.* The following are taken at random from both types.

> *Dāna* is very important. Even if you are reborn as a dog, you need have no concern about food—since you gave *dāna,* people will feed you.

> Everything is ruled by cause and effect; if you repay your debts to others, others will repay their debts to you.

> If you are overly attached to your family or your property, you will be reborn as a demon.

> During the war, many buildings in Mandalay were razed to the ground. From the merit of *kahteing* [special offering of robes to monks], ruined buildings have been repaired, and new ones have sprung up.

> The merit acquired from offering robes to monks will confer upon the donor wealth, wisdom, beauty, health, and strength in his next existence.

> At the time of the Buddha, there was a monk who had a strong attachment to the robe offered him by his sister, an attachment which he retained even on his deathbed. He was reborn as a louse, still clinging to the same robe.

Since, according to this second variant of the first interpretation of karma, different types of acts produce separate, and sometimes specific, inherent natural results each domain in a person's life may be the consequence of different types of good and bad karma. Thus, there may be good and bad karma for education, for politics, for economics, and so on. Take, for example, the cases of U Lum Byei and U Youn, two inhabitants of Yeigyi. Because U Youn's economic karma was bad, and U Lum Byei's good, the former was poor and the latter rich. On the other hand, since U Youn defeated U Lum Byei in the election for village headman, his political karma was good while U Lum Byei's was bad. In short, seen from this perspective everyone's life is a crazy quilt of good and bad karma. U Khant, to cite but one more case from Yeigyi, provides a dramatic example. On a fifty-*kyat* bet he won K1,320 (about $275). Overly excited by his good fortune, he died the following morning, leaving his winnings to his relatives. As a result of his good karma—probably resulting from *dāna*—he won his bet; but as a result of his bad karma—probably caused by a murder committed in the past—he died.

Whatever the disagreements between these two variants of the first interpretation of karma, they both agree that good and bad karma work independently of each other; no good deed goes unrewarded, no bad deed unpunished. Retribution, whether pleasant or unpleasant, is never lost.

Thus, as a consequence of his bad karma, a person may be an animal in this existence, only to be reborn as a *deva* in the next one, in consequence of good karma for which he had not yet enjoyed his proper reward.

The second interpretation of the relations among merit, karma, and retribution differs from the first in that it postulates only one karmic force rather than two. One's karma according to this view represents the net balance, the algebraic sum, of one's accumulated merit and demerit. If the accumulated merit is the larger, one's karma is good and karmic retribution is pleasurable; if the demerit is larger, one's karma is bad and karmic retribution is painful. Thus, for example, one hears that "so-and-so is rich because his karma is good," or that "so-and-so is poor because his karma is bad," meaning that the net balance of his merit and demerit has resulted in either good or bad karma, which in turn has produced either a pleasant or painful retribution. This conception may be diagrammed as follows:

FIG. 10

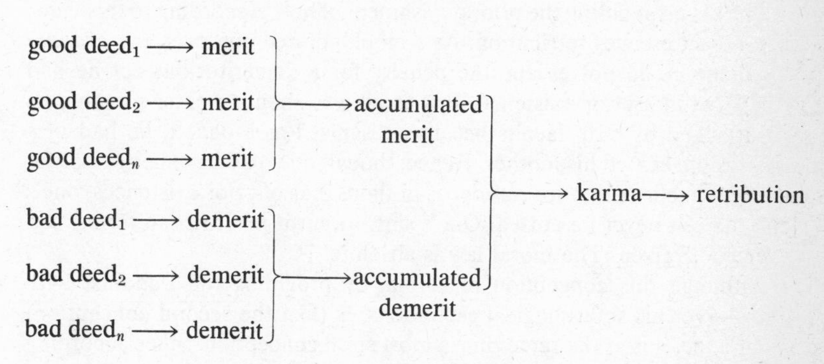

According to this second conception, it will be noted, one's karma is always in flux—it is in a perpetual state of unstable equilibrium. Good karma can be changed into bad karma by the accumulation of additional demerit; bad karma can be changed into good karma by the accumulation of additional merit. Hence the many account books by which the owners are able to assess roughly, for their present existence, their net balance of merit and demerit.

This second conception of karma as representing a net balance of merit and demerit, which renders one's karma susceptible of change, is the basis for many Buddhist practices which are examined in detail in later chapters. It is the basis, too, for that combination of immorality and piety which is found in any legalistic religion. Thus, aware of the karmic consequence of murder, a politician may both plot the assassination of a political opponent and, at the same time, plan the construction of a pagoda—on the assumption that the merit acquired from the latter deed will avert the penalty for the former.[1] This conception of karma is the basis, too, for the transfer of merit, especially at the time of death, to the deceased. The resultant change in the latter's karma is believed to alter the conditions of his rebirth from a painful to a pleasant abode. Finally, this interpretation is the basis for a great deal of popular Buddhism (examined in chapters 6 and 10) in which ritual is employed to avert painful karmic retribution in one's present existence.

Psychological Press and the Neutralization of Karma

The distinction between these two conceptions of karma is of more than metaphysical interest; it has important practical consequences. According to the first conception there is nothing one can do to escape the painful consequences of his evil deeds. A person may have been saintly for a hundred generations, but having at some time committed an evil act whose retribution, say, is rebirth in hell, he has no way of escaping this consequence. He may, because of his saintliness, go directly from hell to heaven; but there is no avoiding the prior punishment of hell. According to this view, then, no act escapes retribution. As a monk pointed out, even the *arahant* Mogallana could not escape the penalty for a demeritorious act he had committed in a prior existence. Just as he was about to enter nirvana, he was attacked by 510 dacoits because, disguised as a dacoit, he had in a previous life beaten his mother. Hence, though one may have performed an infinite number of meritorious deeds in thousands of prior existences, one's demerits can never be erased. One's sins, to put it in Christian terms, can never be forgiven. The moral law is absolute.

Although this conception of karma, by providing the Buddhist with control over his soteriological aspirations, is (like the second conception) one of hope, it is at the same time a most stern conception. Since according to this interpretation karmic retribution for sin is inevitable, it places an enormous burden, both moral and emotional, on the individual, a burden which few persons can sustain. Indeed, this interpretation of karma renders *Theravāda* Buddhism the harshest of all salvation religions. Even without this notion of karma Buddhism is difficult enough. Denying the existence of a divine savior, Buddhism deprives the sinner of the possibility of divine intervention or intercession; it precludes the possibility of grace; it precludes the possibility that the requirement of justice be tempered by divine mercy; it precludes the possibility of atonement and forgiveness. When, in addition, the sinner must face the inexorability of the karmic law of retribution, the burden becomes almost too difficult to bear. Immutable and relent-

[1]A somewhat less extreme example is found in those Thai farmers who debated the use of poison to cope with the rats who were ruining their crops. Some opposed it on the grounds that killing is sinful. The majority, agreeing that killing is sinful, nevertheless favored the use of poison. They argued that its attendant demerit could be offset by the additional merit acquired through the *dāna* paid for by the sale of the surviving crop. (Pfanner and Ingersoll 1962:346.)

less, this interpretation of karma leaves him with no loophole of any kind; even the mitigation of sin, let alone its absolution, is impossible.

The tension induced by this burden is very great indeed, and, except for a handful of moral virtuosos, one would expect it to produce a strong psychological press for the softening of the harshness of the doctrine of karmic inexorability. In fact, this has occurred. The second interpretation of karma, by providing an escape hatch from the seeming inevitability of karmic punishment, may be viewed as a response to this psychological press.

Although, even according to this second conception, one's sins are neither erased nor forgiven, they can be neutralized. The accumulation of merit cannot reduce one's demerits, but by changing one's karmic balance it can stay the actual arm of retribution. Thus, if despite the magnitude of one's demerits, they can be counterbalanced by an even larger store of merit, erstwhile bad karma can thereby be transformed into good karma, which produces only pleasant consequences. To be sure, the potential reward for meritorious deeds may be considerably diminished when merit is neutralized by demerit. Still, since one's karma is good, reward there will be; and the larger one's store of merit, the greater the reward. What is important, then, about this second conception is that, since demerit can be neutralized by merit, it is possible to escape retribution for demerit, or at least to diminish its intensity and/or duration.[2] Suppose, for example, that one is bitten by a snake, and suppose that, given the present state of his karma, the victim would ordinarily die as a result; then, karma can be changed by the neutralization of demerit, it is at least possible that, by means of some meritorious action, he can alter his karmic balance so as to escape death.

In Burma, the primary motivational basis for belief in the neutralization of demerit is the desire, specifically, to escape the punishment of hell, or at least to reduce its duration and/or intensity. For the Burmese, hell is not merely a place name on the Buddhist cosmological map. Translated into a belief within the actor's own cognitive map, it has acquired intense motivational value; to avoid hell is one of his strongest desires. And it is little wonder. There are eight hells in Buddhism, each of which is eighty thousand years in duration, and for all that time there is not even one moment free from torture and pain. These tortures are vividly described in popular literature and graphically portrayed in murals and sculpture in most pagodas.[3] If demerit can be neutralized by the acquisition of merit, then, having violated one or more of the Buddhist precepts (for which hell is the retribu-

[2]Obeyesekere (1968:25) labels the corresponding and identical Sinhalese belief "counter-karma."

[3]The most horrible tortures are meted out in the lowest hell, which is reserved for those who commit the five heinous sins: the murder of father, mother, a Buddha, an *arahant,* or a monk.

tion), a person may be unable to acquire sufficient merit to neutralize his demerit, but may yet be successful in reducing his stay in hell by thousands of years. Moreover, the building of a pagoda or a monastery may produce merit of such enormous magnitude that the demerit is completely neutralized, and he may escape hell altogether.

Although the neutralization of (bad) karma violates the normative Buddhist conception of karmic retribution, this theory is held by monks as well as laymen. Thus, in my sample, some two-thirds of the monks argued for the second conception of karma (according to which demerit can be neutralized), while only a third defended the first (according to which demerit cannot be neutralized). The latter were firm in their insistence that every act—and especially every demeritorious act—has its individual consequence. According to them, even one violation of any of the five precepts will lead to hell; nothing can be done to avoid retribution. And since every being, no matter how pious, has violated at least one of these precepts at least once, it follows ineluctably—so they insisted—that everyone must spend some time in hell. Even the Buddha, one of these monks pointed out, had to spend time in hell. In one of his lives, prior to becoming a Buddha, he had killed his younger brother. For this deed, despite his infinitely great merit, he suffered in hell. "If, then, even the Buddha spent time in hell, it is obvious," he concluded, "that no one can escape it. The only question is the duration of the stay. Like a jail sentence, some spend more, some spend less time."

The majority accept the second interpretation of karma. Unlike laymen, however, at least some of these monks deny that neutralization can be achieved by giving or morality (two of the three means by which merit is achieved); only meditation, they insist, can have that effect. Moreover, most of them insist that *persistent* evil-doing cannot be neutralized; neutralization applies only to temporary lapses from an otherwise moral life. Interestingly, however, many draw no distinctions with respect to the magnitude of the moral lapse. If committed only once, murder—no less than lying—can be neutralized, if the countervailing merit be sufficiently large.

As usual, a scriptural charter was frequently offered to justify their position, and as usual it was found in the *Jātaka*s. One monk offered the following story, purporting to be a *Jātaka*, in evidence.[4] It seems that there was once a man, too poor to have performed any meritorious act (neither charity, nor morality, nor meditation), who was found sleeping in a monastic compound. The monk who found him had a premonition that within seven days the sleeping man would die, and that being without merit he would surely go to hell for all his demerit. Having compassion for him, the

[4] I cannot find this story in the standard *Jātaka* collection. Moreover, although it was offered in support of the second, it may more properly be viewed as supporting the first interpretation of karma.

monk awakened him, and asked if he would not like to perform a charitable deed (and thereby acquire merit). The man replied that he was too poor to offer charity. The monk refused to accept this answer. For seven days, so he advised him, he should scatter part of his meals on the ground and part in a fish pond for the insects and the fish to eat. At the end of the seventh day he died, and, because of the merit acquired in this brief time from these acts of charity, he became a *deva*.

For every Buddhist charter offered for one side of a dispute, however, one may be found for the other side. Thus, the following story was told by a monk who held that demerit cannot be neutralized. It seems that a certain monk was visited by a fellow monk who, unknown to his host, was a saint *(arahant)*. When the laymen who supported the monastery invited the host and his guest for a meal, the former was reluctant to bring the guest lest, enjoying his stay, he decide to tarry in the monastery. Hence he arranged to depart in the early morning while his guest was sleeping, and in order not to waken him used a straw rather than a mallet to sound the morning bell. Whenever this happened, and he arrived at the house where he was to have his meal, he would inform his hosts that his fellow monk would not be eating with them, since he was still asleep. When his hosts offered him food for the other monk, he would cast it into the fire.

For these demeritorious acts, the monk—despite his many merits—was made to suffer in many of his later rebirths. In one he was poor and could find only a minimum of food. In another he was a dog, and his only food was what his master vomited. In another he was an ogre, and ate only discarded placentas. In still another he was a monk, but when he went on his begging rounds, his alms food would disappear from his bowl. All these difficulties were retribution for his acts of selfishness, the demerits of which could not be neutralized by his many meritorious acts.

Although both these conceptions of karma are found in Burma, it should not be thought that they are viewed as competing conceptions, held by different sects or theological schools, or that the second, being the clearly preferable interpretation, is held by the largest number of people. On the contrary, both are believed to be true by almost all Burmese, and despite what has already been said, to hold to the first is sometimes more advantageous than holding to the second. Since clearly both conceptions cannot be acted upon simultaneously, which one the Burmese choose to act upon varies with their specific situation. In general—and who would fault them? —they wish to have it both ways: to benefit from the advantages of both interpretations. Thus for their demerits they act upon the second: rather than suffer karmic retribution, they perform meritorious deeds with the hope that their demerits may thereby be neutralized. For their merits, however, they prefer to believe in the first: having acquired sufficient merit for rebirth as a wealthy human or as a *deva*, they prefer that it not be neutralized by demerit.

Merit Transfer and Karma

Even on the theory of karmic neutralization, the doctrine of karma is a stern doctrine in that it places on each individual the exclusive responsibility for his own salvation. Unlike the case in some other salvation religions, in which the individual can be assisted by a variety of human and divine agents, the Buddhist must attain his soteriological goal by his own unaided efforts. It is by his own meritorious deeds alone that the Buddhist is saved; if his store of merit is inadequate to the task, the immutability of the karmic law precludes any consequence other than just retribution. This requirement that each individual pull himself up by his own meritorious bootstraps proved to be so harsh that even canonical Buddhism found it necessary to reduce its severity. In the very face of the normative theory which insists that the karmic consequences of merit can attach only to the actor himself, Buddhism has long sanctioned two practices which significantly qualify this theory. These practices are found in contemporary Buddhism and, as we shall see, the precedent for their practice is found in Scripture. I am referring, of course, to the sharing and transfer of merit, practices in which the merit acquired by one person can be used to enhance the karma of another.

Following any collective act of merit, a prayer—known in Burmese as the *ahmya. wei-jin:*—is intoned in which the congregation shares its merit with all other creatures, be they on earth, in the heavens, or in the hells. Thus:

> May all creatures suffering torment in the four states of punishment reach the happy abodes of the *deva.* May all my relatives, friends, and all other beings inhabiting this earth and the ten thousand worlds, share the benefits of this meritorious act.

This ritual raises a most vexatious problem for the metaphysics of karma: how can merit be shared when, according to karmic law, retribution for one's acts devolves exclusively on the actor? The problem becomes even more vexatious in those ceremonies in which merit is not only shared with the living, but transferred to the dead. The latter ceremonies are of two types. Based on the belief that the spirit of the deceased is not reborn until the seventh day after death, meritorious acts are performed during that period whose merit is then transferred to the deceased. Any merit that can possibly be acquired within that interval, it is believed, may importantly improve the latter's chances of a good rebirth. Typically, monks are invited to chant scriptures, for which they are feasted and offered other kinds of *dāna.* The resulting merit acquired by the living is then transferred to the deceased. In addition to this immediate postdeath period, *dāna* may be offered for deceased relatives at any other time, and some people do so regularly and at fixed intervals throughout their lives. Since, after the first seven days, the deceased have already been reborn, the merit is intended either to prolong their stay in their heavenly abode (if that is where they are), or to shorten their stay in one of the painful abodes (if that is where they are).[5]

Even more than in the case of merit sharing, then, merit transfer seems to contravene the law of karma: if a person's karmic retribution is rebirth in hell, or as a demon, or as an animal, how can his fate in any way be affected by acts performed on his behalf by someone else after his death?[6]

Most Burmese make no attempt to resolve these apparent contradictions. Like most devotees of any religion, they have little difficulty in sustaining contradictory beliefs. The more sophisticated, however, and especially Buddhist monks are apt to be fully conscious of the contradiction (though some are unaware of it). As one monk put it, "strictly speaking, the transfer of merit is impossible." This being so, although monks perform these rituals, they reinterpret them in a manner compatible with the karmic doctrine. According to one reinterpretation—confined almost exclusively to very sophisticated monks—although merit can neither be shared nor transferred, the ritual is nevertheless useful as a form of spiritual discipline for the actors. The sincere intention to share one's merit is an expression of compassion and concern for others which, in turn, serves to purify one's mind. A second reinterpretation of the ritual allows for benefits to accrue to the recipient as well as the actor, in a manner which does not violate the karmic law. For by this ingenious interpretation, actor and recipient acquire merit through their own action. Let us first consider the actor.

Crucial for the notion of merit (and action in general) in normative Buddhist thought, is intention. As I have already stressed (chapter 2), merit is acquired and karma improved, not by an act itself, but by the intention behind it. An unintentional or mechanical act of giving produces no merit because it has no effect on the mind or volition of the actor. Conversely, if the actor intends to accomplish some end, the intention is meritorious even if the end is not realized. So, too, in the case of merit sharing. This is a special form of giving, and although it cannot achieve its stated end—since merit cannot be shared—the *intention* of conferring benefit on others is in itself meritorious. The desire to share his most precious possession (merit) with others is an expression of love *(mettā)* by which the actor is mentally and morally purified; and anything that purifies his mind produces beneficial karmic consequences for him.

[5]Merit transfer, as well as merit sharing, is also found in Thailand. Thai males, for example, may enter a monastery for a limited period so that their merit may be transferred to their deceased relatives. (Cf. Wells 1960:12.)

[6]The obverse belief—that merit performed by parents before the birth of their children is transferred, sometimes unwittingly, to their offspring—is also encountered in Burma, although much less frequently. Thus, a Burmese trader told me that he was wealthy because of meritorious deeds performed by his parents in their previous existence.

If the actor acquires merit by his volition, his intended recipient can acquire merit in the same way. Thus, at the completion of Buddhist ceremonies, including merit-sharing ceremonies, the audience says *tha-du* ("Well done!"), three times. When pronounced sincerely, this response confers merit on the one who utters it because, since intention is crucial, applauding the desire of another to share his merit is itself meritorious. In this manner the recipients of merit sharing, if they are present, may acquire merit, and the same principle applies to unseen recipients. Upon witnessing or hearing a meritorious act (performed by humans), the latter too—spirits, demons, *deva,* and so on—can acquire merit by saying *tha-du.* In short, although merit cannot be shared with them, the ritual gives them opportunity to acquire merit by performing a meritorious act of their own.

The more sophisticated monks interpret this process in a less mechanical way. It is not, they point out, the recipient's saying of *tha-du* that is important, but rather the change in his psychological or volitional state—for it is the person's mental state that determines his karma. To "prove" this point, a monk recounted the following *Jātaka.* At the time of the Buddha there was a hunter who, alarmed in his old age by his many demerits—for there is no greater sin than killing—became a novice in a monastery in which his son was a monk. As his death approached, realizing that for his sinful life he would spend his next existence in hell, he appealed for help. Concerned for his father's welfare and hoping to avert the impending disaster, his son instructed his novices to offer flowers to the pagoda in his father's name. By observing their efforts on his behalf, the father's mind was immensely purified, so much so that instead of descending to hell, he was reborn in heaven.

The transfer of merit to the dead is explained in similar ways. Thus, as a village elder pointed out, a person who dies with strong attachment to worldly things—to wife, family, property, or status—will necessarily be reborn in one of the "states of woe" regardless of how great his merit may be. If, during the seven-day interval prior to rebirth, he is witness to acts of *dāna* performed on his behalf, his mind is purified of his worldly attachments, so that his karma is changed by his own mental act. For one already born in a state of woe, the transfer of merit has a similar effect. Hearing the recitation of the merit-transfer ritual, he is cognizant of the meritorious act performed on his behalf and, thereby reminded of his own demerits, is led to atone for them. His mind being purified, his rebirth into a better abode is hastened.

Although these various attempts on the part of a sophisticated minority to resolve the contradiction between merit sharing and transfer, on the one hand, and the immutability of the karmic law, on the other, are offered with much sincerity, they are obviously strained—indeed, they create as many metaphysical problems as they solve. The fact that this sophisticated minority—aware of the conflict and yet loath to give up the rituals—must resort to fanciful casuistry in order to resolve the contradiction, together with the fact that most Burmese perform the rituals without bothering about the contradiction—if, indeed, they are even aware of it—would seem to support my thesis that we have here yet another example of a normative nibbanic doctrine succumbing to psychological press. The faithful are incapable of following the inexorability of the karmic doctrine to its logical conclusion. "Although" (it is as if the Buddhist were saying) "neither god nor savior—nor even an intercessor to god or savior—can help us to attain a better rebirth, we can still be helped in this attempt by the meritorious efforts of others. Hence," he seems to be arguing, "despite my sins I need not despair for myself; and despite the sins of my loved ones, I need not despair for them." For in both cases, the sharing and transfer of merit provide him with some hope of reducing, if not avoiding, karmic retribution for sin.

The psychological necessity for such an escape hatch from the stern consequence of the doctrine of karma need not be argued on theoretical grounds only, but may be inferred from the fact that, despite its inconsistency with the entire structure of Buddhism, merit sharing entered *Theravāda* Buddhism very early in its history.[7] Known as *patti-dāna*, it is found explicitly as early as the second century A.D., both in the Commentaries and in *King Milinda* (cf. Rhys Davids 1912). Less explicitly, it is found even earlier in Scripture itself. As La Vallée Poussin puts it (1917:33), although the Buddha, in opposition to certain Hindu notions, insisted on the strictly personal character of merit,

> [a] doctrine of the transfer of merit was tacitly lurking in some Buddhist circles and found expression in several passages of the Scripture. We are told that the right means of helping the dead is not to give them offerings, but to make gifts to the living for the benefit of the dead; that the right means of rendering homage to the deities is not to worship them, but to give them a share in our own pious works.

With these historical precedents, it is understandable that in Burma merit sharing is as ancient as Burmese Buddhism itself. Not only do the inscriptions of ancient Pagan provide evidence for both the belief and the practice (cf. Pe Maung Tin 1936:64-65), but some of them are associated with the great Anawrahta (1044-77) himself, the king who brought *Theravāda* Buddhism to Pagan and established it as the state religion. For months, we are told, Anawrahta could not sleep because of remorse for slaying his foster brother. Appearing to him in a dream, Thagya:min: (the Buddhist *deva* who is the king of the *nat*) suggested the following method for handling his guilt.

[7]Needless to say, it is a central doctrine in *Mahāyāna*, in which *parivarta*, the turning over of one's merits to others, is a necessary part of the *Boddhisatva* tradition. (cf. Suzuki 1963:283.)

O king, if thou desirest to mitigate thine evil deed in sinning against thine elder brother, build many pagodas, caves, monasteries, and rest houses, and share the merit with thine elder brother. Devise thou many wells, ponds, dams and ditches, fields and canals, and share the merit with thine elder brother. [Tin and Luce 1923:65]

The Dynamics of Belief in Karma

Salvation and Karma

It is apparent from the last two chapters that the doctrines of merit and karma (and the corollary doctrine of rebirth) comprise the core of kammatic Buddhism, with karma constituting the fulcrum on which the whole structure rests. In attempting to explain the shift from nibbanic to kammatic Buddhism, we must explain why, when other doctrines of nibbanic Buddhism have been rejected, these doctrines in particular have been retained with strength and conviction.

Following Weber (1946:275), most sociologists of religion have seen the primary function of the belief in karma as providing a solution to the problem of theodicy. This, to be sure, is one of its functions, and I shall deal with it below; but it is only by separating karma from merit, and by ignoring the motivations of the religious actors themselves, that one can take this to be its primary function. Isolated from the doctrine of merit, the karmic doctrine seems to be oriented to the past and the present; i.e., it serves to explain the present by means of the past, and—since one of the characteristics of the present is the differential and inequitable distribution of status and privilege—it provides a compelling resolution of the theodicy problem.

From the discussion in the last two chapters, however, we have seen not only that the doctrine of karma is inextricably related to the doctrine of merit, but that for practicing Buddhists it is important precisely *because* of its lawful and predictable relationship to merit. In short, when the doctrine of karma is studied as a belief of religious actors, rather than as a doctrine in a religious treatise, it becomes evident that Buddhists have cathected this doctrine not because it explains the present, by reference to the past, but because it offers the promise of affecting their future rebirths by action in the present. To be more precise, the dominant motive among the Burmese for believing in karma is not so much to discover the "meaning" of suffering as to do something about their own suffering. Indeed, although the doctrine of karma *is* used by the Burmese as an explanation for suffering, they just as frequently resist this karmic explanation—as I have shown elsewhere (Spiro 1967)—offering instead competing, antikarmic explanations for it. Moreover, it is because the doctrine of karma precludes the possibility of alleviating present suffering—not because it is defective in explaining it—that, as we shall see below (chapter 7), there has developed within Buddhism itself an ideology which, in effect, subverts the karmic explanation for suffering. For the same reason—viz., the desire better to alleviate suffering, not the better to explain it—the Burmese, as described above, have tinkered with the normative doctrine of karma, twisting its metaphysical structure to permit the neutralization of demerit and the sharing and transfer of merit.

In sum, the Burmese (and other Buddhists) are motivated to believe in the Buddhist doctrine of karma and its associated doctrine of merit because it provides them with a guaranteed means for satisfying their desire to transform present suffering into future pleasure, i.e., to achieve salvation.

Since, however, salvation (for the most part) is achievable only in a future life, the doctrine of karma is soteriologically relevant if, and only if, death is merely a transition to another birth. Hence, the same wish constitutes the motivational basis for accepting the doctrine of rebirth, viz., the wish for salvation. It is for this reason, of course, that Buddhists are motivated to believe in many rebirths (in contrast to the Judaeo-Christian-Muslim belief in only one afterlife), for since the amount of merit required for salvation is enormous, it is improbable that the soteriological task can be achieved in only one lifetime.[8] To be sure, the doctrine of rebirth is motivationally ambiguous; as we have seen, it is a source of anxiety as well as hope. Since, according to Buddhism, rebirth can take place in any of thirty-one abodes, one may be reborn as an animal, a demon, or a denizen of hell rather than as a rich human or a *deva* (the two most desired rebirths); and this possibility, especially that of rebirth in hell, is a persistent source of anxiety for many Burmese. Nevertheless, combined with the doctrines of merit and karma, the doctrine of rebirth is, on balance, a source of hope, for according to these other doctrines one's future rebirths are not a result of accident or blind chance; rather, they are causally determined and, what is more important, by one's own acts. Since each person, and he alone, controls his own action, he creates his own karma and thereby determines his own salvation. Hence, if not in one's next rebirth, then in another—hopefully not too far removed—happiness, wealth, beauty, success, may yet be achieved. In sum, to believe in merit, karma, and rebirth is to believe that, regardless of its magnitude, one can overcome present suffering and achieve salvation in the future.

Although (the wish being father to the thought) the motivation for the Burmese belief in the doctrine of karma stems from their desire for salvation, their belief (man being a rational animal) is anchored in what is for them compelling evidence. On the assumption that the world is ethically meaningful, and the Burmese make that assumption, the seeming inequita-

[8]Conversely, since the chances of being reborn in hell are high, it is comforting to believe that, rather than being a final destination, the Buddhist hell is merely a way station to other, including blissful, rebirths. The Burmese are shocked by the Christian belief that the sins committed in the brief compass of one life lead to an eternity of hell. The disproportionate relationship between the crime and the punishment is, for them, morally incomprehensible.

ble distribution of good and bad fortune is in itself for them a convincing argument for the truth of the karmic doctrine. How else, if it is *not* just retribution for behavior in previous rebirths, can one explain this often flagrant inequity? When to this tautological argument they add the accounts of rebirth and karmic retribution found in Scripture, the proof for karma is unassailable. The following tale, recounted by a villager and attributed by him to the *Dhammapada,* is typical of both the genre and its logic.

There was once a villager who, after famine befell the countryside, decided to seek a new life for himself, his wife, and his infant son in the city. Setting upon their journey, husband and wife alternated in carrying their son until, after traveling for four days without food, the man, having lost his strength, was prepared to abandon his son in the bushes. Although the woman persisted in carrying the child, he nevertheless died from lack of food. When man and wife came to the outskirts of the city, they approached a dairy where monks were being offered milk and cheese, and they too were offered food to eat. Not having eaten for a long time, they were attacked by indigestion soon after completing their meal, whereupon the husband, seeing a dog being fed by the dairymen, grew bitter: "That dog is more fortunate than we are; he has had good things to eat while we almost starved to death." Because of these thoughts, the man was reborn in the womb of a bitch. "And," my informant concluded, "this proves that there is rebirth."

But the Burmese have even more direct forms of evidence for the belief in rebirth, and hence of karma. One form consists of various kinds of anomalies which, it is argued—and no one is deterred by the circularity of the argument—can only be explained by rebirth. These anomalies are widely reported in the Burmese press. The following news item is the caption for a (front-page) picture of a Burmese couple and their two seemingly albino children.

> ALBINOS OR REINCARNATED EUROPEANS?
>
> Most visitors to Kyaukpyu will hear about two little boys, sons of a poor couple, who are to all appearances albinos but who the local population believe to be Europeans reincarnated.
>
> The couple are extremely poor but have turned down offers by missionaries and well-to-do people to adopt their children.
>
> Like others in the locality, they are convinced that the boys are reincarnated Europeans. They said that before being delivered of the boys [the mother] dreamt, on both occasions, that a British soldier came up to their house and asked for permission to stay there. [*The* [Rangoon] *Nation,* August 17, 1960]

Anomalies, of course, are highly subjective and relative. For my friends in Yeigyi it was most anomalous that I, an American professor, should have left home and country to travel thousands of miles in order to live and work in Burma; it was even more anomalous that, of the thousands of villages in Burma, I should have chosen their village. The obvious explanation, as I was repeatedly informed, is that in a previous life I had been a Burmese Buddhist, living in or adjacent to the village of Yeigyi.[9]

A second, and the most compelling, direct evidence for rebirth consists of the numerous alleged cases of rebirth found in any village and town. In Yeigyi, for example, almost 10 per cent of all its households include a person who "remembers" having lived in the village in a previous life. Perhaps a few examples will suffice. The son of one couple claimed that, in his previous existence, he had been the wife of his present father (in the latter's previous existence). Another young boy claimed to have been the husband of a neighbor in his previous existence. When only three years old, he entered her home, told her how many children she had (though they were grown up and married), and correctly chose the sarong which had belonged to her deceased husband. Again, a six-year-old girl claimed to be the mother of the village headman in her previous existence. At his invitation she entered his house and correctly identified the rings and sarongs that had belonged to his mother. Similarly a twelve-year-old boy from the village told the monks of a monastery in Mandalay that in his previous life he had been its abbot. (Since as the abbot he had been his present mother's favorite monk, upon his death he was reborn in her womb.) Although he had never previously entered the monastery, he not only identified each of the monks by name, but correctly told them where, as abbot, he had buried some of the monastic treasure. Numerous other such cases from Yeigyi, as well as other villages and towns, might be cited.[10]

These, then, are the kinds of "evidence" which, for the Burmese, constitute proof for the doctrines of karma and rebirth. But the proof for any religious doctrine is only convincing to those who have (as William James put it) the will to believe, and the will to believe in the doctrine of karma is motivated, I have argued, by the desire for salvation.

In addition, however, to the will to believe, a normative religious doctrine, as I argued above, (chapter 3), must also be consistent with the

[9]Waddell (1967:567) encountered the same explanation for his sojourn in Tibet.

[10]These cases are as convincing to the sophisticated as to the untutored. Thus, for Lu Pe Win, a distinguished Burmese scholar, rebirth is not only a "basic belief" in Burma; it is a "well-established fact."

> For instance my wife still remembers her former self. She was a boy in her previous birth, born as the only son of a wealthy landlord at Toungoo and died very young while yet a school-boy. In her childhood, she often told her parents at Pegu about her joyful boyhood days in her last life and she could locate her old home and identify her widower-father, who died at Toungoo just before the war.
>
> Her elder sister, however, was a Chinese lady from Latter Street at Rangoon. My elder daughter is my mother reborn, while my younger daughter is her maternal aunt, the eldest sister of my wife. As soon as they became articulate, they began to relate to other members of their family their last stops in the several stages of *Samsāra* (their restless rounds of repeated rebirths). [Lu Pe Win 1966: Vol. 2, 95]

Evidence of this kind is reported for all Buddhist societies. For a striking case from Tibet, see David-Neel 1932:126-30.

perceptual and/or cognitive structure of the faithful. The Burmese acceptance of these doctrines of kammatic Buddhism is an excellent case in point. For, granting the strength of their desire for salvation, it may still be asked why, having rejected nibbanic salvation, the Burmese could not, with equal impunity, have rejected the merit-karma-rebirth road to kammatic salvation in favor of some other route—that, say, of a redeeming savior, divine compassion, petitionary prayer, and so on. That they have not done so can be explained, I believe, by the cognitive requirement for the acceptance or rejection of normative doctrine: the merit-karma-rebirth route to salvation is entirely consistent with the Burmese perceptual-cognitive structure, while the way of the divine savior is inconsistent with it. To argue alternatively that it is because Buddhism precludes development of the latter path is to ignore the popular Mahayanist *Bodhisattva* doctrine, or the widespread appeal of the Pure Land sect in China and Japan, with its belief in the saving power, achieved through faith and worship, of the Buddha Amitabha.

In Burma and other Buddhist societies of Southeast Asia the Mahayanist belief in savior gods is, for the most part, nonexistent, despite the fact that Burma has been exposed to Mahayanist influences for centuries. Indeed, Buddhism first struck roots in Burma in its Mahayanist form. Although, as we shall see in chapter 7, the Burmese attempt to enlist supernatural protection for their present lives, they deny that any supernatural power can assist them to achieve a better future life. Moreover, even for protection in this life, their notions concerning protective agents (*deva),* how and under what conditions they protect, and so on, are vague in the extreme. Whatever else can be said of these agents, their protection (unlike the assistance of *Bodhisattvas*) does not spring from compassion, but is instead a response to the utterance of spells, the performance of meritorious acts, and so on.

If, for this life, the belief in divine assistance is vague, for the future life it is nonexistent. Nibbanic salvation, of course, must be achieved by one's unaided effort (meditation) alone, and this exclusive emphasis on the unaided effort of each individual characterizes kammatic salvation—in which merit has replaced meditation—as well. Even those Burmese who believe that the Buddha is alive insist, to quote one villager, that

> there is no one to answer your prayers (for salvation). You can rely only on yourself to fulfill your [soteriological] wishes . . . . There is mind and there are acts; there is no other agent . . . . All the myriads of Buddhas, with all their *myitta* [love] cannot help. You can only rely on yourself; no one else can help you.

In sum, if one is to be saved, one must save oneself by means of one's own meritorious efforts. "The only thing you can rely on," the Burmese repeat over and over again, "is karma."

From a psychological point of view, this emphasis on karma as the sole soteriological agent is notable in two related senses which we have already seen: first, one can rely only on oneself for salvation; second, there is no divine figure who, from love, mercy, or compassion, serves as savior. Both of these attributes of Buddhist soteriology, I submit, correspond to convictions deeply rooted in the cognitive structure of the Burmese. In order to believe that one can be saved by the efforts of a compassionate savior, it is necessary—so at least it seems from available evidence—to have had the experience of *persistent* love and emotional nurturance in childhood. This experience, which assures the child that he is not alone, that his parents (and parent surrogates) care for him and are concerned for his welfare, creates a cognitive structure on the individual level which is isomorphic with the cognitive structure of savior gods on the cultural level. In short, such an experience produces a person with a cognitive structure which, when exposed to a soteriology of divine saviors, can accept it and believe in it with conviction.

Such a cognitive structure would be difficult to acquire in Burma, where the socialization system and pattern of child care is rather different from the one just described. In the beginning the Burmese infant is treated with the greatest nurturance. His need for affection is almost constantly satisfied, and his dependency (both physical and emotional) continuously indulged. As he grows older, however, this nurturance is (from his point of view) unpredictably withdrawn. Parents only rarely exhibit physical expressions of affection to children who have outgrown their infancy. This is true in the village, at least, where parents say that too much affection leads to a spoiled child and to the creation of vanity and self-pride. For this same reason they only infrequently praise their children or exhibit other forms of verbal affection for them. But this is not all. At approximately the same age that the child may begin to be the victim of teasing by parents and other adults, he is expected to assume a variety of chores, may no longer sleep with his parents, is trained in rather strict obedience, and—probably most important—may be severely punished by his parents. Thus, in a sample of 32 village children, ranging in age from five to twelve, not only did all of them express fear of parental punishment and temper, but with two exceptions, all alluded to beatings, received from one or both parents, and to the physical pain and shame they suffered.[11]

Put schematically, Burmese socialization is characterized by an important discontinuity between the indulgent nurturance of infancy and its rather serious withdrawal in childhood. This pattern, I submit, does not provide the growing personality with the kind of experience necessary for

[11]This account of one aspect of socialization in Yeigyi (whose detailed description must await publication in a more appropriate volume) is consistent in general outline with other accounts from other parts of Burma. (Cf. Gorer 1943, Hanks 1949, Hitson 1959, Sein Tu 1964.)

the development of a cognitive structure consistent with the belief in a divine savior.

In the absence of such a structure it "makes sense" that neither the Buddha (who, although showing the Way to salvation, remains detached from man's soteriological efforts) nor any other supernatural being should serve as a savior. There simply is no experiential model for the development of such a notion. The only soteriological notion consistent with this cognitive structure is the notion that if one is to be saved, he must save himself, for there is no one else who can or will save him. Hence, "the only thing you can rely on is karma [i.e., yourself]."

But, although you cannot rely on anything *except* karma, you *can* rely on karma. The Burmese do believe that they can, by means of their own karma, save themselves. And if Burmese socialization, as I have argued, creates the cognitive structure that gives rise to the first attitude, it also creates the cognitive structure that gives rise to the second. Until he experiences the withdrawal of nurturance, the Burmese infant experiences almost complete indulgence; his every want is satisfied. Now if Ferenczi (1952) is correct in his reconstruction of the ontogenetic development of the sense of reality, this early indulgence of the Burmese infant, experienced prior to his development of a self separate from other selves, should give rise to the infantile belief that his wants are satisfied, by his own (magical) efforts. He has merely to cry, gesture, or indicate his needs in some other way in order to have them gratified. In the infant's phenomenology, his own behavior can effectively produce the blissful state of the satiety of all desire. It is this cognitive structure, developed by the Burmese in early infancy, which is isomorphic with the Buddhist doctrine that man *can* save himself, just as his later childhood experience creates a cognitive structure consistent with the doctrine that he *must*, if he is to be saved, save himself.

But I think we can carry this argument even further. Granted that in Buddhism man can and must be saved by his own karma, it is notable that in the Burmese view the most effective way to create good karma is by the feeding of monks, symbolically the structural equivalents of young children (see chapter 14). It is not implausible, then, if early experience provides the paradigmatic model for later belief, that this view is related to Burmese experience in infancy. For the Burmese adult, infancy was a blissful period, one in which his every want was immediately and abundantly indulged and in which his greatest pleasure was experienced as satiety of his hunger drive. From this experience it is plausible to believe that infantile satiety would become the (unconscious) symbol of salvation (i.e., the fulfillment of all wants) and the feasting of monks its instrument. Based on the well-known (unconscious) fantasy of magical reciprocity, the adult might expect by the feeding of monks to reconstitute his own infantile bliss. Having experienced complete gratification of his own wants when, as an infant, he was fed by his mother, he hopes to reinstate that condition by the food he offers monks, symbolic infants, to gratify their wants. This expectation would provide the (unconscious) cognitive basis for the cultural belief that merit is most effectively acquired in exchange for food offerings to monks.

To summarize, if the primary motivational basis for the Burmese belief in the doctrines of merit, karma, and rebirth consists in their desire for salvation, this particular soteriological route is acceptable to them because it is consonant with their personal cognitive structures.[12]

Theodicy and Karma

In Western philosophy and theology "theodicy" refers to the efforts to justify both the omnipotence and omnibenevolence of God in the face of the suffering of the righteous and the prosperity of the wicked. In this restricted sense, of course, the problem of theodicy does not arise in Buddhism. But following Weber (1946:271-75), who expanded the notion to include any religious attempt to cope with the "meaning" of suffering, we can agree that Buddhists, too, have a problem of theodicy.

In addition to existential suffering, which all people are concerned to alleviate, I would suggest that the ubiquity of suffering poses three cognitive problems for anyone who, in any sense, regards the world as "meaningful." First, the very fact of suffering poses the simple intellectual puzzle of why it exists at all. Second, its unequal distribution sets up the further puzzle of why some people suffer more, or less, than others. Third, its seemingly inequitable distribution creates the intellectual-moral problem—the Jobian problem—of why the wicked prosper and the righteous suffer. In their attempts to deal with the question of "meaning," all the world's great religions provide answers to these problems. In Buddhism, however, all three problems find a resolution in one doctrine, that of karma. Whether we view the last of these problems alone as the theodicy problem or see them all as jointly constituting it, we may agree with Weber (1963:145) that the doctrine of karma provides "the most complete formal solution of the problem of theodicy . . . " And although their primary motive in believing in karma is to satisfy their wish for salvation, Buddhists do in fact employ this doctrine as one of their solutions to this problem.[13]

In Burma, to advert to the last and most troublesome of the three facets of this problem of suffering, if the wicked are observed to prosper, it must be—the Burmese say—their just reward for merit acquired in previous lives. Similarly, the suffering of the righteous is explained as just punishment for the demerit of *their* previous lives. But karma, as it were, cannot be fooled.

[12]The theoretical model on which this explanation rests was first developed, of course, by Kardiner (1945); it was subsequently supported cross-culturally by Spiro and D'Andrade (1958).

[13]For a discussion of karma in relationship to the problem of theodicy in *Theravāda* Ceylon, see Obeyesekere (1968:19-25).

Just as the wicked are now reaping the harvest of the merit sown in earlier lifetimes, in a future life they will surely reap the harvest of their demerit in this life. The converse, of course, holds for the righteous.

The doctrine of karma is used to explain all problems arising from suffering. Gambling losses, accidents, illness, droughts, freaks, premature death, the loss of an animal, the burning of a house—these and countless other forms of suffering find their explanation in karma. This is not to say that the Burmese are unaware of natural causation: of course crop failures, for example, are caused by drought, heat, and other natural causes. But why did the rains fail this year? And why in the north, and not in the south? Or why did the oxen destroy U Youn's seedbeds but not U Htein's? Or why did the fire burn U Pain's crop but not U Kyi's? Why else, if not for differences in karma?

Having emphasized that the doctrine of karma provides the "most complete formal solution of the problem of theodicy," one must also emphasize that it solves one problem only to create another. For the very logic that enables it to answer intellectual and moral questions concerning the problem of suffering creates grave anxiety concerning the possibility of one's own suffering. I have already alluded to a similar paradox inherent in the soteriological function of karma. Since one's next rebirth depends on one's balance of merit and demerit acquired in past rebirths, even a completely meritorious life does not guarantee a happy rebirth; one may still have to suffer retribution for the demerits of previous births of which one knows nothing. In short, although the law of karma is a law of cause and effect, in the absence of complete knowledge of one's previous lives, the chances of salvation are likewise unknown. And this uncertainty, as we have seen, is a source of grave anxiety for the Burmese.

The same uncertainty that characterizes the karmic theory of salvation pertains to karmic theodicy. Since no one knows from moment to moment what his karmic balance will be, or when it may change, the very theory that provides a rather deterministic explanation for the distribution of fortune and misfortune creates grave uncertainty for the individual. Although I am now enjoying the fruits of my past merit, I may in the very next moment suffer a dramatic reversal of fortune as retribution for my past demerit. In short, it is precisely because the karmic explanation of suffering is completely deterministic that the Buddhist, ignorant of his previous rebirths, is anxious about his future fortune. Although on the macroscopic level everything is determined, on the microscopic level uncertainty reigns.[14]

To be sure, this uncertainty concerning one's karmic balance has its positive as well as its negative side. For if, in the case of the fortunate, the belief in karma is a source of anxiety, for the unfortunate it is a source of hope. As one villager put it: "Karma cannot be foreseen. I am poor because I did not give *dāna* in one of my past rebirths; but because of the *dāna* I

[14]Obeyesekere (1968:21) makes the identical observation in the case of Ceylon.

may have offered in another rebirth, I might yet win the state lottery and be rich." Indeed, it is at least possible that this dimension of their belief in karma is one of the reasons for the well-known capacity of the Burmese to absorb adversity with unexpected equanimity. Nevertheless, the latter dimension does not erase the former; the fact remains that, as a solution to the problem of suffering, the doctrine of karma, intellectually and morally satisfying as it is, also creates considerable anxiety.

If the cognitive explanation I have proposed for the Burmese acceptance of the karmic theory of salvation is correct, it will also explain their acceptance of this "uncertainty principle" in the karmic theory of suffering. For this, like the former, is completely isomorphic with the Burmese own expectations concerning the world, derived (according to our theory) from their early socialization experience. We have seen that in his early years the Burmese lives in a highly uncertain and unpredictable world. Following a period of nurture, the infant, for no apparent reason to himself, experiences its unpredictable withdrawal. Childhood is an equally uncertain period. At one moment the object of parental attention, in the next the child may be unpredictably shunted aside. For him, fortune and misfortune alike follow each other inexplicably and unpredictably. But since his parents provide him with no clue to their behavior, one would expect him to develop the notion that *he* must be its cause: *he* must have done something—though he doesn't know what—to evoke now this, now that, response. Typically moreover such notions, as psychoanalysis has taught us, are talion in character, so that in his explanatory structure (his) good evokes (their) good, (his) bad evokes (their) bad.

According to this theory, then, Burmese socialization produces two dimensions of the Burmese cognitive structure—the expectation of uncertainty and the belief in personal responsibility—which, I suggest, form the cognitive bases for their acceptance of the karmic explanation for misfortune and fortune. The Burmese (as we have seen) expects to go unpredictably and inexplicably from fortune to misfortune and back again. But the Burmese adult, like the child, does not know what causes these reversals. And here the doctrine of karma is useful: it provides him with a causal explanation, one moreover which is consistent with his own cognitive structure. He himself is responsible; his own actions, performed in previous rebirths—and therefore unknown to him—are the cause of these reversals in fortune. But though they are unknown, the karmic explanation specifies the nature of his (causal) actions: his good acts (merit) are the cause of his good fortune; his bad acts (demerit) are the cause of his bad fortune.

Childhood Experience and Religious Belief

Before concluding this discussion of childhood experience and Buddhist belief, I should like to indicate more precisely the character of the theory from which these postdictive interpretations have been derived, especially since they represent the type-interpretation which recurs throughout this volume. I refer to them as "postdictive" because the specific (as opposed to the generic) relationships were not predicted prior to inquiry. Since I knew almost nothing about Buddhism or Burma when I began my research, the latter was a naturalistic, not an experimental study. Nevertheless, although postdictive, the interpretations are not ad hoc. They are derived from the theory, outlined here and elsewhere in the volume, which—as was pointed out in the first chapter—guided the entire process of data collection.

I should like now to explicate in particular the logical form of the relationship between childhood experience and religious belief postulated by the theory, and to specify more rigorously the analytic status of the predicted religious, or dependent, variable. I shall begin with the latter.

In arguing that a certain kind of childhood experience is a prior condition for a particular kind of religious belief, the predicted belief does not refer to a concrete, substantive doctrine—such as the doctrine of karma—but to its generic, structural attributes. The theory states, it will be recalled, that childhood experience produces perduring cognitive sets and need dispositions; and that only if the structural attributes of a cognitive set are isomorphic with those of a culturally transmitted religious doctrine, will the need dispositions provide the motivational basis for belief in the doctrine. With respect to karma, for example, the theory does not predict that a particular childhood experience will produce this specific, historically conditioned belief; rather, that it will produce a belief in any doctrine which denies the existence of saviors and affirms that salvation must be achieved through one's own efforts.

The reason that the theory predicts a range of (structurally equivalent) beliefs rather than one particular belief, is obvious. The cognitive sets created by childhood experience consist of cognitive orientations—ways of looking at the world—rather than substantive beliefs. The latter constitute the doctrines of historically developed cultural systems. Unlike the cognitive sets which are developed by the child in social interaction, religious (and other cultural) doctrines are acquired by him through cultural transmission. Hence, which doctrine (among a potential set of structurally equivalent doctrines) is acquired by a group of religious actors is an accident of their geography and history. But whether they internalize it as a personal belief is a function of their childhood experience, for, *ex hypothesi*, belief in a culturally transmitted doctrine depends (among other conditions) on its structural isomorphism with a perduring cognitive set acquired in childhood.

Returning, then, to our example, the doctrine of karma is an element in the historically conditioned religion of Buddhism. My theory proposes that the Burmese believe in this doctrine—but would believe in any structurally equivalent doctrine—because it is consonant with an ontogenetically prior cognitive set. It further proposes that, if exposed to it, they would reject the doctrine of a savior god—as indeed they have rejected it in their persistent rejection of Christianity—because it is structurally dissonant with that childhood-acquired set.

In short, it is the generic notion of responsibility for one's own salvation, not the particular doctrine of karma, that is the predicted cognitive consequence of the Burmese childhood experience described above. That Burmese believe in this parochial expression of the generic notion is a happenstance of their society's religious history; that they have acquired the generic notion is a function of their own early family interaction.

Having indicated the analytic status of the dependent variable in the childhood-religion relationship, I now wish to specify briefly the logical character of this relationship. This is important not only for rendering the theory as precise as possible, but for indicating the conditions under which the specific interpretations derived from it (in this and subsequent chapters) may be tested. In asserting a causal relationship between childhood experience and religious belief, this theory asserts more precisely that, given the existence of a religious world view, the former is a necessary, though not a sufficient condition, for the internalization of the latter. The logical paradigm for this type of relationship exhibits the following form.

1. $x \not\supset y$
2. $\sim x \supset \sim y$
3. $y \supset x$
4. $\sim y \not\supset \sim x$

As this paradigm shows, in order to reject as invalid the interpretations derived from the theory, it is necessary to find societies in which beliefs similar to those of kammatic Buddhism are present although childhood experiences, similar to those of the Burmese, are absent. Such a condition, it will be noted, would violate the second and third conditions of the paradigm. If, on the other hand, similar childhood experiences are present in other societies, although similar religious beliefs are absent, it would be invalid, as the first and fourth conditions of the paradigm reveal, to conclude that the interpretations are false. Since childhood experience, *ex hypothesi*, is a necessary condition for religious belief, our interpretations are disproved only if the religious belief is present despite the fact that the postulated childhood experience is absent.

CHAPTER 6

Apotropaic Buddhism: A Religion of Magical Protection

Introduction

Thus far we have been concerned with the soteriological ideologies of Buddhism. As a salvation religion—leaving aside the marginal soteriology of its esoteric form—Buddhism is characterized by the following features. First, it has little if any concern with the mundane concerns of everyday existence; its concern is rather with such soteriological goals as nirvana and rebirth. Second, although differing in their interpretation, both nibbanic and kammatic Buddhism agree that morality, giving, and meditation comprise the instruments of salvation. Third, they also agree that none of these instruments involves the aid of a supernatural being or savior: although the Buddha points the way, salvation is achieved by the unaided effort of the religious devotee, neither the gods nor the Buddha being of any avail.

Apotropaic Buddhism, whose ideology we are concerned with in this chapter, differs from soteriological Buddhism on all these dimensions. First, its concern is with important matters in this present existence: health and illness, drought and rain, calamity and tranquility. Second, it assumes that the goals involved here can be attained by specific magical acts which, unlike the ideology of soteriological Buddhism, either create *immediate* merit or enlist the assistance of supernatural beings and/or power. For apotropaic Buddhism, Buddhism as a whole—its devotions, ritual, ethics, Scripture—acts as a protective shield against the dangers (in the most general and generalized sense of "dangers") of the present existence. The world as the Burmese, for example, view it is dangerous—ghosts, demons, evil spirits *(nat)*, and evil people are everywhere; one is constantly and unpredictably in danger of being harmed (cf. Spiro 1967). Buddhism serves as a general protection against all these dangers. How this is achieved is—as we shall see—not at all clear; much more important, however, is the fact that it *is* achieved, and by Buddhist means.

Psychological Press and the Reinterpretation of Normative Doctrine

Although suffering and deliverance from suffering comprise the exclusive concerns of soteriological Buddhism, it nevertheless (paradoxically enough) does not cope with the larger part of human pain. Because its conception of the problem is rather limited; because its solution is otherworldly; because its theory of karmic causality leaves little opportunity to escape from the seeming inevitability of present pain; and because (in the cultural context at least of Southeast Asia) there are causes of suffering which are difficult to fit into the karmic mold; for all these reasons soteriological Buddhism is unable to satisfy completely the universal psychological need to cope with suffering. Under the press of this need, various of the doctrines of normative Buddhism have been modified or reinterpreted, and a Buddhist technology for satisfying it has been developed.

It is obvious, if one examines the doctrine of suffering as it is classically expressed in the Four Noble Truths (chapter 2), that the Buddhist analysis of the ultimate cause of suffering is more hortatory than descriptive, more philosophical than existential, more psychological than physical. That is, this doctrine is mainly concerned with making an otherwise unseeing humanity see that suffering exists even when it appears not to exist; that suffering, not pleasure, is the inevitable trait of all sentient experience; and that pleasure when analyzed properly is an illusion, for it either *is* or *eventuates in* pain. In short, Buddhism's classic doctrine of suffering is not addressed so much to those who, in anguish and despair, are seeking for a solution to felt pain, but rather to those who either experience no pain, or who, experiencing it, believe it is transient or adventitious rather than inevitable. For the most part, in other words, Buddhist doctrine is addressed to those who are living, as Buddhism sees it, in a fool's paradise.

To put it in more concrete terms, soteriological Buddhism offers no respite from such immediate stress as the bite of a poisonous snake, lack of food, the frustration of ambition, the illness of a loved one, the attack of a malevolent spirit, and so on. Since suffering, for Buddhism, is an inevitable characteristic of the human condition, coping with these manifestations of it—even if the karmic law that causes them could be circumvented—is like treating a chronic disease by prescribing a palliative for one of its symptoms. Rather than treat the symptoms, Buddhism attempts to uproot the cause. Instead of providing temporary solutions for specific forms of misfortune, it offers an ultimate solution for the generic condition of suffering. And since this (as Buddhism analyzes it) is caused by attachment to, and therefore rebirth in, the world, its solution consists in deliverance from the former and thereby release from the latter. Until this ultimate solution is achieved—and, indeed, as a means of hastening its achievement—the specific manifestations of the generic condition of suffering can be alleviated by renouncing the world in favor of the monastery.

This treatment of the problem of suffering, it is apparent, can only have been created by—and can only continue to appeal to—a sated and world-weary social stratum. Indeed, as we have already seen, one part of this treatment—its analysis of the problem of suffering and proposed solution for it—has found little resonance among the Buddhist masses for whom pain is the consequence, not of desire, but of its frustration, and for whom the ultimate solution to the problem of suffering is the attainment of a condition in which pleasures are maximized. *Their* soteriological goal consists of blissful and near-blissful future rebirths. They are able to sustain the discomfort caused by the frustration of present desire—for status, for power, for material pleasures—because of their belief that present deprivation is only temporary, that the gratification of desire is merely deferred.

But even kammatic Buddhism (as I have been calling this approach to Buddhist soteriology) does not cope with yet another basis for dissatisfaction with classical Buddhism in the matter of suffering. Although the solution to pain of frustrated desire may be deferred to a future rebirth, there are other forms of stress—a crop-destroying drought, a critical childbirth, an attack by an evil spirit, an astrologically caused epidemic—which are not caused by desire and whose solution cannot be deferred. Heaven can wait, but the bite of a cobra must be cured (or even better averted) now; and although the doctrine of karma may explain the cobra attack, it leaves the victim impotent to deal with it. What he wants is not an explanation for his suffering—let alone one that precludes the possibility of coping with it—but a cure. And however sound it may be philosophically, however consistent it may be logically, the doctrine of karma as an explanation for present pain is frustrating emotionally. Man not only seeks an explanation for his suffering, but wants to do something about it; he is unwilling merely to be resigned to it.

In short, even kammatic Buddhism does not satisfactorily cope with the problem of suffering so far as the masses are concerned. For, as Weber has observed, "it in no way satisfied the . . . need for . . . emergency aid in external and internal distress." And this unsatisfied need, as he further commented, is "always decisive for the psychological character of religion of the masses . . . ." (Weber 1958:237) It was in response to the strong press from this psychological need, so I assume, that apotropaic Buddhism was developed. In order to satisfy this need its first ideological task, as we shall see, was to modify the doctrine of karma so as to soften its harshness and allow for mutability in it. Indeed, this modification is more properly interpreted as an attempt to legitimize a series of practices which, for the most part, clearly repudiate the implications of the doctrine. For even prior to this ideological modification there had developed, within *Theravāda* Buddhism, a host of rituals—recitation of spells, worship of images, performance of rites, and so on—for protection against pain and danger. In brief, in response to an irrepressible psychological need, *Theravāda* Buddhism has come to include nonsoteriological goals within the domain of legitimate Buddhist concern, and in doing so it has added magical ritual to its previous inventory of legitimate Buddhist action.

The Noble Eightfold Path, the Buddhist Path to salvation, is devoid of ritual of any kind: acts of loving-kindness, of morality, and of meditation are the exclusive means to salvation. Although this is still the case—the above three types of action, and they alone, are the instruments of salvation—the development of nonsoteriological Buddhism has meant the development of another type, viz., ritual action. And regardless of its interpretation, this action is, by any definition of "magic," magical. What is most interesting about this Buddhist magic is that its legitimacy, contrary to the claims of many Buddhists and Buddhist apologists, is of an ancient vintage. Indeed, although the modifications one finds in the classical doctrine of karma are modifications held by Buddh*ists*, rather than changes incorporated into the structure of normative Buddh*ism*, the concern with apotropaic goals and the development of apotropaic ritual was legitimized as early as the canonical era. The legitimacy of both is scriptural. In short, apotropaic Buddhism is properly called "Buddhist," not only because its rituals employ almost exclusively the symbols and sacra of Buddhism—the words of the Buddha, the image of the Buddha, the relics of the Buddha, and so on—but because it rests on a scriptural foundation.

It is by a generalization from one canonical model that the other rituals of apotropaic Buddhism have been legitimized. Since this model, the *paritta* ritual, comprises the central core of apotropaic Buddhism, and since *Theravāda* Buddhism is almost uniformly described (both by its westernized spokesmen and by Western converts) as free of magic,[1] it is important to portray the canonical basis for this ritual in detail. To be sure, the fact that *paritta* are prescribed by Scripture and attributed to the Buddha does not necessarily mean that they were, in fact, practiced by the primitive church.

[1]The following quotation is typical of the genre.

> There are no prayers in Buddhism. Instead of prayers there are meditations for purifying the mind in order that truth can be realized. According to Buddhism, the universe is governed by everlasting, unchangeable laws of righteousness—not by any god or any Supreme Being who can hear and answer prayers. These laws are so perfect that no one, no god or man, can change them by praising them or by crying out against them.
>
> . . . for a Buddhist, the laws of righteousness which govern the universe are the same for all, the same forever. A man's duty, therefore, is not to break those laws, nor to try to change them by prayers or any other means . . . .[U Thittila, in Morgan (ed.) 1956:76]

It is certainly possible, rather, that this type of magic was absent from primitive Buddhism and that it entered much later, especially since most of the sermons attributed to the Buddha were not written down for about three centuries after His death. Still, although this is an important historical question, it is an unimportant problem for us. Since the use of *paritta* is authorized by the canon, this ritual, even if later than the primitive church, is certainly part of normative *Theravāda* Buddhism.

The Canonical Basis for Apotropaic Buddhism

Paritta are spells—or, as Rhys Davids calls them, wardrunes—consisting of chapters or sections of chapters taken from various books of the canon, mostly from the *sutta*, which are chanted for protection against danger. Although not all of the *sutta* which are used as *paritta* were composed for that purpose, at least one of them was (allegedly) composed as a spell by the Buddha Himself, and with only two exceptions, all the other *sutta* that comprise the classical collection (Pali, *mahāparitta;* Burmese, *payeigyi*) must have been used as spells very early in the history of *Theravāda* Buddhism, for their use is both referred to and authorized by *The Questions of King Milinda,*[2] that authoritative (though noncanonical) Theravadist text of the first century.

The spell allegedly composed by the Buddha Himself is the *Khanda paritta.* According to the *Vinaya* source (*Kullavagga* V, 6), when the Buddha was informed that a certain monk had died of snakebite, He said that this would not have happened had the monk ". . . let his love flow out over the four royal breeds of serpents." All monks, he continued, can be protected from snakes if they "let their love flow out . . ."—an end which can be achieved, He promised, by reciting the *paritta* which He then

[2]See Book IV, 14th Dilemma. For the anthropological field worker, the most interesting feature of the dialogue which constitutes this text is its contemporaneity. The rationale for the use of *paritta,* which the monk Nāgasena expounds for King Milinda, is almost identical with the rationale offered in contemporary Burma. The power of these spells, Nāgasena points out, cannot change one's karma; if, according to his karma, a person is fated to die, they cannot protect him. If, however, death is not a karmic necessity, the chanting of *paritta* can save him from those dangers which might otherwise lead to his death.

> And when Pirit has been said over a man, a snake, ready to bite, will not bite him, but close his jaws—the club which robbers hold aloft to strike him with will never strike; they will let it drop, and treat him kindly—the enraged elephant rushing at him will suddenly stop—the burning fiery conflagration surging towards him will die out—the malignant poison he has eaten will become harmless, and turn to food—assassins who have come to slay him will become as the slaves who wait upon him—and the trap into which he has trodden will hold him not. [*Ibid.*:216]

But it is not enough, according to the Venerable Nāgasena (and his Burmese successors), that one's karmic state permits the spell to be effective; the moral and spiritual state of the person must be taken into account as well. The *paritta* is effective only if the person leads a moral life and has faith. (*Ibid.*:218-19)

composed for them.[3] (The English translations of this, and other spells referred to in this chapter, are found in chapter 11.)

The *Mora* (peacock) *paritta* is taken from the *Mora Jātaka.* (*The Jātaka,* Vol. II, No. 159) According to the story, a monk informed the Buddha that he had broken his vow of chastity because he had seen a woman dressed in "magnificent attire." Sympathetic, the Buddha said that even the holiest of men are tempted by and succumb to the seductive attraction of a woman. Even He, when a Golden Peacock, had so succumbed as the following tale reveals. As a peacock he had been safe from all creatures because, morning and evening, he recited spells in praise of the sun and the various Buddhas and then asked for their protection. When, at the command of six successive kings of Benares, a hunter attempted to trap the peacock, he was unsuccessful because the peacock was protected by these spells. Finally, having observed the peacock's habits, the hunter brought a peahen with him, and before the peacock had recited his morning spell the hunter had her utter her cry. On hearing the cry, desire was awakened in the peacock; forgetting to recite his spell, he went toward the peahen and was captured by the hunter. The spells recited by the peacock comprise the contemporary *Mora paritta.*

The *Dhajagga* (top of the banner) *paritta* is again based on a tale told by the Buddha. (*The Book of the Kindred Sayings,* ch. 11.) When the gods and the titans *(Asura)* were engaged in battle, Sakka, the king of the gods, told them that should they become frightened they need only look up at the crest of his banner (and the banners of some other gods), and "any fear and panic and creeping of the flesh that will have arisen will be overcome." But, said the Buddha to his disciples, this technique may or it may not help because Sakka, although king of the gods, is yet timid and given to panic. Hence He instructed His disciples, when—having gone "into forests, to the roots of trees, to empty places"—they become frightened, they should think of Him (and/or of the Law, and/or of the Order) and at the same time they should recite the verses which He then composed extolling the virtues of each of these three Gems. If they did so, He promised, "any fear, panic, creeping of the flesh that will have arisen will be overcome," because the Buddha, unlike Sakka, is "Supremely Enlightened, is purged of passion, hate, ignorance, is without timidity or panic or fright, and fleeth not."

The basis for the *Āṭānāṭiya paritta* (*Dialogues of the Buddha,* Pt. III, ch. 32) is an encounter between the Buddha and four kings who come to tell him that there were many demons in the land who, neither believing in the Buddha nor abiding by the Five Precepts, frightened and attacked His

[3]The same *paritta* is found in the *Khandhavatta Jātaka.* (*The Jātaka,* Vol. II, No. 103) When, as an ascetic in a previous birth, the future Buddha heard other ascetics complaining about the dangers they encountered from snakes, he instructed them in the recitation of this spell.

followers when they retire to lonely places for meditation. Moved by their complaints the Buddha agreed that the *paritta* which they presented to Him —"whereby [as He put it] both bretheren and sisters of the Order, and laymen and laywomen may dwell at ease, guarded, protected, and unscathed"—should be taught and used by all His followers.

The *Aṅgulimāla* (garland of fingers) *paritta* (*The Middle Length Sayings*, Vol. II, ch. 86) is named after an infamous robber and killer, who took his name from the fact that he wore a garland comprised of the fingers of those whom he had murdered. Although the Buddha had been warned that he would pass through the country where Aṅgulimāla lived at the risk of His life, He deliberately ignored this warning. Seeing the Buddha, Aṅgulimāla attempted to seize Him, but (the Buddha having performed a miracle) was unable to catch Him even when walking in slow motion. Recognizing thereby the greatness of the Buddha, Aṅgulimāla became a convert; and when the Buddha ordained him a monk, he became His attendant.[4] One day, Aṅgulimāla went to Sāvatthī to collect his alms food, and seeing a woman in difficult labor he became disconcerted. Telling the Buddha of his distress, the latter said he should return to the woman and tell her (presumably as a magical means for saving her life) that he had never intentionally taken a life, and that "by this truth may there be well-being for you, well-being for the unborn child."[5] Aṅgulimāla replied that he could not say this to her since he would be telling a lie. The Buddha said that he should then go to her and say instead that from the time he had become a monk he had never intentionally taken a life, and that "by this truth may there be . . . etc." He did so, and the lives of woman and child were saved by this *paritta*.

According to the Commentaries (cf. Malalasekera 1960: Vol. 2, 710), the *Ratana* (Jewel) *paritta* (*Woven Cadences*, ch. 2) was taught by the Buddha to his disciple, Ānanda, when the Licchavis asked him to rid their city (Vesāli) of the many calamities that had been brought upon it by evil spirits. The Buddha instructed Ānanda to recite the Jewel *Sutta*, a hymn in praise of the Three Gems, while walking round the city and sprinkling water from the Buddha's bowl. When Ānanda followed His instructions the evil spirits fled, and the people recovered from the famine, pestilence, and other difficulties that had befallen them.[6]

[4]Although the Burmese versions of all the other scriptural tales from which the *paritta* are derived correspond (except in minor details) to the original text, the Aṅgulimāla story is told with an interesting and (for Burma) significant twist. In my informants' version, Ingulimala (as he is called in Burmese) is a king who cut off the fingers of his subjects. When he was unable to cut off the fingers of the Buddha, he abdicated his throne and became a monk.

[5]This is known in Buddhism as an "act of truth" *(saccakiriyā)*.

[6]The text of this *sutta* is also found in the *Khuddakapāṭha*, VI. The use of the jewel as a magical amulet is, as Waddell observes, an ancient Indian practice. It is found in the *Atharvaveda* and is referred to by the Buddha as a prevalent practice in his day. Hence, according to Waddell (1926:557), this *sutta* was composed as a "luck-compelling charm," based upon the "supposed magical efficacy of the prehistoric wishing gem or amulet."

The *Vaṭṭaka* (quail) *paritta* is also based on a *Jātaka* tale. (*The Jātaka,* Vol. 1, No. 35.) When the disciples of the Buddha fled to Him during a raging fire, they saw Him standing in an area untouched by the fire, which was raging all about Him. When they exclaimed on His wondrous powers, He said it was through no power of His that the fire stopped before it reached Him, but through the power of an "act of truth" which He had performed as a quail in a previous birth. When He was a baby quail, a forest fire broke out. Fearing for their lives all the birds, including his own parents, flew away, and the young quail, unable to fly, was left to his doom. "I am," he thought to himself, "quite alone in the world. I am without protector or helper. What, then, shall I do this day?" He then thought that if he could call to mind the Buddhas of the past and the "efficacy they have won," he could, by an "act of truth," make the flames recede, thereby saving himself and all the other birds by the "true faith that was in him." With these thoughts he composed a spell—the *Vaṭṭaka paritta*—by which the fire was extinguished.

There are other, even more famous *paritta* in Burma, which however (although consisting of canonical *sutta*) are not based on historical or legendary events. (They, too, are reproduced in chapter 11.)

The "Theological" Basis for Apotropaic Buddhism

The Power of Buddhist Sacra

Scripture does not explain either how the *paritta* works—Why does the utterance of these words offer protection against danger?—or how, granted that it works, it can be reconciled with the doctrine of karma. The latter question, which we shall deal with below, is sufficiently problematic to have been raised in *King Milinda.* The former, however, is discussed neither in *Milinda* nor (so far as I know) in any other traditional text. In the absence of traditional answers, Buddhists have had, therefore, to devise answers of their own. From the general reaction of the Burmese to my queries concerning this problem, it is obvious that, for most of them at least, the question is of no concern; it is not problematic. That *paritta* work is all that is important; how they work is for them not very interesting. (That the belief in their efficacy conflicts, moreover, with other doctrines of Buddhism is something which very few have payed any attention to.) Still, it is a question which cannot be lightly passed over. For protection against a variety of dangers, the Burmese not only recite these spells, but they perform a variety of other apotropaic rituals. Thus, they recite prayers and make offerings to special Buddha images and pagodas; they make offerings, as well, to relics of the Buddha and of Buddhist saints; they build pagodas; they tell their beads; they utilize Buddhist talismans; they liberate animals; and perform many other rituals. (All of these are described in detail in chapter 11.)

If, then, the destruction of karma is the ontological basis for the attainment of nirvana (nibbanic Buddhism), and if the acquisition of merit is the ontological basis for a better rebirth (kammatic Buddhism), what is the ontological basis for the efficacy of these protection rituals (apotropaic Buddhism)? From what I have said, it should be clear that there is no single or simple answer to this question. Not only do *different* villagers offer (both by word and by practice) different answers, but even the *same* villager may offer, and act upon, different answers. What I shall describe, then, is a range of answers.

One of the first questions raised by the belief in the efficacy of these rituals is the extent to which it is thought that their performance elicits the protection of the Buddha. There is at least some suggestion that this might be so, and yet it is a paradoxical suggestion, since for the attainment of salvation—whether viewed in nibbanic or kammatic terms—almost all Burmese agree, it will be remembered, that the Buddha is of no avail: the Buddha cannot save. Is it possible, then, that although the Buddha is not viewed as a savior, He is viewed as a protector? But to be a protector, the Buddha must be alive, and this is a somewhat difficult thesis to sustain, since according to Scripture He died and entered nirvana in His eightieth year. Still, when this question was put even to the members of my blue-ribbon panel, the answers were not unequivocal.

Five members of the panel said they definitely conceived of Him as alive. Five said that He could not possibly be alive—the Buddha is dead. The remaining four, although denying that He was literally alive, argued that He was nevertheless alive in some metaphorical sense. Thus, "He is alive in the worshiper's heart"; "He is alive in the *Dhamma,* and in every act of *dāna"*; "He is alive in His Virtues" *(guṇa);* "He is alive in the person's 'insight wisdom.'" In short, although opinion, even in this blue-ribbon sample, seems divided on this question, the majority very clearly view the Buddha as dead. He is, to be sure, the "leader of all creatures," the "noblest of all creatures," the "incomparable," and so on. But since He is dead, the consensus seems to be that "the Buddha cannot help." It would be fruitless to call upon Him in time of trouble. This is not to say, however, that He plays no role in those protection rituals which even they, the members of the blue-ribbon panel, perform. For although it is not the Buddha Himself who attends to the devotees' prayers or wishes, they are granted, many of them argued, by the power of His "Virtues," or His relics. In short, although (for them) the Buddha Himself is not magically active, He radiates magical power.

Although most of the members of this select sample viewed the Buddha as dead, there is some reason to believe that among less educated villagers —less educated in both secular and Buddhist knowledge—a greater proportion believe Him to be alive. For, since the belief that the Buddha is not alive represents the normative belief, this is the first response that even the unsophisticated Buddhist would be expected to give to such a question.

Thus, when sitting at night with a group of ten or eleven men (who were preparing an elaborate ritual offering to be presented at the pagoda the next day), I put this question to them, the unanimous response was that the Buddha is dead. If so, I asked, who is it that comes to their assistance when they perform their various protection ceremonies? After some prolonged discussion within the group (to which I listened without participating) the consensus was that it was the Buddha who assisted the petitioner—from which most of them concluded that He is alive.[7]

Alive or not, most Burmese believe that if the Buddha Himself does not intercede, the efficacy of the protection rituals is guaranteed by His power *(hpoung: dagou:)*—only, however, if the devotee has faith *(thissa:)* in Him; and if not by *His* power, then by the power inherent in His Virtues (for, if one has confidence [*kou:(sa:)jin:(a)ya*] in the Buddha, and concentrates on His Virtues, *their* power will protect him); and if not by the power of His Virtues, then by the power contained in His words. Thus, for example, the worship of a special Buddha image is efficacious for curing snake bites because, by reciting and contemplating various scriptural passages—the doctrine of Dependent Origination, the Five "groups of grasping," the "Virtues," the Love *Sutta,* and so on—protection is achieved by the power of these words. If so, I asked, why is it necessary to perform the ritual at *this* image in *this* pagoda? Why can't the litany have the same effect if chanted at some other pagoda, or for that matter in one's own home? The answer (indicating again that the Burmese do not give much attention to questions of this kind) was that the king who had constructed this pagoda had great faith, and therefore it was important to recite them here.

This, however, is only one type of explanation for the efficacy of these rituals. Since some are performed in the presence of, or as homage to, a Buddha image, still another explanation refers rather to the power *of* the image, or (as some put it) the power created *by* the image, or (as still others put it) the power *in* the image. If one has faith in this power, one acquires a sense of self-confidence *(young-kyi: hmu)* and a change in mental set which, in turn, can protect him. This power, however, is difficult to characterize. Some say, as in the case of the famous image in the Arakan pagoda, that the spirit of the Buddha resides *in* the image, and this gives it its power. But this is not true for most other images. Our data here are insufficient to carry the discussion any further except to say that most Burmese believe that images acquire this power only after they are worshiped. Others add

[7]According to Than Tun the belief that the Buddha is alive was held by at least "some" Burmese in Old Pagan. In the twelfth and thirteenth centuries, he writes (Than Tun 1955: 174-75), ". . . some considered Buddha as God or some form of living deity and dedicated slaves of all professions and articles of everyday use so that Buddha may enjoy them."

Similarly, from an analysis of a Sinhalese consecration of a Buddha image, one scholar has concluded that the contemporary Sinhalese believe the Buddha to be alive and worship Him accordingly. (Gombrich 1966)

that the power is physically perceptible: the image may acquire a halo or give off sparks.

In the case of certain healing ceremonies, it is not the power of (or in) the image that is deemed important—although the ritual is performed in front of it. The curing power lies, rather, in the relics of the Buddha buried in the pagoda where the ceremony is performed.

Some protection rituals, as in the case of *paritta* ceremonies, are entirely verbal, consisting of spells exclusively rather than prayers or offerings. The *Ratana Sutta,* for example, which extols the Virtues of the Three Gems, may be chanted in order to ward off an evil omen, cure a sick patient, avert an astrologically caused danger, tame a wild beast, etc. This spell is efficacious not only because it contains the words, and therefore the power, of the Buddha, but also because of the power it creates in the mind of the religious actor: it creates thoughts which are sufficiently powerful to affect the external world. The following comment on the attitude of the early Buddhists concerning the efficacy of the *Mettā* (Love) *Sutta* characterizes the attitude of many contemporary Burmese towards *paritta* in general.

> The profession of amity, according to Buddhist doctrine, was no mere matter of pretty speech. It was to accompany and express a psychic suffusion of the hostile man or beast or spirit with the benign, fraternal emotion—with *mettā* [love]. For strong was the conviction . . . that "thoughts are things," that psychical action, emotional or intellectual, is capable of working like a force among forces. [C. A. F. Rhys Davids 1921:185-86]

A contemporary Burmese monk expressed the same notion when he informed me (in 1962) that he recited this same *sutta* daily "in order to bring peace between Kennedy and Khruschchev." When I asked how his litany could attain this end he explained that it is achieved through the "power of the mind [*seik dagou:*]. The mind can conquer many things. The mind has conquered wild beasts through the power of love; surely, it can conquer [the anger of] human beings."

Here, then, is one set of notions purporting to explain the efficacy of protection rituals; viz., they work because of power associated with the Buddha—His own power, the power of the physical objects (images and relics) which represent Him, the power of the words spoken by Him, or the psychic power which is created in those who recite them. Power associated with the Buddha is, however, only one source of the power tapped by these rituals. For according to some monks, there are altogether thirteen sources of power *(hse)* whose protection is assured by the recitation of Buddhist prayers or spells. These are: the power of the Buddha, the Teaching, the Order, the Silent Buddhas, one's parents, one's teacher, the weapons of the *brahma deva,* the thunder of (the god) Sakka, the fire of the *sammā deva,* the weapons of the ogres *(bi. lu:),* the clapping wings of the garuda bird *(galoun),* the sparks of the dragons *(naga:),* and the roar of the lion. The monks of a certain monastery in Mandalay, who first introduced me to this list, said that they feel secure because daily, in worshiping the Buddha, they are assured of protection by these powers.

The most important of these powers is the power of the *sammā* (Burmese, *thama*) *deva*, the Buddhist gods. (Cf. Spiro 1967:43-46.) Most Burmese believe that when a Buddhist text—any words related to the Buddha, the Law, or the Order—is recited, these gods, the guardians of Buddhism, watch over and protect those who recite them. In order to be protected, however, one must have faith *(thissa:)* in the Three Gems, for it is because of them that the gods offer their protection; those who do not have such faith are not protected. But faith in the Three Gems is not enough. To be protected one must also live in accordance with Buddhist morality; those who violate the Buddhist precepts will not enjoy their protection. If, for example, a person is bitten by a snake while stealing or lying, the gods will not protect him even if he worships at the Buddha image which cures snake bites. Indeed, those who persistently violate the precepts will be prevented by some unseen force from even entering the pagoda compound to perform the ritual; only the morally pure can walk through the gate.

In any event, if one is a pious Buddhist, the *sammā deva* will come to his aid when he performs the Buddhist protection rituals. Different informants give different reasons for their assistance: because the actor has faith in them; because they respond to the merit he has acquired by the performance of the ritual; because of his piety, which is called to their attention by his ritual action. Whichever reason is stressed, all informants agree that if the actor is pious and moral, the assistance of the gods is compulsory: they *must* come to his assistance.

A third and final explanation for the efficacy of these protection rituals does not invoke notions of power; it is cast in a rather different mode. Since the performance of many of these rituals includes *dāna* (offerings to the Buddha or to the monks), they create merit which, rather than producing a karmic consequence in the actor's subsequent rebirth(s), creates an immediate change in his karmic balance. This in turn has the effect of averting the impending danger, or (if it has already occurred) of bringing it to an end. A most dramatic example of this belief in "instant karma" (as Manning Nash [1965:136] felicitously terms it) was the construction in Burma a few years ago of thousands of sand pagodas in order to avert an astrologically indicated world disaster (see chapter 11). Only a huge amount of collective merit was deemed sufficient to avert the magnitude of the impending calamity.

These then are the three, essentially lay, explanations for the efficacy of apotropaic Buddhist ritual found in Burma. The explanations, it must be stressed, are not viewed as alternative, let alone mutually exclusive. They are not associated with different sects or theological positions—one more, the other less, orthodox. Most laymen, to the extent that they think about such matters at all, hold all three explanations simultaneously. They may, when queried by the anthropologist, offer only one of them—the first that comes to mind; but they readily agree, when the others are mentioned, that they are equally operative. It is of interest to compare them with those of Buddhist monks, which in principle at least should be closer to those of normative Buddhism.

Unlike the laymen, all the monks in my sample insisted that the Buddha was dead, and the scripturally based *paritta* excepted, many were skeptical of the efficacy of protection rituals. Two-thirds of the monks, for example, denied that any Buddha image can cure snake bites, some stating flatly that rituals performed to that end were, as they put it, "useless." Although agreeing that the image did not possess power, other monks, however, said that the rituals were nevertheless worthwhile. In the first place, although neither the image nor the Buddha can offer assistance, one might still be cured, they said, because of the self-confidence *(young-kyi: hmu)*, strenuous effort *(kyou:za: hmu,)* and exertion of strength *(a:to hmu)* that the ritual produces in the patient, a self-confidence which stems from faith in the Buddha and His power. By this faith-based confidence they cure themselves. Second, Buddhist worship, if it includes *dāna*, confers merit upon the worshiper which—as I have already pointed out—may bear fruit in one's immediate as well as a future existence. The image itself, however, is powerless. On the other hand, almost all the monks agreed that the power of the Buddha *is* found in His relics. By worshiping at a pagoda which contains His relics, it is possible to obtain assistance from this power; and though the means by which this happens is obscure, it is typically interpreted as a consequence of an improvement in karma.

For these monks, then, we seem to have—if I may construct a cognitive structure from their disparate and sometimes contradictory statements—the following notion. The Buddha is dead; He cannot help. Prayer invoking His assistance is futile. But still His worship is efficacious because it enhances one's karma, which in turn may produce the sought-for consequences. One may receive aid, but the help comes not from a personal Being but from an impersonal force or process. Comparing Buddhism on this dimension with Christianity, we might say that in both religions assistance requires personal effort: one must perform a rite. For Christianity, this rite (typically a prayer) influences a personal Being to answer one's needs. For Buddhism, the merit acquired through the rite affects an impersonal force (karma), which determines one's fate in a manner that answers one's needs. In both cases, the outcome is problematic. For the Christian, God may or may not assist; for the Buddhist his past karma, conjoined with present karma, may or may not be sufficiently good to produce the desired consequence.

So far as *paritta* are concerned, all the monks believed in their efficacy. Again, however, there was some difference concerning the mechanism by which it works. One-fourth of the monks said these spells are efficacious because they imbue the person with self-confidence. The majority, however, attributed their efficacy to the supernatural power released by the recitation of the text: the words of the Buddha are powerful in themselves. Hence, although neither the Buddha nor any other being intervenes to help or protect, the power of the Buddha continues to reside in His words, and when they are recited *by monks* in a ritual context, this power is liberated. This is so, however, not merely because they are the words of the Buddha, but because He Himself ordained the *paritta* ritual. Like the laymen, the monks also emphasized that these spells do not work automatically; one must believe in their efficacy and live according to the Buddhist precepts.

As for the chanting of spells to enlist the assistance of the *deva,* almost all the monks agree that these gods can and do assist when they are asked to do so—again, however, only on condition that the petitioner is a pious Buddhist. They will not assist immoral persons. As is so often the case, a *Jātaka* was recounted by one of the monks as irrefutable "proof" for the truth of this belief. Once there were two Brahmins, father and son. When the former died he became a *deva,* and seeing that his son was poor, gave him a wishing pot from which he said the son might take anything he wanted. He warned him, however, not to drop the pot. Once, when drunk, the son dropped and broke the pot, and so could no longer obtain his wishes. From the first part of the story, the monk pointed out, it may be inferred that *deva* can render assistance to human beings.

Another monk offered another scriptural proof for the belief that the gods help people. Whenever a certain monk, who was an Embryo Buddha, entered the forest, he always found a monastery prepared for him. These monasteries were built for him by the *deva.*

A Psychological Interpretation

It should be obvious from this rather tedious discussion that the Burmese conception of the entire structure of apotropaic Buddhism is confused and unclear. Not only do different actors have differing and contradictory conceptions of how and why the rituals work, or whether supernatural beings (the Buddha and the *deva*) do or do not offer protection and care, but each actor is vague about his own conceptions—so vague that each harbors various and contradictory answers to these questions. Nor, in the light of our previous discussion of the experiential and cognitive bases for religious belief, is this surprising.

The belief that one can receive supernatural assistance and protection by means of prayer and other ritual represents more than wishful thinking. For although such a belief is, of course, motivated by the *desire* for help and protection, the *conviction* that this desire can be satisfied must be based on experience. According to the theory delineated above (chapter 5) the experience that may produce such a conviction derives from a particular kind of child-parent interaction, one in which the expressed needs and desires of the child are consistently satisfied by his parents. This experience produces a cognitive structure in which the request for help and protection is associated with the expectation of parental assistance. It is the projection of this cognitive structure onto supernatural beings which produces the conviction that prayer and other rituals can evoke *their* assistance. If however, as in Burma, parents do not consistently and predictably attend to the child's needs, so that his expectations concerning parental assistance are vague and uncertain, it may then be assumed that as an adult his expectations concerning supernatural assistance will likewise be vague and uncertain. Since his *motivation* for such assistance will not have diminished, the lack of this necessary cognitive structure will not deter him from the quest; it will, however, render his conception of supernatural beings and supernatural assistance confused and blurred.[8]

This, I suggest, accounts for the confusion and cognitive looseness in Burmese belief. Worship of the Buddha may produce the desired results, but probably not so much because of His assistance as because of the power inherent in His words or relics, or the merit that derives from His worship. On the other hand, the recitation of certain spells may evoke the assistance of the *deva* though this is probably due to the coercive power of the spell rather than the loving care of the gods. Still again, prayer and ritual may be efficacious, not because they enlist the assistance of any being or beings, but because of the power inherent in the words or rites themselves.

It will be noticed that, underlying these loose and vague conceptions of supernatural assistance, there is less of a notion of propitiating supernatural beings than of coercing supernatural power. It is as if the Burmese cognitive model for Buddhist supernatural assistance were derived more from the infantile experience of indulgent nurturance (which, as I have suggested in chapter 5, creates the conviction that one's own behavior and wishes automatically achieve one's desired ends) than from the childhood experience of help, which typically produces the feeling that aid is contingent upon the solicitation of assistance from others. This is consonant with Burmese socialization, in which, it will be remembered, infantile love is abundant but childhood dependency often frustrated. Perhaps, then, this is why the image of the *deva* is so vague. Even when, unlike the Buddha, they are believed to offer direct help, they are only loosely differentiated if at all. It is almost always the unspecified *deva*, rather than a specific or individuated god or group of gods differentiated by name, sex, and so on, who are believed to offer help. This is in marked contrast to the *Bodhisattvas* of *Mahāyāna* Buddhism, who are differentiated by name and sex, or to the malevolent *nat* of Burma who are similarly individuated (as indeed we would expect them to be, since *ex hypothesi* the punitive experiences of later childhood are projected onto them [Spiro 1967:76-80]).

[8]This explanation, of course, is derived from Kardiner (1945).

The Problem of Karma

The persistence and prevalence of apotropaic Buddhism are a measure of the extent to which the Burmese (and other Theravadists) have resisted the full implications of the doctrine of karma, for by its very nature apotropaic Buddhism poses two serious challenges to this doctrine, one cultural and the other psychological. Let us begin with the cultural challenge.

Under the influence of both indigenous and imported cultural beliefs concerning magical causation, the Burmese have been unable to accept the assumption that karma is the exclusive cause of suffering and pain. Included among these nonkarmic results are illness caused by witches or evil spirits, calamities caused by astrologically interpreted planetary influences, dangers caused by a variety of inauspicious events—the entry of a wild animal into the village, the construction of a beehive in the house, etc.[9]—and many others. Since, from a strictly doctrinal point of view, such painful events represent karmic retribution for past behavior, these alternative causal explanations represent an obvious challenge to normative karmic doctrine.

The psychological challenge consists, as we have already seen, in a reluctance to accept the full implications of karmic determinism. Hence, even when a painful event is interpreted as karmic retribution for past behavior, apotropaic ritual is performed to avert or undo this karmically caused event. Since karmic causation, however, is both inevitable and immutable, any attempt to undo its consequences is yet another, and much more serious, challenge to normative doctrine.

The Burmese differ widely in the way they deal with the contradiction between the doctrine of karma and their belief in nonkarmic causation. Many are unaware of, have never thought about, or are unconcerned by the contradiction. Others, aware of and even distressed by it, can neither give up the non-Buddhist belief nor resolve the conflict. This is especially true concerning their belief in the action of evil spirits (cf. Spiro 1967:246-57). Still others label the beliefs in nonkarmic causes for what they are—anti-Buddhist—and will have no truck with them. This was the attitude of the majority of the monks in my sample concerning planetary influence. As one of them put it, "it is completely contrary to Buddhism." This was also the attitude of a tiny minority of villagers concerning the causal significance of inauspicious events. When, for example, the village was concerned about a stag that had entered it—a highly inauspicious omen—one of the villagers said, "It meant nothing. An animal has legs, it can walk wherever it wants.

[9]The Burmese hold, of course, the equally nonkarmic, but obverse, belief in auspicious times and places. The determination of the date for a wedding, the construction of a house, the ordination of a young boy as a novice—these and many other events may only take place at the astrologically determined auspicious time, which as often as not is calculated by the Buddhist monk.

It can cause nothing. It all depends on karma." This same attitude was expressed by a villager when discussing special Buddha images that allegedly cure snake bites. "Others may believe, but I don't believe in it. The Buddha only taught about karma. If your karma says you must die, you will die. Many snake-bite victims have gone to that image, but they are now dead. You can't escape karma."

Most Burmese, however, adopt a different stance. They neither deny the existence of nonkarmic causes of suffering, nor leave unresolved the contradiction between this belief and the belief in karma. When queried (perhaps "pressed" is a better word), the more thoughtful among them reconcile this contradiction by casting their nonkarmic beliefs in a karmic mode. Planetary influences, inauspicious events, and similar phenomena are interpreted, not as the causes of impending dangers, but as their signs. If a wild animal enters a village, or if the planets enter into a certain configuration they do not *cause* the predicted danger (its cause is karma); rather, they are the warning signals, as it were, that the danger is imminent. Alternatively, if a witch or an evil spirit has caused harm or illness to someone, it is because (according to one interpretation) these beings are the agents of his karma, the instruments as it were through which it works itself out; or because (by a somewhat different interpretation) their influence is consistent with their victim's karmic state. It is only when the latter is "bad," that is, when the victim deserves punishment, that it is possible for them to harm him. Were his karmic state good they could not, however much they might attack him, do him harm. (Cf. *ibid.*) There are some who interpret planetary influence in the same manner. Planets can indeed cause trouble, but only to those whose karma is bad. Those whose karmic state is good cannot be affected by planetary danger.

Although these explanations serve to safeguard Burmese Buddhist orthodoxy, further difficulties inherent in them indicate that these magical beliefs, truly extrinsic to Buddhism, are at best only loosely integrated with it. Thus, for example, if planetary configurations are only omens rather than causes of impending danger, how is it that an entire nation or even (as in the case that caused a paniclike alarm while I was living in Burma) the entire world can have the same karma, which produces the same consequence, at exactly the same time? Since everyone's karma, and therefore everyone's karmic retribution, is individuated (a consequence of his own unique personal history extending over myriads of rebirths), this is clearly impossible.

This explanation, moreover, encounters a second difficulty, one (as we shall see) related to the second challenge of apotropaic Buddhism to the doctrine of karma. When dangers are predicted on the basis of planetary configurations, the Burmese do not merely resign themselves to the impending, generally calamitous danger; rather they perform various apotropaic (usually Buddhist) rituals to avert it. But if the planets are merely the harbingers of karma-caused danger rather than themselves being its cause, and if the effects of karma created in previous lives are immutable, how is it possible to either change one's karma or avert its consequences?[10] By the same token, if evil spirits are merely the agents by means of which one's karma is carried out, how is it possible to undo their harm by means of apotropaic rituals?

Although the desire on the part of the Burmese to avoid the strict implications of karmic determinism is strong and understandable, their wish to act in compliance with Buddhist doctrine is equally strong. It is not surprising, therefore, that apotropaic rituals have been interpreted in such a manner, and the karmic doctrine modified in such a way, as to render them mutually compatible. Indeed, attempts to harmonize them did not originate with the Burmese; they are as old as *The Questions of King Milinda.* When the monk Nāgasena is challenged by King Milinda to explain how a *paritta* can cure a sick patient if, according to his karma, he is fated to die, the venerable monk replies that indeed it cannot save the life of such a person. The *paritta* is efficacious only in the case of those who (even when suffering from karmically caused illness) are not destined by their karma to die. It is only in such cases, in which death is a possible rather than an inevitable consequence of karma, that this spell can be effective. The *paritta,* in the words of Nāgasena, is effective for those "who have a period yet to live, who are full of life, and restrain themselves from the evils of Karma." (*Milinda,* p. 214)

Such a conception is clearly compatible with the normative karmic doctrine, and following the lead of Nāgasena it is applied in Burma, not only for the restricted case of the *paritta,* but for all other apotropaic rituals as well. The rituals are effective only in the case of pious Buddhists whose karma does not destine them to death, to permanent incarceration, to the loss of their crops, and so on. Similarly, only such people will be assisted by the *deva* when their help is solicited.

But other conceptions are also found in Burma which, by claiming that these rituals can prevent karmic retribution, clearly stretch the karmic doctrine beyond its normative limits. Even this antikarmic claim, however, is based on a karmic argument. As we have seen in connection with *dāna,* according to this way of thinking, although one cannot change the fruits of one's past action, one can change one's present action and thereby *its* fruits.

[10]The question, of course, is rhetorical; without rejecting or modifying the doctrine of karma, it is obviously not possible. But the whole point of apotropaic Buddhism is precisely to modify the doctrine of karma so that its consequences can be averted. If this is so, then the use of astrology for its predictive value is entirely understandable, for as we have seen, the karmic theory of suffering, though deterministic, has no predictive value. If, then, the doctrine of karma is modified so that its consequences can be averted, it becomes important to be able to predict impending dangers before they occur. Used in this way astrology is consistent with, and of great assistance to, this modified theory of karma. I am indebted to Obeyesekere (1968:21) for this observation.

Thus if one performs acts of merit *before* the retribution for some demerit has come about, the accumulation may sufficiently alter one's karmic balance so as to render the retribution invalid. By virtue of this new karmic balance, the formerly scheduled retribution is no longer appropriate.[11] This argument assumes that apotropaic ritual is primarily an act of merit-producing *dāna* (to the *deva*, the Buddha, the monks). On this argument, of course, planetary configurations and inauspicious events, interpreted as signs of an impending disaster, may be helpful. Knowing that one is approaching a period of karmically caused danger, one can then perform various kinds of meritorious acts by which the karmic balance can be improved and the danger averted. (Similarly, auspicious days are not in themselves automatically lucky days, but by performing acts of merit on these days one's karma, so to speak, can be propped up.)

This karmic interpretation of apotropaic Buddhist ritual is an obvious attempt, after the fact, to legitimize a practice which is at great variance with normative Buddhism. This is even more evident when one looks at clear cases of non-Buddhist rites which are interpreted in this same karmic mode. Thus, for example, a monk informed me that he had prevented a calamity from befalling a villager when a snake entered his house (I have noted that entry of a snake into a house is a very bad omen) by performing the following *ya.da.ya* ritual. This is a ritual intended to avert impending danger. He instructed the owner of the house to distribute a hundred snake-shaped cookies among the children of the village. Upon receiving his cookie each child exclaimed *"Pou kaung:de!"* ("It's better!"), so that instead of being an omen of misfortune the serpent became an omen of good fortune. This is an obvious case of sympathetic magic, in which external events are thought to be changed by a ritual simulating the change. It is interpreted in Buddhistic terms, however, to render it compatible with the belief in merit and karma. Thus in response to my query, after admitting that the snake itself was not a cause but a sign of impending danger, the monk again affirmed, in response to my further query, that karma cannot be altered in this primitive magical manner (so reminiscent of the biblical story of Rachel and the mandrakes). Rather, he said, by distributing these cookies among the children, the villager had performed an act of *dāna* whose merit importantly changed his karmic balance. This merit, he explained in an interesting metaphor, "is like providing supports for a weak structure that is about to fall. Without the supports it would certainly fall; the supports prevent this from happening." The metaphor, given the monk's belief in the neutralization of karma, is appropriate, but his use of the karmic idiom to legitimize a primitive magical rite is an obvious rationalization.

Following the lead of a great number of monks, and putting their views

[11]This interpretation, it will be noted, is based on the theory of karma which assumes that merit can neutralize demerit, rather than on the theory which assumes that each act carries its specific karmic retribution.

in somewhat more abstract terms, we might summarize the karmic interpretation of apotropaic ritual thus: One should not rely exclusively on the working out of one's past karma. The Buddha Himself, as we have already seen, stressed the importance of wisdom *(nyan)* and effort *(wiriya).* In times of danger—a snake bite, for example—wisdom would dictate that one make the effort to worship at the special pagoda that cures snake bites. For observe: if a person's karma is sufficiently bad so that the increment in merit cannot change his karmic balance, then, although his effort does no good so far as the snake bite is concerned, his augmented merit will be important in his future existence. If, on the other hand, his karma destines him for life, so that the newly acquired merit is not necessary to save him, the same logic applies. If his karma, so to speak, is of the borderline variety, then one has to take two kinds of karma into account: the accumulated total from his past lives *(adeik kan),* and that produced in his present life, including the immediate present *(pitsoukpan kan).* Given a borderline former karma, the increased merit acquired through the apotropaic ritual may tip the karmic balance so as to cure the patient.

Religion, Magic, and Buddhism

As one moves from nibbanic through kammatic to apotropaic Buddhism, one seems to be moving (to use a conventional distinction) from the religious to the magical pole of the Buddhist ideological continuum. To refer to this as the Little and to the religious as the Great tradition is, however, to misrepresent Buddhist history and civilization alike.

Whatever may have been the beliefs of the historical Buddha or the *Weltanschauung* of the primitive Buddhist church, the fact is that apotropaic Buddhist ritual and the religiomagical ontology on which it is based are at least as old as canonical Buddhism (according to which the Buddha Himself is the founder of apotropaic ritual), and are sanctioned by it. Hence, it is simply not true (to quote only one distinguished exponent of the contrary thesis) that "in its relation to the laity ancient Buddhism was relatively, perhaps even absolutely, inimical to magic." (Weber 1958:237) It is true that in ancient Buddhism the monk was "devalued" as a "magical helper and therapist" and that he was forbidden to boast of his "superhuman abilities." *(Ibid.)* This, however, is not because of Buddhism's disbelief in magic but because of its normative emphasis on salvation. Although magical *(paritta)* rituals were practiced by Buddhist monks, and although some were alleged to possess superhuman power, normative Buddhism, which—then as now—emphasized worldly renunciation, viewed magic no less than economics or politics or sex as a worldly rather than an otherworldly activity. It is in this sense and this sense only that magic was (and is) devalued in Buddhism: not because it is wrong, not because its ontological basis is false, but simply because it is irrelevant to the Buddhist quest for salvation. Although magic is perfectly appropriate for the attainment of worldly goals, and—despite its seeming conflict with the doctrine of karma—although its ontological basis is accepted as true, it is of no avail in the quest for deliverance from the Wheel of Rebirth.

Even devout Buddhists, for whom Deliverance is a primary motivational orientation, and who have renounced the sociopolitical world, must live in the physical world. Even they, therefore, suffer the pains and ills and fears of ordinary worldlings, and even they must cope somehow with these forms of suffering. This was as true of those ancient monks for whom allegedly the Buddha Himself created the *paritta* ceremony as it is of contemporary monks—not to mention ancient and contemporary laymen. The former, no less than the latter, not only turned to magical ritual for alleviation of stress, but also attributed much of their suffering to the action of supernatural powers of various types—demons, evil spirits, planetary influences, and so on. Scripture (the *Vinaya*), of course, explicitly forbids any monk to practice any of the magical arts current in ancient India, but then—as now—some chose to disregard this injunction.

Apotropaic Buddhism not only has deep historical roots, but it has played an important role in Buddhist civilization. It is difficult to know, of course, whether it was as important in ancient Buddhism as it is today, but it certainly seems to have been no less important in the classical periods of Burmese or Thai or Sinhalese history than it has been in the more recent periods of these civilizations. Then, as now, these peoples were no less involved in the goals and technology of apotropaic Buddhism because they had strongly cathected the soteriological goals and discipline of kammatic (or even nibbanic) Buddhism. Their world view was and is informed by the ontological and metaphysical postulates of the one, no less than the other.[12] Indeed, whatever their conflicts and contradictions, these postulates form one world view, not two. The evil spirits and the demons, the witches and the ogres, against whom so much of magical Buddhist ritual provides protection, are no less important features of the behavioral world of Buddhists than are the Buddhist sacra. It is precisely because they are important that apotropaic Buddhism looms so important in the minds of Buddhists. Indeed, although in all Buddhist countries there exists, side by side with Buddhism, a magical technology to deal with worldly suffering (and specifically, the suffering caused by these supernatural beings and forces), the magical technology of Buddhism (which invokes the power of Buddhist sacra) is deemed to be much the more powerful. (Cf. Spiro 1967) And Buddhism is valued not merely because it is sacred, not merely because it provides the means for salvation, but also because of its powerful magical technology. That this magical technology has remained an integrated part of Buddhism, rather than fissioning off into a separate cultural system, is attributable (at least in

[12]The world view of apotropaic Buddhism, it need not be emphasized, is hardly unique to Buddhism or to Burma. Structurally viewed, it is highly comparable with that, for example, of medieval Christendom. A Burmese Buddhist would have little difficulty in empathizing with the world view, for example, of St. Gregory the Great. (Cf. Duckett 1961: ch. 4)

part) to its assimilation within the moral and ontological framework of nibbanic and kammatic Buddhism. Buddhist magic, as we have seen, is believed to be efficacious only for those who live according to the moral precepts of Buddhism, and its efficacy is interpreted—albeit by fancy intellectual footwork—in terms of its normative karmic doctrine.

This brings me to my last point. Even when its efficacy is interpreted in terms of the doctrine of karma, Buddhist magic is believed to work because it invokes the assistance of supernatural helpers, viz., the Buddhist gods or *deva.* This must be emphasized here because, just as some interpreters of Buddhism have shorn it of its magic, others—and Durkheim has been the most influential in this regard—have shorn it of its gods. The Buddhist, writes Durkheim, ". . . is an atheist, in the sense that he does not concern himself with the question whether gods exist or not." (Durkheim 1954:46) Although this statement most certainly characterizes the position of the Buddha—as reflected, at any rate, in many scriptural passages attributed to Him—it most certainly does not characterize the bulk of the Scripture, let alone the beliefs of most postcanonical Buddhists.

It is true, as Durkheim observes *(ibid.),* that the Buddha is not a god in the sense of being either a Creator or a Savior; nor do Buddhism or Buddhists believe that any other being or beings have either or both of these attributes. For the most part Buddhism and Buddhists are indifferent to the former question and deny the latter. If, then, "atheism" is defined as the absence or denial of a Creator and a Savior, Buddhism is most certainly atheistic. But gods, even the Judaeo-Christian God, have other attributes as well—they answer prayers and respond to rites that invoke their assistance in worldly matters—and these attributes may be as crucial for their devotees as their soteriological function (and more crucial than their creative function). Without, however, evaluating the relative importance of these various functions, it can be firmly stated that Buddhists are indifferent neither to the existence of the *deva* (gods) nor to their worldly (protective) functions. If, then, Buddhism is atheistic with respect to the former attributes of godhood, it is most certainly theistic with respect to the latter attribute. Without the gods and their protective functions the ideological structure of apotropaic Buddhism—which, as we have seen, is a crucial part of the entire Buddhist fabric—would collapse.

But Buddhism is a theistic religion not only in its belief in the existence of benevolent superhuman beings who assist and protect, but also in its belief in malevolent superhuman beings, who attack and harm. Moreover, to the canonical inventory of such malevolent beings as Māra, *yakkha, bilu,* and so on, postcanonical Buddhists have added a variety of indigenous malevolent spirits (cf. Spiro 1967). Indeed, one of the primary functions of the benevolent Buddhist gods is, as we have seen, to protect the faithful from the harm caused by these evil spirits. In sum, to define Buddhism as an atheistic, or antimagical religion is surely to invoke a highly arbitrary definition of atheism and of magic.

CHAPTER 7

Esoteric Buddhism: A Religion of Chiliastic Expectations

The Major Features of Esoteric Buddhism

All of the great religions have spawned esoteric sects devoted to occult doctrines which, though related to normative religious ideology, are marginal and peripheral, if not heterodoxical, in relation to it. Burmese Buddhism is no exception to this generalization. In addition to the exoteric systems discussed in the foregoing chapters, there exist in Burma two related but distinct esoteric systems.

Like nibbanic and kammatic Buddhism, the ideologies of these two esoteric systems are clearly soteriological, and as such should logically have been described immediately after these two soteriological systems. On the other hand, there are two reasons for describing these esoteric systems here, following rather than preceding the discussion of apotropaic Buddhism. In the first place, unlike all three exoteric systems which are clearly derived from normative or scriptural Buddhism and incorporate its major doctrines, the ideologies of esoteric Buddhism are only marginally related to that normative tradition. Essentially, they represent a syncretism of occult (Indian, Chinese, and indigenous) beliefs, with an overlay of Buddhist doctrines, with which, in order to legitimize them, they are loosely integrated.

The second reason for separating the soteriological ideologies of esoteric Buddhism from the normative Buddhist soteriologies (and even from the nonsoteriological, apotropaic Buddhism) is that while the latter are the public property of the entire Buddhist "church," the former—as the esoteric designation suggests—are associated with and institutionalized in a variety of quasi-secret sects. Hence, although some of their doctrines are known to a surprisingly large number of Buddhists, and even held by them, it is only by initiation into these sects that one can acquire complete knowledge of these doctrines or the skill to use them for traffic with supernatural and occult powers. According to one authority, there are over a hundred of these esoteric sects (known in Burmese as *gaing:*), with a total membership estimated in the thousands (Mendelson 1960:115).

Common to them all is the quest for a more immediate and/or a somewhat different form of salvation than, or in addition to, those promised by the soteriologies of exoteric Buddhism. This, of course, is not an uncommon phenomenon in any of the salvation religions. In all of them, salvation (regardless of the condition the term denotes) is a goal which can only be achieved in a future existence. The present, whether it be the present life of the individual, the present epoch in history, or the present condition of nature, is never believed to be the temporal locus of salvation. Thus, in Buddhism salvation is located in one's next rebirth (kammatic Buddhism) or at the termination of one's cycle of rebirths (nibbanic Buddhism). In the history of all these religions, however, there have been some individuals, and in some cases groups of individuals, who have been unwilling to defer their soteriological aspirations to some future existence; for them, salvation is an imminent goal to be achieved in the present and immediate existence. In order to satisfy their pressing desire for it, they have in some cases reinterpreted the traditional soteriological goal and in others elaborated new and borrowed techniques for its achievement.

The esoteric sects of Burmese Buddhism are a case in point. Since however Buddhism, like Hinduism, has not been an exclusive religion, these sects have not rejected the more traditional forms of Buddhist soteriology; rather, accepting the more traditional forms, they have added yet another soteriological system or systems to those already in existence. In addition to the doctrines and practices of exoteric Buddhism, which they share with their coreligionists and by means of which they hope to attain some future transcendental salvation, they also subscribe to a system of esoteric doctrines and practices which offers them imminent and immanent salvation. With due allowances for the differences between Buddhism and Christianity, we might with some justification characterize the soteriology of these sects as chiliastic in orientation.[1]

Although these esoteric sects are characterized by a variety of beliefs and doctrines, they constitute, in essence, two major ideological systems. Common to both is the belief in a mythical magician or *weikza* who, supposed to possess enormous supernormal powers, and having overcome death, is the presiding genius or spiritual master of the sect. For one of these systems, sect initiation is the means for the adepts to become—as their Masters have already become—*weikza.* To be sure, neither *weikza* nor the aspiration to *weikza* are Buddhist in character (indeed, as we shall see

[1]Two of the essential attributes of chiliastic salvation, even in the restricted Christian meaning of "chiliasm," are the "enjoyment of a 'better' world" as an event which occurs "within history." (Cf. Tuveson 1964: ch. 1.)

below, they are anti-Buddhist); and in themselves they do not render the esoteric sect a *Buddhist* sect. The sect becomes Buddhist only when the *weikza* belief is integrated with the Buddhist beliefs in a Future Buddha, or a Universal Emperor, or (as sometimes happens) both.

Briefly, according to Buddhist belief, the Buddha Gautama (who lived in the sixth century B.C.) is the fourth of five Buddhas to appear in this world epoch; and it is almost universally held in Burma that the fifth or Future Buddha will appear five thousand years after the demise of this Buddha. Similarly someday, according to Buddhist belief, there will appear a Righteous Emperor who will bring the universe under the rule of Buddhist Law. One of these beliefs is a component element of the ideology of every esoteric Buddhist sect—sometimes both of them—though the belief in the Universal Emperor has been transfigured into a belief in the Future King of Burma.

But just as the *weikza* belief, in itself, is not Buddhist, so these two latter beliefs in themselves are not esoteric; rather, they are more or less normative doctrines of *Theravāda* Buddhism. It is only when they are integrated with the belief in *weikza*, and form component elements in a larger configuration of chiliastic beliefs and practices, that they become distinctive doctrines of esoteric Buddhism.

In esoteric sects, these three fundamental beliefs of esoteric Buddhism are combined in two major ways to produce the two esoteric ideologies of chiliastic salvation. When, as in some sects, the emphasis is on the founding master *weikza* of the sect, this belief is conjoined to the utopian belief in the Future King to produce what might be termed "millennial Buddhism." When, as in other sects, the emphasis is on the aspirations of the adepts to become *weikza* themselves, this belief is conjoined to the belief in the Future Buddha to produce what might be termed "eschatological Buddhism."[2] Each of these systems may now be described in detail.

Eschatological Buddhism

Alchemy and Its Goals

Eschatological Buddhism in Burma is based on alchemical techniques and practices (*eggiyat* - the work with fire) which, in the first instance, have

[2]As in the case of "chiliasm," the terms "millennial" and "eschatological," associated as they are with historically defined Christian meanings, are not altogether satisfactory. Still, one must use *some* labels to designate these systems, and these terms are probably more appropriate than others. (Mendelson's "messianic Buddhism" [Mendelson 1961*a*:560] is, I believe, even less appropriate, and in any event lumps together two systems which must be kept separate.) The use of "eschatological" to characterize the second system has the advantage of stressing the end-of-days dimension of this system of esoteric Buddhism as well as its emphasis on individual salvation. The use of "millennial" for the first system is already sanctioned by comparative usage (cf. Thrupp 1962). It is not coincidental that the generic attributes of millennialism, as defined by a leading authority of these movements (Cohn 1962:31), find a point-for-point correspondence in this system.

no relationship to Buddhism. These techniques, on the one hand, are similar to but distinct from European alchemy. On the other hand, they are not only similar to, but at least in part probably derived from Chinese and Indian alchemy.[3] As in the case of European alchemy, Burmese alchemy too includes techniques for the transmutation of base metals into gold. Of much greater importance in Burmese alchemy, however, are the goals of achieving magical power, especially—as in the case of Chinese (that is, Taoist) alchemy—of immortality. These powers are acquired by means of the alchemic stone *(datloung:)* whose absolute purification or refinement is the aim of all alchemic experiments. Whenever one sees a bellows and a crucible in Burma, one may be sure that much of the time and the major part of the financial resources of their owner are devoted to this end. In some cases, the medium employed for the achievement of such power is not the alchemic stone, but a magical square *(in:)* which, filled with cabalistic symbols, is cast over and over again until the goal is achieved. To simplify matters, however, most of our discussion will be confined to the alchemic technique.

Together with most Asian peoples, the Burmese believe that all matter consists of four elements: earth, air, fire, and water. Although these elements change and decay, Burmese alchemic theory holds that there is an essence, underlying them, which is eternal. (This of course, is an anti-Buddhist belief, contradicting the Buddhist doctrine of impermanence.) Burmese alchemic practice is based on the premise that if this essence can be extracted from the alchemic metal—in Burma, mercury and iron are the favorite metals—and injected into a human being, he too can become eternal.

However, a properly fired alchemic stone may acquire magical power even before the final stage of a perfect stone is achieved. In the first stage of this process, the metal is fired over and over again until it undergoes no further perceptible chemical or physical changes. At this point it is believed to possess magical, and especially protective, powers. In the villages in which I worked, alchemic practitioners, laymen and monks alike, were forever recounting the magical powers of their own, or someone else's, stone. Thus, one monk told me that he had formerly possessed a stone—which he has since lost!—which preserved the freshness of milk for over twenty-four hours. Moreover, when he carried it with him, he could walk with such speed that even his young novices could not keep up with him. Another monk, recounting the powers of his stone, said that when it was placed in a cup of petrol, the latter would not burn, no matter how many matches were used in the attempt. A Township Officer, a Christian, pos-

[3]For general surveys of alchemy which particularly stress its occult dimensions, cf. Burland (1967), Eliade (1962), Jung (1953), Taylor (1962). Chinese and Indian alchemy, and especially its occult aspects, are summarized in Eliade (1958: ch. 7; 1962: chs. 11-12), Johnson (1928), Taylor (1962: ch. 6). For Burmese alchemy, see Htin Aung (1962: chs. 4-5).

sessed a stone which he claimed could subdue any cobra. He once held it over the head of a hooded cobra, and the latter lowered its hood. When it was held over a cobra for a sufficiently long period, the creature would die. Other stones afford protection not only against snakes, but against witches, sorcerers, bullets, and other forms of deadly power.

A fully purified stone not only has power in itself, but confers great power on its possessor. Although no one that I interviewed either possessed or knew of anyone who possessed such a stone, they all knew what these powers consist of: to fly through the air and through the earth, to make oneself invisible, to pass from one place to another in a moment, and to satisfy all one's desires almost instantaneously.[4] One monk, abbot of a monastery in Mandalay, informed me that although he has not seen the display of such power with his own eyes, it is "well known" that in 1930 some German teachers at the Mandalay agricultural college had seen some alchemists flying over Mandalay. It was later established, he said, that these alchemists were also monks.

Thus far, the alchemic power I have been describing resides in the alchemic stone. As noted above, however, the ultimate aim of the alchemist is to incorporate this power into his own body so that he himself may possess it. This is achieved when, as part of a dangerous and frightening initiation ceremony described below, he swallows the stone.[5] If the ceremony is successful, the alchemist himself—without the aid of a stone—can, by his own power, fly through the air, become invisible, and so on. Much more important, like the stone itself, he acquires the attribute of eternal life and, more specifically, eternal youth. He has become a *weikza.*[6]

[4]These powers are also guaranteed by certain types of Yoga (cf. Eliade 1962:127); indeed, the Burmese alchemist who achieves these powers is called a *zawgyi,* the Burmese corruption of *yogi.* These same powers, incidentally, may be achieved by means of *jhānas,* those ecstatic states which sometimes accompany Buddhist meditation.

[5]That the power inherent in an object—or a person—can be incorporated by another is, of course, a very widespread belief; it constitutes one of the motives for cannibalism. The following quotation indicates that, until recently, the latter practice was an alternative means in Burma for the acquisition of power which could otherwise be obtained only through alchemy.

> The notorious bandit Twet Ngalu had been a monk and a magician and was elaborately tattooed; when he was killed in 1888, nothing would satisfy the nearest Shan chief but to dig up the body and boil it down into a concoction which he persisted in wanting to share with the English Chief Commissioner so that they both might become invincible. Burmese and Shan legends are full of stories about eating corpses to obtain magical powers such as flying. Similarly in 1907 Saya I, a Burmese wizard doctor, was convicted at Hanthawaddy Sessions for a shocking act of murder and cannibalism—*mulierem grauidam occidit, puerumque utero exsecuit coxit, deuorauit;* and while I was at Bassein in 1914 a Burman was tried and convicted for disinterring a corpse in the town cemetery, apparently with the same object. [Harvey 1925:318]

[6]In India the desire for immortality is one of the aims of certain forms of tantra (cf. Eliade 1962:133-35) as well as of alchemy (cf. Eliade 1958: ch. 7). In China, too, it is the primary motive for alchemy, which of course finds its basis in Taoism. (Cf. Taylor 1962:63-69.) This

Having become a *weikza*, the adept no longer remains within human settlements; even the smell, let alone the sight, of human beings—they are meat-eaters, and he disdains the eating of meat—is repulsive to him. (In anticipation of their future state, many alchemists become vegetarians.) Hence, *weikza* generally live on the remote Himalayan slopes. In order to satisfy their sexual appetites, they have intercourse with a type of fruit ("fruit maiden") which is remarkably similar in appearance to a human female. Being meat-eaters, women, of course, are repugnant to *weikza*.

Burmese villagers—those, at least, in the section of Upper Burma in which I worked—believe that alchemy and weikzahood had their origins in the early Burmese capital of Pagan. The following tale is recounted as the charter for this belief.[7] In the kingdom of Pagan there lived a hermit who hoped to become a *weikza* by means of his alchemic stone. On his way to "victory," the hermit enlisted the support of the king, who financed his alchemic experiments from the royal treasury. When, after many unsuccessful experiments, the treasury was almost depleted, the king became angry with the hermit and as a punishment took out his eyes.

Actually, the stone required the addition of only one more liquid in order to achieve victory, but the hermit did not know that. Unhappy with his fate, and disgusted with his stone, he instructed his disciples to cast it into a latrine pit. When it touched the bottom of the pit the stone immediately became "victorious"; the liquid required for victory was human excrement. When his disciples reported the wondrous colors being emitted from the latrine pit, the hermit knew that his stone had been completed. He ordered them to bring him two eyes—of either a bull or a goat—from the butcher shop. Because of a shortage of eyes, however, they brought him one goat's eye and one bull's eye. He touched them with his alchemic stone, the eyes entered the hermit's sockets, and his sight was restored. He then informed his disciples that he could now become a *weikza*. Before retiring from the world, however, he instructed the people to smelt all their bronze, iron, and lead in huge pots. Subsequently, he touched the pots with his stone, and their contents all turned into gold. Thus all the people became wealthy.[8] He then retired from the world to become a *weikza*.

---

theme of death and resurrection is also central to European alchemy, as Taylor (*ibid.*:53) and Jung (1953) have shown.

[7]The Burmese specialist will be interested in comparing the differences between the version of the tale told to me and that recorded by Htin Aung (1948:155-59), in his classic collection of Burmese folk tales.

[8]In Htin Aung's version, this tale is used to explain how it is that Pagan acquired the wealth to construct its numerous magnificent pagodas. By adding a sequel to the story which we need not recount here, my informants used it variously to "prove" that women as well as men can become *weikza*, to explain how *nat* cause trouble to humans, and to account for the origin of the Burmese belief that tugs-of-war can cause rain.

Alchemic Sects

In Yeigyi, only eight laymen (all males) are members of an alchemic sect. The monastic percentage, however, is much higher; two of the four village monks practice alchemy. An important (but not the only) reason for the small number of lay practitioners is that this is a very expensive enterprise. One of the means of purifying the alchemic stone is to "feed it" (as the Burmese say) with gold, and the cost of this process can be exorbitant. I met many formerly wealthy Burmese who have become destitute from their alchemic experiments. In any event, many Burmese do practice alchemy—extrapolating from Yeigyi, their members would run nationally into many thousands, especially when it is noted that the percentage of alchemists in the city is, if anything, higher than in the villages—and in order to do so they become members of one or another esoteric sect *(gaing:)*.

Although different informants classify these sects differently, and although the sects themselves differ in aims and techniques, their ultimate aim in all cases is to achieve the occult goal of *weikza.* Despite their goal, these are not merely *occult* sects; they are also *Buddhist.* Whatever their origins may have been—and they have, no doubt, deep roots in Burmese and probably pre-Buddhist Burmese history—they have acquired certain Buddhist characteristics, including a Buddhist charter. Recognizing that immortality is an anti-Buddhist notion, for according to Buddhism nothing is permanent, and that the desire for even the prolongation of life is non-Buddhist, since a true Buddhist aspires to release from the Wheel of Life, these sects have adapted the quest for eternal youth to the constraints imposed on them by these Buddhist doctrines. Weikzahood, they say, does not mean eternal life. Rather it means the prolongation of life for a certain stipulated, admittedly extensive duration—according to some, of 2,500 years; according to others, of 80,000. Moreover, they argue, this extension of life is not an end in itself, but is motivated by eschatological aims related to the belief in a Future Buddha. It is here that the idea of *weikza* is conjoined with, and hence legitimized by, Buddhist doctrine—a conjunction which transmutes this occult belief into eschatological Buddhism.

The Future Buddha, the fifth and last in this world cycle, is the Buddha Maitreya (Pali, *Metteyya;* Burmese, *Arimadei:ya*) of normative Buddhism. (See the *Cakkavattī Sīhanāda Suttanta* of the *Digha Nikāya,* in *Dialogues of the Buddha,* Part III.) According to a widespread Burmese belief, the Buddha Maitreya is to appear 5,000 years after the death of the Buddha Gautama—i.e., in about 2,500 years from now. The Burmese believe that many changes will take place both before and after His appearance. Thus, before He arrives, the present world will be destroyed by fire, water, and storms, so that when He appears there will be a new world. Moreover, although most of the inhabitants of the present world, being wicked, will be destroyed by the holocaust, a few—the pious ones—will survive until after the arrival of the new Buddha, whose dispensation will last for 80,000 years.

The tenuous relationship between *weikza* and the belief in the Future Buddha may now be unraveled. Sect members aspire to *weikza,* they say, so that they may live until the arrival of Maitreya (2,500 years) or until the end of His dispensation (80,000 years). Remaining alive until His arrival, they will be able, by worshiping the "physical body" of the Buddha Gautama—which will be formed, immediately prior to the arrival of Maitreya, by the recombination of His relics—to enter nirvana. This is known as *da-tu. neikban* (from the Pali *dhātu,* or essence, substance, or element).[9] Those who hold that the *weikza* will remain alive for the entire dispensation of Maitreya stress that it is the continuous worship of Him as well as the study and practice of Buddhist Law that will then assure the attainment of nirvana.

In addition to the desire to attain nirvana through the worship of the Buddha, some sect members legitimize their desire for a prolonged life by still another Buddhist argument. To say that Buddhism teaches that all life is suffering, they argue, is a misreading of the Buddha's teachings. The Buddha, they point out, spoke of the four inevitable causes of suffering—conception, sickness, old age, and death; He spoke, too, of the sufferings attendant upon remaining with a person whom you dislike and being separated from one you like; finally, He spoke of the suffering attendant upon the frustration of desire. This means, in the words of their spokesman in this instance—a Buddhist monk—that "although there are many things that cause suffering, there still remain many things that are pleasurable. The life of the *weikza* is a life in which the suffering is abolished, and only the pleasure remains."

It should be noted, before proceeding, that the conjunction of nirvana and weikzahood is not as bizarre as it appears; for, psychologically viewed, they are opposite sides of the same coin. Nirvana is a state characterized by the absence of desire, and hence, according to Buddhist psychology, by the absence of pain. Similarly weikzahood, too, is a state characterized by the absence of pain; not, however, because of the absence of desire, but because all desire is instantaneously satisfied. Doctrinally poles apart, psychologically these beliefs are all but identical.

But the sects are "Buddhist" in yet another way.[10] Since weikzahood is

[9]In most discussions of *weikza* (cf. Mendelson 1960:115; Htin Aung 1962:131), it is the worship not of Gautama, but of Maitreya which will assure the attainment of nirvana. This belief is also found in Ceylon. (Ames 1964:26, Obeyesekere 1968:36.) Although some of my informants held the same view, they represented a small minority. The majority, who stressed the worship of the Buddha Gautama, were divided however into those who held (at least by implication) that the recombined relics of Gautama will in fact constitute the new Buddha, and those who held that the two Buddhas are distinct. I could not discover from the latter what, in their view, then happens to Gautama.

[10]The notion that nirvana can be achieved by ritual and worship is, of course, completely contrary to normative (*Theravāda*) Buddhist doctrine.

a means to the attainment of nirvana, initiation into a sect entails a commitment to the practice of Buddhist discipline. The initiate must agree to observe the moral precepts of Buddhism and to perform Buddhist devotions. In addition, many sect members practice Buddhist meditation (not so much, to be sure, as a means for the attainment of nirvana, as for acquisition of the superhuman powers of *weikza*). Finally, sect members place themselves under the protection of one or more of the Buddhist gods or *deva.*

Sect members known to me are still at the bottom of the alchemic hierarchy; at best, they have succeeded in refining their alchemic stone to the point where it can protect them from snakes, witches, and so on. None has refined his stone to the degree where he can, with its help, perform superhuman feats, let alone achieve *weikza*. Nevertheless, as most of them hope to attain that state, they all know what the requirements for weikzahood are. Having created an alchemic stone whose possession enables him to perform superhuman feats, the alchemist must swallow the stone so that its powers become his. But it is not so simple. He must enter the forest with a brave and trusted disciple. There a pit is dug; after swallowing his alchemic stone, the alchemist, while in a trance state, is buried in the pit for seven days. His disciple is then put to a series of severe tests by wild animals, evil spirits, witches, seductive maidens—all of whom successively attempt to lure him from the pit. If they succeed, his Master will die. If he stands his ground, however, his Master will emerge from the earth as a full-fledged *weikza.*[11]

Although, typically, sect members do not become *weikza* or attain supernormal power, many achieve other forms of alleged power. Sect members may be trained not only in alchemic techniques, but in techniques for controlling supernatural beings. Some use this power for malevolent ends; some for benevolent. The latter, who employ their skills to exorcise evil supernatural beings (spirits and witches), are believed to possess much power, both because of their ability to control these sinister forces and because, in the process, they are able to enlist the power of benign Buddhist gods. (Spiro 1967: chs. 11 and 13) Famous exorcists *(ahte:lan: hsaya)* are rewarded for their efforts by the acquisition of great wealth. Most of them, however, are not wealthy, since their income is used to support their experiments in alchemy.

[11]In this connection, F. K. Lehman (by personal communication) has raised a number of perceptive issues. First, the Buddha was put to these same tests as he attempted to achieve enlightenment. Moreover, the retreat from the world—which the *weikza* shares with the Buddha, the hermit *(yathe),* the Buddhist monk, and the Hindu mendicant—entails in all cases a return in power and/or merit. And in all cases there is the death-rebirth theme: monks and hermits being spiritually reborn from a civil death, the *weikza* from the earth, an important mother symbol in Indian thought. In all cases, too, this spiritual rebirth exalts the adept's status within *saṃsāra,* even while it places him beyond the relativities of all civil status. As for the *weikza* himself it may be speculated whether, on a deeper symbolic level, these practices (which are believed to prolong life) are believed to achieve their end by substituting symbolic rebirth for death.

Although there are other relationships between them, it is in the exorcist role especially that esoteric and apotropaic Buddhism intersect. Many of the rituals of apotropaic Buddhism are performed by the exorcist, who, though a functionary in the latter system, learns his craft (and acquires his power) in the former. Almost always, moreover, the exorcist establishes his credentials by reference to his membership in an esoteric sect, and almost always, too, he calls upon the assistance of the master *weikza* of his sect during a ceremony of exorcism. There is finally a crucial cash nexus between the exorcist and the alchemist. It is through his role as exorcist that the alchemist—unless he is wealthy or a monk—acquires the funds necessary for his experiments.

Millennial Buddhism

The Idea of the Future King

The Buddhist notion of a Universal Emperor *(Cakkavattī)* and the utopian age which he will usher in (see the *Cakkavattī Sīhanāda Suttanta* and the *Aggañña Suttanta,* both of the *Dīgha Nikāya,* in *Dialogues of the Buddha,* Part III) has had a long history in Burma. Even today it continues to inform Burmese politics and Burmese socialist aspirations. (Cf. Sarkisyanz 1965.) During the Burmese kingdom it was manifested in the claims of some Burmese kings that, as world emperors, they had the right to conquer foreign lands, and in the claims of still others that as world emperors they should also be recognized as Embryo or Future Buddhas. Indeed, the founder of Burma's last dynasty took as his reign-name, *Alaung-hpaya:,* i.e., Embryo Buddha.

In normative Buddhism, it will be recalled, there is an intimate relationship between a Buddha and a Universal Emperor. Thus, in one of his lives as an Embryo Buddha the present Buddha was allegedly a Universal Emperor. It is perhaps for that reason that any king (insofar as he can be recognized as a Universal Emperor) can become (or aspire to become) a Buddha or an Embryo Buddha. More important, the essential prerequisites for becoming either a Buddha or a Universal Emperor are identical: both possess the thirty-two marks of the superman. (*Lakkhana Suttanta* of the *Dīgha Nikāya,* in *Dialogues of the Buddha,* Part III) One who is born with these marks can choose only one or the other of these two careers. Should he choose the latter, he becomes a Turner of the Wheel (a *Cakkavatti*), for as an emperor of righteousness he brings the world under the Wheel of the Law *(dhammacakka).*[12] Because of his righteousness the Wheel (or discus) precedes him through the air, causing everything before it to submit to the Law.

[12]This Buddhist belief was later adopted by orthodox Hinduism, and is found as well among the Jains (Cf. Basham 1954:83), and of course in contemporary Buddhist countries other than Burma. For Thailand, see Wilson (1962:86-90).

Distinct from this Buddhist belief in the Universal Emperor, but later merging with it, is the Burmese belief in the Future King. After the British conquest of the country, many Burmese continued to hope for restoration of the monarchy, a hope which in some cases looked for its incumbent to descendants of the former royal dynasty, but in other cases turned to a number of royal pretenders. In any event, it was the British abolition of the monarchy that gave rise, in the minds of some Burmans, to hope for the appearance of a Future King who would drive out the British and restore Burmese independence.

Millennial Buddhism represents the conjunction of the Buddhist notions of a Universal Emperor and a Future Buddha with the Burmese notions of a Future King, weikzahood, and occult power. During the British rule, many peasant revolts were inspired by a configuration of these beliefs. Galvanized into action by an Embryo or Future King, whose legitimacy was often based on his barely concealed charismatic claim to be an Embryo Buddha, these rebels were inspired not only by the nationalist aim of abolishing foreign rule. Their hopes included, in addition, the restoration of the traditional Buddhist monarchy because enjoyment of the goals of the utopian Buddhist society could only be assured by the rule of a future *Buddhist* emperor. At the same time, their courage—with sticks and stones they believed they could prevail against the enemy's rifles—derived from their conviction that the alchemic and other forms of occult power transmitted to them by the Future King (not the least of whose accomplishments was *weikza*) would render them invulnerable in battle.[13] Although Saya San, whose abortive revolt occurred as late as 1930, was the most famous of these Future Kings (cf. Cady 1958:309-321), pre-Independence Burma witnessed the rise and fall of dozens of royal pretenders of this type.

In post-Independence Burma, overtones of millennial Buddhism continue to reverberate in the country, especially among the peasantry. In 1961-62, when I was conducting field work there, many (but not all) Burmese peasants firmly believed in the coming of a Future King. Moreover, most of them placed this belief within a Buddhist context. Thus, in a detailed study of the belief in a sample of twenty-two males in Yeigyi, fifteen agreed that the belief in a Future King was sanctioned by Buddhism, five denied it, and two said they did not know. Of the fifteen, ten said they would welcome his arrival, three said they preferred a democracy, and two said they were undecided. Despite the existence of some skeptics, it is fair to conclude that the belief in a Future King is held by a large percentage of the Burmese lay population. (Among Burmese monks there was much greater skepticism. Although believing in the Buddhist Universal Emperor, many of them dismissed the notion of the coming of a Burmese Future King as a "bazaar rumor.")

[13]For comparable beliefs of medieval Christian millenarian movements, compare Cohn (1961:71).

Peasant beliefs in a monarch to come relate more to the Burmese notion of a Future King than to the Buddhist notion of a Universal Emperor. To be sure, he will be a pious Buddhist, turning the Wheel of the Law—indeed, his Burmese title, is derived from the Sanskrit *Cakravarti* (Pali, *Cakkavattī*)—but more important, he will be the king of Burma, restoring law and order to that country, driving out the foreigners, and bringing prosperity and wealth to the Burmese people. In coming to power he will conquer all his enemies, turning their weapons into sticks. During his regime even human nature will change. Not only will there be no greed or corruption, anger or lust, but people's minds will also be improved. Thus, for example, monks will not be required to study Scripture, since they will know the entire canon by heart. His reign will be as utopian as the society he governs: righteousness and compassion will be its marks. For once, a Burmese government will not be, as it has been in traditional Burmese sentiment, one of the Five Enemies.

Unlike the Future Buddha, who is not to appear until five thousand years after the death of the present (i.e., last) Buddha, the Future King—so these Burmese believers hold—will arrive at any time within the second half of the latter's dispensation. Since 1961 (the year of my study) was already four years into the second half of His dispensation, the king in theory might appear at any time, and indeed most of my informants believed he would appear in their own lifetime. On the basis of complicated Pythagorean calculations, involving the assignment of numerical values to various Buddhist symbols, it was widely believed he would assume power in the year 2509 of the Buddhist Era, or in 1965 A.D.

But this set of beliefs, whether or not related to the Buddhist doctrine of the world emperor, does not in itself constitute what I am here calling the millennial dimension of esoteric Buddhism. As part of esoteric Buddhism, millennial Buddhism combines two additional features. First, on the belief level it stresses that the Future King, or at least the herald of the Future King, is already here. Second, on the social level, it entails membership in an esoteric sect *(gaing:)* which is devoted to him and to his alleged powers.[14] Moreover, since no esoteric Buddhist sect represents a "pure type" of either millennial or eschatological Buddhism, these messianic sects also contain many eschatological features. Thus, typically, the putative Future King, or his herald, is believed to be a *weikza* as well, and more

[14]When these features are added to the other beliefs of millennial Buddhism, its correspondence to the five generic attributes of any "millenarian" ideology (Cohn 1962:32) is almost complete. It is:

a. Collective, in the sense that it is to be enjoyed by the faithful as a group;

b. Terrestrial, in the sense that it is to be realized on this earth and not in some otherworldly heaven;

c. Imminent, in the sense that it is to come both soon and suddenly;

d. Total, in the sense that it is utterly to transform life on earth, so that the new dispensation will be no mere improvement on the present but perfection itself; and

e. Accomplished by agencies which are consciously regarded as supernatural.

importantly, he is believed to be the incarnation, or the persistence, or both (these beliefs can become very confused) of one of the two famous master *weikza* of the past: Bo Bo Aung and Bo Min Gaung.[15] These sects have been described in great detail and with such insight by Mendelson (1960, 1961*a*, 1961*b*, 1963*a*) that I can do little more than add a few ethnographic footnotes to his accounts.

Two Future Kings

Since, unlike those esoteric sects whose primary emphasis is eschatological, messianic sects are rare, and since moreover they are even rarer on the village level, it was by accident that I encountered the existence of two of them in Upper Burma. In the midst of a discussion of the Future King notion in Yeigyi, one of the villagers noted that a putative Future King was living in Mandalay. Neither he nor any of the other men with whom I was engaged in conversation placed any credence in this Future King—none of them (nor any other inhabitant of Yeigyi) was a member of a messianic Buddhist sect, nor did any of them know where he lived. Nevertheless, with the assistance of a young Mandalay monk who did know his address but had never been there himself, I was able to spend a day in what turned out to be the "palace" of this royal pretender, where I interviewed him and some of his devotees. By chance, this particular "palace" had been visited a few years earlier by Mendelson, and although he was unable at that time to interview the king, his description of the establishment and of the ideology of this sect obviates the necessity of repeating what he has already set forth (Mendelson 1961*a*).

The ground floor of the "palace," a building in the center of the city, consists of rooms for secular activities of various kinds—eating, sleeping, study, discussion, and so on. The two upper stories include the chambers of the king; administrative offices; altar rooms for various gods, spirits *(nat)*, *weikza*, Buddhas, and so on; and a throne room with all the regalia, including the throne, associated with the traditional Burmese court. This is the throne of *bou:do sakya* (hereafter anglicised Bodaw Setkya) Future King of Burma.[16] Although he denied, in our interview, that he himself was that person, this man is referred to by his followers as Bodaw Setkya, and it is by that name that I will refer to him.

[15]The latter, a twentieth-century *weikza*, is often identified with, or viewed as an opponent of, Dhammazedi, the famous fifteenth-century king of Burma, who is believed to have been not only a *weikza* but the putative founder of what is probably the most famous of the esoteric sects, the Dhammazedi *gaing*. Dhammazedi's role as a *weikza*, and the story of Bo Bo Aung, a nineteenth-century *weikza*, are both described in Htin Aung (1962:55-60). A detailed summary of the life of the modern Bo Min Gaung is given in Mendelson (1963*a*:798-803).

[16]*Bou:* designates a grandfather, and by extension, an old man. *Daw* is a royal honorific. *Sakya* is the Burmese corruption of the Sanskrit, *cakra* (Pali, *cakka*), the Wheel or discus, which (as the king said) "circumambulates the globe and destroys all enemies in its way."

Although disavowing any claim to be the Future King, Bodaw Setkya admits to being a powerful exorcist *(ahte:lan: hsaya)* and a Master of Buddhist meditation. In short, rather than making any admissions that would render him liable to charges of treason, he established instead, and in one sentence, his *bona fides* as a wonderful being: he has power over the supernatural world, and as a master meditator he is a contender for nirvana (claims traditionally associated with the statuses of Buddhahood and emperorship). In general, both Bodaw Setkya and a second king (described below) spoke circumspectly, by means of indirection and allusion, and neither granted me permission to take notes during our interview. Their followers, however, are not as circumspect as their Masters. With respect to nirvana, for example, Bodaw Setkya's followers claim explicitly that (to render the Burmese expression literally) he has "found a way out to a blissful place," a discreet way of saying that he has attained nirvana.

Bodaw Setkya is a short, plump man, flabby and effeminate in appearance, who gives the appearance of great shrewdness. Before attaining his present position he had been, so he claimed, an electrician and a trustee of the pagoda adjacent to the "palace" in which he now resides. Hoping to become a Buddha, he began some years ago to recite the Virtues *(goung:do)* of the Three Jewels, and giving up his electrical work he devoted full time to meditation. Indeed, for a year he meditated while sitting on top of the pillar which is now enshrined in the courtyard of the "palace." As a result of these activities, he is now under the protection of the *deva* whose images are in the various altar rooms. Ten years ago, having "completed" his meditation (another indirect way of saying that he had achieved the aim of his meditation, either Buddhahood or nirvana), he entered the present building, which he has never left. All these years he has continuously observed the Nine Buddhist Precepts; hence his yellow robe—yellow, he pointed out, being the sign of purity. Since in adhering to the Nine Precepts it was necessary to abstain from all sexual behavior, he also abandoned his wife. He is attended instead by a woman who sat in his room with us during the entire interview, whom he identified as his "sister," but whose sensuous appearance did not at all accord with the sibling role he imputed to her.[17]

From his present chambers, the Bodaw conducts his occult medical practice; and it is a lucrative practice indeed, for it permits him, he said, to feed his many poor followers. But his fees are not his only source of wealth; in addition, he has been successful in making gold by means of his alchemic skills. (This was his only allusion to the possibility that he might be a *weikza*, although his followers had no reticence in telling Mendelson that he was

[17]It is of interest to compare the miraculous details of his life provided by his followers (Mendelson 1961*a:* 566-71) with the rather pedestrian summary provided by the Bodaw himself.

the incarnation of Bou: min: gaung.) He leaves his chambers only four times a year, on the four important Buddhist festivals, when—carried on a palanquin—he grants an audience to his followers in the throne room.

Royal symbolism—Burmese kings, too, did not touch the ground, and they too were carried on palanquins—was practiced by those few members of the sect who were privileged to enter his chamber during our interview. Prostrating themselves when they entered the room, they bowed themselves out when they left his presence, their backs always away from him, which of course was the stylized manner of approaching and leaving the presence of the Burmese king.

In order to become a follower of Bodaw Setkya it is necessary, he stressed, to adhere to Buddhist discipline in detail. His followers must observe the Five Precepts, practice meditation, cleave always to the truth, practice both love and tolerance, and do homage to the Three Gems. This is why, he explained, so many monks, in addition to recognizing his "greatness," are included among his followers. Indeed, the day before our interview he had fed, so he claimed, five hundred monks in a special dining room set aside in the "palace" for monks. As for lay followers, he estimated their numbers at a hundred thousand! (His steward told Mendelson that their number was five thousand.)

What can we make of all of this? Piecing together the information Mendelson elicited from his followers with what I obtained from the Master himself, and in both cases reading between the lines, it is fair to conclude that this Bodaw Setkya claims to be and/or is viewed by his followers as a master *weikza,* probably the incarnation of Bo Min Gaung, who either already is—or in a future rebirth will become—the Future Buddha and/or Future King. This conclusion, moreover, is supported by a description in a Burmese language newspaper *(Bahosi)* of a *nat* ceremony held in the "palace" in which he is referred to, alternatively, as Dhammazedi Min Gaung and as Bodaw Setkya.[18]

This meeting with Bodaw Setkya took place soon after I began my field work and some months before I knew enough about esoteric Buddhism to be able to probe beyond the obvious. (Unfortunately, becoming involved in many other research problems which I then considered of greater importance, I did not find an opportunity to return.) Although my second encounter with a Future King was also confined to a single interview, it took place some months after I had been in Burma, by which time I had acquired sufficient information about esoteric Buddhism to ask intelligent questions. As with Bodaw Setkya, my encounter with the second King—Bo Min

[18]The same article, incidentally, emphasizes that the participants in the ceremony were preponderantly Shan peasants. That Shans, being Buddhists, should be involved in these messianic sects is not surprising, especially when it is noted that even non-Buddhist hill tribes have been infected by the same beliefs. Stern (1968:297-327) has provided us with a remarkable account of a sect of this type among the Karen, a non-Buddhist Burmese hill people.

Gaung *weikza* himself, as some of his followers referred to him—was almost entirely due to chance.

Close to Mandalay, on the highway leading to the Shan States, is a large spirit shrine holding the images of certain local as well as national spirits *(nat)*. Travelers frequently stop before the shrine to do homage to them. Behind this shrine, and situated on a lower plot of land, is a small but especially lovely pagoda, with a tall brick tower near by. One afternoon I stopped my car by the side of the road in order to explore this religious complex, which I passed every week on my trip from Yeigyi to Mandalay. Walking through the pagoda compound, I noticed a typical resthouse *(zayat)*, which it turned out was the dwelling of a very old, very friendly monk. This man was deeply involved in esoteric Buddhism. The tower, he explained, was a receiving station, which took messages transmitted by distant *weikza*. He invited me inside the resthouse, where I noticed on his bed a large photograph of a handsome man dressed in white. To my query he responded that it was a picture of Bo Min Gaung, the famous *weikza*, in whose behalf he (the monk) had built the pagoda. At the beginning of our conversation he said that Bo Min Gaung had died, or left the world, some years earlier; later he said that Bo Min Gaung was living on Mt. Popa; still later he said that Bo Min Gaung was even now living among men, and that I could find him in Mandalay. When I expressed an interest in meeting this famous *weikza*, who was both dead and alive, and who lived simultaneously both in Mandalay and on Mt. Popa, the monk not only gave me his address but provided me with a letter of recommendation.[19]

The following day, I set off for Bo Min Gaung's residence in Mandalay. I arrived with my assistant at a fairly large house, surrounded on all sides by a high wall. In order to get into the compound, we had to pass through a guardhouse where, despite our letter of recommendation from the old monk, we were detained for quite some time while the guards held a long conference among themselves. Finally, after an exchange with messengers called from the house, we were allowed to pass and were ushered directly into the *weikza's* consulting room. When we entered he was holding a consultation with two women traders who, he later told us, had come for advice concerning their business. On the floor were various offerings the women had brought him.

Sitting on the floor and wearing the pointed hat of a *weikza*, Bo Min Gaung appeared to be an effeminate, middle-aged man—younger than Bodaw Setkya—with very light skin and a soft voice. On the wall behind him were three copies of a curious photograph, showing a normal-sized man

[19]For the importance of Mt. Popa, as a center for esoteric Buddhism, see Mendelson (1963*a*). As F. K. Lehman has pointed out (by personal communication), a true Buddhist monarch controls the country insofar as he controls the *nat* spirits of its constituent territories and/or replaces them with those of his own appointment. That this Bo Min Gaung resides on Popa is, therefore, of the utmost symbolic significance.

sitting in the meditation posture, holding a much smaller man, about one-fourth his size, on his lap. The large man was the putative *weikza* seated before us, and the small one was the man in the photograph owned by the monk who had sent us to this *weikza*, whom he had identified as Bo Min Gaung. To my query, the man seated before us immediately resolved the problem. He, so he claimed, is not Bo Min Gaung; rather, the spirit of Bo Min Gaung is inside of him. In short, he was claiming to be the reincarnation of Bo Min Gaung (which resolved the apparent contradiction in the monk's statements that Bo Min Gaung was both dead and also living in Mandalay. The physical body of Bo Min Gaung was dead, but his spirit survived in this man who—and this was physically exemplified in the picture—is self-consciously aware that he is the reincarnation of the former).

When I asked him directly if he were a Future Buddha or a Future King —he did not conceal the fact that he was a *weikza*—he circumvented the question by saying, "I have only come to advise people on how to live a Buddhist life." I tried again, this time indirectly, by asking whether he knew of Bodaw Setkya or had any relationship with him. To this he said in a flat tone that he had nothing to do with him.

While we talked, he kept pouring hot tea into small cups which, after blowing into the cup, he would give us to drink (thereby imparting some of his power to us—a cherished privilege). Before we left him, he also gave us an *in:*, a cabalistic square which he said would protect us from all harm.[20]

As we were ushered out, our host told us he could see us again in about an hour if we wanted to wait, which we did. Later, after receiving the message that he would see us, we were taken to another room in a different part of the house. When we entered this small and simple room, the man we knew as Bo Min Gaung was seated with a monk and was no longer wearing his *weikza* hat. When we had seen him earlier, he explained, he was Bo Min Gaung (an ellipsis, I assume, for the notion that the spirit of Bo Min Gaung had been inside him); but now Bo Min Gaung had (temporarily) left his body and we could speak to him as Ba Pwa (his proper name), the ordinary mortal, rather than as Ba Pwa the reincarnation of, or one possessed by, the mighty Bo Min Gaung.

In answer to my question, he said that the first time Bo Min Gaung came to him, he appeared in physical form, and they had slept together in the same bed. Since then the ancient *weikza* has possessed him—i.e., his spirit enters into him—every day.[21] (So we now have still another interpretation

[20]Like most magical power, *in:* too can be harnessed for both benevolent and malevolent ends. In itself, its power—essentially amoral—can become manifest in destructive ways. When, a few weeks after this incident, I offered this *in:* to a Western-educated professional woman, she (literally) expressed horror. "You must stay away from *in:*; even good ones can do harm! I might take it into my house today, and then someday it might blow up."

[21]In the Burmese *nat* religion, shamans (typically females) are possessed by various spirits or *nat* (typically male), whom they marry and with whom (typically in their dreams) they have coitus. (Spiro 1967: ch. 12.) Ba Pwa's possession by Bo Min Gaung is reminiscent of this type

of the relationship between Ba Pwa and Bo Min Gaung. Alternatively: Ba Pwa *is* Bo Min Gaung, he is the reincarnation of Bo Min Gaung, he is the body in which the spirit of Bo Min Gaung resides, he is the body whom Bo Min Gaung regularly possesses.) When Bo Min Gaung first possessed him, he ordered him to live with love and concentration, and to help people to observe the Buddhist precepts. He taught him all his occult arts in subsequent possessions.

When the interview ended and we began walking down the stairs, we were approached by a follower of Ba Pwa (alias Bo Min Gaung), a philosophy graduate of the University of Mandalay. He was eager to talk about his Master, and we were eager to listen. When we first saw Ba Pwa, he said (as Ba Pwa himself had said), he was possessed by Bo Min Gaung. The latter, he said, had the choice, after becoming a *weikza,* of becoming a Buddha or of entering nirvana. Because of his love for others and his desire to help them, he chose instead to stay in the world. (Here, then, is the Mahayanist *Bodhisattva*, and indeed the young devotee used that term in connection with Ba Pwa.) Bo Min Gaung, he continued, is both an Embryo Buddha and a *weikza,* and like all *weikza* he is immortal. Although his physical body is in the Himalayas—like Popa, the abode of *deva*—his spirit travels. Hence it is that he possesses Ba Pwa.

But Ba Pwa is also *weikza.* Many people, including many monks, have become apprenticed to him in order to become *weikza.* Ba Pwa himself was a mill-owner when he was possessed by Bo Min Gaung twenty-three years earlier. Forsaking his mill and all his other property, he had lived ever since on alms and donations from his followers. He was—and still is—married, but after his first possession by Bo Min Gaung, he repudiated conjugal life forever.

Ba Pwa, our informant continued, has followers all over Burma, including university graduates like himself, because they all recognize his power. When I asked about Bodaw Setkya, he not only said he knew of him, but immediately identified him as a competitor to Ba Pwa. Bodaw Setkya, he admitted, is "powerful," but "we will soon see who is the more powerful. Within the year strange things will occur." I asked if these "strange things" referred to the appearance of the Future King. He said he could not divulge such information, but he did say, in answer to my direct question, that neither Bodaw Setkya nor Bo Min Gaung is the Future King, although "Bo Min Gaung has a plan to be followed by the Future King."

This suggested rather strongly that Ba Pwa—he who has followed Bo Min Gaung—is viewed as the Future King. When I put this to him directly, he was reluctant to talk about it. Finally, however, he admitted that it was

---

of *nat* possession, except that in this case the relationship is homosexual rather than heterosexual. This is consistent with my first impression of Ba Pwa as being highly effeminate.

so. "In a year or two," he said, "Bo Min Gaung—[or did he mean Ba Pwa?] —will show his power, and everyone will worship him." But what about the present government, I asked. Will they oppose him or submit to him? "All of them," he said, "including [Premier] U Nu, will bow down before him and worship him."

Motives and Functions of Belief

Although—whatever their actual numbers—the total membership in esoteric sects is small, the dominant themes of esoteric Buddhism are the common property of a large percentage, perhaps an overwhelming majority, of the Burmese people. More interesting, the belief in *weikza* and/or the hope for a Future King is found not only among simple peasants but among educated and westernized Burmese as well. When I expressed some skepticism concerning the existence and alleged powers of *weikza* to the sophisticated headman of Yeigyi, a devout believer in alchemy, he said that he had just returned from a meeting with the leaders of his political party at Mt. Popa, where among others they had consulted with a famous master of alchemy, an alleged *weikza*. "If," he continued, "important people like U Nu [then prime minister] and U Kya Nyein [leader of the opposition party] and other officials and important businessmen believe in him [the alleged *weikza*], then I am prepared to believe, too."

In my own rather limited experience I came to know civil servants, university professors (both humanists and scientists), Buddhist abbots, wealthy businessmen, and members of the bar and the bench who not only believe in, but are practitioners of, alchemy. One of the most famous believers is the Stalin Prize-winning writer, Thakin Kodaw Hmaing.[22]

This is not to say that there are no skeptics; there are. Thus, when I asked

[22]In the past, too, alchemy has been a favorite practice of Burmese literati. "No branch of knowledge," writes Malcom (1839:326), "is cultivated with avidity but alchemy, in which absurd pursuit nearly every person, pretending to literature, engages more or less." Similarly, Crawfurd (1834:114) writes:

> In reference to the state of Burman knowledge, I ought not to omit an intense passion for alchemy, of which the object is to transmute the baser into the precious metals. From our earliest acquaintance with the Burmans, they seem to have been tainted with this folly: persons of all ranks, who can afford to waste their time and money, engage in it: and even his present Majesty and his predecessors have not disdained thus to occupy their leisure hours.

Crawfurd adds the following in a footnote:

> The search for an elixir of immortality forms no part of Burman alchemy. This would be contrary to their religion; for, according to their system, immortality, or even longevity, would be a misfortune and not a blessing.

This shows the pitfall of assuming that a people's nonreligious beliefs can be validly deduced from their formal religious doctrines. In fact, as we have seen, immortality rather than gold is the primary goal of Burmese alchemy—a goal which, moreover, can be traced as far back as ancient Pagan.

an abbot in Mandalay why so many Burmans believed in *weikza*, he said contemptuously that he was "not responsible for the beliefs of every fool in Burma." Similarly, a village monk said that if he wanted to fly through the air he could do so very easily: he could purchase a ticket at the UBA (Union of Burma Airways) ticket office. Again, a villager said that he could see no point in worshiping the Future Buddha. "Why isn't the present Buddha sufficient? This is like asking for a stepmother, when you already have a real mother." It should be noted, too, that the beliefs as well as the leaders of the esoteric sects are often attacked in Burmese newspapers. These attacks, however, have not influenced true believers; for them the belief in alchemy persists with undiminished intensity.

What is most remarkable, as I have already pointed out, is the hold which these beliefs have on the educated Burmese. The intensity of their involvement in these occult phenomena may be inferred from the time and the wealth which they invest in alchemic experiments—many, as I have noted, have lost fortunes in their unsuccessful attempts to fashion a "victorious" alchemic stone—and it may be directly observed in the heightened affect which accompanies any discussion or activity relating to these phenomena. Perhaps one example will suffice to convey the flavor of their involvement.

U Tein, a government official of medium rank in Upper Burma, is a native of Rangoon and a graduate of the University of Rangoon. Of all his possessions and accomplishments, none gives him greater pride than the two alchemic stones he has fashioned in his own forge. While talking with me in his home he proudly recounted that some very experienced alchemists had remarked to him that he had accomplished in only a few weeks with his forge what they had been unable to achieve in years of practice. The rapture that came across his face when he showed me his stones cannot be captured in words; it had to be seen.

Later, when I accompanied U Tein to an outlying village, where he was to supervise a headman election, one of the first things he did was to inquire about the alchemists in the village. Introduced to three of the four living there, he engaged them in lengthy discussions of alchemy while the voters were passing in and out of the polling booth. Each one displayed his stone to the others and described its special power. When U Tein passed his around for their inspection, he became elated—it is the only word to describe his reaction—when the leading alchemist in the village praised its attributes. "Hey, Mel, did you hear what he said? He said my *datloung*: is so beautiful that if I stopped [alcoholic] drinking [alchemists are expected to observe the Buddhist precepts] I could become a *weikza*!" Further discussion with the alchemists revealed that one of the local monks was a famous alchemic expert. Telling his assistant to take over, U Tein left the polling booth to have "a few words" with the monk. When he finally returned, more than two hours later, the balloting had ended and the villagers were eagerly awaiting the counting of the ballots in what had been a hotly contested election. Instead, however, U Tein persisted in questioning the alchemists about some of the more technical information he had received from the monk. He knew, of course, that this was a dereliction of duty, but by this time his involvement had reached such a pitch that nothing, including his administrative duties, would deter him.

This quality of involvement obviously demands some kind of explanation. On one level it is simple enough. The dream of achieving immortality and eternal youth is a universal human dream; it is found on both the personal and (in religion, myths, and folk tales) the cultural level. That the Burmese, who share this dream, should be involved in a set of beliefs and practices by means of which it might be realized is hardly surprising,[23] especially since for most Burmans the scientific picture of the world and man has not yet demythologized their own traditional world view. That in principle immortality can be achieved by some men is, for them, a no more fanciful belief—though its achievement is much more miraculous—than that rebirth is achieved by all men.

But the "victorious" alchemist, it will be recalled, can also achieve lesser supernormal goals: power over malevolent beings and—much more important—over the constraints imposed on all of us by nature. Achievement of the latter kind of power—that of flying through the air, of passing through the earth, of satisfying all one's desires instantaneously, and so on—would, of course, appeal to any human being; it is an expression on the adult level of every child's self-fantasy of omnipotence. Moreover, if those observers of Burmese character who stress their inordinate concern for power and autonomy are correct (cf. Gorer 1943, Hagen 1962: ch. 8, Hanks 1949, Hitson 1959, Mendelson 1960, Pye 1962, Sein Tu 1964), the achievement of such power would be especially appealing to the Burmese. These superhuman powers of the *weikza* would satisfy even the most intense drive for power and autonomy.

In addition to its general appeal to the Burmese, the powers of weikzahood make separate appeals to the different social and cultural strata in Burmese society. For the lower stratum, attainment of weikzahood is more than adequate compensation for the wide chasm between their aspiration to, and almost total deprivation of, power and autonomy in their present lives. This deprivation is as characteristic of these strata today as under the

[23]Refined through the constraints imposed by Buddhist doctrine, weikzahood, to be sure, means the prolongation, rather than the immortalization, of life. There is little question in my mind, however, that the alchemist's claim that weikzahood is a means for the attainment of nirvana through the worship of the Buddha is a facade for his true desire for eternal youth. Moreover, the 80,000 (or even 2,500) years to which he aspires are, for most human minds, tantamount to immortality. It should be added that many Burmese Christians are as much involved in aspirations to weikzahood as Burmese Buddhists, and it can hardly be contended that *their* motive is the attainment of nirvana.

British rule in Burma and before that under the Burmese monarchy. For the upper (westernized) stratum, the belief in and attempt to achieve weikzahood has, if anything, a more important—albeit a latent—function. Latent functions are, of course, difficult to prove, and I shall be content here merely to display the argument in its behalf.

The Burmese in general, but more particularly the westernized intellectuals, politicians, and government officials, have suffered two serious narcissistic blows attendant, first, upon the colonial conquest, and second, upon Burma's post-Independence national experience. The British conquest revealed to the Burmese how impotent they were, and how inferior their technology was in the face of Western power and technology. At the same time, the British presence created a Burmese demand for the products of modern technology—a demand, however, which could only be satisfied by importation from the West. All this was to be changed as a result of independence. After driving out the colonial oppressor, Burma, it was believed, would take its rightful place—denied it by the colonial master—in the modern world. Controlling their own destiny, in charge of their own polity, the Burmese would achieve ever higher levels of technological and economic achievement.

These high hopes, however, were soon turned to ashes. Post-Independence Burma has been characterized instead by political and economic disaster, even aside from the military coup and its calamitous aftermath, which occurred only at the end of my research in Burma. The history of post-Independence Burmese economy has been one of industrial failure and agricultural stagnation. Continuing to want the products of modern technology, the Burmans have been unable to satisfy this desire of their own efforts; to the extent that these wants have been satisfied at all, they have been satisfied by the importation of foreign products. Indeed, were Burma to be cut off from its foreign markets, its people would be reduced, so far as consumer goods are concerned, to the level of a preindustrial economy. And with the British gone, there is no apparent scapegoat on whom to blame these failures and shortcomings.

The result has been disillusionment and humiliation. One cannot talk very long with Burmese of any stratum without realizing the depth of their bitterness and frustration. These feelings are especially intense, however, in the upper stratum. As many of them expressed it to me, while the rest of the world—by which, of course, they mean the Western world—has undergone vast economic and technological changes, Burma has stood still. Everything seems hopeless to them; their high dreams have turned into nightmares. It is out of desperation, therefore, a desperation stemming from the discrepancy between what they have and what the West has been able to create, that, in my opinion, these upper-class Burmese turn to alchemy and the belief in weikzahood. They may not be able (as their erstwhile

Western masters are) to manufacture autos, but as *weikza* they are able to travel even faster than the speed of autos; they may not be able to manufacture planes, but as *weikza* they are able to fly through the air without them; they may not be able to manufacture bullets, but as *weikza* they are able to become invulnerable to them; they may not be able to manufacture radios, but as *weikza* they are able to communicate over long distances without them.

This interpretation, it must be stressed, is not merely the speculation of a psychological functionalist; it is at least hinted at in the explicit statements of some upper-class informants. When a government official, to offer but one example, was explaining how *weikza* fly through the air, he suddenly interrupted his explanation and, looking at me gleefully, said: "You see, they are much better than Americans who [if they want to fly] must use airplanes." In short, through alchemy these westernized Burmese can have all the things the West has—and more!—without having to acquire them from this hated (because envied) model.

My argument, then, is the reverse of the conventional argument concerning the persistence of magical beliefs in modernizing societies. Such beliefs persist, it is usually held, despite the increasing knowledge of modern science and technology. I am arguing, rather, that they persist *because* of increasing knowledge of modern science and technology. Because, in an era of science, Burma remains backward; because, in an era of technological miracles, Burma remains underdeveloped; because, therefore, desiring the fruits of science and technology, Burma cannot achieve these fruits by the natural methods of science and technology—because of these conditions, many educated Burmese have turned instead to the supernatural method of alchemy. This method, moreover, will not only enable them to attain the goals achieved by science and technology, but it is their own method, one that has been neither borrowed from nor shared with the West.[24]

Similar motives explain in part the Burmese hope for a Future King, although few Burmans believe that any of the current royal pretenders, such as those discussed in the last section, is the manifestation of this hope. Like the belief in weikzahood, the hope for a Future King stems, I believe, from universal human aspirations, which however have been intensified by the unique Burmese historical experience. To the extent that the Future King of Burma, though dressed in Burmese garb, is the Buddhist Universal Emperor, he is a politically powerful and at the same time a morally perfect Buddhist ruler (he is after all the herald, if not an embryonic manifestation, of a Buddha); and this belief satisfies a deeply ingrained, probably universal human need to have goodness, power, and authority combined in a single person. Like the rest of mankind, however, the Burmese know (and have

[24]The similarities and differences between this function of Burmese alchemy and primitive cargo cults, though immediately apparent, deserve extensive discussion.

known) many leaders and institutions who possess one, perhaps even two, of these attributes, but never all three. Typically power and goodness, with authority associated sometimes with one, sometimes with the other, have always been dissociated in Burmese historical experience. In their contemporary experience, for example, the Burmese have known the good but weak U Nu, on the one hand, and the powerful but not very "good" military rulers, on the other. To expect these three attributes to be embodied in one person, however, is obviously to expect the ideal; and the Burmese, aware of the utopian quality of this expectation, have projected it onto a Future King rather than requiring it from ordinary politicans.

The hope for a Future King, therefore, can only be viewed as a utopian, a messianic hope. In him are combined the dominant values of both the secular and the religious domains of Burmese culture, viz., the Burmese secular values of prestige *(goung:)*, power *(hpoung:)*, and authority *(o-za)*, and the Buddhist values of love *(mettā)* and adherence to the precepts *(sīla)*.[25]

But utopian hopes, though universal, are usually dormant in human history; they generally become activated in periods of stress and crisis. As I have already indicated, post-Independence Burma has been experiencing an acute psychological crisis which stems from profound disillusionment with the political fruits of independence itself. If anything, the post-Independence political experience of the Burmese has been even more disastrous than their economic experience. The history of post-Independence Burmese politics—again, even aside from the military take-over—has been a history of insurgency *against* the government and factionalism, misgovernment, disunity, and corruption *within* it. It would be difficult to exaggerate the bitterness and disillusionment attendant on this experience, a disillusionment which is variously expressed in such disparate forms as cynicism, political apathy, new forms of insurgency, nostalgia (and expressed desires) for the return of British rule, and finally, hopes for the appearance of the Future King.[26]

In short, although the belief in a Future King is a manifestation of utopian aspirations which are almost universal in distribution and appeal, its salience in contemporary Burma, and especially among the peasantry, is both a manifestation and an index of the profound political crisis in Burmese

[25]It is the latter dimension that is missing in Mendelson's otherwise superb account of these sects. Although he is undoubtedly correct in stressing their power dimension, he errs, I believe, in neglecting to stress the moral one. Whatever the character of the actual royal pretenders may be, this moral quality is attributed to them by their followers—for it is an important ingredient in the traditional beliefs concerning the Future King—and indeed, it must be present if the belief is to be characterized, as Mendelson insists, as messianic.

[26]Many of my friends in the business community in Mandalay expressed, in addition, a hope for an army take-over. When, however, the hope was actualized (the army coup took place in 1962), it became another source of disillusionment. Rather than bolstering their position, as they had expected, the army dispossessed them.

society. By 1962, the second year of my study, the Future King was much more than the object of a nebulous utopian belief; he was a person whose expected arrival was imminent. Indeed, for thousands of Burmese, it will be recalled, he was to appear in 1965; and this prediction, however justified by cabalistic calculations, was motivated by the belief that he and he alone could save them from chaos and disaster. For the vast majority of the population these beliefs remain unfulfilled aspirations; for sect members, a tiny percentage of the population, they have come true. For them the king —or if not the king, then his herald—has arrived; he is living in their midst. Soon, when he makes his power manifest to all, they will reap the rewards of their early discipleship.

Esoteric Buddhism and Burmese Religion

Esoteric Buddhism, it is apparent from the foregoing sections, is deeply involved in the indigenous Burmese spirit *(nat)* religion. *Nat* images are as prominent as Buddha images in the shrines of esoteric sects, and the propitiation of *nat* and of *nat-weikza* is as much a part of their cultus as worship of the Buddha. In view of the debate that has long raged over the importance of the *nat* in the total religious life of the Burmese, it is important at least to touch upon this debate before passing on.

There is a long tradition of Western scholarship which has insisted that Buddhism is essentially a veneer, only barely concealing the true religion of the Burmese, which, animist and magical to the core, is essentially concerned with spirit *(nat)* worship. Another tradition has maintained that Burmese religion is an amalgam of various elements, and that, although Buddhism and animism can be isolated as "pure" or "ideal" types, they really comprise one syncretistic Burmese religion. I have argued, in opposition to both traditions, that Buddhism and animism exist side by side both in Burmese society and in Burmese personality. In the former they are expressed in distinct institutionalized forms, while in the latter they are compartmentalized, with Buddhism—in both cases—enjoying primacy. (For a discussion of these conflicting views, see Spiro 1967: ch. 14.)

If esoteric Buddhism represented the religion of most Burmese Buddhists—if, that is, most Burmese were members of the sects described in this chapter, there is little question that the view (most persuasively argued by Mendelson) that animism and Buddhism represent one syncretistic Burmese religion would be correct.[27] For those who belong to the sects *(gaing:)*, Buddhism and magico-animism in all its forms have become one indistinguishable religion. For in the sect, the beliefs and practices of the Burmese *nat* cultus and those of *Theravāda* Buddhism in all its phases (nibbanic, kammatic, and apotropaic) have become all mixed up. Indeed I would go

[27]Mendelson (1961*b*, 1963*a*, 1963*b*) erred, I believe, in generalizing too widely from esoteric Buddhism—his special research interest—to Burmese Buddhism as a whole.

even further, as does Mendelson, to argue that esoteric Buddhism comprises not only these two traditions, but also various Hindu (especially yogic), Mahayanist, and tantric elements, as well. Given this admixture, the *gaing:* would seem to be much more at home on the Himalayan slopes than in the Irrawaddy valley.

But the *gaing: is* in the Irrawaddy valley, and the religion of the *gaing: is* a syncretism of diverse and even conflicting religious elements. If this syncretistic religion—esoteric Buddhism—were the dominant religion of Burma, Buddhism might perforce be viewed as only analytically distinguishable from the total configuration of beliefs and practices that comprise Burmese religion. In fact, however, although almost all Burmese are as much caught up in the religion of the *nat* as in the religion of the Buddha, not only are these two religions typically compartmentalized, but the latter enjoys a position of primacy in the value system and behavior of the Burmese (Spiro 1967: ch. 14). Esoteric Buddhism, in which these diverse religious elements are combined into a total configuration, is the Buddhism of the *gaing:* alone, and as I have indicated, most Burmese are not part of the *gaing:* world, which is confined to a small minority.[28]

[28]For Burmese specialists, I would like to summarize once again my arguments for the "two religions" thesis. First, the Burmese themselves make a sharp distinction between Buddhism and the *nat* cultus. Moreover, introspective Burmans not only distinguish them, but view them as mutually incompatible, and, as devout Buddhists, experience guilt over their continuing participation in the *nat* cultus. The incompatibility does not consist in Buddhism's denial of the existence of spirits and supernormal beings; as we have seen, their existence is explicitly affirmed by Buddhism. Hence, it is not the belief in *nat*, but participation in their cultus, which is inconsistent with Buddhism.

So far as salvation Buddhism is concerned, the *nat* cultus is orthogonal to, rather than incompatible with, Buddhism; Buddhist soteriology is concerned with one's future lives, whereas the *nat* cultus is concerned with the present existence. This in itself renders the *nat* cultus and soteriological Buddhism (in both its nibbanic and kammatic forms) distinctive religions. Distinctive, but not incompatible. What renders them incompatible is that the attempt to achieve this-worldly goals by the propitiation of *nat* is (like much of apotropaic Buddhism) an implicit denial of the karmic law, and contains behavioral elements—such as consumption of alcohol and bacchanalian dancing—which are in direct opposition to both the precepts and ethos of Buddhism.

In short, the *nat* cultus is in conflict with the metaphysics, the ethics, and the spirit of Buddhism. This in itself, however, renders them two religions only in a logical and typological sense. Most syncretistic religions contain equally pronounced incompatible elements, and it could be assumed that, like them, Buddhism and the *nat* cultus also comprise one syncretistic religion. That they are, rather, two religions must be argued therefore on other grounds. And this I attempted to do in my *Burmese Supernaturalism.* First, as I have already observed, the Burmese themselves view them as different religions. Second, unlike a truly syncretistic religion, such as folk Catholicism, Buddhism and the *nat* cultus have separate religious specialists, separate places of worship, separate days of worship, separate modes of worship, etc. Contrast this with the cult of a local god-turned-saint whose cultus is performed in the *Catholic* church, on a recognized *Catholic* feast day, as part of the *Catholic* Mass, celebrated by a *Catholic* priest. None of these possibilities is even thinkable in Burma, where *nat* and *deva*, shaman and monk, *nat* festival and Buddhist holyday, spirit shrine and pagoda are separate and distinct both in fact and in conception.

III

BUDDHISM
AS A RITUAL SYSTEM

CHAPTER 8

The Buddhist Cultus: Its General Attributes

A Typology of Ritual Action

Although the ornate and complex ritual system of *Mahāyāna* Buddhism has often been remarked upon, *Theravāda* ritual has been less frequently described.[1] Indeed, for those who conceive of the latter form of Buddhism as a precursor of modern humanism (or even of analytic philosophy!), its rich ritual system comes rather as a shock, or is viewed as a late degeneration from a pristine state of ritualless purity. Either attitude is consistent with the major premises of nibbanic Buddhism, viz., that Buddhism is a salvation religion; since there is no savior (the Buddha is dead), salvation must be attained by man's unaided efforts; and these efforts consist of three types of action: charity, morality, and meditation. Although these premises would seem to preclude the development of a ritual system, the fact is that even canonical Buddhism, as we have seen more than once, found a place for ritual. Scripture, not only sanctions the use of instrumental ritual for the attainment of nonsoteriological goals, but (as we shall see) also sanctions its use for the attainment of proximate soteriological goals. If, then, even instrumental ritual is legitimized by Scripture, it is hardly surprising that *Theravāda* Buddhism contains expressive and commemorative ritual as well.

These three concepts—instrumental, commemorative, and expressive ritual—describe most of the types constituting one of the *cultural* dimensions of ritual, that is, the goal or purpose of ritual action. Although religions differ in the relative weights they assign to these types, there is

[1]Except for Wells' (1960) detailed description of Thai ritual, there is no book-length description of the Buddhist cultus of any *Theravāda* country.

probably no religion which does not include all three.

"Commemorative ritual" is performed in remembrance or celebration of some event, historical or mythological, sacred in the annals of the religious tradition. In the case of religions with sacred founders, they generally celebrate some event in the founder's life. Many Buddhist rituals, for example, commemorate an event in the life of the Buddha.

"Expressive ritual" serves as a vehicle for manifesting emotions, attitudes, and sentiments felt toward the religious sacra. In Buddhism, for example, the Buddha, the *Dhamma*, and the *Saṅgha* are objects of intense reverence, and the performance of many Buddhist rituals is a means for expressing veneration, homage, and devotion to these Three Jewels, as they are called in Buddhism.

"Instrumental ritual," performed to achieve some goal or end, is rather more complicated. The end may be some extrinsic goal—physical (health, beauty, and so on), social (wealth, honor, fame, power, and so on), natural (rainfall, plentiful crops, and so on)—which could be attained either in the present life or not until after death. In Buddhism, future goals are achieved by meritorious action, while present goals are attained by a combination of meritorious and ritual action. Sometimes, however, the end to be achieved by instrumental ritual is an intrinsic goal, i.e., a spiritual or psychological change in the self. In Christianity this is the purpose of a sacrament, a ritual which confers grace. Buddhism, having no notion of grace, is like most religions nonsacramental. Change in the self is, of course, the goal of the central act of nibbanic Buddhism: the practice of meditation. But meditation falls outside the domain of ritual as the latter is usually conceived. Within the Buddhist cultus proper, the closest approximation to the notion of an intrinsic goal is found in the Buddhist initiation rite, which, among other ends, purports to induce some change in the spiritual state of the initiate.

For this ritual typology to claim to be exhaustive, it will be necessary to include still a fourth type, i.e., "expiatory ritual," performed to atone for sin. Although this is found in most other salvation religions, it seems to be absent from Buddhism. To be sure, some Buddhists believe, as we have seen, that demerit, or sin can be countered or neutralized by merit, but the belief that in itself it can be expiated or atoned for is foreign to Buddhist thought.

Ritual Types and Buddhist Ideological Types

Although the culturally defined goal of any ritual,[2] to say nothing of private goals, frequently represents a mixture of these pure types, it is especially

[2]Cultural defined purposes of institutional action are usually—though not always—internalized by social actors to constitute at least one of their motives for performing the prescribed act. Religious ritual is no exception to this generalization. The culturally defined purposes of Buddhist ritual have indeed been internalized by the Burmese, and they do indeed constitute one, perhaps the most important, motivational basis for their performance. But they are not

important in a discussion of Buddhism to attempt, at least analytically, to sort them out. It is particularly vital to try to relate these pure types of ritual to the three pure types of Buddhist ideology discussed in the last section. Typologically at least—and to some extent even empirically—it would be rather strange if there were no systematic relationships among them.

Although even instrumental ritual is sanctioned by Scripture, the rituals of nibbanic Buddhism are essentially expressive and commemorative in character. Offerings to the Buddha, His relics, and His symbols (pagodas or images) are certainly encouraged, but these offerings (flowers, incense, water, food) can in no wise affect one's hope for nirvana. They are expressions of veneration *(vandanā)* and of honor *(pūjā)* to Him who has discovered the Way. Prayer, if that term may be used to designate a simple expressive statement, consists of the following Confession of Faith, the *Buddham saranam gacchāmi*, a Confession which is as ancient as Scripture itself.[3]

> I take refuge in the Buddha
> I take refuge in the *Dhamma*
> I take refuge in the *Saṅgha*
> For the Second Time, I take refuge in the Buddha, (etc.)
> For the Third Time, I take refuge in the Buddha, (etc.)

This Confession of Faith is the one indispensable ritual of nibbanic Buddhism. All other ritual forms may be dispensed with. For, as the Buddha tells Ānanda, although it is proper for a Buddha to be given homage, it is not through ritual and offerings that He is

> rightly honored, reverenced, venerated, held sacred or revered. But the brother or the sister . . . who continually fulfills all the greater and the lesser duties, who is correct in life, walking according to the precepts—it is he who rightly honours, reverences . . . and reveres the *Tathâgata* [Buddha] with the worthiest homage. [*Mahâ Parinibbâna Suttanta* V, 3, in *Dialogues of the Buddha*, Pt. II: 150]

Hence, so the Buddha admonishes his disciple: "Hinder not yourselves, Ânanda, by honoring the remains of the *Tathâgata.*" (*Ibid.*:154)

This theme is taken up in *Milinda*, when Nāgasena tells the king:

> Paying reverence is not the work of the sons of the Conqueror, but rather the grasping of the true nature of all compounded things, the practice of thought, contemplation in accordance with the rules of *Satipatthâna* [meditation], the seizing of the real essence of all objects of thought, the struggle against evil, and

---

the *only* motivational basis. Burmese ritual action is based on a variety of other motives as well: prestige, display, sociability, power, and so on. These will be described in succeeding chapters as we come to specific ceremonies and festivals.

[3]This Confession is found in the *Khuddaka-Pāṭha*, in *The Minor Readings*, ch. 1.

> devotion to their own [spiritual] good. These are things which the sons of the Conqueror ought to do, leaving to others, whether gods or men, the paying of reverence. [*The Questions of King Milinda,* IV, 3, 25]

This same point of view finds an echo among some contemporary Buddhists, even among a tiny minority (monks and laymen) of Burmese villagers, those whom, ingeniously, my Burmese assistant characterized as "Protestants." As one monk put it,

> Learned and sophisticated Buddhists can dispense with the Buddha statue completely, and concentrate instead on His teachings. The statue is only a crutch for ordinary people who require a visual symbol.

A layman expressed the same thought when he said,

> If you wear shoes in the pagoda you will not go to hell. It is just a tradition. So, too, with ritual. The Buddha discarded music, flowers, and all other worldly things. So why should we offer such things to Him now?

Similarly, in discussing the worship of Buddha images, one layman put it this way.

> The Buddha image is only a piece of wood, like a doll. It is not to be worshiped.

Although they are not prepared to discard Buddhist worship—as one monk put it, "People show respect to ordinary mortals; how much more should we pay respect to the Buddha?"—more than half the monks in my sample agree with this ritual attitude of nibbanic Buddhism. Buddhist worship, for them, is not instrumental, at any rate for extrinsic ends, but expressive. From their point of view, the worship of the Buddha is a means primarily for cleansing or purifying the mind. Buddhist devotions lead one to concentrate on the Buddha and His teachings (which in turn promotes proper moral and spiritual conduct), but they cannot aid in the attainment either of nirvana, which requires meditation, or of a better rebirth, which requires merit. Some of these same monks point out, however, that although Buddhist worship is not conducive to immediate utilitarian ends, its psychological consequence may be. By giving the devotee peace of mind it increases his self-confidence, thereby providing him with the emotional strength to pursue his more immediate worldly goals.

This ritual attitude of nibbanic Buddhism is represented in Burma by a small minority. Worship of the Buddha's relics, at least, is widely practiced not only as a form of homage to the Buddha but as a means for a better rebirth. And, contrary to some interpreters of *Theravāda* Buddhism, this practice is explicitly legitimized by Scripture. The *Suttapitaka* especially abounds in passages referring to the efficacy of worshiping the Buddha, the pagoda, and the relics of the Buddha. Thus whereas, in the *Dhammapada*, *pūjā* refers to an attitude of reverence, in these later works it means an instrumental act producing future fruits. In one *sutta*, the Buddha Himself tells Ānanda that a cairn (pagoda) should be erected to a Buddha (as well as to a silent Buddha, a "king of kings," and a "true hearer" of a Buddha) at the "four crossroads."

> And whosoever shall there place garlands of perfumes or paint, or make salutations there, or become in its presence calm in heart—that shall long be to them for a profit and a joy. [*Mahâ Parinibbâna Suttanta* V, 11, in *Dialogues of the Buddha,* Pt. II:156]

What is meant by "profit" and "joy" is spelled out in the next verse. By performing these rituals,

> the hearts of the many shall be made calm and happy; and since they there had calmed and satisfied their hearts they will be reborn after death, when the body has dissolved, in the happy realms of heaven. [*Ibid.:* V, 12]

Lest these passages give rise to misunderstanding, however, three comments should be made concerning their import—observations, I should add, which are frequently made by Burmese monks, though infrequently by laymen. First, the rewards referred to in the text are the consequence of the worship of the Buddha, not a boon vouchsafed by Him. Second, they do not include the attainment of nirvana. Third, they are not an automatic result of the offerings per se, nor of any merit they produce, but a consequence, rather, of the psychological change—a calm and happy heart—that accompanies the offerings. This, as we shall observe again, is a crucial notion in Buddhism: one's future rebirth is importantly influenced by one's state of mind, and especially by one's state of mind at death.[4]

[4]Despite these observations, it is obvious that the following comment of a contemporary Sinhalese monk, published in a book intended for Western intellectuals, represents a conception of Buddhist worship designed to appeal to Western humanists rather than an accurate description of canonical Buddhism, let alone of Buddhism "on the ground."

> The respect paid to the Buddha image is *nothing more* than the general practice of cultured people to honor a statue or monument of a great personage with flowers, incense, and similar signs of veneration. The words said by a Buddhist before the image are a meditation on the virtues of the Buddha, an expression of aspiration for similar virtues. The respect and honor paid to a bodhi tree, also, is an expression of gratitude, for it was under the shadow of a bodhi tree that the Bodhisattva attained Buddhahood. [Ānanda Maitreya Nayaka Thero, in Morgan (ed.) 1956:130—italics mine]

The same comment applies to the remarks of a Burmese monk in the same volume. True Buddhists, he writes,

> do not worship an image nor pray before it expecting any worldly boons or sensual pleasures while they are living or a pleasurable state of existence, such as heaven, after death. [U Thittila in Morgan (ed.) 1956:75]

A later source, the *Mahāvastu,*[5] is much more extravagant, both with respect to the types of offerings which might be made to the Buddha and the promise of the rewards to be received. Since the Buddha's merit is inexhaustible and His qualities of goodness infinite, offerings made to Him are "infinite, unending, inconceivable, immeasurable, illimitable and ineffable." Hence, "it is not possible to determine the merit of him who shall render him honor with flowers, garlands, perfumes, flags and banners, music, and ointments" (*Mahāvastu,* Vol. 2:329). By worshiping a pagoda, the text continues, the devotee becomes (among other things) wealthy, affluent, ablaze with splendor and glory, a mighty universal king, an inhabitant of heaven, a king of *deva,* renowned for his beauty, and so on. These rewards, described in the greatest detail, require twenty-five pages (*ibid.*:329-54) to complete.

Milinda, a later but more orthodox text, is less extravagant. Since the Buddha is dead, clearly He cannot accept gifts; yet—so Nāgasena assures Milinda—the construction of a pagoda yields important fruits.

> The Blessed One, O king, is entirely set free [from life]. And the Blessed One accepts no gift. If gods or men put up a building to contain the jewel treasure of the relics of a Tathâgata [a Buddha] who does not accept their gift, still by that homage paid to the attainment of the supreme good under the form of the jewel treasure of his wisdom do they themselves attain to one or other of the three glorious states [rebirth as a man, a god, or an *arahant*]. [*The Questions of King Milinda,* IV, 1, 11]

The same point is made somewhat later in the text.

> As fans and punkahs are means of producing wind, so the relics and the jewel treasure of the wisdom of a Tathâgata are means of producing the threefold attainment. And as men oppressed by heat and tormented by fever can by fans and punkahs produce a breeze, and thus allay the heat and assuage the fever, so can gods and men by offering reverence to the relics, and the jewel treasure of the wisdom of a Tathâgata, though he has died away and accepts it not, cause goodness to arise within them, and by that goodness can assuage and can allay the fever and the torment of the threefold fire. Therefore is it, great king, that acts done to the Tathâgata, notwithstanding his having passed away and not accepting them, are nevertheless of value and bear fruit. [*Ibid.*]

It will be noticed that the rewards promised by *Milinda* are based on the same mechanism stressed by the *sutta,* which (in both cases) differ from that stressed in the *Mahāvastu.* The latter text emphasizes that the rewards are a consequence of the merit derived from the worship of the Buddha. The former two texts emphasize, rather, that these rewards result from the

[5]Although the *Mahāvastu,* a *Vinaya* text, is not part of the Theravadist canon, it belongs to a school that was contemporaneous with the *Theravāda,* one which drew from the same traditions. (Cf. Thomas 1960:256.)

psychological changes produced by His worship: the *sutta* speak of a "calm heart," *Milinda* of the "goodness" that will "arise within" the worshiper. In contemporary Burma, both mechanisms are stressed.

Scripture legitimizes not only Buddhist worship as a means for a better rebirth, but it similarly legitimizes Buddhist pilgrimage. Thus, four types of pilgrimage centers, and the reward for making a pilgrimage, are specified by the Buddha.

> And there will come, Ânanda, to such spots, believers, brethren and sisters of the Order, or devout men and devout women, and will say:—"Here was the Tathâgata born!" or, "Here did the Tathâgata attain to the supreme and perfect insight!" or, "Here was the kingdom of righteousness set on foot by the Tathâgata!" or, "Here the Tathâgata passed away in that utter passing away which leaves nothing whatever to remain behind!"
>
> And they, Ânanda, who shall die while they, with believing heart, are journeying on such pilgrimage, shall be reborn after death, when the body shall dissolve, in the happy realms of heaven. [*Mahâ Parinibbâna Suttanta,* in *Dialogues of the Buddha,* Pt. II:154]

Given this authoritative sanction, it is hardly surprising that most Burmese laymen and about half the Burmese monks in my sample should have stressed the instrumental, as well as the expressive value of Buddhist worship. (Surprisingly, however, none of them even alluded to Scripture to justify their attitudes, let alone invoking its authority.) According to them, Buddhist worship can enhance one's chances for a better rebirth in two ways. First, the worship of the Buddha consists of offerings as well as homage. The merit derived from these offerings enhances one's chances for a better rebirth. Second, worship is conducive to a good mental state; and as we have noted, one's rebirth is to a great extent dependent upon one's mental state. If a person dies in a state of tranquility, compassion, detachment, and so on, he will achieve a happy rebirth.

Thus far, instrumental ritual has been discussed exclusively in the context of kammatic Buddhism, its goal being an enhanced rebirth. For apotropaic Buddhism, as we have seen, ritual is exclusively instrumental, its goal being protection in this birth. The actual rituals that constitute this type, as well as the two other types, of Buddhism are described in subsequent chapters.

A Note on Children

On the assumption that the religious beliefs of adults develop out of beliefs they have held as children, and on the assumption too that the latter beliefs leave some residues in the mind of the adult, it is of more than passing interest to know what beliefs children hold about ritual action. In order to obtain at least some preliminary answers to this question, nineteen children —twelve boys and seven girls, ranging from seven to twelve years of age—

were interviewed. They were asked four simple questions: *(a)* Do you ever worship *(shi.khou)* the Buddha? If so, how often? *(b)* Why do you worship Him? *(c)* Do you ever pray to the Buddha? *(d)* Is there any goal you hope to achieve by your prayers? The children's responses, and the developmental trends revealed in them, are highly instructive.

Worship of the Buddha—i.e., prostration before the Buddha image or some other symbol of the Buddha—is a universal practice among these children. The frequency of their worship, however, is variable. Of the nineteen, eight worship Him nightly before retiring; ten worship Him irregularly; and one worships Him twice daily, in the morning after awakening and in the evening before retiring. For the majority (twelve of the nineteen) the purpose of worship is to obtain merit. For a smaller number, worship is motivated by a more specific aim: to become a *deva*, to avert dangers of various kinds, to achieve some material boon, to escape from hell.

Overwhelmingly (fourteen out of nineteen), the children recite the Buddhist Common Prayer (see chapter 9), as part of their worship. A few recite other traditional prayers, such as the "Three Disasters" ("Lord, help me to escape from the three disasters [disease, war, and famine].") In addition to these formal prayers, a large majority of the children had composed their own prayers for help in achieving some personal goal or end. Almost invariably these prayers are addressed to the Buddha, and almost invariably they take one of two forms: "Lord, may I attain (or achieve) . . . ," or "Lord, please help me to attain (or achieve) . . ." The goals for which they pray are of interest: nine had prayed for such material objects as fountain pens, rings, watches, food, clothing, and so on; three had prayed to escape from a particular threat or danger; two had prayed for the health of a sick parent; and one each had prayed that a father should give up drinking, that his parents (who had gone on a trip) should return, that he (the child) might obtain nirvana, that he might be wealthy in his next existence, that she have her ear-boring ceremony soon.

It is instructive to note the developmental trends in children's prayers, of which six can be delineated. Until the age of ten, there are no cases of children praying for a specific goal (i.e., there are no petitionary prayers); until the age of eleven it is believed that the Buddha Himself will answer petitionary prayers; after eleven, it is believed that either the Buddha or the *deva* answer petitionary prayers; after the age of twelve, it is believed that if the Buddha answers prayers, He does not answer them directly, but rather helps them to achieve their goals; after twelve, petitionary prayers have reference to goals in the next rather than the present existence; finally, after the age of twelve it is believed that Buddhist worship automatically results in merit, rather than merit being something the Buddha bestows. In short, by the age of twelve, these children have outgrown their idiosyncratic conception of Buddhist worship and prayer, and have acquired the normative conceptions held by the adults.

The Forms of Buddhist Ritual Action

As I am using it here, "ritual" is the generic term for any kind of cult behavior, regardless of its degree of elaboration or complexity. As a global concept, however, ritual must be broken down into its component units. For our purposes, the *rite* is the minimum significant unit of ritual behavior. Rarely, however, does a single rite exist as an independent and complete ritual event. Typically, rites are part of larger ritual configurations, which for lack of better terms I shall designate as "ceremonies" and "ceremonials." A *ceremony* is the smallest configuration of rites constituting a meaningful ritual whole, and *ceremonial* is the total configuration of ceremonies performed during any ritual occasion. The totality of its rites, ceremonies, and ceremonials constitutes the *cultus* of a religion. Sometimes these are performed at specifically designated sacred days known as *holydays* or *festivals.*

Although the ceremonies and ceremonials which comprise the Buddhist cultus are classified below into three types, they all include the same type of rite. A description of these rites is, therefore, a description of the basic forms of Buddhist ritual action. Hence, before describing the ceremonies and festivals of Buddhism, it will be useful to outline the rites that constitute the basic units of these larger ritual configurations.

Offerings. Almost without exception, Buddhist ritual includes some form of offering. Daily devotions before the Buddha image, prayers at the pagoda, and so on almost invariably include the offering of lighted candles, flowers, water, and food.[6] Although all but one member of my blue-ribbon sample made these offerings as part of their Buddhist devotions (the one exception said he never made such offerings because they are not the mark of a true Buddhist), their motives for doing so (except in an apotropaic context when the motive is uniform) are varied. For seven of the fifteen, the motive is soteriological—to obtain nirvana, to achieve a better rebirth, to avoid hell, to acquire merit (for their next birth). Some of them mention the conventionally ascribed soteriological benefits of the offerings: flowers are a means to health and beauty; water is a means to a "cool" mind—peaceful and free from worry; food assures adequate nourishment; the lighted candles are a means to enlightenment and glory. Those who hope for rebirth in a higher abode admit that these offerings in themselves are not sufficient to guarantee the outcome; still, their importance they say cannot be minimized. As one informant put it, although his karma may destine him for rebirth as a dog, the merit from these offerings will

[6]Although the Buddha, monks, and spirits are all offered food as a sign of respect or as a means of worship, the lexicon of feeding the three is different. In the case of the Buddha the term for feeding is *tin-de;* for monks, *laung:de,* for *nat* spirits, *bali natsa.* The food, too, is referred to differently. Alms food for the monks is *hsun:;* for the Buddha, *hsun:do* (*do* being a royal honorific); for the spirits, *poukthou:de.*

enable him to have a rich man as his master.

Two informants interpret these offerings commemoratively—they recall the Buddha and His attributes to the mind of the devotee. If, while making them, one does not contemplate the qualities of the Buddha, they are in vain. "It is no better than giving food to the crows, or lighting candles so the rats can see."

Four said that offerings are made because it is the duty of a Buddhist to do so, or because it is a Buddhist custom. Some went so far as to say that, although these offerings are opposed by the Buddha, it is a Burmese tradition and they must comply with it. One informant gave a simple psychological answer: he makes them "because it makes me feel better." One informant could give no reason at all.

Regardless of their differences, all but one of these informants said that these offerings are neither desired by the Buddha nor useful to Him. Whether He is alive (as some think) or dead (as most view Him), He neither eats the food nor smells the scent from the flowers, etc. Only one demurred: the Buddha, he said, wants food just as human beings do. Even he agreed, however, that the Buddha does not reward those who make offerings to Him. The benefits received are automatic—in the form of increased merit.

Whatever his conception of this ritual may be, when the devotee makes his offerings, he recites a standard prayer.

> I offer this good food in honor of the Lord of the World. May I, by this meritorious act, avoid the pains of hunger.
>
> I offer this good water. . . . the torture of burning.
>
> I offer this good light. . . . a great darkness.
>
> I offer these fragrant flowers. . . . the smell of raw flesh.

Another type of offering, restricted to important celebrations and festivals, is the *kadaw pwe*—three bunches of bananas surrounding a coconut.[7] Although displayed to the Buddha (and to the Buddhist gods), these food offerings may be consumed by humans. The *kadaw pwe* may not be touched for seven days, after which the coconut is eaten raw and the bananas (usually) fried. The bits of food offered at the pagodas are taboo to everyone except pagoda slaves and their contemporary descendants.[8]

[7]Spirits are also propitiated by means of *kadaw pwe;* for them, however, only two bunches of bananas are used. Once used, moreover, the latter cannot be taken to a Buddhist monastery, a cemetery, or a house in which a woman is in labor.

[8]During the Burmese monarchy prisoners of war, and others too, were dedicated to pagodas where they and their descendants after them served as custodians. Although this form of "slavery" has been legally abolished, the descendants of these "slaves" remain an outcast group, many of whom continue to make a living by caring for pagodas, operating stalls in the

Motor Behavior. An integral part of all Buddhist worship is the act of physical prostration *(shi.khou)* before the Buddha image, the pagoda (His symbol), or the mental image of Him. Indeed, this is such a basic part of worship that Burmese bilinguals invariably translate *shi.khou* as worship, the part standing for the whole; *hpaya: shi.khou,* for example, is translated as worship of the Buddha. To perform this act, the worshiper kneels, places his clasped hands to his forehead, and three times touches his forehead to the floor (or ground). This is the ultimate form of obeisance, indicating reverence, homage, subjection. Henceforth, in this book, "to do obeisance" or "physical prostration" will always refer to this act of *shi.khou.*

The Buddha, in Burmese lore, is one of "five objects of worship," i.e., one of five objects worthy of prostration, the others being the Teaching, the Order, one's parents, and one's teachers. Hence the identical form of prostration is displayed toward all of them—by a layman when he comes into the presence of a monk; by young children when they greet their parents upon returning from school; and by adults when, on special Buddhist holydays, they go to their parents' homes to pay them special respect. It is also displayed, of course, when entering the presence of royalty and nobility. Peasants also prostrate themselves, even today, before important government officials.

Although the act of worship is performed by means of prostration, other forms of motor behavior are also required in the presence of Buddhist sacra. Shoes and sandals must be removed at the entrance to the pagoda or monastic compound. In the presence of a Buddha image or a monk one either sits or rests on one's haunches so that one's head not be above the head of the monk or the image. Under no circumstances may one's feet be pointed in the direction of the sacred object: the legs are always turned backward, away from it. When reciting or listening to a litany, the hands, palms touching each other, are held to the forehead in the case of men and to the chest in the case of women. The completion of the litany, like its inception, is marked by physical prostration performed three times.

Verbal Behavior. "Verbal behavior" is a better expression than "prayer" since it includes petitions, devotions, spells, incantations, and so on. Most closely related to the notion of petitionary prayer is the Burmese *hsu.taung:* (*hsu.* - boon or reward; *taung:* - to request). As is frequently the case, the Burmese redundantly combine a Pali and Burmese term in one expression. Thus *hsu.taun pa.hta.na* is to ask for a boon. But the meaning of this expression is tricky, at least within the framework of soteriological Buddhism, for the mere request for some boon is useless in a system in which rewards are retribution for deeds performed rather than the undeserved consequence of a request or petition. Thus the prayer quoted above, which

---

pagoda compounds, or scavenging and begging there and elsewhere. Pagoda slaves, it should be noted, are also found in Thailand (Rajadhon 1961:67).

accompanies an offering, ends with the wish that the worshiper be free from hunger, burning, and so on. But it does not ask for these things as a free boon, but rather expresses the hope that they may be the consequences of the meritorious deeds the worshiper has already performed.

Objects of Ritual Veneration

The pagoda is the most sacred structure in Buddhism. Neither a church nor a temple, it is in the most technical sense a relic chamber, and in the least technical sense a symbol of the Buddha. In either case it is a triangular or cylindrical structure of solid stone or brick, which (if it is a true pagoda) is an object *of* worship rather than a structure *for* worship.[9] Most probably antedating Buddhism (Dutt 1962:182-83), pagoda worship is an ancient Buddhist practice, prescribed (as we have seen above) by the later *Theravāda* texts for Buddhist reliquaries, and therefore proper.

There is probably no Buddhist society in the world in which the pagoda (Burmese, *hpaya:*) is more popular than in Burma.[10] Almost nowhere in the entire country can the eye scan the landscape without lighting on a pagoda—usually three or four, often scores. For, in addition to the inhabited village or crowded city, there is no place too remote and no mountain too high to dampen the zeal of the pagoda builder. Although pagodas differ in numerous details and size—they may range from a few feet in height to the 326-foot *Shwe Dagon* in Rangoon—they conform typically to the same basic plan. At the bottom is a square terrace, usually made of brick or masonry, on top of which is the polygonal plinth on which the bell-shaped body rests. This latter is divided into two parts by an ornamental band. Capping the structure is a cone-shaped spire made up of a number of lotus-leaf rings. Attached to the top of the spire is an "umbrella" *(hti:)* made of metal (in the case of famous pagodas, inlaid with precious metals and stones), from which hang

[9]Structures of the latter type—temples rather than pagodas—are restricted almost exclusively, so far as Burma is concerned, to the ancient capital of Pagan, where they stand as a mute witness to its former glory. Unlike a true pagoda, whose purpose is to contain relics, the purpose of the temple is to contain a huge Buddha image. Although found primarily in Pagan (which, of course, contains solid pagodas, as well), there are also a few contemporary Burmese Buddhist temples. Indeed, the most fantastic Buddhist structure I have seen in Burma is a contemporary temple—the Thambouktei—outside Monywa, a town in Upper Burma. A huge, rambling, cavernous building glittering with stone and glass, its inner chamber is filled with five hundred thousand Buddha images which form decorative patterns on its walls and vaults. It was erected by a wealthy Chinese merchant in honor of a famous abbot, the Monywa *hsaya-daw.* In one of its rooms is a life-size statue of the abbot in meditating position. On one side of the temple is a tomb, ready to house his remains when he dies. This abbot, seventy-eight years old at the time I visited the temple, is alleged to have attained various supernormal powers.

[10]The word "pagoda" (probably an English hysteron-proteron of the Sinhalese *dagoba,* in turn derived from the Sanskrit *dhātu garbha,* or relic container) is not, of course, a Burmese word. Nor do the Burmese use the Indian *stupa* to refer to these structures. Some use the term *zeidi,* derived from the Pali *cetya* (offering place), but mostly they use *hpaya:* (Lord), a term which is also used for the Buddha, a monk, or a king.

the sweet-sounding pagoda bells. Pagodas are usually painted white, but the more famous ones are covered with gold leaf. As they ascend to the pagoda platform, the faithful purchase one or more pieces of gold leaf which they apply to the structure.

Pagoda architecture is given a variety of symbolic interpretations. According to one, the base of the pagoda represents Mt. Meru; the plinth and the two parts of the bell-shaped body represent the three worlds of sense, form, and shapelessness; and the spire represents the Buddha. According to another interpretation the bell-shaped body represents an inverted monk's bowl. In still another, the base represents the heavens of the four World Guardians; the plinth represents the Tusita heaven (where Buddhas reside before they descend to the earth), and the spire represents nirvana. The symbolism of the other parts is equally complicated and overdetermined; space does not permit further elaboration here.[11]

At the entrance to the pagoda compound one usually encounters two huge leogryphs made of brick. These are meant to guard the pagoda. In the compound, and close to the pagoda itself, one usually finds images of ogres *(bi. lu:)* and winged half-lion, half-human creatures *(manoukthi-ha).* These, too, are guardian figures. Adjacent to the building is a larger pillar holding a streamer *(tagun-daing)* on top of which rests an image of a Brahminy goose *(hin-tha),* while attached to each of its four sides are images of the protector gods of Buddhism *(sammā deva).* The bird is said to represent the wife of the Buddha, who at her death became a Brahminy goose and in that form worshiped her husband. Frequently a pagoda contains many niches with small Buddha images made of brick or plaster. In addition, the platform on which it is built may have on it a number of large bronze images of the Buddha. Some pagodas have a central Buddha image as well. The Arakan pagoda of Mandalay, for example, is famous not for its relics but for its *Mahamuni* image, which over the years has been so heavily gilded by the faithful that its original shape is no longer recognizable.

A true pagoda, as I have mentioned, is a Buddhist reliquary. Preferably it contains a relic of the Buddha Himself (or in some instances, like the famous *Shwe Dagon* pagoda in Rangoon, of a previous Buddha); or, in lieu of that, a relic of a holy monk or of a saint. In Burma the relic, together with numerous other sacred objects, such as Buddha images, and treasure (gold and jewels, for example), is buried in a vault deep inside the structure, forever sealed from the human eye. Hence, the religious rather than social

[11]The manifest sexual symbolism associated with the pagoda in Ceylon (cf. Yalman 1963:-30) is, so far as I can discover, absent in Burma. The Sinhalese interpretation aside, however, it is not hard to imagine that historically pagoda architecture was derived from the Hindu *lingam,* or that even today it evokes unconscious phallic imagery in the perceiver. On a conscious level, moreover, at least one pagoda in Burma, a rounded Sinhalese-style *dagoba* outside the town of Sagaing, is associated with breast symbolism. According to legend, its royal patron instructed the architect to construct a pagoda modeled after the most beautiful object he knew, the breast of his queen.

motive for pagoda worship is fairly clear: since there is a relic of the Buddha, He Himself is present there in more than a symbolic sense. This is why the Buddhist does not worship *at* the pagoda; rather, he worships the pagoda. It is not only a memorial to the Buddha but in some important sense an embodiment of Him. This accounts in part for the reverence with which it is treated, and the enormous wealth lavished upon it.[12]

Although there are probably as many putative relics of the Buddha as of Christ, there are nevertheless many more pagodas in Burma than there are known relics of Him. Most of them, therefore, although symbolic of the Buddha, are not worshiped. Some may nevertheless be celebrated centers of Buddhist devotion and the sites of famous pagoda festivals for other reasons: they may contain a sacred Buddha image (such as the one in the famous Arakan pagoda in Mandalay); they may have been constructed on the occasion of a miracle (as was the famous pagoda in the little village of Shweizayan); and so on. Most pagodas, however, enjoy no such distinction. Constructed so that their donor may acquire merit (no act confers greater merit than the construction of a pagoda) and prestige (no symbol confers greater prestige than the formal title, Pagoda Donor—*Hpaya: Taga*), the vast majority are of no significant devotional significance. Thus, although almost every village in Burma probably contains at least one pagoda, it is not an important place or object of worship, although it is a reminder of the Buddha.

The true pagoda is not the only form in which the Buddha is worshiped. In addition to those buried in the pagoda, *Theravāda* Buddhists worship relics of greater visibility. Although none of these is found in Burma, at least one—the sacred tooth—is located in Ceylon, where it is worshiped at the famous Temple of the Tooth in Kandy. Periodically it is removed from its special vault and paraded through the city. Another sacred Buddha tooth is found in China. In 1961 the Chinese government sent it by plane on a two-month loan to Ceylon. En route, the plane landed in Rangoon, where it was worshiped by a large delegation of Buddhists, both lay and monastic.

Buddhists worship symbols of the Buddha as well as His relics. In early Buddhism there were three special symbols in whose form He was adored:

[12]Because it contains sacred relics, the pagoda is said to have a "heart," which can send forth visible aura. In our terms, it possesses mana, or uncanny power. Other Buddhist sacra —monks, the Buddha, kings—also possess mana, which in my opinion accounts for the fact that they are all, together with pagodas, called *hpaya:* in Burmese. Any other object that possesses uncanny power is also a *hpaya:*, or at least is treated like one. Thus if one did not know a cannon was being described below, one might imagine it was a Buddha image or pagoda.

The army of King Alaungpaya (Burma's famous eighteenth-century empire builder) had a three-pound cannon which, according to Harvey,

> was the pride of the day, because when fired it went off, and when it went off it was the enemy whom it hit, and the enemy whom it hit died; because of these things, it was coated with goldleaf, and men made offerings of spirits to it, reverently perfuming it with scents and wrapping it in fine raiment. [Harvey 1925:232]

the lotus, the Wheel, and the bo tree. This is the pipal *(ficus religiosa)*, a species related to the banyan. It was under a pipal that the Buddha attained Enlightenment *(bodhi)*. Hence, that specific pipal is the *bodhi* tree, and the entire species (by a corruption of the Pali) are bo trees.[13] Although all three remain sacred symbols, only the latter continues to be an object of worship.

The most prevalent and favorite symbol of contemporary Buddhist worship is, of course, the Buddha image, of which there are three forms in Burma: the seated image (by far the most common), representing the Buddha in the act of meditation; the standing image, showing Him in the act of preaching; and the reclining image, which reveals Him as about to attain nirvana. Historically Buddhist image worship arose several centuries later than pagoda worship—indeed, it encountered more than a little resistance among early Theravadist monks, even as late as the fifth-century Pali commentaries.[14] (Cf. Rahula 1956:125 ff.) Today, Buddha images are found in many forms and sizes. Small ones are frequently placed in the domestic shrine found in almost all Buddhist homes. Images both large and small are found in, and often clutter, the monasteries.[15]

Needless to say, not every piece of sculpture in the form of the Buddha is a ritual object. Unless or until it is consecrated, it may be an aesthetically beautiful sculpture, but it is not ritually sacred. The consecration of an image *(ane-kaza tin-thi)* consists in two things: first, verses from the *Dhammapada* (153 and 154) are recited over it—preferably, but not necessarily, by a monk;[16] second, its eyes must be painted, thereby giving it "life."

[13]For the meaning of these symbols, cf. Coomaraswamy 1935.

[14]The parallel to Jainism is striking, as the following quotation indicates.

> As the Jaina laity had been drawn away from Hinduism by their adhesion to Mahavira [the founder of Jainism], they were left without any stated worship. Gradually, however, reverence for their master and for other teachers, historical and mythical, passed into adoration and took the form of a regular cult. Finally, images of these adored personages were set up for worship, and idolatry became one of the chief institutions of orthodox Jainism. The process was precisely parallel to what happened in Buddhism. It is not known when idols were introduced, but it was probably in the second or first century B.C. [Stevenson 1915:11-12]

[15]Caves and caverns were famous sites for Buddha images—witness the famous Ajanta and Elora caves in India—and today they are sometimes used for this purpose in Thailand and Burma, as well. The most notable Burmese example, in my own experience, is an image found in a cavern in the Sagaing hills of Upper Burma. Entering a small passageway, one climbs a series of steps cut into rock which lead to a pitchblack, labyrinthine maze whose passages are so narrow that at times one can only proceed by walking sideways. After what seems like an interminable climb, one emerges into a large airy room, in the midst of which stands the massive Buddha image. The entire experience is reminiscent of the Upper Paleolithic caves, especially that of the Trois Frères.

[16]I have run through a course of many births looking for the maker of this building and finding him not; painful is birth again and again.

> Now are you seen, O builder of the house, you will not build the house again. All your rafters are broken, your ridgepole is destroyed, the mind, set on the attainment of nirvana, has attained the extinction of desires.

According to Radhakrishnan (1950:110), these verses are alleged to have been recited by the Buddha at the moment of his Enlightenment. The "builder of the house," he comments, refers

Relics and symbols of the Buddha are not the only objects deemed worthy of Buddhist devotion. Relics of famous monks and of saints are similarly worshiped, and in some cases boons are requested of them. Images of these sacred persons may also be worshiped in pagodas and monasteries. Sometimes these are of well-known historical persons, such as the founder of one of Burma's monastic orders, whose life-size statue is in a glass case in the national headquarters of the order in Mandalay. Offerings of flowers and water are made to this image, as to that of the Buddha.

A Cultic Typology and a Classification of the Buddhist Cultus

Although the purpose of ritual is a useful criterion for the construction of a typology of ritual action, it is not very useful for the classification of a religious cultus. To classify a cultus from an action framework would result in many overlapping and ambiguous classes, whether viewed from a cultural perspective or from that of the actor. From the former perspective many of the rites and ceremonies which comprise the religious cultus partake of more than one purpose: the same ritual—especially when found in different contexts—may have, for example, both instrumental and expressive goals, and one ceremony or festival may simultaneously partake of two or more purposes. Similarly, when the cultus is viewed from the actor's perspective, the same ritual act—especially in religions which claim the allegiance of a wide array of devotees—may be instrumental for one person and expressive for another. Moreover, there are few ritual acts which are viewed, even by the same person, as exclusively one or the other. More frequently the actor's motives are diverse; his motivation, as we say, is overdetermined. What is required, therefore, at least from the cultural perspective—and any cultus is, in the first instance, a cultural phenomenon—is a typology by means of which the various elements of the cultus can be unambiguously classified. Basing such a typology on the dimension of *occurrence*, anthropologists and other students of religion have been able to achieve this end without violating intracultural classifications.

From the point of view of any individual life span, the rituals which comprise a religious cultus may be classified (using occurrence as the classificatory criterion) into those which are *recurrent* and *nonrecurrent*. Nonrecurrent rituals are those that mark regular events—birth, adolescence, marriage, death, and so on—which represent a transition from one status (biological and/or sociological) to the next in the life cycle. Typically, therefore, these events occur only once in a particular life span. (In some societies, marriage is an exception to this nonrecurrent pattern.) Recurrent rituals are those which, in principle at least, occur repetitively. Their recur-

to craving, the cause of rebirth. Hence, the verses are a symbolic summary of the basic Buddhist truth that with the extinction of craving "there is nothing to bind us to the wheel of existence."

rence, however, is of two types: *cyclical* and *noncyclical.* Recurrent, noncyclical rituals are those related to irregular events in the individual life cycle (illness and other kinds of personal trouble), in nature (droughts, storms, and so on), and in society (wars, coronations, and so on). Typically recurring by chance, these events are *a*periodic, happening at nonfixed and irregular intervals. Recurrent, cyclical rituals are tied to a ritual calendar or to the regular rhythms of nature (seasonal changes of various kinds), economy (agricultural and other cycles), and society (periodic changes in leadership, and so on). These events are periodic, recurring at fixed and regular intervals.

On the basis of this typology of the occurrence of ritual occasions, rituals which comprise the religious cultus may be classified into three relatively unambiguous classes. First there are the recurrent cyclical rituals—periodic, fixed, and regular—which comprise the *calendrical cycle.* Second, there are the nonrecurrent and noncyclical rituals, associated with the transitional events in the life cycle. These comprise the *life-cycle* rituals. Finally, there are the recurrent noncyclical rituals, associated with the dangerous events, actual or potential, that punctuate the lives of both individuals and groups. These comprise the *crisis* rituals.

The anthropological reader will notice that this classification differs from the conventional ritual classification in a number of ways. Instead of the conventional dyadic classification—rites of passage and rites of intensification—this one is triadic. Then, its terms are descriptive rather than (as in "rites of intensification") functional: at this stage in the scientific study of religion, functions are still to be discovered rather than imputed. Finally, it distinguishes two types of events in the life cycle (which accounts for the triadic classification), rather than lumping them, as is conventionally done, into one type. The reasons for this are threefold. First, it seems important to distinguish those events which mark a transition from one status to a succeeding status in the life cycle—and for which the rituals, therefore, are truly *rites of passage*—from those which do not constitute such a transition. The former, whether dangerous or not, are nonrecurrent transitional points in a life trajectory; the latter are recurrent and dangerous events, which moreover are not tied to either a biological or a sociological trajectory. Finally, it does not seem important to distinguish events dangerous to groups from those dangerous to individuals. To assume, a priori, that the cultus assigns certain rites to individual danger and others to group danger is to beg the empirical question.[17]

[17]To be sure, some of the rituals included in the first two classes are also associated with danger. Mortuary rituals for example, which according to our classification are life-cycle rituals, may be related to the danger created for a group by the death of one of its members. They are, nevertheless, distinguished from crisis rituals in that they mark a transitional event in the life cycle, an event moreover which (even if viewed as dangerous) is nonrecurrent. Crisis rituals, on the other hand, are associated with recurrent though irregular events.

With this classification, we may now turn to the rites, ceremonies, and festivals that constitute the Burmese Buddhist cultus. With few exceptions, the rituals of its calendrical and life cycles are those of nibbanic and kammatic Buddhism. Their purpose, both individually and severally, may be expressive, commemorative, or instrumental. When their purpose (or one of their purposes) is instrumental, their goal is almost always soteriological —rebirth or nirvana. Crisis rituals, on the other hand, are exclusively associated with apotropaic Buddhism. They are without exception instrumental, and their goal is always protection from danger. In the following three chapters I shall describe, respectively, the calendrical, life-cycle, and crisis rituals of the Buddhist cultus.

CHAPTER 9

The Ceremonial Cycle: I. Calendrical Rituals

Many of the ceremonies and festivals of the Buddhist cultus, like those of almost all other religions, are tied to the calendar—the lunar calendar, in the case of Buddhism. This being so, they are cyclical: they are performed on predictable occasions, at fixed periods and periodic intervals. The Buddhist ceremonial cycle, however, as is the case in other religions, consists not of one but of a series of cycles, each of a different duration. Specifically, there are in Buddhism daily, weekly (and biweekly), monthly, and annual cycles. Before attending to them it must be noted that in all, participation is voluntaristic; failure to participate is in no sense sinful or demeritorious. Nevertheless, almost without exception every adult Buddhist (children do not participate as actors, as contrasted to observers, until they reach their teens) takes part to some extent in every type of Buddhist ceremony, performed at every structural level of Burmese society: home, village, district, and nation.

The Daily Cycle

For a pious Buddhist, the first and last acts of the day consist of devotions performed in front of the small shrine found in almost every Burmese household. Always on the eastern (auspicious) side of the house, and always above head level (for to be placed below another's head is a grave insult, while to be placed above it is a sign of respect), the shrine consists, minimally, of a shelf for a vase, which usually contains fresh flowers to honor the Buddha. In some cases, a polychrome picture of the Buddha or of a Buddha image is found on the shelf. Ideally, of course, an image itself is found there, but in Yeigyi only one in five households has one; the others, so they claim, lack funds for its purchase.

In addition to the flower offerings, candles are lit and/or food offerings placed on the shelf as part of the daily devotions. Typically, these are brief, consisting only of the famous *Okāsa* (Burmese, *o-ka-tha*), the Buddhist Common Prayer (as Pe Maung Tin [1964] properly calls it) and the Five Precepts. The former, named after its opening phrase—*Okāsa, Okāsa, Okāsa*—has two parts. The first part (known as the *kado gan*) is an expression of reverence.

> I beg leave! I beg leave! I beg leave! By act, by word, and by thought, I raise my hands in reverence to the forehead and worship, honor, look at, and humbly pay homage to the Three Gems—the Buddha, the Law, and the Order—one time, two times, three times, O Lord [Buddha]!

The second part (known as the *hsu.taun: gan*) is more strictly a prayer.

> By this act of worship may I be free from the four States of Woe [rebirth in hell, as an animal, a ghost, a demon (a monster with a huge head and slender body)], the Three Scourges [war, epidemic, and famine], the Eight Wrong Circumstances of Birth [rebirth in hell, as an animal, a ghost, a *Brahma deva,* or a human remote from human habitation, with heretical views, incapable of understanding the Buddhist doctrines, or outside Buddhism] the Five Enemies [king, thief, fire, water, foe], the Four Deficiencies [tyrannical kings, wrong views about life after death, physically deformed, dull-witted], and the Five Misfortunes [loss of relatives, wealth, health, proper belief, morality], and may I quickly attain Nirvana, O Lord!

In reciting the Five Precepts, the devotee pledges to abstain from taking life, from stealing, from drinking intoxicants, from lying, and from sexual immorality.

Especially pious Buddhists—typically, the elderly—conclude their evening devotions by saying their beads. In Yeigyi a majority of the other villagers also say their beads, frequently if irregularly, at this time. The Buddhist rosary *(seikbadi:)* consists of 108 beads, that number being interpreted as representing the 108 markings on the feet of the Buddha.[1] The beads are said while reciting *dukkha, anattā, aneissa* or Buddha, *Dhamma, Saṅgha,* or some other such litany, in minimal units of three and maximal of nine. Some say that these units represent the twenty-seven planets (twenty-seven being the multiple both of nine and three). Others, that the three represents the Three Gems (Buddha, *Dhamma, Saṅgha*), nine merely being its square.[2]

In addition to these daily private devotions, public devotions are held

[1]The Buddha is believed to have visited Burma during his lifetime. Throughout the country, on hilltops adjacent to pagodas, there are replicas in plaster of his footprint showing these 108 markings.

[2]On Sabbath days, pious Buddhists wear their rosary about the wrist or around the neck. Sitting in the monastery or in the pagoda compound, the faithful move their lips (in silent litany) and click their beads even while listening to or participating in the day-long conversations.

every evening after sunset in the village chapel *(dhamma.young).* Located in the center of the village, the chapel is a shedlike structure open to the air on three sides, the fourth enclosing an ark containing an image of the Buddha. Typically, attendance at chapel service is sparse, consisting of the same two or three men in their fifties, a group of six or seven old women, and ten to fifteen teen-age and younger girls. This number is substantially increased, however, during Lent and in times of crisis. The more sophisticated villagers, those who stress meditation as the central Buddhist activity, are somewhat disdainful of the chapel service, saying that this kind of piety, with its magical overtones, is irrelevant to the Buddhist life.

Unlike pagoda worship, which even on holydays is private, each worshiper saying his own devotions, chapel worship is congregational; there is a fixed service, taken from a popular prayer book (the *Dhamma Gīti* or Song of the *Dhamma*), parts of which are recited or chanted in unison, others responsively. It must be stressed, too, that the chapel devotions are exclusively a lay activity; monks never participate, let alone officiate, at these services, which typically last about an hour. They are led, instead, by male elders.

Despite the fact that participation in the daily chapel is limited, the service is summarized here in some detail for two reasons. First, with exceptions to be noted below, most of it (unlike devotions at which monks officiate) is conducted in Burmese rather than Pali. This, then, is one of the occasions in which young boys and girls—and the latter especially are regular chapelgoers—are exposed to Buddhist doctrine in a language they understand. Second, this service includes some of the core elements of the Buddhist cultus, such as the water libation, the sharing of merit, and so on, found in all Buddhist ceremonies, as well as a large percentage of the total Buddhist litany. Having described them here, I shall not find it necessary to repeat the account when we meet them again. The component parts of the service are set forth below in the order in which they typically occur.

Invocation of the gods *(nat pin:)*: this is the prelude to worship. The Buddhist gods *(deva)* who, when the Buddha was alive, worshiped him collectively, are requested both to hear the prayers about to be offered and to participate in the ceremony: "Attend to us, all ye *sammā deva,* as we worship the Buddha; attend to our chanting, and worship with us."

Invocation of the presence of the Buddha *(nei-ya-daw hkin:)*: A velvet cloth is placed in front of the Buddha image, and before the service begins freshly cut flowers are placed in a vase on top of it. The Buddha is requested to descend to this "throne" so that He may be worshiped. "May Thou, O Glorious Buddha, who hast conquered the Five Inner Forces (*man nga:ba:*; alternatively, *a:twin: an-jin.*[3]) be pleased to

[3]Alternatively translated as "hindrances," "obstacles," and "entanglements," these Five Forces consist of worldly lust, ill will, torpor and sloth of heart and mind, flurry and worry, and suspense. (Cf. *Tevijja Sutta,* in *Dialogues of the Buddha,* Pt. I:312.)

descend to the place we have prepared for Thee."

Permission to worship the Buddha *(hpaya: pin.)*: "May the incomparable Buddha, who possesses supermundane powers beyond all other creatures, whose wisdom is greater than the sun and the moon, who has six kinds of halos, Thou, the discoverer of the Four Noble Truths and the Noble Eightfold Path, permit us to worship Thee."

Prayer *(hsu.taung: gan)*: "As a result of worshiping the Buddha we pray that we may enjoy nirvana and the higher abodes."

Request of the precepts *(thi-la. taung:)*: "May the Buddha, who has conquered the Five Inner Forces, offer us the Five Precepts, so that we may have an auspicious victory and attain nirvana." The Five Precepts are then recited.

Prayer *(hsu.taung:)*: "By helping us to understand the meaning of 'suffering,' 'nonself,' and 'impermanerce,' help us to attain supermundane powers and thereby nirvana."

Offering of flowers, candles, and water: The offering is accompanied by the following words: "We possess name and form; therefore, we offer water, flowers, and candles unto Thee—water for cleansing and drink, flowers and candles for whatever Thou mayest desire."

Recitation of the Five Objects of worship *(ānanda nga:ba:)*: "There is no object more venerable than the Buddha. We give endless veneration to the Buddha, the Law, the Order, our parents, and our teachers. By worshiping these five objects may we attain nirvana and be free of all hindrances." (This is recited in Pali.)

Recitation of two *paritta*—the *Mangala Sutta* and the *Mettā Sutta*—in Burmese translation: Known in Burmese as the *Mingala Thouk* and the *Myitta Thouk,* respectively, these *sutta* are translated in chapter 11.

The recitation of the Virtues of the Buddha and of the *Saṅgha* (for a translation, see chapter 11): Their recitation protects the worshiper from all evil creatures.

The dissemination of love *(myitta pou.de)*: "May all creatures, all living things, all beings, all persons, all individuals, all males, all females, all Aryans, all non-Aryans, all gods, all mankind, all spirits be free from enmity, from care, and from oppression. May they all live happily. May they all be free from trouble and adversity. May they all enjoy prosperity. May they all help themselves through the law of karma." (This is recited in Pali.)

Recitation of the doctrine of Dependent Origination (Pali, *Paṭiccasamuppāda;* Burmese, *Pateiksa-thamoukpa*): This is the Buddha's famous analysis of the ontological basis for being and becoming (rebirth), found in the *Majjhima-Nikāya* (*Middle Length Sayings,* Vol. 1:180). According to this analysis, rebirth is a link in the following causal chain: the cause of death and suffering, rebirth, in turn is caused by the process of becoming, which is caused by attachment, which is caused by craving, which is caused by sensation, which is caused by contact, which is caused by one's sense organs, which is caused by a mind-and-body, which is caused by consciousness, which is caused by karmic formations, which is caused by ignorance of the Four Noble Truths. (This is recited in Pali.)[4]

Recitation of the "last words" of the Buddha (known in Burmese as *patan chan*): This is the famous line addressed by the Buddha to his disciples immediately before entering nirvana. "Decay is inherent in all component things! Work out your salvation with diligence." (*Mahâ Parinibbâna Suttanta* vi, 7, in *Dialogues of the Buddha,* Pt. II)

Recitation of the five *khandhā:* These are the five "heaps" into which human individuality is analyzed by Buddhism (matter, feeling, perception, impulse, consciousness). It is believed that by their recitation the devotee will be protected by the Buddhist gods. (This is recited in Pali.)

A prayer to the eight planets for protection from evil: This being a non-Buddhist notion, some villagers suggest that since there is a Buddha for each planet, this is really a prayer to the eight Buddhas of the eight points of the compass.[5]

Confession of Faith *(hsu.taung: imaya damanu)*: "I take refuge in the Buddha; I take refuge in the *Dhamma;* I take refuge in the *Saṅgha,* " etc.

Recitation of the life of the Buddha and of the Buddhist church in a Burmese folk version *(tha-thana shauk).*

Water libation rite *(yei-zetcha.)*: While water is poured drop by drop from a glass into a vase, and thence onto the ground, the congregation recites, "We have offered candles, flowers, and alms food to the Buddha; we have observed the Five Precepts and have practiced giving and meditation. May the *deva* and Withou-daya [see below] bear witness to our meritorious action. May I, as a result of this merit, attain nirvana, and may all intoxicants [āsava] be destroyed."[6]

This water-libation ceremony, as the Burmese call it, is an intrinsic part of all public ceremonies and public acts of meritorious giving.[7] As the formula indicates, it calls the merit of the worshipers to the attention of an earth goddess, known in Burma as Withou-daya (alternatively, Wathoung-daye), and in ancient India as Vasundhara. Although little known in ancient Indian Buddhism, this goddess is widely known in Buddhist Southeast Asia. Indeed, it is a myth associated with her that provides the Buddhist charter for the water-libation ritual, which is no doubt older than Buddhism in

[4]To include this highly abstract metaphysical treatise in a Buddhist devotional service and to recite it in Pali, is like including a chapter of Aristotle's *Metaphysics* in a Christian service and reciting it in Greek.

[5]According to Htin Aung (1962:8-11), these are not Buddhas, but *arahants.*

[6]The "intoxicants" are the characteristics of "worldlings" which must be destroyed before nirvana can be attained. They include sensuality *(kāma);* existence—or, less literally, lust for life—*(bhava);* speculation *(diṭṭhi);* and ignorance *(avijjā).* In Burmese, these Pali terms are rendered respectively as *kama, bwa, deiti,* and *aweiza.*

[7]It is found in most, but not all *Theravada* societies. Cf. Lévy (1957:12) for a description of this ceremony in Cambodia, and Wells (1960:118-19) and Rajadhon (1961:78) for Thailand.

Southeast Asia. This myth, known to every Burmese schoolboy,[8] may be summarized as follows.

When Māra, the Evil One, arrives with his hosts to oust the Buddha from under the *bodhi* tree, he points to his army as validation for his claim. The Buddha, in turn, points to the Earth, as witness to his many meritorious deeds, to validate His claim. Thereupon, the Earth appears in the guise of a woman (Withou-daya), and to display the Buddha's accumulated merit she squeezes from her hair the water that had been poured on the earth to commemorate His meritorious deeds.[9] They are so numerous that the water creates a flood, causing Māra and his hosts to flee.

Like the Buddha, then, the Burmese commemorate their meritorious acts by pouring water on the ground, calling upon Withou-daya to witness (and according to some, to record) them. As in many rituals, however, the symbolism is overdetermined. The "intoxicants" for whose destruction the worshiper prays while performing the libation are also compared to floods which, if not controlled, wash one away (from the path).

Release of the *deva (nat pou.de)*: "The gods who have worshiped with us may now return. Having proclaimed 'Well done!' [*tha-du*] for these meritorious deeds, may they return to their heavenly abodes."

Sharing of merit *(amhya. wei)*: Two girls, almost screaming, proclaim the following on behalf of the group, "We share this merit with our parents, friends, relatives, spirits, and all sentient beings." Thereupon, a large gong is sounded so that its vibrations, which spread to the corners of the earth, will announce to men and gods alike the merit they have just performed.[10] With this the service is ended.[11]

The Weekly and Monthly Cycles

Although the Burmese year is solar, the month is lunar,[12] and four days in each lunar month—the full and new moons and the eighth day after each

[8]According to Duroiselle (1921-22), this myth is found in no written work in Burma, although it is recorded in Thailand and Cambodia in a Pali text.

[9]A favorite sculpture on many pagoda platforms portrays Withou-daya squeezing this water from her hair.

[10]In worship at a pagoda a similar ceremony, with the same meaning, is performed. The worshiper concludes his devotions by sounding with an antler horn, one of the heavy bells found on every pagoda platform, thereby announcing his meritorious act to the gods. This at least is the interpretation of my Upper Burma informants. Nisbet (1901:160) has a variant interpretation for this practice. It is intended, he says, to call one's merit to the attention of Vasundhara, who normally records all acts of merit, since he *(sic)* may be otherwise engaged at the time. King, basing his interpretation on westernized Rangoon informants, says that the sounding of the bell is a symbolic act, sending waves of "good will and benevolence" to all creatures. (King 1964:52) This, of course, is the *myitta pou.de* described above.

[11]In addition to their daily devotions, there is yet another, and much more important, daily expression of Buddhist piety. This is the morning offering of alms food to the monks, described in a later chapter on monasticism.

[12]Calendrical adjustments are made by periodical additions of intercalary months.

of these—are duty days, or Sabbath days, as the Pali, *uposatha,* is variously translated. Canonically based, these devotional days were appropriated by Buddhism from the religion of pre-Buddhist India, in which the days of the full and new moons were regarded as sacred. They were, appropriately, the sacrificial days. (Dutt 1924:100) The day preceding the sacrifice was a sanctified day, the sacrificer observing abstinences of various kinds—from food, labor, sexual intercourse, and so on. The day of sacrifice (the *upavasatha*) became the Buddhist Sabbath *(uposatha),* known in Burmese as *u.bouk nei..*

Typically, the Sabbath observer arrives in the monastic compound early in the morning and spends most of the day in the resthouse *(zayat).* If he observes the day at a remote pagoda, he arrives on the Sabbath eve, and the resthouse is his lodging for the night. As in any Buddhist ceremony, his first act of piety and merit is to offer alms food to the monks, after which he joins the other laymen assembled in the resthouse for his own meal. Typically, each person or family brings their own food, but sometimes a wealthy villager will feed the entire assembly (thereby acquiring merit). Following their meal the faithful enter the monastery, where the important rituals take place. First, in the presence of a monk, the laymen chant the Common Prayer (see above, p. 210). Then, repeating after the monk, they chant the Buddhist Confession: "I take refuge in the Buddha; I take refuge in the Law; I take refuge in the Order," etc. Following this, the monk "offers" them the Ten Precepts: he chants the precepts, and they repeat them after him and vow to observe them.

The rest of the day the laymen spend quietly in the monastic compound, the resthouse, or the pagoda compound,[13] where they "observe the Sabbath" *(u.bouk saun.),* i.e., live in accordance with the precepts they have vowed to observe. Some spend the day in conversation with the monk, who sometimes discusses various aspects of Buddhist doctrine, or more rarely delivers a sermon. Others may spend the day saying their beads, intoning silent prayers, or reading one of the many popular Buddhist homilies. Mostly, however, they rest and talk. At sunset they return to their homes.

Unlike the Christian Sabbath, observance of the Buddhist Sabbath is optional. Although merit is acquired by observing it, there is no demerit as a consequence of omitting to do so. Hence only the very pious, the aged, and those who are otherwise free from economic obligations are seen at the monastery or pagoda compound. Indeed, even the pious tend to restrict their observance to the two important Sabbaths, the full moon *(la.byi.)* and

[13]Although in the village the Sabbath is observed in or adjacent to the monastery, in the city it is observed at the pagoda. A monk is invited there, and is fed by the laymen and in turn offers them the precepts. This urban-rural difference in observing the Sabbath explains why it is that laymen are seldom seen in city monasteries on the Sabbath, whereas this is the one day on which they will be found in village monasteries.

the dark of the moon preceding the new moon *(la.gwe).* In Yeigyi, for example, a little more than a third of the villagers—twenty-six in a sample of eighty-four—observe the Sabbath regularly. Almost without exception, however, all villagers observe the Sabbath on the three major Buddhist holydays, which almost always fall on a full moon, while few observe more than six or seven Sabbaths a year. Only one villager, a middle-aged woman, reported herself as never having observed the Sabbath—but she seemed somewhat subnormal; for example, she claimed not to have heard of nirvana![14]

Aside from the question of motivation, to which we shall turn below, there are obvious situational constraints on regular Sabbath observance. Dependent as it is on the phases of the moon, the Sabbath occurs on different days of the week; and since it is difficult, even in a pious country, to run a modern economy in which the day of rest changes each week, business and government offices in Burma are closed on Sunday rather than on Buddhist Sabbath days. So it is difficult for an ordinary city dweller to observe the Sabbath regularly.[15] The villager encounters a different problem: it is difficult to leave his fields in the middle of the agricultural cycle to spend a day at the monastery.

For Buddhism the Sabbath day is not primarily a day of rest and abstention from secular activity—although it is that as well—but chiefly an opportunity for the layman to live according to the Rule of the Buddha: to observe the Sabbath means to observe not only the five lay precepts which prescriptively govern the daily routine of the faithful, but also the additional five precepts which are the mark of a monk. These include abstention from food after midday, from worldly amusements (such as plays, sport, gambling, and so on), from the use of perfume and other bodily ornaments, from the use

[14]Sabbath observance does not begin until adolescence. Although young children may accompany their parents to the monastery, they do not observe the Sabbath because they "do not understand the meaning of the precepts."

[15]In preindustrial and precolonial Burma, when Buddhism was the state religion, the Sabbath was a legal holyday, so that these contemporary constraints on urban Sabbath observance were not operative. Indeed, in the eighteenth century at least (according to one report), regular Sabbath observance was primarily an urban phenomenon.

> The eighth day of the increasing moon, the fifteenth or full moon, the eighth of the decreasing moon, and the last day of the moon, are religiously observed by Birmans [*sic*] as sacred festivals. On these hebdomadal holidays no public business is transacted in the Rhoom; mercantile dealings are suspended; handicraft is forbidden; and the strictly pious take no sustenance between the rising and the setting of the sun; but this latter instance of self-denial is not very common, and, as I understood, is rarely practised, except in the metropolis, where the appearance of sanctity is sometimes assumed, as a ladder by which the crafty attempt to climb to promotion. [Symes 1800:335]

With the British conquest Sunday became the legal day of rest, and this pattern was continued after Independence as well, until 1962, when with the passage of the State Religion Act the Buddhist Sabbath day became the legal day of rest. A few months later, when the Army seized power, one of its first decrees was to restore Sunday as the day of rest.

of high beds for sleeping, and from the handling of money (i.e., business transactions). These five, unlike the first, are incumbent upon the layman for the duration of his vow only, i.e., for the twenty-four-hour Sabbath. He may, of course, observe them for a longer period—even for life—if he chooses, and there are laymen who, unwilling or unable to observe the 227 rules of the monastic order, lead the semimonastic life entailed by perpetual observance of the Ten, or—if they live in the world and must handle money —Eight Precepts.

Although the monk alone lives according to the complete Buddhist Rule, the layman who lives in accordance with only the Five Precepts also lives under the Rule of the Buddha. It is this that renders him an *upāsaka* (female, *upāsikā*), which, as La Vallée Poussin (1918:716) points out, connotes more than "layman" or "worshiper." Since he lives his life under a Rule, he is "a 'religieux'; he is actually a member of the third order, a tertiary." If this is true of the Buddhist who observes the Five Precepts only, it is surely true of the Sabbath observer who, for the period of the Sabbath at least, observes the monastic precepts. Appropriately, therefore, the Burmese restrict the use of *upāsaka* (Burmese, *u.pa-tha.ka* [fem., *u.pa-tha.-ki*]) to those who regularly observe the Sabbath.[16]

Although Sabbath observance, like most human action, derives from a number of motives, most important religiously is the desire for merit. Next to religious giving *(da-na.)*, the vow to observe the precepts *(u.bouk saun.)* is the most effective means for acquiring merit. For most villagers, compliance with the precepts is not in itself meritorious, though their violation is demeritorious; it is only when their observance is accompanied by the vow to observe them that compliance is meritorious. And more merit, obviously, is acquired through the vow to observe the Ten than the Five Precepts. Over and over again one is told, "I don't know when I will die, or to which abode I shall go after death. Therefore, I must observe the Sabbath so that I can acquire merit."

This emphasis on the vow, however justified by the Burmese, is related of course to the importance of *intention* in normative Buddhism. For the Burmese, it is the vow to observe the precept that establishes intent. Since, then, the unintentional violation of the precepts does not produce demerit, and since their unintended observance does not produce merit, the crucial means (as they view it) for acquiring morality-derived merit is the vow to observe them. Yet this is not to be taken lightly, for consciously to violate a precept is then doubly demeritorious. That is, when a vow has been taken to observe the precept, its violation involves not only that precept, but also the precept against lying, for the vow is made to the Buddha.

[16] *U.pa-tha.ka*, however, is rarely used for such persons. Instead, pious devotees are called *hpaya: lu-gyi:* (for males) and *hpaya: lu-gyi: gado* or *hpaya:gyi: mein-ma.* (for females). While observing the Sabbath the layman—whether an *u.pa-tha.ka* or not—is an *u.bouk* (Sabbath [observer]).

Since this vow is viewed as a central ritual for the Burmese laymen, it is important to note that half the monks in my sample deemed it unimportant; for them, it was an unnecessary ritual. The other half, however, stressed its importance on two grounds. First, it is an important source of merit—though, they hastened to add, there is no merit for those who then violate the precepts. Second, to vow in the presence of a monk—a Son of the Buddha—to observe the precepts is a psychologically impressive act and therefore highly conducive to their observance.

Although Sabbath observance is an important source of merit, as we have seen, on a regular basis it is not widespread. This is related not only to the situational factors discussed above, but to certain motivational factors related to the very desire for merit. This variable is demonstrated most easily when Sabbath observance is related to age, sex, and economic status; the resultant correlations show that those who most desire merit are the most regular Sabbath observers. Thus, to begin with age, all twenty-six persons in Yeigyi who observe the Sabbath weekly are over fifty. Partly this is because they have fewer economic responsibilities, but partly it is because the aged, being closer to death, are increasingly concerned about their next rebirth and the acquisition of merit. This concern explains, too, why the daily chapel services are attended primarily by elderly rather than middle-aged or young adults. I was frequently told by elderly and pious Burmese men that in their youth they had been indifferent to religion, that they had violated the precepts against drinking and adultery, and that it was not until their late middle age that they had become pious. This is consistent with the Burmese ideal-typic stage theory of the life cycle—reminiscent of, though not identical with, the Brahmanic stage theory. In the first stage, till about twenty-five, one is concerned with physical pleasures; in the second, till about fifty, one is concerned with domestic and economic responsibilities; in the third, after fifty, one is concerned with religion and meritorious deeds.

Not only do the elderly observe the Sabbath much more frequently than the young, but females observe it much more often than males. Of the elderly residents of Yeigyi who observe the Sabbath every week, 70 per cent are female. Similarly among the younger people, and especially the adolescents, females are again preponderant, as they are in the daily chapel services.[17] Women are more concerned with merit because, among other reasons, they aspire as we have seen (chapter 3) to rebirth as a male. Their greater concern is shown not only in ritual, but also in meditational activity. In two lay meditation centers—a village center in Upper Burma and a large Rangoon center—women outnumber men by more than two to one. Because of their greater piety, so the Burmese hold, there are five hundred

[17]Ryan (1958:95 ff.) and Mulder (1969:9) found the same situation in Ceylon and Thailand, respectively.

female *deva* to every male. (One monk raised the ratio to a thousand to one.)

The poor comprise the third group of frequent Sabbath observers. When they can escape from their economic burdens, they observe the Sabbath more often than the wealthy. As one villager put it, "Poor people have more trouble than the rich, so they are more eager to find out what the Buddha taught." I suspect, however, that there is another, equally important reason. The rich can acquire more merit by giving; the poor, for whom this possibility is less prominent, turn to other means to supplement their store of merit.

The Annual Cycle

Introduction

Buddhist holydays always fall on a Sabbath day. It is as if, for example, Easter, Christmas, and all other Christian holydays always fell on Sunday. A Buddhist holyday is a Sabbath day which is especially sacred because, putatively, it commemorates some event in the life of the Buddha. And, since the Full and Dark moons are especially sacred, these holydays always occur on one of those Sabbaths, especially the first. One does not have to look too closely to realize that, as with all the great religions, the Buddhist holydays probably derive from an older religion. They all fall at obvious transitional points of either the agricultural or the climatic year: the beginning or end of the monsoon, the beginning or end of the paddy cultivation cycle, and so on. Many of them, despite their Buddhist superstructures, continue to retain non-Buddhist elements as prominent features of their observance. It is not unduly rash to assume that they or things like them were originally celebrated as part of earlier nature and/or spirit cults, which even today are a prominent feature of Burmese religious life (cf. Spiro 1967). This is probably true not only of the nonscriptural holydays, but of the scriptural ones (the inception and conclusion of Lent and the *kahteing*) as well.

Even if non-Buddhist in origin, these holydays have been legitimized as Buddhist—as Christmas and Easter have been legitimized as Christian holydays—by basing them on a myth concerning the life of the founder. Their observance is viewed as commemorating and symbolically reenacting the myth. Often, however, the myth only barely conceals not only the pre-Buddhist origin of the day, but the partially non-Buddhist quality of many of its ceremonies. This is especially true, for example, of the Water Festival and the Festival of Lights, described below.

Its origin aside, the Buddhist annual cycle is clearly tied to the natural (especially astrological-divinatory) and agricultural cycles. Buddhist holydays do not occur during the plowing, transplanting, or harvesting seasons, nor do pagoda festivals occur during the rainy season when travel is difficult.

They all take place during those months which, economically and physically, are most conducive to the expenditure of the time and effort required for the planning and organizing of the holydays, and the travel required for the festivals.

Before describing this annual cycle of holydays and festivals, it must be stressed that their central *religious* ritual consists in the offerings made to monks, the Buddha, and the pagoda, and that their primary *religious* motive consists in the merit derived from these offerings. This being so, it is important to observe that merit is primarily acquired as part of a social act, "social" in that it is either public or cooperative, or both. That is, in some cases the meritorious act, though performed by an individual, nevertheless occurs in a public context. In other cases, as with the offering of a robe, or the feeding of monks, it is performed conjointly by a group of devotees. This may be an extended kin group, an entire village, or even an entire district.

We may now turn to a description of the annual ceremonial cycle, beginning appropriately with the first month of the Buddhist calendar.

The New Year

The Burmese New Year *(Thin:gyan)* falls in the month of April (usually the Burmese *Tagu:*), and its celebration lasts for three or sometimes four days. This celebration is a mixture of religious piety and boisterous fun. Although Buddhicized, this most popular of all Burmese festivals is scarcely more Buddhist in spirit than the Western New Year is Christian.

According to the myth (which, for all its obvious reworkings, seems still to be a combination of at least two separate mythic traditions), the king of the gods, known to the Burmese as Thagya:Min: or the Chief Thagya (= Sakka = Śakra = Indra), annually descends to the earth, where he remains for the last two days of the old year. He notes the doers of good and the evildoers, and records their names in two separate books. Completing his work, he returns to his abode in the Ta-wa-deing-tha (Pali, Tāvatiṁsa) heaven on the third day, his return marking the beginning of the New Year. According to another myth the Chief Thagya: once in the remote past engaged a *brahma deva* in debate, and both agreed to take the dispute to an earthly sage for arbitration with the understanding that the loser would forfeit his head. Thagya:, having been declared the winner, decapitated the *deva* and was immediately confronted with a problem: what to do with the head? Were he to bury it, the earth would dry up in a terrible drought; were he to cast it into the ocean, the waters would dry up. To forestall both calamities, he ordered seven goddesses to hold the head, in turn, each for a year. At the end of the year the goddess in charge washes it and passes it to the next goddess, and so on. The New Year begins when the head is passed from the old to the new goddess.

The first two days of the New Year celebration comprise the Burmese (and more generally the Southeast and South Asian) Water Festival. In village Burma people offer pots of cool water to their elders on these two days, and water is thrown in fun at all passersby. Both practices are interpreted, normatively, as washing away the dirt, physical and moral, accumulated during the year. In the cities, the water throwing is much more elaborate. Stalls are erected throughout the city from which passersby are inundated with water, either from pails or from hoses. Trucks loaded with teen-agers cruise the streets pouring water on all pedestrians. An integral part of the frivolity is the series of insulting remarks leveled by the water-throwers, not only at their victims, but at public figures: politicians, officials, businessmen, and so on.[18] Both sexes seize this opportunity to douse each other, and the physical and verbal encounters that accompany the dousing border (from the Burmese point of view) on the obscene. In general, the clowning, the disrespect for authority, the aggression, the transvestism, the sexual banter—and more recently, the rowdy and drunken behavior (cf. *The* [Rangoon] *Guardian,* April 17, 1962)—mark the urban celebration of the Water Festival as singularly un-Buddhist in tone and character.

While all this is taking place on the streets, the elderly and the pious are often found in the monasteries and pagodas, where they may be observing a three-day Sabbath. On the third day of the festival—the New Year proper—the boisterous celebrants, both urban and rural, abandon the carnivallike carrying-on of the festival and turn, like their elders, to the more Buddhist-seeming behavior of the New Year. After the traditional washing of the hair, young and old alike engage in various meritorious activities: they worship at a pagoda, observe the precepts at the village monastery, make offerings to monks, and offer gifts and obeisance to older relatives and to the aged in general. Many, too, acquire merit by freeing animals and fish. The latter are caught and placed in special ponds where fishing is prohibited; the former are purchased and transferred to special animal enclosures where they are fed and cared for until they die. In Yeigyi every villager, almost without exception, observes the New Year as a Sabbath day.

Buddha Day

The full moon of May *(Kahsoung)* is commemorated as the day on which all Buddhas attain Enlightenment and on which the present Buddha, Gautama, was born, attained Enlightenment, and died. In addition to the central ritual of any Sabbath—the observance of the precepts—the day is marked by watering the bo tree, the tree under which Enlightenment came to the Buddha. As at the New Year, merit is also acquired by capturing fish in the dwindling ponds and lakes, for this is the very end of the dry season, in which many lakes and riverbeds dry up, and releasing them in fresh water.

[18]Although officials are criticized and derided, and may even have water gently poured on them, they are never handled in Burma as they are in Laos, where according to Halpern (1958:121) even provincial governors may be pitched into the Mekong during the festival.

Strangely enough, Buddha Day, despite its important mythological associations, is not one of the popular festivals in Burma. In the villages it comes at the beginning of the agricultural season, and few villagers find time to take part in its various observances. Not having witnessed its celebration in the cities, I cannot be sure of its popularity outside the village. From the small amount of newspaper space devoted to it (compared to the much greater coverage given to other festivals) I would guess that in the cities, too, it is not one of the more popular holydays.

Lent and the Inception of Lent

The three-month period from the full moon of July *(Wa-zou)* through the full moon of October *(Thadin:jut)* might be called the Buddhist Lent (Burmese, *wa*; Pali, *vassa*). In addition to its monastic importance—monks may not travel for that period—it is a solemn season for laymen. Marriages cannot be performed, plays and other forms of public entertainment are forbidden, and pious Buddhists attempt to observe the Sabbath as frequently as possible during this time. Together, therefore, with the New Year, the full moons that mark the beginning and the end of Lent are occasions for the two most important holydays in the Buddhist calendar.

The religious significance of *Wa-zou* (the Burmese use the names of their months as names for some of their holydays) is enhanced by the fact that it marks the beginning, not only of Lent, but of two seasons: the rice production and monsoon seasons. The villagers have passed from an economically slow to an intensely busy period, planting and transplanting rice; and the climate has changed from the oppressive heat and drought of the dry season to the welcome rain and relative coolness of the monsoons.

Unlike ordinary Sabbaths and most other holydays, which are celebrated by individuals or by families, *Wa-zou* is celebrated by the village as a corporate entity. The village transforms itself, as it were, from a secular residential settlement into a sacred Buddhist congregation. Various task groups, elected by the village, are activated at this time to perform the variegated tasks necessary for the celebration. Food must be prepared, offerings for the monks must be collected, the village orchestra must be brought together for rehearsal, and so on. If, as I shall argue below, one of the main functions of a Burmese village is the performance of collective activities that promote individual salvation (especially those related to the maintenance of a monastery and its monks), this function is never more evident than on *Wa-zou.*

On *Wa-zou* eve a procession, accompanied by the village orchestra, proceeds from the village square to the resthouse adjacent to the village monastery. The celebration takes place in the resthouse-turned-chapel. In the procession the men carry to the resthouse the various offerings that are to be given to the monks on the next day. There they are arranged. On the morning of *Wa-zou* the meal that from early hours has been prepared for the monks by another male task group is placed on the table at which they are to eat. Families begin arriving at the resthouse at sunrise; as they arrive the men eat their breakfast, sitting around the huge pots in which food has been prepared by still another task group, the "bachelors' association." Seated at a table to greet the arrivals is the secretary of the arrangements committee, who records each contribution, both in money and in kind, made by each family to the collective offering for the monks. In addition, some families make personal contributions to their favorite monks.

Two lotteries take place as part of the total ceremony. Prior to *Wa-zou*, a lottery is held for the laymen to determine who shall use the gilded begging bowl, owned by the village and used only on *Wa-zou*, for making his offering to the monks. This is a highly cherished prize.[19] On the day of the festival, a lottery is held for the monks to determine the distribution of the collective offerings. Were this not done, favorite monks would receive the bulk of the donations. Eleven monks, from the three village monasteries and the neighboring forest hermitages, were invited to the ceremony the year of my study. Each monk receives a ticket with the name of a donor written on it. When his ticket is called out by the master of ceremonies, the monk, followed by the student or novice who will carry his offerings, walks through the two rows of kneeling laymen to the table where they are displayed and receives his tray of alms. The trays are laden with food, money, toiletries, and other items of personal use. As the monks in turn walk solemnly to the table, the congregation, in contrast, is surprisingly informal—talking, joking, witty, gay. On receiving their offerings the monks leave the resthouse and, except for the senior monk present, return to their respective monasteries.

This part of the ceremony completed, the senior monk (monastic seniority is determined by the number of successive Lents spent in the robe) leads the congregation in the recitation of the precepts. Those who have to work that day, and who therefore cannot fast, do not take the precepts. For this part of the ceremony, the men sit in front, the women behind. The men squat on their heels, hands together raised to the forehead; the women sit with their legs folded behind them, hands together resting on the chest. Following the recitation of the precepts, the monk delivers a sermon. Typically, these sermons both exhort the people to observe an austere Lent and emphasize the rewards for liberality in giving. As they listen—the women more attentively than the men—many of the congregants click their beads. Following the sermon, some of the prayers described in the daily prayer service are chanted responsively, always including the Confession of Faith. In fifteen minutes the ceremony is completed.

Except for the gaiety which marks the distribution of alms, the congre-

[19]In gratitude for winning this prize the year in which I conducted my study, U Thein, a wealthy landowner, promised to defray the expenses of the loudspeaker. An invariable part of every public ceremony and festival, the loudspeaker is used to play popular Burmese music —the louder the better being the prevailing sentiment.

gation (as on all Buddhist holydays) is restrained. It is, as I noted in my diary, a bland group, displaying no special fervor or religious emotion. It is also an informal one. Young babies are nursed by their mothers at any time during the service; older children run about and talk or play with impunity. They are too young, it is claimed, to understand the meaning of the holyday, and their informal behavior bothers no one; so why shouldn't they do what they like?

At the conclusion of the service, the congregation is dispersed. Those who are not observing the precepts return to their fields—primarily the young men in their twenties and thirties. The others, the women and older men whose sons or sons-in-law care for their fields, proceed to a variety of pious activities. Some spend the day in their favorite monastery in the village. Others go to one of the two forest hermitages whose monks are regularly supported by the village. Still others proceed to a famous pilgrimage center about two miles away, which (like most such centers) is a hill covered with pagodas and monasteries whose resident monks are especially known for their meditation. (Meditating monks choose such remote places precisely because they can live without being interrupted by laymen, except on those special holydays and Sabbaths when the faithful come to offer them alms.) On their ascent to the top, the pilgrims stop at each pagoda and at each Buddha image; after saying their beads, while silently intoning one of the ritual formulae, they move on to the next one. Arriving at the top of the hill, they spend the rest of the day in one of the two monasteries at the summit, returning to the village before sunset.

In general, the village is a relatively austere place during the three-month Lent, and characterized by an obvious quickening of religious activity. First, more time is spent in private daily devotions and in the saying of beads. Second, attendance at evening chapel about doubles during this period. Third, an attempt is made to observe at least one or two Sabbaths during the Lenten period. Fourth, women cook food to be offered to the Buddha. Fifth, and related to this, on every Sabbath eve *(ahpeiknei.)* the village sodality *(ayoung:do)* walks in formal procession through the village, collecting food and cash offerings to be used for its various religious undertakings (the upkeep of the chapel, the purchase of utensils used in the preparation of religious feasts, and so on). The food is offered to the Buddha on the Sabbath day, after which it is distributed among the children and the poor. The procession of the sodality is a solemn one. Preceded by a sounding gong and led by its officials, who are dressed in white shirts and sarongs, the group marches to a measured beat through the village. Each time the gong is sounded the leader chants, "For giving *dāna,* one becomes rich; for morality, one achieves coolness of mind; for meditation, one reaches nirvana."

The Lenten period, finally, is the favorite season for representatives of outside organizations to solicit donations in the village. They come from other villages, from Mandalay, and from other towns as far as fifty miles away. Contributions are solicited for the construction of a monastery, the restoration of a pagoda, the replacement of a monastery roof, and so on. Money is exchanged for talk; almost always the emissary is a former monk who is only too happy to offer a learned discourse on the "nine meanings of *dāna*" or the "four kinds of sacrifice," or the "twelve types of renunciation," etc. In addition, these emissaries are important media through which the villagers receive news from the outside world and establish a network with other villages.

The First Festival of Lights

Coming at the end of the monsoons, the full moon of October *(Thadin:-jut)* is one of the three specially sacred days in the Buddhist calendar, together with the New Year and the inception of Lent. For the Burmese, this day, which signals release from a three-month period of mild abstention, commemorates the descent of the Buddha from the *Tāvatiṁsa* heaven. The myth has it that a few years after attaining Enlightenment, the Buddha ascended to heaven on the full moon of *Wa-zou,* where he spent the entire Lent expounding the intricacies of Buddhist metaphysics and ontology *(abhidhamma)* to the gods, and especially to his mother. Completing his discourses at the end of Lent, he descended to the earth on *Thadin:jut,* preceded by myriads of heavenly torches which lit his way. This, of course, is the mythological charter for the lights. Special oil lamps are burned before Buddha images and Buddhist shrines. Oil lamps and candles are lit in the house. Oil lamps are placed at the base and at each of the succeeding levels of a pagoda, so that the entire structure is outlined in light. In the cities, the same end is accomplished by circling the pagoda with electric bulbs. As in the Christian West, however, lighting displays are not restricted to the home or to holy places. In the cities, both private and public buildings are illuminated with candles and electric bulbs. In Mandalay, for example, Mandalay Hill and the former palace walls are ablaze with lights.

Like the New Year, the Festival of Lights lasts for three days. On the first day, as on New Year and the beginning of Lent, elders—parents and relatives—are "worshiped." After presenting a parent, an uncle, a grandparent, and so on with food or clothes, the donor makes obeisance to him and asks for his blessing: "If at any time I have wronged you, either in word or in deed, please forgive me." The elder responds by wishing the donor health, wealth, and long life.

On the eve of the first day of the festival, the men are busy in the monastic compound and resthouse. As on the inception of Lent, *Thadin:jut* is observed by the village as a corporate unit. In addition to individual contributions, public funds are solicited for the corporate observance of the day: for the cooking of the festive meal for the monks, the offering of other alms, and the observance of the precepts. Gathering at the resthouse, the village "bachelors' association" works long into the night preparing the food that is to be offered to the monks—thirty monks were invited the year of my study—and to the Buddha. Some of the men sleep in the resthouse, for the food is ritually presented to the Buddha at 4:00 A.M.

On the following day, the full-moon day, the congregation assembles in the resthouse for the distribution of alms to the invited monks, a distribution again determined by lot. Again the monks walk through rows of kneeling women to the far end of the resthouse, where they receive their trays filled with cigarettes, cheroots, matches, soap, towels, fruit, and money. Although they walk on a path of mats, many women spread towels before them—so that their feet need not touch even the mats—and after they have walked by, the women touch their own bodies with the towels, as if to absorb the monks' mana. For the same reason, when the women offer the trays filled with alms to the monks, they touch the latters' robes with the trays before handing them to the students who will carry them.

After the precepts are received, the ceremony is ended, and the people observe the day in the same manner as described for the beginning of Lent.

For many villagers the third day of *Thadin:jut* is the most exciting, for that is when they travel to Mandalay to participate in one of its numerous pagoda festivals, described below.

The Robe-Offering Ceremony

During the one-month period from the first waning of *Thadin:jut* to the full moon of the month of *Tazaung-moun* (November), the Burmese are busy with the celebration of *kahteing* (Pali, *kathina*) ceremonies. Scripturally based, this ceremony consists of the public offering of yellow robes to the monks. Needless to say, these and all other public offerings are accompanied by a large feast for the monks *(hsun:jwei)*. Although individual monks are supplied with robes throughout the year by the faithful, those offered during this season fall into a special category: they are given collectively rather than individually, and they are offered to an entire chapter of monks rather than to an individual monk. The ritual importance of the robe ceremony for the monks is discussed below (chapter 12); here I am concerned with its significance for the layman.

The Burmese believe that special merit attaches to the offering of a *kahteing* robe—merit which leads, variously, to respect from men and gods, wealth, physical beauty, power, influence, long life, health, and so on. In their sermons which accompany the robe-offering ceremony, monks invariably expatiate on these rewards. Because of their fidelity in performing this ceremony, so a village monk announced, the people of Mandalay were able to repair the destruction which followed in the wake of World War II. For the same reason, so another monk promised, those who continue to participate in the ceremony will enjoy wealth, wisdom, beauty, health, and strength in all their future lives, and will eventually attain nirvana. If, according to a third monk, the participants in a robe ceremony are reborn in heaven, they will enjoy unheard of pleasures. They will wear beautiful and precious garments. Females will require no makeup, since in heaven they are naturally beautiful. Their life span will be indefinitely long. They will be free of greed and anger. And so on.

Although originally conceived as a robe-offering ceremony exclusively, the robe ceremony has become an occasion for providing the monks with all their needs and wants: canned food, medicine, umbrellas, begging bowls, toiletries, tobacco, blankets, money. Rather than being offered in the usual manner, in begging bowls or on trays, they are hung from, or placed under, an artificial "tree"—a wooden structure in the form of a Christmas tree. Known as the *padei-tha* (Pali, *padesa*) *bin*, this "wishing tree," as it is called, is reminiscent of the trees found in the mythical Southern Island which, according to Buddhist cosmology, supply its inhabitants with all their wants merely for the plucking. (Cf. Sarkisyanz 1965:88-90.) A typical expression of the display emphasis in Burmese culture, the *kahteing* gifts (purchased from public contributions) are hung from the wishing tree before the faithful arrive for the ceremony and remain on display for the entire day. In electrified villages and towns, offerings and tree are displayed on the eve of the ceremony and remain under floodlights for the entire evening. The names of the donors, usually, are conspicuously displayed. The dimensions of the wishing tree and the wealth it represents in consumers' goods depend on the size of the participating group. Thus, I have seen small robe ceremonies performed for one village monastery, large ones for the monks of an entire township, including fifty villages, and mammoth ceremonies—sponsored by wealthy businessmen, factories, government offices—for the monks of a ward in Mandalay.

The township robe ceremony, to take but one example, cost close to K10,000 (more than $2,000), the funds being raised by an assessment of about one *kyat* from each villager. A monk from each of the sixty-four villages in the township was chosen by lot to participate in the ceremony. Each monk received donations whose value was approximately K150, and the wishing tree, drawn by lot, was worth K1500. Like all large celebrations of this kind, the ceremony took place in a collapsible structure *(pandal* or *mandat)*, modeled after the royal palace on earth and (supposedly) the divine palaces in heaven. The presents and the wishing tree were on display all day, the monks and then the lay participants were fed, the assembly received the precepts from the monks, and the presiding monk delivered appropriate homilies.

The *pièce de resistance* of this robe ceremony was the transport of the wishing tree to the monastery of the monk who had won the lottery. Although the journey by truck normally takes about forty-five minutes, this trip, because of the Burmese penchant for display, took three and a half hours. So that everyone along the route might see their act of merit, the committee in charge had the tree, laden with presents, placed upright on the truck. As if this were not enough, it was topped by the ritual finial, an "umbrella" *(hti:)* which, as the symbol of royalty, tops all pagodas, royal thrones, and other sacred objects. Extending horizontally from the tree were two large poles from which gifts of blankets were hung. The result, predictably, was chaos. In order to accommodate the truck and its cargo, telephone wires had to be loosened and restrung, branches of living trees all along the route were severed to make way, and so on. Not only was the countryside thereby despoiled as if a tank had lumbered through it, but most of the offerings were scratched, bent, torn, or destroyed by the end of the journey. When the truck finally arrived at the village, the tree had collapsed!

This one-truck procession was a minor affair compared to the *kahteing* parades in the towns. In Mandalay one may see processions extending for as many as two city blocks, of cars, jeeps, trucks, carts, bicycles, all carrying *kahteing* offerings on their way to a monastery. Typically the parade will wind through many streets on a circuitous route before reaching its destination. The prestige *(goung:)* acquired in this world may not be as significant as the merit *(ku.thou)* acquired for the next, but its immediacy is just as compelling, if not more so.

The Second Festival of Lights

On the full moon of November *(Tazaung-mon:)*, at the onset of the cool season, the Burmese celebrate a second festival of lights, *Tazaung-daing* ("pillar of light") when, as on *Thadin:jut*, pagodas are brilliantly illumined. *Tazaung-daing* marks the dramatic end of the *kahteing* season, for it is on this night that a special robe is prepared for offering to the monks. This is commemorative of the robe offered by His mother to the Buddha. When the latter was still a prince—so the myth tells us—His mother, a *deva* in the *Tāvatiṁsa* heaven, realized that her son would discard his royal garments on the very next day in order to become a mendicant monk. Wanting to be the first to provide him with the required robe, she stayed up all night weaving it, and next morning sent it to him by a heavenly messenger. It is in commemoration of this event that, on *Tazaung-daing*, village groups sit up all night stitching a robe to be offered to a monk. Beginning with the act of symbolically preparing the thread they continue through all the other processes, until the robe is completed. This robe, the *mathou:thin-gan:*, is especially precious and especially meritorious. If the task is too burdensome, many families together prepare instead a smaller robe to be draped around a Buddha image—either a small image in their family shrine or a larger one in a pagoda or monastery.[20]

[20]Reported as late as the second decade in this century, but (so far as I can tell) no longer practiced, *Tazaung-daing* was the occasion for the Burmese "Thieves' Night." On the eve of the festival, both in Upper (Brown 1914) and Lower (Than Maung 1915) Burma, people would play pranks on each other, removing furniture and other domestic belongings of neighbors and depositing them at varying distances from the house. As Brown describes the situa-

The Full Moon of February (Tabou.dwe:)

For reasons which are obscure to the villagers, special offerings are made to the Buddha on this Sabbath day. Many villagers travel to Mandalay to celebrate the holyday at one of its famous pagodas. The special offering made on this day consists of pieces of scented wood which are lit and placed before the Buddha images in the pagoda compound. The villagers say that, since this Sabbath occurs during the cold season, the wood is lit to give warmth to the Buddha, commemorating those occasions during his life when he warmed his hands at a fire.

Pagoda Festivals

In addition to holydays which commemorate some event in the life of the Buddha, the Burmese religious calendar is marked by a cycle of pagoda festivals which commemorate the founding of a pagoda. Unlike those described above, these festivals do not occur on a Sabbath—hence their festive mood is not constrained by the observance of the precepts, and their celebration always takes place only at a particular pagoda. In the villages of Upper Burma in which I worked, almost everyone attends at least one pagoda festival annually—in Mandalay, in Monywa (a town about forty miles distant), in Kyaukse (a town about the same distance) and in the village of Shweizayan. In Yeigyi, forty-three of the fifty households sampled attend two or more pagoda festivals a year; the remaining seven attend only one.

Pagoda festivals not only do not fall on Sabbath days, but are different both in tone and in quality from Buddhist holydays. Indeed, it would be wrong to assume that the most important, let alone the exclusive, motive for participation in a pagoda festival is "religious"; motivation aside, there are important extrareligious consequences attendant on participation. Pagoda festivals are gay, colorful events. After paying homage to the Buddha, which requires no more than a few minutes, the participants spend their time (and money) making purchases in the temporary bazaar, eating at the food shops, attending dramatic performances, etc. Indeed, the pagoda festival has many of the attributes of a county fair, and as such brings a welcome surcease, not only from labor but from the monotonous routine of village life. The social and political features of these occasions, which also contribute to their spirit, are discussed in another context.

Perhaps one example will suffice to give the flavor of these festivals. The pagoda festival of the remote village of Shweizayan is held in March. According to the legend that serves as its charter, King Anawrahtha, founder of the Pagan dynasty, was married to a Shan princess whom he divorced and banished from Pagan because his courtiers accused her of

---

tion in Mandalay, roads were rendered impassable because piled high with purloined furniture.

being a witch. Although their accusation was based on the fact that her earring shone as brightly as fire, the real reason for its extraordinary brightness was that it contained a relic of the Buddha. After her banishment the erstwhile queen, Sawmunhla, began her long return journey to the Shan country. When she came to what is now the village of Shweizayan, her earring fell into the Myitnge River, which it borders. Although it shone through the water, none of the men who dived into the river to retrieve it were able to seize it. Then, looking into the sky, Sawmunhla saw the earring suspended in midair, surrounded by singing birds. For this miracle she did obeisance to the earring, whereupon it descended, and she ordered that it be enshrined in a pagoda which she constructed on that spot.[21]

The special sanctity of this pagoda is apparent even today. Although thousands of pilgrims pass through grounds during the six-day festival, there is no need—so the villagers insisted—to clean up the rubbish left in their wake, for the *nat* spirits perform this task for them. It is further alleged that even animals, recognizing the sanctity of the pagoda, come to worship the Buddha on this festival.

Arriving at the pagoda grounds, the pilgrim buys flowers at the large bazaar set up next to the village, places them in a jar at the pagoda, and after a few minutes of worship, spends the rest of the day roaming about the bazaar, eating, gossiping, and so on, before performing yet another ritual. Hiring a boat, he and his friends travel down-river for about half an hour to a hooded-serpent *(naga:youn)* pagoda. Its name derives from the form of its seated Buddha image which, resting in an opening inside the pagoda, depicts him as protected by a hooded cobra who, as it were, forms an umbrella over him. Such pagodas, as we shall see below (chapter 11), are believed to have special magical power against snake bites. The devotee purchases flowers at the pagoda, which he hands to a male attendant, who places them against the image and in exchange gives the devotee a bouquet from among the flowers already piled up there. Deriving mana from the image, these flowers are later used for both therapeutic and prophylactic purposes.[22] If they are tied about the wrist, the wearer is protected from snake bites; if a victim of a snake bite drinks from the water in which the flowers have been immersed, he is cured of the bite.

Typically, after worshiping at this pagoda, the pilgrim tarries a while to eat and gossip. He returns to Shweizayan by way of still another pagoda,

[21]This is the version I obtained at Shweizayan. For a somewhat different but more detailed "official" version, see Tin and Luce (1923:83-85).

[22]This technique is identical with that used in Burmese spirit *(nat)* worship. At the famous Taungbyon *nat* festival, the devotee offers leaves of the eugenia tree to the female attendant of the *nat* image (the attendant at a pagoda is always male), who places them against the image and in exchange gives him a sprig of leaves from the pile already touching it. These leaves provide him with protection against punitive *nat* and other evil supernaturals.

where he does obeisance to an image of the former queen which stands in the pagoda compound.

On one level, the pagoda festival *(hpaya: pwe:)* is very similar to a *nat* festival *(nat pwe:).*[23] In addition to the ceremonial offerings to the images (in the one case to the Buddha, in the other to the *nat*), both have the same extracultic features: the temporary bazaar, the feasting, the sideshows, and so on. There are, however, two important differences. *Nat* propitiation tends to be frenetic, frenzied, Dionysian; Buddhist devotions are subdued, restrained, Appollonian. A similar contrast holds for the extracultic behavior at the respective festivals. *Nat* festivals are often disrupted by rowdiness and by drunken and obscene behavior which, for all its country-fair atmosphere, would be unheard of at a pagoda festival.

Still, participation in pagoda festivals is based, as we have seen, on important social, material, and recreational motives. And indeed, for many people these may supersede in importance their religious motives. It is no accident that, in a survey of Burmese converts to Christianity, it was found that what they missed the most in their new religion was the "festive and social element [of Buddhism] . . . the show and noise, the excitement of Buddhistic social functions." (Purser and Saunders 1914:52) This is true not only of pagoda festivals, but of the Buddhist holydays (described above) as well. The Burmese are fully aware of the multiplicity of motives which lie behind festival and holyday behavior; indeed they distinguish three typical motives for cult *(ba-tha)* behavior in Buddhism. The first type is *Boukta* (Buddha) *ba-tha,* in which the motive for the celebration of the holyday or festival is to follow the teachings of the Buddha. The second is *Myam-ma* (Burma) *ba-tha,* in which the motive is to follow the customs of Burma, to conform with the general community norms. One celebrates, so to speak, because it is the thing to do. The third type is *apyo* (enjoyment) *ba-tha.* Here, the motive is the pleasure to be derived from the orchestra, the bazaar, the theater, the conviviality, and so on. My bilingual Burmese assistant coined the following terms, respectively, for these three motives: *Buddhism, Burmanism,* and *joyism.* According to informants in Yeigyi, their rank order is Burmanism, joyism, Buddhism. But in my opinion very few if any Burmans exemplify these types in pure form. Most, if not all, are admixtures of all three, and they vary considerably in the relative proportions of the mix.

[23]For a description of some *nat* festivals, see Spiro 1967: ch. 7.

CHAPTER 10

The Ceremonial Cycle: II. Life-Cycle Rituals

Introduction

Canonically, Buddhism is not at all involved in the changes of status that sociologically mark the individual's passage through the life cycle. Although contemporary Buddhism pays greater attention to these points of transition, it too has less involvement in them than is characteristic of other religions. Except for the Buddhist initiation rite (for adolescent boys) and certain death ceremonies, Buddhism is only peripherally concerned with the life cycle. It is not that birth, marriage, and so on, are not marked in Burma and other Buddhist societies by rites of passage; they most certainly are. In Burma, as we shall see, thirteen nonrecurrent events in the life cycle have been selected for ritual treatment. It is rather that for the most part these rites are not Buddhist; they are not sacralized by Buddhism. This is a most curious phenomenon. One of the few generalizations that can be made about religion—one that takes in the primitive as well as the great world religions—is that it is involved in the crises that mark the career of the individual from birth to death. It is difficult to understand why Buddhism should constitute such a notable—perhaps a singular—exception to this generalization. The usual explanations offered for the indifference of Buddhism to these events are, first, that as an otherworldly religion it is unconcerned with worldly matters, and second, that there is no canonical basis for their ceremonial observance.

Neither explanation is convincing. Most of the calendrical festivals described in the last chapter are noncanonical, as well as the Buddhist initiation, the most important ceremony in Burmese Buddhism, which moreover probably originated as a non-Buddhist ceremony. Similarly, the argument that life-cycle ceremonies are outside the purview of an otherworldly religion can be countered with the observation that the worldly orientations of many of the Buddhist calendrical ceremonies did not prevent them from receiving the stamp of Buddhism. Moreover, the life-cycle ceremonies can as easily be provided with an otherworldly message as the former. If it is then argued that the ceremonies of the calendrical cycle are communal while those of the life cycle are private, it must be said that the Buddhist initiation ceremony violates the implication of this generalization. Or, if it is argued that life-cycle ceremonies are "magical," while Buddhism eschews magic, the vast domain of magical Buddhism (described in the next chapter) must then be explained. In short, I know of no satisfactory answer to this question, and having said so, can only move on.

As already mentioned, there are thirteen nonrecurrent rites of passage in Burma. Twelve of these consist of what the Burmese term "meritorious" or "auspicious" *(min-gala)* ceremonies. (The thirteenth is the funeral ceremony.) Of these twelve, eight occur in infancy, one in childhood, two in early adolescence (one for males and one for females), and one in late adolescence. Only one of the twelve is Buddhist. Five, although non-Buddhist, contain peripheral Buddhist elements, and seven are entirely devoid of Buddhist content. Almost all of them, on the other hand, include the propitiation of *nat.*

1. The pregnancy ceremony, for the safety of mother and child, has no Buddhist elements. It is not, incidentally, held in Yeigyi.

2. The birth ceremony, performed during labor, assures the mother of an easy and safe delivery. Sometimes, if the delivery is especially difficult, monks are requested to recite *paritta.*

3. The head-washing ceremony is held a few days after the birth of the child. It has no Buddhist elements.

4. The hair-shaving ceremony, celebrated about a month after birth, is not observed in Yeigyi. It involves no Buddhist elements.

5. The cradle ceremony, which occurs when the infant is placed in a new cradle, is performed at any time from the second to the twelfth month after birth. Prior to the ceremony, but not as an integral part of it, the parents may invite one or more monks to their home for a special feast. When this happens one of the monks—as is the practice in Burma—offers a short homily to the assembled guests.

6. The naming ceremony, often observed at the same time as the cradle ceremony, is performed during the child's early months. There are no Buddhist elements involved.

7. The cloth-wearing ceremony is not observed in Yeigyi; it, too, includes no Buddhist elements.

8. The rice-feeding ceremony is held when the infant, a month or two after birth, is first fed cooked rice. Since it is given three mouthfuls of cooked rice, some informants infuse this part of the ceremony with Buddhist symbolism: the three mouthfuls, they say, symbolize the Three Gems—the Buddha, the Law, and the Order.

9. The ear-boring ceremony, for girls, is almost always performed at the

same time as the *shin-byu*, the male adolescent initiation ceremony, and will be discussed with it. In itself it contains no Buddhist elements.

10. The hair-tying ceremony, for boys, also takes place (at least in the villages) as part of the male initiation. It contains no Buddhist elements.

11. The male adolescent initiation is definitely Buddhist—indeed probably the most important of all Buddhist ceremonies. Described below.

12. The marriage ceremony is entirely secular. In itself it contains no Buddhist elements. On the morning of the wedding day, however, monks are invited to the home of the bride, where they are offered a special feast. Usually, but not always, they are asked to recite *paritta* to protect the prospective bride and groom from danger. The monks return to their monasteries before the marriage ceremony begins: they do not even witness the ceremony, let alone take part in it.

With the exception, then, of the male initiation ceremony, none of the other "auspicious" ceremonies of the Burmese life cycle is Buddhist. In addition to these ceremonies, however, the Burmese perform two other rites of passage, and they do include important Buddhist elements. These are the house-construction and funeral ceremonies. The former being very brief, the initiation and funeral ceremonies alone will occupy our attention in this chapter.

Buddhist Initiation

The young boy's Buddhist initiation is by far the most important of all Burmese Buddhist ceremonies.[1] Any ceremony by which merit is acquired is called an *ahlu* (lit., "offering") and, say the Burmese, "Of all *ahlus*, the most important is the Buddhist initiation." Indeed, when *ahlu* is used without a qualifier or contextual designation, it always refers to the Buddhist initiation, the *shin-byu*.

In the initiation the young boy—normatively the ceremony is held when the boy reaches puberty—is temporarily inducted as a novice into the Buddhist monkhood. Almost without exception, every Burmese male has this nuclear and prototypical Buddhist experience of abandoning the world and donning the yellow robe. (In Yeigyi only three adults had not gone through this experience.) Although with the exception of Ceylon, where it seems to be a much less frequent occurrence, the custom of spending some time in the robes is widespread in all *Theravāda* societies, in Burma alone has it been elaborated into the complex ceremony described below. And in Burma alone has this custom been transmuted into a ritual drama with all the overtones of true initiation; in Burma alone it has become *the* central

[1]Many of its components, however, which are now interpreted as symbolic of various themata of the Buddhist myth, according to Htin Aung (1962: ch. 8) are neither Buddhist nor religious in their origin.

Buddhist ceremony; in Burma alone the boy's temporary ordination as a novice is celebrated with much more pomp than the man's ordination as an intended permanent monk. Although this contrast between Burma and the other Buddhist societies of Southeast Asia has not been commented on, it is surely one of the most intriguing, yet unresolved, problems in the comparative study of Buddhism.

Although the initiation is usually celebrated when the boy reaches puberty, in fact the age at which this ceremony is performed varies widely. In a sample of sixty adult males in Yeigyi the range was from two to eighteen years, the mean age being eleven. The contemporary situation is somewhat different. Thus in a sample of twenty-four students at the township school, the oldest age for the *shin-byu* was twelve. The upper age limit is usually a function of poverty: poor families require many years to save the requisite capital for the ceremony, and indeed some may never be able to do so. The three men in Yeigyi who had never had a *shin-byu* came from such poor families. The lower limit may be caused by a number of factors. If the family is wealthy, it may decide to perform two initiations, one at an early, one at a later age. Sometimes the early age is determined rather by the fact that the boy's sister has reached the appropriate age for the ear-boring ceremony; and since the two are always held conjointly, the brother may have an early initiation so that his sister's ceremony—without which she cannot be married—is not unduly delayed.

The religious significance of the *shin-byu* is both symbolic and instrumental. Symbolically, it denotes the passage of the boy from the status of a biosocial being to that of a spiritual person. No Burmese male is truly human—not to mention Buddhist—unless he has worn the yellow robe. Indeed, for the period in which he is in the robe, the boy—like the fully ordained monk—is not an ordinary human *(lu);* rather he is a "Son of the Buddha." Hence, although the spiritual inferior of a fully ordained monk, he is the spiritual superior of all secular human beings. As a secular being he is by virtue of his youth subordinate in status to all his seniors in the age-graded, hierarchical Burmese social structure. When he dons the yellow robe, this status hierarchy is reversed: he is now their superior. This reversal of status is symbolized by a dramatic reversal in roles. Thus, prior to the initiation ceremony, the boy acknowledges the superiority, for example, of his parents by the act of physical prostration. After he puts on the yellow robe, however, his parents acknowledge the boy's superiority by prostrating themselves before him. For the outside observer it is a touching, albeit somewhat incongruous, thing to see a father prostrate himself reverently before his yellow-robed, five-year-old son.

Instrumentally, the initiation is the means par excellence for acquiring merit, not so much for the boy (though it goes without saying that he gains merit for his participation) as for the sponsors of the ceremony, typically his parents. "Among all types of *da-na.*," say the Burmese, "the promotion of Buddhism by means of the *shin-byu* is the noblest *da-na.*, " (Being the "noblest" *da-na.*, it confers the greatest amount of merit on its sponsor.) Hence the mutual responsibility: on the one hand, of every parent to see that his son is initiated, so that he may reap the rewards of Buddhist initiation; on the other, of every child to be initiated, so that his parents may reap the merit accruing from the sponsorship of the ceremony. By wearing the robe, the Burmese saying has it, the boy repays his mother for the milk he imbibed from only one of her breasts. It is because of the merit that the initiation confers on parents and son alike that, normatively, the boy is expected to spend a minimum of three Lents in the robe: one for his mother, one for his father, and one for himself.[2] As we shall see below, however, few initiates comply with this expectation.

The merit gained through sponsoring an initiation is so great that wealthy Burmans will frequently sponsor more than one: in addition to their son's, they will sponsor the initiation of a boy whose parents cannot afford the very heavy expense which the ceremony entails. Similarly, a couple with no sons of their own will sponsor the initiation of a relative's second or third son. (The relative, having already acquired the merit from one initiation, cannot refuse the request.) Sometimes, too, a boy may undergo more than one initiation, so that a relative without sons may acquire merit from the sponsorship. (Similar customs are found in Thailand. Cf. Rajadhon 1961:-68.)

The great concern over the sponsorship of a *shin-byu*, although the Burmese do not put it this way, gives one the impression that the merit is not only quantitatively larger, but somehow qualitatively different from other kinds of merit. It is as if the merit derived from the initiation had no functional equivalent; no matter how much one may accumulate by other means, one must nevertheless acquire this *type* of merit as well. Just as a boy is not a Buddhist until he has been the recipient of the *shin-byu*, an adult, it seems, is not a Buddhist until he has sponsored one. This sentiment appears implicit in Hla Maung's peculiar remark that Burmese parents "cannot afford to die" without performing the *shin-byu*. (Hla Maung, n.d.:14) This sense of urgency impels some parents to perform a token initiation for their infant son at the time of the naming ceremony. He is wrapped in a piece of yellow cloth, lest he or they die before he reaches the age of a regular initiation.

Although the initiation ceremony can be held at any time during the

[2]Similar notions are found in other *Theravāda* societies. Thus in Cambodia a young man enters the novitiate "in honor of his mother's care" and the monkhood "in honor of his father's care." (Lévy 1957:4) In both cases, merit accrues to his parents. In Thailand, where the same belief is found, the merit acquired from a son's novitiate can save his mother from hell; that acquired from a son's monkhood can save his father from hell. (Rajadhon 1961:68)

year, it is typically performed in the interval after the harvest and before Lent. There are at least two reasons, religious and secular, for preferring this time. First, by holding the ceremony during this season, the probability of the boy's remaining for the minimally expected duration of one Lent is enhanced. Second, the *shin-byu* is a most costly occasion, and by holding it after the harvest the family will have a chance to accumulate some capital from the sale of the year's rice crop. The specific date, of course, is determined by its astrological auspiciousness. In general, villagers in Upper Burma consult their monk for the calculation of auspicious dates, while in Mandalay Hindu astrologers *(pon-nas)* are consulted.

A few weeks before the initiation, printed invitations are sent to relatives, friends, and acquaintances. Since frequently they are distributed among seven or eight or more villages and towns as well as in Mandalay, the initiation provides an opportunity for persons from widely scattered areas and diverse social backgrounds to participate in a common ritual. The ceremony in itself does not require the presence of a large group—indeed, requires no group at all—so the large guest list is a function of the fact that *secular* success is directly related to the size of the participating group. The size of the group is also important economically because each guest helps to offset the cost of the ceremony by offering a cash contribution to the sponsor; and generally his contribution is larger than the cost of feeding and entertaining him.

Initiation invitations, like wedding invitations in America, are fairly standard in form. Extended not only on behalf of the sponsoring couple but of their close relatives as well, they invariably stress that the sponsors *(ahlu daga)* will render offerings to the Buddha and the Order so that they may eventually attain nirvana, and that the ceremony for the sharing of (this) merit will be performed. In short, although the ceremony is in principle performed for the boy, the invitation stresses the almsgiving of the sponsor, *his* anticipated merit, and *his* intention of sharing his merit with others, as if he rather than the boy were the central actor of the drama.

This emphasis on the sponsor is consistent with the display aspect of the ceremony, which again redounds to the glory of the sponsor, not the initiate. I have noted that the initiation is a very expensive event. In Yeigyi, in which the average annual income per family was approximately K1,000, the cost of a *shin-byu* ranged from K200 to K5,000. These are staggering sums, not only in themselves, but in relation to the objective requirements of the ceremony: shaving the head of the initiate, his recitation of his faith in the Three Gems, his request of the monks that he be initiated as a novice, and his donning of the yellow robe. Since no Buddhist ceremony is conceivable without feeding at least a few monks, the total expense involved here, for purchase of the robe and feeding the monks, could hardly be more than K50. The difference, therefore, between K50 and K5,000 represents the outlay for nonessential elements, irrelevant to the initiation of the boy but crucial for the prestige—and to a lesser extent the merit—of the sponsor. For in general the amount of prestige *(goung:)* heaped up by the sponsor is (like the amount of merit) directly proportional to the money he spends. Since a modest ceremony, therefore, represents a loss of face, this explains why the Burmese are reluctant to undertake an initiation unless they can amass the sums required for these display aspects of the occasion. It also explains why it is that the sons of very poor parents are either not initiated (unable to afford the display, their parents are unwilling to lose face by performing a simple ceremony) or have their initiation sponsored by someone who can afford all the trimmings.

Without meaning, therefore, to minimize the religious aspect of the initiation—the Burmese, after all, are as much concerned with merit as they are with prestige—one can sympathize with the Yeigyi monk who complained that

> . . . today, people give a *shin-byu* only for prestige [this, in contrast to the past, when piety reigned!]. The initiate can scarcely recite the precepts properly, but yet there is a huge ceremony. The sponsors always want to have a huge *man-dat*, a dramatic performance, to spend lots of money. They do this only for the prestige, not out of religious conviction.

Although the basic structure of the initiation is identical throughout Burma, there are minor differences in its performance even from village to village. Differences are especially marked, as might be expected, in its display aspects. The following is a description of one initiation I observed in Yeigyi. Costing K4,000, it was more elaborate than a typical village ceremony in its display elements; K4,000 is not a typical outlay for a village initiation. Otherwise, however, it differs little from the other village ceremonies which I saw in the course of field work. (For comparison, cf. Htin Aung 1962: ch. 8; Nash 1965:124-31; Shway Yoe 1896: ch. 3.)

The total ceremony typically extends over a period of three days, and this one was no exception to the rule. On the day before the initiation itself, the imitation palace in which part of the ceremony takes place was completed, and an orchestra performed throughout the day.[3] The sponsor was performing the ceremony for his son, as well as for two sons of a younger and less affluent brother. On the morning of this first day, the three boys to be initiated were taken to the shrine of the village spirit, where offerings were made to ensure a peaceful occasion. If the spirits *(nat)* are not properly appeased, they may disrupt the ceremony.

On the morning of the second day, that of the initiation proper, all the

[3]The village "Protestants"—as my assistant called them—object to the orchestra on the grounds that it is Hindu, not Buddhist, in derivation.

monks in the village, and others invited from surrounding villages, were offered a special meal inside the palace. When the monks had eaten, the invited guests, numbering approximately two hundred, were fed. (A very large proportion of the expense of the ceremony is for the feeding of these large groups of monks and laymen.) As each group of diners completed their meal and thence proceeded to the *pandal*, their eyes would fall immediately on the boys to be initiated and the girls who were to have their ears bored, all of whom were seated on a raised platform.

The ear-boring ceremony *(natwin)*, performed only for girls, although historically unrelated to the Buddhist initiation is now inextricably associated with it and rarely performed without it, except in the case of the poorest families. Indeed, the two ceremonies are so deeply associated in the minds of the villagers that they say, "Without an ear-boring ceremony, there can be no *shin-byu.*" Typically, the girl's ear-boring is performed at her brother's initiation, but if she has no brother, or if their ages preclude the combination (the ear-boring is held for girls between roughly four and seven), then it is held in conjunction with the initiation of a cousin or some other relative.

The ear-boring itself is a simple thing—the lobe is pierced with a golden needle—and has no religious significance. It confers no merit either on the girl or on her sponsor. Being held in conjunction with the initiation, however, it does provide the girl with her moment of glory. Although eclipsed by the boy's greater importance, she nevertheless gets to sit on the platform with her brother, and like him wears the costume of royalty: she is dressed like a royal princess, he like a prince.

Whatever the origin of this court regalia, its contemporary interpretation invokes the imagery and symbols of the central Buddhist myth, which the initiation explicitly commemorates. Having found the pleasures of the court unsatisfying, Prince Siddhartha, it will be recalled, abandoned the royal palace and renounced the throne in order to seek Enlightenment as a wandering mendicant. In the initiation the young boy, like Siddhartha before him, is a royal prince—which is why the ceremony takes place in a palace—who in the course of the ceremony renounces the world and its pleasures for the robes of the mendicant monk. While still a prince, however, he enjoys the privileges of a prince. He sits on an elevated platform; he wears royal dress; in the procession through the village, as befits royalty he rides a horse while the guests walk; and again like royalty, he is shielded from the sun by a royal—i.e., white—umbrella.

To go back to the actual events of the day, when the guests completed their meal, they were entertained by a dancing "elephant"—four men, each fitting into one of the legs of a huge papier-mâché elephant—put through his paces by his trainer.

The entertainment ended, a procession was formed to accompany the young princes and princesses to the monastery, where offerings were taken to the monks and where the monastic requisites of the novices-to-be *(maung shin-laung:)*,[4] in anticipation of their renunciation of their princely status for that of mendicants, are deposited. The procession was led by village elders, carrying the offerings to the monastery; immediately following were the "village belles" *(kun:daung-kaing)*,[5] who carried betel boxes; they in turn were followed by the young "princes," their horses led by their attendants; following them and riding in a gaily decorated oxcart were the young "princesses." Bringing up the rear came the invited guests, the orchestra, and the elephant. The procession first proceeded to the monastery where the boys would reside as novices, then to the other two village monasteries in turn. At each, the members of the procession entered the main hall, where they made obeisance to the monk, recited the Buddhist precepts, and offered their gifts. Although the precepts are recited responsively, it was almost impossible to hear the litany above the orchestral music coming from the courtyard outside, whose blare drowned out everything else.

Having made the round of the monasteries, the procession returned to the palace. However, as the future novices attempted to enter, their passage was obstructed by a group of young men menacing them with long mallets in mock battle, who prevented them from entering until the sponsor of the initiation paid them a proper toll.[6]

[4]*Maung* is the most common epithet prefixed to the name of any young boy; *shin* is a novice; *alaung:* refers to the embryonic state in which anything is brought to incipient readiness for something.

[5]The betel box is a *kun:daung;* the girl who carries it to the monastery is the *kun:daung-kaing*. In every village there is at least one *kun:daung-kaing*—I have encountered as many as six. To qualify for the position, a girl must be single, chaste, between the ages of 18-21, and a village beauty. In addition both parents must be living. To be so chosen is a mark of great prestige.

[6]A variant in other initiations is for the young boy to be "kidnaped" while visiting the monastery, and not returned until he is ransomed. Either variant, seen as the blocking of a consummatory act, is structurally analogous to the Burmese wedding custom in which young men block the entrance of a newly married couple into their home until they are paid off.

This blocking of the ceremony is not restricted to Burma. An identical custom, though more highly elaborated, is also found in Cambodia, where, however, it occurs as part of the ordination for the monkhood. (For the analogous Thai ritual, see Wells 1960:140-41.) There, when the procession makes its way to the monastery, it is led by a mask-wearing group who represent the army of Māra, the Evil One. Having attempted to prevent the Prince Siddhartha from attaining Buddhahood, he now attempts to prevent the novice from entering the monastery. Unlike the case in Burma, however, Māra and his host are not bribed—the forces of evil cannot be bribed—but, as in the original myth, they are overcome by the superior spiritual power of the future monk. (Cf. Lévy 1957:8.)

Here, then, we have themes which, in the context of ritual, require theoretical exploration: the themes of interruption, prevention of consummation, and ransom or bribe as a condition for continuation to climax. This thematic sequence is found in other ritual traditions. One obvious example is the ritual interruption of the Jewish Passover Seder, in which the young boy who has "stolen" a piece of the ritual *matzo* prevents the ceremony from reaching its conclusion until his father agrees to pay a ransom.

Paid their toll, the obstructors removed themselves from the entrance to the palace, and the entire procession was free to go in. Spontaneously, however, two men accompanied by the orchestra performed solo dances highly reminiscent of the dancing at spirit festivals. (Cf. Spiro 1967:120-22.) Again, when the people had taken their places inside the palace, two women, quite spontaneously, were moved to do the same. Since I did not see this kind of free expression of emotion at any of the other initiations I attended, I was especially interested to observe it here. The fervor, zest, and sensuous feeling tone displayed in their dancing, rare enough in a secular Burmese context, is normally never seen in a Buddhist context. Indeed, the only other time I witnessed such intense affect was in the famous Taungbyon spirit festival (cf. *ibid.*:113 ff.). It was as if the emotions which had been controlled during the long agricultural season were suddenly released in these dancers by the festive situation. And their release seemed to be contagious; for suddenly, as the women were dancing, one felt the entire assembly being caught up in their excitement. It had so many of the overtones of bacchanalian temper, foreign to Buddhism but congenial to the *nat* religion, that one felt as if the two were struggling for domination before one's very eyes. At a signal, however, from the Master of Ceremony, the orchestra stopped playing and the dancers, responding to this cue, returned to their places exhausted.

Now that all was calm once again, the ritual inside the palace could begin. This, which for most Burmans is the core of the initiation, but which from a normative point of view is Buddhistically irrelevant, is conducted by a professional Master of Ceremony *(bi.theik hsaya).* With minor variations, the basic pattern of ritual is the same in all the initiations I attended. It is primarily a virtuoso performance by the Master of Ceremony, who for about two hours entertains the assembly with religious chants, secular songs, dialogues (both serious and humorous) with the orchestra leader, several short sermons, homilies, Buddhist legends and myths, and even off-color jokes. These are all woven into a dramatic fabric. Periodically, *shin-byu*-specific rites are performed. From the point of view of the audience, the success of the initiation is almost exclusively dependent upon the virtuosity of the Master of Ceremony.

For this part of the ceremony, the boy(s) and girl(s) to be initiated sit on a mat toward the middle of the palace. Seated on another mat opposite are their parents, sponsors, and relatives. The Master of Ceremony takes his place facing the center of this grouping (see FIG. 11); geometrically, then, he is at the apex of an equilateral triangle, in which the initiates occupy one end of the base and their family the other end. The orchestra is seated at one side of the palace behind the Master of Ceremony, and the seated guests surround the *dramatis personae* seated in the center. Thus:

FIG. 11

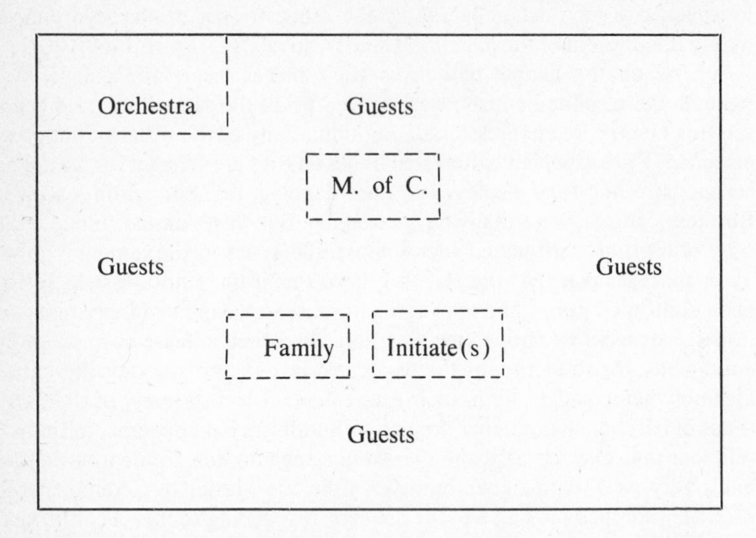

Since the initiate is still dressed in the costume of a royal prince, the ritual begins appropriately with the orchestra playing a tune which, in the days of the monarchy, heralded the arrival of the royal presence. When the music is ended the Master of Ceremony does obeisance, respectively, to the Buddha, his own Master, his parents, and all his teachers—to all those, that is, who "have helped me to become a good person." He then turns to the orchestra leader as if to engage him in dialogue.

In the actual ceremony described, he began his remarks by saying the Burmese people are a noble people because they know and believe in the Three Gems. He then announced his own bona fides by recounting first the biography of his Master and then his own biography. Having established his qualifications, he prepared the yarn which would later be placed around the necks of the initiates to serve as a talisman. While thus engaged, he announced that although he was not an accomplished Master of Ceremony, he was a fairly expert actor and would entertain them with a song. Describing the thirty-eight beatitudes *(min-gala)* he then sang the "Victory Song," accompanied by the orchestra.[7]

He then preached a short sermon. Usually, he said, sponsors of an

[7]This is the *Jaya Mangala Gāthā*, a medieval poem probably composed in Siam. It consists of eight stanzas, each recounting one of the eight famous conquests of the Buddha over Māra (the Evil One), Ālavaka (a child-devouring demon), Nālāgiri (an elephant who tried to kill Him), Angulimāla (a robber), Ciñca (who claimed He had seduced her), Saccaka (the false teacher), two demons (in the guise of serpents), and Baka (a Brahmin). (For a translation of some of these stanzas, see Slater 1951:127.)

initiation preferred that he tell them that in consequence of their sponsorship they would become wealthy. This might be, he admitted, but nevertheless it was only half the story. Like everyone else, they must guard against the four kinds of grasping,[8] including of course grasping after wealth. In order to escape from the tyranny of grasping, they should concentrate on the three truths of suffering, impermanence, and nonsoul. They should take as their model the example of a certain king, who, rather than accumulating wealth, gave it away in the form of charity. . . . In the olden days, nobody wanted to become a king; today the reverse is true. They did not want to become kings because they knew that they would then give little thought to the Three Gems, the Buddha *(Hpaya:)*, the Law, and the Order. Today *Hpaya:* is used indiscriminately; people not only use it to address the Buddha or the monk; they use it to address government officials and even the lowly Township Officer. . . . It is difficult to escape from the Wheel of Rebirth; therefore one should always pray for this Liberation.

With the completion of his sermon, he asked the orchestra to play an interlude. When they finished, he continued with his colloquy. Everyone wants to satisfy his five senses—to taste pleasant tastes, smell pleasant odors, listen to pleasant sounds, and so on. But it is in vain, for we must realize that whatever we see, whatever we hear, whatever we taste is created by our perceptions (i.e., essentially they are all illusions). . . . In the past everyone was pious; even women competed for knowledge of the Law. . . . It would be unfair, he said, to compare him with other masters of ceremony, because he is still a neophyte. He only recently became one and it takes a long time to become an expert.

It was now time to invite the Buddha to the palace. The orchestra played a special tune, and an invocation *(hpaya: pin.)* was sung by a male soloist. At this time the initiates were instructed by the Master of Ceremony to do obeisance to their parents—first the mother, then the father—and to their relatives sitting across from them. Then he gave a short disquisition on the Buddhist concept of karmic retribution *(wut)*, which he classified into various subtypes. Looking at his watch, he announced that it was now past noon; so, too, the dispensation of the present Buddha is past the halfway mark (of 5000 years).

Following another orchestral interlude, he addressed the young "princes." The mother, he said, should be placed on the right shoulder, the father on the left. The mother is given the place of honor because of the suffering she undergoes during pregnancy. On the other hand, the father too must be revered, for he must work in the sun and the rain in order to support his family.

[8]Buddhism views attachment, desire, grasping *(upādāna)* as the basis of demerit, suffering, and rebirth. It classifies grasping into four types according to its source: from physical desire, from speculation, from belief in the efficacy of rites, and from belief in the soul theory.

Turning to the audience, he now praised the women present. They are all beautiful, their hair is soft, their makeup attractive, and so on. But withal, they should always refrain from the three kinds of sin—by thought, by word, and by deed—for beautiful as they are now, they will be even more beautiful if they remain pure in thought, in word, and in deed. Then (in a witticism which the audience greatly appreciated) he remarked that the girl who carried the betel tray was selected because of gold and relatives (i.e., by bribery and political connection, rather than for her beauty). Still on the same subject, he alluded—as a warning—to the case of one queen, who was arrogant because of her renowned beauty and refused to do obeisance to the Buddha.

He now turned to the initiates, and instructed them to do obeisance to their grandparents. Following another orchestral interlude, he instructed them to do obeisance to their teacher. In between he continued to intersperse his own comments. In the past, he said, he had sung on radio, together with Shweiman Htin Maung (a famous Burmese singer and dancer). But now, he said, his voice was failing because he had conducted so many initiations.

He now instructed the initiates to do obeisance to the kings—but not, he cautioned, to drunken kings—even though, he observed, the initiate is more powerful than a king. Thus there was once a king, *Setca.wadei:* by name, who had the power to fly through the air; but he was unable to fly over the *man-dat* where the boys to be initiated were sitting, because the latter were about to become Sons of the Buddha. This shows how noble the initiates are; they are more powerful than kings!

The time had now come for the "feeding" ceremony. Cooked rice mixed with water was fed to the initiates—first to the boys, then to the girls. This is to protect them from danger. Then the thread of cotton yarn, over which the *paritta* had been chanted, was placed around their necks—also to protect them, especially from attack by evil spirits who, jealous of their glory, might wish to harm them. Holding in his hands a conch shell and a eugenia leaf, respectively, the Master of Ceremony again sang the Victory Song so that the initiates should be victorious over all danger). He then sprinkled water from the shell on the heads of the initiates and placed eugenia leaves in their hair. (The eugenia is the Burmese victory flower—*aung gyi:.*)

All spirits—both the Buddhist *deva* and the Burmese *nat*—were now invited to the palace, in a ceremony known as *nat theik.* They were offered food and drink from one of three bowls in front of the Master of Ceremony. Each bowl contains the usual offering *(Kado.pwe:)* of coconuts and bananas.

A member of the orchestra now came forward as a clown, in a bisexual costume, dressed on one side like a man, on the other like a woman, and imitating a *nat,* walked up to the sponsor of the ceremony and asked him for twenty-five *kyat.* (The latter gave him only two.) He then solicited contributions from other members of the audience, and returning to the orchestra read aloud the names of the contributors and the amount of their contributions—usually a few pennies. Still acting the clown he announced that the sponsor, having given as much as two *kyat*, will most certainly go to nirvana (this is said with mock sarcasm), but that his wife, who gave nothing, will most certainly not. It is, he said, like buying a railway ticket. The sponsor bought his ticket to nirvana (by making his contribution), but this ticket is for him alone; his wife cannot travel on the same ticket. He then read a list of names of people present from whom he still expected a contribution; they ought, he said, to give large sums because they were all relatives of the sponsor and, like him, all wealthy landowners, brokers, and merchants. With this, another member of the orchestra then approached each of the persons named and received a contribution from each.

The money collected, the Master of Ceremony pricked the lobes of the girls' ears with his needle. He then announced that the ceremony was complete. The real masters of ceremony would not appear, he said, until the afternoon, when the Buddhist monks arrived. With that, two hours after the ceremony had begun, people began to leave. In those two hours, although the Master of Ceremony had alluded to Buddhist doctrine, legend, and myth, almost nothing took place that was intrinsic to the *shin-byu.*

After the guests departed the young boys were taken from the palace to have their heads shaved and to change from royal dress into the yellow robe. The head and eyebrows are shaved with a razor, and although this is not unpainful, the boy is expected not to cry. Since he is now sacred, his hair is not allowed to fall on the ground; instead, it is caught in a sheet. Generally a monk begins the shaving of the boy's head and a layman then completes the job. Only the sponsor and the parents are present. When the hair has been cut and the boy is robed, he recites, following the monk, the Ten Precepts and the Buddhist Confession of Faith. This is the core of the initiation; he is now a novice *(kou-yin).*

When this ceremony is finished, the initiate is returned to the palace for the concluding ceremony; having left a prince, he returns a mendicant. In the palace now are very few people: the parents of each boy, close relatives, the village headman, and a few of the village elders. Unlike the morning ceremony, which was performed by a layman, this one is conducted by a group of Buddhist monks. The senior monk preaches a short sermon stressing the various benefits to be derived from the ceremony. When he has finished, he asks the sponsor whether he has a wish he would like fulfilled, to which invariably the answer is that he wishes to attain nirvana. Then the water libation is performed, the sponsor and his wife pouring the water jointly. After announcing their merit, they then share it with others. They conclude by reciting: "May we, as a result of this *shin-byu* ceremony, attain nirvana." The ceremony ends with the monks chanting *paritta,* and especially the *Mangala Sutta.*

On the following morning, the final rituals are held. First, the monks are again feasted in the palace. Then, in the presence of the postulants, their parents, and a few elderly people the monks chant *paritta,* following which the postulants are given their new names. Based on astrological calculations, this—a Pali name—must be used as long as the boy wears the robe. When he returns to the world, he resumes his secular name; but should he reenter the monastery—and Burmese men frequently do so for varying periods during their lives—he will again resume his Pali name.

Finally, and for the last time, the water libation is performed again, after which the senior monk delivers a short sermon. In the particular ceremony described here, the monk compared the sponsor to the Buddha: just as the Buddha by virtue of his merit had been able to combat Māra, the Evil One, so the sponsor, by virtue of merit acquired from the ceremony, has become invulnerable to harm. At the close of the sermon the monk sanctified a Buddha image which the sponsor had recently acquired, and with that the occasion came to an end. The people filed out of the palace and into the eating sheds, where they ate the final meal offered them by the sponsor of the initiation.

With the great emphasis on display and on the acquisition of merit and prestige by the sponsor, the young postulant sometimes seems almost forgotten. Still, the formal purpose of the ceremony is to induct him into the Order, and when the pomp and ceremony are over, his connection with the secular world has been severed. Unless he is very young he now resides in the monastery, and under the tutelage of the resident monk receives his Buddhist education, together with the other novices. With them he leaves the monastery every morning to receive alms from the villagers, including his parents. When the group of novices and monks file past his parental home, neither he nor his parents may show by their demeanor that he has any special relationship to them. As a member of the Order, he is officially indifferent to the ties that bind him to them; he has passed from the secular order, in which emotional bonds and the norms of kinship obligations are binding, into the sacred order in which these worldly ties and norms are abrogated. Similarly, although he is their son, his parents offer him the same obeisance as they offer to a distinguished or revered member of the monkhood.

Normatively, as I have noted, the initiate is expected to spend three Lenten seasons in the robe. In fact, however, although some do spend three years in the monastery (and a few of course remain for life), very few exemplify this norm. The variability in the time spent in the robe makes it difficult to draw a single generalization. As Table 8, based on a sample of fifty-two Yeigyi adults, reveals, the duration ranges from a few days to many years, the average being somewhat more than a year.

There are a number of reasons—few of them "religious"—for this wide variation found in the sample. Young sons of poor families frequently remained in the monastery for a long period because, all their economic wants

TABLE 8
DURATION OF STAY IN MONASTERY FOLLOWING INITIATION

DURATION	*N*
One day to two weeks	8
Two weeks to one month	3
One month to six months	4
Six months to one year	11
One year to two years	10
Two years to three years	11
More than three years	5
Total	52

being cared for, it relieved the strain on a meager family income. On the other hand, older sons of poor parents were taken out early because, as able-bodied males, their work was necessary to augment the family income. Very young boys, whether from rich or from poor families, remained no more than one night (sometimes only a few hours) in the monastery because they were too young to be separated from their parents, especially—as was stressed—from their mothers.

The contemporary situation presents a somewhat different picture. In a sample of twenty-four boys (all students at the government school) the amount of time spent in the robes ranged from two to fifteen days. When asked the reason for such a brief stay, the boys' responses tended to fall into three categories. One group spoke of their longing to return to their parents, and (as noted for the older sample) especially to their mothers. A second group emphasized their hunger pangs and their desire to eat after the prohibited hour of noon. A third group, of only a few cases, were taken out of the monastery by their parents in order to help in the fields.

Sometimes, of course, a lengthy stay in the monastery stimulates the novice to consider the monastic life as a career. Some discover that they have a religious vocation; others are attracted by the relative indolence and comfort which is theirs in the monastery. The latter group accounts, in part, for the high percentage of Burmese monks who obviously have no "calling" at all. In the sample of twenty-four boys alluded to above it is interesting, in this connection, that the majority viewed their monastic experience as a happy one, so much so that (as we shall see) many of them hope some day to return to the monastery as monks. A smaller group said that, bored by their monastic experience, they had no desire to repeat it by joining the Order. Although some few monks are harsh disciplinarians (cf. Hanks 1949), none of these boys expressed dissatisfaction with their monastic experience for this reason.

Death and Burial

Although Buddhism is scarcely involved in one's entry into the world, it is involved in many ways in one's exit. If birth and childhood ceremonies are primarily concerned with *nat,* death ceremonies are the concern primarily of Buddhism. Since these are somewhat elaborate, and since the Buddhist elements are related to the non-Buddhist as web is related to woof, it will be necessary to give a detailed (albeit schematic) description of the total complex of death rituals, rather than singling out the Buddhist elements alone.

Before describing them, however, and as a means for assessing the discrepancy between kammatic and nibbanic Buddhism, on the one hand, and between Buddhism as a salvation religion and Buddhism as magical technology, on the other, the teachings of normative Buddhism concerning death and rebirth should be reviewed. In normative Buddhism there is no soul; hence, nothing survives the death of the body. Rebirth is caused by the deceased's craving for existence; the nature of his rebirth is determined by his personally created karma. This being so, the deceased has no power to do good or ill for the deceased. Keeping these normative Buddhist assumptions in mind, it will be noted that they are all inverted by the assumptions underlying the Burmese death and burial ceremonies, described below.

Wherever possible, Buddhism in Burma becomes involved with death, not after a person dies, but in the process of his dying. For, according to certain Buddhist teachings, a person's rebirth is importantly determined by his state of mind immediately prior to his death. If he is in a state of agitation, if he harbors hostile feelings to others, if he is attached to worldly objects (be they persons or things), his chances of attaining a happy and pleasurable rebirth are slim. If, on the other hand, his mind is at peace, if his attitude to others is one of kindness, if his attachments to the world are minimal (if not completely severed) his chances of a happy rebirth are good. In order to achieve these latter states of mind, it is necessary to concentrate on Buddhist ideas—especially the concepts of suffering, impermanence, and nonself—and to repose one's faith in the soteriological virtues of the Three Gems. To achieve this end, Buddhist devotions are recited at the deathbed by friends or relatives, and frequently monks are invited to chant *paritta.* The less sophisticated believe that these rituals have the power, on the one hand, to overcome satanic powers which wish to deliver the soul of the nether world, and on the other hand, to send the soul to a heavenly abode.[9]

After death, the deceased lies in state in his own house for a minimum

[9]This belief is not restricted to the unsophisticated. It was held, for example, by a former president of the Union of Burma (Ba U 1959:80).

of three days before he is buried or cremated. This, informants claim, is to permit relatives from distant places to attend the funeral. Immediately after death, the corpse is washed: typically, by relatives, and always by males. Women do not wash the corpse because, so it is claimed, they are afraid that its ghost *(tasei)* might harm them. This is confusing—to the anthropologist, that is—because many Burmese seem to be holding several notions simultaneously, all anti-Buddhist. On the one hand, it is believed that the soul *(leikpya)* remains near the house until it is finally exorcised five to seven days after the funeral. It is also believed that the soul may be hostile, angry, or evil, and rituals are performed to protect the family from its hostility. But it is held, simultaneously, that the soul may already have been reborn as a ghost—this being its karmic retribution. In any event, much of the Burmese mortuary ritual is concerned with the disposition of the (non-Buddhist) soul, an end which is accomplished by Buddhist means. Minimally, it is hoped that the soul can be induced to leave; and these rituals are a means to that end. The reason the soul does not depart—so the villagers believe—is that it does not know that the body has died. It is only after it is finally sent away that it is then reborn, either by entering the womb of a human being or an animal, or by being transported to one of the nether or heavenly realms.

From the time of death until the day of the funeral, a steady stream of visitors passes through the household, and from the time of death until seven days after the funeral (the period of formal mourning) the immediate family of the deceased are never alone. They are fed by relatives, who not only cook their meals but also make the arrangements for the funeral, feed the guests, feast the monks, and so on. They continue to offer these services until the monks perform the *paritta* ceremony on the seventh day after the funeral.[10]

Every night, beginning with the first night after death and continuing until the monks recite the *paritta* which permanently expel the soul from the world of the living, the house and courtyard of the deceased are filled with groups of men who gamble at cards until dawn. One of these groups always plays in the room where the corpse is laid out. The explanation given for this custom is that it protects the bereaved from the deceased's ghost or the fear of it. For the same reason lanterns are hung around the courtyard, not only to provide light for the gamblers, but to keep the ghost away.

Although the ghost is feared, it is not ignored. Before the burial, for example, jaggery (a form of molasses) and rice are placed in a bowl at the cemetery for the ghost to eat, and when the corpse is buried the bowl is placed with the body inside the coffin. Similarly, the day before the monks

[10]Surprisingly, relatives of the deceased observe very few taboos and comply with very few restrictions. One of these—its reason is obscure—applies to the relatives who care for the bereaved. If they sleep in the latter's house on the burial day, they must continue to sleep there until the *paritta* ceremony is performed.

are called in to recite the *paritta* which finally send the soul to its next abode, the spouse of the deceased calls the ghost to the house to be witness to the ceremony.[11]

That the nightly presence of groups of men gives courage to the fearful family is understandable. What is not explained, however, is why women are never present at night; or why, if the men are present to provide protection for the family, they play cards; or why, if they play cards, they gamble. There is little to indicate from the demeanor of the card players that a death has occurred. They eat and drink (the expenses are defrayed by the relatives of the deceased, as well as by contributions from the men themselves), talk and joke, and in general behave in an entirely casual manner.

While lying in state the deceased is swathed in burial clothes, his thumbs and big toes tied together with hair cut from the head of one of his children. In his mouth is placed a coin, known as ferry fare *(kadou.ga.).* There is some vague notion that the soul, in passing from its present to its future abode, must cross some river on a ferry, and the coin is used to pay its passage. A vase, holding a flower, is placed by the head of the corpse so that, the villagers say, the ghost may use it to worship the Buddha. It remains there until the funeral is over, and is then broken.

If the family can afford it, monks are invited to the house every morning before the day of the funeral and, after they are feasted, recite *paritta.* This ceremony (known as *yetle taya:na*) has three functions. It is intended to keep the soul from returning to the house; it is hoped that the soul, listening to the chanting of the Buddhist Scriptures, will achieve a peaceful mind; and it is hoped that the merit acquired by feeding the monks, subsequently transferred to the deceased, will aid him in being reborn into a happy abode.

Although the gambling is restricted to the night hours, the bereaved are not left alone during the day. Throughout the mourning period men and women alike visit the family. One would term these visits "condolence calls," except that condolences in the Western sense are not offered. People enter the house, talk with each other or with the bereaved, but formal sympathy is not expressed. Indeed the death is scarcely mentioned—although the body is lying in the middle of the room.[12]

On the morning of the funeral wealthy villagers invite monks to the house for a feast. When, for example, the mother of my landlord died, ten monks—six from Mandalay and four from the village—were invited to the house. The feast is offered with the specific intention of transferring the merit to the deceased, thereby enhancing his chances of a better rebirth.

[11]The more knowledgeable Buddhists point out that according to Buddhism there can be no ghosts, since immediately upon death the "spirit" is reborn. They are, of course, only half right: according to normative Buddhism nothing of the deceased is reborn.

[12]The same absence of affective expression is also characteristic of joyous celebrations. At weddings, for example, none of the guests offers congratulations to the bride or bridegroom or to their respective parents.

If the monks are not feasted, the funeral is always held in the morning so that the monks can have their meals before noon, as required by their Rule. Villagers comment caustically on the urban practice of holding funerals in the afternoon "after the custom of the Christians."

When the body is taken from the house to be carried to the cemetery, it is removed through a back door or a window, since moving it through the front door will bring bad luck to the household. It is carried on a bier or a bed borne by four men, one at each corner. Sometimes a bed is specially purchased as a bier, and when the funeral is over it is donated to the monastery. As the corpse is lifted to the shoulders of the pallbearers, there is brief ritualized wailing by the female relatives. This is the only outward sign of mourning, ritualized or spontaneous, that can be seen. The funeral procession walks in single file, the men following the bier and the women walking behind them. When the procession reaches the cemetery, the body is taken by a small group of men to be buried or cremated. (Burial is usual, but especially pious people or parents of monks and monks themselves, of course, are generally cremated.) The other members of the procession proceed to the resthouse *(zayat)* at the entrance to the cemetery, where the monks are waiting to conduct the ceremony. This is held without the corpse, for burial is completed about the same time this ceremony ends.

There being no professional morticians or gravediggers in the village, the male relatives of the deceased dig the grave or prepare the funeral pyre. Before burial or cremation, the flowers that have been in the room with the body at home are scattered in the cemetery, symbolizing, so the villagers say, the separation of the deceased from the living. Similarly, if the body is cremated, the food for the ghost which is usually buried with the corpse is scattered in the cemetery.

If the body is buried, still another ritual is performed to prevent the ghost from returning to the village. In the coffin is placed one piece of string for every living member of the household, each piece of string measuring in length the height of the surviving relative. Known as *leikpya kwe:de,* this is intended to separate the soul (or ghost) from any attachment (positive or negative) to the living. Moreover, gravediggers must request permission from a spirit of the earth—the *boung-ma. de-wa.*—to bury the corpse. This spirit is appeased with rice dyed in turmeric.

The ceremony in the resthouse takes from half to three-quarters of an hour. The number of monks present depends on the wealth of the family of the deceased; the greater the wealth, the larger the number of monks invited, for each monk is presented with alms. To three of the village funerals I attended only one monk was asked; to one, ten were invited; and to another, thirteen. The preference, of course, is to invite as many monks as possible. First, the merit transferred to the deceased is proportionate to the alms presented to the monks—the more monks present, the greater the merit. Second, the *paritta* chanted by the monks are intended to help the deceased, and again it is believed that their efficacy is proportional to the number of monks who chant them. Hence, so she informed me, one elderly rich widow has arranged in her will for seventy-five monks to be present at her funeral.

Placed before the monks is a ritual offering *(kado pwe:)* consisting of bananas and coconuts. Each monk is given a fan, with a bank note (five to ten *kyat*) placed in the stem. Monks, of course, are forbidden to touch money, and the fans are carried by their monastery pupils.

The funeral ritual is little different in content from any other Buddhist ceremony. First, the Five Precepts are offered to the assembly, after which the *deva* are invoked. The monk then chants two or three *paritta* (always including the Love *Sutta* and the Beatitudes), the Virtues of the Three Gems, and the Five Inner Forces. Typically, at the conclusion of these "prayers," he preaches a short sermon. Following the sermon, the water-libation ceremony is performed, and the announced merit is then transferred to the soul of the deceased. The monk then concludes the ceremony by pronouncing *aneiksa wutta samkaram*—"all is impermanent."

Funeral sermons (those at least which I heard) all stress the same themes. The following is a summary of one such typical sermon. Mourning is useless, for illness, old age, and death are inevitable; there is no way of avoiding them. Everyone should give up his attachments and strive, instead, for nirvana. Everyone believes in karma, and in order to improve one's karma one should observe the precepts and offer charity. While reflecting on the deceased, everyone should reflect also on the meaning of impermanence. May the Withou-daya *nat* be witness to the merit that is being performed for the deceased, so that he may go to a pleasant abode and from there to nirvana, where there is no death and no rebirth, no old age and no illness.[13]

As I have noted earlier, on the seventh day after the funeral[14] monks are invited to the home of the bereaved to recite *paritta*—of course, after they are feasted. Again, the number invited varies with the wealth of the family. Poor households may invite only one or two, wealthy families many more. For this day thirteen were invited, both from Mandalay and from surrounding villages as well as Yeigyi, after the death of my landlord's mother, and each monk was presented with a five-*kyat* note (attached to his fan) as well as a meal.

[13]The funerals I observed differed only in detail from descriptions found in the older literature. The most important difference is the absence of an orchestra, which according to Shway Yoe (1896:585) and Bigandet (1912: Vol. 2,19) was a regular feature of older funerals. The orchestra played intermittently at the house of the bereaved and accompanied the funeral procession to the cemetery.

[14]The Burmese are no more compulsive in their religious than in their secular behavior. Although the *paritta* ceremony traditionally occurs on the seventh day, it may occur before that if there is some pressing reason for it. Thus I missed one ceremony because the death occurred during the harvest season and the family, wishing to get it over with so that they could return to their agricultural labors, had it performed on the fifth day.

This ceremony has two intended functions. First, if the ghost is still lurking in the village, it serves finally to drive it to its new abode. Second, it confers merit on the bereaved, which they transfer to the deceased with the hope of enhancing his chances of a happy rebirth. By this time, it must be admitted, it is difficult to know where the soul might be. As we have seen, various rituals are performed at the funeral with the intention of severing its relationship to the world of men and hastening its rebirth wherever this is to be. Nevertheless, when the funeral procession returns from the cemetery, one of the relatives breaks a branch from a tree and brings it to the house, where the soul or ghost may rest for seven days until the monks recite *paritta.* At the same time, though fearing the possible malevolence of the ghost, the spouse of the deceased invites him to attend this *paritta* ceremony as if he were not already in the house. It is obvious that various traditions, pre-Buddhist, Buddhist, post-Buddhist, and anti-Buddhist have been joined, as it were, and all are observed simultaneously. These inconsistent beliefs and practices do not disturb the Burmese, nor—unless they are pointed out to them—are they even aware of the contradictions. In neither regard are they different from the devotees of any other religion.

At this as at any Burmese ceremony, all participants are fed. As usual, of course, both the number of people invited and the plentitude of the feast vary with family wealth.[15] As usual, too, the merit derived from this feeding is transferred to the deceased as part of the merit-transfer ceremony performed when the chanting of *paritta* is ended.

It should be obvious from this general description that the Buddhist rituals which comprise the bulk of Burmese death and funeral ceremonies have two intended functions. First, fearful that the ghost of the deceased may cause them harm, the survivors hope that the rituals will speed the ghost on its path to its next rebirth.[16] Second, desiring to provide the deceased with the best possible rebirth, the survivors attempt to acquire, and then transfer to the deceased, merit sufficient to ensure this possibility.

[15]In the case of one well-to-do village family, three hundred people were fed rice, pork curry, pickled mangos, fried chili, and sweetmeats.

[16]The more fearful they are of the ghost of the deceased, the more careful they must be of its disposal. Ghosts of women dying in labor before the baby is born are believed to be especially malevolent. Crawfurd (1834:484) describes a funeral for such women. I do not know whether the customs he describes are observed today.

> The belief is, that the souls of women dying under such circumstances would become evil spirits, haunting the towns or villages to which the deceased belonged, if a certain ceremony were not practiced to exorcise them. The horrid ceremony in question is as follows: —The husband, with dishevelled hair, and bearing a Da, or sword, in each hand, goes before the coffin, in the procession, from his house to the funeral ground, using the gestures of a maniac, and cutting the air with the weapons in every direction. When the procession has arrived at the place, the case is inquired into by the public officers, and a regular deed of divorce between the husband and the deceased is drawn up. The body is then opened by one of the burners of the dead, the foetus extracted, and held up to the spectators. The husband, after this, walks thrice around the coffin, goes home, washes his head, and returns when the corpse is burned with the usual ceremonies.

To complete this description of Buddhist rites for the dead it need only be added that merit is also transferred to the deceased on the annual anniversary of his death. Close relatives—parent or child, sometimes spouse—perform some type of meritorious act (from offering flowers to the Buddha to building a pagoda), after which the merit transfer ceremony is held. The following notice, which appeared in *The* [Rangoon] *Nation*, describes this type of ceremony. Its scope is beyond the means of an average villager—though it is consistent with and appropriate to the great stature of this particular sponsor—but its motive and spirit are no different from those I observed in Yeigyi.

IN MEMORIAM

Today being the anniversary of the death of our only son (Timmie) Mg Tin Maung Thant (aged 21 years) at the Rangoon General Hospital, my wife and I, in accordance with Buddhist belief, are performing on behalf of our dear departed son the following deeds of merit: Offering of *Navakamma* alms in the form of cash donations and refreshments to 10 members of *Sangha* from *Sasana Yeiktha* headed by Agga Maha Pandita Mahasi Sayadaw: offering gold-leaves, votive candles, Bo-water and flowers at the Great Shwedagon Pagoda: sanctuary for fish and goats: cash donations to relatives and acquaintances; and recitation of Buddhist scriptures, at the residence of U & Mrs. Thaung, Wingaba Avenue, Bahan, Rangoon at 5 P.M.

May the late Mg Tin Maung Thant rejoice "Sadu, Sadu, Sadu" and reap the full benefit of these merits in whatever plane of existence he now is. May he be happy therein.—U Thant-Daw Thein Tin, Secretary-General, United Nations Organisation, New York. 21-5-63.

CHAPTER 11

Crisis Rituals

Causes and Occasions of Crisis

If the rituals described in the last two chapters may properly be characterized as comprising the cultures associated with nibbanic and kammatic Buddhism, those described in this chapter may be characterized as the rituals of apotropaic Buddhism. The motivation for their performance is neither commemorative nor expressive, but instrumental; and, unlike the instrumental rituals of the former two types of Buddhism, their goal is neither soteriological nor even the attainment of some positive boon in this life, but protective. That is, they are performed to extricate the actor from a calamity which he is presently suffering, or to save him from one which is or may be impending. Hence, before describing the rituals, we must first examine the causes and occasions of these calamities.

First, there is a class of ills, dangers, and troubles whose causes are natural and/or (from a Buddhist point of view) karmic. Automobile accidents, imprisonment, certain kinds of illness (such as snake bites), droughts, losses due to theft and banditry, the beginning of a new venture, attacks by enemies, and so on, are examples of this first class. These actual or imminent occasions and causes of crisis are handled in a variety of ways, which at least in the first instance may have no relationship to Buddhism. Doctors, both Western and indigenous, are used for the treatment of illness; irrigation canals are dug to afford protection against droughts; legal and political means are used to help those who have fallen foul of the law; and so on. Sometimes, however, these naturalistic means of coping with these forms of danger are ineffective. Sometimes, too, although these means are presumed to be effective, extra insurance is deemed wise and proper. In both contingencies the rituals of apotropaic Buddhism—as well as a set of non-Buddhist magical rituals—are both available and widely used.

There is another class of dangers, however, for which naturalistic techniques are ineffective. These are troubles whose causes—from our point of view—are supernatural. Even if, in the Burmese view, their distal cause is karmic, their proximate cause is a more immediate agent: witchcraft, spirits, planetary influence, evil omens, and so on. Sometimes, too, no specific cause is ascertainable, and the misfortune is attributed to bad fortune. After Daw Myan, for example, suffered from a series of acute problems, including the death of her husband, she moved from her home because, she was advised, it was an unlucky, an inauspicious *(a-min-ga-la)* place.

Illnesses, losses, storms, accidents, and other troubles caused by the agents mentioned above cannot be coped with by naturalistic techniques. For protection against them the Burmese have recourse to three sources of assistance, and frequently all three are used simultaneously. First, there is the elaborate ritual apparatus associated with the *nat* cultus, which affords protection from evil spirits and witches. Second, there is a wide array of magical rituals, integral neither to the *nat* cultus nor to Buddhism, but partaking of both. Third, there are the rituals associated with apotropaic Buddhism. Since *nat* and witch causation, and the rituals associated with them, have been described elsewhere (Spiro 1967), this discussion will be confined to the Buddhist and (to a lesser extent) non-Buddhist magical ritual. First, if only briefly, I must describe two other supernatural agents of danger which are combatted by these rituals, viz., the influence of the planets and evil omens.

Astrology is firmly entrenched in Burmese culture;[1] without his horoscope it is almost impossible for the ordinary Burman to find his way through the maze of life. It determines the day and the time for a marriage, a *shin-byu*, the construction of a house, the beginning of a business venture, the declaration of national independence—and almost every other event, large and small, in the private and collective life of the Burmese. Life is lived under auspicious and inauspicious planets and planetary constellations whose influence on human affairs is self-evident to almost all Burmese.

Burmese astrology, like that of the other societies of Southeast Asia, was imported of course from India. And to this day, although some Burmese—most notably Buddhist monks—do practice astrology, most astrologers are

[1]For those Westerners who believe that (in the modern world) astrology is a peculiarly Oriental phenomenon, the following facts should prove rather sobering. In the United States alone it is estimated that astrology has ten million hard-core adherents and another forty million fellow travelers. Moreover, 1,200 of the 1,750 newspapers in the United States publish brief daily horoscopes, and almost every major woman's magazine publishes an extensive monthly version. In addition, this country supports 5,000 professional astrologers. (*Newsweek*, 1/13/69.)

Indians. The most famous astrologers in Upper Burma—under the monarchy they were employed as court astrologers—are the Manipuri Brahmins, known as *Pon-na.*

Planetary influence is, of course, both beneficent and maleficent. Here we are concerned only with the latter type, which is sometimes seen as potentially very harmful indeed.[2] Thus, beginning in October, 1961 astrologers in Burma (and of course in India and the other Indianized states of Southeast Asia) were predicting that a great calamity—full-scale wars, bombings, fires, widespread devastation—would commence sometime between February third and fifth, 1962. This calamity was to be caused by the congregation of eight of the nine heavenly bodies which—according to astrological theory—affect human destiny within the constellation of Capricorn. The reaction to a predicted disaster of this magnitude was, understandably enough, one of grave, almost traumatic, concern. Hence the enormous efforts described below to prevent it from occurring.

Omens *(nameik),* like planetary constellations, may augur either good or bad consequences. The latter alone include a number of major types. Prominent among them is belief in the evil effect of a wild animal's entering a place of human habitation, especially a house. Sometimes the effect is unspecified; sometimes, however, it is specific. Thus, if a reptile enters the house, the inhabitant will lose all his property. If a vulture alights on the house, it is also inauspicious but the danger is unspecified.[3] If a beehive is built on or near the house, this is especially inauspicious; if combined with some other bad omen, the danger may be grave indeed. Thus the death of my landlord's mother was attributed to the conjunction of a beehive found on a tree in her courtyard and a vulture landing on the roof of her house. Had her house been dismantled, so the villagers claimed, she would not have died.[4] The appearance of an undomesticated mammal inside a village

[2]Important as it is in Burma, planetary influence as a cause of trouble seems to be even more significant in some other *Theravāda* Buddhist societies, and most especially in Ceylon. For descriptions of the important *bali* ceremony, used for coping with planetary causes of danger, cf. Sarathchandra 1953:31; Gooneratne 1866:12; Ryan 1958:116 ff.; Wijesekera 1949:157-58.

[3]As already mentioned, not all forms of danger are coped with by means of Buddhist ritual. Thus, there is a specific antidote for the danger caused by the vulture, viz., to hang a peacock doll—for the peacock is auspicious *(min-gala)*—in the house. Sometimes the bad omen is handled by verbal magic. If a reptile enters the house, images of reptiles are made which are then called *pou kaunde.* This verbal reversal is believed to avert the danger. The Burmese use other forms of verbal reversal as well. Thus there is a species of lizard, known in Burmese as *hput,* which is believed to be an omen of scarcity. To avert the misfortune, when they encounter such a lizard the Burmese refer to it as *Zaw:tika,* after the name of a well-known wealthy person in the *Jātaka.*

[4]As in many other magical beliefs, the beehive, depending on the context, can be both auspicious and inauspicious. Thus, when an extraordinarily large beehive was discovered on the famous *Shwemawdaw* pagoda in Pegu, some interpreted this to mean that "peace will be restored in the country, poor people may have to face hardships, rice can be scarce, and that the omen as a whole portends good." (*Union Express,* May 20, 1962.)

Similarly, when as a young barrister the former President of Burma discovered three beehives under his house, he consulted

or town is especially serious, a sign that the place will turn into a wilderness.[5]

We may now turn to the Buddhist rituals employed for protection against these and all other types of supernaturally caused dangers. One may classify them according to their predominant content—some emphasize the use of Buddhist sacra, some Buddhist spells, while still others consist of the practice of *dāna.*

The Use of Buddhist Sacra

The Rosary

It has already been noted that the rosary, when said as part of the daily devotions of the pious Buddhist, serves as a generic prophylactic against danger. "So long as I say my rosary," said a Yeigyi informant, "I have no fear of witches and ghosts. For if you say your rosary, you are invulnerable to attacks by evil beings, whether natural or supernatural." The rosary is also used, however, as an antidote against specific troubles. During World War II, for example, when Mandalay and its environs were bombed by the Japanese, many people said their beads to be protected from the bombing. Again, when my Burmese assistant was unemployed, he said his beads in the hope of finding employment. (His faith in this ritual was vindicated when I hired him.) Similarly, a village headman told me that when he was imprisoned on the (false) charge of having aided the insurgents, he said his beads, among other magical steps taken, so that he might be freed. A few months later he was released.

The Pagoda

To avert the dangers caused by planetary influence and terrestrial omens, the most effective defense is to build a pagoda. (This ritual, like all rituals performed in order to avert an impending calamity, is known in Burmese as a *ya.da.ya.*) Thus, believing—on the basis of many omens—that world peace was seriously threatened, the Burmese Government in 1952 constructed the famous World Peace Pagoda in Kaba-Aye, a suburb of Rangoon.[6] For Westerners, this pagoda is interpreted as a symbol of peace.

---

a well-known phongyi as to the portents of these beehives. He said that they meant I would get a promotion soon. Right enough—I do not know whether it was a case of coincidence or not—soon after the prediction, I received a letter from the Registrar, saying that a notification would soon be out confirming me as a District and Sessions Judge and that I could go on leave if I wanted to. [Ba U 1959:96]

[5] According to Scott (Shway Yoe 1896:478), it was the discovery of a tiger and some deer in the environs of Amarapura which led to the decision to shift the capital from that city to Mandalay.

[6] According to G. P. Charles (1955:61), one Hsaya Htay was meditating near Pakoku in 1948 when an old man came down from the hills and gave him a staff, on which was engraved *Shri Mangala.* (*Shri* is an honorific and *mangala* is "auspicious," "good fortune.") He re-

For the Burmese, however, it is not a symbol but a *condition* of peace; it was constructed to avert impending war.

Since the construction of a real pagoda is too expensive for the ordinary person, as well as too time-consuming to be completed in time to prevent the predicted calamity, one of two alternative strategies is employed. Sometimes a regular brick pagoda is erected whose dimensions are sufficiently small so that it can be completed in a short time. Thus, when a friend in Mandalay was told by an astrologer that her daughter would die unless something was done to avert the danger, she constructed a small brick pagoda. (Her daughter, as predicted, regained her health.) Sometimes, however, a miniature pagoda is built, of sand. This of course can be completed in a very short time, and its material—sand—is "pure."

The most dramatic example of such an attempt to avert danger took place in December 1961, two months before the scheduled world calamity which was predicted by astrologers throughout Asia. Under a directive from the government's Ministry of Religious Affairs, sixty thousand sand pagodas, each consisting of nine tiers and standing nine cubits high, were built, scattered through every district of the Union of Burma. The pegging of the pagodas occurred, in accordance with astrological calculations, between 6:00 A.M. and 8:24 A.M. on Saturday, December 9. Moreover, since each planet has its own point on the compass, and since the days of the week (which are named after the planets) have the same directional points as their planets, each pagoda had to be built on the "Saturday" or southwest corner of the chosen site. Following the completion of each, nine monks were offered a vegetarian meal by the participants; and for three days following its construction nine laymen and laywomen recited *paritta.* (Needless to say, when the predicted calamity did not occur, it was believed to have been averted by this ritual, as well as by others described below.)

A Buddha Symbol

According to Buddhist mythology, the Buddha was a fish in one of his many rebirths. Burmese peasants in villages near Yeigyi believe that He lived as a fish in a nearby lake. In commemoration of this circumstance, a pagoda situated on a sacred hill adjacent to the (now dry) lake contains three carved fish, each about three feet long, gilded with gold leaf. These fish not only represent the Buddha in a previous incarnation, but also have the magical power to bring rain.[7] Hence, each year at the beginning of the

quested that the staff be given to U Nu (then prime minister) and that the latter be requested to build a pagoda, to be completed before 1952. This pagoda and its surrounding buildings would, he said, bring peace to Burma and to the world. This was the basis for the decision to build the Kaba-Aye pagoda. The site, it was later discovered, had been known in the past as "Shri Mangala."

[7]Animals are widely used in magical rain rites, as Frazer (1920: Vol. 1, 287-96) has shown.

planting season—or whenever there is a drought, or a predicted drought[8] —one of the fish is carried in a royal procession through all the fields of the villages in that area. As befits royalty, it is seated on a palanquin carried by four men and shaded by two white umbrellas (insignia of royalty). It is preceded by an orchestra and two female dancers who, accompanied by the musicians, dance in front of the image; and it is followed by the villagers, some riding in oxcarts, others walking. The mood of the procession is serious. While the laymen march in solemn parade, monks from a number of villages who have assembled in one monastery chant *paritta.* Returning to the village, the people assemble at this monastery, where they feast the monks. Following their meal, the monks chant the *Mangala Sutta.* The fish is kept in this monastery until it rains, when it is returned to its home on the hill.

Laymen and monks alike observed to me that this ritual always works;[9] and in the case that I witnessed, rain fell two days after the procession. Most villagers, if asked to explain the efficacy of the rite, resort to a simple magical explanation: being a representation of the Buddha, the fish image has the power to cause rain. Some of the more learned monks offered a different explanation: out of respect for the Buddha, Indra (the Lord of Heaven), commands Monatha (the rain god) to send the rain.[10]

[8]If the first day of the waxing moon in the month of *Tabaung* is hazy, this is an omen that there will be sufficient rain during the rainy season. But if it is bright, this means there will be little rain.

[9]When I pointed out to a Western-educated monk that this is not very surprising since the ritual always occurs at the beginning of the rainy season, he was visibly impressed. He had never thought of that, he said. On the other hand, he pointed out, it also works when the ritual is performed during a drought.

[10]It is not only in Burma that the fish serves as a Buddhist symbol or is the object of veneration. The following news story appeared in the *New York Times.*

> Tens of thousands of rural Vietnamese are reported to be making pilgrimages to a small pond to see a giant fish that they consider to be the miraculous reincarnation of a disciple of Buddha.
>
> The pond is in Quang Nam province about 30 miles west of Danang in an area where animosity between Buddhists, who number about 80 per cent of the population, and Roman Catholics is strong.
>
> According to usually reliable sources, the "miracle" began about two months ago, in the middle of the Buddhist crisis, when word began to spread throughout the countryside that there was a giant fish, apparently a carp, swimming in a small pond, and that it was a Buddhist disciple. The fish was so big and could be seen so easily that it had attracted the attention of villagers. Soon Vietnamese from all over the region began going to the pond to see the fish.
>
> FISH IS IN OPPOSITION
>
> At this point the district chief, who is a Catholic, worried. The pilgrimage, he told one American, was an act of opposition. He decided to clean the pond. Nothing happened.
>
> They placed 10 mines in the pond and set them off. As one informant said, "They blew up and killed everything in that pond except the fish. The fish kept swimming."
>
> Then they started feeding the fish bread, to train it to come to the surface. They

The Buddha Image

In the village of Lethit, about ten miles from Yeigyi, there is a small hollow pagoda which contains a special image of the Buddha. About a foot high, it portrays a seated Buddha, hooded by one large and six small serpentine heads, representing mythical serpents known as *nāga.* Hence, this pagoda is known as the "hooded-Buddha" *(naga:youn:)* pagoda. According to tradition it also contains Buddhist relics. Although it is not known exactly when it was constructed, it is said to be very old: the village monk says that it was already repaired as early as the twelfth century by King Minshinsaw (of Pagan). For the entire Mandalay district, the image in this pagoda and its counterpart at Shweizayan, play an important magical role in the prevention and cure of snake bites. It is prayed to before working in the fields; special ceremonies are held in the pagoda compound preceding the planting and harvesting seasons; and victims of snake bites are brought to the pagoda for cure. Since poisonous snakes are prevalent in the area, the image plays an important role in peasant thought and life.

The representation of a serpent-hooded Buddha is interpreted by local informants in terms of both Buddhist and Burmese traditions. According to Buddhist tradition, the Buddha, caught in a rainstorm while meditating, was protected by a *nāga* king, Muchalinda, who wound his body around the Buddha and covered Him with his hood. (Cf. Thomas 1960:85.) According to Burmese tradition, the young and future King Kyanzittha, fleeing from the wrath of the then King Sawlu (eleventh century), slept the night in a pasture where he was protected by a young *nāga.* (Tin and Luce 1923:108) On both accounts, then, the hooded-serpent image represents protection—and by Frazer's principle of sympathetic magic, offers protection specifically against snakes.[11]

---

followed the bread with a hand-grenade pitched into the water. Twice this was done, twice there were terrific explosions, and twice the fish continued to swim.

TOO DANGEROUS TO KILL

This convinced the villagers that in fact a miracle was taking place. When an officer suggested another way of killing the fish the district chief said it had become too dangerous. He feared there might be a violent reaction among the population if the fish was killed.

At this point the pilgrimage began in full force. People started coming from all over Vietnam. Buses from as far away as Saigon were chartered. The road to the pond was lined with people on bikes. The pilgrims carried away water from the pond. Army helicopters mysteriously landed, soldiers got out and filled their canteens with the magic water.

One American said tens of thousands of people were visiting the little pond. To them the fish was a disciple of Buddha. The Government, unable to kill the fish or stop the pilgrims, contented itself with printing in the local newspaper a report that the water in the pond was poisoned, and that many people died from drinking it.

[11]The *nāga,* whose importance in Indian symbolism is well known, also plays an important role in Buddhist symbolism throughout Southeast Asia, where it is represented sculpturally in pagodas and monasteries, as well as in these Muchalinda-Buddha images, as Zimmer (1962:68) calls them. Its importance no doubt preceded the introduction of Buddhism, as traces of *nāga* worship indicate. In Burma for example an image of a *nat,* representing a *nāga,* was worshiped in Tagaung as late as 1917. (Cf. Brown 1917.) More recently, in 1962, a *nāga* was

As mentioned above, this particular Buddha image figures in three types of ritual. Every morning during the harvest season, farmers recite the following prayer to the image. "If I am bitten by a snake, please help to save my life."[12] Moreover, while working in the fields, farmers tie dried flowers which have been offered to this image around their wrists or attach them to their hats. The flowers which serve as a talisman to protect them from snakes, have been offered to the image during the biennial pilgrimage to the hooded-Buddha pagoda. Before embarking on their pilgrimage, the villagers collect food (in Yeigyi and three other villages) to be used for feasting the monks living near the pagoda. Thus, those who do not make the journey can also acquire merit. The pilgrims not only observe the precepts at the pagoda as they would on an ordinary Sabbath, but stay awake most of the night chanting Buddhist prayers. Before their return they drink the water from the vase in which they have offered their flowers to the Buddha image.

Sometimes, despite his pilgrimage to the pagoda and/or wearing the talisman, a person may nevertheless be bitten by a snake. When this happens he is again taken, if at all possible, to the pagoda. The following account of the ritual performed for one village woman is typical.

When the group accompanying Ma Than—the victim of the bite—arrived at the pagoda, one of the men had her recite the precepts after him. She then informed the Buddha (image) of how she had been bitten and asked Him to cure her. Flowers and water taken from a vase next to the image were given her to eat and drink. Although ordinarily victims of snake bites must not drink water—they drink coconut milk instead—because it is believed that water increases the potency of the poison, *this* water, having been offered to the hooded Buddha, has powerful curative qualities. When Ma Than had consumed the water and flowers, a relative rubbed her wound with flowers from the same vase and then massaged her entire leg (from the wound to her toes) to draw out the poison. The local monk, who was watching the proceedings, told Ma Than that until she recovered she should not eat until she had first offered food to the Buddha. All this time, Ma Than, lying on her back, was moaning over and over again, "O Buddha, help me, cure me, give me your assistance!"

---

reported to be observed in a pool in the Northern Shan States, and according to *The* [Rangoon] *Nation* the pool became a pilgrimage focus for the area.

The Burmese, moreover, believe that the entire world is surrounded by a huge *nāga,* which circles the earth in perpetual motion. Before starting out on a journey the traveler must discover the direction in which it is moving, since to move in the direction of its head would be to encounter danger—one might be swallowed up by its jaws. Similarly, in making a substantial purchase—a bull, for example, or a cart—the object of the transaction is handed over either from the position of the *nāga's* tail to its head, or across its body. If, for instance, the *nāga* is facing east, the object is passed from south to north.

[12]During the harvest season, the guardian *nat* of the fields is propitiated for the same reason. Every morning, after he is offered food, the following prayer is recited: "With this food we offer you this meal. For doing so, let me be free from disaster, snakes, scorpions, insects, and dangers, and let me have pleasantness."

By this time some local villagers had stopped to talk, about both this case and the many other victims who had been cured by this image. On the basis of these past cures, they pointed to the signs indicating that Ma Than, too, was on her way to recovery. Thus, when she was brought to the pagoda she had been moaning badly, but now her moans had stopped; she had been unable to move, but now she could move; she had complained (when they gave her the flowers to eat) that she could not eat, but now—after the ritual—she was eating ordinary food with obvious appetite. They also observed what a "strange" case this was. Thus, although Ma Than had been walking with her husband when the snake had struck, it had made no attempt to bite him; and when he sought to capture the snake it was nowhere to be found. It was pointed out, too, that when we were driving in my car to the pagoda at Lethit, and the car stuck in the mud, we finally got free, although we all believed at the time that we would never get there. This, everyone agreed, was a good omen.

When Ma Than completed her meal, one of her male relatives offered food to the image and chanted some prayers. With this the ritual was ended. Ma Than, it should be noted, recovered.

The Yellow Robe

The yellow robe of the monk has great magical power. It is especially potent as protection against evil supernaturals—witches, spirits, demons, and so on—for few of them would have the audacity to harm a "Son of the Buddha." Hence the ultimate protection for a victim of spirit possession or witchcraft who anticipates yet another attack is to take the monastic vows and don the yellow robe.

The Use of Buddhist Spells

"Spell," here, means any verbal formula (of whatever length or from whatever source) whose utterance is believed to achieve a desired goal by creating or harnessing magical power, or by enlisting the assistance of superhuman beings. Buddhist spells, known as *gāthās* (literally, verses or stanzas), typically consist of scriptural passages ranging in length from a few sentences to an entire chapter. In Burma, the most famous of the short spells is the collection of the "Virtues" (Pali, *guṇa;* Burmese, *goung:do*) of the Three Gems. Although the *Dhajagga paritta* comprises these three sets of Virtues, the Burmese do not regard them as *paritta;* they are a group apart.[13] Since these verses, divided into stanzas and describing the distinctive fea-

[13]When used as part of a *paritta* ceremony, these verses from the *Dhajagga Sutta* are called in Burmese *Dazet Thouk;* when used for the specific ends noted below, they are referred to as *goung:do.* In the former case the Virtues of all Three Gems are recited as a group; in the latter, only one set—usually the Virtues of the Buddha—is recited.

tures of the Buddha, the *Dhamma,* and the *Saṅgha,* were originally recited by the Buddha following His narration of a martial story,[14] they are of course used as protection in battle and in time of war. But this is not their only or even their most important use. When treating a patient, Burmese native doctors recite the Virtues as well as prescribing medicine in order to cure him. Or, in an entirely different domain, prisoners (both criminal and political) may recite this spell as a way of obtaining their release. Often it is recited while saying the rosary.

The following translations of these three sets of Virtues, as found in the original *sutta,* are taken from the *Book of the Kindred Sayings* (Vol. I:282).

Virtues of the Buddha:

> the Exalted One, Arahant, supremely enlightened, proficient in knowledge and in conduct, the Blessed One, who understands the world, peerless tamer and driver of the hearts of men, the Master, the Buddha for gods and men, Exalted One.

Virtues of the *Dhamma:*

> Well proclaimed by the Exalted One is the Norm, relating to the present, immediate in its results, inviting all, giving guidance, appealing to each, to be understood by them that can understand.

Virtues of the *Saṅgha:*

> Well practised is the Exalted One's Order of Disciples, practised in integrity, in intellectual methods, in right lines of action—to wit the four pairs, the eight groups of persons—this is the Exalted One's Order of Disciples worthy of offerings, oblations, gifts, salutations, the world's peerless field for merit.

More powerful even than the Virtues is the spell known in Burmese as the *Tham-bouktei* (Pali, *Sambuddha* = Perfect Buddha).

> With my head bowed, I worship the twelve, the twenty-eight, the one thousand, the five thousand, the seven thousand perfect Buddhas. To the innumerable Buddhas, as many as the sands of the Ganges, to the Buddhas who have attained Nirvana, the Conquerors. To them, and to their Law and their Monks, I do homage. By virtue of this act of worship, may I acquire the power to discard this body [i.e., to attain nirvana], and may all misfortunes perish without residue.

Villagers recount numerous anecdotes telling of the power of this spell.

[14]The Buddha, in the original *sutta,* prescribes their use merely as a means for overcoming fear. If, He promises the monks, any of the Three Gems are "call[ed] to mind" by reference to their respective Virtues, "any fear, panic, creeping of the flesh that will have arisen will be overcome." (*Dhajagga Sutta,* in *Book of the Kindred Sayings,* p. 282.)

Shipwrecks have taken place in which those who recited the *Tham-bouktei* were saved; airplane crashes occur in which those who recited it are miraculously uninjured; and, closer to home, when insurgents killed and plundered the villages, those who recited this spell were spared.

The third and most important category of spells is the collection of *paritta* whose scriptural basis was discussed in chapter 6. The eleven *sutta*, which in Burma comprise the basic collection, may be recited either individually or collectively. Some or all may be recited as part of ordinary Buddhist devotions, serving as protection against generalized "danger." More important, they are recited on some special occasion to deal with a specifically known danger—either to remove it (if it has already appeared) or to prevent it (if it is imminent). The recitation of these spells afford defense against dangers of all kinds, both natural and supernatural. Although any *paritta* serves this protective function, each has a specialized function as well: one serves as a protection against dangerous childbirth, another against snake bites, another against evil spirits, and so on.

Paritta are the core of Burmese crisis ritual,[15] constituting an indispensable element in the Burmese personal security system. No crisis can be faced without them, and all crises can be dealt with by them. The chanting of these spells (together with the public recitation of the precepts) constitutes one of the few ritual acts which the Buddhist monk performs on behalf of the laymen. For a monk to refuse an invitation from a layman to perform a *paritta* ceremony would be as inconceivable as for a doctor to refuse to attend a patient in his care.

Taught as part of the core curriculum of the village monastery school, many *paritta* are known to the laymen. Memorized in Pali, however, a language which the students do not understand, they are only barely grasped. (Their ritual use is nevertheless justified by some monks on the ground that even if the students knew Pali, they would still not understand the texts because Buddhist concepts are too difficult for them to comprehend.) Most of the *paritta* have been translated into Burmese, however,

[15]This generalization holds for Thailand and Ceylon as well, and most probably for all other *Theravāda* societies. For Thailand, see Wells (1960:268 ff.). In Ceylon (cf. Gogerly 1908:327 ff.; Hardy 1850:240-42; Hackman 1910:122-23), *paritta* rituals are, if anything, even more highly elaborated than in Burma. A typical Sinhalese ceremony may continue uninterrupted for seven days and nights, and for an especially serious crisis may last (as the following quotation indicates) as long as a month.

> Dalada Maligawa Sacred Temple of the Tooth in Kandy, Ceylon's hill capital, will today inaugurate a month long Pirith ceremony (invocation of blessings of the Gods) to ward off any evil influences that may result from a conjunction of eight planets which astrologers have said will occur on February 2. The temple's chief High Priest said that 30 monks would conduct round the clock ceremonies for thirty days and that they would plead with the Gods to bring about harmony in the world. [*The* [Rangoon] *Nation*, December 28, 1962]

and it is in that language that they are recited in the lay devotions held in the village chapel.

With this general description of their ritual use[16] we may now consider, in translation, a sample of the main *paritta.* In studying these texts it will be noted, as has already been indicated (*supra,* ch. 6), that although they are used for magical protection, few of them have either the form or the content of a spell, and in any event their cognitive meaning almost never has any relation to the specific protective function they are intended to serve.

Khandha Paritta

This *paritta* is recited for protection not only against dangerous snakes, for which it was originally composed, but from other dangerous beasts as well. When recited in the house all the windows are opened, so that all creatures may hear the love *(mettā)* that is being expressed for them.

> I love Virûpakkhas, the Erâpathas I love.
> I love Khabyâputtas, the Kanhâgotamakas I love.
> I love live things that have no feet, the bipeds too I love.
> I love four-footed creatures, and things with many feet.
> Let no footless thing do hurt to me, nor thing that has two feet.
> Let no four-footed creature hurt, nor thing with many feet.
> Let all creatures, all things that live, all beings of whatever kind,
> Let all behold good fortune, and let none fall into sin.
> Infinite is the Buddha, infinite the Truth, infinite the Order. Finite are creeping things; snakes, scorpions and centipedes, spiders and lizards, rats and mice.
> Made is my safeguard, made my defence. Let living things retreat,
> Whilst I revere the Blessed One, the Buddhas seven supreme.
>
> —*The Vinaya* 6:75-77

[16]*Paritta* have been used ritually in Burma from the earliest, even pre-Pagan times. Thus according to the *Sāsanavamsa,* when Soṇa and Uttara, Asoka's alleged missionaries to Lower Burma, were told of the demon who devoured all boys born in the royal palace, they vanquished the demon by means of a *paritta.* (*History of the Buddha's Religion,* p. 43.)

For the Pagan period the evidence is less legendary. Thus, as Luce (1940:326) informs us,

> Recitation of protective charms (*paruit rwat,* Pali *paritta*) was an important part of a Pagan dedication, eight or more of the leading clergy taking part, sometimes headed by the mahāthera. It was even more important at the lengthy ceremonies connected with the building of Kyanzittha's palace, full details being given of the recitation of the parit mangal and pouring of *paritta* water at an all-night ceremony of March 1st-2nd 1102 by 4108 monks headed by the mahāthera Arahan. On every fastday while the palace was being built, Arahan and other leading monks, assisted by scholars and children of Mon and other chiefs, would hold midnight services and sprinkle holy water all round the palace.

In early Pagan, these spells were also used as a means for the expiation of sins. By reciting an appropriate *paritta,* "corrupt and cynical monks" (probably the *Ari*) taught that all crimes (including matricide) "need bring no retribution if the guilty man recited (or engaged someone to recite) an appropriate *paritta.*" (Bode 1909:12) I have never heard of the *paritta* being put to this use in contemporary Burma.

Mora Paritta

The recitation of this *sutta* is believed to be especially efficacious in protecting those in danger of arrest, and in freeing those who have been arrested.

> There he rises, king all seeing,
> Making all things bright with his golden light.
> Thee I worship, glorious being,
> Making all things bright with thy golden light,
> Keep me safe, I pray,
> Through the coming day.
>
> All saints, the righteous, wise in holy lore,
> These do I honour, and their aid implore:
> All honour to the wise, to wisdom honour be,
> To freedom, and to all that freedom has made free.
>
> —*The Jātaka,* Vol. 2:23

Ātānāṭiya (Burmese, Atanariya) Paritta

This *sutta,* which runs to five printed pages (*Dialogues of the Buddha,* Pt. III: 189-194), is especially used to combat dangers caused by evil spirits and supernatural beings.

Aṅgulimāla (Burmese, Ingulimala) Paritta

This *paritta* is for difficult and dangerous childbirths.

> I, sister, am not aware of having intentionally deprived any living thing of life since I was born of the ariyan birth. By this truth may there be well-being for you, well-being for the unborn child.
>
> —*Middle Length Sayings,* Vol. 2:289

Vaṭṭaka (Burmese, Wuda) Paritta

This *paritta* is especially efficacious as a protection against fire.

> With wings that fly not, feet that walk not yet,
> Forsaken by my parents, here I lie!
> Wherefore I conjure thee, dread Lord of Fire,
> Primeval Jātaveda, turn! go back!
>
> —*The Jātaka,* Vol. 1:90

Bojjhanga Sutta (Burmese, Boukzin Thouk)

This *paritta* is recited for protection against illness.

"Monks, these four deeds I have myself comprehended, realized and made known. What four?

"There is a dark deed with a dark result; a bright deed with a bright result; a deed that is both dark and bright, with a dark and bright result; and the deed that is neither dark nor bright, with a result neither dark nor bright, which being itself a deed conduces to the waning of deeds. These four deeds . . . I have made known.

"And of what sort, monks, is the deed neither dark nor bright . . . ?

"The limbs of wisdom that is mindfulness, that which is dhamma-search, that which is energy, that which is tranquillity, that which is concentration, and the limb of wisdom that is equanimity. This is called. . . ."

—*Gradual Sayings,* Vol. 2:238, 241-42

Pubbaṇha Sutta (Burmese, Poukpana Thouk)

This is recited for protection from epidemics, and especially from all dangers caused by the twelve planets.

"Monks, whatsoever beings at early dawn, at noon and at eve practise righteousness of body, speech and mind,—such have a happy dawn, a happy noon, a happy evening."

"Auspicious, festive, happy, blessed dawn,
Fair day, glad time is that when alms are given
To holy men: when righteous acts, words, thoughts,
Right aspirations bring auspicious gain
To those who practise them. Happy are they
Who get such gain, and prosperous in the Way.
So be ye also prosperous in the Way,—
Free from disease and well with all your kind."

—*Gradual Sayings,* Vol. 1:272

Mangala (Burmese, Min-gala) Sutta

The *Mangala* (luck) *Sutta*—also *Mahāmaṅgala Sutta*—is alleged to have been composed by the Buddha when requested by a *deva* to tell him what the "highest blessing" might be. The Buddha's answer, which comprises the text of this *sutta,* is probably the most famous of all *paritta* in Burma. It is recited not only for protection from danger, but as a means to attain almost any problematic end—a good harvest, good grades in school, victory in competition, and so on. Together with the *Ratana* and *Pubbaṇha Suttas,* it is always chanted by the monks after they are feasted by the faithful.

2. Buddha said: "Not cultivating (the society of) fools, but cultivating (the society of) wise men, worshipping those that are to be worshipped, this is the highest blessing.

3. "To live in a suitable country, to have done good deeds in a former (existence), and a thorough study of one's self, this is the highest blessing.

4. "Great learning and skill, well-learnt discipline, and well-spoken words, this is the highest blessing.

5. "Waiting on mother and father, protecting child and wife, and a quiet calling, this is the highest blessing.

6. "Giving alms, living religiously, protecting relatives, blameless deeds, this is the highest blessing.

7. "Ceasing and abstaining from sin, refraining from intoxicating drink, perseverance in the Dhammas, this is the highest blessing.

8. "Reverence and humility, contentment and gratitude, the hearing of the Dhamma at due seasons, this is the highest blessing.

9. "Patience and pleasant speech, intercourse with Samanas, religious conversation at due seasons, this is the highest blessing.

10. "Penance and chastity, discernment of the noble truths, and the realisation of Nibbâna, this is the highest blessing.

11. "He whose mind is not shaken (when he is) touched by the things of the world (lokadhamma), (but remains) free from sorrow, free from defilement, and secure, this is the highest blessing.

12. "Those who, having done such (things), are undefeated in every respect, walk in safety everywhere, theirs is the highest blessing." [*Sutta-Nipāta*, pp. 43-44][17]

Mettā (Burmese, Myitta) Sutta

Like the previous *paritta*, the *Mettā* (love) *Sutta* is not associated with any myth or tale. The Burmese believe that its recitation is especially efficacious for protection from evil spirits because, as one monk put it, "for reciting the *Myitta Thouk* all the *Brahma* and *sammā deva* will love [and therefore protect] you."

1. Whatever is to be done by one who is skilful in seeking (what is) good, having attained that tranquil state (of Nibbâna):—Let him be able and upright and conscientious and of soft speech, gentle, not proud.

2. And contented and easily supported and having few cares, unburdened and with his senses calmed and wise, not arrogant, without (showing) greediness (when going his round) in families.

3. And let him not do anything mean for which others who are wise might reprove (him); may all beings be happy and secure, may they be happy-minded.

4. Whatever living beings there are, either feeble or strong, all either long or great, middlesized, short, small or large,

5. Either seen or which are not seen, and which live far (or) near, either born or seeking birth, may all creatures be happy-minded.

6. Let no one deceive another, let him not despise (another) in any place, let him not out of anger or resentment wish harm to another.

[17]This *sutta* is also found in the *Khuddakapāṭha*, ch. 5.

7. As a mother at the risk of her life watches over her own child, her only child, so also let every one cultivate a boundless (friendly) mind towards all beings.

8. And let him cultivate goodwill towards all the world, a boundless (friendly) mind, above and below and across, unobstructed, without hatred, without enmity.

9. Standing, walking or sitting or lying, as long as he be awake, let him devote himself to this mind; this (way of) living they say is the best in this world.

10. He who, not having embraced (philosophical) views, is virtuous, endowed with (perfect) vision, after subduing greediness for sensual pleasures, will never again go to a mother's womb. (*Sutta-Nipāta*, pp. 24-25) [18]

Ratana (Burmese, Yadana) Sutta

Another famous *paritta*, this long *sutta* (*Woven Cadences*, pp. 35-38) is recited in any situation of danger, but especially for those that are supernaturally caused.

It is time now to flesh out this collection of *sutta* by describing an actual ceremony. One morning it was announced in Yeigyi that a stag had come through the village the previous night since (as we have noted) it is a very bad omen for wild animals to enter a village or town, a *paritta* ceremony was to be performed to avert its "dangers."[19]

The ceremony was held at the boundary of the village and was performed by three monks seated on a raised platform. Vases filled with flowers were placed in front of the monks as offerings to the Buddha. Also displayed on the platform were offerings to the monks—who, prior to the ceremony, had been feasted by the villagers—consisting of trays of rice, matches, candles, and soap. The chanting by the monks lasted about an hour, for although the core *sutta* for this type of danger is the *Pubbaṇha Sutta*, other *paritta* were also recited. As the monks chanted, the congregation (three-fourths of whom were women) faced them, sitting on the ground in the traditional devotional pose. When the chanting was completed, a representa-

[18]This *sutta* is also found in *Khuddakapāṭha*, ch. 9.

[19]*Paritta* are recited in the cities for the same purpose, as the following news story from Lashio, a large town in the northern Shan States, indicates.

> Recitation of *paritta* (holy scriptures) by Presiding Monks of the town to dispel evil spirits were made at the Town Hall on May 24 evening. Among those who attended the function were the Deputy Commissioner, Headquarters Assistant (Civil) and Elders of the town.
>
> About two weeks ago, a *gyi* (barking deer) entered Lashio as far inside as Kaladan quarter, in the heart of the town. The entry of a jungle animal into town was considered a bad omen especially as evil spirits might visit the place in its wake.
>
> Recently, many deaths had occurred round about Lashio of persons losing their lives at the hands of gangsters, dacoits and rebels. The townsfolks fearing visitations of bad spirits of those who lost their lives in tragic circumstances, had organized the recitation of the holy scriptures to drive them away. [*The* [Rangoon] *Nation*, May 31, 1961]

tive from each household was given one piece of string and one flower from the vases that had been placed in front of the monks. The string, which had acquired the power of the *paritta,* was tied around the walls of the house to prevent the impending danger from penetrating the house; and the flower, which serves the same function, was tied to one of the walls. Finally, a member of each household was instructed to throw a handful of sand against the house, which (for reasons I was unable to discover) has the same function.

The Use of *Dāna*

The efficacy of Buddhist apotropaic ritual, we have seen in chapter 6, is interpreted in a number of ways: assistance from the Buddha, assistance from the *deva,* the tapping of the power of Buddhist sacra, and immediate change in karma brought about through an instant increase in merit. Since almost all these rituals include offerings to the Buddha, merit accrues from the *dāna* they represent. Since, however, the amount of merit may not be sufficient to cope with the magnitude of the crisis, two other forms of *dāna* are performed if time permits. First, special meals are offered to the monks—the more elaborate the meal and the greater the number fed, the greater the merit; though if necessary, of course, even a single monk will do. This is one of the reasons that no village can afford to be without a monk. *Dāna* offered to the monk is not only the Burman's most important investment for a happier rebirth, but a crucial means of protection against the dangers of his present existence. The monk may be viewed as the Burman's insurance policy, as it were: his daily feeding of monks represents his regular premium payments, and the special feasts offered in times of crisis represent special assessments. Thus on the day the planetary disaster was to occur all the monks in the village, and in other villages and towns throughout Burma, were given special meals with the hope of averting the impending disaster.

A second and more expensive form of merit-producing *dāna* is the purchase of domestic animals in order to save them from slaughter. The protection of animal life in order to acquire merit is, of course, a well-known Buddhist practice. I have already noted that during certain Buddhist holydays fish are transferred from the stagnant pools left by previously swollen rivers to the regular riverbed. Similarly, pagoda and monastery compounds often contain ponds in which turtles and fish, protected for life, are fed by the devout in order to obtain merit. The freeing of domestic animals is a much more dramatic act—it releases an animal destined for slaughter and therefore produces a great amount of merit. Indeed, since the saving of life is the positive expression of the Buddhist precept against killing, and since it is the ultimate expression of the Buddhist virtue of *mettā* (loving-kindness), the merit acquired from such an act is, according to some informants, even greater than for feeding a monk—especially since the sacrifice, measured by the cost, is greater. Precisely because it is so expensive, this ceremony is performed only in the face of great danger, and generally as a collective ritual. Thus, in yet another attempt to cope with the impending world calamity described above, the Burmese Government not only ordered all slaughterhouses closed for the three-day period of the predicted disaster, but itself freed 602 animals. Threes and nine being auspicious numbers, nine classes of animals were ransomed in three and in multiples of three. As reported in the press, they were bought off in the numbers noted below.[20]

Cattle	3
Pigs	3
Goats	9
Sheep	9
Fowls	60
Ducks	60
Pigeons	120
Fish	120
Crabs	218
Total	602

As he freed the animals on behalf of the government, U Nu, then premier,

> exhorted them not to avenge themselves of the wrongs if the people, in their previous existences, had either ill-treated or slaughtered them and that the people would reciprocate by forgiving them [the animals] if they had similarly done such wrongs against them [the people] in *samsara* (round of births). [*The* [Rangoon] *Guardian*, 2/5/62.]

Before closing this section, it should be explicitly emphasized—although this has already been indicated in passing—that only rarely is one of these rituals performed by itself. Even for relatively minor crises at least two are performed, and for major crises (as in the case of *nat* possession) many of these Buddhist, as well as some non-Buddhist, rituals are performed simultaneously. During a seance of exorcism—probably the most important ceremony of apotropaic Buddhism—all the Buddhist sacra are worshiped, almost all the Buddhist spells are chanted, and various forms of *dāna* are offered. In addition, sundry forms of non-Buddhist magic are employed and the *nat* responsible for the illness propitiated. Since this ceremony has been described elsewhere (Spiro 1967: ch. 11), I shall not repeat it here.

[20]Other magical notions, too, were involved in this ceremony. Not only was the time of the release—7:00 A.M.—astrologically calculated, but each day of the week was represented by at least one class of animals astrologically associated with that day. Thus fowls, crabs, and fish are Monday animals, goats are Tuesday animals, pigs are Wednesday animals, and so on.

The Use of Meditation

One of the most fascinating means for coping with crisis—fascinating because of the transformations that have occurred in the technique—is Buddhist meditation. We have already noted that in kammatic Buddhism, meditation was transformed from a means for the extinction of craving to a means of acquiring merit. But this is only one of its changes. In contemporary Burma, meditation is viewed as a method for dealing with various of life's problems. It is used to cope with such minor difficulties as dissatisfaction with life, insomnia, and a variety of psychosomatic complaints (cf. Tin Swe 1965); as a technique for determining the identity of one's enemies; and as a method for curing heart trouble, ulcers, hypertension, chronic migraines, mental illness, and even cancer. When I queried him on the last category, a lay meditation master in Rangoon produced sworn affidavits and letters from former meditators, all claiming to have been cured of these various ailments by the meditation course they undertook under his guidance. What is most interesting about these letters and sworn statements is that they were written, not by village peasants, but by a middle-class and educated urban clientele, both Burmese and Western. It would seem—although additional research is required to sustain this argument—that in the absence of trained psychiatric resources, many urban Burmese turn to meditation centers for the kind of assistance which in the West is offered by psychotherapy. Indeed, without using the concepts of modern psychiatry, this particular meditation master interprets his putative results in psychological terms: through meditation, the mind can control the body.[21]

However it be interpreted, it is the case that an increasing number of Burmese attempt to overcome the anxieties and tensions of normal life by periodic retreat to meditation centers. Indeed, under the civilian regime of U Nu—who himself frequently retreated for long periods of meditation, especially when faced with political crises—government officials were given leave with pay in order to spend time in meditation centers. The significant thing about putting meditation to this use is that the peace of mind which, in nibbanic buddhism, is a means for achieving the concentration necessary for insight meditation has become, in these modern centers, either an end in itself or a means to cope with physical and emotional problems or achieve worldly success.

[21]From these letters and affidavits I gained the strong impression that, among other factors involved in the meditators' improvement, there was a strong transference relationship with the meditation master; and that, rather than gaining independence and self-reliance, they acquired a deep sense of emotional dependence on him.

Non-Buddhist Magic

Certain kinds of danger, as we have seen, may be coped with alternatively by non-Buddhist or by Buddhist ritual, and sometimes by both. Magic of the former type consists almost exclusively of talismans. Typically, the talisman consists of an amulet *(lethpwe.)* worn about the wrist or neck, made of string or a strip of bamboo or metal, over which an incantation—most often a Buddhist spell—has been chanted. (Spiro 1967:35-36) To this extent, of course, it is infused with Buddhist power. These amulets, which afford generic protection from attack by witches, spirits, snakes, and so on, are almost universally used, at least in rural Burma.

Until recently tatooing, also, was very widely used as a talisman. From the waist to below the knee, the male was tatooed with representations of tigers, *nāgas,* demons, and other dangerous creatures, as well as with *in:,* those cabalistic symbols which are used in many Burmese ceremonies. (Spiro 1967:175 ff.) Today it is rare to see tatooing in a male under forty.

A third type of talisman which I have not seen, although I suspect it is still used today, but which was importantly used in the past, is an amulet inserted under the flesh in the upper part of the arm. These charms, made of gold or silver, render one invulnerable. (Cf. Sangermano 1893:148; Trant 1827:88.) According to Winter (1858:219), a special group of Burmese soldiers known as the "invulnerables"—because they were armed with these talismans—fought against the British troops in the first Anglo-Burmese war (1824); these same type of talisman played a prominent role in the Saya San rebellion of 1930. Because of their power, and that of other charms and amulets, the followers of Saya San believed that they would be rendered

> invulnerable, invisible, their bodies would rise and fly through the air, they could cause a hostile army to drop its weapons by merely sounding their enchanted gongs, and if they pointed their fingers at an aeroplane it would crash on the spot. They advanced on to our machine guns believing these things, and they continued to believe even after they were wounded. [Harvey 1946:73]

Unlike the talisman, which overlaps in function a variety of Buddhist rituals described above, there are other forms of non-Buddhist magic whose protective equivalent is not found in the rituals of apotropaic Buddhism. Thus, to take but one example, there is a belief in the villages in the vicinity of Yeigyi that the first villager to die during the Buddhist Lent will bring misfortune to the village unless his corpse is cut into three parts, each part being buried separately. This form of burial is the only means by which the village can be protected. In 1962, as I was preparing to leave Burma, a neighboring village suffered inexplicably from a disproportionately high number of deaths during and after Lent. The village monk dreamt that they resulted from the negligence of the village to perform the appropriate magical ritual for the first person who had died during the previous Lent. When he informed the village elders of his dream, they ordered the corpse disinterred and the proper ritual performed.

All these forms of magic, it will be noted, are "non-Buddhist" only in the sense that they are not legitimized by some scriptural charter. From the perspective of the average Buddhist, however, they are most certainly Buddhist in that their efficacy lies in their harnessing of Buddhist power and their use of Buddhist symbols. In addition, their Buddhist legitimacy is guaranteed when they are performed, as they sometimes are, by Buddhist monks. Monastic involvement in these and other forms of magic is discussed in chapter 14.

IV

BUDDHISM AS A MONASTIC SYSTEM

CHAPTER 12

Monasticism: I. The Normative Structure

The Monk as Religious Virtuoso

From its inception Buddhism was conceived as a virtuoso religion. A true Buddhist, one who accepts the message of the Buddha, is one who follows in His Path. Having accepted the truth of the Buddha's teachings, his only consistent attitudinal response is to seek salvation; and having committed himself to this goal, his only consistent behavioral response is to renounce the world in order to extinguish all craving *(taṇhā).* To renounce the world, according to Buddhism, means to renounce all ties—parents, family, spouse, friends, and property—and to "wander alone like the rhinoceros." (See the *Khaggavisanasutta* of the *Sutta-Nipāta.*) In short, the true Buddhist is the *bhikkhu,* the monk.

Although "monk" is the conventional English gloss for the Pali *bhikkhu,* the latter term has no precise equivalent outside of Buddhism, and even within it one seeks in vain for a satisfactory definition. Take, for example, the following passage from Scripture (in the *Suttavibhanga* of the *Vinaya-Piṭaka*).

> *Bhikkhu* means: he is a *bhikkhu* because he is a beggar for alms, a *bhikkhu* because he submits to wandering for alms, a *bhikkhu* because he is one who wears the patchwork cloth, a *bhikkhu* by the designation of (others), a *bhikkhu* on account of his acknowledgment; a *bhikkhu* is called "Come, *Bhikkhu,*" a *bhikkhu* is endowed with going to the three refuges [the Buddha, the *Dhamma,* and the *Saṅgha*], a *bhikkhu* is auspicious, a *bhikkhu* is the essential, a *bhikkhu* is a learner, a *bhikkhu* is an adept, a *bhikkhu* means one who is endowed with harmony for the Order . . . with actions (in accordance with

> *Dhamma* and the discipline), with steadfastness, with the attributes of a man perfected. . . . [*The Book of the Discipline*, Pt. I, p. 42][1]

Although this passage does not assist us in deciding on a proper English equivalent, it does help us to rule out certain of the terms that are currently used. Thus, although most writers on Thai Buddhism use "priest" to designate the Thai *bhikkhu*, it is obvious from this passage—and, as we shall see, from empirical observations of contemporary *bhikkhus*—that whatever else he may be, the *bhikkhu* is most certainly not a priest (not, at any rate, as that role is conventionally understood). Thus, he is not an intermediary between man and the supernatural; he administers no sacraments; he does not minister to a congregation, whether as the celebrant of a divine service or as a pastor. Although when requested he performs rituals on behalf of laymen, this is not his essential function, which, so far as laymen are concerned, is to serve as a "field of merit," i.e., as a means by which (through the offerings they make to him) they can acquire merit.

If "priest" is a poor translation, "monk" (the typical gloss) has certain limitations as well, especially when Christian monks are taken as the implied institutional model. As wandering mendicants, the early *bhikkhus*, at least, were more like friars than monks. This is not the case nowadays, for though mendicants they are settled in permanent domiciles. But even today *bhikkhus* (unlike Christian monks, who, following the Benedictine Rule, take a vow of stability) are not bound to any particular house. Still, most of them, it must be admitted, remain more or less permanently in one location. Finally—and perhaps most importantly—though rejecting the world and all its works, they are not cloistered. Living in monasteries at the edge of a village or in the middle of a town, they maintain daily intercourse with laymen. The latter are free to enter the monastery at will, and the *bhikkhus* emerge from it, not only for their daily alms-rounds but also to perform rituals, to be fed at the homes of lay devotees, and so on. Unlike the Christian monk, therefore, who is neither in the world nor of it, the *bhikkhu* is not of the world but is frequently in it.

Despite these difficulties, however, it is not stretching the term unduly to render *bhikkhu* as "monk." If, generically, a monk is one who renounces the world in order to attain salvation, then the *bhikkhu* is most certainly a monk. Moreover, he not only renounces the world, but like monks everywhere, lives according to a rule and practices a life of asceticism in order to achieve his goal. Henceforth, therefore, I shall render *bhikkhu* as "monk."

Although monasticism is the core institution of Buddhism, it was not, of course, invented by the Buddha: Buddhist monasticism, as is well known,

[1]In her translation of this text, Horner consistently renders *bhikkhu* by "monk." So as not to prejudge the issue, I have deliberately left the Pali term untranslated.

had its origins in the pre-Buddhist religious movements of ancient India. When the Buddha Himself became an ascetic almsman, the almsmen's community was already in existence. Most scholars view the Upanishads, with their emphasis on renunciation *(tyāga)* as the supreme virtue, as the philosophical source of those Indian ascetic movements which preceded Buddhist asceticism;[2] and the ritual of *pravrajyā*, or "going forth," is viewed as the basis for the monastic institutionalization of asceticism. *Pravrajyā* entailed the rejection, not only of home life, but of "the whole system of Vedic social practice and religious culture and all its signs and symbols. It is therefore called *sannyasa*, the 'complete casting off.' " (Dutt 1962:41) In Buddhism this practice is known as the passing from "home into homelessness" *(agārasmā anagāriyam)*. By the sixth century B.C., those who had performed this ritual of "going forth" comprised a community of wandering religious ascetics, known as *parivrājaka*.

> They live by begging, have no settled dwelling (except during the rains, when the observance of the rain-retreat is a common custom among them), move about from place to place, and are either ascetics practicing austerities or are, in the words of Rudyard Kipling, "dreamers and babblers of strange gospels." [*Ibid.*:40-41]

The Buddhist monastic order, or *Saṅgha*, probably originated as a sect within the *parivrājaka* community, differing from others of its sects in recognizing the Buddha as their Master, and in accepting His *Dhamma* as their teaching.

Unlike the present *Saṅgha*, the original *Saṅgha* viewed itself as following the mission layed down by the Master, viz., to go forth ". . . on tour for the blessing of the manyfolk, for the happiness of the manyfolk out of compassion for the world, for the welfare, the blessing, the happiness of *deva* and men" (*Mahāvagga* I, 11, 1, tr. in *The Book of the Discipline*, Pt. IV, p. 28). With this mission, the members of the early *Saṅgha* (like other

[2]Many explanations have been offered for the prevalence of asceticism in India. The following speculations by Mrs. Stevenson (Stevenson 1915:2) are an example of the speculative genre.

> To understand the creeds of India one must, of course, remember its climate: over a large part of the country except during the rainy season, when ascetics suspend their wanderings, it is always fine: no drenching rain and (in the greater part of India) no biting frost compel men to provide themselves with houses or fires. The intense heat discourages exertion and robs men of energy, till rest seems the greatest bliss and meditation an alluring duty. And then, as we know only too well, the influence of the climate breeds pessimism eventually in the blithest European or Indian. In the east death and disease come with such tragic swiftness, and famine and pestilence with such horrifying frequency, that the fewer hostages one has given to fortune, the happier is one's lot. To the poor and unaided in ancient India justice was unknown and life and property but ill secured, just as we may see in many native states to this day. All these influences, creed, climate, pessimism and injustice, pressed men more and more towards the pathway of the professed ascetic's life. . . .

members of the *parivrājaka* community) lived the lives of hermits, as Scripture clearly indicates. Gradually, however, the eremitical practice—though not the ideal—gave way to a more settled life, a transition which may have been accomplished as early as the fourth century B.C. According to Dutt (*op. cit.*:57) the consequence of this transition was twofold. First, the *Saṅgha* became independent of, and distinguished from, the wanderers' community; second, it marked the beginning of the Buddhist coenobium.[3]

Whatever the origin of Buddhist monasticism, the monk has been normatively viewed as the true Buddhist from the very inception of this institution. This conclusion not only follows from the very nature of the Buddhist message, but is clearly implied in all three "baskets" of Scripture. With some few exceptions, the *sutta* are addressed to monks or to potential converts to monkhood. In the entire *Sutta* only one discussion is addressed to the social ethics of the layman,[4] and only one sermon—the *Mangala Sutta*—deals with relationships in general among laymen. Moreover, the abstruse and arid philosophy of mind which comprises the bulk of the *Abhidhamma*, the second "basket," is hardly calculated to appeal to the masses. Finally, the rules and regulations found in the *Vinaya* are intended to govern the behavior of the monastic order only.

The reason for the normative emphasis on the monk as the Buddhist par excellence is stated by the Buddha Himself (in the *Sāmañña-Phala Sutta*, 42). Although it is possible for the householder to live as a true Buddhist, it is, He says, extremely "difficult"; rather, renunciation is most conducive to the Buddhist life.

> When he has thus become a recluse he lives self-restrained by that restraint that should be binding on a recluse. Uprightness is his delight, and he sees danger in the least of those things he should avoid. He adopts, and trains himself in, the precepts. He encompasses himself with good deeds in act and word. Pure are his means of livelihood, good is his conduct, guarded the door of his senses. Mindful and self-possessed he is altogether happy. [*Dialogues of the Buddha*, Pt. I, p. 79]

[3]Dutt (*ibid.*:124-27) sees the origin of the Buddhist coenobium in the custom of the rain-retreat. Whether, as he believes, this custom began as a practical response to the virtual impossibility of wandering about in the tropical monsoon, and the necessity to seek shelter, or whether it began because wandering in this season resulted in harm to the young crops and to animal life, as other scholars (cf. Horner 1938:xlvi), following Scripture (*Mahāvagga* III, 1-3), believe, it was during this three-month rainy season (the *vassa*) that the monks settled in temporary colonies known as *āvāsa*. Although originating as temporary settlements of three-month duration, the *āvāsa* became semipermanent and eventually permanent settlements; the monks, heretofore strangers to each other, developed a collective life during this three-month retreat. Then, as Dutt (*op. cit.*:55) observes, "with donations coming in a liberal measure for the monks' maintenance, the rule of wandering almsmanship lost its urgency and much of its mandatory character."

[4]This is the *Sigālovāda Suttanta* of the *Dīgha Nikāya* (ch. 31, of *Dialogues of the Buddha*, Pt. III). Characterized by Buddhaghosa as the "Vinaya of the Houseman" (C. A. F. Rhys Davids, 1921:169), it spells out the reciprocal duties of parent-child, husband-wife, friend-friend, master-servant, teacher-pupil, monk-layman.

But it is not only in conception that Buddhism is a virtuoso religion. Psychologically only a small minority in any society could be expected to follow the Buddha's path. The number of persons who might be convinced by its world-rejecting attitudes is small; the number (even from among those so convinced) who might be willing to abandon the world is yet smaller; while the number among the latter who are intellectually and emotionally qualified to lead the contemplative life is smaller still.

If psychological considerations preclude the possibility of world renunciation becoming a mass phenomenon, its sociological consequences render such a possibility absurd. For consider: if the philosophy of world renunciation were to be popularly adopted, there could be no state; and if the rules governing the monastic order were to apply to all men, there could be neither a society—for monks are celibate—nor an economy—for Buddhist monks perform no physical labor. For these same reasons, if all men were to become monks there could be no monastic life, since without a laity to support them the monks could not exist. Indeed, lay Buddhism is most essentially expressed in supporting the monastic order, thereby making it possible for this small group of religious virtuosos to follow the path of true Buddhism. In an important sense, their support of these virtuosos is a measure of the laymen's devotion to the values and principles of Buddhism which the former embody in their lives.

Structurally viewed, then, a Buddhist society consists of a small core of world-renouncing religious virtuosos surrounded by a large mass of the religiously unmusical, who although living in the world cherish and support this otherworldly minority. The size of the minority varies of course both in time and in space. In Thailand, for example, where the population of ethnic Thais was estimated in 1957 to be 18,000,000, the monastic population in 1954 was 157,000. (Blanchard 1958: 101) In contrast, the monastic populations in 1894 of Sikhim and Bhutan have been estimated as comprising a tenth, and those of Tibet and Ladak as a sixth, of the total populations, respectively, of those societies (Waddell 1967:171).

Nobody knows how many monks there really are in Burma, not only because of the difficulties in obtaining a reliable estimate of a population which is inherently unstable—since monks may and do freely enter and leave the Order—but also because the Burmese Order has long resisted any governmental attempt to take a monastic census. Their resistance stems from two fears: first, that a census constitutes government interference and would lead to even greater intrusion into monastic affairs; second, that by revealing the large number of bogus monks ("humans in yellow robes") who inhabit monasteries, a census would bring discredit on the monkhood. Naturally enough, the bogus monks themselves are especially obdurate on this issue. Resistance is so strong that, responding to strong monastic pressure, even the present military government withdrew its 1965 plan to conduct a monastic census. This being so, all figures concerning the monastic population of Burma, including those listed below, represent crude estimates.

On the basis of an unofficial census taken in Mandalay in 1960 by the local office of the Ministry of Religious Affairs, the monastic population of that city was estimated to be 9,881.[5] For the same year the officials of the Department estimated the total monastic population of Burma proper (exclusive of the constituent states) to have been 850,000. This is close to the figure of 800,000 which Tinker (1959:168) quotes from a 1954 government statement to Parliament. If these estimates are reliable, monks would constitute approximately 5 per cent of the total and 10 per cent of the male population.

If, again, these estimates are reliable, the monastic population of Burma has if anything increased in modern times—compared, at least, to the earliest available historical data. Thus, a century and a quarter ago Malcom, admitting that it was impossible to give any "exact number" for the population of Burmese monks, nevertheless estimated that "their proportion to the people is about as one to thirty."[6] (Malcom 1839:264) As is the case today, however, then, too, monks were distributed unevenly through the population. Thus while the town of Ava was estimated to have had 20,000 monks in a population of 200,000, the province of Amherst had 1,000 monks in a population of 36,000.

Fifty years later, according to the 1891 Census (Government of India: 1902), the monastic population was estimated at 137 to every 10,000 males, a sharp decline from Malcom's estimates: from 3 per cent of the *total* population, to 1½ per cent of the *male* population. (The Census also estimated the number of monasteries at 15,371, or one to every 93 houses, and 1.9 for every village and town. On both indices, the proportions were much higher for Upper than for Lower Burma.) Ten years later the number of monks seems to have increased again. According to the 1901 Census, their number was 91,500, 2½ per cent of the male population, but the number of monasteries remained the same. Twenty years later, the monastic population of Upper Burma was estimated as 3 per cent of the total population. (Scott and Hardiman 1900:3) In Mandalay, where they were estimated at 13,227, they would have constituted 8 per cent of the population.

The Function of Monasticism

"Function" is a fuzzy term in the social sciences. When it refers to a social institution, it has been used to designate either its purpose or its conse-

[5]The head of one of the national monastic associations said that his survey estimated their number to be closer to 12,000. According to the same survey, there were 4,000 estimated monks in Rangoon and 3,000-4,000 in the small town of Pakoku.

[6]The estimate of one to thirty for Burma contrasts sharply with the estimate given for Ceylon—one to four hundred—for the same period. (See Hardy 1850:309).

quences; and whether the one or the other, it sometimes refers to collectivities, sometimes to individuals. Moreover, in either case it is sometimes used for those putative functions of which the actors may be aware (manifest function), and sometimes for those of which they are unaware (latent function). Given these ambiguities I wish to state at the outset that this section is concerned exclusively with the normative function of Buddhist monasticism. That is, not with its social or psychological consequences, but with its purpose; and by "purpose" is meant, not the personal motives which lead to monastic recruitment, but the culturally stipulated end or ends for which monasticism is the culturally prescribed means.

TABLE 9
FUNCTIONS OF THE BUDDHIST MONK, AS REPORTED BY BURMESE MONKS ($N = 20$)

FUNCTIONS		Σ
For Laymen		6
Teach Buddhism	5	
Perform religious ritual	1	
For Self		19
Meditate	5	
Study	4	
Strive for nirvana	4	
Live in compliance with Rule	3	
Say beads	2	
Strive for supermundane power	1	
		25

An examination of the Buddhist monastic life (see below, chapter 13) reveals that the monastic role subsumes two sets of activities: those that serve the needs of laymen and those that serve the needs of the monks themselves. All monks insist, however, that the latter activities are of much greater importance, for they hold, as we have otherwise abundantly seen, that the main function of Buddhist monasticism is to promote the monk's spiritual welfare. Thus in response to the question, "What are the functions of a monk?" not even one monk listed service to laymen as a major, let alone *the* major monastic function. (See Table 9.) The six who mentioned it proposed it as of secondary importance. In addition to seeking their own spiritual welfare, they said, monks should also attempt to promote the spiritual welfare of others (by teaching Buddhism or performing rituals). But even for them the primary function of the monastery is to provide the monk with optimum conditions for pursuing his own salvation—in that pursuit the needs of laymen are secondary.[7]

[7]Although Christian mystics, unlike these Buddhist monks, stress unselfish and altruistic motives for their renunciation, Leuba discovered that they "fell far short of their ethical goal and approached it no nearer than did a host of inconspicuous Christians." (Leuba 1925:189)

This is not to say that monks are indifferent to the salvation of the layman. The Buddhist virtue of *mettā* (loving-kindness) is not lacking in the monks, and although most of them may not have studied the *Sigālovāda Suttanta* they would certainly agree with the sentiment expressed in verse 33 that monks display this virtue in the following ways.

> They [monks] restrain him [the layman] from evil, they exhort him to good, they love him with kindly thoughts, they teach him what he had not heard, they correct and purify what he has heard, they reveal to him the way to heaven. [*Dialogues of the Buddha,* Pt. III, p. 183]

Still, even when agreeing with this passage, they would say that their primary function is the pursuit of their own salvation, not that of laymen. The following examples are typical. While discussing Buddhism with a village monk I asked him why it is that despite centuries of Buddhism the Burmese—according to him—continue to be characterized by greed, lust, and anger. The answer, he said, is that the Burmese are really ignorant of Buddhism; they pay no attention to it. "But," he continued, "I can't be concerned about that. I have to look after my own nirvana."

Again, in talking with another monk, I asked him whether it was possible, as many laymen had claimed, to attain nirvana without meditating. This, he said, is "absolutely impossible." But, he went on, "it is none of my responsibility to inform them that they are wrong. My only responsibility is to myself; I must look after my own salvation, not that of others."

In sum, so far as the monks are concerned, the primary duty of the monk is to practice a discipline by which he can accelerate his attainment of his own salvation.[8] In this case, of course, their motivation is entirely consistent with the metaphysics of Buddhist soteriology. Except as a passive agent, serving as the recipient of their alms, the monk can do nothing to assist laymen to achieve salvation because each Buddhist must save himself. Their motivation is consistent, too, with the orthodox position of *Theravāda* Buddhism concerning the monkhood. When King Milinda asked the purpose of the monk's renunciation, the Venerable Nāgasena answered:

He summarizes his findings as follows.

> We are to recall that if the establishment of God's Will in them, and of His Kingdom upon earth, came to occupy the first place in the concern of our great mystics, it played quite an inconspicuous role in their determination to enter the religious life. Self-regarding motives, egoistic in character, were the main determinants of their decision to renounce the World for the companionship of God. [*Ibid.:* 189-90]

[8]In this sense, the *bhikkhu* is similar to the Christian (Benedictine) monk. For, as Butler (1962:29) informs us:

> A man became a monk precisely because he felt called to be a monk and for no other purpose or object whatever, nor as a preparation for anything else—except Heaven. The monk's object is to sanctify his soul and serve God by leading a life in community in accordance with the Gospel counsels. Works of various kinds will be given him to do; but these are secondary, and no one of them is part of his essential vocation as a monk.

> Why do you ask? Our renunciation is to the end that this sorrow may perish away, and that no further sorrow may arise; the complete passing away, without cleaving to the world, is our highest aim. [*The Questions of King Milinda*, p. 49]

Nor would the layman have it otherwise. The view expressed in the above passage is held not only by the majority of Burmese monks, but is entirely shared by Burmese laymen. Almost unanimously, the latter hold that the function of the monk is to meditate, study, and live according to the Rule. To be sure, the monk is expected to perform those ritual functions which laymen request of him, but this aspect of the monastic role is of secondary importance, both descriptively and normatively, in their eyes. This is not to say that the layman does not need the monk; on the contrary, he needs the monk desperately. He needs him, however, so that he (the layman) may serve him, rather than being served by him. For it is primarily by offering *dāna*—food, robes, housing, and so on—to the monk that the layman acquires the merit necessary for *his* salvation. And that is why the layman, from his point of view, holds that the primary function of the monk is to seek his own salvation. For it is only by making offerings to a pious monk, one whose life is devoted to soteriological action, that merit is acquired.

As the Burmese see it, then, the monk's duty is to save himself; and laymen's duty is to provide him with the physical requirements by which he can devote his energies to that end. From their point of view, the monk-layman relationship, so far as salvation is concerned, is the obverse of the priest-layman relationship. Whereas in Christianity, for example, it is the duty of the priest, by his sacramental functions, to assist the layman to achieve salvation, in Buddhism it is the recognized duty of the layman to assist the monk to achieve salvation.

If, then, the monk is not expected to be primarily dedicated to the religious welfare of laymen, it is not surprising to learn that he is not expected to be concerned with their secular welfare. Buddhist monasticism, to employ a critical Buddhist distinction (which we have encountered before) is concerned with otherworldly *(lokuttara)*, not with worldly *(lokiya)* goals. All those worldly concerns which in the West have become associated with the clerical role—social service, community welfare, economic justice, public relations, and so on—are foreign to both the letter and the spirit of Buddhist monasticism. The Christian clergyman who addresses the Kiwanis Club, serves as the chaplain for the Elks' Lodge, raises funds for a charity drive, arranges for a church social, or serves on the mayor's beautification committee, has no counterpart in the Buddhist clergy. It would be unthinkable for a monk to be interested, not to mention participate, in such worldly concerns. As the monks, when queried about such matters, put it: "What have they to do with nirvana?"

This same attitude holds for their concern with village morality. Monks certainly preach about morality in their (occasional) sermons, but they almost never apply the abstract moral concepts of their sermons to specific moral, let alone social, issues confronting the villagers. The monk as moralist, to say nothing of any role as prophet, is as rare as the monk as pastor.[9]

This same negative stance holds, as well, for those activities which have come to be referred to as "nation-building." Although it has sometimes been suggested that the Burmese Government might better achieve its development goals by enlisting the active participation of the monks, the monks themselves will have no part in village or national development programs, such as the construction of roads, improvement of sanitation facilities, building of schools, and so on. The monks' reactions to this suggestion are unanimous: they would refuse to play any role in the encouragement or execution of such programs. "What," they ask, "does this have to do with the life of the monk? These are worldly matters; the monk is concerned with otherworldly goals." Moreover such participation, almost all of them added, is in violation of the monastic Rule, or *Vinaya.* Similar attitudes are found among monks in Lower Burma (cf. Pfanner 1966), and for the most part they are shared by monks in other *Theravāda* societies as well.[10]

Although the attitudes expressed in the foregoing paragraphs character-

[9]In a survey of twelve villages, I discovered only one exception to this generalization. In one village, an irascible monk was reported to have reprimanded and even beaten villagers who squandered their income on drinking and gambling. During the Japanese occupation, when such behavior was especially prevalent, he ordered five of the more flagrant cases to appear before him in the monastery. Commanding four of the five to hold the fifth on the ground, he beat each one in turn with his cane. This case is interesting not only because this monk's concern with village morality is atypical, but because the villagers conceded that he had the right to administer a beating to grown men. The monk is supreme!

[10]In Thailand the picture is not entirely clear. According to Ingersoll (1963:92-93), monks in central Thailand do not themselves participate in the manual aspects of village development programs, but they do play an active role in their encouragement. Moreover, unlike Burma, abbots are often viewed as community leaders.

In northeast Thailand, according to Klausner (1964), monks not only take part in all aspects of village life, but physically participate in the building of roads, the construction of schools, and so on. (Cf. Klausner 1964.) Moreover, unlike the case in Burma, their laymen expect them to share in these activities. Similarly, monks in that politically sensitive area are frequently used by government and other agencies to stimulate developmental programs (with the financial assistance, it should be added, of the [American] Asia Foundation).

To the extent that Thai monks are involved in nation-building, it is primarily a response to deliberate attempts by the Thai government to stimulate their interest. Their involvement, as a recent study indicates, ". . . is a neologism in Thai Buddhist history, and almost contrary to the traditional and orthodox idea that monks should be far apart from mundane affairs . . ." (Mulder 1969:2). In Bangkok, especially among the junior and learned monks, the attitude to monastic involvement in such worldly affairs is signally hostile. The monks interviewed, writes Mulder *(ibid.),* ". . . felt amazed by my interest in their potential welfare activities, and most were vehement in denying that the monkhood should engage in such activities. . . . They viewed their roles as religious *per se.* . . ."

ize the overwhelming majority of monks, there are a small number who, so far as social service is concerned, feel otherwise. Thus for example one group, concerned with performing acts of charity, have established orphanages in their monasteries. In 1956 they organized the Social Service *Saṅgha* Association *(Parahitta Saṅgha).* By 1962 there were 77 orphanages, scattered throughout Burma and the Shan States, affiliated with their monasteries, with more than 6,000 resident (male) orphans.[11] As might be expected, however, from the foregoing discussion, little interest has been shown in its work, either by other monks or by the laity. Financial support for its activities was mainly provided by the (American) Asia Foundation until its expulsion from Burma in 1962. Indeed, one of the moving spirits in the work of these monks, and in the founding of their association, was a Burmese employee of the latter foundation, a Western-educated Buddhist who, exposed to and influenced by Christian missionary work, was obviously attempting to cast the Buddhist monk in the latter mold. To be sure, he admitted, the goal of the monk is the attainment of nirvana, but, he argued, nirvana can only be achieved by service to others, because only through service can one achieve the necessary selflessness.

Since the small number of monks who participate in this organization are atypical in their attitudes to social service, it is of some interest to examine the Buddhist rationale for their deviance. In a seminar held with twenty of them who had arrived in Rangoon for the annual conference of the association, the following conclusions emerged. (1) Working for and with orphans is not an expression of attachment, which they admitted is a serious obstacle to the attainment of nirvana; it is rather an expression of love and compassion, sentiments enjoined on all Buddhists and necessary for the achievement of nirvana itself. (2) Those monks who criticize them are mistaken in saying that theirs is a worldly activity; it is otherworldly, because its object is nirvana. By working for the orphans, they obtain merit, and by this merit they can eventually attain nirvana. (3) Contrary to what others say, working for others is *the* way to nirvana. But obtaining nirvana for oneself is not enough; one must also help others to attain this goal. In caring for these boys they also teach them about Buddhism, so that they too can achieve nirvana. (4) Contrary to what others say, meditation is *not* the only way to nirvana. Nirvana can only be achieved by abolishing the belief in a permanent self or ego. Meditation is one, but not the only way by which this end can be achieved. Social service can also lead to this end, for in serving others one reduces the concern for oneself. (5) By engaging in social service one emulates the Buddha who, having achieved detachment, nevertheless continued to work ceaselessly for all sentient beings.

These, however, are the sentiments of a tiny minority. For the vast

[11]The nucleus of the *Parahitta Saṅgha* is the Tiger School of Kamayut, in the Insein District of Lower Burma, which pioneered in providing its boys with vocational training.

majority of Burmese monks, social service is viewed not only as irrelevant but as an obstacle to their quest for salvation.

The Rule

Ordination

Although renouncing the world in order to seek his salvation, the Buddhist monk does not pursue this goal anarchically. Even when he lives in physical isolation, he is yet implicated in a social order—the Buddhist Order of monks—and his behavior is governed by a set of norms and regulations—the monastic Rule. Having abandoned the world, the monk has not become a social isolate; he has merely exchanged one social system for another. To be a monk is not merely to be an almsman, even when his alms are a means for the pursuit of a soteriological goal; rather it is to live in accordance with the norms and regulations of the Rule. Unless he follows it, neither his alms collecting—if, indeed, anyone would offer him alms—nor his pursuit of nirvana stamps him as a monk.

Before one can follow the Rule, one must become a candidate for admission to the order of monks, the *Saṅgha.* The first and most important qualification for candidacy is that one be of the male sex. In the early history of Buddhism there was an order of female monks *(bhikkhuni),* parallel to that of male monks, which the Buddha Himself, bowing to the pressure of his disciples, reluctantly agreed to create. This female order, however, disappeared fairly soon in the history of Buddhism and was replaced by a lowly order of nuns.[12] Today, then, only males are eligible.

Being a male, however, does not suffice for admission to the Order. In addition, the candidate must be free from communicable diseases and from debts, he must be neither illegitimate nor a slave, and he must have the consent of his parents and (if he has one) his wife. Certain educational qualifications are also necessary, but they are simple. In principle, a male who possesses the above qualifications and is at least twenty years old can be ordained into the monkhood, although he possesses only the most elementary knowledge of Buddhism.

[12]For the most part, the tiny population of Buddhist nuns have neither religious nor social position in Burmese society. With some few exceptions, their social origins are humble and their educational attainments meager. Typically, they are former spinsters, widows or social rejects who have become nuns for lack of other means of economic support. Typically, too, they receive no religious training, nor do they serve any religious or social function. Observing the same five or eight precepts observed by Buddhist laymen, nuns do not live according to a rule. It is no accident that, although many village boys said they would like to become monks, only one girl said she would like to become a nun. Hence it is that Crawfurd's comments on Burmese nuns are as relevant today as they were when he made them over a century ago.

> The profession of a nun is not much respected by the people, and in general may be looked upon as little better than a more reputable mode of begging. A p'hun-ghi, or priest, never begs; he only expects charity. The nuns, on the contrary, go about begging from house to house, and are to be seen in the public markets openly asking for alms. [Crawfurd 1834: 130]

Ordination as a novice—the lower ordination *(pabbajā)*—is necessary before the candidate can receive the higher ordination for the monkhood. A novice (Burmese, *kou-yin;* Pali, *sāmaṇera*) must be at least eight years old, so that, should he remain in the robes until he receives the higher ordination, he will have had twelve years of monastic experience before becoming a full-fledged monk. In Burma, as we have seen, almost every boy becomes a novice at some time, not in preparation for taking the higher ordination, but as part of the Buddhist initiation ceremony. In either case, the novice is not bound by the 227 rules that regulate the monk's life, but is bound by 105 of them, and like the monk must constantly observe the Ten Precepts.

Since the monk, in essence, is a homeless, ascetic mendicant, the core of the higher ordination ceremony consists in taking the monastic vows of poverty, chastity, and homelessness. (It is to be noted that, unlike the Catholic monk, the Buddhist monk does not take a vow of obedience.) The ordination (Burmese, *yahan:gan* or *pazin:gan;* Pali, *upasampadā*) must take place in a special ordination chamber (Burmese, *thein;* Pali, *sīmā*) which laymen are not permitted to enter; indeed, they may not approach closer than the small stone stakes that surround the chamber. The time and date for the ordination are set by astrological calculation, as is the candidate's monastic (Pali) name, which supersedes his lay name.

Together with monks of the surrounding villages who participate in the ceremony—a minimum of four is mandatory—the candidate listens while one monk, selected for the occasion, chants the ordination ritual from the *Kan-ma-wa sa,* the ceremonial compendium used in ordination ceremonies. This is inscribed on palm leaf and usually enclosed within beautifully ornamented and gilded covers. The one ceremony I observed lasted about forty-five minutes and was almost identical with that described for the eighteenth and nineteenth centuries, respectively, by Sangermano (1893:124-28) and Bigandet (1912:275-81). Kneeling in front of the assembled monks, the candidate—head and eyebrows shaven, and dressed in the yellow robe—affirms, in response to the questions addressed to him by the presiding monk, that he is a human being of sound body and mind, of legitimate birth, free of debts, a freeman, at least twenty years old, in possession of robes and begging bowl, and has the consent of his parents. Then, instructed by the presiding monk to approach, the candidate sits before the assembled monks and asks them to admit him to the monkhood. Before complying with his request, the presiding monk asks three times if any of his colleagues has any objection to the candidate. There being no objection, he is pronounced a monk, and his new name is bestowed upon him. At this time the first section of the Rule (the *pārājika*) is read aloud to the new monk, first in Pali and then in Burmese, and after each regulation is recited, he promises to comply with its provisions. With this, the ceremony is ended.[13]

[13]As might be expected, the ordination is witnessed by relatives, friends, and fellow villagers of the candidate. In the ceremony I witnessed in Yeigyi there were about seventy-five

Ordained into the Order, the monk dies a civil death. Before the ceremony, he both divests himself of all his possessions and relinquishes title to any inheritable property (cf. Maung Maung 1963:125). He brings to the ordination, as gifts offered by the faithful, the only property which, as a monk, he may possess, viz.: the two parts of the yellow robe *(thin-gan:)*, a begging bowl *(thabeik)*, a girdle, a small razor, a needle and thread, a water strainer, and a palm-leaf fan. To destroy all vanity the razor is used for shaving not only his beard, but his hair and eyebrows as well. The water strainer is used as a filter so that, even unwittingly, the monk will not destroy insect life.

The Rule

The monastic Rule is contained in compendium form in the *Pāṭimokkha*,[14] a short treatise which monks recite twice a month on Buddhist Sabbath days. As a compendium it brings together the various rules which (allegedly formulated by the Buddha Himself) are scattered throughout the *Book of the Discipline*, the *Vinaya-Pitaka*, as the third "basket" of the Buddhist canon is called. As *Theravāda* Buddhism counts them there are 227 regulations in this Rule, which are classified according to severity into eight categories.[15] Expectedly, in a list so long, these regulations range from seemingly trivial and arbitrary conventions to basic norms which touch the very heart and essence of the monastic life. Clearly, the first four rules, the *pārājika*, are the core of the Rule, since their violation alone entails expulsion from the monkhood: as the formula has it, the monk who violates any of these four "is defeated." These four are simply stated. (1) A monk may not have sexual intercourse either with a human being or with an animal.

---

women in attendance, but except for the men who cooked the food for the meal that follows the ordination, very few men were present. (The attendance was small largely because a wedding was being celebrated in the village on the same day and people preferred to attend the wedding, where they would have a full meal instead of the simple tea and snacks served at the ordination.) With some few exceptions, most of the audience, showing only slight interest in the ceremony, talked and joked in the same manner as at a less solemn event. It must be explained, however, that this was the ordination of an elderly man who was donning the robes after a long life as a layman. The general feeling tone is very different, so I was told, in the ordination of young men who enter the monkhood directly from the novitiate.

[14]For an English translation, together with brief explanatory notes, see the *Pāṭimokkha*.

[15]The first, and most important, category comprises 4 *pārājika* (Burmese, *Pa-ra-zi.ka.*) rules whose violation leads to expulsion from the monkhood. Next in importance are the 13 rules comprising the *sanghādisesa* (Burmese, *thin-ga-di thei*) which, if violated, lead to a probationary period followed by penance. Two rules comprise the *aniyata*, or unclear category. Depending on the evidence, their violation may lead either to expulsion, to probation, or to penance. There are 30 *nissaggiya* (Burmese, *neikthagi*) rules whose violation requires forfeiture (of property improperly acquired) and expiation. Ninety-two *pācittiya* (Burmese, *thou-da:*) rules involve expiation. The 4 *pātidesaniya* (Burmese, *padi.dei-thani*) rules require confession only. There are, finally, 75 *sekhiya* (Burmese, *thei-khi.ya.*) rules of conduct and 7 rules concerning the settlement of litigation, known as *adhikaraṇasamatha* (Burmese, *a.di.ka.ra.-na.thamata.*).

Should he do so, he is like a "head which is severed from the body." (2) A monk may not take any object which is not freely given to him. Should he do so, he is like a "leaf severed from its branch, which can never be green again." (3) A monk may not intentionally destroy life. Should he do so he is like a "slab of stone that has splintered." (4) A monk may not make false claim to have achieved supernatural power. Should he do so he is like a "palm tree whose top has been severd in the middle."

The second category of thirteen rules—whose violation entails probation and penance—are close to the core of Buddhist monasticism. They, too, are simply stated. (1) A monk may not intentionally emit semen. (2) He may not hold the hand of a female or embrace her in any way. (3) He may not engage in sexually suggestive conversations with a woman. (4) He must not talk to a female about his desire for sexual intercourse. (5) He must not act as a go-between for any couple. (6) He must not have a monastery built for his personal use without obtaining formal consent for its site from other monks. (7) He must not have constructed for himself a monastery whose length and width exceed certain specified limits (40' x 25'). (8), (9) He must not groundlessly, directly or indirectly, accuse other monks of violating one of the *pārājika.* (10) He must do nothing to create a schism in the monkhood. (11) He must not support other schismatic monks. (12) He must not reply disrespectfully when admonished by other monks for violating a rule. (13) He must not perform errands or other favors for laymen.

The remaining rules, sometimes in the minutest detail, govern almost every aspect of the monk's life—eating, excretory behavior, relations to other monks, relations to laymen, norms of propriety and etiquette, monastic architecture and furniture, and so on. Some of the latter, although the penalties for their infringement are less severe, are more conspicuous than those listed above, and—from the laymen's point of view—much more onerous. Thus, although Burmese laymen say that one of the most difficult aspects of the monastic life is to refrain from eating after the hour of noon—according to many former novices, this was one of the basic reasons for their not becoming monks[16]—this is a minor rule, its infraction merely requiring expiation, without probation.

When one examines the entire compendium of regulations comprising the Rule, it is seen that it governs three behavioral domains: the monk's relationships with laymen, his relationships with other monks (especially those in his own monastery), and the proper expression of his various needs, wants, and drives. Putting aside those rules of propriety, etiquette, and simple good manners which are required by any civilized community[17]—and a large percentage of the regulations in the *Pāṭimokkha* are of that

[16]The same finding is reported for Thailand. (Ingersoll 1963:156)

[17]Weber has shrewdly observed that many of the monastic regulations reflect an attempt of the early *Saṅgha* to protect its upper- and upper-middle-class sensibilities from the crude behavior of the lower-class recruits who later invaded the Order. (Weber 1958:225)

order—and ignoring, too, those rules which are necessary for maintaining nondisruptive social relationships in any group, it is hardly surprising to discover that the basic concern of the Rule is with the regulation of the monk's physical desires and temptations, especially of lust. I say "hardly surprising" because this concern is but the institutionalized expression of the *raison d'être* of Buddhist monasticism, viz., to provide the framework which is most conducive to overcoming desire and achieving detachment.[18] By observing the Rule, the monk learns not to succumb to desire; by meditating, he learns to extinguish desire; by the extinction of desire he attains Liberation.

As we have already seen, the roots of Buddhist otherworldly asceticism are deeply embedded in the Indian religious soil. So, too, its anticipated fruits are almost identical with those sought by other types of Indian asceticism. Although the magical power which is attained by means of Indian asceticism—and which is remarked upon in the following quotation—was disdained by the Buddha as a normative goal, it was certainly acknowledged by Him as a by-product of asceticism. Essentially, however, the ultimate goal of Indian asceticism was Liberation, which is the explicit goal of Buddhist asceticism as well. Basham's remarks on Indian asceticism apply without qualification to its Buddhist variant.

> As he advanced in his self-training the hermit acquired powers beyond those of ordinary mortals. He saw past, present and future; he mounted the heavens, and was graciously received at the courts of the gods, while divinities descended to earth and visited him in his hermitage. By the magical power acquired in his asceticism he could work miracles—he could crumble mountains into the sea; if offended, he could burn up his enemies with the glance of his eye, or cause the crops of a whole people to fail; if respected, his magical power could protect a great city, increase its wealth, and defend it from famine, pestilence and invasion. In fact the magic potency, formerly ascribed to the sacrifice, now began to be attributed to asceticism. In the succeeding age the idea that the universe was founded and maintained through sacrifice slipped into the background; in its place it was widely believed that the universe depended on the penances of the great god Siva, meditating forever in the fastnesses of the Himalayas, and on the continued austerities of his human followers.
>
> If asceticism had its charms even for the less spiritual, they were still greater for the questing souls who took to a life of hardship from truly religious motives.

[18]This is the *raison d'être* of Christian monasticism as well. Thus, according to Father Augustine Baker, the "duty" of a Christian monk

> is to love nothing at all but God. . . . All adhesion to creatures by affection, whether such affection be great or small, is accordingly sinful, more or less; so that, if being deprived of any thing or persons whatsoever, or being pained by anything, we find a trouble and sorrow in our minds for the loss or suffering of the thing itself, such trouble, in what degree soever, argues that our affection was sinful, not only because the affection was excessive, but because it was an affection, the object whereof was not God. [Quoted in Butler 1962:54.]

> As his mystical exercises developed his psychic faculties, the ascetic obtained insight which no words could express. Gradually plumbing the cosmic mystery, his soul entered realms far beyond the comparatively tawdry heavens where the great gods dwelt in light and splendour. Going "from darkness to darkness deeper yet" he solved the mystery beyond all mysteries; he understood, fully and finally, the nature of the universe and of himself, and he reached a realm of truth and bliss, beyond birth and death, joy and sorrow, good and evil. And with this transcendent knowledge came another realization—he was completely, utterly, free. He had found ultimate salvation, the final triumph of the soul. The ascetic who reached the goal of his quest was a conqueror above all conquerors. There was none greater than he in the whole universe. [Basham 1954:244-45]

Before pursuing the goal of Buddhist monastic asceticism, we must first examine its characteristics.

Ascetic Orientation

As an otherworldly ascetic, the Buddhist monk not only possesses no property, but he abstains from sex, abstains from food after the noon hour, and in general reduces his physical pleasures to the barest minimum. Thus, with respect to the four monastic requisites—food, clothing, shelter, and medicine—his attitude must be strictly utilitarian. With respect to each he must think: "I eat this rice, not to please my appetite, but to satisfy a want of nature"; "I wear this robe, not for vanity, but to cover my nakedness"; "I live in this monastery, not for glory, but for protection from the elements"; "I take this medicine so that, by recovering my health, I can pursue my devotions and meditation with greater diligence."

Nevertheless, concerned as it is with the suppression of desire, the asceticism of the Buddhist Rule is far removed, both qualitatively and quantitatively, from the asceticism, say, of Christian and Hindu monasticism. Buddhist monasticism, as fashioned by the Buddha, represents the Middle Way, the Path between, on the one hand, the material indulgence of the worldly, and on the other, the bodily mortification characteristic of other monastic orders of his (and our) day. Indeed, the Buddhist Rule expressly prohibits the practice of those physical austerities and bodily tortures which are found in certain Hindu (and Christian) orders. It is no wonder that, from the very beginning of Western contact with Burma, those Europeans who had had prior experience in India were almost unanimously struck with this dramatic difference between Buddhism and Hinduism.[19]

[19]Symes' comments, written in the eighteenth century, are typical. Although noting that the Burmese ". . . deem it meritorious to mortify the flesh by the voluntary penance of abstemiousness and self-denial. . . ." he is quick to observe that "the Birmans do not inflict on themselves disgustful tortures, after the manner of the Hindoos." (Symes 1800:272) Symes' characterological explanation for the absence of torture in Burma is worth recording. The Burmese, he writes, ". . . are in general blessed with a disposition too cheerful to retire from the world in hopeless despondency, or sullen discontent. . . ." (*Ibid.*)

To say, however, that Buddhist monasticism is devoid of austerities characteristic of monasticism elsewhere is not to deny that it is ascetic. Since its asceticism is based on a different premise, its form is correspondingly different. Desire, from the Buddhist point of view, is not a *sin*, requiring atonement and penance; it is rather, a "hindrance," an "obstacle," a "fetter" (as it is variously referred to in Buddhism) which must be removed if salvation is to be achieved. But desire cannot be extinguished by bodily torture, as the Buddha discovered in his various abortive attempts to achieve Enlightenment. It can only be extinguished by meditation and compliance with the Rule. In short, Buddhism is not opposed to bodily mortification on principle; it is opposed to it, rather, because it does not achieve its ostensible aim, the extinction of desire.

The latter aim is the goal of Buddhist monasticism because the body and bodily lust constitute the crucial obstacle to Liberation. Indeed, the extinction of sexuality is, alone, one of the sure signs of sainthood. There are, it will be recalled, three stages of sainthood on the path leading to Liberation. A mark of the first stage is that sexual intercourse is desired no more than a few times a month; in the second stage, desire is reduced to once a month; and in the third stage it has been utterly extinguished. It is only after this stage that one becomes an *arahant* and attains nirvana.[20]

Although the Buddhist attitude to the body, which comes close to being phobic, is well-known, it is yet necessary to adumbrate it here in order to achieve a better understanding of the monastic norm (as well as of the selective personality recruitment to the monastic institution). "Buddhism," said a monk in Mandalay, "is a catabolic institution; it aims at the destruction of the body." Scripture repeatedly announces that the body, as the seat of desire, is in essence a loathsome, stinking mass of repulsive tissue and excrement. Once this insight concerning the true nature of the body is achieved, one will then—it is assumed—withdraw all cathexes from one's own body, and more important, lose all desire for the body of a woman, that greatest of all temptations.

If sexual desire is the greatest of all temptations, succumbing to that desire is, for the monk, the greatest of all derelictions. Admonishing a monk who had had sexual intercourse with his former wife, the Buddha tells him (*The Book of the Discipline*, Pt. 1, p. 36):

> It were better for you, foolish man, that your male organ should enter the mouth of a terrible and poisonous snake, than that it should enter a woman. It were better for you, foolish man, that your male organ should enter the mouth of a black snake, than that it should enter a woman. It were better for you, foolish

[20]This relationship between sexuality and sainthood is taken very seriously in contemporary Burma. Many villagers argued that U Nu, the former prime minister, was a saint because of his sexual asceticism.

> man, that your male organ should enter a charcoal pit, burning, ablaze, afire, than that it should enter a woman.

Sex is to be avoided, in the Buddhist view, because there is a fundamental opposition between sexual activity and spiritual power. Sexual activity precludes the attainment of spiritual power, and once that is attained, leads to its destruction. As proof for this thesis, a village abbot told the following *Jātaka.* In a former life, the Embryo Buddha was a hermit who, through the power of his meditation, was able to fly through the air. Once, when collecting his alms in Benares, he was invited by the king to come and live in his garden. When the king went off to war, he instructed the queen to offer alms to the hermit. One morning, flying to the palace to collect his alms, the hermit spied the queen lying naked on her bed. Although he had practiced meditation for hundreds of thousands of years to reach his state of spiritual power at the time, all his "impurities" returned when he gazed upon the queen's nudity. Seized by lust, he had sexual intercourse with her, and at that moment his spiritual power left him and he could no longer fly through the air. After some time he realized his folly, gave up the queen, and his powers returned. Refusing to live where he could even smell a female, he flew away to the Himalayas. "Thus," concluded the abbot, "Even an Embryo Buddha can be reduced to the state of a layman by sexual desire."[21]

As a defense against sexual temptation, classical Buddhism, as Conze observes, "cultivated a certain contempt for women. The monk was warned to be perpetually on his guard. . . ." (Conze 1953:58). But contempt in itself is not a sufficient defense. The best protection against the temptress is to avoid her. Hence, when asked by Ānanda, his beloved disciple, how monks are to conduct themselves with regard to women, the Buddha answered:

> "As not seeing them, Ânanda."
> "But if we should see them, what are we to do?"
> "No talking, Ânanda."
> "But if they should speak to us, lord, what are we to do?"
> "Keep wide awake, Ânanda."
> —*Mahâ Parinibbâna Suttanta,* in *Dialogues of the Buddha,* Pt. II, p. 154.

This epigrammatic expression of the Buddhist attitude toward women is expanded more fully in another text. A monk should never look at women because ". . . through the eyes concupiscence finds its way into the heart, and shakes its firmest purposes." Even when they come to bring food to the monks, no conversation is to take place with them. For, as the Buddha admonishes Ānanda,

[21]This is the *Mudulakkhana Jātaka,* No. 66 in the Cowell edition.

> Safer and better it would be to hold conversation with a man who, sword in hand, would threaten to cut off our head, or with a female Biloo [ogre] ready to devour us the moment we open the mouth to speak. By conversing with women, one becomes acquainted with them; acquaintance begets familiarity, kindles passion, leads to the loss of virtue, and precipitates into the four states of punishment. It is, therefore, most prudent not to have any conversation with them. [Quoted in Bigandet, 1912: Vol. 2, 52]

But, Ānanda persists, what if a woman asks the monk to instruct her in the teachings of Buddhism. Must he ignore her search for the Truth? In such a case, the Buddha replied, he should consider her as sexless.

> Let him consider as mothers those who are old enough to be mothers, as elder sisters those who appear a little older than he, as younger sisters or children those that are younger than he. Never, O Ânanda, forget these instructions. [*Ibid.*]

The Rule contains many regulations whose aim is to minimize the occasions for interaction with females. Thus, monks are forbidden to sleep under the same roof with any female (including female animals!), to travel alone with them, or to accept anything directly from them. They are not permitted to touch the clothes of a woman, to caress a little girl, or to handle a female animal. When preaching or chanting before a mixed congregation, monks must keep their eyes fixed on the fans held before their eyes so that they not be tempted by the sight of an attractive woman. The prohibition on touching a woman extends to the monk's mother. Should she fall in a ditch, if others are present to help her he must not go to her assistance; if others are not present, he may offer her his robe or a stick (but not his hand), and he must think to himself that he is only pulling out a log of wood.

Avoidance is, at best, a negative defense. More important is to consider what the body really is; for once one penetrates behind the veil of appearance, so that the body is seen in all its loathsomeness, desire is extinguished. The real body, as the Buddha sees it,

> is composed of 300 bones, of 900 veins, and as many muscles, is full of intestines, phlegm, and mucus; from nine different apertures disgusting matter is discharged; a stinking perspiration exudes from all its pores, and yet there are people so foolish, as not merely to cherish their own bodies, but also to fall in love with those of other persons. This body, which even when alive is so disgusting, when it is dead becomes a carcase, which its own relations cannot look upon without horror. After two days it begins to swell, on the third it becomes green and black, worms come from it in every part, and, when in the grave, it is gnawed by the most despicable insects. Whoever considers these things will be persuaded, that in the body there is nothing but decay and misery; and, therefore, he will cast off all affection to it, and turn all his desires to the Niban [nirvana],

where these evils do not exist. [Quoted in Sangermano 1893:137. See also *Vijayasutta* in *Sutta-Nipāta.*]

To achieve this attitude to the body is one of the basic aims of Buddhist meditation, especially of that type known as *asubha-bhāvanā.* In this type, the monk (often aided by contemplating a picture of a skeleton or by contemplating a dead body in a cemetery) must reflect that the body is

composed of thirty-two impurities; that as the worm is bred in the dunghill, so it is conceived in the womb; that it is the receptacle of filth, like the privy; that disgusting secretions are continually proceeding from its nine apertures; and that, like the drain into which all kinds of refuse are thrown, it sends forth an offensive smell.[Hardy 1850:247]

The main object of the Rule, then, is to lead to the suppression, and ultimately the extinction, of bodily—and especially sexual—desire. This is the canonical view, and also the contemporary Burmese view, of monks and laymen alike. The monks were asked to adduce reasons for the interdiction of sexual behavior, or of eating after the noon hour, the reasons for these rules being especially examined since laymen say that they are the most difficult to comply with. The rationale at the basis of their admittedly widely ranging responses was the extinction of desire. Thus, food is prohibited after noon because it is a Buddhist regulation, it helps to control the mind, it decreases mental impurities, it promotes meditation, it provides more time for spiritual activities, it serves to distinguish monks from laymen. The same reasons, and more, are offered for sexual abstinence. It is instrumental in the acquisition of supermundane powers, it kills lust, it promotes the Buddhist religion, it promotes the attainment of nirvana, it decreases craving; it decreases emotional attachment; sexual intercourse is an animal act, it leads to misery and worry over family affairs, is an expression of pride and lust. The ban on private property stems from the above reasons and more. The possession of property leads to greed and increases the temptation to become involved in worldly affairs.

In glancing at these rubrics and in reading the longer interview protocols it is evident, so far as the monks are concerned, that the main basis for these rules (and for monastic asceticism in general) is to decrease the passions and the attachment to worldly things, and hence purify the mind (thereby freeing it for meditation and other nirvana-pursuing activities). As one monk put it, the various desires are "like wild elephants which, enclosed in a stockade, must be tamed. Only after they are tamed is a person psychologically prepared for meditation. They can be tamed only through observing the precepts, especially abstinence from food, sex, and so on."

Lay opinion is identical with that of the monks. When asked why monks should comply with the Rule, laymen exhibited a scatter of responses, similar to the scatter exhibited by the monks: to refrain from eating provides more time for meditation, not attending plays distinguishes the monk from the layman, not possessing property kills worldly pride, and so on. But preponderantly they said that monastic prohibitions serve to kill desire and the mental impurities. Like the monks, laymen too view the sexual rules as the most important; if impurities are to be destroyed, the sex drive above all must be extinguished.[22]

Since all Buddhists *qua* Buddhists must aim at destroying their "impurities," sensual indulgence is not only strictly forbidden to monks, but, say the Burmese, should be avoided as much as possible by laymen. Sexual behavior should be reduced to the barest minimum—sex precludes the possibility of attaining nirvana;[23] gluttony is decidedly anti-Buddhist—one should not eat beyond subsistence; property is not to be coveted—one may own but not be attached to it. In short, the layman, like the monk, is bound by Buddhist notions concerning physical desires. The monk must suppress them altogether; the layman—unable to suppress them—must limit their expression.

Structural Elaboration

Although the regulations comprising the Rule were designed to implement the ascetic ideal, there gradually developed—as all normative and legal systems gradually develop—an elaborate set of subregulations designed to further the initial regulations. In short, from an original Rule there has developed a system of what might be termed ecclesiastical law. To illustrate this development, we may instance some of the elaborations of only one set of monastic regulations: those concerning the robe.

The yellow robe (*thin-gan:*), one of the requisites of the monk, is one of the few objects the monk can own. It is the symbol of his poverty, the badge of the monastic office. When laymen do homage to an impious monk, they say they are showing respect not for the man—he is merely a "human in a yellow robe"—but for the robe. Indeed, for laymen the robe is believed to possess quasi-magical properties: one who wears the robe is immune to attacks by ghosts, witches, and so on. As with any sacred object, there are numerous regulations concerning its use, its wear, its bestowal, and so on. One of the main disagreements between rival monastic orders throughout the Buddhist world is whether the robe should be worn over both shoulders or only one.

[22]Some informants traced the rule prohibiting sex to an incident occurring during the life of the Buddha when a certain monk, Shin Thou Dein, had intercourse in the cemetery with his wife's corpse. His penis was caught in her vagina, and it was only removed by the efforts of one Withaka, a laywoman.

[23]The consequences of lust may be seen in somewhat extreme terms. The Burmese tell the legend of one Sougadei, whose blood, as a result of his lustful life, turned into semen. He was brought to his senses only when he saw that one of the five hundred women with whom he had consecutive sexual relations was his mother.

Burmese monks distinguish six kinds of robes. The *kahteing* robe, which is offered only during a one-month period—eight days after the full moon of *Thadin:jut* to eight days after the full moon of *Tazaung-maung:*—refers to the robe offered during the *kahteing* ceremony, described in chapter 9. The *mathou:* robe, which is offered in the month of *Tazaung-maung:*, is unique because it must be woven within one night. Beginning with a ceremonial imitation of the agricultural processes—plowing, harrowing, planting, reaping, etc.—necessary for the production of the raw material, the yarn is then spun into cloth and the cloth woven into a garment in a single night (also described in chapter 9). The *kya* robe, so-called because it is decorated with a water-lily (*kya*) pattern, is usually offered to the Buddha and may be offered at any time. The *thin-gan ji:*, or great robe, is the robe a monk receives at his ordination, although it may be offered at any other time as well. Larger than the ordinary robe, it consists of small patches of yellow cloth stitched together—as is indeed required by the *Vinaya*—rather than of one piece of woven cloth.[24] The offering of a "great robe" is always accompanied both by an offering to the Buddha and by a merit-sharing ceremony. Frequently, too, it is an occasion for the sponsoring of a feast. The *shwei:*, or golden, robe is also offered to the Buddha. It consists of a white cloth with gilded flowers painted on it, so as to resemble a yellow robe. It may be offered at any time. Finally there is the *pan-thagu* robe, which, paradoxically, is offered to a pious monk who has taken a vow not to accept a robe from anyone. *Pan-thagu* means ownerless. Offering a robe to such a monk—whose piety assures the donor of much merit—is accomplished by placing it on the path he is known regularly to take. Having found the robe rather than received it as an offering, the monk does not violate his vow when he takes it for himself. Such a pious monk, incidentally, will otherwise stitch his own robe from a shroud obtained in a cemetery. (Although this is the method prescribed by the *Vinaya*, I know of only one monk in the entire area in which I worked who made his robes in this manner.)

From the standpoint of the monk, the *kahteing* robe is the most important, not only because by custom it is accompanied by many other offerings, but because by ecclesiastical law it confers many privileges upon him. In the first place, unless a monk has received a *kahteing* robe, he may not travel during the five-month period, from *Thadin:jut* to *Tabaung*, without carrying all three parts of his robe with him, even though he may intend to be away for only one night. Indeed, a monk who has not received a *kahteing* robe may never be more than two and a half arm-lengths distant from his ordination robe. Second, the monk who does not have a *kahteing* robe may not leave the monastery without the consent of his abbot. Third, should a monk receive an ordinary robe he must recite a special ritual formula within ten days after its receipt or else forfeit it to another monk. If, however, he

[24]Requiring much cloth and effort to make, this robe is three times as expensive as an ordinary robe—while the latter costs thirty *kyat*, or about $6.00, the former costs ninety *kyat*.

has already received a *kahteing* robe he need not recite it during the five-month period from *Thadin:jut* to *Tabaung.* Fourth, should a monk who has not received a *kahteing* robe be invited to a meal by a layman who does not use the correct ceremonial formula,[25] he may not accept the invitation. If, however, he has received a *kahteing* robe, he may accept the invitation despite the layman's bad form, but only during the five-month period alluded to above. Fifth, during this same five-month period, a monk who has received a *kahteing* robe is permitted to violate the rule which prohibits him from informing a layman of his wants or desires. Finally, although ordinary robes offered to a monastery are the common property of its monks, and may be worn by visiting monks as well, the *kahteing* robe may be worn by the recipient alone.

Confession

Given the importance of the Rule, it is not surprising that institutions should have been developed to insure compliance with its requirements. There are two such: regular recitation of the *Pāṭimokkha* within each chapter, and regular confession of violations of its constituent rules. There is some evidence that, from the very beginning of the *Saṅgha,* Buddhist monks—perhaps as an institution prescribed by the Buddha Himself—have met together for the collective recitation of the Rule. (Cf. Horner 1938; Sobhana 1966). This recitation, which may be viewed as the monastic parallel to the recitation of the eight precepts by laymen on the Sabbath, occurs twice a month, on the full and new moons. Called *u.bouk pyu-de* in Burmese, it takes place in the ordination hall.[26]

Some time after the institution of this ceremonial recitation of the Rule, there was introduced the practice of simultaneously confessing any violation of its individual regulations. Hence, the ceremonial recitation of the Rule became in effect a confessional service; and as Dutt (1962:106) has observed, this confession became the "centre point of monastic discipline, an adventitious solemnity [being] given to it by prescribing the performance of this duty on the ceremonially sacred days." Impressed with the "practical character" of Buddhist monastic confession, Dutt is surprised that it did not persist. "Curiously enough," he writes, the confessional service "evaporated" and "the original idea of a mere ceremonial observance reasserted itself." (*Ibid.*:107)

Although confession may have been dropped from the ceremonial reci-

[25]The formal expression for inviting a monk to dine is: "Please come to give merit (or honor) to the cooked rice, my lord."

[26]Since Burmese monks do not agree on the terminology by which various aspects of this institution are to be designated, I have arbitrarily chosen to follow the terms provided by an abbot in Mandalay who is acknowledged to be very learned in these matters. If fewer than three monks are present in the ordination chamber, the recitation is known as *pouk-ka.la ubouk;* if there are three, it is *ga.na. ubouk;* and if there are four or more, it is *than-ga ubouk.*

tation of the *Pāṭimokkha*, it has not disappeared from the monastery; it is found in Burma as well as Thailand (cf. Ingersoll 1963) to this very day. Known as *dei-thana kya:de*, monastic confession takes place twice a month. In the case of infractions of the minor rules (the last three sections of the *Pāṭimokkha*), it is sufficient that they be confessed to one monk in the monastery. For these infractions confession is frequently reciprocal, two monks confessing to each other; moreover, no penance is required, the confession itself being sufficient expiation. For the graver offenses (all other sections of the *Pāṭimokkha*), confession must take place in the ordination chamber on the very day of the violation, and in the presence of at least three other monks, who prescribe a proper penance. (There is no penance, of course, for violation of the regulations comprising the first section, the *pārājika;* instead, it will be recalled, the derelict monk is expelled from the monkhood and—according to Burmese monks—he will suffer even more by being reborn in hell.) Having confessed his violation, the monk sits to one side while two of the other monks recite appropriate sections of the *Pāṭimokkha*, and the third listens. (This is called *kan-ma-wa hynatta;* alternatively, *kam-ma patte.*) Should the monk confess his violation when it first occurs, the ceremony occurs once. Should he wait a day, it takes place on two separate days, and so on up to the maximum of fifteen days.[27] Although in the monasteries in which I worked no penance is prescribed, the offending monk is suspended for as many days as the ceremony is performed, i.e., as many as elapsed between the violation and the confession. He is isolated from his fellow monks and in some cases forbidden to sleep with them under the same roof.

Should a monk refrain from confessing his offense, it is believed that his personal guardian spirits[28] will inform the *deva*, who in turn will punish him in his next existence. Until they confess their offenses monks are in an "immoral state" (*alisi*). After confessing they are in a "moral state" (*lisi*).

In addition to the confession of single offenses, a ceremony is performed at rare intervals for the confession of all offenses which may have been committed over a period of three or five or ten years.[29] In the one I witnessed, the monk performing the ceremony was approaching his sixtieth birthday and felt that his demerits, accumulated in forty years in the robe, should be abolished. This, he said, was done not only for his benefit, but for that of his lay supporters as well. The Burmese believe, it will be recalled, that the merit acquired from supporting a monk is proportional to his piety.

[27]A one-day ceremony is known as *pari wut* (or *so ti.de*), the longer one as *mana ti.de* (or *so ti.da*).

[28]For a description of these spirits, see Spiro 1967:54-55.

[29]Again, we must note the lack of agreement concerning both the term for the ceremony and its nature. A group of nine monks assembled for the recitation of the *Pāṭimokkha* provided me with the meaning, as well as the term, I am using. A monk who was himself undergoing the ceremony gave me a different term and a somewhat different explanation.

Hence, it confers less merit on a layman to support a monk whose demerits have not been abolished than one who is pious or whose demerits have been cancelled. This ceremony requires a minimum of six days (the ceremony I witnessed lasted for eighteen days), and must take place in the presence of at least three other monks. Twice a day, morning and evening, the monk must confess his offenses to the other monks. Moreover, except for four hours sleep, he is required to recite the *Pāṭimokkha* continuously from dusk to dawn.

CHAPTER 13

Monasticism: II. The Social Structure

The Daily Routine

Having examined the culture of the monastic community, we may now describe its social structure. Since the monk, although ordained into the Order as a whole, lives in a particular monastery *(hpoung:ji caung:)*, it is appropriate to begin our discussion of the social structure of the Order with this, its smallest unit. Starting with the daily routine of the monk—typically, there is only one ordained monk in the village monastery—we shall proceed to the physical setting and the group structure within which his behavior takes place.

Although usually the monk is found in or near his own monastery, this is not always the case. For unlike Christian monks who, following the Benedictine Rule, take a vow of "stability," Buddhist monks may move about. It is only during the three-month Lent that they must remain within the monastery; otherwise, they may travel anywhere. They visit colleagues in other monasteries, make pilgrimages, attend conferences, deliver sermons in other villages and towns, and so on. The only constraints on a monk's travel are that his journey be undertaken for a serious purpose, that he carry no money with him, that he not travel alone with a female, and that he not remain outside a monastery after sunset. (Hence, having reached his destination, the monk spends his time in a monastery.)

Whether he lives in his own or in another monastery, the monk's daily schedule is more or less predictable, not only because the routine is, within broad limits, prescribed by the Rule, but because it transpires (with some exceptions) within the physical limits of the monastic compound. The village monastery is always outside the village fence, and although monks are not cloistered, they are prohibited from entering the village except for the fulfillment of a specific religious duty, such as collecting alms, chanting *paritta* or officiating at a funeral. For a monk to stroll through the village merely to chat with the villagers or sip a cup of tea at the local teashop, or even to pay a pastoral call—such behavior is prohibited in theory and unheard-of in practice.

The following daily schedule, based on behavioral observations in twelve monasteries, represents the routine of the average village monk. Rising at approximately 5:00 A.M.—but never after sunrise—he sweeps the monastic compound or has it swept by his novices and lay students. This brief exercise, together with the walking required for his alms rounds, is the only form of physical labor which he is permitted. Unlike the rule of various Christian orders, in which labor is either permitted or prescribed, the Buddhist Rule prohibits the monk from earning his living, repairing his monastery, tilling the soil in the monastic compound, cooking his meals, or engaging in any other form of physical work. Indeed, he may not so much as pour his own tea or lift a serving bowl to fill his plate with food. Even these acts must be performed for him.[1]

Shortly after rising, the monk says his daily devotions *(hpaya:wutte).* Then, for approximately an hour, from 5:30 to 6:30, he takes his morning tea while the novices, who have prepared the tea for him, say their devotions in their own quarters, usually on the ground floor of the monastery.

About seven o'clock monks and novices leave the monastery to collect alms food. Then, sometime between nine and ten, after their morning bath, the monks take their main meal of the day, normally served by the novices. Not being permitted to serve himself, if a monk does not have a lay steward *(hpou:thu-do)* to care for his needs, he requires a novice to serve him. Seated on a mat in front of a low table, he eats from several bowls of curry set on the table before him. While eating, he does not talk, except perhaps to inform the novice—by indirection—of his desires.

From ten to eleven, while the novices and lay students prepare their

[1]If Hamilton's observations are correct, Burmese monks did not always refrain from manual labor. Writing in the early eighteenth century (1930:29), he observed that every layman

> has free liberty to build a Baw or temple, and when it is finished, purchases or bestows a few acres of ground to maintain a certain number of priests and novices, who manure and cultivate the ground for their own sustenance, and in the garden the priests and novices have a convent built for their conveniency of lodgings and study, and those are their settled benefices, for they are no charge to the laity, but by their industrious labour in managing their garden, they have enough for themselves and something to spare to the poor indigent of the laity; but if their garden is too small or sterile for the sustenance of their family, they send some novices abroad [to collect alms food].

Nor does the interdiction on physical labor apply to contemporary rural Thailand, where monks may not only cut the grass and tend the gardens in the monastic compound, but may even engage in heavy construction and repair work. (Ingersoll 1963:159) In the large monasteries in Bangkok, monks serve as masons, electricians, plumbers, and so on.

lessons, the monk is free. He may study or stroll in the compound, or talk with anyone who comes to visit, or nap. From eleven to twelve he has a morning snack. Since from noon until the following morning he may take no food, this is his last meal of the day. (For some these two meals are reversed—the snack coming first and the heavy meal second.) He is then usually free until the middle of the afternoon when, around three, he teaches the boys who, rather than study in the government school, attend the monastery school. Formerly the monastic school was the only school in Burma, and all education was provided by monks. Today only a tiny fraction of city children receive a monastic education, but in the villages at least half of all school children continue to be taught by monks. Hence, in the villages the monk continues to serve as schoolmaster.[2] His teaching function, however, takes very little time, the daily lesson lasting approximately an hour. During his free period from noon on, he may nap or study or, if he is so inclined, meditate.[3]

After his pupils leave for their homes, the monk again is free until five or six o'clock, when, if he has novices in his monastery, he may either study with them or instruct them. Shortly before eight, monk and novices say their evening devotions, and by nine they are all in bed. In theory, at least, the day has been spent in study, meditation, and (to some extent) teaching.

It will be noted from this account of his average day that, generally speaking, the monk has little interaction with the village. Even on a typical day, his contact with and services on behalf of laymen are minimal. On Sabbath days and holydays he leads them in recitation of the Buddhist precepts; on special occasions—a wedding, a funeral, a personal or collective crisis—he chants *paritta;* three or four times a year he presides over a Buddhist initiation ceremony *(shin-byu);* periodically (usually at the time of these special occasions) laymen come to the monastery to serve him a special meal; and sometimes, especially during the Lenten season, he preaches a brief sermon, either in the monastery or in the village chapel. Sometimes, too, laymen come to the monastery for advice and instruction.

[2]The traditionally high literacy rate in Burma is a testimonial, of course, to the Buddhist monk as national schoolteacher. The Burmese literacy rate in the premodern period was probably the highest in Asia, and one of the highest in the world, since almost every male child spent at least some time studying at the feet of his village monk. This, no doubt, was one of the latter's sources of authority and prestige. There is of course no necessary relationship between education and the Buddhist monkhood. In traditional China, education was almost a Confucian monopoly, Buddhist monks playing no role at all in the secular process. Moreover, many Chinese Buddhist monks, like the Taoist priests, were themselves illiterate. (Cf. Yang 1967:337-38.)

[3]In fact, as we have seen, very few village monks ever meditate, and only a handful even claim that they do. Typically, they plead lack of time. The situation differs little in the large urban monasteries. In Mandalay, according to an official of the Ministry of Religious Affairs, no more than 15 per cent of the monks spend any time at all in meditation. In rural Thailand, according to Ingersoll (1963:99) no monks meditate. Usually, as in Burma, they say they have no time.

In a random sample of twenty-five adults in Yeigyi, twelve indicated that they consult with their village monk from time to time. Two each have gone to him to discuss the meaning of such Buddhist concepts as nirvana, merit, and demerit. Two have gone to him to obtain advice concerning meditation, and two have gone for astrological advice. One has sought information concerning Buddhist philosophy. One wished to discuss the possible karmic reason for his poverty, and another has sought advice concerning escape from his poverty. It is to be noted, however, that none of them consulted the monk on matters which in our culture would be termed "pastoral." The monk, as I have already stressed, is not a pastor.

The above account, even including the atypical days, of his daily routine does not exhaust the monk's activities. Some monks engage in alchemy, astrology, exorcism, healing, and other occult arts; some, too—but this is confined to the cities—participate in politics. Since, however, these activities are practiced by only a minority, and since they fall outside the role-set of the monk *qua* monk (being expressly forbidden by the monastic Rule), they will be described in a separate section.

In general, as this schematic description reveals, Buddhist monastic life is far from onerous. In contrast to the villager, who toils in the fields under a hot tropical sun, the monk not only leads a life of comparative ease, without labor, but the physical austerity and rigorous spiritual exercises often associated with monasticism elsewhere are, typically, absent from the Burmese monastery. Indeed, almost the reverse is the case; for although formally recruitment to the Order means renunciation of the world and acceptance of an ascetic regime, life in a Burmese monastery is, paradoxically, a life of material abundance—even, as compared to the life of the average layman, luxury. Laymen may wear the same clothes for years; monks receive many new robes annually. Laymen may eat their daily rice with a simple curry; monks typically enjoy three or four different curries at each meal. Although normatively they are expected to eat the mixture of foods found in the begging bowl (a practice known as *tu-din*), in fact, all but a few very pious monks deviate from this rule. Food, to be sure, is still collected in the begging bowl, but it now contains a set of small aluminum cups, so that each kind of food—rice, curry, sweets, and so on—is placed by the housewife in a separate cup. Moreover, although the monk is enjoined to collect his own food, only the most pious comply with this injunction. Claiming that they do not have the time to go on daily alms rounds, most monks have their novices and lay students collect their alms food for them.[4]

[4]The daily alms procession follows a regular route, so that housewives, knowing when the procession will be passing through their section of the village, wait outside of their houses with rice and/or curry which they place in the begging bowls.

In the city, collection of alms food presents a serious organizational problem. It is obvious that a monastery which houses one or two hundred monks cannot obtain its food exclusively from the quarter of the city in which the monastery is located. This economic burden must

Equally important, no monk subsists exclusively on the food collected in the begging bowl. Laymen are forever preparing special meals which they themselves bring to the monastery and serve to the monks. Sometimes, though more rarely, monks are invited for such a special meal to the home of the layman. On such occasions, of course, the monks eat by themselves, while the laymen who serve them eat only after they have finished. Sumptuous meals, consisting of the most expensive foods the layman can afford, are offered on every ceremonial occasion—initiation, wedding, funeral, house-warming, and so on—and whenever the layman wishes to acquire additional merit. Some monks, moreover, are never dependent on the begging bowl, the more wealthy among the faithful taking it upon themselves to supply them with their meals daily.[5] In Yeigyi, for example, thirty families in rotation offer a monk his daily meal one day a month.

From all of this it may be seen that, although the begging bowl (next to the robe) is the symbol of the Buddhist Order, it retains its original instrumental function for only a small number of monks—those who are very pious and those whose monasteries are in poor villages. Still, the ritual of begging alms food persists, even among those whose meals are brought to the monastery, for it is by their offerings that laymen acquire merit. Hence, every morning the alms procession passes through the village, and if the monk himself does not eat the food in the bowl, he distributes it among his novices and the poorer lay students in the monastery; if any is still left over, it is scattered on the ground for the insects, the birds, and the pi-dogs.[6]

The monk not only enjoys better food and raiment than most laymen, but his housing, too, is far superior. Typically, the villager lives in a small one-story house, with coconut-thatched walls and split-bamboo floors. The typical monastery, on the other hand, is a large two-story building, constructed with plank walls and wooden floors. Wealthier establishments are built of teak or brick, in some cases adorned with fine carvings on their walls and gables. Although the typical house is bereft of all furnishings, the typical monastery contains a few easy chairs, fine mats and even carpets, bookcases and desks, large grandfather clocks, and sometimes—where electricity is available—radios.

The monastic compound is, if anything, more impressive. The spacious and airy monastery is usually located in the midst of a campuslike garden,

---

be shared by pious laymen from other parts of the city as well. Usually a monk or one of his representatives will go to various parts of the city, inquiring whether this or that household or households will be willing to supply him regularly with daily alms. His lay supporters, rather than being concentrated in one quarter, therefore, may be scattered throughout the city, and in order for him or his novices to collect the food, they must ride by bus to the various districts. To facilitate their task, bus companies provide free transportation for monks during the early morning hours when alms food is collected.

[5]This is an old practice in Burma, commented upon by Bigandet (1912:293).

[6]In a study of a village in northeast Thailand it was discovered that, because food is brought to the monks in the monastery, no monks go on alms rounds. (Tambiah 1968:66)

surrounded by shade trees. The setting is not only pleasing to the eye, but compound and monastery alike are one of the few refuges from the tropical Burmese sun.

Contrary, then, to any expectation which might be aroused by the monk as wandering mendicant or almsman, the standard of living of the average members of the Order is surpassed only by that of the wealthiest laymen. Aside from sexual deprivation, the monk suffers no other; the quantity and quality of gifts he receives at a *kahteing* alone is staggering. Technically a pauper, he finds his physical desires (again, except for sex) abundantly satisfied. This paradox of abundance and even luxury,[7] in an institution dedicated to renunciation is readily resolved in the context of Burmese Buddhism and its complex emphasis on monastic giving as the most effective means for acquiring merit.

The Structure of the Monastery

Although the Buddhist monk does not take a vow of stability, he is however attached to a particular monastery. Technically, a newly ordained monk spends his first ten years in the robes in the monastery in which he is ordained, sitting at the feet of his ordination master *(u.pa-zin: hsaya).* After that he may, theoretically, leave for any monastery of his choice. Unlike the Christian monk, he is neither assigned to a monastery by his superior nor does he require the latter's permission to transfer from one monastery to another. Of the twenty monks for whom we have data on this topic, only five remained in the monastery of their natal village. That 75 per cent should have transferred to other places provides a fair measure of the geographical mobility of the monkhood. Further, a breakdown of these fifteen cases indicates that the monks are one of the main agents of internal cultural diffusion. Only three of the fifteen are in monasteries relatively close to their natal villages; ten are remote from their home villages, and two came to their present monasteries from as far away as Lower Burma.

Although the monastery is a democratic institution in that the avenues of monastic recruitment and promotion rest on universalistic criteria—secular distinctions of family, status, wealth, and rank are extinguished with the donning of the yellow robe—it is nevertheless hierarchically organized, the hierarchy being marked by a set of status terms. At the bottom is the

[7]Hardy, on the basis of his observations of Sinhalese monasteries in the early nineteenth century, commented on the same paradox. From a study of the Buddhist texts, "it is evident," he wrote,

> that the situation of the priests of Ceylon is at present very different to that which was intended at the commencement of their order by Gótama Budha, as they must have degenerated therefrom in proportion to the extent of their lands and of their social and political privileges. Professedly mendicants, and possessing only a few articles that are of no intrinsic value, they are in reality the wealthiest and most honoured class in the nation to which they belong. [Hardy 1850:69-70]

young boy, under eight, who is too young to be ordained as a novice, but who wears the yellow robe as a consequence of the initiation ceremony *(shin-byu).* He is known as a *kou-yin galei:,* a "small novice." Above him is the novice, or *pyit-shin,* most frequently referred to, however, as *kou-yin.* (Only rarely is the Pali, *sāmanera,* used.) The fully ordained monk, who must be at least twenty years old, is an *u.pazin:.* After ten years in the robe, he is a *hpoungi:ji:* or "great glory."[8] The presiding *hpoung:ji:* or abbot, of the monastery is a *hsaya-do* (literally, royal teacher), whether he be the exclusive inhabitant of a small village monastery or the head of a large city monastery inhabited by hundreds of monks.[9]

In village monasteries, the *hsaya-do* is selected in one of two ways. The incumbent may designate his successor before his death, or, should he fail to do so, the laymen of the village, and more particularly the chief supporters of the monastery, may invite a monk of their own choosing to be his successor. The former method is known in Burmese as *thin-ga keiksa*—"the concern [literally, the business] of the monks"; the latter is known as *lu keiksa*—"the concern of the laity" (literally, humans).[10] Which of these two methods is adopted depends on whether the monastery is "owned" by the monk or by the Order. We shall return to this distinction below.

Symbolic of this status hierarchy, deference must be shown to each monk whose status is superior to one's own. Deference is expressed both ritually, in the traditional act of obeisance *(shi.khou),* and instrumentally, in the performance of some service. This deference structure is most clearly observed in the order in which monks take their meals. After the food is prepared, it is placed before the presiding monk, who in the presence of the others eats his fill. When he has finished, the other ordained monks eat whatever remains in the serving dishes. When they have completed their meal, the novices and postulants eat what is left.

Within each status position in the hierarchy, hierarchy is determined by the number of years or (as the Burmese put it) the number of Lents spent in the yellow robe. Thus, unlike the Burmese secular order, in which status

[8]In addition to *hpoung:ji:,* the Burmese refer to the monk as *bhikkhu, yahan:da,* and *rahanda.* Although *hpoung:ji:* is certainly the term most frequently used by both laymen and monks, it is, interestingly enough, a relatively modern designation. At the time of the Burmese monarchy this title was only applied to the king, and it was not until the demise of the monarchy (in 1885) that it became attached to the Buddhist monks. (Cf. Cochrane 1904:37)

In technical usage, *hpoung:ji:* is not an undifferentiated term; it too, is divided into subcategories. Thus, from one to seven years—or, as the Burmese say, for seven Lents *(wah)*—the *hpoung:ji:* is a *nwa htei;* from eight to twenty years, a *mitzi ma.htei;* for more than twenty years, a *maha htei.*

[9]Originally, this title was conferred exclusively on monks who served as tutors to the king. Its present usage has its roots in the mid-nineteenth century when it began to be applied to all monks of wide learning. (See Htin Aung 1966:18-19.)

[10]The Sinhalese system by which a monastery becomes in effect the property of a particular descent group, passed on from maternal uncle to nephew (cf. Evers 1968), is not known in Burma.

is graded by chronological age, deference being accorded the older by the younger, monastic status is graded by ecclesiastical age, and older monks must accord homage to the younger if the latter have spent more time in the robe.

In principle, at least, the presiding monk of a monastery is subject to the authority of the administrative head of the district. For administrative purposes the country is divided into districts, and all the monasteries of a district are under the jurisdiction of a superior known as a *gaing: ouk* (who in turn is assisted by a *gaing: htauk*). Unfortunately I do not know how these officials are chosen nor what their powers or functions are. Although nominally subordinate to the *gaing: ouk*, the presiding monk of the monastery is relatively autonomous in his domain. This is especially true of the village monastery, which invariably consists of one building, inhabited at most by several monks. In the towns and cities, however, the organizational structure is somewhat more complicated, for there the monasteries consist of a complex of buildings each of which houses a group of monks headed by their own presiding monk. This monastery complex (known as a *kyaung:taik*) is enclosed in a common compound. Its affairs are regulated by an abbot *(taik ouk)* chosen from one of several residing in the monastic complex, and by his executive officer *(taik kyat)*. Both of these elective offices are, at least in theory, bestowed upon senior monks known for learning and piety as well as for administrative ability.[11]

In general, then, there are two main types of monastery in Burma. The village monastery *(ywa caung:)* consists of a single building, inhabited by its presiding monk and at most several other monks and a small number of postulants and novices. The monastery may sometimes house a few boarding students in addition to the day students taught there, and sometimes, too, the compound may contain a small hut inhabited by a pious layman *(hpou:thu-do)* who has retired to the monastery and looks after the needs of the monk. The city monastery usually consists of a monastic complex *(caung: taik)* inhabited by many monks—sometimes hundreds of them. Some of these monasteries serve also as centers for higher study or meditation.

[11]Sarkisyanz, quoting Gard and Gokuldas, finds the roots of the Buddhist monastic structure in the structure of the republican state communities of ancient India. Moreover,

> long after the small republican state communities of ancient India succumbed, their principles of government were preserved in the Buddhist monastic community and through it transmitted to other parts of Asia. Thus, historically speaking, the Buddhist "copy has long outlived its secular models". In founding his monastic community [Samgha] "the Buddha adopted the name as well as the constitutional form of the political Samgha of the Sâkya and adjoining republics. . . . Although the Buddha renounced a possible future government position, he remained throughout his life an adviser to neighboring states and . . . founded his monastic organization upon existing political practices." The Buddhist Samgha was copied from the political Samgha [of the Indian republics]. The procedure was secular first and became Buddhistic afterwards. [Sarkisyanz 1965:21]

In addition to these two main types, there is a third type of monastery in Burma: the forest hermitage *(to-ya. caung:)*. A monk primarily concerned with meditation and desiring to remain aloof from all lay responsibilities—such as the performance of rites or the teaching of schoolchildren or novices—may retreat to the jungle, where although living in isolation he is supported by nearby villages.[12] In addition to the rules that apply to an ordinary monk, the anchorite is subject to yet another set. Thus he must devote his time to meditation; neither relatives nor strangers are permitted to live with him; he must not ask for alms; he must not have guests at his monastery; he must not build pagodas or bridges; he must not loiter or roam; he must not permit novices to live in the monastery; he must cure any illness immediately; he may not teach students; he may not, as a result of meditation, enter into trance.[13]

Although forest hermitages are only infrequently found today—I knew of five in the district I studied—there is some reason to believe that they have been in greater evidence in the past.

Despite the marked difference between, say, a simple forest hermitage and an elaborate urban monastic complex, there is no difference in the regulations governing monastic property. Theoretically, of course, this is limited to the eight "requisites" of the monk stipulated by the Rule. These of course are supplied by the faithful. In addition, however, monks are permitted to receive other gifts if these are deemed necessary to meet their needs, and since the interpretation of "necessary" has changed with changing historical and economic circumstances, monks and monasteries have inevitably accumulated a great deal of property, and an elaborate code has developed for its regulation. The need for such a code became evident even in the early history of Buddhism, with the transition from eremitic to cenobitic monasticism, when conflicts began to arise over the technical possession of monastic gifts, viz., do they belong to an individual monk or to his chapter?

In general, Buddhist law recognizes two types of monastic property: corporate (*sanghika;* Burmese, *thinghika*) and personal *(poggalika)*. The latter consists of gifts (capital goods, such as land or monasteries, as well as personal effects) that are offered to an individual monk for his personal use. As such, it is transferable under certain conditions: if of a nonreligious kind, it can be transferred to either a monk or a layman, but if it is of a religious nature it can be conveyed to a monk only. Should the monk leave the Order, however, he can neither retain the property nor is he free to dispose of it. Should he die without making provisions for its disposal, it

[12]The cenobitic, cave-dwelling ascetics of Ceylon (cf. Yalman 1962) are not found in contemporary Burma, although Symes, writing in the eighteenth century, alludes to caves of hermits, presumably hermit monks. (Cf. Symes 1800:272)

[13]This set of rules was obtained from an anchorite who read them aloud from a published text. I had no chance to check this list.

automatically passes from personal to corporate status.

Corporate property belongs to the monastic order rather than to an individual monk. Although village informants knew of only one kind of corporate property, Burmese Buddhist law distinguishes three. (Cf. Maung Maung 1963:125-27.) The generic *sanghika* refers to property which belongs to the entire monkhood—"*Saṅgha* of the four quarters [of the globe]." *Aramika sanghika* refers to property which belongs to monks residing in a particular locality, and its control is invested in the presiding abbot of that locality. *Ganika sanghika* refers to property which belongs to a particular branch of the Order, its control being vested in the presiding monk of the order.

In the case of a monastery, the distinction between personal and corporate ownership is a crucial one, and most monastic conflicts, as we shall see, hang on that question. For a monk to occupy a privately owned monastery without the consent of its owner is not only a violation of Buddhist ecclesiastical law, but in the Burmese mind has serious punitive consequences. Consider, for example, the following case.

On my way to attend the funeral of a monk in a village distant from Yeigyi, I was informed by a group of men from still another village that the original incumbent of the monastery of the deceased monk had become a demon. How else, they asked, could one explain the curious coincidence that the deceased was the fifth incumbent to die within a very few years. Arriving in the village in which the funeral was to take place, I asked the headman whether it was true that three incumbents of this monastery had died within a short time. Visibly embarrassed, and explaining that it was a source of great shame for the village, the headman admitted that this was so. Following the death of the original incumbent, his four successors had died after incumbencies of two, three, three, and eight years, respectively. Much as I tried to draw him out, however, the headman refused to comment any further on this matter. It should be added that the monks who had been invited to the funeral and had heard our discussion did not perceive anything untoward in this coincidence; everything is impermanent, they said, and death is inevitable.

As we began to walk to the monastery, however, the headman's assistant, anxious lest I be offended by the headman's refusal to answer my question, explained that the villagers were indeed alarmed by these premature deaths, which they interpreted as having been caused by the ghost of the original incumbent. It seems that this monastery had been owned by him as personal property. Dying suddenly, he had no time either to appoint a successor or convert it to corporate property. This being so, the monastery, in theory, still belongs to him, and by right should have remained vacant. All his successors, therefore, are technically usurpers. Angered by this usurpation, the monk had become a ghost and had caused the death of all four. To appease his anger, the village has constructed a new monastery for their newly appointed monk, and the old one will be abandoned.

Since it will no longer be inhabited by a monk, and since monastic property cannot be transferred to or used by a layman, the above-mentioned monastery (like all abandoned monasteries) will be left to decay. This is one of the reasons that all over Burma many often beautiful monasteries may be seen rotting in the jungles.[14] The legal difficulties entailed in attempting either to use or rehabilitate them is exemplified in the following incident that occurred in Yeigyi in the course of my field work. When the headman proposed to make a Buddhist chapel out of an abandoned and decaying village monastery, his proposal was hotly debated at a village meeting. His opponents argued that a monastery cannot be used by laymen even for a chapel, and anyone who would so misuse it would surely go to hell. When it was pointed out that, in the past, a decaying monastery had been used for the construction of a bridge, the opposition contended that precisely because of that sinful act Yeigyi had changed from an amicable and peaceful village to one torn by conflict and dissension. The headman's proposal was finally withdrawn after its proponents were advised by one of the village monks that it was in clear violation of the *Vinaya.* Their only alternatives, he said, were either to allow the monastery to decay, or to dismantle it and build a smaller monastery (on the same spot) with the materials. The headman saw no point in the latter alternative since the new monastery, like the old, would also remain uninhabited. The monastery was left to decay.

The Structure of the Order

In no Buddhist country is the *Saṅgha* a homogeneous group of monks. From its very beginnings the Order has been subject to splits and divisions. One of the earliest and most important ideological splits, which survives into the present, was the division between *Mahāyāna* and *Theravāda* Buddhism. Within each of these, however, there have been further divisions based on both sociological and ideological grounds. Thus—confining our discussion to *Theravāda*—the Sinhalese *Saṅgha* is divided by caste; recruitment to its largest and most powerful branch (the *Siam Nikaya*) is restricted to the highest caste, while the lower (and minority) castes are recruited to yet another (the *Amarapura Nikaya*) branch. A third branch, young and small, admits recruits from all castes. In Thailand, the Order is split into two divisions, the major division (the *Mahaanigai*) being less strict in its interpretation and observance of the Rule, the minor (the *Tamayud*) requiring a strict observance.

The Burmese *Saṅgha* has been no exception to this fissiparous tendency; it has almost always been split into at least two groups, each having its own hierarchy of monastic officials. Known in Burma as *gaing:*, these groupings

[14]There are other reasons, too, the most important being the relative lack of prestige accruing to the repairer of a monastery.

have been termed "sects" by Western writers on Burma. This term, however, is both misleading and confusing, for the monastic *gaing:* is most certainly not a sect in either the technical meaning of that concept or in popular usage.[15] Taking our cue from the fact that they are monastic rather than lay groupings, the obvious solution, following the lead of Christian monasticism, is to call these *gaing:* "branches." This term, too, is not without its difficulties, because, among others, the differences among them are not nearly so great as between, say, the Benedictines and the Trappists. Nevertheless, "branch" is certainly preferable to "sect"; for, like most of the monastic branches in Christianity, the *gaing:* represent changes in, and sometimes reformations of, monastic practices which stem from one original Rule.

The contemporary Burmese Order is divided into four branches. The *Thu.dama* is the largest, comprising 85 to 90 per cent of the entire monkhood. *Shwei-jin,* the next largest, has about fifty thousand monks; *Dwāra* has three to four thousand; and *Hngettwin:* even fewer. (These estimates were supplied by the Ministry of Religious Affairs.) The differences that divide the two larger branches consist primarily of minor details concerning monastic discipline. Breaking with its parent branch in the mid-nineteenth century, and founded by an abbot from the village of Shweigyin, the reformist *Shwei-jin* branch differs from *Thu.dama* in forbidding smoking, betel chewing, the consumption of beverages after the noon meal, and the witnessing of popular entertainment. The latter, majority, branch takes its name from the Ecclesiastical Council or *Thu.dama* which, founded in the latter part of the eighteenth century by King Bodawpaya, exercised supreme control over the entire Order until the British conquest. Hence those monks (the overwhelming majority) who continued to recognize the council's authority in the face of the innovations introduced by the newer branches, became known as *Thu.dama.*

The *Hngettwin:* branch, founded by the abbot of the *Hngettwin:* ("cave of birds") monastery of Sagaing, came into being during the reign of King Mindon in the mid-nineteenth century. According to the abbot of the main *Hngettwin:* monastery in Mandalay, this differs from the two major branches both in its conception of Buddhist morality and in its approach to Buddhist ritual.

With respect to morality, all branches of the Buddhist Order demand that the Five Precepts be observed both in word *(wezigan),* referring to the injunction against lying, and in deed *(ka-yagan),* the latter referring to the injunctions against the consumption of alcohol, stealing, killing, and forbidden sexual practices. *Hngettwin:,* in addition, demands that they also be observed in thought *(mano-gan);* the thought of violating any of the pre-

[15]For the classic treatment of religious sects in the sociology of religion, cf. Troeltsch 1931:328-49; Weber 1946: ch. 12.

cepts is in itself a violation. So far as its approach to ritual is concerned, *Hngettwin:* views most of the rituals associated with Buddhist worship as "Hindu" and inconsistent with Buddhist doctrine. Hence it is opposed, for example, to the following conventional Buddhist practices: the striking of triangles during Buddhist ceremonies, the elaborate ceremonial which normally accompanies the *shin-byu,* and theatrical performances or financial contributions at religious ceremonies. Finally, it is opposed to the worship of Buddha images, insisting, rather, that His spirit alone be worshiped. By the same token, it denies the efficacy of prayers offered to the gods. Although believing in their existence, *Hngettwin:* teaches that they have no power to affect human affairs; prayers and offerings to them are futile.[16]

Although placing somewhat less emphasis than *Hngettwin:* on the importance of meditation, *Dwāra* differs in very little else from the latter branch. Founded in Lower Burma by the abbot of the Okpo monastery, a contemporary of the *Hngettwin:* abbot, *Dwāra* also insists that the mental attitude underlying an act is the crucial criterion for its moral or spiritual evaluation (Htin Aung 1966:23). Hence its name, for *Dwāra* means source.

The existence of rival monastic branches in the Burmese *Saṅgha* is as old as Burmese Buddhism itself; and, as in the contemporary difference between *Thu.dama* and *Shwei-jin,* the disagreements between them have usually been based on minor differences in monastic discipline. As early as 1190 Chapata, a Burmese Mon monk returning from a ten-year sojourn in Ceylon, brought with him four foreign monks who had also been ordained in Ceylon, and established a monastic chapter near Pagan. Regarding the Burmese ordination as invalid, he and his Ceylon-ordained companions refused to participate with Burmese monks in the performance of monastic duties, and so in 1192 established a new monastic branch. Monks who had been ordained in Burma were known as the *Maramma Saṅgha,* or the Former Order, while those ordained in Ceylon were known as the *Siṅhala Saṅgha,* or the Latter Order. (Harvey 1925:56; Ray 1946:254-57)

As time passed and the number of branches increased, the rivalry among them increased in intensity, while their knowledge of the canon decreased

[16]Buddhist reform in Burma has been almost exclusively confined to monastic Buddhism. The only exception (to my knowledge) was an eighteenth-century lay reform movement whose doctrines, so far as I can tell, were remarkably similar to those of *Hngettwin:*. As described by Malcom (1839:270), this sect was called *Kolan,* after the name of its founder.

> Kolan was a reformer, who lived about fifty years ago, and taught a semi-atheism, or the worship of *Wisdom.* Homage was to be paid to this, wherever found; of course not a little was to be rendered to himself. Preachers and teachers of this sect, always from among the laity, frequently rise, and gain many followers. Many of the nobles are said to be of this sentiment. Most of this sect are near Ava, and in the towns on the Irrawaddy. They are called *Paramats,* from a word which signified "the good law." They discard the worship of images, and have neither priests nor sacred books. Kolan took the Be-dam-ma, (the first part of the Bedagat), and, after revising it, adopted it as a good creed; but it is not much copied among his followers. Until lately, the Kolans have been greatly persecuted; but at present little notice is taken of them.

commensurately. The differences among them included such matters as the consecration of an ordination hall and the character of the ordination ceremony, each branch performing the ceremony in its own way. (Cf. Ray 1946:184.) In the fifteenth century, with the accession of Dhammazedi to the throne an attempt was made to reform and unify the *Saṅgha.* Turning to Ceylon, Dhammazedi reintroduced the *upasampadā* ordination from the famous Mahavihara monastery. This had the twin effect of restoring unity to the Order and establishing the supremacy of *Vinaya* orthodoxy. From that time, writes Ray, "strict conformity to the rules of the *Vinaya* according to orthodox interpretation was ever the character and ideal of the religion in Burma." (*Ibid.*:257)

The unity achieved by Dhammazedi did not last long. By the beginning of the eighteenth century the Burmese *Saṅgha* was again divided into two opposing camps, and the feud between them lasted for a century. As in earlier feuds and those that were to follow, this too involved relatively minor differences in monastic discipline rather than disagreement as to ethical or metaphysical questions. Around 1700 a certain monk, one Gunabhilamkara, instituted the practice of covering his head and carrying a palmyra fan while making his daily alms rounds. Even more important a breach, from the point of view of monastic orthodoxy, he wore his upper robe (the *uttarasanga*) over one shoulder only, leaving the other uncovered. Soon others followed his practice, and they became known as the *Ekamsikas,* i.e., those who cover one shoulder only. The orthodox monks, the majority, became known as the *Parupanas* because they continued to cover both shoulders. (Cf. Bode 1897:pp. 37 ff.; 1909:ch. 5.) Although both sides attempted, and alternatively succeeded, in obtaining royal support during the reigns of successive kings, the controversy was not finally resolved until the eighteenth century with the accession of King Bodapaya, who ruled in favor of the traditionalists.

Again whatever unity may have been achieved was only temporary. By the end of the nineteenth century Lower Burma, at least, was again confronted with two branches, the reformist *Sulagandi,* representing strict monastic discipline, and the much larger *Mahagandi,* whose discipline was much more lax. (Cf. Hackman 1910:140-41; Shway Yoe 1896:149-50.) Their differences became so intense as to lead to street fighting, and intervention by the English authorities was required to restore peace. The reform branch denounced the wearing of silk monastic robes, which by that time had become frequent. They opposed, too, the practice of sorting out the alms food collected on the daily round before eating from the bowl, and they especially denounced the practice by which the monks would distribute the food so collected to the poor, eating instead meals specially cooked for them. They were opposed, too, to the practice of wearing sandals and of carrying an umbrella while on the alms round, to taking money (however indirectly), to the performance of plays *(pwe:)* on feast days or near pagodas, and to the saturnalian demonstrations that marked the end of the Buddhist

Lent in many monasteries, especially in Rangoon.[17]

Despite the differences that exist among the contemporary branches of the Burmese Order, their relationships are amicable. Unlike conditions in earlier times, monks of different branches cooperate in the performance of Buddhist ritual, as well as in all other monastic activities. By the same token, recruitment to the several branches of the Order is neither competitive nor based on missionary effort. Typically, the novice is ordained in the branch of which his village monk is a member. Typically, too, the villagers care little about these monastic differences. It is usually by happenstance rather than village choice that a local monastery is occupied by the representative of one or another of these branches. By tradition, the incumbents are chosen from the same branch as the founder of the monastery.

Despite the slight behavioral differences among these monastic branches, they are unified by their allegiance to, and almost identical interpretation of, a common religious and monastic ideology. In the days of the Burmese monarchy, when Buddhism was the state religion, they were unified organizationally as well, by the existence of a primate for the entire monastic order (and—if one may speak of such a thing—for the Burmese Buddhist church). The Primate, known as *tha-thana baing* (Pali, *Saṅgha rāja*), was appointed by the king and was assisted in his duties by an Ecclesiastical Council which he himself appointed.[18] After the British conquest of Upper Burma, this office was allowed to lapse, so that the Burmese Order—unlike the Thai Order which is still headed by a *Saṅgha rāja*—has been without a head for about seventy-five years.[19]

Cutting across these four branches of the Order are three monastic

[17]For the sociology of Buddhism it is not irrelevant to emphasize what I have already observed, viz., that monastic splits in other *Theravāda* societies have also been based, not on philosophic issues, but on relatively minor matters of ritual or monastic discipline. In Ceylon, for example, the three branches of the Order differ, among other matters, in the following respects (cf. Copleston 1908:429-33; Hardy 1850:328; Morgan 1956:128-29): (1) covering of one or of both shoulders with the robe; (2) the utterance or nonutterance of a blessing after receiving a gift; (3) using one or two monks for reading and interpreting the Scriptures to laymen; (4) the use or nonuse of a certain formula in offering a gift to monks; (5) cutting of the monk's eyebrows; (6) questions over the ownership of monastic property and the use of luxuries. In the past the hostility between the two earlier of the three branches has been so great that they denied nirvana to each other, each calling the other *duk-silayas*, or "priests without sanctity." (Hardy, *loc. cit.*)

[18]It is worth noting that Buddhism has never achieved organizational expression beyond the level of the national *Saṅgha raja*. There is not, nor has there ever been, even an approximation to the office of Pope.

[19]Although the post of Primate has lapsed, each of the monastic branches continues to be headed by at least a nominal leader. Following Independence the government has conferred the highest ecclesiastical title, *Abhidhaja Maharattha Guru*, on one venerated monk from each of the three large monastic branches. In all three cases the appointee had already received the prior title of *Agga Maha Pandita*, had worn the robe for a minimum of forty years, and was the author of well-known Buddhist tracts. Immediately under the *Abhidhaja* is a council consisting of ten monks and an executive officer known as the *Maha Maiyaka*. Jointly, they comprise the nominal governing body of the branch. In theory the council is an elective body, but I have never met a village monk who claimed to have participated in its election or who, incidentally, either knew or cared about its powers or functions.

political organizations (or were, until the 1962 military coup), each loosely affiliated with a parliamentary political party. However, since they have had little effect on village monks, who almost without exception are either indifferent or hostile to their interests, and since in any event their activities are political rather than religious, they will be discussed elsewhere.

Also cutting across these monastic branches is a national system of ecclesiastical courts which was brought into being by the post-Independence Burmese Government. According to the law each township (roughly equivalent to a county) has such a court, its members elected by the monks of the township. It is empowered to hear cases involving violations of monastic regulations, as well as disputes among monks and monasteries. As we shall see below, these are not infrequent.

CHAPTER 14

The Monk: I. Recruitment Structure

Introduction

Having outlined the normative and formal structure of the monastic order, I should now like to explore the bases for the persistence of this unique institution. Sociologists and anthropologists usually attempt to explain the survival of institutions by reference to the social functions they serve. Such explanations however are only partial, since they assume, without explaining, a normal rate of recruitment of personnel to the institution. The assumption begs the very question which must be answered. Since the putative functions of the institution cannot be served unless social actors are recruited to its various statuses and perform their prescribed roles, it is necessary in the first instance to understand—particularly in the case of achieved statuses—the basis for recruitment. Since, in the last analysis, the problem of recruitment is a problem in motivation, any attempt to explain the persistence of Buddhist monasticism must explain the motivational bases for recruitment to the monastic order.

In attempting to answer this question, I shall limit our discussion to those monks who are, or intend to remain, permanent members of the Order. Buddhist monastic vows, it will be recalled, are not binding for life; many men who have no intention of spending their lives in the monastery can and do spend varying periods of time in the yellow robe. It would be unduly complicated to include these monks—temporary dropouts from the lay life—in a discussion of the permanent members of the Order. Since they have not truly renounced the world, they are not included in this assessment of monks.

By the same token, this assessment does not include those monks—and their number apparently is not small—who have entered the monastery for nonmonastic reasons. Such monks—"humans in yellow robes," as the Burmese refer to them—use the monastery as a refuge from justice, as a base for political agitation, as a means of gaining an easy livelihood, and so on. These bogus monks cannot be excluded from a discussion of the personal functions of the Order and its role in Burmese society, but it would be improper surely to include them in an assessment of those who have genuinely renounced the world. It is the latter alone—those who have embraced the monastic life as a vocation—who are the subjects of this and the next chapter.

A few words of caution are necessary. Although, theoretically, one would expect monks to be different from other men, it must yet be remembered that (analytically speaking) they are men before they are monks. In an important sense therefore, Burmese monks are Burmese men, with the same desires, fears, hopes, anxieties, and aspirations as other Burmese men. In one sense, then, to describe the characteristics of Burmese monks—or more accurately, of those Burmese men who become monks—is to describe the traits of Burmese men, a task beyond the compass of this chapter, nor indeed, even if it were possible, would it be very helpful. For, granting their overriding similarities, Burmese monks are not identical with other Burmese men; if they were, monks presumably would have remained laymen, or laymen would have become monks. There must be some differences between those Burmans who have abandoned the world and those who remain in it. To identify these differences, which have led the former to enter the monastic order, is not easy; none of the answers—at least the obvious answers—is entirely satisfactory.

When the Burmese, monks and laymen alike, are asked why men become monks, they offer a set of stereotypic responses. There are, they say, three motives for entering the monkhood. First there are those who do so from religious motives. Such a one is called *thada pappazi.ta.* Second are those motivated by the desire to escape the difficulties and miseries of human life. This is known as *baya pappazi.ta.* Third are those who wish to obtain an easy living. This is known as *taṇhā pappazi.ta.* Let us examine each in turn, beginning with the last.

The more cynical Burmese—and those, too, who are not so cynical—say that the last-mentioned motive accounts for the preponderance of the inhabitants of monasteries. Thus a village headman said that if the monks were not "spoiled" by being provided for so liberally, there would be far fewer recruits to the Order. "Because of their easy living, there are five times as many monks as there would be otherwise. This is a terrible economic drain. Why support five monasteries when one will do as well?"[1]

[1]That the monastery may attract persons for base motives is already recognized in the extracanonical *Questions of King Milinda.* When Nāgasena explains to Milinda the religious basis for monasticism, the King asks if it is for such "high reasons" that all monks have joined the Order. To this, Nāgasena, with great candor, answers:

Bigandet, writing in the nineteenth century, records identical charges made in that period. The monastic life, he says (Bigandet 1912:271),

> is often looked upon now as one fit for lazy, ignorant, and idle people, who, being anxious to live well and do nothing, put on the sacred dress for a certain time, until, tired of the duties and obligations of their new profession, they retire and betake themselves anew to a secular life.

There is no question that some, perhaps many, monks enter the Order from this cynical motive. Nevertheless, this explanation does not answer our question for at least two reasons. First, we are concerned with genuine rather than bogus monks. Second, and more important, since all Burmese aspire to lives of comfort, indolence, and prestige, yet relatively few become monks, it is obvious that other motives also must be the basis for monastic recruitment.

What, then, about the first motive mentioned by the Burmese, viz., that monks are more religious than other men. Although this would seem to be an obvious explanation, it is no explanation at all unless we know what "religious" means. Surely, we can no longer speak of a specifically *religious* impulse, drive, instinct, motive, and so on. For instead of constituting an irreducible concept, the religious attitude or motivation is itself comprised of a number of psychological elements which have yet to be identified. We might, of course, delimit the scope of this suggestion by arguing that those who become monks are characterized by a strong drive for salvation. But even granting that this is true, the question remains: What is there about these men that accounts for the greater intensity of their salvation quest?

Nor is the task made any easier by phrasing the question in uniquely cultural rather than universally psychological terms. One might have said, for instance, that those who become monks place a higher value than their fellows on the attainment of nirvana. But this answer, too, not only begs the question but is hardly consistent with the facts. There is little doubt that the percentage of laymen who desire nirvana is as high as the corresponding percentage of monks. On the other hand, the percentage of monks who desire a better rebirth rather than nirvana, is—we shall see—as high as the corresponding percentage among the laymen. Why, then, have not the former become monks, or the latter remained laymen?

Well, then, it might be argued, those Burmans who (although desiring nirvana, a better rebirth, comfort, and prestige) prefer to live as laymen are those who are unwilling to make the other sacrifices required by the monastic life. I would agree with this argument, and indeed it is precisely what

---

Certainly not, Sire. Some for those reasons, but some have left the world in terror at the tyranny of kings, some have joined us to be safe from being robbed, some harassed by debt, and some perhaps to gain a livelihood. [*Ibid.:* 49-50]

the Burmans themselves say. But notice, then, that the answer to our question is no longer sociological or cultural; it has become rather a characterological one. For if this is true, then neither a knowledge of the culture—the soteriological goal of nirvana—nor of the social structure—the monastic society and economy—can help us in distinguishing potential monks from laymen. Rather, in order to answer the question we must identify instead the character traits of monks which, despite the sacrifices required, are conducive to, and lead them into, monastic life. Perhaps the third motive suggested by the Burmese may help us in explaining monastic recruitment; perhaps, that is, future monks are motivated to join the monastery in order to escape the suffering and misery of human life. Perhaps, too, they are distinguished from those who are essentially and permanently laymen by needs which find unique satisfaction in the monastery. Since these needs, whatever they may be, develop out of the monk's premonastic life experiences, we must first examine the social matrix within which they arise.

The Sociological Background

Macrosociological Influences

The single most important sociological characteristic of Burmese monks is their predominantly, indeed almost exclusively, rural background. With one exception (and even he was raised in a "small town" rather than a city), all the monks in our sample were born and raised in villages. This finding is consistent with data obtained from the Ministry of Religious Affairs, which show that the entire Order, urban as well as rural, is overwhelmingly rural in origin. In the city of Mandalay, for example, only an infinitesimal number of monks—ten out of a total of ten thousand—had urban backgrounds. Although the Ministry had no statistics for Rangoon, its officials were of the opinion that the situation in that city was not very different, and their expert opinion coincides with the information obtained in my admittedly superficial research in Rangoon. A spot check of ten monasteries there revealed that not one of their monks was himself born in a city, nor did they know of any who were.[2]

In discussing this rather extraordinary finding with Burmese monks themselves, they typically offered one of two explanations. Some said that urban youth, being exposed to the material pleasures of the city, are unwilling to suffer the privations of the monastery. Others said that village families are more religious and more interested in nirvana than urban families, and that these attitudes are passed on to their children.

[2]From the little information available to me from Thailand, the situation there appears to be identical with that in Burma. A Thai scholar in Chiengmai, who had himself spent twenty years in the robe, said that no monk of his acquaintance in Chiengmai had an urban background. Moreover, although he had taught in the Buddhist university in Bangkok for almost ten years, he had never met a monk in that city who came from an urban background.

A different set of explanations was offered by an abbot in Mandalay. His perceptions are consistent both with my own observations and with an explanation I received for the same phenomenon in Thailand. His first point was that "villagers are poor; knowing the meaning of *dukkha*, the poor are more likely to enter the monastery than the rich." Now it is certainly not the case that all villagers are poor, but all available evidence indicates that the great majority of monks come not only from village families, but from *poor* village families. The twenty-one monks in my own sample, for example, were either from landless families, their fathers working as farm hands and unskilled workers (eight out of twenty-one), or from families of small, poor landholders (eleven out of twenty-one). Only two were from large and wealthy landholding families (in one case the family owned fifty, in the other eighty, acres). In short, for nineteen of the twenty-one monks in the sample, life in the monastery offered a much higher standard of living than would have been available to them in the world, and of course a much higher social status.[3]

But obviously poverty is not the only explanation for the urban-rural imbalance in monastic recruitment. After all, there are poor in the cities as well, and even poor boys from the urban setting do not take vows. Moreover, in former times the monasteries were able to obtain recruits—if not full-fledged monks, then at least novices—from the cities, which today do not provide even novices. There must be other factors, then, to account for this differential recruitment, and indeed the Mandalay abbot had a second explanation. It is to be found, he said, in the difference between the educational experience of urban and rural boys: typically, the latter receive their education in monastery schools, the former in state schools. What, then, does this educational difference suggest for the problem at hand?

[3]These data are also remarkably similar to the data available from Theravadist Thailand and Mahayanist China. According to the Thai scholar and former monk mentioned above, Thai monks, too, are mostly recruited from poor families. If his data are reliable, the motivation of poor Thai boys for entering the monastery is somewhat different from that of the Burmese. For the former, the monastery is not only a haven, but for the ambitious among them also their only means for acquiring an education, which in turn is their only vehicle for *secular* mobility. Those monastery boys and novices who perform well in their home monasteries are recommended for admission to the teaching monasteries in provincial towns, and from them they have entree to the Buddhist universities in Bangkok. With degrees from the latter institutions, they can hope to obtain teaching posts or other secular positions which will permit them to leave the monkhood. Those who are not qualified to climb this monastic educational ladder, and for whom therefore there is no release from the monastery, are—according to the same informant—unhappy and frustrated. Not being religiously "musical," they turn to extrareligious pursuits such as electricity, carpentry, etc., within the scope of monastic life.

In China, too, the Buddhist monastery has been a refuge for the "economically destitute." That, at least, is the conclusion of one student of Chinese religion. He goes on to say:

> Priesthood and the monastic orders claimed a large number of converts from socially and economically helpless individuals, giving them in effect not so much spiritual as material salvation. Thus, most of the priests came from poor families or were orphans and widowers, without intimate family ties. [Yang 1967:332]

Until the British conquest, the monastic school was the only educational institution in Burma. To this day the monastery is termed *caung:*, school; any family, from peasant to king, which was interested in providing its sons with an education, sent them to the monasteries.[4] Following the conquest, however, the private schools established by missionaries and the colonial government, and the state schools established still later by the post-Independence Burmese Government, gradually emptied the urban monastery schools of their pupils. Indeed, the situation is so critical that urban monks most frequently obtain their monastery boys—necessary for performing those many tasks which are forbidden to monks—from village families, who from either piety or poverty are willing to part with one, at least, of their sons. It is significant in this regard that among urban children there is a stigma attached to monastery students. The former, studying in private or state schools, poke fun at them, referring to them tauntingly as beggars.

The secular school system, then, has become an obstacle—perhaps *the* great obstacle—to monastic recruitment, for it is from the monastery pupils that the Order has traditionally drawn its novices, and the latter in turn have supplied its monks. Our data are entirely consistent with this explanation. Except for one monk, who had studied through the sixth standard in a Mandalay state school, all the others in our sample had received an exclusively monastic education.

If these explanations for differential rural-urban recruitment to the Order are sound, they suggest that urbanization and affluence, jointly, constitute a powerful threat to the numerical strength of the Order. Thoughtful Burmese agree that this is indeed the case.[5]

The situation in Thailand is even more deteriorated. Despite the population explosion in that country in the past ten years, the number of novices entering the monastery has remained constant. Or, to cite another measure of the problem, while the population rose 178 per cent from 1927 to 1966, the number of monks (both temporary and permanent) in monasteries during Lent increased only 35 per cent. The ratio of monks to total male population declined from 1:16 to 1:34 in that forty-year period. (Mulder 1969:35)

[4]Some observers have remarked on the democratic implications of this facet of traditional monastic education. For Cady the monastery was "socially important as a democratic leveling agency. The sons of princes and fishermen enjoyed the same status at the monastery, for entrance was open to all alike and all were subject to the same discipline." (Cady 1958:61)

[5]Traditional Burmese say that the weakening of the *Saṅgha* is entirely consistent with the teachings of the Buddha Himself. As we approach the end of Gautama's era—we have already passed the halfway mark of the five thousand years of His dispensation—Buddhist practice will become more and more attenuated, and the number of monks will become fewer and fewer, until just before the appearance of the Buddha Maitreya they will all but disappear. Officials in the Ministry of Religious Affairs pointed to other indices of this progressive degeneration of Buddhism. Thus, during the reign of King Mindon a century ago there were, they claimed, ten thousand lay stewards in monasteries; today there are only a handful.

Microsociological Influences

It would seem evident from the foregoing discussion that a particular socioeconomic and educational background is especially conducive to monastic recruitment. This, however, provides us with only a partial answer for our problem, for it is equally evident that, although monks from poor and rural origins, monastically educated, are disproportionately represented in the Burmese Order, it is still the case that most men from this socioeconomic matrix do not become monks. We must therefore attempt to delimit our inquiry even further. Since the majority of monks (if I may generalize from our sample), even including those who defer joining the Order until middle age and later, make their decision to become monks sometime before the end of their teens, it seems reasonable to seek additional explanations for monastic recruitment in the influences impinging on them in childhood and adolescence. First, however, let us look at the data.

For the twenty persons for whom we have information, one knew from his early childhood that he would become a monk (he had decided when he was nine years old), half had decided between the ages of twelve and fifteen, and one quarter had decided between the ages of sixteen and twenty. Although some, as we shall see, did not execute their decision until they had become adults, the great majority of these men had decided to enter the Order while they were monastery students or novices—this is consistent, of course, with our previous observation concerning the importance of the monastery school—while only 20 per cent came to their decision as adults. Among the latter, interestingly, none had made their decision in their twenties, three had decided in their thirties, and one in his forties. These findings are summarized in Table 10.

TABLE 10
AGE AT WHICH DECISION WAS MADE TO ENTER THE ORDER

AGE	*N*
0-12	1
12-15	10
16-20	5
21-30	0
31-40	3
40-	1
	20

Since, with one exception, all the monks in our sample had received their primary education in the monastic school, it is not unreasonable to assume that their decision had been influenced in some degree by their teachers. It is not implausible that their parents, too, affected it. Although both influences are important, it would seem, on the basis of interviews with these monks, that the former influence is the more significant.

So far as family is concerned, we might distinguish two types of family influence on occupational choice: the family might actively encourage the child's decision, or one of its members might constitute a role-model for the child. In our sample, both types of family influence have been operative. In every case the monk's parents either encouraged and/or approved of his decision to become a monk. In no case did they disapprove of his choice. In addition to parental approval, the majority of the monks had family role-models; two-thirds of the monks in the sample have relatives—elder brothers, cousins, uncles—who are monks, by contrast with the lay population, for which the corresponding figure is 25 per cent.

But this is not all. It is extremely unlikely for an adult to become a monk if he has never had the experience of living in a monastery during his early, impressionable years. Hence, today—as in the past—it is the village boy, educated and often living in the monastery, who may come to identify with and prefer the monastic way of life. From earliest childhood, he is not only imbued with the ethos and tone of the monastery, but is exposed to no other competing intellectual or cognitive, let alone experiential, structure. The city boy does not have this background. Although the monastic life may offer a poor boy from the city, as it does his rural counterpart, a much higher standard of living, the economic incentive is not salient, for, lacking the requisite socialization, he is psychologically unqualified for the monastic life.

But this monastic experience is crucial for another, perhaps more important reason: the influence of the monastic teacher. All the monks said that his was a very important influence, not because he attempted to direct them into a monastic career, but because his behavior and personality was for them a model to be emulated. As one monk put it, as a child he came to respect and love the monks he knew, and he wanted to become a monk in order to be like them.

It seems reasonable to conclude, then, that for a young boy studying in the monastery school, identified with a kindly monk and imbued with the overriding importance of Buddhism in village society—impressed, too, with the authority attached to the monastic robe, and perceiving the great prestige accruing to that status (even a king, let alone ordinary mortals, must prostrate himself before the monk)—such a setting would be optimally conducive to monastic recruitment. If, in addition, he is a poor boy, who can compare the hardship and poverty of his parents' lives—"we are like animals," say the villagers, "toiling in the mud up to our knees"—with the physical ease and relative luxury of the monastic life, the wonder is that there are not many more monks in Burma rather than, as many visitors exclaim, that there are so many. For clearly, from the standpoint of almost any of the conventional socioeconomic bases for occupational choice, the monastery would seem to offer the village boy a most desirable career. Indeed, from this perspective, the difference between the monastic careers of the Buddha and of the contemporary "Sons of the Buddha" is illuminating. Whereas the Buddha was a prince who, in order to become a monk, renounced the wealth and high status of his position, his Burmese "Sons," stemming from a depressed social stratum, enhance both their status and their standard of living inestimably by becoming monks. That, despite these obvious incentives, only a small minority of village boys do choose to enter the Order, indicates of course that there are important opposing influences.

Countervailing Influences

Among the many possible obstacles to monastic recruitment, one may mention three. First, the monastic teacher is not always a kindly figure with whom the boy can identify or whom he may desire to emulate. Although I only rarely observed the strict authoritarian monk-pupil relationship that others have described, it cannot be denied that some monks are indeed harsh with their students—especially, as Hanks (1949) observes, by comparison with the treatment which the younger ones, at least, receive at home. Even the milder monks, however, are sometimes feared by their pupils: in one monastery in which I worked, it was sufficient for the novice-teacher to indicate by sign language that the monk was approaching to energize the entire class to a hasty return to their recitations. Hence, although the monks I observed were not the harsh taskmasters that Hanks describes for the Arakan (southwest Burma), or that Lévy (1957:5) describes for Laos (where monks may beat the students and tie them up), still, many of them are not the kind of person to whom a young child would respond happily.

A second obstacle to monastic recruitment is that the monastic life, although providing both comfort and ease, is nevertheless difficult in other respects. Former novices, and those current novices who have decided not to pursue a monastic vocation, emphasize three negative aspects of the life. Almost without exception, they complain that the life is boring; the monastery, they say, is a dull place in which to live.[6] Indeed, even among ordained

[6]Monastic boredom, as might be expected, is not a uniquely Burmese phenomenon. It is found to the same degree in Thailand despite the fact that Thai monks can, at least to some extent, alleviate their boredom through manual labor. In northern Thailand, where (according to Moerman) about 80 per cent of the boys who become novices leave the monastery before becoming monks, and those few who are ordained return to a secular life after a short time, boredom is the primary obstacle to monastic commitment. Thus,

> The difficulty of being a priest comes not from the rigors of temple life but from the blandishments of the secular life outside. Boys who have been in the temple for any length of time complain about "boredom" and "loneliness." They fret that they cannot join their lay peers in farming, courting, and earning money. The longer they have been in the temple, the duller life seems there. [Moerman 1966:154]

monks boredom remains one of the difficult problems in monastic adjustment. Prohibited by the Rule from engaging in physical labor and deprived of even the mild exertion of walking on their alms rounds—having neither an aptitude for scholarship nor a vocation for the contemplative life—it is little wonder that many of them are visibly bored by a daily routine that offers little exercise for either body or mind. St. Benedict was well aware of the perils of idleness. "Idleness," he wrote, "is the enemy of the soul: therefore at certain times the bretheren should be occupied in manual labor, and at certain times in religious reading." (Butler 1962:373) Hence, the Benedictine Rule assigns six hours of the monk's day to work, and three and a half to reading. The Buddhist Rule on the contrary interdicts manual labor, and although it certainly encourages, it does not prescribe either reading or meditation. It is not surprising that the average Buddhist monk suffers from boredom.

Boredom, no doubt, accounts for the inordinate amount of sleeping one sees in monasteries—monks are forever taking naps—as well as for the dullness and apathy frequently encountered in them. I suspect, too, that those (as we shall see, they constitute a large number)—who practice alchemy, medicine, exorcism, and—in the cities—politics, do so not only for the intrinsic interest of the subject, but as an escape from the tedium of monastic living.

Similarly, boredom probably accounts for the great interest monks display in visitors. Although it seems that many have little interest in a genuine clash of ideas, still they almost invariably welcome conversation and discussion. With one exception all the monks I had hoped to interview were most cordial; instead of meeting resistance—as many Burmese had warned—I encountered instead a great desire among them to talk and answer questions. Much of this cooperation may be explained by the genuine desire to be helpful, but much of it also, I am sure, by the desire to alleviate their boredom. If one discounts the obvious bias and loaded vocabulary of a Catholic missionary, Bigandet's description of nineteenth century Burmese monks (Bigandet 1912:317-18) characterizes the contemporary situation as well. Monks, he writes,

> remain during the best part of the day sitting in a cross-legged position, or reclining, or sleeping, or at least attempting to do so. They occasionally resume the vertical position to get rid of *ennui,* one of their deadliest enemies, and by repeated stretching of arms and legs, and successive yawnings, try to free themselves from that domestic foe. The teaching of their scholars occupies a few of them for a short time in the morning and in the evening. They are often relieved

---

The same picture holds for central Thailand. According to Ingersoll (1963:250) boredom—followed by the desire for food, money, family, and sex—is the most important reason given by young men for leaving the *Saṅgha.*

> from their mortal *ennui* by visitors as idle as themselves, who resort to their dwellings to kill time in their company.

But boredom is not the only hardship in the monastic life. Another complaint of Burmese novices, former and current, is the difficulty of complying with the ascetic aspects of the life. The curtailments of the monk's sensuous pleasure—his exclusion from almost all forms of popular entertainment, the prohibition against eating after midday, and especially the vow of celibacy—serve to dishearten many young men who would have otherwise been attracted to the monkhood.[7] Many novices say that, were it not for their sexual frustration, they would have found the monastery a most congenial place in which to live.

But the Rule is an impediment to monastic recruitment in yet another sense. Monastic regulations are not only difficult to comply with, but their violation entails serious karmic consequences. Former novices frequently speak of the anxiety they felt concerning their ability to comply with them. As one of them put it, "it is better to be a layman, and observe the precepts of the layman, than to become a monk and violate the precepts of the monk." Or, as another expressed it,

> Violation of the precepts is much more serious for the monk than for the layman. The monk's investment is much greater, and therefore he can lose much more. The investment of the layman is very little; therefore he cannot lose very much. But the monk must be very careful; he cannot violate the precepts [lest he go to hell]. It is hard, very hard.

To conclude, then, in the case of most villagers the motivational dispositions to monasticism produced by the sociological conditions discussed in the previous section are not ordinarily strong enough to overcome the countervailing influences discussed here. Still, since a significant number do become monks, our task is to identify the additional motives which, when combined with those produced by these structural conditions, lead to their decision. These motives, presumably, arise out of specific, perhaps idiosyncratic, experiences of the incipient monk.

Some Motivational Bases for Recruitment: Conscious

World-Renunciation

When monks themselves are asked why they decided to enter the Order, most of them—consistent with the normative ideology of Buddhism—say it was because of suffering, the desire to escape suffering, or the hope of acquiring the means (merit and good karma) by which the latter goal can

[7]Pfanner (1962:315) reports the same finding in Lower Burma.

be achieved—either by a better rebirth or by the attainment of nirvana. Some of them, too, as Table 11 indicates, stress the comfortable life of the monastery—escape from suffering in this existence—while some, in addition, emphasize the opportunity to teach and disseminate the teachings of Buddhism.

TABLE 11
MOTIVES FOR BECOMING A MONK ($N = 20$)

MOTIVE	Σ
Disgust with the world and its misery	8
To avoid labor/to have easy life	6
To achieve nirvana	6
To acquire merit and good karma	4
To promote and teach Buddhism	3
	27

It is obvious from their responses that these monks are, as indeed Buddhist monks are thought to be, world-rejectors. This does not mean, of course, that they are all otherworldly, as we have been using that term. Some, as practitioners of kammatic Buddhism, reject the present world in order to enjoy worldly pleasures in a better future rebirth. Others, the minority, as practitioners of nibbanic Buddhism, reject the world in any form, so as to achieve nirvana. But in order to understand the motivational bases for their world-rejection in either case, it is important to distinguish between those—known as *hge-byu*—who enter the Order directly from their apprenticeships as monastery students and novices (and who, therefore, have never experienced the lay life), and those—known as *to:dwet*—who enter the Order as adults after having lived in the world.

In general, the latter monks became world-rejectors as a result of personal pain and suffering experienced in the world. For them the monastery is their means of coping with existential suffering; they also view it, of course, as a means of reducing suffering in their future rebirths. Those, however, who have entered the monkhood directly from the novitiate do not specify any personal misfortune as the motive for their decision. They rather refer in abstract terms to the desire to avoid misery or achieve nirvana. Their renunciation, in short, is ideologically rather than experientially inspired. This is not to say that they, too, have not known pain—most of them, as I have pointed out, come from poor families—but for the most part they have not known personal tragedy, suffering, or misfortune; and living in the monastery both as students and as novices, they have led lives of relative ease and contentment. For many of these latter monks, therefore, *dukkha* was a theoretical concept, an ideological commitment, whose experiential truth was not known or deeply felt. Moreover, only a small number discovered its meaning while living in the monastery. Thus the seventy-three-year-old abbot of one monastery admitted quite candidly that until he was fifty he "payed little attention" to the Buddhist "truth" that "birth, old age, sickness, and death cause suffering"; they were words he had "learned and affirmed," but which he "had not felt." At fifty, he became personally aware of their truth, and having long practiced Buddhist meditation, he is now even more convinced of it.

For those who have entered the monkhood after previous experience in the world, the pattern is quite different. For them suffering has been an existential fact (not merely a scriptural teaching), the experience of which led them, first, to the personal realization of the truth of Buddhist *dukkha*, and thence into the Order. Since the latter monks are preponderant in our sample, the motives classified in Table 11 are obviously skewed in their direction. Of course, if the sample is representative, this skewing effect would hold for the Order as a whole, but on the basis of our present information I am not prepared to say which of these two types of monk is preponderant in the total monastic population.[8] In any event, whether it constitutes a minority or a majority, it is important to examine the motives of this group in detail, not only for the light they can shed on monastic recruitment, but also for their implications for the functions of monasticism.

For these monks, three classes of motives led them to renounce the world for the monastery: the desire to escape from a difficult and stormy life, the weight of social (and especially domestic) responsibility, and the pain of personal frustration or tragedy.[9] These may best be illustrated by actual cases.

Desire to escape from a difficult life. Monk *A* had decided when he was only twelve that he wanted to become a monk, but deferred acting upon his decision because he was obliged to support his widowed mother. He joined the Order at the age of twenty-one, the year his mother died. After eleven years in the robe, however, he left the monkhood because he was "not feeling well" and for twenty years he worked as a farm laborer. He never married. At the age of fifty-one, he decided that he could no longer perform physical labor. Moreover, since "an old man should not forget religious matters," he once again donned the yellow robe.

[8]In the villages I surveyed, the majority of monks had entered the Order after leading lay lives. For these villages, therefore, the sample is representative. According to an experienced abbot in Mandalay, most monks in that city, however, had entered the Order directly from the novitiate.

[9]In China, according to Yang, very similar motives were the basis for recruitment to the priesthood and the monastic order. Noting that one of the main functions of these two institutions was to provide a "refuge for disillusioned individuals," Yang (1967:330) goes on to observe:

> Thus, many a thwarted statesman, a frustrated scholar, a bankrupt merchant, a jilted lover, a person who had failed to withstand the onslaught from life . . . would suddenly waken to the futility of the struggle and "flee into the door of emptiness," the traditional phrase for conversion to Buddhist priesthood.

Monk *B* entered the monastery when he was thirty-nine years old. Before that he, too, had been an agricultural laborer and a bachelor. (Being a bachelor, he said, the monastery was "fit" for him.) Even in his youth he had wanted to become a monk, but being in debt, he was disqualified for ordination. Prior to working as a farm laborer, he had worked in a quarry and had seen many deaths due to accidents. Deeply impressed with the reality of suffering, he was confirmed in his desire to become a monk. When eventually he accumulated sufficient funds to purchase his robes and other essentials, he entered the monkhood.

Monk *C*, a fifteen-year-old novice, is an exception to the generalization that monks who enter the Order from the novitiate have not experienced suffering. This novice had lived a life of constant instability and struggle until deciding to enter the monastery. When he was only three months old, his mother divorced his father because of the latter's infidelity. Without a father, his early life was one of stark poverty, his mother barely earning a living by working in a variety of menial jobs. In his early teens, when his mother remarried and he was ill-treated by his stepfather, he moved to the home of his mother's sister. This, too, proved an unhappy experience, since he did not get along with either his aunt or her husband. "Disgusted with secular life," he decided to enter the monastery.

Monk *D* had for years suffered an abusive, nagging wife. Finally, in his forties, deciding that he had had enough, he left her to enter the monastery. In accordance with the Rule, he had, of course, to receive her prior consent.

For all these monks, then, the monastery was sought as a refuge from a difficult world. Sometimes the difficulty consists of what in other societies would be perceived as a petty annoyance, which would be handled in a less drastic fashion than abandoning the world. Take, for example, the following incident, quoted from *The* [Rangoon] *Nation* (May 26, 1961).

> A landless manual worker has sought the sanctuary in the Buddhist Monastic Order as he was unable to carry out the order of the local Headman to dismantle a home which he had constructed with the help of kindly neighbours.
>
> Taking compassion on landless labourer Ko Soe Myint and family, the Land Committee at Natmaw (Chaungzon Township) told him he could occupy a vacant site on the outskirts of the village. Overjoyed, Ko Soe Myint pawned what little he had, borrowed the rest and put up a small home costing about K150.
>
> Last week, U Suppana and Daw Mar Mi, who claimed ownership of the plot of land, sought the help of Headman U Maung Thaung to evict the poor family. The Headman ordered Ko Soe Myint to dismantle his home within 24 hours, and brusquely dismissed the poor man's appeal for a one-year stay.
>
> Too depressed to carry the bad news back to his family, he forsook this mundane world and sought sanctuary at the nearby monastery. There he entered the Order of the *Sangha*.
>
> Meanwhile, sympathetic neighbours are looking after the family.

Although the monks described here pointed to stormy and difficult personal lives as their motive for entering the Order, it is not implausible —although there are none in my small sample—that today, as in the past, some men become monks to escape from the social and political unrest in the larger society. Thus, in describing a sixteenth-century adviser to the king who abandoned the comforts of the court in order to retire to a monastery, Harvey observes that ". . . in those days of violent contrasts a cloister was the only place on earth where existence was bearable to a man of finer nature." (Harvey 1925:109) Similar motives operated in the seventeenth century when, as Ray observes, ". . . not unoften members of the laity joined the Order in numbers not always for the love of monastic life, but just to escape from the stormy and calamitous days in which their lot was cast." (Ray 1946:216)

The weight of social and especially of family responsibility. Cady, in a historical discussion of Burmese monasticism, remarks that "the desire to escape onerous service demands which were levied on the population generally may have contributed something to the popularity of the life of the monk, as did, no doubt disinclination to undertake the responsibilities for supporting a family" (Cady 1958:50). These same motives, especially the latter, are operative today.

Monk *E*, after twenty-six years of marriage, informed his wife that he desired to enter a monastery. He had supported and lived with her for many years; life was hard, they were poor, and there was "no purpose" to remaining in the world. She granted permission for him to do so. "I was happy," she told me, "that he had decided to follow the Good Path."

Monk *F*, a father of three, entered the Order after contemplating this decision for four or five years. As a layman he had constantly to be concerned with satisfying his wife, both sexually and materially, and after almost twenty years of family life he no longer wanted this responsibility. Hence, although still attached to his wife, he entered the monastery at the age of thirty-seven.

Married and the father of six, monk *G* was ordained at the age of forty-two. An impoverished farm laborer, burdened with "suffering," he suddenly decided, without previous warning, to enter the monastery. When I first visited his village he was a layman working in the paddy fields. Two weeks later, when I returned to the village, he had been received as a monk.

Monk *H*, a sixty-year-old man, was also a layman when I first met him. At that time he was married to his sixth wife, by whom he had had a five-year-old daughter. His previous wives, some of whom had also borne him children, were either divorced or dead. When I interviewed him he told me that he was fed up with the world; his life was hard and his work tedious. He had decided to become a monk because, he said, "the life of the monk is easy." Three months later, when I returned to his village, he was wearing the robe.

Here, then, we have a group of men who, suffering from nagging wives or from the burden of irksome family responsibility, have decided to reduce their suffering by entering the Buddhist Order. Although this might not be an accepted motive for taking vows in a Christian order, it is of course a perfectly legitimate motive for Buddhist monasticism. The realization of the truth of suffering is the first aim of Buddhism. The reduction of suffering is its essential goal. The desire to reduce suffering, regardless of the experiential basis involved, is a legitimate—nay, *the* legitimate—motive for recruitment to the Order. From a Buddhist point of view, these men have become monks from genuine motives.

Personal frustration and/or tragedy. In some cases the decision to enter the monastery followed some frustration which either in itself was too difficult to bear, or which served to confirm the conviction (always apprehended but not before acted upon) that suffering is the characteristic of existence.

Monk *I* was a wealthy landowner and trader who, at the age of forty-five, was the victim of an auto accident which left him crippled. Contemplating his life, he realized how sinful it had been—among other things he had been a hunter—and, filled with remorse, he decided to become a monk. Selling his land and other properties and distributing the proceeds to pagodas and monasteries, he entered the Order. His wife, whom he has not seen for seven years, became a nun.

Monk *J* had a very different background. Before entering the monastery at the age of fifty-eight he had been a farmer; he was married and the father of four children. By his own negligence he lost his land, and as a result became severely depressed. At the recommendation of a friend, he began to practice Buddhist meditation with the guidance of the abbot in whose monastery he now resides. Through meditation he "discovered the impermanence of worldly things, the difficulties of existence, and the truth that one cannot control one's fate." The "difficulties of existence" refer especially to the hardships entailed in working and in supporting a family. Discovering these truths, he decided to become a monk, a decision which met with the disapproval of his wife. After a few years, however, she acquiesced, and bequeathing his remaining property to her, he entered the monastery.

Monk *K*, formerly a bookkeeper in the Irrawaddy Transport Company, became a monk at the age of thirty when his wife, to whom he was deeply attached, died. To escape from the "misery of existence" he entered a monastery.

Monk *L*, forty years old, has been wearing the robe for six years. As a boy he had never contemplated becoming a monk, and as a teen-age novice he longed to leave the monastery, for when he did not know his lessons he was beaten by his monastic teacher. When his parents died, he left the novitiate and became a farm worker. Later he married and became a father. Shortly after the birth of his daughter, he discovered his wife in an adulterous affair. Bitter, he divorced her, and following the divorce began to frequent the village monastery, attending the sermons of the monk and practicing meditation under his guidance. After a year, he compared the monastic with the lay life and decided that the former was superior. Had his wife remained faithful he would never, so he claimed, have considered it; but now, having discovered the benefits of monasticism, he is grateful for her infidelity.

Monk *M* is the only man whom I knew very well both before and after his joining the Order. Hence, in his case alone was I able to observe personally the accumulation of ego-frustrations which eventuated in his renunciation of the world. A landless farmhand, this man had attempted to satisfy his intense need for prestige in a variety of ways: he performed as a clown in an itinerant theatrical group, he practiced traditional medicine as well as exorcism, and was known as an authority on Buddhism. All these roles served to some extent to satisfy his need for attention and public acclaim. Then, within a three- or four-month period, he lost them all. The theatrical troupe was dissolved; he suffered severe humiliation when, publicly failing in his attempt to exorcise an evil spirit, he was forced to call in another exorcist to treat his patient; finally, his brother, who had been studying Buddhist meditation, had begun to supersede him locally as a Buddhist authority. In many discussions with him, prior to becoming a monk, it became apparent that each of these events was a heavy narcissistic blow; the combination resulted in a serious depression. Persisting in his depressive state for a few weeks, he suddenly appeared at my house to announce that he had made up his mind to become a monk. He had been working in the field, he said, thinking about the "misery" of existence, and there and then decided to enter the monastery. A month later, with the consent of his wife, he was ordained.[10]

Some Motivational Bases for Recruitment: Unconscious

Introduction

Although the above discussion of its conscious bases is necessary for our understanding of monastic recruitment, it is not sufficient. Personal tragedy, for example, was an important factor in the decision of these monks to enter

[10]It is interesting to compare these conscious motives for monastic recruitment, as they are constructed retrospectively by monks now in the Order, with those of young boys (between the ages of seven and eleven) who look forward to becoming monks. In a sample of twenty-four boys at the government school at the township seat, ten said they wanted to become monks—for one or more of the following reasons: because the life of a monk is easy—as one boy put it, "monks only sit and eat"; because of the great merit which monks acquire; because of the desire for nirvana. Those who did not wish to become monks were motivated by the desire for some other occupation, the wish to escape the boredom (as they put it) of the monastic life, or the unwillingness to give up food after noon. (They complained that, as postulants, they were constantly hungry.) One boy was disinclined to become a monk lest, if he violate any of the precepts, he end up in hell.

the Order, but surely many Burmese men—many more, at any rate, than have become monks—suffer personal tragedy, yet do not enter a monastery. In addition, then, to their conscious motives a complete explanation for monastic recruitment must attend to the monks' unconscious motives as well. In saying this I assume that it goes without saying that recruitment to any achieved status is motivated by unconscious as well as conscious needs, that monks constitute an example of, rather than an exception to, this generalization. All of us have unconscious needs and wishes—unconscious because, their expression being culturally prohibited, they are repressed—which demand expression and satisfaction. Just as the performance of social roles permits the direct fulfillment of conscious motives, so too it permits the simultaneous, but disguised fulfillment for our forbidden, unconscious motives. To put it somewhat differently, since almost all social roles may be viewed as providing an opportunity for the institutionalized sublimation of forbidden drives and wishes, the latter are important motivational bases for recruitment to their associated statuses. It is this combination of conscious and unconscious motives that constitutes the necessary and sufficient motivational set for recruitment to any achieved status.

At the present state of our knowledge, we cannot pretend to accurately identify the unconscious needs which contribute to monastic recruitment. Still, if asked to name those emotional characteristics which, either qualitatively or quantitatively, distinguish monks as a group from nonmonks as a group, I would emphasize dependency, narcissism, and emotional timidity. These characteristics, I suggest, provide at least part of the unconscious motivational dispositions for recruitment to the Order.

Need for Dependency

By "need for dependency" I mean the desire to avoid responsibility (for others and self) and instead to be taken care of and nurtured by others. Although this need is found in its most extreme form in the child, it is also found in a less intense (and often unconscious) form among adults as well. To conclude, therefore, that Buddhist monks have a strong need for dependence is not to say that they are distinguished by a unique craving which is absent from other human beings, but that they exhibit an intense form of a generic human need. Many men, no doubt, wish to be relieved of the burden of domestic responsibility, but in few of them is this need so strong that they do, in fact, abandon their families. Many men, too, suffer from tragedy and frustration, but for few of them is the resultant trauma so great that they cannot face up to their problems with independence and self-reliance. No doubt many men, too, would like to be cared for by others and to be relieved of worry and insecurity, but in few of them is this need so intense that they do, in fact, permit others to assume this burden for them. Buddhist monks, on all these dimensions, are among the few; the three, above-mentioned conditions characterize almost all the monks described in the last section. These conditions, by their own admission, are what lay behind their decision to enter the Order. Given their strong dependency needs, the decision was no accident, for it is my thesis that the Buddhist monastery is by its very nature an institutionalized and culturally sanctioned means by which such needs can be satisfied.

Strong dependency needs not only lead men into the monastery, but their persistence is one of the basic reasons for their remaining. Although the life is one of comfort and security, there are after all many frustrations attached to it. *Dukkha*, as the monks point out, is not transcended by joining the Order; it is as characteristic of life in the cloister as in the world. Still, although they stressed the difficulties inherent in the monastic life, none of the monks indicated (in response to my query) that they regretted their decision. If they had had regrets they could, of course, have left the Order, since they do not take permanent vows. Instead, they said that although there is suffering in the monastery, it is not like the suffering they would have in the world. Thus, if they lived in the world, they would have to work in the fields, stand guard at night in the village, obey numerous governmental regulations, take on onerous financial burdens, assume responsibility for wife and child, for mother or brother. The emphasis on these forms of suffering and their desire to avoid them, is a pervasive theme in the interviews with all the monks. Hence, although as many as a third said that the monastic life is a lonely life, they added that it is better to be lonely than to face all the responsibilities alluded to above.

The wish to avoid the *dukkha* of responsibility is one of the reasons, too, that monks will not participate in village welfare or development activities. Their participation, to be sure, would be contrary to the Rule, but in addition to this normative reason, many monks also offer a psychological reason for nonparticipation. The following is fairly typical.

> It is too complicated. Those monks who want worldly prestige [*lo:ki goung:*] will participate. But for others there are too many worries involved in managing the villagers. The monk will constantly have to agitate his brain: should the cart go this way or that way? Should Maung Youn or Maung Maung Gyi supply the oxen? And so on. He would lose his freedom. The *doukkha.* is too great.

That the monastic life constitutes a means for avoiding responsibility and satisfying the need for dependency is apparent from even the schematic description of the monastic life in chapter 12. Almost all his needs are satisfied by others, without his doing—or being permitted to do—anything on his own behalf. As we have seen, he does no work; he does not earn his own bread; even if he wants to, he cannot so much as pour his tea or lift his serving bowl, let alone tend his garden or repair his monastery. Everything he needs must be given to him by others; everything that he desires must be provided him by others. Moreover, others not only *must* provide for the monk, but in fact they *do* provide for him, and—as we have seen —with a lavish hand. As parents may deprive themselves in order to provide for their children, so Burmese laymen stint on nothing in satisfying the needs of their monks. Food and gifts, goods and services are theirs for the asking—and even without asking, for technically monks are not permitted to ask for anything. The monk, in short, lives in a state of complete security. He need never be anxious about being cared for, provided for, taken care of.

There are class and status groups in many societies, of course, and unspecified individuals in most, who like Buddhist monks are both dependent on others for the satisfaction of their needs and handsomely provided for. Almost always, however, their relationship with their benefactors is reciprocal. The reciprocity may not—at least from our point of view—be symmetrical, but nevertheless there is reciprocity: *A* receives goods or services or women or honor from *B*, and *B* reciprocates by giving something in return to *A*. In the case of the monk, however, his needs are satisfied by others without his (actively) doing anything for them in return. This does not mean, I hasten to add, that from the layman's point of view, the relationship is not reciprocal. From his point of view, he provides for the needs of the monk, and the latter by his asceticism is in turn the means by which he, the layman, acquires merit. (See chapter 16.) Nevertheless, though the relationship is profitable for the layman, the fact remains that on the monk's side it is not viewed as symmetrical: from his point of view, his asceticism is for his, not the layman's, benefit. From his point of view, their relationship —like any true dependency relationship—is asymmetrical: the monk is dependent and he expects his dependency needs to be satisfied by the layman.

This almost absolute dependency, which is structurally built into the monastic role, is not only observed in behavior, but finds symbolic expression as well. The only term, in addition to their proper names, by which monks address or refer to laymen is *daga* (masculine) or *dagama.* (feminine), literally, a donor, provider, or benefactor (Pali, *dāyaka*). These terms are used even in reference to strangers whom the monk may have never met and who have never contributed to his support. Psychologically viewed, I take this to mean that, from the monk's perspective, every layman is essentially a giver of nourishment, a provider of nurturance. For the monk this is the salient characteristic of the layman, the "figure," as it were, against which his other characteristics are merely "ground." And this can only be so because the converse is equally true, viz., the salient characteristic of the monk is his need for dependence and his perception of others as agents for its satisfaction. The emotional quality of this need for dependency is manifest, albeit in an extreme form, in the following letter, written by a village monk to his special *dāyaka.*

DEAR X,

I am writing these lines to inform you of the stroke of ill luck that has befallen me. I have been laid up with a serious headache, as well as indigestion, so that I can hardly eat my meals; and besides my mother has been sent to the General Hospital. Almost all the duties and responsibilities have fallen on my shoulders. At present I am tortured by suffering from indigestion and migraine headaches, and I can hardly eat anything. I would therefore like to solicit your kind favour and help as my *dāyaka*, and friend, to please try and bring a doctor and some medical requirements for myself. I can hardly eat anything. I feel squeamish, and am constantly vomitting and ejecting up whatever food I may eat. I would be very glad and extremely grateful if you could get a doctor to see me and treat me with whatever is required or essential as I am in a rather dismal and sorrowful plight; and solitary as well as abandoned.

Thanking you immensely for your kindness
I am Yours Sincerely in the *Dhamma*.

In a society in which modally, according to the perceptive analysis of a Burmese psychologist, the dependency need is an "acute and salient feature in the personality organization" (Sein Tu 1964:278), it would be of interest to discover why the dependency needs of men who enter the Order are especially strong. Although our data, unfortunately, do not permit us to answer this question with assurance, there are bits and pieces from which we might venture a speculation. First, compared to laymen, the monks in our sample are from large families. Of the nineteen for which we have information on family size, five were from families with less than three children, only one was an only child, while thirteen came from families ranging from three to nine children. This (the latter figure) is to be contrasted with the average village family of two children. In addition to their large families, most of the monks were middle children, very few being either the oldest or the youngest. Finally, a third of the monks had a disruptive relationship, either physical or emotional, with their parents: six were orphaned, one came from a broken home, and one believed he had been rejected by his parents.

Taking one or more of these variables into account we might, perhaps, offer the following partial explanation for the monks' strong dependency needs. Raised in a large family, in which parental love and care are diffused—and hence diluted—among a number of siblings; being a middle child who, in a Burmese family, is typically frustrated by older siblings and, with the birth of a younger sibling, ignored by parents; deprived by orphanage of parental nurturance—any or all of these conditions might result in the frustration, and consequent intensification, of the need for dependency.

Whatever the ontogenetic causes may be, however, the fact is that the monks are characterized by strong dependency needs; and, whatever the historical causes, the rules governing the monk-layman relationship place the former, so far as dependency is concerned, in the structural position of child. Indeed, the one universally found paradigm for this dimension of the monk-layman relationship is the relationship between parent and child. Hence it is no accident, in my opinion, that the parental image is explicitly and especially invoked in the monk-sponsor dyad. Before he is ordained every monk acquires a lay "sponsor" who undertakes the expense of the ordination and who, for as long as the monk remains in the robe, continues to provide for his welfare by supplying him with special meals, building him (if possible) a new monastery, caring for any special needs, and so on. This sponsor acquires the title of "father of the monk" *(yahan: apha)* or "mother of the monk" *(yahan: ama)*, depending on sex, and the monk refers to his sponsor as "my father" or "my mother." Notice then that while in Catholicism the priest or monk is "father" to the layman, in Buddhism the reverse is the case.

But we can, I think, go even farther. If, so far as dependency is concerned, the monk is symbolically the structural equivalent of a child, the specific period of childhood evoked by his dependency longings and the manner in which they are satisfied is the period of infancy. As in the case of the Burmese infant, most of the monk's needs are anticipated and generously satisfied even before he expresses them. The reinstatement of that (real or fancied) blissful period of infancy, in which all needs are anticipated and satisfied by the all–nurturant mother, is a recurrent wish, conscious and unconscious, of mankind, appearing (disguised and undisguised) in fantasy, dream, and myth. In societies such as Burma, in which there is a sharp discontinuity between indulgent satisfaction of dependency in infancy and its frustration in childhood, one would expect this wish to be especially powerful, and the monastery may be viewed as an institutionalized means for realizing that wish. The monk can regress and reenact the role appropriate to that infantile period. This regression is symbolized in the very physical appearance of the monk. With his shaven head and eyebrows (required by the Rule) he acquires a foetalized appearance consistent with the psychological foetalization we have been discussing. And is not the constant feeding of the monk reminiscent, and perhaps a reenactment, of that same period?

To a great extent, then, the monastic recruit can satisfy his dependency needs in the monastery—but not without a price. Indeed, he must pay a very heavy price: he must renounce sexual satisfaction and suffer the burdens of all the other monastic restrictions. From this perspective the monastic role may be viewed as an institutionalized and symbolic resolution of the Oedipus complex. The monk renounces any sexual claim not only on his mother, but in compliance with the demands of his "father"—monks, it will be recalled, are "Sons of the Buddha"—on all other women as well. For the monk all women are (forbidden) mothers. In exchange for this renunciation he can even as an adult continue to enjoy the dependency of early childhood. In short, by obeying the commands of the "father," including the command of not sleeping with the "mother," the monk can enjoy that state to which he (and probably most of mankind) aspires—the stage of absolute succorance. For him, unlike the Buddhist layman, the price is not too high to pay.

We must speculate on the reasons why the monk is willing to pay this price. In a perceptive, and "blind," analysis of the Rorschach tests of the monks in my sample, Steele (n.d.) concluded that these monks are characterized by (among other things) latent homosexuality and an above-average fear of female- and mother-figures.[11] If his analysis is correct—and it is certainly consistent with Sein Tu's analysis of Burmese laymen, in whom he finds with diminished intensity the same traits (Sein Tu 1964:276-78), and with my own clinical impressions of the monks—it may be argued that they are willing to pay this price because, at least for many of them, celibacy is really not a price. On the contrary, recruitment to the monastery allows those among them who have these characteristics to resolve what would otherwise be a pressing and unresolved conflict: the monastic role permits a person characterized by fear of women to lead a life of female-avoidance, and the all-male monastery permits the sublimated expression of latent homosexuality. Both of these character traits, moreover, receive cultural support from the phobic antisexual and antifeminine ideology of monastic Buddhism described in chapter 12.

Narcissism

Concern for oneself and one's needs, even at the expense of the needs of others, is a human characteristic, which however is especially pronounced in the case of these monks. The egocentric quality of the monastic personality has already been implicit in our discussion of the basis for monasticism: the monk is exclusively concerned with his own salvation. It is implicit, too, in our discussion of monastic dependency. To desire to be taken care of by others, especially when this desire is not associated with a willingness to assume a reciprocal responsibility, is of course an extreme

[11]Steele's Rorschach analysis of monastic personality, and my analysis, based on interviews and behavioral observations, though undertaken independently, are remarkably congruent. Steele identifies six salient features of the monastic personality. (1) A high degree of "defensiveness," (2) "regressed" expression of aggressive and oral drives, (3) cautious avoidance of affective situations, (4) "hypochondriacal self-preoccupation" and "erotic self-cathexis," (5) latent homosexuality, (6) fear of female- and mother-figures.

Although employing different vocabularies, the two analyses, it will be noted, overlap in their identification of some of the same traits. Where I say "dependency," Steele says "regressive expression of oral drives." Where I say "emotional timidity," he says "avoidance of emotionally laden situations." Where I say "narcissism," he says "self-preoccupation" and "erotic self-cathexis."

form of egocentrism, for which I am using the term "narcissism." One might, instead, use the colloquial "selfish," but this expresses a value judgment which I have attempted to avoid in this analysis, and which is obviated by the more technical term.

By "narcissism," then, I mean an overriding preoccupation with self, regardless of its consequences for the welfare of others. This does not so much betoken an overestimation of one's self-importance—connoted, for example, by "egotism"—as it does a lack of sensitivity to, or concern for, the needs of others. Monastic narcissism may be observed in both the unofficial and the official behavior of monks—if one can make this distinction in a role which is so monolithic and undifferentiated. In their unofficial behavior they constantly make demands on laymen with (seemingly) no concern for the price—in time, effort, money, or inconvenience—it may cost them. It is rare that a layman visiting the monastery is not requested by the monk to do something for him; to run an errand, make a delivery, drive him to some destination. That the visitor might be busy, might not have the time, might be going in the opposite direction—these possibilities seem never to enter his mind.

This concern for self is observed not only in episodic events of this type. In one of the villages in which I worked, to give a fairly usual example, the pupils in the state school had the task of collecting the monk's alms food (which, of course, is an important means for acquiring merit). After collecting the food, they would serve the monk his meal and clean up when he finished. Only then did he permit them to go to school. As a result they were deprived of at least an hour's schoolwork in the morning, and the teachers could do nothing but mark time until they arrived. The inconvenience for the teachers and the educational deprivation for the students presumably never entered the monk's mind.

Despite such examples, villagers seem to be less put upon in this regard than townspeople. Usually villagers' schedules are more flexible, and they are less inconvenienced; usually, too, they do not have the means—automobiles, for example, or taxis—for certain requests to be made. The situation is different in the cities, and many urban laymen, as we shall see, are quick to complain about this respect of the monks' narcissism.

In the monks' official role behavior the same situation obtains. At a funeral, especially, what might be called the "institutionalized narcissism" of the monk is clearly to be seen. Although they have just suffered the loss of a loved one, it is not the bereaved but the monk whose needs must be attended to. In accordance with his role requirements the monk expresses no sympathy to the bereaved for their loss, he offers them no consolation and in general shows no special concern for them. Rather it is *he* who is the object of concern. It is he for whom food is bought; it is he who is fed; it is he who must be brought from and returned to the monastery. This behavior, to be sure, is institutionalized, and for their behavior the bereaved receive merit. Nevertheless, the tone required and conveyed by this institutionalized narcissism is consistent with the monk's personally narcissistic attitude described above. One might characterize the tone as follows: "Although you are suffering, it is proper that I, not you, be the object of concern, that my wants, not yours, be attended to. It is not for me to enter into your suffering or your tragedy."

The narcissism of monks is seen in its most blatant form, however, in the process of monastic recruitment. As we have already seen, a large percentage—perhaps the majority—of monks have already founded families when they decided to join the Order. Although they must obtain their wife's prior consent, for them to enter the monastery is to abandon wife and children. Often families are left not only without husband and father, but also destitute, with no one to care or provide for them. Nevertheless, such considerations do not serve as deterrents; their own needs, say the would-be monks, must take precedence above all others.

When *A*, a Mandalay merchant, decided to become a monk, his personal physician—an Indian—remonstrated with him in my presence. Surely, he said, he was being "selfish"; surely, he should think of his wife and children. But *A* was adamant; his decision had "nothing to do with selfishness. I want to enter nirvana, and that's all that counts."

When *B*, a village farmer, decided to become a monk, he came to inform me of his decision. I asked him what would happen to his wife and children (who would be destitute). "They will have to look after themselves." he said. "This is not my responsibility; I must think of my own nirvana. If they have good karma, they will be able to get along."

Monk *C* left behind a five-year-old daughter when he entered the monastery. I asked him if he felt no attachment for her or for his wife. "No, I have cut off attachment, because if I have attachment I cannot obtain nirvana. My wife and child will have to take care of themselves. That is no longer my worry."

The degree of narcissism implicit in the recruitment of married monks may further be gauged by the fact that, most often, these men enter the Order without first granting their wives a divorce. In such a case, the latter may not only be left destitute, but of course may not remarry. To be sure, if the wife wishes it the village elders—this, at least, is the case in Yeigyi—will grant the divorce even over the opposition of her husband. But this does not alter the fact that the husband himself is quite prepared to leave her in this untenable situation. Although the Burmese, as we shall see, do not censure those who leave their families in order to enter the monastery (on the contrary, they admire them for their ability to cut off their attachments), they are critical of men who do not divorce their wives prior to ordination. This, for them, is a mark of selfishness. As one villager put it, "Even if the husband wishes to enter the Order for seven days, he should divorce his wife; otherwise it shows his craving [*taṇhā*]. It is like giving up a meal, but still keeping a bit of food on the side."

Just as the monastery is an institution wonderfully adapted to the personality with strong needs for dependency, so too recruitment to the monastery is a perfect institutionalized solution for the personality whose narcissistic needs permit—perhaps motivate—abandonment of wife and children. Simply to abandon one's family would provoke intense social disapproval in Burma; similarly, to obtain a divorce on the grounds that one wishes to be relieved of domestic responsibility would be impossible. To abandon one's family in order to enter the monastery, however, is not only to escape the onus of social disapproval, but to become the object of strong admiration. Men who adopt this course are viewed as having entered upon a holy life. If their wives were to protest their action, it is they and not their husbands who would become the objects of disapproval: how can they object to their husbands' search for salvation? Hence, by becoming monks, such men not only escape the unwanted burden of domestic responsibility with impunity,[12] but are acclaimed for their action. Rather than being disdained for shirking their obligation to their families, they are praised for having had the strength to cut their attachment to them. Not only are they not censured, but—having donned the yellow robe—they are worshiped.[13]

Social approval for their decision is strengthened by strong religious support as well; the decision is sanctioned by an impressive historico-mythological charter. Thus, as the Prince Gautama, the Buddha Himself in order to seek salvation abandoned wife and children to become a monk. In an earlier incarnation too as the Prince Vessantara, He gave up His wife and children in order to obtain salvation. The latter story, found in the *Vessantara Jātaka,*[14] is the most popular of all Buddhist myths in Burma. When Vessantara was asked by a Brahmin for his children, he exclaimed (p. 282):

> Come hither, my beloved son, my perfect state
> fulfil;
> Come now and consecrate my heart, and follow
> out my will.
>
> Be thou my ship to ferry me safe o'er existence'
> sea,

[12]The wish to achieve "complete freedom from worldly cares and fears" has been a ubiquitous theme, according to Basham, in Indian asceticism. "This sense of freedom, of a great load lifted from one's shoulders by casting aside one's family and possessions, is evident in many passages of calm joy in the religious literature of India." (Basham 1961:224)

[13]This attitude is found in the other Buddhist societies. According to Ames (1964:26),

> The most highly venerated person in Sinhalese society is the one who leaves behind his family and retires to a forest to spend his remaining days in solitary meditation. He is striving for his own salvation, and that is precisely why he is respected.

[14]This is No. 547 in the Cowell (1957) edition of the *Jātaka.* All page references below refer to that edition.

> Beyond the worlds of birth and gods I'll cross
> and I'll be free.

Despite the tears of his children at being separated from their father, and without having an opportunity even to say farewell to their mother, Vessantara "comforts" them by saying, "Don't you know that I have gladly given you away? So do that *my desire* may attain fulfillment [my italics]." Although the *Jātaka* makes clear that his love for his son is strong, in order to satisfy his own desire for omniscience he is willing for his son to become the servant of the cruel Brahmin. Saying, "Dearer than my son a hundredfold, a thousandfold, a hundred thousandfold is omniscience," he gives his children to the Brahmin.

When his children, beaten and oppressed by the harsh Brahmin, manage to escape and come crying to their father, "dire grief" arises in Vessantara.

> His heart grew hot within him . . . from his mouth he sent forth hot pantings; tears like drops of blood fell from his eyes. Then he thought: "All this pain comes from affection, and no other cause; I must quiet this affection, and be calm." Thus by power of his knowledge he did away with that keen pang of sorrow, and sat still as usual.[P. 286]

As if this were not enough, when he finally disposes of his children, Vessantara is requested by another Brahmin to give him his wife—she who left the palace with him, and who, while they lived in the jungle, gathered food for him that he might devote himself to meditation. Nevertheless, the *Jātaka* emphasizes, Vessantara did not reply that, having only the day before given away his children, he could hardly be expected now to give away his wife. On the contrary, he not only gave her to the Brahmin, but parted with her with no more thought than he would have parted with a "purse filled with coins." He was "indifferent, unattached, with no clinging of mind. . . ." For, although

> Not hateful is my faithful wife, nor yet my
> children are,
> But perfect knowledge, to my mind, is something
> dearer far. [P. 293]

In abandoning wife and children in order to seek his salvation as a monk, the Buddhist, moreover, is not only emulating the model of the Buddha both as Vessantara and as Gautama, but is following His explicit words, as recorded in the *Khaggavisâṇa-sutta.*

> Just as a larger bamboo tree (with its branches) entangled (in each other, such is) the care one has with children and wife; (but) like the shoot of a bamboo not clinging (to anything) let one wander alone like a rhinoceros.

> Removing the marks of a gihin (a householder) like a Kovilâra tree whose leaves are fallen, let one, after cutting off heroically the ties of a gihin, wander alone like a rhinoceros.
>
> Having left son and wife, father and mother, wealth, and corn, and relatives, the different objects of desire, let one wander alone like a rhinoceros.
>
> Removing the characteristics of a gihin (householder), like a *Pârikhatta* tree whose leaves are cut off, clothed in a yellow robe after wandering away (from his house), let one wander alone like a rhinoceros. *(Sutta-Nipāta,* verses 4, 10, 26, 30).

In sum, then, the narcissistic attitude reflected in the abandonment of wife and children is sanctioned by Buddhist myth and even prescribed by the Buddha Himself, if it issues in the decision to join the monastic order. Buddhist monasticism, in short, not only provides a marvelously institutionalized expression for a character trait which would otherwise find no sanctioned outlet, but Buddhist culture affords the narcissist a legitimate motive to justify his abdication of responsibility.

Emotional Timidity

Monks not only have a strong desire to be dependent on others, and those who join the Order as adults are not only narcissistic enough to drop their responsibility for others—but they also avoid establishing emotional relationships with others. This does not mean that monks are emotionally indifferent. On the contrary, many of them, on one level at least, desire emotional relationships. Thus, at least one-third of the monks in our sample, it will be recalled, not only complain that the monastic life is a lonely one but report that loneliness is their most important problem. And yet rather than establishing social relationships, they prefer to live alone, for they say such relationships cause attachment, and attachment causes suffering. I refer to this interpersonal stance as "emotional timidity."

This stance is implicit in many of the interviews with monks, and is explicitly stated in connection with questions concerning their natal families. Some monks have not seen their parents and siblings for ten or fifteen years, and though many say that they miss them, they nevertheless prefer it that way. If, so they reason, they don't see their families, they can remain affectively indifferent to them. Were they to see them, they would develop an attachment *(than-yo:zin)* which could only cause suffering. It is best, therefore, to remain aloof.

This self-analysis by the monks applies, I would submit, not only to their attitude to their families but to their other relationships as well. The monk is afraid not only of familial but of all attachments; for him, they all cause *dukkha.* This interpersonal attitude is, as we shall have occasion to observe in another place, a generic Burmese attitude. Burmese laymen as well as monks are extremely wary about establishing emotional relationships, for fear of being hurt. Nevertheless, they do in fact establish and sustain at least some relationships. They marry and beget offspring and maintain some degree of affective investment in their wives and children, even when holding attitudes of affective indifference toward other persons.

From this perspective it may be said that Burmese monks carry the generic Burmese attitude about emotional involvement to its extreme. Their cathexes, except for their extraordinary self-cathexis, seem to be directed to such objects as the Buddha and other Buddhist sacra. These objects, of course, are emotionally safe: a friend may disappoint, a lover may betray, a wife may be unfaithful, but the Buddha remains firm and absolute. Having restricted the depth and breadth of his emotional involvements, the monk, as some Burmese say, is "aloof," or as one villager complained, "he stands on his dignity." Both statements have reference, in my opinion, to the same genotypic monastic stance, viz., emotional detachment. The monk retreats to the monastery because there he can avoid attachments; he remains detached because detachment is safe. The isolated life of the monastery may be viewed as an institutionalized defense against emotional involvement.

It is not only Buddhist monasticism, however, that serves this purpose; the entire ideology of Buddhism and its outlook of worldly abnegation support the attitude of noninvolvement. For Buddhism, to be detached is not a vice but a virtue. It is only through detachment that nirvana can be achieved. Hence, detachment *(upekkhā)* is a quality to be cultivated, a goal to be attained; the entire monastic discipline, especially the contemplative life, is a means to that end. But this Buddhist emphasis on detachment can stem from two different attitudes to the world. It may come, on the one hand, from an heroic attitude in which, in order to achieve Enlightenment, one is willing to sacrifice all the pleasures which ordinary worldlings cannot give up. On the other hand, it may also come from an overcautious orientation according to which, since all worldly pleasure (including that of emotional attachment) may entail sorrow, one is unwilling to risk the pain in order to achieve the pleasure. It is the latter attitude that underlies the detachment of most of the monks in our sample—a timid rather than an heroic outlook.

If these impressions of Burmese monks are sound, it may be concluded that they are detached, not because they have achieved the Buddhist goal of ego-extinction, but out of fear of ego-frustration; not because they have overcome affection, but because they are afraid of it, and these fears are the basis of their emotional timidity.[15]

[15]This, of course, is a modal description. It must be added that some monks of course are detached, not through fear of affection, but because of the extinction of their capacity for it. These are the monks who impress some observers as being "cold fish."

We may conclude, then, that the Buddhist emphasis on redemption from suffering permits the monastery, in addition to its other functions, to serve as an institutionalized solution to the problems of all kinds of men including those who, from a secular perspective, are (or would become) misfits, neurotics, and failures.[16] Deprived of this solution, these men would probably reveal many forms of pathology and some of them constitute a serious problem for Burmese society. The Buddhist message, which permits them to conceptualize their problems in religious terms, and the existence of the monastery, which permits them to resolve them in a highly honored manner, obviate the development of both possibilities.[17] It is probably because the monastery satisfies their needs so well that, among other reasons, the dropout rate from the monastery is so low. My own survey in a small district in Upper Burma and national figures compiled by the Ministry of Religious Affairs indicate alike that it is extremely rare for a monk who enters the monastery as a vocation to leave the Order.

[16]It is perhaps not surprising to discover that similar men were attracted to the *Saṅgha* from its very inception. The early monastic community in India, we are informed by Dutt (1962:47), was recruited

> from all ranks of society and from widely different cultural and social backgrounds. Of those who passed into its fellowship, it was only perhaps the more serious and more cultured who had a realization or even awareness of the purpose and dignity of the calling. With a good number, the spiritual quest *(Brahmacarya)* must have been just a colourable motive. Among them were those who had left home, not of their own choice, but under compulsion of circumstances—fugitives from justice, bankrupt debtors, vagabonds and idlers, loath to shoulder the responsibilities of a householder's life, disgruntled or frustrated men who had left the world in disgust.

[17]For an extended analysis of the use of the monastery as a culturally constituted defense against serious pathology in the context of a theoretical discussion of psychopathology in cross-cultural perspective, see Spiro (1965).

CHAPTER 15

The Monk: II. Character Structure

Persistent Characteristics of the "Worldling"

Introduction

Many people entertain exaggerated notions of the emotional qualitites of *religieux.* It is often assumed that, dedicated to the spiritual life, they are not only striving for, but have in fact attained the character traits which are the goals of that life. It is important to know, then, whether the Buddhist monastic life produces changes in the monk which are consistent with (or, at least, in the direction of) its goals, changes which would differentiate him from what Buddhism terms the ordinary "worldling" *(puthujjana).*

In general, one comes away from an extended encounter with Burmese monks with the feeling that the monastic life has produced a certain emotional quality in the typical monk—a quality of warmth, innocence, and naïvete—which is somehow "different." I, at least, found a positive and engaging difference. Certainly one of the first qualities exemplified by the average monk is (to employ a Buddhist concept) that of *mettā,* or kindliness. One is constantly impressed, for example, with the great courtesy monks display to strangers and the hospitality and generosity with which they receive all guests. And this open and cheerful reception greets the foreigner as well as the Burman. In an earlier period in Burmese history, monks saved many foreigners from slavery, as they saved many Burmans from the gallows. During the Burmese kingdom, many persons condemned to be hung were spared, as is well known, by the intervention of monks at considerable risk to their own lives. Little known, however, is the charity they have displayed to foreigners. The following eighteenth-century account describes it well.

> And now, since I must leave Pegu [Lower Burma], I must not omit giving the clergy their due praises in another particular practice of their charity. If a stranger has the misfortune to be ship-wrecked on their coast, by the laws of the country, the men are the king's slaves, but, by the mediation of the church, the governors overlook that law; and when the unfortunate strangers come to their baws [monasteries], they find a great deal of hospitality, both in food and raiment, and have letters of recommendation from the priests of one convent to those of another on the road they design to travel, where they may expect vessels to transport them to Syriam; and if any be sick or maimed, the priests, who are the Peguers' chief physicians, keep them in their convent, till they are cured, and then furnish them with letters, as is above observed, for they never enquire which way a stranger worships God, but if he is human, he is the object of their charity. [Hamilton 1930:34]

Contemporary foreigners have no need for this extreme expression of kindliness, but they are almost uniformly the recipients of its modern expression. Every Westerner who has visited a Burmese monastery recounts the good humor, the choice food, and the Buddhist homilies he has received from monks in all parts of the country. For myself, I experienced (with one exception) only the warmest hospitality and sincere cooperation from the scores of monks whom I visited and interviewed, and in whose monasteries I lived.

This, however, is not exactly what one wants in a chapter devoted to the monastic character. Friendliness, warmth, hospitality, cooperation—these are qualities which one encounters in most Burmans; and though it is important to know that they are also found in Burmese monks (for they are, after all, not always found in other monastic and ascetic communities) we want to know more. Specifically, we want to know the fate of those emotional characteristics—pride, vanity, worldly attachment, and so on—whose extinction, according to Buddhism, is the goal of monasticism. To this it may be immediately replied that, with some exceptions, they are found among monks in about the same degree as they are found among ordinary worldlings.

Nor is this a surprising finding. Monks, as I have already emphasized, are men like other men. They may have entered the Order to pursue the path to Liberation, but they do not claim to have achieved Liberation. Hence, not unlike those who live in the world, monks too are characterized by craving, by clinging, by attachment, by the temptations of the world and the desires of the flesh. Like other men, too, monks are vain and arrogant, envious and worldly. To be sure, they may strive for deliverance from all human foibles—especially from those three "cankers" (as Buddhism describes them) of avarice, ignorance, and delusion; but it would be altogether naïve to expect that the mere donning of the yellow robe, or living in accordance with the monastic Rule, or even the performing of spiritual exercises, would enable the average monk to achieve this goal. Although everyone knows, or knows of, a select few who have succeeded, their number is very small. Nor does Buddhism expect that more than a few will achieve this goal. Indeed, Buddhism is profoundly realistic about the possibility of eradicating the Adam in man. The *arahant* alone has achieved Liberation, and although the monk—by the very fact that he has been able to renounce the world—is certainly on the Path, he is far from an *arahant*. If the Buddha Himself, even after vowing to become a Buddha, required hundreds of rebirths to achieve arahantship and Buddhahood, the average monk can hardly be expected to achieve it in less time.

It is precisely because monks are men, like other men, that the regulations and prohibitions comprising the Rule were instituted early in the history of the Order. Even a cursory reading of the *Vinaya* indicates that the founders of Buddhism were well aware that, except for the few, the characterological dispositions which monks share with all men are not extinguished by the donning of the yellow robe. And it is precisely because they are not extinguished that the Rule was required.

Recognizing, then, that monks like other men have their fair share of human virtues—kindness, honesty, compassion, tolerance—this section is concerned rather with identifying those "cankers" which, despite their monastic regimen, continue to be part of the behavior and personality of monks. In the last chapter, we were concerned with psychological characteristics conducive to monastic recruitment, which therefore distinguish Burmese monks from other Burmans. Here we are concerned with traits which, despite the fact that their extinction is the goal of Buddhist monasticism, Burmese monks share with other Burmans—indeed, with human beings everywhere.

Vanity

Vanity is a prominent characteristic of Burmese monks. Self-praise—the recounting of personal erudition, piety, adherence to the Rule, the respect paid them by others, their popularity as preachers—is a characteristic feature of almost all our interviews with them. This quality is frequently accompanied by the need for praise. Thus, after receiving a disquisition on doctrinal matters by a monk, I would inevitably be asked whether I liked what he had told me; whether it was not true that his explanation was lucid; and so on. Moreover, while seeking praise from me, monks would persistently praise themselves, more especially by making invidious comparisons between themselves and other monks. Thus, almost invariably, each monk would stress that, among all monks, he alone knew the answers to my questions; he alone could resolve the difficulties that were being raised; he alone knew the texts; and so on. Not infrequently my interview notes end with the same personal gloss: "Like the others, he is very vain"; or, "Like the others, he takes almost a childlike glee in being praised"; or, "He repeated for the nth time that no *hpoung:ji:* [monk] can compare with him in his knowledge of Buddhism."[1]

Hostility

A theme which runs through all the interviews with monks is their hostility, especially directed to and expressed in a generalized criticism of other monks. This theme is repetitive to the point of compulsiveness. The best way to illustrate the point is by direct quotation from interview notes.

> He [monk *A*] warns me to make sure that the monks with whom I speak are learned because, unlike him, many monks will not be able to answer my questions. Not all monks are learned, some are empty vessels. Only he, among all other monks, will tell me the truth because only he is learned. Moreover, all the others are avaricious.

> When, after a brief interview, I decided to leave, he [monk *B*] said I should stay and talk with him because no other monks are as learned as he is. Since most of them joined the Order at an advanced age, their knowledge is limited. By talking with them, I will acquire a bad impression of the *Saṅgha.*

> As we talked, he [monk *C*] said there are no true monks in Burma. All are politicians, i.e., they cannot be trusted.

> He [monk *D*] spent two hours attacking the other monks for being ignorant, unlearned, incapable of answering my questions, and so on. They are only interested in prestige.

[1]One might speculate on the basis for the monks' vanity, which I am inclined to view as a defense against feelings of inferiority, but we lack the data to test any explanations.

Bigandet, who in his usual hostile fashion also comments on monastic vanity—monks "entertain a very high idea of their own excellence" (Bigandet 1912:316)—finds an explanation in "the great respect paid to them by the people . . . [which] make[s] them believe that nobody on earth can be compared to them. . . ." *(Ibid.)* This is a plausible but, I believe, false interpretation. Most monks contend—and their claim has a true ring—that they receive little ego satisfaction from the obeisance they receive, because it is really for the robe they wear, or for the Buddha whom they represent, and not for their own qualities.

Bigandet is not the only early observer to comment on monastic vanity. Symes, a much more sympathetic observer, comments on the vanity displayed even by an especially revered abbot whom he had been anxious to meet. In meeting him Symes was, he writes,

> disappointed in the expectations I had formed; he betrayed a worldly pride inconsistent with his years and sacred function; he announced, with much pomp, that he was the head of the church at Rangoon, and ostentatiously displayed his sacerdotal titles, engraven on iron plates, that had been conferred on him by the present and the late king. . . . I left him impressed with much less reverence than I had entertained for his character before our interview. [Symes 1800:213]

> Most monks who serve on the ecclesiastical courts are only interested, he [monk *E*] said, in getting their names in the newspapers. They know nothing about the essence of Buddhism, but merely want to make themselves popular among the laymen. Moreover, they have no right to organize into associations because they then dictate to others. The majority of monks are not pious, so why should they dictate to others?

> He [monk *F*] said he has traveled throughout Burma and the Shan States and he can say that the *sāsana* [the Buddhist Teaching] is dying because the monks are not educated; they are interested only in having an easy life. . . . The monks preach about the importance of meditation in order to get fame and money. Although most of the monks are not pious, he must forgive them, just as, in the Buddha's day, the pious monks forgave the impious ones.

Rivalry and Conflict

The monks' hostility toward other monks is expressed not only in generalized criticism of them, but also in personal rivalry and conflict between them. Rivalry most frequently concerns the relative prestige and status of two or more monks inhabiting different monasteries within the same village. Conflict, on the other hand, is most frequently occasioned by competition over the incumbency of a particular monastery. This, which occurs in both village and city, is sufficiently frequent so that, according to the president of the Buddha *Sāsana* Council (a government-appointed lay commission, charged with promoting the cause of Buddhism), the main reasons for the establishment of government-sponsored Ecclesiastical Courts was to adjudicate these disputes.

The necessity for such courts becomes apparent when it is realized that sometimes contentious monks commit physical assault and even bloodshed. I did not see, or hear of, such violence among village monks, but cases are not infrequently reported in towns and cities. Thus, in a three-month period during which I surveyed the English language press, three cases were reported for Rangoon alone. In one, a disputant beat his rival over the head with an iron rod; in another, one of the disputants led a charge of sixty monks, armed with clubs, against the incumbents of the contested monastery, with the result that three monks were hospitalized; in a third, each disputant, assisted by two colleagues, "came to blows" over the contested monastery.

Although conflict between village monks over possession of a monastery did not in my experience result in violence, it did lead to enmity, backbiting, mutual accusations and recriminations, request for governmental interference, social withdrawal, and the involvement of laymen in what amounts to, a socially divisive and enduring factional dispute. All these elements are found in the following rather complicated set of interlocking disputes in Yeigyi.

U Thuta is the most respected monk in Yeigyi, allegedly the most pious, and certainly the most learned. When the incumbent monk of an adjacent village died, the monk who had looked after him during his illness took possession of the monastery, claiming that the incumbent had designated him as his successor. U Thuta, however, together with the headman of the village, had proposed another monk to be the successor, and since the monastery was corporate rather than personal property, the new resident of the monastery, they claimed, had taken possession of it illegally. They appealed, therefore, to the Ecclesiastical Court (which however had not handed down a ruling before I left Burma, although they had been presented with the case almost a year before I arrived).

In the meantime the enmity between U Thuta (as well as the headman) and the resident monk became intense. U Thuta charged him with ignorance of Buddhism, with various violations of the *Vinaya*, with absconding with monastic property, and a variety of other derelictions. Neither monk will attend an ecclesiastical meeting or preside at a Buddhist ceremony if he knows that the other will also be present.

This dispute, however, must be viewed as primarily a skirmish in the ongoing battle between U Thuta and U Pandeisa, senior monk of a second monastery in Yeigyi and an active supporter of the other monk in the matter just described. U Pandeisa had already opposed U Thuta in a conflict over the possession of still another monastery, this being in Yeigyi itself. There had apparently long been disagreement between U Thuta and a former incumbent of that monastery, who claimed some land in U Thuta's compound, which bordered his own. In that dispute, which was adjudicated by the District Commissioner's office, U Thuta's rival—who had a long history of similar disputes over other monasteries—was supported by U Pandeisa.

But the conflict between U Thuta and U Pandeisa did not end there, for when the incumbent died (shortly after the land dispute), a conflict arose over his successor. U Thuta again proposed the same monk he had supported for the monastery in the nearby village, while U Pandeisa promoted the candidacy of two young monks whom the incumbent had designated as his successors. These were brothers and—it so happened—nephews of the incumbent. Before his death he had apparently invited his nephews—poor woodcutters—to the monastery and ordained them as novices with the promise that they would succeed him. Since the monastery was corporate property, he had no authority to designate his successors without first changing its status to privately owned. A document was produced showing that the sponsor and builder of the monastery had, in fact, agreed to this change in status. This person—a wealthy, but illiterate peasant woman—said however that she had not known what she was signing—that she had merely, at the monk's request, affixed an *X* to the document he placed in her hand, and that she had never intended to change the status of the monastery. The dispute was adjudicated by a committee of three monks, presided over by U Pandeisa, who ruled against the candidate proposed by U Thuta and in favor of the two brothers.

This conflict between the senior monks of the two chief village monasteries concerning monastic succession was merely a symptom of a more general rivalry between them for local influence and prestige. This first erupted into the open as a result of a monastic funeral. U Pandeisa, as the senior monk in the village, was appointed chairman and U Thuta a member of the funeral committee for a certain deceased monk. Annoyed because U Pandeisa did not consult him on the plans for the funeral, U Thuta resigned from the committee and later charged in an anonymously circulated letter that U Pandeisa had embezzled a large sum of money collected for it. From that time, about four years prior to my settling in the village, the conflict between them was in the open.

Their rivalry is expressed in a number of ways. Both accuse each other of various real or alleged forms of misbehavior. Neither will attend ceremonies performed in the other's monastery, even when invited and when propriety demands that they attend. During my stay, for example, neither would attend the *kahteing* performed in the other's monastery. U Thuta would not even attend the ordination of a local villager because it was held in U Pandeisa's monastery, and refused to participate in the special penitential ceremony performed by U Pandeisa. This, it will be recalled, is held to atone for the violation of all *Vinaya* regulations accumulated after many years in the monastery. There are certain regulations, however—the *pārājika*—for which there is no penance; their violation requires expulsion from the Order. U Thuta charged that U Pandeisa had in fact violated the *pārājika*, and on the first day of the three-day ceremony posted an unsigned public notice to that effect on the village chapel.

> I defy anyone to prove that the monk who violates a *pa-ra-zi.ka.* can still be a *beikkhu.* Not even one hundred monks reciting one hundred *kan.ma.wa* [the palm-leaf book containing the 227 regulations which comprise the Rule] can enable him to remain a *beikkhu* if he has committed such an offense. I am offering a reward of K500 to anyone who can prove that it is possible for such a monk to remain in the *Saṅgha.*
>
> I am not naming anyone; I am a member of no organization [i.e., this is not politically inspired]. I am only reporting the words of the Buddha. I am a Son of the Buddha. Oh friend, do not be angry for what I have written.

When I asked U Thuta about this notice, he said that, since it is against the *Vinaya* to create dissension in the Order, he accused no one and cited no names; the people were free to draw any conclusions they pleased.

The rivalry between the monks spilled over into, and served to exacerbate, a factional dispute among the village laymen. Each appealed to a different faction, and each faction in turn became associated with one of them. Thus when a village woman sponsored a pagoda festival, she invited U Thuta, but not U Pandeisa; the former was associated with her faction. In revenge, when U Pandeisa arranged for a robe ceremony to be held for him, he did not invite the members of the opposing faction. (Even a member of his own faction was critical of him for this—he should have permitted anyone to share in the merit of the ceremony.) The factional alignments of the laymen with each of these monks was so strong that I was cautioned, after I had begun my monastic investigations in U Thuta's monastery, to spend less time with U Thuta because the members of the opposing faction would resent it. Rather than discouraging this kind of factionalism, the monks helped to sustain it.

Sometimes, as in this particular rivalry, monastic conflict has paranoid overtones. U Thuta, for example, has accused the two brother monks (who, of course, have sided with U Pandeisa), of conspiring against him; many of the villagers, he claims, are trying to drive him from his monastery and have sent laymen to spy on him; a group of laymen, he alleges, has joined with a group of local monks in an organized attempt to drive him out; the monks, he says, are against him because he is originally from a different district, and he has requested the headman to take legal action against one of these monks, who he claims insulted him because he is a stranger.

Worldly Values

Although renouncing the world, many monks yet retain the values of the world. A large majority, for example, view salvation in *kammatic*, rather than in *nibbanic*, terms. Many of them, too, are concerned with prolonging their present existence, as we shall see in our discussion of the occult. These same monks are not only interested in *kammatic* salvation for themselves, but stress the rewards of a pleasant rebirth in their sermons to laymen. Repeatedly, in emphasizing the importance of giving, they underscore the worldly benefits—wealth, beauty, and long life—accruing to those who practice this virtue. Monks frequently end their sermons with the hope that all their listeners may attain nirvana, but that first they may be reborn as millionaires. They also stress the pleasures of the *deva* abodes, promising that these, too, await those who offer *dāna*. A local monk, an adept in alchemy, expressed the wish in one of his sermons that he might discover the alchemic secret by which he might take all the villagers with him to these heavens.

Nor are material pleasures projected into future existences alone. Many monks actively pursue them in present life. Although not permitted to ask directly for material gifts, they may—and do—use circumlocutions to do so. One monk, in the presence of laymen, told me that the quality of the food he receives is not very good—but of course, he said, he never complains about this to the villagers. Another—in a speech to a group of laymen—said that, unlike other monks, he did not complain because he was not offered a radio; indeed, had he been offered one, he surely would never have used it. Many monks, too, hoping to increase their material wealth, buy tickets in the state lottery. One told me that he had recently stopped this practice because, if he won, his greed might be increased and he might be tempted to return to the world!

Monks are attached to worldly values in yet another sense, as one may see by a few examples. Those living in wealthy urban monasteries would proudly display their modern plumbing facilities to me. (The typical monastery, like the typical home, makes do with an outhouse.) Urban monks with famous friends or supporters would proudly announce the fact; a Supreme Court justice offers one his meals, a foreign dignitary was brought to the monastery of another, and so on. This high valuing of worldly success is found in village monasteries too, but of course on a less pretentious scale. The supporters of one monk, so he informed me, are the wealthy people of the village; those who come to another monk for advice, that one proudly announced, are the people of prestige, and so on. These men may have left the world physically, but it is by the values of the world that they assess their own worth and importance.

Intellectual Level

Just as the average monk retains many of the characteristics and values of the layman, so, too, his educational attainment and intellectual orientation differ little from the latter's. For the typical village monk this is hardly surprising, since he receives his entire education in the village monastery; and this means that, typically, it is mediocre. The secular curriculum of the monastery school consists of the three R's plus a smattering of Burmese history. Instruction in the sciences is, for the most part, confined to the ancient geography, cosmology, and cosmography of traditional Buddhism. The Buddhist curriculum is not much better. Even if the young boy remains in the monastery as a novice, his Buddhist education is more or less confined to the rote learning of a core of religious texts in a language—Pali—which he does not understand. Historical interpretation, linguistic exegesis, and philosophical analysis are conspicuously absent.

The core of the monastic curriculum includes the following texts: the Buddhist Beatitudes *(Mangala Sutta);* the *Jaya Mangala Gatha,* a poem recounting the Victories of the Buddha; the collection of *sutta* used as *paritta;* two collections of prayers, the *Ratana Shwei Cauk* and the *Nama Kara;* a compendium of secular wisdom, the *Loka Nitti;* and selected *Jātaka,* especially the last ten. Should the student remain as a novice, he also studies Pali grammar, parts of the monastic Rule *(Vinaya),* and a smattering of scriptural metaphysics *(Abhidhamma).* Since these subjects have been studied only by monks who spend many years in the novitiate, it will be noted that the majority (those who are ordained in their maturity, after long periods in the world) have typically acquired no more Buddhist knowledge than their erstwhile fellow laymen.

But even this low-level curriculum does not tell the full story of the intellectual level of the village *Saṅgha.* Boys who enter the novitiate and then the monkhood directly from the monastery school are, in general, not among the most gifted of the village children. According to village monks, the most gifted boys are not permanently enrolled in the monastery school. If they are bright, and if their parents have high aspirations for them, after a few years in the monastic school they will be entered in the consolidated Middle School run by the government. Only the duller boys are sent to the monastic school. As the Burmese proverb has it, *makaung: caung:bu:*—"What is not good is sent to the monastery."

In addition to these obstacles to intellectual attainment, one must mention yet another, the learning environment. Daily instruction in the monastery school is confined to an hour at most, in mid-afternoon. The rest of the day is spent in self-study in the classroom, usually the bottom floor of the monastery. Typically, each student sits on a mat, reciting his lessons from a textbook. Seated in front of them (with his back to them) is the eldest novice, who divides his time between reciting his own lessons, and attempting to keep the lay students at their lessons. In order to achieve the latter end, he periodically strikes the floor or (if he believes a student is not studying) a student with a bamboo switch. In one two-hour session, I saw a novice twice circulate among the students, striking each child at least once.

The lesson recitation is seeming chaos. Each student may be reciting a different text—there are no age-graded classes—at a different rate, and as loudly as he possibly can. Indeed, loudness seems to be the one criterion for intellectual diligence. When their voices fall, the novice turns to the students with a scowl. When, once again, they resume their screaming—this is the only appropriate word—he appears satisfied and returns to his own equally loud recitations.

While students and novices are chanting their lessons downstairs, the monk is chanting *his* lessons upstairs. If a novice is absent, the monk himself indicates his displeasure with the lack of student diligence—as indicated by the absence of loud chanting—by knocking on the floor with his stick, and the din once again increases. In general, when the monk does not pound, or when the novice's back is turned, the students do almost no reciting, most of their time being spent in talk and subdued play. In one three-hour study session, I estimated that the students devoted about fifteen minutes to their lessons.

In mid-afternoon, the students go upstairs for their lesson with the monk. Sometimes he gives them some instruction; sometimes he listens to them recite from their books; sometimes he asks them to recite by heart.

In any case, the goal of study is rote memory. Having memorized one text, the student passes on to the next.

It is little wonder, then, that the Buddhist education of the typical village monk is elementary—no greater, and in many cases less, than that of the educated layman. In a discussion of the Order one villager, perhaps with undue arrogance, commented as follows:

> Don't talk to me about monks. I feed them and get merit, but my knowledge of Buddhism—except for U Thuta's—is much greater than theirs.

Since the average village monastery is not renowned for the scholarship of its monks, few novices receive the quality of education available in the teaching monasteries in the larger cities. (From my sample, only three monks had studied in one of these.) Even in the city monasteries, however, the educational emphasis is on memory rather than analysis or inquiry. Sangermano's comments, describing the situation a century ago, apply without change to the contemporary situation.

> The study of the Talapoins [monks] is however rather an exercise of the memory than of the understanding. They do not esteem the faculties of reasoning and discoursing, but only that of committing easily to memory; and he is esteemed the most learned man whose memory is most tenacious. [Sangermano 1893:181]

The traditional emphasis on the memory of texts also characterizes the government-sponsored scriptural examinations, described below, in which prizes are awarded solely for rote memory of texts, the greatest kudos going to those—known as *Tipitikas*—who have achieved the incredible feat of memorizing the entire Scripture by heart.

Small wonder that, although historically the Burmese Order has made notable contributions to Buddhist scholarship,[2] this contribution, according

[2]For many centuries after the introduction of Buddhism in Pagan, the monasteries, according to Ray (1946:259),

> had been busy centres of scholarly activities; there in the darkness and solitude of the library-hall of the monastery generations of monks strove hard, day in and day out, to master the sacred texts of their religion and other works most suited to their lines of study. No subject was too unworthy for their pursuit and attention; and though naturally Buddhism in all its various aspects and branches demanded the most serious and careful attention, subjects like grammar, logic, medicine, astrology, astronomy, philosophy, polity, law, prosody, metres and even military science claimed their time and labour, grammar of course being one of the most important and favourite. But studies alone did not satisfy the scholarly craving of the monks; they were authors as well and produced works, mostly commentarial, on Buddhist ethics and metaphysics, myths and legends, morals and law, on grammar and prosody, on logic and astrology, on medicine and astronomy and other arts and sciences. The Sasanavamsa, the Gandhavama, the Pitakatthamain and other chronicles give long lists of such monk-scholars and philosophers.

For a general survey of Buddhist scholarship in Burma, see Bode (1909).

to a leading authority on the subject, has not been "creative." Thus, according to Ray (1946:262),

> Burma has hardly any creative contribution to Buddhist logic and metaphysics to her credit. Buddhism as an intellectual and emotional discipline certainly engaged their attention; but there is hardly any evidence throughout the centuries of their having ever made any conscious attempt to expand or interpret creatively the Buddhist way and philosophy of life. There have been recent attempts toward such contribution, but on the whole Buddhism in Burma remained and still does remain a colonial religion.

Still, rote knowledge is better than no knowledge,[3] and in order to upgrade the education of the Order, the Burmese Government, although unable to increase the formal educational requirements for ordination, has attempted to improve the educational level of the monks by means of a postordination incentive system.[4] Prizes and honorific titles are awarded to individual monks for demonstration of Buddhist knowledge in competitive

[3]It must be remarked that the monastery has no monopoly on rote knowledge. This emphasis pervades the secular educational system as well, right through the university level, as in almost every other country in South or Southeast Asia.

[4]As far back at least as the seventeenth century, the government has sponsored annual scriptural examinations, a tradition that was maintained by the British Government and later expanded by the post-Independence Burmese Government. During the monarchy "the successful were duly recognized and rewarded, the outstanding scholars being elevated forthwith and given popular acclaim." (Tha Myat, mimeo:27) Successful candidates may pass the examination, which consists in the rote recitation of texts, at four different levels. (Ranging from the lowest to the highest, they are termed *pahtamin-nge, pahtamin-lat, pahtamin-ji:, pahtamin-jàw:.)*

Building on this examination system, the post-Independence government passed the Pali University Act, according to which any monastery or monastic complex *(caung:taik)* which contains ten monks who have passed the scriptural examination at the *pahtamin-ji:* level can constitute itself as a Pali "university." (If two neighboring monasteries or monastic complexes have five monks each who have passed at this minimum level, they can jointly constitute a "university.") For each group of ten monks, the "university" is provided with three "professors," and an additional professor is appointed for each additional group of ten. These teachers receive a monthly salary from the government of K60 (about $12); the principal receives K80. To become a *dhammacariya* (or professor), the monk must pass the scriptural exam at the highest (the fourth) level, exhibiting mastery of all three sections ("baskets") of the Scripture.

In addition to the honor afforded to those who pass these examinations, the government, under this act, also provides the candidates with a financial incentive: those who take the exam in Burmese receive K50, K75, and K100, for passing at each of the three levels respectively. For passing the exam in Pali an additional K25 is added to the prize. For passing the *dhammacariya* exam the candidates receive K100 for each of the three tests comprising the examination, and K500 for passing with honors.

From an intellectual point of view—regardless of all other, essentially political considerations for the passage of the act (Mendelson 1964)—the need for the establishment of these universities was and is urgent. It was hoped that the educational level of the monks and monasteries could be improved by such inducements as financial prizes, honorary titles and degrees, free railway passes, the prestige of belonging to a "university," and so on. Withal, the act has not yet had an important impact. As late as 1962 only forty-two monasteries—thirteen in Mandalay, twelve in Rangoon, and seventeen distributed in other sections of the country—had acquired the status of "universities."

examinations, and those monasteries which have a minimum number of such monks are designated as Pali "universities." It is, perhaps, too early to evaluate the impact of this program on the intellectual attainments of the Order as a whole.

Given the low educational qualifications for admission to the Order, the relatively low level of educational instruction in the typical monastery, and the relatively low intellectual motivation of the typical monastic candidate, one can hardly be surprised if the intellectual and scholarly level of the average monk—obviously there are notable exceptions—is not very high. Nor can this be blamed on the heritage of colonialism. Bigandet's nineteenth-century observations, (1912:315) when stripped of their missionary bias, could have been made today.

> I have met with a great number of laymen who were incomparably better informed, and far superior in knowledge to them [monks]. Their mind is of the narrowest compass. Though bound by their profession to study with particular care the various tenets of their creed and all that relates to Buddhism, they are sadly deficient in this respect. They have no ardour for study. While they read some book, they do it without attention or effort to make themselves fully acquainted with the contents. There is no vigour in their intellect, no comprehensiveness in their mind, no order or connection in their ideas. Their reading is of a desultory nature, and the notions stored up in their memory are at once incoherent, imperfect, and too often very limited.[5]

Bigandet is, if anything, less critical than King Bagidaw, the eighteenth-century king of Burma. Cox (1821:229-30) reports the following conversation with His Majesty.

> The conversation had taken a religious turn, in consequence of the examination of some of the heads of keouns, or priests, which had passed the day before. It appears they had been found very ignorant, and his majesty was much dissatisfied with them. Among the observations that were made by him on the subject, he said, that he feared too many resorted to a religious life from a love of indolence, that he did not pretend to be learned in these matters himself, but, as the head of the religion of his dominions, it was his duty to see that those immediately intrusted with its rites were well informed; and in consequence he gave orders that candidates for the superiorities of keouns should in future undergo a more strict examination. His courtiers maintained a humble and profound silence, except when occasionally answering in the affirmative. It appears that his majesty is much dissatisfied with the present state of religion in his dominions, and meditates some great changes. He has found the priesthood in general miserably ignorant; even his arch-priest he doubts. He says they read over their canonical books, when they first enter on the monastic life, as

[5]Hardy's description of the Sinhalese Order for the same period is even more critical. (Hardy 1850:311-12) His missionary bias, however, is even stronger than Bigandet's.

> a task imposed on school-boys; and although they have no other employment to engage their attention, they never afterwards investigate or inquire into the mystical meaning of their rites; so that they are totally unfit to instruct the people. Hence the various abuses that have crept into their religion; the building of small pagodas, the use of beads, etc., all of which are cloaks for hypocrisy, and unauthorized by the tenets of their ancient faith.

Their rural education, together with their rural background, have left an indelible stamp on the monks. Intellectually and culturally their horizons are little different from those of the peasants with whom they live. The essentially medieval world view which informs the peasant mentality—with its spirits and demons, miracles and magic, animism and supernaturalism—similarly informs the mentality of the monk. The occult arts, as we shall see, are as widely practiced in the monastic compound as in the village square. Nor are the political and social views held in the monastery different from those held in the peasant's house. The average monk's view of the larger society, of the social and economic forces that have brought it into being, and of the changes that it is undergoing are those of the unsophisticated peasant. By the same token, and for the same reasons, his geography is pre-Columbian, his astronomy pre-Copernican, his biology pre-Darwinian.

These observations, though relatively unimportant in themselves, become pertinent when it is recalled that in contemporary Burma, as in all other *Theravāda* countries, the three important national institutions are the monkhood, the army (especially the officer corps), and the civil service. Together, they represent most of the cultural and national values of Burmese society. Their importance for nation building, modernization, and economic development—either as leading and promoting or as obstacles and impediments—cannot be exaggerated. In Burma, as in almost all the so-called developing societies, the army is the most important modernizing influence, and since the military coup in 1962 the Burmese army has become the most powerful institution in the country. It is instructive, therefore, to compare recruitment to the Order—the most traditional institution in Burma—with recruitment to the officer corps of the army.[6] The differences are dramatic. Unlike recruitment to the monkhood, most recruits to the military academy are urban in background (90-95 per cent come from cities and towns); they are generally from middle-class families, sons of traders, doctors, teachers, etc., and all are high-school graduates. Moreover, the curriculum of the military academy is the intellectual equivalent of a university curriculum; the army officer, in effect, is a university graduate. The officer corps, then, is a highly select group, university-trained, middle-class in its values, urban in its outlook. Compare this with the monkhood, which has little if any secular education, and which is lower-class in its values and rural in its outlook.

[6]I am indebted to Colonel Lwin, Commandant of the Defense Services Academy in Maymyo, for information on the recruits to the officer corps.

Using these same variables, the monkhood is removed from the civil servants and national politicians as well. The civil service is upper-middle-class in background, highly educated and highly anglicized. The politicians are lower-middle-class, and although rather less educated and acculturated than the former (Pye 1962: Section V), they are nevertheless more sophisticated than the monks. Since the monks, then, are much closer in world view to the peasants than are these other leadership groups, it is not astonishing that all post-Independence governments, including the present military government, have attempted to enlist their cooperation if not their active support.

Before concluding this section, it must be stressed that all the generalizations I have been making have notable exceptions. Although typically the intellectual level of the monks is low and their intellectual motivation small, there are deeply learned men among them, not only in the cities, but in village monasteries too. The following comments, quoted from my field notes, describe some of these village monks.

> He [monk *A*] lives here [in the forest] because he does not wish to become involved in the secular—or even the religious—affairs of a village. He is one of the few *hpoung:ji:* I have so far met who has impressed me with his piety, his integrity, and his learning.

> This [monk *B*] is obviously a serious monk. He has written at least two pamphlets on Buddhism; he prepares charts and diagrams illustrating the basic principles of Buddhist philosophy; and he still spends much time in meditation. Unlike most of the village *hpoung:ji:* we have met, he certainly uses his time profitably—mostly in intellectual activity.

> This [monk *C*] is a learned *hsaya-do.* This conclusion emerges from his conversation, and it is strengthened by the impression one receives from his facial expression. Unlike many monks who give one the impression of lethargy, he gives the impression of intellectual vigor, of a man who has spent much time with books and in thought.

Monastic Morality

Introduction

From the Buddhist point of view, the most important measure of monastic morality is the extent to which a monk complies with the regulations comprising the Rule. These regulations, as we have seen, are not intended to extinguish nonmonastic drives—that, rather, is the aim of meditation—but to channel their expression in certain desirable paths. These paths are often radically different from those on which ordinary humans travel. This being so, it is important to assess the degree to which the behavior of the monks follows the paths ordained by the *Vinaya.*

My general impression, based on interviews with both monks and laymen and on personal observation in literally scores of monasteries, is that in general village monks are remarkably true to the demands of the Rule. There are exceptions of course, but the great majority of monks—those, at least, whom I know—can be said to live in accordance with at least the major regulations of the *Vinaya.* Although Burmese laymen, as we shall see, are quick to recount the foibles and weaknesses of their monks, they almost never complain of major violations of the Rule, and this is not because of ignorance. Almost every layman has spent at least a few months—in some instances many years—in a monastery. They have had a chance to observe the monks in their daily behavior and in the most intimate detail. The fact that they have seen so little to criticize and continue to hold the monks in the highest veneration is, I would submit, the most persuasive evidence for their conformity with the demands of the Rule. Still, I should like to examine monastic behavior in some detail in two rather different domains which are of concern to the *Vinaya:* sexual behavior, on the one hand, and the practice of occult arts on the other.

Sex

I have chosen to examine the degree of adherence to monastic sexual regulations for three reasons. We have assumed that the Rule does not extinguish basic human drives, especially the demands of the flesh. Indeed, if the lessons of monasticism in the West are applicable as well to its Eastern counterpart, it may be taken for granted that the demands of the flesh are often even more imperious inside the monastery than outside. It is all the more interesting, therefore, to try to assess the degree to which monks comply with the *Vinaya* regulations concerning this, one of man's most basic drives. The Rule itself, moreover, stresses celibacy as its most important regulation, and violation of this injunction leads to expulsion from the Order. Finally, the Burmese themselves, following the emphasis of the Rule, stress the overriding importance of chastity as the essential trait of monastic morality.

Since sexual behavior can be practiced in private, one can never be absolutely sure that monks are indeed celibate. Nevertheless, since Burmese laymen are quick to criticize them, and since the Buddhist unlike the Christian monastery is always open to the public, it would be difficult for sexual derelictions to remain undiscovered. This does not mean that all monks are chaste, but it is probably fair to say that cases of unchastity—among village monks, at least—are extremely rare. I discovered only one in my investigations. This was a village monk who is said to have had an affair some years ago with a woman of the same village. It came to an end when the woman became pregnant, and had an abortion. The same monk is alleged to have later taken up with another woman, and only when his behavior became flagrant did he terminate the affair. When I arrived in his monastery, he was carrying out a special penitential ceremony which (so some of the villagers informed me) was an attempted atonement, four or five years later, for his sexual derelictions.

This, however, is an isolated case. By all accounts village monks do in fact comply with the sexual prohibitions, both homosexual and heterosexual, of the Rule. And they do so, it must be added, in the face of temptation. Of the twenty monks who were intensively interviewed on sexual matters, only three said they were not bothered by their vows of chastity. Twelve said that the vow was "difficult," and five that it was "very difficult," to comply with. We have already seen that sexual frustration is the most important reason for defection from the monastery. Many men, the Burmese observe, simply do not have the proper "qualification" *(pāramī)* for living in a state of sexual abstention; and by "qualification," it should be emphasized, they do not mean the absence of sexual drive, but rather the discipline to overcome it. As one monk put it, "Only an *arahant* [the saint who, about to enter nirvana, has extinguished all passions] is devoid of sexual desire; I am not an *arahant,* I am only an ordinary worldling [*puthujjana*]. For an ordinary worldling it is normal to have such desires; even the Buddha had them." Or, as another monk put it, "Lust is like a serpent; one never knows when it will rise up to strike. Hence, one must always be on one's guard against it."

Typically, then, Burmese monks are not without sexual desire; rather, they are men who must control sexual desire. (Their "fear" of women, alluded to earlier, is an important factor in achieving control.) On the other hand, not a few married men enter the monastery precisely because, having little interest in sex, they find the sexual demands of their wives unduly burdensome. For them the monastery is a face-saving solution for problems of sexual impotence.

So far as we can tell (from our meager historical evidence) Burmese monks have a long historical record of fidelity to their sexual vows. Charges of homosexuality (frequently made against monks of other religions and against Buddhist monks in other societies) are not found in the early descriptions of the Burmese Order, and charges of heterosexual derelictions are also absent. If anything, early writers go out of their way to praise the monks for their compliance with these vows. Bigandet, no lover of Buddhism, admits (in his description of Burmese monks of the nineteenth century) that "the law of celibacy . . . is observed with a great scrupulosity, and a breach of it is a rare occurrence." (Bigandet 1912:291) Again, "they avoid all that could lead them into dissipation. Exterior continence is generally observed, and though there are occasional trespasses, it would be unfair to lay on them generally the charge of incontinence. Their life so far may be considered as exemplary." (*Ibid.*:318) The same opinion is voiced in the eighteenth century by Father Sangermano. "The law of continency, externally at least, is observed with the greatest scrupulosity by these men, and in this respect they might even serve as an example to many of our religious."[7] (Sangermano 1893:115)

There are a variety of reasons for the monks' fidelity to their sexual vows. In the first place there is the fear of karmic punishment: an unchaste monk will be punished in hell for sexual derelictions. Second, there is fear of expulsion from the Order, sexual misbehavior being one of the few grounds for this. Third, there is the fear of public opinion, and especially of public punishment. The Burmese would be outraged by an incelibate monk, not only because of the immorality of his act but also because—since little merit is acquired by supporting an impious monk, especially one who has violated one of the *pārājika*—of the resources they have wasted on him. For both reasons contemporary Burmese opinion is little different from that found in the following nineteenth-century account (although their behavior, no doubt, would be different).

> Popular opinion is inflexible and inexorable on the point of celibacy, which is considered essential to every one that has a pretension to be called a Rahan. The people can never be brought to look upon any person as a priest or minister of religion unless he live in that state. Any infringement of this most essential regulation on the part of a Rahan is visited with an immediate punishment. The people of the place assemble at the kiaong of the offender, sometimes driving him out with stones. He is stripped of his clothes; and often public punishment, even that of death, is inflicted upon him by order of the government. The poor wretch is looked upon as an outcast, and the woman whom he has seduced shares in his shame, confusion, and disgrace. [Bigandet 1912:291][8]

In addition to punitive fears, both natural and supernatural, there are as we have seen some obvious emotional bases for the low incidence of sexual dereliction among the monks. Some have little interest in women, and

[7]The sexual decorum of the Burmese monks and their fidelity to their sexual vows is especially interesting by comparison with contrasting charges made against Buddhist monks in other *Theravāda* societies. Thus, for example, in his nineteenth-century description of Buddhist monks in northwest Thailand (the Chiengmai area), Colquhoun reports that

> . . . women were not only frequenters of the *kyoungs* [monasteries], but in some cases were actually living there. The young monks, and even the novices, were ogling women and maidens, and joking freely, amidst an interchange of amorous glances which were obvious to every chance passerby. [Colquhoun 1885:238]

Similarly in Ceylon in 1959, I was told by a Rural Development Officer that some monks in his district (the Dry Zone) keep mistresses; and I personally know one monk, in the Kandyan highlands, who keeps his mistress in the monastery grounds. Moreover, I was told that homosexuality, too, is not infrequent in the Sinhalese monkhood—between monks and monks, monks and novices, and monks and laymen.

[8]A Catholic priest, Bigandet cannot help but express his admiration for Burmese opinion, nor conceal his bewilderment that such attitudes should be found in a non-Christian culture.

> Such an extraordinary opinion, so deeply rooted in the mind of a people rather noted for the licentiousness of their manners, certainly deserves the attention of every diligent observer of human nature. Whence has originated among corrupted and half-civilised men such a high respect and profound esteem for so exalted a virtue? [*Ibid.*]

indeed are phobic in their attitude toward them; others, latent homosexuals, are confused about their sexual identity.

The Occult Arts

Although normative Buddhism sanctions the use of many kammatic rituals, it is firmly and explicitly opposed to what we would call the "occult arts," which it characterizes as the "low arts." More important for our present purposes, the *Vinaya* explicitly prohibits Buddhist monks from any form of participation in these arts. Hence, from the (normative) Buddhist point of view, a most important measure of monastic morality is the extent to which the monks comply with this interdiction. In addition, it is important for us in assessing the degree to which the monkhood has emancipated itself from older magical beliefs and practices.

The low arts prohibited by the *Vinaya* (and which, from the standpoint of the Noble Eightfold Path, fall within the category of "wrong means of livelihood") are spelled out in great detail in various of the sermons attributed to the Buddha. Included among them are palmistry; divining by means of omens and signs; augury; fortune-telling by means of dreams, marks on the body, and so on; the use of charms; astrology; the determination of auspicious and inauspicious places, and of auspicious and inauspicious times; exorcism; and any form of medical practice, including diagnosis, prognosis, and therapy. (Cf. *Brahma-Jala Sutta,* I, 21-28, in *Dialogues of the Buddha,* Vol. II.)

Despite their prohibition, numerous Burmese monks indulge in many of these pursuits, especially astrology, medicine, and divination.[9] In Mandalay, for example, their number according to reliable estimates is as high as 10 per cent of the monastic population. Equally reliable estimates, however, indicate that the percentage is somewhat smaller in the villages, although in Yeigyi two of the four resident monks engaged in at least one of these practices.[10] It is all the more interesting to note, therefore, that the great majority of the monks in my sample, including those who believe in the practices themselves, were firm in their conviction that such monks are not only in violation of the Rule but should be expelled from the Order. It is equally interesting that, despite their conviction, neither they nor any other group of monks have made any move to act upon this conviction.[11] Let us, then, briefly examine some of these monastic practices.

[9] *Mahāyāna* monks, as is well known, perform many other "arts" as well, including even love magic. (Cf. Goullart 1941:97.)

[10] Nor is this a modern phenomenon. Writing seventy years ago Scott and Hardiman (1900:81) observe that "many of the most noted seers, necromancers, and tatooers are pongyis."

[11] The situation was different in the days of the monarchy when monks who engaged in such practices provoked "immediate intervention" on the part of the civil authorities. (Scott and Hardiman 1900:4)

In the realm of astrology monks may be consulted to determine, for example, the auspicious day for holding a wedding, the proper antidote against business losses, the prognosis in the case of illness, or the reasons for general failure. In all these cases the answer is discovered by reading the client's horoscope. Unlike village monks, who may intermittently engage in astrology, urban monks especially renowned for their astrological skills may be recognized as astrological specialists. One such, for example, saw three clients within the two-hour period that I spent in his monastery, and three more were waiting to see him when I left. The problems brought to him by the first three clients are typical of those with which he deals.

A young man, a petty merchant, complained that he was failing in his business. The monk advised him to refrain from travel and from the eating of pork for two months. After that things would improve.

A young mother was concerned about her sick child. The monk informed her that after a certain date (which he named) the child would recover. In the meantime she was to burn ten candles daily before the Buddha shrine in her home and pray to Him for the child's health. In addition she was to discard the child's old sandals on the southwest side of the house.

An old woman was failing in health and in business. The monk informed her that she was under the baneful influence of a certain planet. Until October, when she would pass out of its influence, she should execute no plans, for they were all bound to fail. She should only stock tea, dried fish, and rice in her store. She must avoid all persons born on certain days, which he stipulated. Beginning with her impending birthday she must offer nine fried bananas daily to the birds. She should only drink water in which gold jewelry has been immersed. Finally, when she washed her face she should think about auspicious things.

These prescriptions are taken seriously by the clients. In Yeigyi, for example, a woman insisted that her husband return an ox he had purchased from a neighbor because this same monk, whose advice she had sought only the preceding week, had cautioned her against purchasing any four-legged animal from the south side of her home, lest the troubles she had been encountering continue.

Some monks practice medicine, both as herbalists *(hsei: hsaya)* and, in cases of witchcraft and spirit possession, as exorcists *(ahte: lan: hsaya).* Even those who do not practice any of the healing arts may dispense amulets and spells to ward off danger. Almost every villager who works in the fields wears an amulet as protection against poisonous snakes. Sometimes it is obtained from a local village monk; sometimes from some monk in Mandalay who specializes in occult and magical matters; sometimes from an itinerant monk who, wishing to raise funds for a special project—repairing a monastery, constructing a pagoda, etc.—dispenses amulets as he travels from village to village. Although spells, too, are employed as protection from such natural hazards as snakes, they are typically used rather against the dangers of witches or evil spirits.[12]

Monks also practice divination. When one of the farmers in Yeigyi lost his bull, he went to a village monk who, by magical means, told him where it could be found. In another case, when a young man believed he had lost his gold studs, his mother went to seek the help of a monk. The latter, invoking the assistance of the *deva*, discovered that they had in fact been stolen. He instructed her to light a candle, over which he had recited a spell, and informed her that before the candle was burned out the studs would be returned. The flame, he explained, causes heat; because of the spell, the heat would cause the thief to be hot inside and, anxious lest his crime be discovered, he would return the studs.

The occult arts cited above are performed by monks on behalf of laymen. There is one art, however, which monks (like many laymen) perform, not for clients, but for themselves. This is that of alchemy, whose practice is widespread in the Burmese Order. One-third of the monks in my sample, for example, either practice alchemy now or had practiced it in the past. Some monks with whom I spoke said this figure was a bit low; in their experience, 40 per cent of the monks in the district in which I worked were alchemists.

Monks, like laymen, practice alchemy from at least three motives: to make gold, to acquire supermundane powers, such as the power to fly, and to achieve an enormously lengthened life, hopefully for 2,500 years. All three motives, it will be noted, are either in violation of the monastic Rule or in contradiction of basic Buddhist philosophy. Thus the monk, *qua* monk is prohibited by the Rule from even handling money (gold), let alone coveting it; he is prohibited, *qua* monk, from performing supernatural feats;[13] and finally, as a Buddhist he surely cannot favor the prolongation of life—if life

[12]In some instances, as the following newspaper account indicates, monks who practice "medicine" may become very famous.

> PEGU,—Villagers from and around Kyaikkasin, about ten miles north of here, yesterday joined in the ceremony of hoisting the pinnacle of a small pagoda which was built with his own hands by a Hindu peasant, Aramun by name.
>
> The miniature pagoda stands in a part of the field owned and worked by Aramun and was erected with the assistance of village elders U Kyaw and U Chit.
>
> Breakfast and other refreshments were provided for the visitors.
>
> The Venerable Sayadaw U Teiktha, Aramun's patron, took the occasion to effect cures of the ill and the sick and treated about 200 patients with water, salt and a *dah* over which he had recited sacred incantations.
>
> The fame of the Sayadaw's cures has spread to outlying villages and patients are flocking to him by car and cart, on foot and litters. [*Working People's Daily*, April 2, 1964]

[13]The Buddha's opposition to wonder-working is not based on His disbelief that some men may acquire such powers as levitation, flying, walking on the waters, etc. On the contrary, He explicitly acknowledges that these powers can be attained and that He himself has attained

is suffering, how can one wish to prolong it? Or, if the true goal is nirvana, how can long life be one's goal?

To these objections, those who practice alchemy (as well as their defenders) have a reply. Although there can be no justification for a monk to desire gold, the other two motives, they argue, may be justified. Thus, some monks desire supermundane power, not for its own sake, but as a means to certain spiritual ends. The alchemic stone *(datloung:)* gives one the power to go for seven days without eating; a monk may wish to acquire this power so that he can meditate uninterruptedly for seven days. Similarly, longevity may be desired, not as an end in itself, but as a means for attaining nirvana. If, so it is believed, one can live until the coming, in 2,500 years, of the future Buddha *(Metteya);* then, by worshiping Him, one can enter nirvana. In short, it is not because they desire life, but because they hope to achieve deliverance from it, that they wish to prolong their lives. Despite these claims, it is my distinct impression that the vast majority of alchemists, monastic and lay alike, are indeed seeking immortality. Since the Buddhist principle of "impermanence" precludes that possibility, the quest has been rationalized to render it consistent with Buddhism: it is for a finite immortality (only 2,500 years) and is linked with a normative Buddhist motive—the attainment of nirvana. (For a more extensive discussion of Burmese alchemy, see chapter 7.)

The Moral State of the *Sangha*

Except for a fairly large percentage who either practice or dabble in the occult arts, Burmese monks, I have contended thus far, live in accordance with the regulations that comprise their Rule. Readers who, either from previous reading or from personal experience in Burma, are knowledgeable about the Burmese *Sangha*, may be rather surprised by this picture of the Burmese monkhood. For they will have seen or heard of many monks who live in violation of both the letter and the spirit of the Rule. Indeed, they will know (as I know) that the worldly involvements of a significant number of Burmese monks is a public scandal. Despite the dimensions of this scandal, I would still contend that the vast majority of them comply with the Rule, for my description has related to genuine rather than bogus monks; i.e., has been concerned with those who are in the Order out of conviction rather than those who use it to further political, material, and other nonmonastic ends. Since, for reasons discussed below, the Burmese Order does not police its own members, it contains a considerable number

---

them. (Cf. *Kevaddha Sutta,* XI, 4, in *Dialogues of the Buddha, Part I.)* His opposition is based, instead, on the grounds that people might say that these wondrous powers were made possible by the use of some charm rather than by spiritual discipline. Such a conclusion, He believes, is dangerous to true religion. Hence, "it is because I perceive danger in the practice of mystic wonders, that I loathe, and abhor, and am ashamed thereof." *(Ibid., XI, 5)*

of these fundamentally ungenuine monks. (This has been just as true in the past [cf. Bigandet 1912:314] as it is today.) Thus, for example, a respected Mandalay monk estimated that one-fourth of the monks in that city are former rebels who entered the Order to escape the law.

Recognizing, then, that the Order contains "phony" as well as genuine members, it would surely be inappropriate, in attempting to describe the behavior of bona fide monks, to lump both types together. On the other hand, in attempting to give a picture of the entire Order, it would be equally false to close our eyes to the fact that it does include men who are essentially pretenders as well as genuine members. So long as these bogus monks are permitted to remain in the Order—either because of the inaction of the laity or the indifference of the true monk—they are officially part of it, and any assessment of the moral state of the Burmese *Saṅgha* must finally consider their behavior as well. Within this wider framework, then, let us consider the following data.

Even the casual reader of Burmese newspapers knows that anyone who advocates a practice, a point of view, or a legislative bill disapproved of by the monkhood may be subject to the following types of reprisal by gangs of urban monks: physical beating, burning of mosques, overturning of automobiles. Scandalous, too, is the naked use of power by some monks in order to maintain their sense of importance. When, for example, a Mandalay bus driver allegedly insulted some monks who were riding in his bus, a large meeting of monks demanded that the driver walk from the Government Building to the Arakan Pagoda—a distance of approximately five miles—with a sign identifying his "crime," hanging from his neck, and that a group of monks ride behind him announcing that this is the price to be paid for insulting a monk. After many negotiations with the management of the bus company, the monks relented, settling for a public request for forgiveness by the bus driver, and of course a special feast.

Even more common, and from the standpoint of the Rule equally scandalous, is the attendance by many monks at movies and theatricals. When the pious owner of a Mandalay cinema announced that he would refuse to sell tickets to monks, a group of them threatened to burn his theater in reprisal.

Lest it be thought that these examples of nonmonastic behavior are confined to urban monks, it must be added that rural monasteries also include their fair share of "humans in yellow robes." To be sure, their nonmonastic behavior is not as blatant as the urban examples cited above, nor do rural monks participate in politics, a topic we shall explore in the following chapter. But their egregious behavior is sufficient to evoke the critical comments of the villagers, who complain especially of the rapacity, greed, and even dishonesty of some of their monks. Two examples of such conduct, one from Yeigyi and another from a neighboring village, may suffice.

A monk in the latter village was accused of cutting down the trees in his monastic compound and taking the proceeds for his own use. He was accused, also, of turning over part of his alms food to his former wife. Finally, he was alleged to have sold monastic property (including Buddha images)—which his predecessor had acquired and bequeathed to the monastery—again taking the proceeds for his own use. Since this was a repetition of behavior in another monastery, of which he had taken possession without being invited, so that he was forced to flee when threatened with violent expulsion, the villagers decided to invite another monk to become abbot here. The incumbent, however, refused to admit him, and the villagers brought the case to the Ministry of Religious Affairs, asking that he be expelled. The Ministry, after investigating the charges, ordered him to leave the monastery, but he again refused. Although the Township Officer was empowered to remove him by force, he was reluctant to do so because, as a Christian, his motives might be suspect. Four months later, when I left Upper Burma, the monk was still in the monastery.

The Yeigyi case concerned a monk who was alleged to have committed the following abuses. First, he was given paddy land by a certain woman with the understanding that the proceeds from the sale of paddy (i.e., uncut rice) were to be used, upon her death, to finance her funeral. Instead, and unknown to her, he sold the land. With the proceeds he purchased another plot in the name of a certain layman, one U Sein, with the understanding that he himself would receive the profits from its rice yield. (U Sein did not keep the bargain but retained the proceeds, and since the land was recorded in his name, the monk had no recourse.) Second, in silent partnership with a layman, this monk operated a trucking business. (Again he was swindled of his share of the profits, and again had no recourse, since the truck was registered in the layman's name only.) Third, he sold utensils that belonged to the monastery, keeping the proceeds for his own use. (As luck would have it, the funds were stolen.) Nor was this all. In charge of a monastic cremation, he allegedly embezzled K800 (about $175) from the contributions. When he was openly accused of absconding with the funds, he replied that he was merely holding them for safekeeping. (This was during the unrest in Upper Burma, when savings were liable to be seized by insurgents.) Finally, claiming that a decaying monastery in the village was his, he contracted to sell it to a monk from another village, who wished to use its materials for a new monastery that was being constructed for him. Before the transaction could be put through, it was discovered that the original claim to ownership was false.

Although the early historical records show no reference to this type of monk, the more recent contain descriptions which have a modern ring. The following quotation describes the Burmese Order at the turn of the century.

> Many of them [monks] are extremely covetous, and are eager for the personal possession of money and presents; indeed, they themselves carry on business transactions. Lawsuits are by no means uncommon, both with one another and with the laity, even in the English law courts. [Hackmann 1910:140]

Sangermano, whose missionary bias however is very strong, describes the eighteenth-century monks as follows. "They are insatiable in their lust after riches, and do little else than ask for them. . . ." (Sangermano 1893: 115)

Similar complaints have been made in the past by the Burmese themselves. In an opinion survey conducted in the second decade of this century, it was discovered (Purser and Saunders 1914:20) that the Burmese exhibited a "very widespread dissatisfaction with the lives of the monks." People complained that they violated their rules, accumulated property, married their female followers, and so on.[14]

Although the Burmese do not drive these fraudulent monks from their monasteries, they are deeply offended by their behavior and have no compunctions about criticizing them. Discounting the hyperbolic "all," the following statements are typical of the criticisms one may hear:

> Today there are no real monks. They are all corrupt, greedy, impious. This is especially true of the *Yahan: Byou:* [an organization of monks, with headquarters in Mandalay]. They are not monks. They carry guns and knives.

> The *Saṅgha* has fallen on evil days. They violate the *Vinaya* because they are greedy for material things.

[14]Other *Theravāda* societies also have (and have had) their share of ungenuine members. The following picture of contemporary Sinhalese monks is drawn by a Sinhalese scholar. The *Saṅgha,* he writes, "is in dissolution. The laymen have lost that ancient and customary veneration for the monks." There is no "unity" or "amity" in the *Saṅgha;* the discipline is "relaxing"; the robes of the Buddha are in some cases used "to veil the identity of the illiterate, and undesirables who parade in the guise of the members of the sangha." The latter are in a state of "pitiable degeneration." (Wijesekera 1949:163)

Colquhoun, whose description (like Sangermano's) is colored by an obvious missionary bias, has the following to say of nineteenth-century monks in (northwest) Thailand.

> The priests are in bad odour with their flocks, because of their evil lives and their rapacity. They have retrograded from the observances required from the priesthood still further than the Maha-gandee sect in Burmah. Not only do they take money openly, but, in opposition to all their vows of abstinence from all cravings of the flesh, they covet and vociferously beg for everything that they think can be acquired by begging. [Colquhoun 1885:103]

Among other things, he notes the following nonmonastic, behavior: loitering in the bazaar, entering houses at night, riding elephants, eating after noon, selling offerings made to the monastery, bowing to the chief, wearing gold and jewelry, drinking liquor, attending cockfights and plays, and listening to music even in the monastery itself. (*Ibid.*:147)

> I will no longer give alms food to the monks. In this area there are only three pious monks. All the rest are rogues.

> Only a few monks are really pious. All the rest are ignorant and corrupt.

Pious laymen refuse to refer to bogus monks as *hpoung:ji:.* Instead, they refer to them as "humans in a yellow robe," or "yellow humans," or "pillars wrapped in a yellow robe." Genuine monks, who observe the *Vinaya* rules, are said to "have discipline" *(theikkha.* [Pali, *sikkhā*] *shi.de);* the others, the bogus monks "do not have discipline" *(theikkha. mashi.bu:).*

Laymen not only criticize derelict monks, but penalize them even when they continue to support them. Their low esteem is expressed in the following ways. Village boys are not sent to study with them, nor do they become novices in their monasteries. Often the level of material support for such monks is low. Sometimes they are even refused a robe ceremony. When this happened to the Yeigyi monk described above, a small ceremony was arranged only after some of his former students pleaded with the other villagers to hold the ceremony.

It may be wondered, in the light of these descriptions, how bogus monks continue to be supported at all by the villagers; for, of course, if the latter did not provide them with food and other requirements they could not survive. It may be wondered, too, why such monks are not expelled from the Order. To begin with the first question, it can be said that laymen are extremely loath to drive a monk from his monastery, for despite his sinful behavior he is still clothed in the yellow robe, the symbol of sanctity. Hence, they say they do not worship the monk but the robe; they do not support the monk, but the *Saṅgha.* There are other reasons, too. For some villagers, the monk has been their teacher in the monastic school, and it is difficult for a Burman to turn against a teacher.

In the cities, of course, the situation is rather different. Since the monastic population is counted in the thousands, there are few primary relationships with laymen, so that the latter feel no constraint about not supporting such monks. The result is that many urban laymen do in fact refuse to support those whom they know to be "yellow humans." Still, the latter flourish even more in the cities than in the villages, since it is difficult to identify them, and they require only one or two wealthy supporters to survive.

If the laymen continue to support bogus monks, it may still be wondered why their fellow monks do not expel them from the Order. In this regard the situation is somewhat more complex, but we can identify a few reasons. One of the important differences between pre- and postconquest Burma is that under the monarchy the monkhood could, and did, police its own members. Although the powers of the Primate *(tha-thana-baing)* were limited, he and his administrative officials were able with the support of the state (ecclesiastical law was recognized by the courts) to expel "phony" monks from the Order. The British, however, not only abolished the office of *tha-thana-baing* but refused to recognize the ecclesiastical code; at least one authority has attributed the moral deterioration of the Order to these facts. (Harvey 1946:26-27) In short, following the British conquest of Burma, the *Saṅgha* was deprived of the institutional means for enforcement of the Rule.

Since Independence, of course, the situation has changed again. The government, as we have seen, has established ecclesiastical courts which are empowered (among other things) to try monks accused of violating the Rule. The inactivity of these courts in this regard is attributable to a variety of factors. In the cities, with their large monastery complexes, pious monks rarely bring charges against derelict colleagues because they are afraid of reprisal. The fear is realistic. Many corrupt monks control goon squads who will not hesitate to harm(physically) those responsible for the expulsion of a comrade. The situation in the village is rather different. If the corrupt monk is the sole occupant (as is usually the case in a village monastery), and the monastery is the only one in the village, there is no other monk to bring charges against him. Given the loose social structure of the Order (described in chapter 13), there is no supervising ecclesiastical body outside the village which has the authority to initiate an indictment. As an alternative, the government would be able to control the situation by its own surveillance of monks, but this would require a registration of the membership, which for fear of government control even pious monks have opposed. The result of inaction from *Saṅgha* and government alike is that the "yellow rogues" do their mischief in society, bringing the entire monkhood into disrepute.[15]

[15]The problem of monastic infiltration by undesirable criminal and political types is not, of course, restricted to Burma. In Thailand, for example, where potentially the problem is as acute, it has been met by strengthening the power of the Primate and the subordinate hierarchy, by licensing all monks permitted to perform ordination rites, and by rather firm governmental supervision. (Cf. Mulder 1969:13-15).

CHAPTER 16

The *Saṅgha* and the State

Introduction

In the last chapter, the political role of Burmese monks was alluded to but not discussed, for this important subject deserves extended attention in its own right. To view the problem of political monks in the exclusive framework of monastic morality is to see it much too narrowly. This chapter attempts to enlarge that framework.

As is well known, political monks are not a recent phenomenon in Burmese history. From the British conquest of Upper Burma in 1886 until the most recent military coup in 1962, monks have almost always been actively involved in secular politics. (Cf. Cady 1958, Smith 1965, von der Mehden 1963.) Because these political monks have been both visible and articulate, the impression has sometimes been created that the Burmese Order was highly politicized, more concerned with political than with religious goals. In fact, these political monks (almost exclusively urban) have always comprised a small minority of the total monkhood.

But political action is only one means by which the *Saṅgha* can be related to the state, and although normatively the monk is supposed to remain aloof from politics, even in Buddhist theory the *Saṅgha* and the state are not expected to exist independently of each other. On the contrary, their relationship is one of interdependence, the state having the responsibility of purifying the Order, and the Order having the responsibility of assuring that the state keep steadfast to Buddhist principles. This indeed was often the actual relationship between the Order and the state in Burma. Contemporary monastic politics, then, are best understood within the broader context of these normative and historical dimensions of the relationship between the *Saṅgha* and the state.

Church and State in Early Buddhism

In classical Buddhist political thought, there is an intimate relation between the state (especially the king and the court) and the Buddhist church. The king (for both normatively and actually, Buddhist political theory presupposes a monarchical government) is the protector of Buddhism, which means of course that Buddhism is the state religion. Obversely, Buddhist ideology is the reservoir from which the monarch derives charismatic authority. As we have seen in chapter 7, the king, in Buddhist thought, may be a Universal Emperor who will bring the world under the Wheel of the Law. He may also be a Future Buddha, who will proclaim the Law. It is not surprising, then, that there should have been a symbiotic relationship between the monastic order (the embodiment of the Buddhist church) and the government (the embodiment of the state), in both theory and practice. This relationship is as old as the Asokan period in Indian (Buddhist) history.

As Dutt has observed (1962:43), Indian monasticism is unique in the history of monasticism, not only because it was in India that ascetics and hermits were first constituted as a separate community, recognized as such by the people, but because, as may be seen in the edicts of Asoka (third century B.C.), it was in India that their separate legal status was first officially recognized by the government. Ancient Indian political philosophy had conceived of society as comprising diverse social (and legal) status groups, each governed by its own traditional law *(samaya)*, and it was the duty of the government to protect these groups from both internal and external disruption, and especially to assure the preservation of their traditional law. Since the Buddhist Order was recognized as one among those status groups, the government was constitutionally bound to protect it and to prevent any infringement of its traditional law *(Vinaya)*. (Dutt 1962:80) In short, the government was not only the protector of Buddhism, but was responsible for the preservation and purification of the Order. In a sense, then, the Order became dependent upon the government, and this dependency was perpetuated to some extent in every Buddhist nation in Southeast Asia after Buddhism became the religion of the country. Reciprocally, the Order became the conscience of the government, ensuring that it ruled, at least to some extent, in accordance with Buddhist ethical principles.

Church and State in Burmese History

Precolonial Burma

From the very inception of Buddhism in eleventh-century Pagan as the state religion, there was a close and reciprocal relationship in traditional

Burma between the government and the monastic Order. Although in the narrow sense the Order was apolitical,[1] it nevertheless had an important influence on the government, and the government in turn accorded the monks much honor, as well as material support.

Aside from any of the ideological considerations alluded to above, the throne was anxious to curry favor with the monks because of their popular support. (Ray 1946:212) Hence, even in periods of political turmoil or social and economic difficulties, "we see kings building new viharas [monasteries] . . . and extending generous bounties to the Samgha." *(Ibid.)* In addition, the government offered special titles and rewards to monks who excelled in the government-sponsored scriptural examinations, and it provided elaborate state funerals to those who died at an especially old age. But even before their deaths monks received special treatment from the government. They received a monthly subsistence allowance, they could be tried only in ecclesiastical courts, they could offer monastic sanctuary to anyone who donned the yellow robe, and their relatives were exempt from taxation. (Scott and Hardiman, 1900:1-3)

To assure monastic support for itself the throne not only provided honors and support for the Order, but—consistent with the establishment of Buddhism as the state religion—appointed the important members of the hierarchy, including the Primate *(tha-thana-baing)* and his ecclesiastical council *(thu.dama).*

The *Saṅgha* not only received material privileges from the government, but were able to exert considerable influence on it. Monks had access to the king and his ministers, and they used this privilege to assist the people in many ways. They frequently interceded on behalf of prisoners condemned to execution,[2] protected the weak from extortion by powerful officials, assisted others in obtaining tax relief in periods of economic distress, and

[1]In his account of the political unrest in the Burmese empire of the eighteenth century, Symes writes: "In the various commotions of the empire, I never heard that the Rahaans [monks] had taken any active share, or publicly interfered in politics, or engaged in war: by this prudent conduct they excited no resentment. . . ." (Symes 1800:212) Writing in the nineteenth century, Bigandet paints a similar picture. Although the monks exerted a "great influence" on Burmese society, they made no attempt to interfere with politics. "It does not appear," he writes, that

> they have ever aimed at any share in the management or direction of the affairs of the country. Since the accession of the house of Alomphra to the throne, that is to say, during a period of above a hundred years, the history of Burmah has been tolerably well known. We do not recollect having ever met with one instance when the Phongyies, as a body, have interfered in the affairs of the State. [Bigandet 1912:303]

[2]Sangermano, who strongly disapproved of the monks' opposition to capital punishment, indicates that sometimes their intercession was based on more than spiritual persuasion. The moment the monks heard that a criminal was to be executed,

> they issued from their convents in great numbers, with heavy sticks concealed under their habits, with which they furiously attacked the ministers of justice, put them to flight and, unbinding the culprit, conducted him to their Bao. Here his head was shaved, a new dress was put upon him, and by these ceremonies he was absolved from his crime and rendered inviolable. [Sangermano 1893:122]

urged the removal or transfer of despotic district officials. They even protested effectively against arbitrary royal confiscation of private land. In short, the Buddhist monk, who, as Scott and Hardiman (1900:2) observe, ". . . theoretically had nothing to do with politics, or things of this world, was really a political power, the only permanent power in a system where office was . . . transient and evanescent."

Although the monk served as a middleman between government and people, it would be a mistake to believe that his influence was exerted solely on behalf of the governed. Governments, after all, do not offer rewards without the expectation of some reciprocal service, and as Scott and Hardiman point out (*ibid.*:2), the monks not only attempted to protect the people from the arbitrary and tyrannical rule of the government, but also tried to reconcile the people to that rule. Needless to say, it was for this latter function that they were rewarded by the throne. If the kings permitted the monks a great deal of freedom in their interference with royal prerogatives[3] —not only because they needed their political support, but of course because to harm a monk would lead to calamitous results in a subsequent rebirth[4]—the monks in turn supported the kings not only because they were the recipients of royal rewards and privileges, but because their entire way of life was indirectly dependent upon royal favor. As Bode (1897:53-54) has observed, under despotic rule—and the Burmese court was an example of extreme despotism—

> no man's property or labour is his own; the means of supporting the Samgha may be withdrawn from any subject who is under the royal displeasure. The peaceful, easy life dear to the Burmese bhikkhu, the necessary calm for study or the writing of books, the land or water to be set apart for ecclesiastical ceremonies (a fitting place for which is of the highest importance), all these are only secured by the king's favour and protection. If this be borne in mind, the general loyalty of the Samgha to the head of the State is easy to understand.

[3]Although there is no record of a monk playing the prophetic role of royal critic—monks, after all, are not prophets—there are a few recorded instances of the display of great courage by monastic critics of the kings. The following anecdote is apocryphal, but no doubt typifies some of them. When King Mindon sent a messenger to discover what the Bhamo *hsaya-do* was doing in his Sagaing retreat, the monk is reputed to have told the messenger: "Your king must take me as a rebel or perhaps he wants to instruct me in the ways of the ascetics. Tell him that a man who lives between the hills does not need instruction from a man who lives between the thighs [of women]." (Than Tun 1955:179)

[4]Not all the kings, to be sure, were deterred from harming monks by these karmic considerations. The sixteenth-century King Thohanbwa not only pillaged the pagodas of their treasures but, viewing all monks as potential rebels, was determined to rid himself of this source of danger. Inviting all the monks in the vicinity of Ava, the capital, to a feast, he had them surrounded and then ordered their wholesale massacre. According to Harvey (1925:107), 360 monks were killed and the manuscripts in their monasteries burned.

In the eighteenth century, the famous *Alaung:hpaya:* ordered 3,000 Mon monks thrown to the elephants on the excuse that they had helped the Mon resistance. Their monasteries were pillaged and their robes, bowls, and other sacred objects desecrated. (Ray 1946: 225)

The kings were not only the patrons of the Order but often intervened, sometimes by invitation, in monastic affairs. The king, after all, was the defender and purifier of the faith; it was only natural that he should attempt to settle monastic disputes, especially when important religious issues were believed to be at stake. Indeed, from the beginning of the monarchy to its end, it was the king who took the initiative in, and provided the means for, all movements of monastic reform. Perhaps a few examples will be illuminating.

The first triumph of the orthodox Sinhalese school *(Simhala Saṅgha),* which became the model for the entire Burmese Order, was assured only after the intervention of King Narapatisithu in the twelfth century. Similarly it was King Dhammazeti, in the fifteenth century, who assured the ultimate triumph of this school by purging the Order of monks who did not strictly observe the *Vinaya*: he banned those who practiced medical and occult arts, who possessed private property, and who in general were "without faith and devotion." (Ray 1946:189) As a measure of the relationship that obtained at that time between throne and monastery, it should be carefully noted that this reform was undertaken at the king's—not the monks'—initiative, and that the monks freely followed his bidding and guidance.

Again, throughout the century-long controversy between the reformist *Ekamsikas* and the traditional *Parupanas* (see chapter 12), both sides invoked the authority and assistance of four successive kings, until the controversy was finally resolved by King Bodapaya.

Royal intervention in monastic affairs continued almost to the end of the monarchy, when Mindon (the penultimate king) became disturbed by the laxity in observance of the Rule—monks carried money, chewed betel after the noon hour, used tobacco and other intoxicants, entered the villages wearing shoes and carrying umbrellas, and so on. The king took "stern measures" to insure conformity with *Vinaya* regulations (Htin Aung 1966: 17). It was Mindon, too, who convened the Fifth Buddhist Council (no previous council had been held since the first century, and then only in India), whose main task was to provide an authoritative recension of Pali Scripture.

To conclude, then, the relationship between state and *Saṅgha* during the monarchy was a reciprocal one. By supporting the monks, on the one hand, while on the other hand purifying the Order of dissident elements, the government minimized the potentiality of the *Saṅgha* for becoming an independent nucleus of political power. On the monastic side, by upholding the legitimacy of the government, while at the same time protecting the people from tyranny, the *Saṅgha* exercised a restraining influence on excessive abuse of power by the government.

Colonial Burma

The British conquest of Upper Burma in 1886 converted many erstwhile politically docile monks into political activists. Indeed, one might date the origin of the political monk from this period. Since the colonial government recognized no responsibility for supporting the *Saṅgha*, and refused to accord to Buddhism the status of a state religion, the traditional reciprocal relationship between church and state collapsed. On their side, recognizing no responsibility to the government, and unconstrained by a traditional hierarchical authority—for the British had abolished the office of Primate—monks who were inclined to political action were freed from the traditional impediments.

It is difficult to know the percentage of monks who participated in the pervasive insurgency which followed the British conquest, as it is difficult to know whether they were impelled by nationalistic, religious, or status motives. One admittedly biased source claims that monks fought the British because their power and prestige were threatened by British rule (Government of India 1902:33). But whatever their numbers and their motives, we do know that Buddhist monks were among the active leaders of the resistance movement. Between 1885 and 1897, in various parts of the country, a series of rebellions against British rule were led by Buddhist monks. As this same official source put it: "There were few more pertinacious and dogged opponents to the British rule in the new territory than the wearers of the yellow robe . . . but for the monks the pacification of the country would have been completed far earlier than was actually the case." *(Ibid.)* This generalization is echoed by a former governor of Burma. "Wherever there was an appearance of organized resistance, Buddhist monks were among the chiefs. No political movement of importance has been without a monk as the leading spirit." (White 1913:161)

As is the case among contemporary political monks, however, it is difficult to know how many of the monastic rebels were true monks and how many were merely disguised in the yellow robe as a cover for their political activities. No less an authority than Crosthwaite, the officer in charge of the pacification program, believed (as I do) that the latter was frequently the case. "I doubt," he wrote,

> . . . if the religious orders as a body had much influence on the course of events, or took an active part in the resistance to us. When a monk became a noted leader, it was a patriot who had been a monk and not a monk who had become a patriot. At the same time some of the most serious and deepest-laid plots were hatched in monasteries or initiated by pongyis. [Crosthwaite 1912:39]

By the beginning of this century, Burma (and the political monks) had become reconciled to British rule, and it was not until the second—but especially the third—decade of this century that anti-British activity and a strong independence movement became prominent once again. Linked with a number of different parties and organizations—each with different orientations, goals, and ideologies—monks played a leading role in the independence movement until the mid-thirties. (Cf. Smith 1965; von der Mehden 1963.) As in the earlier anti-British struggle, it is difficult to know to what extent these were true monks or merely—again—"humans in yellow robes."[5] On the basis of interviews, both in Mandalay and in the villages, I am inclined to believe that for the most part they fell into the latter category. Still, it is certainly the case that monks—or at least persons identified as such—were among the leaders of the independence struggle, especially in the 1920's, when no doubt they "set the tone" (von der Mehden 1963:128) for the movement. This is hardly surprising when we remember that Buddhism—the indignities to Buddhism perpetrated by the British, and the need for its revival—became the rallying cry of the early nationalists.

Although with the passage of time the nationalist movement came more and more to be dominated by secular politicians, monks were nevertheless conspicuous during the two most explosive events in the thirties. The Saya San rebellion—the most famous and extensive of the many led by a "Future King"—was, according to the official *Report on the Rebellion*, "spread mainly by disaffected pongyis." (1931:14) This was also true of the 1938 riots against the Indians which, though not directed explicitly against the British, was an important battle in the independence struggle. Generalizing from a mass of data, the *Final Report of the Riot Inquiry Committee* concludes:

> In our evidence we have a mournful record of these (pounjis) up and down the country promoting meetings in their kyaungs for political or subversive ends, participating in rioting and, arms in their hands, leading or accompanying crowds of hooligans, committing assaults, looting and even murder and in general breaking the civil laws of the country and the laws of their own order. [1939:277]

[5]Whether the one or the other, von der Mehden's (1963:168) estimate that 80 per cent of the monastic order "took part" in the independence movement is, in my judgment, a wild exaggeration, based on his obviously biased source: the "leaders" of the politically active monks. If "took part" means more than being "sympathetic with," I would suggest, on the basis of my interviews, that 8 per cent is much closer to the truth than 80. Most of Burma's monks lived, and live, in villages; but almost all the politically active ones were and are in the cities. Hence, even if all urban monks were as politically active as von der Mehden's estimate suggests—and I am highly dubious about this—it would still leave the majority of the monkhood in a politically inactive category.

Although numerous demonstrations and riots which were led by monks are usually described in a manner that makes them seem spontaneous and unorganized, many of them were planned and led by the Young Monks' Association *(Yahan:byou: Ahpwe.)*, a monastic political organization founded in 1938. All political organizations were inactive during the Japanese occupation, and later, during the postwar independence struggle, politically active monks were not influential, primarily because the new leader, General Aung San, insisted that Burma should become a secular state and that monks confine their activities to religion. But after a rather long period in eclipse, the Young Monks' Association again acquired influence following Independence. We shall return to this organization below.

Church and State in Contemporary Burma

Viewing himself, in traditional Burmese terms, as the protector of the faith and the purifier of the Buddhist religion, U Nu, first prime minister of independent Burma and a very devout Buddhist, embarked on a large-scale program to promote and strengthen the Buddhist religion. (Because of his piety Burmese villagers, who consistently gave him landslide victories, believed that U Nu was, or aspired to become, a future Buddha.) In addition to calling the Sixth Buddhist Council in 1954, U Nu and his government sponsored the restoration and construction of pagodas, the translation of Buddhist texts, and the creation of the Ecclesiastical Courts and of Pali universities, not to mention such devotional acts as the freeing of animals on Buddhist holydays and so on. In addition to these programs, the government formed the Buddha *Sāsana* Council, which (headed by the Chief Justice of the Supreme Court and including other distinguished citizens) was devoted to the promotion of Buddhism in all its aspects.

But a Buddhist ruler must rule over a Buddhist domain, and to cap all these programs and activities on behalf of Buddhism, U Nu (his party enjoying a tremendous parliamentary majority) in 1962 pushed through a constitutional amendment establishing Buddhism as the state religion. This was greeted with enthusiastic, though not unanimous, acclaim by the *Saṅgha*—many of whom were instrumental in persuading the prime minister to take this action—but it was opposed with equal vigor by the representatives of the minority religions. To reassure these groups, U Nu moved the adoption of still another amendment, guaranteeing complete freedom of religion to non-Buddhists. This infuriated many members of the *Saṅgha*, and various of the monastic political organizations (see below) organized both peaceful and violent demonstrations in opposition to it. Indeed, the bitterness and violence engendered by both amendments contributed to the breakdown in law and order which marked the last months of U Nu's regime, thereby providing additional provocation for the 1962 military coup.[6]

But in his concern for Buddhism, U Nu was interested not only in strengthening its hold on the people; he and his government were equally concerned to purify the Order, and especially to place some checks on the power of the political monks.[7] Indeed, this was evident as early as the constitutional convention when, worried about the potential political role of the *Saṅgha*, the makers of the constitution prohibited the monks from voting for, or holding, office. Although the government did not succeed in persuading them to agree to a monastic census and registration—a measure which would have helped in weeding out fraudulent monks from the Order—it did succeed in stimulating the formation of two monastic organizations which, it was hoped, would cooperate in the planning of the Sixth Buddhist Council and also serve as a foil to the Young Monks' Association. These were the Association of Presiding Abbots *(Caung:taik Hsaya-do Ahpwe.),* and the Younger Monks' Association *(Yahan:nge Ahpwe.).*

These three organizations were active to some degree (until the 1962 coup) in attempting to influence legislation—the Ecclesiastical Courts act, the compulsory teaching of Buddhism, the state religion act, and so on—as well as parliamentary elections. Indeed, many observers of the Burmese political scene attributed U Nu's remarkable success at the polls not only to his charisma, his political shrewdness, and his Buddhist piety, but to the active support of one or another of these monastic organizations.

The latter, it should be noted, did not always confine their methods to peaceful persuasion. At least two of them have used, or threatened to use, violence against business firms which had allegedly insulted their members, against politicians who disagreed with them, against members of minority groups and religions who attempted to exercise their constitutional rights of free worship, and so on. Violence and threats of violence were especially prominent during the debate over the state religion bill, when monks went so far as to overturn automobiles of M.P.'s and to burn and seize mosques.[8]

[6]It must be added that U Nu's religious activities were not confined to Buddhism. He was equally active in revival of the government-sponsored spirit *(nat)* rituals.

[7]Mendelson (1964), who has argued the latter thesis most persuasively, believes that this was one of the prime motives in convening the Sixth Buddhist Council.

[8]Although our knowledge concerning the political role of the *Saṅgha* following the 1962 coup is meager, some information is available. Immediately after the coup I interviewed the presidents of the three monastic organizations to ascertain their attitudes to the new regime. One of them welcomed the military take-over as an economic and political necessity; a second said this was a secular matter, of no concern to monks unless the policy of the new government became inimical to Buddhism; the third said the monks could not pass judgment until the new government announced its policies, but that his own organization was opposed in principle to any seizure of political power by force.

As the new regime revealed its policies and methods—confiscation and nationalization of property, imprisonment of opposition leaders, abrogation of civil liberties and civil rights—individual monks, notably in Mandalay, began to speak out against the regime, although the three monastic organizations did not take any official stand. In 1965 about seventy monks were

In short, in post-Independence Burma an attempt was made by the government to restore Buddhism and the *Saṅgha* to their precolonial status, and at the same time exercise a restraining influence on the political monks. On its side, the majority of the *Saṅgha* supported the government—except in situations where it felt its own welfare, or the welfare of Buddhism, was jeopardized—but nevertheless there remained a small but significant group of political monks who continued to pose a threat to law and order. A brief description of the monastic organizations they represented may be useful. Since the Young Monks' Association *(Yahan:byou: Ahpwe.)*, or Y.M.A., was the first to be formed, and since for years it was the only one truly concerned with political action *per se*, we shall be primarily concerned with it.

The Y.M.A., I have already noted, was formed in 1938 to assist in the struggle for national liberation. Prior to Independence, its membership was 32,000, but by 1962 it had dropped to 12,000. This compares with the 20,000-member Presiding Abbots Association and the 3,000-member Younger Monks' Association. Officially, at least,[9] the Y.M.A. is concerned with politics only to the extent that political action relates to Buddhism. Thus, its platform consists of three main planks: to further the Buddhist church *(sāsana)* by stimulating faith in the Buddha and His teaching; to oppose those forces that represent a threat to Buddhism (this of course is an umbrella which could cover almost anything, from Communism to movies); to improve the status and quality of the monkhood, especially through curricular and instructional reforms. As to the last plank, it was the Y.M.A. that first proposed creation of the Ecclesiastical Courts and of Pali "universities."

Of course, the original aim of the Y.M.A. was political independence from Britain, and the independence struggle brought these young monks into contact with Communists and Communist ideas (since, in the words of its president, "many of the young people in the independence movement were Communists"). This contact led them to become deeply anti-Communist, and indeed much of the Y.M.A.'s activity, continuing into the post-Independence period, was especially devoted to combatting Marxism and Communism. After independence, and continuing into the middle fifties, its anti-Communist work was subsidized by grants from the Asia Foundation, which, according to Y.M.A. leaders, supplied them with funds for a printing press, a bookstore, the distribution of anti-Communist tracts, and so on.

imprisoned for antigovernment activities, and since then, so far as we know, there has been no overt monastic opposition to the government. Beneath the surface, however, monastic opposition to the regime exists, including assistance to some of the rebel organizations which are attempting to overthrow it.

[9]All information concerning these monastic organizations was obtained through interviews with their presidents.

In addition to its anti-Communist work, the Y.M.A. has been especially active in establishing Buddhism as the state religion, creating state schools in village monasteries, providing compulsory Buddhist instruction in colleges and universities, and creating ecclesiastical courts. At the same time, it has fought the granting of equal privileges for other religious groups, because "Burma is a Buddhist country."

In attempting to achieve their goals they have used persuasion (from the ward level to the cabinet and the prime minister) and violence. So far as the latter is concerned, they have (together with other monks) looted, burned, and pillaged; they have obstructed traffic, overturned cars, and seized buildings; they have physically beaten their enemies, and (so the latter charge) threatened others with murder.

At one time the leaders of the Y.M.A. exerted a powerful influence at the highest levels of government. They had access, so they claim, to the nation's leaders, demanded hearings from cabinet officers, and met frequently with the prime minister. Their opinions were solicited and often adopted by the government. As monks, they were treated with the deference accorded other members of the Order. They, on the other hand, frequently treated government officials, including cabinet ministers, discourteously. The prime minister became so angry at the behavior of one of their leaders that (so the latter reported) he exclaimed: "I would rather look at the faeces of a dog than at the face of U——." U——, in turn, said he would never again see the prime minister. When the latter made attempts through an emissary to see him, the monk retorted: "I will continue to fight against him in my next ten existences."

By the middle fifties the relationship between U Nu's government and the Y.M.A. had deteriorated, not only because of the personal feud between the prime minister and some of their leaders, but because of important ideological differences. While U Nu deeply believed in democracy and the principle of equal rights for all groups and religions, the Y.M.A. insisted that Buddhism be given preferential treatment in all matters—that Buddhism, but no other religion, be taught in the schools; that a Buddhist chapel, but none other, be constructed at the university at government expense; and so on. When U Nu refused to comply with these demands they began to attack him and abuse his ministers. At the same time, the Y.M.A. had entered into a free-wheeling relationship with the Asia Foundation which the government would not tolerate. The Asia Foundation, according to a Y.M.A. leader, had provided them with funds and programs which were not open to government supervision and which were at times in contravention of government policy. When U Nu ordered the Asia Foundation to clear its programs through him, the Y.M.A. became his "sworn enemy." From that time, it became an active supporter of the anti-Nu, socialist faction in the government party, actively campaigning on its behalf in the last (1960) parliamentary election.

Hoping to counteract the influence of the Young Monks' Association, influential Buddhists in the government encouraged some older and influential monks to launch a new organization of young monks, the Younger Monks' Association *(Yahan:nge Ahpwe.),* or Y.A. Later, when it became evident that these young monks had ideas of their own which were often in conflict with their older sponsors, the latter launched their own organization, the Presiding Abbots' Association *(Caung:taik Hsaya-do Ahpwe).* After obtaining its autonomy, the Y.A. adopted a platform of its own which called for the establishment of Buddhism as the state religion, the cessation of insurgency, the achievement of unity in the country, and an end to inflation (*sic!*).

Although anti-Communist (but not, like the Young Monks' Association, anti-Russian or anti-Chinese), and although, like the older group, opposed to equal rights for non-Buddhist religions, the Y.A. is the more progressive organization. Of the three monastic movements, it alone seems genuinely concerned with social reform, economic development, a higher standard of living for the poor, and the advance of democracy. Of the three, its leadership too is the most interesting; they have given much thought to the role of the *Saṅgha* in modern society, they seem to be the most politically sophisticated and knowledgeable about the outside world, and they are highly intelligent. Their leadership, like their membership, is the youngest among the three groups.

Like the Y.M.A., the Y.A. has not hesitated to use violence and threats of violence to achieve their ends. This was especially evident in its opposition to the Fourth Amendment which guaranteed freedom of religion to all religions in Burma. In attempting to influence policy, it too (like the Y.M.A.) has forged alliances with political parties, changing them, however, according to the issues. From 1955 to 1960 it supported the pro-Communist parliamentary party, partly because it favored some rapprochement with the underground Communist insurgents and partly through favoring its economic programs. After 1960 it switched its allegiance to the government party, which was then attempting to establish Buddhism as the state religion.

Organized and supported by the government, the Presiding Abbots' Association is the organ of the monastic establishment. Politically conservative, it is primarily concerned with advancing the cause of Buddhism through government support and assistance and in defending Buddhism from its two main dangers: Communism and impious monks (including, from its point of view, most of those in the other two organizations). Although establishment in orientation and a staunch supporter of U Nu's government (which, in turn, was its staunch supporter), it broke with the government on the issue of granting equal rights to minority religions—the Fourth Amendment issue. Much less concerned than the two other groups with purely secular politics, the Presiding Abbots' Association was especially prominent in the activities of the Fifth Buddhist Council.

We have already seen that not all politically active monks are genuine members of the Order; many are using the robe to wield political power or achieve certain political goals. Few, of course, will admit to these motives —even those whose primary motive is power wrap themselves in the mantle of Buddhism. There are some exceptions, particularly among those who are really concerned with promoting social welfare and whose aim is political reform rather than personal power. Still, few are as candid as U Pandita, the most colorful monk I met in Burma.

This was a sixty-year-old man living in one of the larger monastic complexes in Mandalay. Under the British he had been convicted for making explosives and had spent six years in prison. He was imprisoned again under the independent Burmese government for counterfeiting bank notes. He needed funds for his continuing experiments with explosives, and since, "unlike researchers in other countries," he had no governmental support for his experiments, his "only alternative" was to raise his own funds through counterfeiting.

It was under British rule that, although a monk and a Buddhist, U Pandita became a revolutionary and an apostle of violence as he grew increasingly impatient with "British exploitation." At that time, he had to choose between the tactics of Marx and those of the Buddha: "If a tiger enters the village, Marx said the village must defend itself; the Buddha said the tiger should be avoided." He decided to follow Marx. Shortly after joining an organization of monks affiliated with the General Council of Buddhist Associations, he was asked to resign for publicly advocating the killing of every official in Burma if that were necessary to drive out the British. It was then that he joined the newly formed Young Monks' Association and became one of its leaders in the independence struggle, making speeches, organizing rallies, and leading demonstrations. After Independence he left the Y.M.A.—because, he claims, its leadership is corrupt—and has ever since remained a political lone wolf. He continues to make explosives, even under a Burmese government, because "all governments are evil" and the people will some day want to use them.

Although hardly consistent with the life of a monk, U Pandita has nevertheless persisted in his political activities because it "is even more important to fight the exploiters." To be sure, it might have been more honest to become a layman, but having lived in the monastery from the age of seven, he remained a monk because—he strongly implied—he had no other way of making a living. (Actually he once tried to earn his daily bread as a hawker, but was unsuccessful.)

U Pandita is not only a political, but also a religious revolutionary. He is a Buddhist skeptic, a stance he first adopted when, after studying Hinduism and Greek philosophy, he came to realize that "the Buddha was not original in His teaching." As he studied other religions he became skeptical of the truth of all religious doctrines, for he came to realize that none could be proved. "Christianity says everything depends on God; Buddhism says everything depends on karma. But neither can prove that his is the case."

U Pandita is a man of high integrity. Not believing in nirvana, he would not accept alms from pious laymen who made their offerings with the expectation of achieving it. Instead, he has been supported through the alms of a small group of "friends" who know of his activities and beliefs. Despite his skepticism concerning Buddhist doctrine, he believes he can honestly remain in the robes because he is carrying out the Buddha's admonition to continuously examine His teachings for oneself, rather than accepting them on faith. That he has not been driven from the monastery is another matter. Whatever his beliefs and political activities, he complies with "the major *Vinaya* rules; and these rules alone are the mark of the monk. So long as the monk obeys the *Vinaya* he is a monk."

Even if obedience to the *Vinaya* were not the mark of the monk, expulsion from the Order for violations of its rules would, in large measure, bring greater discipline into the Order. The almost fantastic aspect of U Pandita's story is not that he holds heretical views while wearing the robe, but that his political activities—inciting to arson and riot and the making of explosives—has led to no disciplinary action from either his monastery, his branch, or the Order. But U Pandita has less reason to be disciplined than many other monks who, though their nonmonastic behavior has been even more flagrant—they pillage Indian shops, burn mosques, beat up businessmen, overturn cars, and so on—have also been spared any punitive sanctions. That they are not punished, let alone expelled from the Order, does not mean that their behavior is condoned by their fellow monks, most of whom view them with contempt. It does mean, however, that in the absence of a church hierarchy empowered to impose sanctions or introduce expulsion procedures from above, the local monastery, as we have seen in other instances, is afraid to proceed on its own for fear of physical reprisals from monks who are often little more than thugs.

It would seem, then, that the abolition of the office of supreme Primate contributed not only to the general moral decay of the *Saṅgha,* as I have suggested, but to its inability to control the disruptive behavior of its political monks. This interpretation is supported by monastic political behavior in *Theravāda* Thailand and Ceylon. In the former country, where the office of Primate has never been abolished and the government maintains strict control over the activities of the monkhood, monastic discipline is relatively high and the phenomenon of the political monk does not exist. In the latter country, on the other hand, which has no Primate, the moral status of the *Saṅgha* and its political involvements are similar to the conditions found in Burma. It should be added, of course, that the absence of foreign rule in Thailand precluded the development of one of the important motives for the early politicization of the Burmese and Sinhalese *Saṅgha,* viz., the desire to rid the country of a non-Buddhist and (as they saw it) anti-Buddhist power.

The Political Culture of the Contemporary Burmese *Saṅgha*

Nonpolitical Monks

Although political monks are highly articulate, and although, having achieved influence and notoriety, they manage to convey the impression—thereby enhancing their power—that they represent vast numbers of monks, they are in fact a very small minority, even in the cities. In the villages, of course, they are almost nonexistent. Most monks and laymen are deeply opposed to the involvement of the *Saṅgha* in political activities. Their opposition is based on the classical Buddhist distinction between the secular and worldly *(loki)* and the sacred and otherworldly *(lokuttara).* As they view it, these are not only mutually exclusive but opposing domains. If, from this point of view, even social welfare activities are excluded from the purview of the *Saṅgha* (because, no matter how noble their goals, they fall within the worldly realm), how much more, then, is this true of political activity?

Without a single exception, the above sentiment was expressed by all the village monks in my sample. They all said, unequivocally, that they themselves would under no circumstances engage in political activity, and were outspoken in their criticism of monks who do. One man, perhaps somewhat more extreme than the others, went so far as to claim that monasticism demands *absolute* indifference to politics. "Whatever the regime or its policies, the monk," he said, "should neither support nor oppose the government. Even if the Communists should seize power, the monks should remain politically aloof. Let them kill us if they want to, but it is forbidden for us to interfere."

Most monks in the sample believe that the involvement of monks in the Burmese independence movement was wrong. Typical of their view is the comment of a distinguished abbot in a rather large village. Monks who participated in the independence struggle, he said, "were not true monks. Protesting, picketing, fighting, and killing—this is not monks' work, regardless of its purpose." Nor were those who supported the movement, even though they did not participate in it, any better in his view. "The sin of killing applies not only to the killer, but it applies as well to those who agree with, encourage, or praise, the act of killing."

Another monk, a simple village monk, criticized those of his fellows who participated in the independence movement on the grounds that "from a Buddhist point of view, independence is useless." Appealing to Scripture, he said that when Māra (the Evil One) asked the Buddha to rule over a certain city, the Buddha refused on the grounds that it would only increase his passions and mental defilements *(kilesa)*. Hence, he concluded, "Buddhism is totally indifferent to such issues as independence and nationalism."

It would be wrong to attribute these otherworldly attitudes to the bucolic quality of rural life. Similar attitudes were expressed by urban monks, the great majority of whom were opposed to any political involvements. Thus, when I queried an abbot in Mandalay about the political activities of the monastic organizations, his first response was: "I thought you were interested in nirvana; those organizations have nothing to do with attaining nirvana." Then, quoting a Burmese proverb, he exclaimed: "A horse who does a dog's work is fated to die." These organizations, he contended, are bad not only because their interests are worldly, but also because they create disunity in the monkhood and quarrels among laymen. "People should not become monks in order to engage in quarrels." Monastic political organizations are absolute obstacles to the attainment of nirvana.

> It is like a log floating on a river—if there are no obstacles, it will eventually float to the ocean. These monks will have a hard time getting to the ocean [nirvana] because their political organizations are an obstacle. In fact, not only will they not get to the ocean for a very long time, but it is even more likely that they will become waterlogged and sink to the bottom of the river. Instead of getting to the ocean, they will end up in hell.

Another Mandalay monk, a very learned abbot, was equally uncompromising about political monks. When I attempted to justify their behavior by quoting one of them to the effect that the monk has three duties: to help himself, his family or nation, and mankind—politics being one of the ways in which the monk helps his family and mankind—the abbot dismissed this justification as "a completely false reading of the teachings of the Buddha." It is true, he said, that a monk, like the Buddha, should try to help his family and mankind, as well as himself; like the Buddha, however, he must help them to attain nirvana, not some worldly goal. The Buddha taught only three things, and the monk, too, should only be concerned with these three:

> to help the ignorant to know the Law, so that they can move from a worldly to an otherworldly plane; to help worldlings to escape from the Wheel of Rebirth; to attain Buddhahood oneself. How are these related to politics? No! Monks who engage in politics do so for fame, for power, and for privileges. They are not Sons of the Buddha.[10]

[10]These sentiments, as well as those to which they are a reaction, were officially represented to the Governor's Legislative Council when, in 1946, it sought the opinions of the monks concerning their own enfranchisement. The Young Monks' Association argued that if the people wished to give the vote to the monks, it should not be refused, for monks were concerned with "service to humanity." The older monks, on the other hand, argued that

> priests should be aloof and isolated from mundane matters; that politics bred anger and ambition and the emotions from which priests should strive to keep free; that, therefore,

These comments, perhaps, convey some of the flavor, both intellectual and emotional, of the attitudes of the great majority of the monks toward political involvements. Still, since there *are* monastic political organizations and political monks, these can hardly be said to represent the views of all monks. Although they are a minority, it is important to comprehend the outlook of the political monks, not only because they have been influential beyond their numbers, but in order to understand how, with their supposedly otherworldly ideals, they justify their very worldly behavior.

Political Monks

Actually there are two types of political monks, each offering a different rationale for monastic political action. One type, represented by the Young Monks' Association, believes that monks should attempt to influence the political process only when Buddhism itself is at stake. Hence they should oppose Communism, work for the establishment of Buddhism as the state religion, and so on. The other type, represented by the Younger Monks' Association, believes that they should attempt to influence the political process in all matters dealing with human welfare. The arguments adduced for each position are rendered below in a paraphrase of its proponents' words.

According to the first view, it was not necessary for monks in precolonial Burma to become politically involved, for governments were pious and fostered Buddhism, and laymen (who were also pious) would rally to the defense of Buddhism if it came under attack. Today, however, governments are not pious, and laymen are busy making money. Hence, since there is no one else to look after Buddhism, the monks must take on this responsibility. To be sure, since this leaves them with less time for study and meditation, they are necessarily deferring their attainment of nirvana. But they should give no thought to this. "It is more important to ensure the existence of Buddhism."

Those who believe that monks should engage in political action even for purely secular ends adopt a stronger argument. Although admittedly study and meditation are the only means to attain nirvana, this is not the only legitimate monastic aim. Monks are supposed to model themselves after the Buddha, and the Buddha pursued not one but several goals. He worked not only for his own welfare (by attempting to gain nirvana), but also for the welfare of the "universe" (mankind) and of his "relatives" (the nation). The Buddha never turned his back on those in distress, and his concern for the welfare of His relatives is well known. When some of them became involved in a dispute over the rights to a certain river, the Buddha darkened the day so that He might preach to them uninterruptedly until He reconciled their

---

they should not have the vote in parliamentary and other elections. [Maung Maung 1959:122]

differences. Like the Buddha, then, monks should not work only for their own welfare, but should emulate Him by laboring for the good of the universe and their relatives. Those who are only concerned with their own salvation, devoting themselves to study and meditation exclusively, are really not following the Buddha.

The example of the Buddha demonstrates, according to this view, that it is possible to attain nirvana even while concerned with worldly matters (i.e., the welfare of others). And the reason this is so is that the attainment of nirvana depends on one's karmic qualifications. Possessing the proper qualifications, one can attain nirvana after even one meditational session; without the qualifications, nirvana is unobtainable regardless of how long and often one meditates.

Still, even if political activity meant the deferment of nirvana, the monk should be willing to make this sacrifice in order to benefit his relatives and the universe. Those only concerned with nirvana are like businessmen who, indifferent to others, are only intent on becoming rich themselves. Politically concerned monks wish to help others as well as themselves, even if they have to delay attainment of their final goal.

To be sure, a concern for the welfare of others indicates that one is still implicated in the world *(lo:ki nei)*, in suffering and in attachment. Those who are politically involved admit that they have not yet attained that inner state in which suffering and attachment are transcended *(lo:kouktara hei)*. But, they argue, if those monks who are opposed to political action on the grounds that the monk is one who has achieved, or aspires to achieve, detachment, why don't they then abandon the world and repair with their begging bowls to the forest? As long as they remain in human society, they must recognize that they have not transcended their attachment to the world. Hence it is their duty, as Buddhists, to work for the welfare of others as well as themselves.

Monks, they continue, are especially qualified to work for the collective welfare because, living by the monastic Rule and much less subject to anger, delusion, and greed than laymen and lay politicians, they are able to act without consideration for their own advantage or power. Since the monk cannot even become a village headman, it is obvious that he can only be working for the benefit of others rather than for himself. This being so, it is especially important for monks to involve themselves in worldly affairs, and influence others to stop their evil ways. Toward this end, and so long as he is not in violation of the *Vinaya*, the monk may justifiably engage in political action.

CHAPTER 17

The Status of the Monkhood in Burmese Society

Veneration of the Monkhood

The Order of monks is (together with the Buddha and His Teaching) one of the Three Gems through which salvation is sought. In their daily devotions, all Buddhists "take refuge" in the Buddha, in the *Dhamma*, and in the *Saṅgha*. As one of the Three Gems, the Order no less than the Buddha is characterized by extraordinary Virtues *(guṇas)*. The Order is

> Well practiced . . . practiced in integrity, in intellectual methods, in right action . . . [it is] worthy of offerings, oblations, gifts, salutations, the world's peerless field for merit. [*Kindred Sayings*, Vol. 1:282]

The normative importance of the Order in Buddhist doctrine is paralleled by its importance in the Burmese mind. There is probably no other clergy in the world which receives as much honor and respect as are offered the Buddhist monks of Burma.[1] This respect, which amounts to veneration, is expressed in numerous ways. Let us consider only some of them.

The Burmese term for monk, *hpoung:ji:*, means literally "the great glory." As "Sons of the Buddha" monks are addressed in the same terms

[1]In general, monks are highly respected in any Theravadist society. This is not the case, however, in all Mahayanist societies. In traditional China, for example, Buddhist monks enjoyed a "generally low social status." (Yang 1967:333). Recruitment to the monastery ". . . represented no improvement of social status for the poor and it meant class degradation for members of the middle and upper classes." *(Ibid.)* In the early years of this century, a family that would frequently invite Buddhist monks to perform religious ceremonies would be "despised."

as the Buddha and the pagoda (the representation of the Buddha): *hpaya:* (sacred, holy) or *shin-hpaya:* (sacred Lord). *Hpaya:* clearly connotes a status or category of being—a sacred supernatural or superhuman being—which sets off any of its incumbents from the category of *lu*, or human being. Thus one hears such expressions as, "When [a certain monk] was a human being, . . . but now that he is a monk. . . ." or "When he [a certain layman] was a monk, . . . but now that he is a human being. . . ."

Like "God" and "man," *hpaya:* and *lu* are not merely different terms for designating different objects on a continuum; they are rather reciprocal terms, designating categorically different objects. If the latter designates the secular or profane, the former designates the sacred; if the latter designates the natural, the former designates the extraordinary; and so on. It is hard to suggest the precise meaning of *hpaya:*; the point that is relevant for our present purposes is that, whatever its meaning, it—and therefore the monk—is something radically other than *lu*, or an ordinary human being. This difference is reflected in numerous ways in the layman's interaction with a monk.

In conversing with a monk, the layman refers to himself as *dabe.do*, your royal disciple (*do* is a royal honorific). The monk, in addressing the layman, refers to himself as *hpoung:ji:ga.* (*ga* being the nominative), or as *coukka.* The latter term, a first-person pronoun which emphasizes the inferior status of the other person, is used by parents, for example, in relation to their small children or by masters to slaves.

The reverence afforded monks is symbolized not only in their honorific titles of address and reference, but in the special respect language used in talking to or about them. Thus a layman eats rice *(htamin: sa:de)*, but a monk "gives glory to the alms food" *(hsun: hpoung:pei:de)*. Again, the layman sleeps *(eikde)*, but the monk curls in repose *(kyeing:de)*. More important, the layman dies *(thei-de)*, but the monk "makes his return" *(pyan-do mu-de)* to some state of blessedness or auspiciousness in one of the nonmaterial realms. (Similarly, the king "ascends to the abode of the *deva*"—*nat ywa san-de*—while the Buddha "ascends to His final nirvana"—*pari.neikban san-de.)* In short, at death as in life, the veneration shown the monks, and the symbols by which it is expressed, are reminders of the veneration and symbols appropriate to kings and Buddhas.

Together with the Buddha, the pagoda, and the king, the monk is approached by the layman only after the latter "worships" *(shi.khou)* him, by kneeling and touching his forehead to the floor or ground three times. The king himself "worships" the monk, as do the latter's own parents. Since they are one of the Five Objects of worship, parents of course are ordinarily worshiped by their sons. In the case of a monk, however, the status hierarchy of parent and child is reversed, the child becoming superordinate to the parent. Hence the seeming anomaly of a mother kneeling before her son, a teen-age novice, while offering him alms; or a father "worshiping" his ten-year-old son who, following the initiation ceremony, has donned the yellow robe.

But anomaly is a function of context, and within the Burmese context there is nothing anomalous about this behavior. For the Burmese there are three types of *nat,* or supernatural powers, who—each for a different reason—are worthy of worship. First, there is the Buddha, the *wi.thoukdi* or pure *nat,* who is worshiped out of desire for merit. Second, there is the king—the *lo-ka. thamu.di.* or conventionally designated *nat*—who is worshiped out of fear. Third, there are the gods *(deva)*—the *u.pa. pa-ti,* or self-produced *nat*—who are worshiped for protection. Since, as the Burmese explain, monks, like the Buddha, are worshiped because of merit, they are superior not only to the king but to the gods. Indeed, the gods themselves, like kings and ordinary men, must worship the monks if they wish to acquire merit and hence improve their karma.[2] That monks are superior to the gods is expressed at times in rather exaggerated ways. Thus the Burmese proverb has it that, "if a monk observes one precept only, gods and men must worship him." Similarly, the Burmese say that although all gods and men must pay homage to the Lord Sekka (the king of the gods), He in turn must pay homage even to the lowliest novice, not to mention a fully ordained monk.

Reverence for monks is expressed in other ways, as well. No layman may stand in the presence of a monk—it is an insult for a subordinate to be higher than his superordinate—nor may he sit with his feet pointed in the latter's direction. At public gatherings the monk sits above the laymen on a platform or dais; if this is not possible, he sits on a special mat which symbolically raises him higher than the laymen. Similarly, when during the monarchy the royal chaplain was invited to the palace, the king would offer him his own position on a raised carpet. (Cf. Bigandet 1912:269.)

In addition to reverence, monks are and have always been afforded many privileges. During the monarchy, for example, sumptuary laws forbade commoners from building multiple-story dwellings or carrying umbrellas (the insignia of royalty); the monks, however, could and did do both.[3] Similarly, they were and are exempt from taxes, corvées, military service, and other forms of national service—"an immense favour," as Bigandet observes (1912:313), in a society in which "the rulers look upon their subjects as mere slaves . . . for executing the absolute orders of their capricious fancy." Their parents, similarly, were exempted from taxes.

The treatment of a dead monk is, if anything, even more exaggerated. Formerly, the celebration of a "monk's return" *(hpoung:ji: byan)*—as the

[2]At the same time the monks, being superior even to the gods, need not fear, let alone propitiate, those lesser *nat*—the nature spirits and the Thirty-seven Lords—whose cultus plays such a prominent role in Burmese religious life.

[3]The latter privilege was permitted them in Ceylon as well. (See Knox 1911:118.)

monk's funeral is called—was one of the most dramatic ceremonies in Burma. (Cf. Bigandet 1912: Vol. 2, 78-80; Sangermano 1893:122-24; Shway Yoe 1896: ch. 63.) Although much of its drama has since been removed, because certain practices have been banned, it remains even today a most impressive event. Here I can describe it only briefly.

Since the monastic funeral (especially that of a famous monk) involves heavy expenses, it cannot be performed until the necessary funds are collected, and this may take many months. Moreover, it may be even further delayed because the funeral may not take place during Buddhist Lent. But whatever the delays, it must take place during the calendar year in which the death occurred. In premodern times, the corpse was embalmed prior to its final cremation and lay in state in a temporary structure, gilded and decorated with tinsel. After embalming, the body was swathed in cloth, covered with gold leaf, and placed in a coffin hollowed out of a log. The latter, in turn, was placed in a heavily ornamented casket, sometimes covered with an elaborately designed tapestry, embossed with semiprecious stones. While lying in state the body was visited by pilgrims, who would make offerings to it much as they might make offerings to a pagoda. Periodically, classical dramas *(zat pwe:)* and orchestral music would be performed, lending a fairlike quality to the extended mourning period. Only after this extensive period of mourning was the body cremated.

Today, because the body is permitted to lie in state only until it begins to decay, this traditional procedure has been modified. The body is cremated shortly after death and prior to the long mourning period, during which funds are collected for the performance of the final rites. During this interval the charred bones are kept on display in the monastery, and all the surrounding villages are solicited for contributions—of money, food, and services—to help defray the expenses of the final rites. As in earlier times, dramatic and orchestral performances take place during the mourning period, but except in the case of very famous individuals they are usually restricted to the last two or three nights before the final rites. Typically, but not always—for, as the headman of one village put it, "today the people do as they like"—the dramatic performances are appropriate to the occasion, emphasizing the Buddhist messages of impermanence, the importance of detachment from self and wealth, and the inevitability of death.

Today, as in the past, the funeral pyre for the cremation may be as high as twenty feet, and is covered by a bamboo canopy which may be fifty or sixty feet in height. In earlier times, when the cremation and final rites were performed on the same occasion, they must have been an imposing spectacle. Thousands of people, in their holyday best, would assemble at the site, carrying seven-tiered spires *(pyathat)*—representing the seven-tiered *deva* heavens—which they would place around the pyre, and Buddhist "wishing trees" *(padei-tha bin)* which, laden with gifts, they would present as offerings to the invited monks. (Today, too, the faithful bring spires and wishing trees, but the former are brought to the cremation, as before, while the latter are not brought until the final rites, which are performed later.)

In premodern times there then followed two spectacular events which have since been banned. Prior to removing the body from its mortuary structure to the funeral pyre, there took place a frenzied tug of war between two opposing and randomly recruited teams, for possession of the huge four-wheeled cart on which the casket was transported to the pyre. Motivated by the merit which might be obtained by transporting the monk's body, each team pulled at the cart by means of ropes attached to its side. The winning team—and sometimes it would take up to three days to decide the battle—would then pull the cart to the pyre.[4] Today there is no special cart to transport the body, and no tug of war.

The second spectacular event consisted in the lighting of the pyre. Today it is set alight by torches, but formerly it was lit by rockets fired into it. Since most of the rockets were homemade, and their creators amateurs, the occasion was not only loud and frenzied but dangerous. All the older descriptions tell of at least a few people killed, and numerous others injured, by poorly guided rockets and flying debris. The monks, who had already recited the litany for the deceased, did not participate in this show of rocketry, having already returned, laden with offerings, to their monasteries.

Today the cremation and the final ceremony (known as *daranagoung:*) are held separately. On the morning of the final rites, professional mourners are hired to wail and chant over the bones of the deceased. These are placed in a cradlelike structure filled with flowers—hence known as a *pan: thahket,* a flower cradle—which is rocked to and fro, much as an infant is rocked in its cradle; and a prayer is recited expressing the hope that the monk will achieve a happy abode. This service is in the charge of monks. In the only such ritual I observed, a very modest one for an ordinary small village monk, thirty-one monks had been invited to participate.

The final rites take place in the afternoon. First, the Buddhist precepts are offered to the laymen, after which the offerings from the wishing trees are presented to the monks. The latter then chant two *paritta* (the *Mangala Sutta* and the *Mettā Sutta*). Finally, the announcement of the merit and the transfer of merit to the deceased by means of the water libation (*yeizetca.*) are performed. As usual, a public announcement is made concerning the amount of funds collected—K1,180 for the above ceremony—and refreshments are served to the participants. The ceremony ended, the bones are usually interred. In the case of very famous monks, they are—or at least used to be (Shway Yoe 1896:583)—pounded into paste, from which a Buddha image was fashioned and placed in the monastery of the deceased.

[4]Tugs of war are not infrequent ceremonial events in Burma. They are practiced in some parts of the country, for example, as a means of bringing rain. They are practiced, too, in some *nat* ceremonies, in which teams of males oppose teams of females in obtaining possession of the palanquin on which the *nat* image rides. (Cf. Spiro 1967:111-12.)

That in a small, thirty-family village as much as K1,180 should be collected for the funeral of an undistinguished monk is an example of yet another, perhaps the most important, measure of the veneration of monks, to wit, the incredible amount of wealth offered to and expended on them. The sum just cited may be more meaningful when it is noted that the average annual family income in such a village is about K1,000. So far as this measure is concerned, Crawfurd's observation is as true today as a hundred and fifty years ago. The prosperity of any section of Burma, he wrote, is to be judged "... not by the comforts or luxuries of the inhabitants, or the reputable appearance of their habitations, but by the number, magnitude, splendour, and actual conditions of its temples and monasteries." (Crawfurd: 1834:79) And though he was undoubtedly correct in pointing out that religious expenditures were the only safe ones in Burma—"insecurity of property [due to dacoity, warfare, social unrest, and confiscation] forbids that the matter should be otherwise"—there is also no doubt that monastic offerings were and are to a great extent a measure of the veneration felt for the monkhood. In this regard my own observations support, without qualification, the record of Bishop Bigandet (1912:307) made in the nineteenth century.

> The best proof of the high veneration the people entertain for the Talapoins [monks] is the truly surprising liberality with which they gladly minister to all their wants. They impose upon themselves great sacrifices, incur enormous expenses, place themselves joyfully in narrow circumstances, that they might have the means to build monasteries with the best and most substantial materials, and adorn them with all the luxury the country can afford.

Today, as in Bigandet's day, a "poor and wretched" house may be inhabited by one whose "pious liberality" has been responsible for the construction of a "lofty and roomy diaong [monastery], adorned with fine carvings." (*Ibid.*: 308) Indeed, I received my first lesson in monastic veneration when a monk who had recently moved into a new and luxurious monastery in Mandalay asked me to drive him to the home of his "mother," who had constructed the monastery at a cost of K45,000. I was astonished to find her living in a basha hut which could not have cost more than two or three hundred *kyat*.

From the Burmese point of view, their veneration of Buddhist monks follows from the latter's *hpoung:* their spiritual charisma, or as it is usually translated, their glory (hence, their title, *hpoung:ji:*, great glory). It is their *hpoung:* that accounts for the monks' prestige (*goung:*) in Burmese society, and for their high position in the Burmese stratification system. To be sure, the assessment of their position in the latter system raises some tricky analytic problems. The Burmese distinguish between two types of prestige —secular or worldly *(lo:ki goung:)* and religious or otherworldly (*lo:kouk-tara goung*:). For many Burmese, otherworldly prestige ranks higher than worldly prestige; for them monks (who have the highest otherworldly prestige) occupy the highest rank in the social stratification system. For others, however, the two types of prestige are incommensurate; they pertain to two distinctive and parallel stratification systems. For them, to compare the rank of monks and, say, military officers makes no sense; their relative rank simply cannot be measured by means of a common instrument. Typically, this latter position is held by the more sophisticated urbanites, the first by less sophisticated peasants.[5]

Nevertheless, whatever view may be adopted with respect to monastic prestige, all Burmese hold the monk in high veneration. This attitude is sufficiently pervasive to be found among children as well as adults. Thus when children (between the ages of nine and fifteen) were asked whether they would prefer to be monks or laymen, the great majority—forty-four out of sixty-five—said they would prefer to be monks. Still, even among these there were interesting differences between peasant and nonpeasant children. As Table 12 reveals, peasant children, male and female alike, overwhelmingly expressed a preference for the monastic life. Among nonpeasant children, on the other hand, the boys' preference for the monastic life was only slightly greater than their preference for the lay life, and among the girls the order was actually reversed.

TABLE 12
RELATIVE PREFERENCE AMONG CHILDREN (AGES 9-15) FOR THE MONASTIC VS. THE LAY LIFE

	Male		*Female*	
	monk	layman	monk	layman
Peasant children	20	6	8	2
Nonpeasant children	13	8	3	5
	33	14	11	7

The Burmese veneration of monks may be observed in bold relief in the case of those especially pious monks who, it is believed, have achieved special spiritual power and/or those states characteristic of the *ari.ya,* the saint destined for nirvana. The fame of such monks is nationwide, people coming to pay them homage from all parts of the country, as well as from

[5]Pye (1962:191) believes that his sample of urban-based politicians and administrators demonstrated their ambivalence toward monks because they could easily shift their ranking of monks from the top to the bottom of the prestige hierarchy and back again. This is an erroneous interpretation, in my opinion, stemming from Pye's lack of attention to the important *lo:ki-lo:kouktara* distinction. Using a *lo:ki,* or secular scale, sophisticated urban respondents would inevitably place monks at the bottom of the prestige hierarchy. The same respondents, using a *lo:kouktara,* or sacred scale, would place them at the top. Pye is correct in seeing the Burmese as ambivalent to monks, but his evidence is misplaced.

foreign countries. Perhaps the most famous of such monks is the Weibu *Hsaya:do,* abbot of the Weibu monastery. Periodically, he travels to the larger towns and cities in Burma, where for a few days or a week he holds special devotional meetings at which he delivers sermons, leads the faithful in prayer, and offers them the precepts. For the period when he is resident in the town, he himself collects his daily alms on foot. It is on these daily alms-rounds that the veneration of monks is expressed in its most dramatic, even ecstatic, form.

In Rangoon—Burma's capital and largest city—his rounds take place each day in a different section of the city. His announced itinerary draws such large crowds that—as with an American presidential cavalcade—motor traffic through that part of the city comes to a halt: streets are cordoned off by traffic police as the monk and his entourage walk through them between rows of the faithful who are lined up for one or two miles to do homage to the holy man.

Leaving his temporary residence in the early morning, he is driven to the place where he is to commence his alms-collections. Following behind is a motorcade of cars, buses, and trucks, all of which are required to hold the food and other gifts with which he is inundated. Prior to his arrival, the faithful spread mats strewn with flowers over the entire stretch of streets on which he will walk. One layman holds a white (royal) umbrella over the abbot's head while he walks; another fans him; others carry large baskets for collecting the *dāna* offered to him, for although he carries his begging bowl, it obviously could not begin to hold the tons of gifts he receives. When the baskets are filled, they are emptied into the trucks that follow the procession; as one basket-carrier moves to the truck, another takes his place beside the abbot. The alms are later distributed among the poor.

As is incumbent upon any monk, the Weibu *Hsaya:do* walks with eyes to the ground, unsmiling, looking to neither side. The thousands of laymen —and especially women—who line the streets try to make physical contact with him as he slowly walks past them. Some, for example, try to touch him. Others strew flowers on his path and, after he treads on them, retrieve them, taking them home and placing them in a vase for good luck. (Ordinarily, anything touched by feet is polluted; even to point one's feet at another person is a deadly insult.) Even more abasing, in terms of ordinary norms, is the practice of spreading their hair in front of the holy man as he walks by, so that he must walk on it in order to pass. (The head is the most sacred part of the body, and the hair the most sacred part of the head; ordinarily they are inviolable.) Others, again, attempt to touch the holy man's feet with flowers or with scarves. Some mothers place their babies on the mats so that, as he passes, he must step over them (again, ordinarily a deadly insult).[6]

[6]This blatant reversal of normal patterns of respect and dignity is demonstrated, sometimes even more dramatically, in the case of other holy monks as well. Thus the Burmese newspaper,

Here then is an outpouring of devotion and reverence, an expression of piety and magic—for, of course, the attempts to touch and be touched are efforts to acquire the holy man's mana—which can only be believed when seen. The obeisance shown in this case—reminiscent of the obeisance shown a despotic ruler by his lowly subjects—is, to be sure, extreme; it is extraordinary behavior displayed toward an extraordinary monk. Nevertheless, it is shown *only* toward an extraordinary monk—not toward an extraordinary politician, athlete, or movie star. As such, it is I believe a valid measure of the unique place which the monkhood occupies in the Burmese mind. The discrepancy between the honor accorded the ordinary layman and the ordinary monk is no less than the discrepancy between that accorded an extraordinary layman and an extraordinary monk.

I may conclude this section by recounting a Buddhist myth popular among the Burmese. Because Dewata, the Buddha's brother-in-law, insulted Him, he was reborn in hell, where he was pierced with three spears. There he was asked whether now he believed in the Buddha, and when he said he did, one spear was removed. Again, he was asked whether he believed in the Law, and when he said he did the second spear was removed. When, however, he was asked if he believed in the Order, he answered in the negative. For rejecting the Order, he continues in hell to this very day, the saints themselves being impotent to help him.

The Bases for Veneration: Expressive

Monastic Asceticism

To explain the intense, indeed extraordinary veneration which the Burmese show their monks we can do no more than add some theoretical footnotes to the explanation offered more than half a century ago by Bishop Bigandet. His is not a complete explanation—although certainly true as far as it goes—but no better one is available in our present state of knowledge.

> Two chief motives induce the sectaries of Buddha to be so liberal towards the Talapoins [monks], and to pay them so high a respect; viz., the great merits and abundant rewards they expect to derive from the plentiful alms they bestow upon them, and the profound admiration they entertain for their sacred character, austere manners, and purely religious mode of life. The first motive originates from interested views; the second has its root in that regard men naturally have for persons who distinguish themselves from others by a more absolute self-denial, a greater restraint and control of their passions, a renouncement of permitted pleasures and sensual gratifications from religious motives. [Bigandet 1912:311]

The Guardian (4/15/62) described a monk in the Shan States, alleged to be an *arahant*, whose disciples paid five *kyat* for a bottle of water in which he washed his feet!

Bigandet, then, stresses two motives for the Burmese veneration of the monkhood. One responds to what the monks *do* for the faithful; this their instrumental value, will be discussed in the next section. The other, based on the monks' expressive and symbolic value, i.e., on what they *are* and what they *mean*, I shall touch upon here.

When queried directly about their devotion to the monkhood, the Burmese most often offer a traditional explanation: monks possess very rare and special qualities. These—known as *pāramī* or perfections—are acquired as a result of huge amounts of merit accumulated over numerous previous existences. To be born an ordinary human being, with all the merit that implies, is itself one of the Five Rarities. To achieve, in addition, the "perfections" necessary for monkhood (another of the Five Rarities) requires, *a fortiori*, incalculable amounts of merit. Surely, a person who possesses these "perfections" is worthy of the greatest respect and veneration.[7]

What, then, are these perfections? They consist, as closer questioning reveals, in those qualities of mind and spirit which enable the monk to renounce the world and take on the heavy burdens of the monastic Rule. Thus, when our select sample was asked why monks are venerated, their answers, summarized in Table 13, referred either to the renunciation of the world and its pleasures, or to the fact that the status they occupy symbolizes this renunciation ("they wear the yellow robe"; "they are Sons of the Buddha").

TABLE 13
REASONS FOR VENERATING MONKS

REASONS	*N*
They observe the precepts/meditate	8
They wear the yellow robe	5
They are Sons of the Buddha/*arahant*	4
They have renounced sex	2
Because of their *guṇa* (Virtues)	1
	20

To renounce the world for an ascetic life is, for the average Burman, an incredibly difficult thing to do. Many men, referring to the incalculable advantages, so far as one's future rebirths are concerned, in donning the yellow robe, say that this is their great desire; and yet, they say, it is

[7]Technically, *pārami* refer to the perfections—of which there are ten—necessary for becoming a Buddha. Colloquially, however, this term is used in Burma to designate the karma required to be or achieve almost anything. When a layman asserts that he does not have the necessary *pārami* to become a monk, he means that he lacks the proper karma. With respect to the monkhood the colloquial use of the term is not entirely misconceived, since monks require some, at least, of the *pārami* requisite for Buddhahood.

impossible for them to fulfill it, for they do not possess the qualifications for this act of renunciation. "I could not be a monk for even seven days," said one pious villager. How, he asked—and in this echoed the sentiments of all the others—could he "give up my attachment to my wife, my children, my worldly pleasure?"

Again, many who now talk about becoming monks were once before on the verge of entering the Order, when at the last moment they withdrew. They describe the experience as if some magical barrier or impediment had stood in their way. When analyzed, this barrier seems typically to have consisted of their own desires and lusts, which they knew would be frustrated by the monastic life.

For these men, then, and for the Burmese in general, the fact that the monks—Burmans like themselves—can withstand the frustrations which they themselves could not face is for them both a continuous source of wonderment and an achievement worthy of the highest reverence. It is because they themselves are unable to make the sacrifices demanded by the monastic life that the Burmese venerate so highly those few who can and do make them. And for the Burmese these sacrifices are great indeed. They are a people of strong passions, whose uncontrolled expression (by their own admission) is kept in check primarily by their fear of the bad karma—and especially consequent rebirth in hell—attendant upon such expression. To control their passions is difficult enough; to frustrate them completely is to suffer beyond any normally acceptable threshhold.

This is especially true for sexual privations, which almost uniformly Burmese laymen take to be the most frustrating of all, and therefore the most important single obstacle to monastic recruitment (see chapter 14). For the Burmese, sex is a constant and ubiquitous temptation, so much so that to be alone with a woman is presumptive evidence for sexual activity. As one informant put it in discussing the relative importance of the Five Precepts, adultery is the most important precept because it is the only one he really desires to violate. "I must restrain myself because I always have the desire to violate it." Or, as another, a knowledgeable and sensitive villager, put it: "When men say that they do not have the proper qualifications for the monkhood, they almost always mean that they cannot give up sex." If chastity were not required of monks, almost everyone, he claimed (with perhaps some exaggeration) would join the Order, for "it would be easy to be a monk."

It is the willingness of the monks to accept the suffering entailed by physical, and especially sexual, frustration, and thereby give up what other Burmans deem so important, that is perhaps the single most significant basis for their veneration.[8] As Hall rather dramatically but still accurately has put it, the monastic life, the Burman's ideal, is

[8]One of the important sources of the prestige of the former Prime Minister, U Nu, was his public renunciation of sex. Although he continued to maintain a home with his wife, he announced that he had taken a permanent vow of celibacy.

> a very difficult ideal. The Burman is very fond of life, very full of life, delighting in the joy of existence, brimming over with vitality, with humour, with merriment . . . . To them [the Burmese] of all people the restraints of a monk's life must be terrible and hard to maintain. And because it is so, because they all know how hard it is to do right, and because the monks do right, they honour them, and they know they deserve honour. [Hall 1903:132-33]

The Burmese appreciation for the monk's achievement in overcoming the temptations of the flesh is frequently based, it should be noted, on personal experience. Since almost every adult male has sometime in his life lived in a monastery, either as a novice or as a monk, he knows from his own experience how difficult it is to subdue the demands of the flesh: after all, he himself was unable to do so. Thus, when asked why, given their wish to be monks, they left the monastery after brief apprenticeships, the majority of our select sample said they were unable to sustain the privations entailed by monasticism. Their responses (summarized in Table 14) were differently expressed—they did not have the *pāramī*, or they could not give up sex—but in almost all cases they voiced the same sentiment; the monastic life requires that the pleasures of the world be forfeit, and they did not have the strength to give them up.[9] It is precisely because the monks are able to make those sacrifices which they themselves proved to be incapable of making that they are so highly revered. As one of them put it, "it is difficult enough to observe the Five Precepts [incumbent on laymen], while they [the monks] must observe two hundred and twenty-seven."

TABLE 14

LAYMEN'S REASONS FOR LEAVING THE MONASTERY

REASONS	*N*
Sexual/sensual needs	7
Lack of desire for monastic life	5
Lack of *pārami*	4
Family responsibility	3
Boredom of monastery	1
	20

For Burmese laymen, then, monks have achieved what they would have liked to be, but could not—and cannot—become. And the greater the discrepancy between the monks' achievement—especially in the case of very holy monks—and their own lack of it, the greater their respect and

[9]Their inability to make the sacrifices necessary to become a monk—or, for that matter, their lack of interest in doing so—occasions no feeling of guilt or personal inadequacy, for it can be (and is) rationalized by the belief that they lack the requisite qualifications. This lack is not their fault; it is a result, rather, of their past karma, over which they have no present control. They can, of course, influence their future karma; and many men say that although they lack them now, they hope to accumulate sufficient merit to acquire them in a future life.

devotion to these monks. Conversely, the monk who is careless in his observance of the ascetic requirements of the Rule has lost his prestige (*goung:*) and forfeited his right to veneration. Because he is in the yellow robe he is offered formal obeisance, but is deemed unworthy of respect.

That the Burmese should revere the monk because of the latter's renunciation is, in an important sense, a measure of the great distance between nibbanic and kammatic Buddhism. For nibbanic Buddhism, monasticism is the most important avenue for release from suffering. Having demonstrated his detachment from worldly enjoyment by his act of renunciation, the monk—according to the ideology of nibbanic Buddhism—should suffer less, not more, pain than the layman. For the Burmese, however, renunciation leads, not to a reduction but to an increase in suffering; for—consistent with their ideology of kammatic Buddhism—suffering is decreased by the achievement of physical pleasure and not by detachment from it, let alone complete deprivation. If the worldling suffers, who at least to some extent satisfies his desires, how much greater is the suffering of the monk whose ascetic regime frustrates most of his? And precisely because the monk complies with this ascetic regime, despite the suffering which this putatively entails, he is venerated.

Monastic Power

If the monks' ability to withstand the temptations of the flesh and sustain the frustrations attendant upon monastic asceticism is one expressive basis for their veneration by laymen, their superhuman power, i.e., their alleged miraculous attainments, is another. Although all monks, by virtue of the power inherent in the yellow robe, are believed to have some degree of power, certain of them are thought to possess extraordinary power, and the latter especially are the objects of special respect and awe. Such monks are favorite subjects of discussion; the Burmese are eager to recount and hear recounted their miraculous powers.

Monastic power is achieved and expressed in a number of ways. Its most important source, however, is asceticism. There are, especially holy monks —such as the Weibu *Hsaya:do* discussed above—who are believed to have conquered desire *(taṇhā)*—in whom, indeed, it is not merely controlled, but has been extinguished. Technically, they are believed to be saints *(ari.-ya)* who have achieved Liberation. Interestingly, however—and consistently with the Burmese stress on magical Buddhism—these monks, venerated above all others, are revered not so much for their attainment of Liberation as for the magical powers they are believed to have acquired. It is probably correct to say that their alleged superhuman power is the sign that they have achieved Liberation. Thus, for example, one is told that the Leidi *Hsaya:do* was able to write in two minutes any document which, in the case of an ordinary person, would have required fifteen. Or, one hears of the levitation powers of the Weibu *Hsaya:do.* As he walks up and down his monastery compound while meditating, his feet, it is said, remain two or three inches above the ground. Again, this same abbot is alleged to levitate from his monastery to the top of a nearby mountain—a forty-minute hike—in a minute or two. Such feats are not only told from mouth to mouth, but many witnesses claim to have seen them with their own eyes.

Other powers, less magical but equally impressive, are attributed to other monks. For example, there are those few known as *Tipitakas* who have accomplished the incredible feat of memorizing the entire Scripture (*tipitaka*). The feat, understandably enough, is attributed to their special powers. Villagers are fond of telling the story of a young novice of Upper Burma who, born of poor parents, was a cowherd until he entered the Order. While grazing his cows, he engaged in Buddhist meditation. One day he announced to his parents that he had decided to enter the Order, and then, although he had had no previous education, it was discovered that he knew the entire Scripture by heart.

Compared to these special cases, most monks are believed to possess rather ordinary power. One hears of monks who, divining the evil intention of witches, escape from their clutches by declining to eat the poisoned food they had been offered. Or one is told of monks who have the power of discovering lost objects, or of ascertaining the identity of thieves, and so on.

Finally, all monks are believed to have the power of immunity from supernatural attack. They need not propitiate *nat,* because their power is greater than that of these malevolent spirits. Frequently this power is believed to inhere in the yellow robe rather than in the monk himself. Thus, victims of spirit possession are often advised to enter the monastery, for by donning the robe they can become immune from attack. Often, too, monastic power is believed to derive from the monks' sacred knowledge; having learned the words of the Buddha, they have acquired power.[10]

The Bases for Veneration: Instrumental

Respect for their asceticism and their power are not the only bases for Burmese veneration of the monkhood. When manifested in worshipful obeisance and in alms-giving, this veneration is not merely expressive; it is also instrumental. That is, these motions are not merely the outward signs of an attitude of reverence, but (especially the alms) are the means par excellence for acquiring merit. Thus the feeding of monks yields numerous rewards: protection from harm and misfortune, great wealth (without the necessity

[10]Mendelson, too, believes that the putative power of monks is a primary—indeed *the* primary—reason for the Burmese veneration of the *Sangha.* His analysis, however, is rather different from mine. According to him, the primary aim of the Burmese "is some kind of unfettered power, placing him above all criticism and attack, combined with the highest honour. . . ." This being so—his argument continues—the monk is revered because he is the "living symbol of that aim." (Mendelson 1960:118. See also Mendelson 1963*b* and 1965.)

for work), an abundance of fine food and utensils of silver and gold on which to eat it, honor and prestige, and many other forms of contentment and happiness. Merit acquired by sponsoring a *kahteing* or building a monastery yields the even more desirable reward of rebirth in one of the heavens and all the delights and pleasures that fill the life of the *deva.* It is little wonder, then, that from the laymen's point of view the most important function of the monk is that he exist. His mere existence provides the laymen with what Buddhism terms "a field of merit," and this is for the laymen by far the most important attribute of the Order.

Because the monk is a field of merit, no Burmese village can exist without a monastery. A village can do without electricity and tractors, without radios and dispensary—and most villages do—but it cannot do without a monk. For by accepting their alms the monk makes it possible for the villagers to acquire what they desire above all else: merit. That is why, of course, he does not express gratitude to his benefactors, who receive more benefit from the giving of alms than their object. The layman is grateful to the monk for accepting them, rather than the other way around. If a monk strongly disapproves of the behavior of a layman, his most punitive recourse—one which is almost never exercised—is to invert his bowl when passing the latter's home on his alms-round. Even to an impious monk the layman continues to offer alms, and is reluctant, if a substitute is not handy, to drive him from the village. In this instance, his benefaction is an expression of reverence not for the monk himself, but for the robe and the Order, and in that sense still a means of acquiring merit.[11]

As might be expected, this instrumental view of the monkhood is stronger in children than in adults, whose veneration is (as we have seen) expressive as well as instrumental. Children, on the other hand—the oldest child in our sample was twelve—are too young to understand the meaning of renunciation or the reverence for it; still lacking the needs and desires frustrated by monasticism, they cannot appreciate the strength required to withstand their frustration. Perhaps, too, children are less ashamed to indicate their naked instrumental motives. In any event, when asked why they worship (*shi.khou*) monks (since the abstract notion of "veneration" was too difficult for them to grasp), their answers were almost unanimous: in order to acquire merit. Thus monks are esteemed not for qualities *they*

[11]In defense of this position, the following story—alleged by the Burmese to be a *Jātaka* —was recounted by a group of informants. A king of Benares, while on tour, saw a monk sitting under a bo tree. Returning to his palace he instructed his servants to take the monk an offering of food. When they came to the tree they saw that he was in lay clothes, fishing. As they approached, he put down his rod and donned his robe. Having observed his shocking behavior —the taking of life is, of course, strictly prohibited by Buddhism—the servants returned to the palace without feeding him. When they informed the king, he said they had behaved improperly: so long as a monk is in his yellow robe, he is to be fed, however great his infidelity to the Rule. In short, these informants concluded that "one acquires merit for one's *dāna* regardless of the piety of the monk."

possess, but for the benefits to those who venerate them.

Adults, too (monks as well as laymen), stress the instrumental value of the veneration of monks. When queried directly, half of even my select sample, consisting of the most pious and knowledgeable Buddhist males in the village, said they offered alms to monks in order to acquire merit. (*All* the children, on the other hand, gave this answer.) The other adults referred to their duty as Buddhists to support the Order, or to certain deserving qualities of monks. Even some of these, however, said in response to my query that, were they to gain no merit for their offerings, they would not feed the monks regardless of their qualities. To the same question only three children answered that they would feed the monks nonetheless.

That the lavish support of monks is motivated by the donor's concern for his own merit rather than the welfare of the monks is best seen in the superfluity of monastic giving. The most dramatic example, as we shall see below, is afforded by those few cases in which monasteries are constructed for monks who, it is known, will not inhabit them. Although less dramatic, there are more frequent examples. Most monks are offered more food, more robes, indeed more of everything than they can conceivably consume. Not only are most monks given much more food on their alms rounds than they can possibly eat—and since nothing offered to a monk may be used by laymen, the superfluity is thrown out, to be eaten by dogs and birds—but very often they eat none of the food offered them on their daily rounds. Rather, ordinary monks are frequently provided with a specially prepared meal in commemoration of a birth, a death, a wedding, and so on, and famous monks are often exclusively supported by one or more wealthy laymen who provide them with their daily meal, warm and freshly cooked, in the monastery. In either case the monk has no need of—and indeed, does not eat—the food placed in his begging bowl. Nevertheless, he or his novices will make his daily rounds, not for his own benefit but for the laymen's. The latter acquire merit by their food offerings even though the monk neither needs the food nor eats it.

I must now make explicit two propositions—one theological, the other sociological—which have been implicit throughout this discussion. Theologically, it may be observed that, although there is no Savior in Buddhism, the monastic order inadvertently serves that function. Since, by accepting the alms that are offered them, monks enable laymen to acquire the merit necessary for (kammatic) salvation, the Order may indeed be viewed as a collective savior. Deprived of the merit derived from alms-giving, it would be difficult to be reborn even as a human, let alone as a *deva*. Is it any wonder, then, that monks are esteemed so highly? Or that alms are offered to them so lavishly?[12]

[12]In the light of this analysis of the instrumental value of Buddhist monks it is rather difficult to understand Ames' (1966) contention that Buddhist prestations are expressive and nonreciprocal.

The latter point leads to my sociological proposition. Despite many arguments to the contrary, monastic offerings are not merely a free outpouring of gifts without expectation of receiving something in exchange. This is not an asymmetrical system in which laymen give and the monks receive. It is, on the contrary, a perfectly symmetrical system, exemplifying the general pattern of reciprocity and exchange which, as Mauss (1967) has shown, characterizes all gifts. The layman provides the monk with all the physical requirements—and more!—necessary to pursue his salvation-oriented goal, while the monk in turn provides the layman with the spiritual requirements (merit) necessary for *his* salvation-oriented goal. At the same time, the monk acquires merit by accepting the prestations through which the layman acquires merit.

Viewing this *dāna* system as an exchange system—alms offered in exchange for merit—we can better understand the Burmese insistence on the purity of their monks; for this, too, is based on the notion of reciprocity or exchange. As they view it, the amount of merit acquired from alms-giving is proportional to the piety of the recipient. Indeed, some Burmese—dissenting from the view that alms-giving even to an impious monk is meritorious (being offered not to the man but to the office)—go so far as to say that, despite the fact that he wears the yellow robe, no merit is acquired by giving alms to an impious monk. This is a minority view, but everyone agrees that the greater the purity of the monk, i.e., the stricter his observance of the Rule, the greater the merit accruing to the donor.[13]

Hence, in addition to the symbolic reasons for the laymen's insistence on monastic asceticism, they have another, more practical reason: by offering alms to worldly monks they are squandering their resources, for they are receiving a much poorer return on their investment.[14] Thus worldly monks are very naturally both despised and hated by the Burmese.

This instrumental concern of the Burmese with monastic purity was shown very clearly when I asked them why the monks should observe the *Vinaya* regulations governing the behavior of monks. The question was intended to elicit lay opinion concerning the meaning of the Rule for the monastic life. But most of the lay respondents, even in this select sample of devout Buddhists, answered by reference to the consequences, not for the monks but for themselves. As Table 15 reveals, most of them said that monks should comply with the Rule so that they, laymen, could acquire

[13]That is why laymen are unconcerned about the monk's absorption in his own salvation and his lack of special concern for their welfare. On the contrary, the more interest he shows in otherworldly concerns, the more pious he is; and the more pious, the greater the merit accruing to those who support him.

[14]Rahula makes the identical observation for traditional Ceylon.

> If the Sangha was impure, the charity bestowed on them would bring poor results, and the donors must naturally be unhappy about it. That was one reason why the kings and the people were so anxious about the unblemished purity of the Sangha. [Rahula 1956:259]

merit (when they offered them alms). Others expressed the same notion in the form of an ultimatum: if monks did not observe the Rule, laymen would not feed them. Only three respondents in this sample of pious Buddhists answered the question—as did the monks themselves, when asked—by reference to the meaning of the Rule for the monastic life. Observance of the *Vinaya* regulations, these three pointed out, helps the monks to destroy desire, is conducive to meditation, and promotes Buddhism. (One respondent offered a cynical rationale: its true value is to enable the laymen to brag about the piety of *their* monk.)

TABLE 15
REASONS GIVEN BY LAYMEN FOR MONKS' COMPLIANCE WITH THE RULE

REASONS	*N*
To enable laymen to obtain merit	6
So that laymen will feed them	4
To destroy desire	1
To facilitate meditation	1
To promote the Buddhist religion	1
So that laymen can brag about the piety of their monk	1
	14

Here, then, we may see the active—in addition to the passive—dimension of the reciprocity intrinsic to the *dāna* system. The acquisition of merit for the offering of alms may be viewed as passive exchange when the layman expects nothing from the monk himself other than to accept his alms. But when, in addition, the layman insists upon monastic purity, the resulting reciprocity may be viewed as active exchange. The layman's alms are offered in exchange for the monk's asceticism. Alternatively, for the monk to receive alms from the layman, the latter demands in exchange that he renounce his desire for material and sensuous pleasure.[15]

Notice, however, that this type of exchange gives rise to the most ironical and paradoxical consequences. The monk establishes his worthiness to receive alms by the purity of his renunciation; but the greater his renunciation, the more worthy he is, and therefore the more alms he is given. The more otherworldly the monk, the more he is rewarded with the very worldly goods he has renounced. Hence the paradox: the most ascetic

[15]It is for this reason that I cannot agree with Mendelson when he writes that the Buddhist monk serves as ". . . a model of nonreciprocity; he is the person who, within *Vinaya* limits, always receives and never gives; a material illustration of his [the layman's] own perpetual drive to self-enhancement." [Mendelson 1965:217]

monks, who least desire any possessions, are those who receive the most impressive monasteries, the finest food, the most luxuries, including even automobiles (a rare luxury in Burma). The irony is just as poignant: the greater his rejection of worldly goods, the holier the monk is deemed to be, but the holier he is, the more lavishly he is supplied with worldly goods. Thus reverence for monastic austerity is expressed in a form which is the very antithesis of the basis for reverence; while the attainment of austere self-control is rewarded by ever-increasing temptations to worldly enjoyment. Both the paradox and the irony, needless to say, flow from the layman's desire for merit.

Of all such cases known to me, the most dramatic is that of a monk living in the Sagaing hills, a monastic enclave and pilgrimage center some twenty miles west of Mandalay. An austere monk, he has long abandoned his monastery to take up residence in a natural cave. For the great merit to be acquired from contributions to such an obviously holy monk, the faithful, over the years, have constructed three new monasteries for him adjacent to the one he abandoned. There are now four uninhabited monasteries in this monk's monastic compound, for of course he will live in none of them. Indeed, it is precisely because he will not live in them that they were built. His refusal to live in a comfortable monastery is a sign of his holy life; by giving to a monk of such holiness, the benefactor is assured of great merit.

Ambivalence and Hostility to the Monkhood

If ambivalence is characteristic of any intense social relationship, it would be rather surprising if, despite their profound reverence for the monks, there were no negative qualities in the layman's attitude to them. Ignoring the *unconscious* Oedipal feelings evoked by the relationship, I shall comment only on the *conscious* resentment which the monks arouse in laymen. I have already remarked upon their narcissism and the inconvenience this often causes (chapter 14). Urban laymen especially suffer from this egocentric quality, and it is they, therefore, who complain about it most frequently. Thus, many of them say that they try to have as little as possible to do with the monastery. This attitude holds for even the most pious Buddhists. A prominent leader of the Buddhist "revival," for example, pointed out that monks know very little about the affairs of the world. Without meaning to, therefore, they exploit laymen, "asking them to do things for them, or to give them things, without taking into consideration that they may not have the money or that they may be busy." Except when required for the performance of a ceremony or for the offering of *dāna*, "it is better," he said, "to keep one's distance from monks." This sentiment was echoed by a village headman. "The less you have to deal with them," he observed, "the better."

But even apart from personality traits, the monastic status itself evokes ambivalent feelings; and it is with their status that we are concerned here.

To persistently treat a class of human beings as semigods, to serve their every whim, to observe them living in veritable luxury and ease while you (the observer and contributor) toil in the mud under a hot sun, to be constantly informed of their exceptional virtues—all this and more is bound to engender ambivalence toward the members of this class, and in fact it does.

Thus to say, as many Burmans do, that in paying homage to the monk they are really worshiping the robe or the wisdom of the Buddha, rather than the physical monk, is one rather subtle indication of this. Less subtle is the persistent litany of criticism directed against the monks—monks are greedy, monks do not observe the *Vinaya,* monks do not understand the layman's troubles, monks are corrupt, and so on. The very exaggeration of the criticism indicates, on the one hand, that it is not entirely serious, but on the other, betrays the ambivalence underneath.

Even more important, however, than these essentially ritualistic expressions of hostility are the derogatory folk sayings which one hears in conversation and when people are queried about their attitudes to the monks. Consider the following conundrum: "What three sons *(tha:)* are to be feared?" Answer: *"caung:tha:* (students), *siṭtha:* (soldiers), and *hpaya:tha:* ("Sons of the Buddha")." Or consider the following riddle (attributed by the Burmese to the *Jātaka,* though I could not find it there).

> One is ill-treated by the other, and yet does
> not hate him. Who can it be?
> One gives orders to the other, but the other
> does not obey. Who can it be?
> One is teased by the other, but does not
> become hostile. Who can it be?
> One always gives to the other, but the other
> squanders what is given and still asks for
> more. Who can it be?

The first refers to mother and infant; the infant makes demands on the mother, who nevertheless loves him. The second refers to mother and child; she no longer controls him. The third refers to spouses, and the fourth to the layman and the monk.[16]

Consider, finally, the following quatrain.

[16]That some monks, especially in the city, deserve this criticism was underscored by my assistant from Mandalay who, after listening to a group of villagers complaining about the rapacity of certain monks, remarked

> When I was rich [before his land was nationalized] they [monks] always came to my house. I used to feed them and give them money. When I lost my land, they stopped coming to me. That is the way they are in the city. I prefer the village monks; they do not stand on their dignity.

Bodi koukkou / Nyaung tou.tou.
Lu-byou hpaya: / Ma hpyit nya:

Literally:

Under the bo and acacia tree
All Buddhas attain Enlightenment.
This tree, that tree,
The bachelor will never attain Buddhahood.

As explicated by informants, the meaning of this quatrain is something like this. To become a Buddha one must first understand the meaning of suffering; understanding it, one attempts to achieve release; in this attempt, a Buddha discovers Enlightenment. Since a bachelor does not know the responsibilities of wife and children, he does not know what worry and misery are, and has no reason to pursue Liberation. Hence the monk—at least he who has never been a husband and father—has less chance of attaining Buddhahood than the layman.

These and other traditional expressions of ambivalence toward monks were quoted by laymen during spontaneous discussions of Buddhism in order to support their own critical attitudes. The Burmese—adult village males, at any rate—spend hours on end discussing points of Buddhist doctrine, and such debates frequently lead to discussions of monks and monasticism. It is in the latter especially that the full flavor of their ambivalence toward the Order can be savored. I can do no better than to quote at random from some of these conversations.

In one instance U Sa Mya was saying that Buddhism has only one aim, the extinction of the passions. I asked him why, then, he did not become a monk. To this he replied that, because of his bad karma, he is a widower and must care for his motherless children. Still, he continued, although he does not wear the robe, he is as good as any monk: *he* should be called a monk, for he has as complete knowledge of Buddhism as any member of the Order. When I observed that, unlike the monks, he does not follow the 227 rules of the *Vinaya*, he said that the Ten Precepts only are really important, and that he who observes those Ten, be he layman or monk, is truly pious. Since *he* observed them, he was as pious as any monk.

In the same discussion, Kou Ahlu said that the only difference between monks and laymen is that the former wear the yellow robe. I took exception to his argument, observing that monks, for example, are celibate whereas he is not. To this he replied with some asperity: "Sex has nothing to do with it. One can attain nirvana without overcoming the passions; all that is required is wisdom. . . . The monk is a member of the *Saṅgha* only in appearance. The *Saṅgha* is a reality. One who acquires wisdom [whether or not he is in the yellow robe] is the real *Saṅgha.*"

In another discussion U You Sou argued that a layman can attain nirvana as readily as a monk if he practices Buddhism. "A monk is merely a human being in a yellow robe." The real difference between monk and layman is that "monks have less worry than laymen; they don't have to make a living. The only thing they have to worry about is the observance of the *Vinaya.* The life of the monk is easy." In the very next breath, however, he said (in answer to my query) that he could not become a monk even for seven days, because he does not have the qualities to face all the difficulties of the monastic life. Some time later in the discussion, he attacked the monks for their impiety and argued that Buddhism would be saved not by the monks but by pious laymen (like himself).

Perhaps one more example will suffice. U Pain, in yet another talk, argued that "we"—he and his colleagues—"are as good as any monk. Anyone can obtain nirvana so long as he meditates; there is no need to be a monk in order to meditate." But he went even further, arguing that for the true Buddhist—one who aspires to nirvana—there is no need for monks at all, for although feeding of the monks gives merit, such merit *(da-na. ku.-thou)* cannot lead to nirvana. "Only meditation can lead to nirvana. As long as one meditates that is all that is required [i.e., there is no need to offer *dāna* to the monks]."[17]

Conflict Between Laymen and Monks

The veneration which the Burmese feel for the Order as a Buddhist institution is much too strong to be seriously affected either by the ambivalence that characterizes their perception of the monastic status or by the hostility they feel for the narcissistic and exploitative dimensions of monkish personality. On the other hand, Burmese Buddhists (laymen and monks alike) are not only Buddhists but also Burmese, and human. It should not be surprising, that sometimes the relationship between layman and monk exhibits serious tension and even overt conflict. It remains to describe some of the bases and forms of such conflict.

Peasant villages are almost universally known for their factionalism, and village Burma is no exception to this generalization (Spiro 1968). The relation between monks, too, is often attended, as we have seen, by factionalism and conflict. On the basis of my limited data, it seems that conflict between monks and laymen, when it occurs, is most often the by-product

[17]These sentiments are reminiscent of the teaching of a nineteenth-century Buddhist sect which is briefly described in the 1901 census. Insisting that the *Saṅgha* is "a mere excrescence," it "repudiated the obligations of the laity to supply the monk with the four necessaries. . . ." (Government of India 1902:32) Man, it taught, can attain his salvation without any need for monks. These teachings, which first arose in Upper Burma, "spread like wildfire" until they were proscribed by the Burmese Government. Later they spread to Lower (British) Burma as well.

of factionalism between villagers (the monk siding with one of the lay factions) or between monks (the villagers siding with one of the monastic factions). Then, in typical schismogenic fashion, the conflict escalates: monks accuse the opposing laymen of immorality and impiety, and laymen attempt to force the monk from the monastery by withholding alms. In some instances, monk and laymen live, as it were, in a state of armed truce for years, even decades.

Factionalism, although the most important, is not the only basis for conflict. Since the monk-layman relationship is governed by norms of reciprocity, conflict may ensue when reciprocity breaks down. In one village close to Yeigyi, the narcissism of the monk exceeded the implicit normative bounds of the permissible. He was very demanding toward the villagers, and when his demands were not met would become excessively insulting. The villagers retaliated with the only, and most extreme, means available to them: they refused to offer him alms food. Although he succeeded in obtaining a monastery in another village, his personality did not change. He insisted that the villagers come to the monastery for meditation, despite the fact that it is a rare villager who meditates. When they persisted in their refusal, he took it as a personal insult and in pique abandoned the village.

This monk's experience in the first village illustrates the club which a village holds over a monk, should he exceed the limits of reciprocity. Just as a monk can punish the laymen by refusing to accept their alms food, so they can punish him by withholding it from him. This is never done, of course, unless the provocation is intense, and even then only if there is more than one monk in the village. If he is the sole monk there, the laymen put up with him, at least until they can obtain a substitute, in order to continue to receive merit by supporting him. But if the offending monk is not the only monk in the village, withholding of alms food is both a possibility and (for him) a source of potential anxiety. Thus in one such conflict in Yeigyi, the leader of the lay opposition persuaded ten families to withhold alms food from the monk. Concerned that the boycott might expand, this monk issued a public announcement: he would preach for seven consecutive nights in the village chapel. This was for him a dramatic gesture, for he had always remained aloof from the village—it was one of the complaints against him—rarely attending religious ceremonies and never before preaching in the chapel.

This particular monk is one of the most learned and pious in the area—this even his opponents concede. Yet, even in his case, the stereotypic picture of the serene monk, remote from the petty concerns of the mundane world, is not apt. The monk *is* sensitive to the opinions of the villagers, and *is* concerned to remain in their good graces.

It is of some interest, I think, that in the cases of conflict I knew best—those that occurred in Yeigyi—the monks not only openly discussed the disagreement with me, but had no hesitation in making serious, even criminal charges against their lay opponents. The laymen, on the other hand, not only refused to discuss the conflict but denied that one existed. In order to get their side of the story it was necessary to interview laymen who were not party to the conflict. I suspect that their notions of propriety concerning monastic respect would not permit them to discuss their quarrel with a monk, for they certainly had no compunctions about discussing their feuds with laymen. To take but one example, Kou Ahlu, leader of the opposition to the village monk, U Thuta, and instigator of the boycott against him, refused even to visit U Thuta when the latter was ill. Yet when I asked him why he was opposed to this monk, Kou Ahlu denied the existence of any conflict between them; indeed, he said, he was on the best of terms with U Thuta. He did not visit U Thuta when he was ill, and did not attend his series of sermons because, he claimed, he did not wish to show partiality: there were three monasteries in the village, and he wished to treat all monks with equal consideration. Similarly, the headman too, who was also in opposition to U Thuta, said he knew of no conflict between the monk and the villagers. There is no ill will toward U Thuta, he insisted; on the contrary, he is a respected monk.

U Thuta's willingness to criticize his lay opponents is in sharp contrast, therefore, to their refusal to criticize him. They never came to his monastery, he said, because they were afraid of his superior knowledge. They talked about impartiality, but they were partial. They talked about Buddhist morality, but they slaughtered cattle and killed fish. Only if they could make a profit would they work for a monastery or for the promotion of Buddhism. They swindled money from everybody; they became friendly with others until they got what they wanted, and then turned against them. In addition, he accused them of a number of crimes, including stealing merchandise from a Mandalay merchant and demanding bribes from village landowners in order to save their lands from nationalization. The real reason they hated him, he claimed, is that he reprimanded them for all these immoralities. This claim, however, I later discovered was only partially true. We can redress the balance and at the same time provide an example of a lay-monk controversy by pursuing this one case.

It turned out that two groups of laymen were in conflict with U Thuta. In one case, the difficulty had a long history, going back at least ten years to the funeral of U Thuta's predecessor—the same funeral that led to the conflict between U Thuta and his monastic rival, discussed above (chapter 15). The four men who were in charge of arrangements, and who now comprise the core of opposition to U Thuta, complained that he did not have the courtesy to take part in the funeral service. To this U Thuta replied that he was not formally invited to the ceremony, and it is against the *Vinaya* rules for a monk to participate in a ceremony unless he is explicitly invited.

U Thuta, in turn, complained that neither his students nor his novices were invited to partake of the funeral meal, although hundreds of others had been invited and although it took place in the very courtyard of his own monastery. To exacerbate matters, when his opponents came to him to protest his ostensible boycott of the funeral, he asked them for an accounting of the money they had collected. This angered them, either (as they claimed) because he impugned their integrity, or (as he claimed) because he thereby prevented them from embezzling a great deal of money.

Viewed somewhat more objectively, this conflict seems to have derived from the laymen's resentment against a monk whose behavior only barely falls within the permissible bounds of monk-lay reciprocity noted above. U Thuta is a pious monk and certainly fulfills that dimension of the reciprocity rule; but he does not assume his full share of the ceremonial obligations that are also part of the monastic role, except for those who reside in a forest hermitage. His nonattendance at his predecessor's funeral was only the first instance of a long history of nonparticipation. U Thuta, who readily admits that he does not participate, lays it to the "immorality, impiety, and greed" that have come to characterize this village and its monks; so long as this condition continues, he says, he will continue to remain aloof. His opponents, however, accuse him of being too "proud" to attend the ceremonies, and it is this perceived arrogance that they find so offensive. It was after his refusal to attend yet another funeral (which occurred after I settled in the village) that the boycott began.

The other conflict in which U Thuta was involved has a more specific but more complicated basis. I have noted earlier the dispute which arose between U Thuta and the monk of an adjoining monastery over the boundaries of their respective grounds. At this time U Thuta was approached by a group of four laymen who offered their support in the ensuing litigation. Since the government officials who would decide the case were (so they claimed) corrupt, it would be necessary, they told him to bribe these officials in order to get a just decision, and they asked him for K200 for this purpose. U Thuta gave them the money, only to discover later that no bribe was required. Some time after, when another group of laymen came to the monastery to observe the Sabbath, U Thuta informed them of the transaction, and one of them reported his charge to the four conspirators who, shamed by the revelation, offered to return the money to him. U Thuta, so his followers maintain, refused to accept their offer on the grounds that they had attempted to cheat him; it had always been their intention, he said, to keep the money instead of using it to pay the bribe. Indeed, he claimed that, rather than helping him, they worked against him: that they forged a letter from the District Commissioner advising him to withdraw his complaints against the neighboring monastery on the grounds that it was without foundation. He further claimed that one of the four conspirators sent his wife to the monastery for an additional K50, ostensibly to advance his cause, even after these facts had become known. Actually, there is some reason to believe that she was really sent to blackmail him: if he would not give her the money, her husband would inform the authorities of the attempted bribe.

The result of all these charges and countercharges—whose accuracy was impossible to verify—was the eruption of a feud between U Thuta and these four conspirators which, even after two years, showed no sign of abating. His opponents would not invite him to officiate at Buddhist ceremonies, nor would they participate in ceremonies, such as *kahteing,* held at his monastery. The feud affected not only the religious life of the village, but spilled over into its secular life as well. U Thuta played a prominent but clandestine role in the headmanship election, trying to defeat the leader of the four conspirators; which in turn exacerbated the feud between him and his rival village monk, who supported the candidacy—etc.

V

BUDDHISM AND THE WORLD

CHAPTER 18

Buddhism and the World: A Critique

The Problem

The relation between religion and the world is a two-way street. On the one hand, man's experience in society, by forming his personality orientations, determines his susceptibility to the acceptance or rejection of traditional religious doctrines, and the creation of new ones. For this dimension of the relationship the world is the independent variable. But there is also another dimension, in which religion is the independent variable. In the preceding chapters, primarily concerned with explaining the persistence of and changes in a Great Tradition, I have treated Buddhism as the dependent variable in this relationship. Now I should like to treat it as the independent variable, i.e., to examine its possible effects on the society in which it is embedded.

Typically, it is the latter dimension of the relation between religion and the world that has generated the most interest among social scientists. Durkheim's concern for religion as an instrument of social solidarity, Malinowski's interest in it as a charter for institutional legitimacy, Weber's interest in it as a fulcrum for (or a brake on) social change—these are not only classic examples of the scientific study of religion, but continue to represent some of the abiding religious concerns of the social sciences.

But it is one thing to assert that religion has a specified influence on one or another of a society's social or cultural institutions, and another to demonstrate it; and the ratio of assertion to demonstration in this field has been distressingly high. Students of Asia have been especially prone to interpret many features of society and culture in that part of the world as a consequence of religion: caste, poverty, conservatism, pessimism, spirituality, egalitarianism—these and a host of other real or imputed characteristics of Asia have been variously attributed to the influence of Hinduism and Buddhism. Usually these attributions are less than convincing, relying as many of them do on two types of specious argument.

One type, usually advanced by scholars who assume that the religion of the texts is that of the people, takes its departure from some normative religious doctrine and proceeds to deduce from it a consequent characterological or motivational consequence which, in turn, is postulated as the cause of some observed social variable. Thus, for example, the conservatism of traditional Buddhist societies has been attributed by some scholars to the pessimism of their populations, which in turn they attribute to such Buddhist doctrines as suffering or karma.

The fallacies in this type of argument are twofold. First, it assumes without proof that the normative religion has been internalized, so that the inferred motivational disposition is in fact present in the population; second, it ignores the fact that in most Asian societies the normative religion is not the only one. As concerns the first fallacy, there is no use in deducing from the normative doctrine of suffering that the Burmese, for example, are a pessimistic people, when (it will be recalled) few Burmese agree with this doctrine. The fact is that the Burmese are not a pessimistic people at all, but if they were, the cause would have to be sought in some other ground than Buddhism. Moreover, as to the second fallacy, most Buddhists have not internalized much of nibbanic Buddhism, while they have internalized much more of that other religion—kammatic Buddhism. And since in some respects these two forms of Buddhism are drastically different, the *actual* influence of the latter form may be entirely unlike the *deduced* influence of the former.

The second type of argument for the influence of religion on Asian society and culture avoids the fallacies inherent in the first type, only to fall into another. Having determined empirically the coexistence of a religious variable (a doctrine, a belief, or a ritual) and a social variable (a political institution, an economic form, or a stratification system), it then assumes as self-evident that the former must be the cause of the latter. The fallacy here, of course, is that the putative causal relationship is only one of four possible relationships between the variables in question: the causality may be in the reverse direction, they may not be causally related at all, or they may both be related causally to a third variable. In the absence of persuasive evidence to the contrary, and/or a powerful theory from which the first relationship alone can be deduced, there are no *a priori* grounds, surely, for arguing the causal efficacy of the religious variable. (Cf. Spiro 1966, 1968).

We may now examine some concrete instances of each of these arguments.

Nibbanic Buddhism and the World

In his monumental sociology of religion, Max Weber argued that certain doctrinal characteristics of Buddhism, specifically its soteriological doctrines, are inimical to worldly action (and hence to the development of rational, bureaucratic capitalism).

> For characterization of the influence upon external behavior of the Buddhistic type of salvation the following is decisive. Assurance of one's state of grace, that is, certain knowledge of one's own salvation is not sought through proving one's self by any inner-worldly or extra-worldly action, by "work" of any kind, but, in contrast to this, it is sought in a psychic state remote from activity. This is decisive for the location of the *arhat* ideal with respect to the "world" of rational action. No bridge connects them. Nor is there any bridge to any actively conceptualized "social" conduct.
>
> Salvation is an absolutely personal performance of the self-reliant individual. No one, and particularly no social community can help him. The specific asocial character of all genuine mysticism is here carried to its maximum. [Weber 1958:213]

Now if the textual doctrines upon which Weber based his argument were indeed internalized by Buddhists, and/or if they comprised the only form of Buddhism practiced by Buddhists, his argument would be flawless. Indeed, so far as these doctrines are concerned I would go even further than Weber and argue that there is *no* point at which any of the doctrines of nibbanic Buddhism articulate with the secular social order, either to give it value, on the one hand, or to provide a fulcrum by which it can be changed, on the other.

For nibbanic Buddhism, it will be recalled, all life in any form entails suffering; surcease from suffering can never be achieved in the world of rebirth *(saṃsāra)*, regardless of what changes may be effected in the social order. Nor can any form of secular behavior bring the individual to the ultimate goal of release from suffering (nirvana). This goal can be achieved only by certain transformations of the self, effected by the practice of meditation in retreat from the world. Involvement in the world is more than religiously neutral, it is religiously perilous. Even moral behavior is an obstacle to salvation, since it leads to the accumulation of merit and hence to a continuation of karma and the cycle of rebirth. The true Buddhist (as we have seen) is one who abandons all ties and attachments and "wanders alone like the rhinoceros."

If the *Dhamma*, the basic message of nibbanic Buddhism—suffering and release from suffering—provides no point of articulation with the world, the same is true of its two other Gems—the Buddha and the Order of monks—in which daily the Buddhist takes refuge. Unlike Jahweh or Allah, who represent activity, the Buddha—obviously the most important element in this trinity—represents passivity: He is a contemplative, world-negating being. He teaches the Way to redemption, but does not redeem; and His Way is the way of worldly renunciation. Indeed, His own renunciation of the world (as the Prince Gautama) and His ultimate attainment of enlightenment and salvation (as a wandering mendicant) are the nuclear experience for Buddhism—as the Crucifixion and the Passion are the nuclear experience for Christianity, or the Exodus and Sinai for Judaism. Implicit in this nuclear experience of Buddhism are some of its basic lessons, all prejudicial to worldly endeavor: *(a)* power and wealth, pomp and luxury—these are experiences to be disdained, not goals to be desired; *(b)* the attainment of salvation requires great struggle—not with the external world but with one's own desires and impulses; *(c)* above all, one must overcome one's attachment to the world and all it contains.

If, then, sacred beings are not merely objects of devotion, but also—and, for the purposes of the present discussion, even more important—models for emulation, the imitation of the Buddha can only lead to retreat from and renunciation of the world. This symbolic value of the Buddha, as a renunciatory model, is underscored in all Buddhist festivals, for they commemorate His renunciation of the world and/or His attainment of deliverance from the realms of desire and attachment. Moreover, the single most important ceremony of Buddhism—the male initiation ceremony—is a reenactment, it will be recalled, of the Buddha's transformation from prince to mendicant. The ritual begins with the young initiate dressed in court costume and ends with his donning of the yellow robe and his entry into the monastery.

The third element of the Buddhist trinity, the Order of monks, is both an exemplification of the world-renunciatory orientation of the Buddhist message and the model for it. Although it is not absolutely necessary to become a monk in order to achieve liberation from suffering, the chances of attaining it as a layman are exceedingly remote. If, moreover, one remains a layman (because one lacks the qualifications for the monastic life), one's chief responsibility as a Buddhist—and best hope for ultimate release—is to support and provide for the monastic order. The lay community is not only devalued relative to the monastic community, but the latter, a model for worldly renunciation, provides no model for the organization of lay society. In principle at least each monk—or at any rate each monastery—is an autonomous entity, each man or group seeking salvation in their own way, constrained only by the Rule laid down by the Buddha. The true monk, as the Master stressed, must "wander alone like the rhinoceros," remaining "an island unto himself." The monk must not only save himself, for the Buddha cannot save anyone, but must be saved *by* himself. The monastic community cannot help in his efforts. The salvation quest in Buddhism is an individual matter.

Just as the Buddhist sacred trinity provides no articulation with the secular social order, so soteriological action in nibbanic Buddhism provides no support for action in the world. Nibbanic salvation, as we have seen, is salvation through knowledge, not through works. To be sure, morality *(sīla)* is demanded as a way station *en route* to soteriological knowledge, but it is neither a means nor a sign of salvation. Any action, moral or immoral, builds karma; and karma, whether good or bad, is inimical to salvation, leading to the perpetuation of the cycle of rebirth rather than to its extinction (nirvana).

All of which, as Weber correctly indicated, means that assurance of one's own chance of salvation cannot be found in *any* type of action; neither in work, nor in art, nor in politics, nor even in monastic action. The ultimate aim of the nibbanic Buddhist—and the only sign of his own salvation—is nonaction, or more accurately, a state of mind characterized by nonattachment, the absence of craving, and the extinction of desire. Only by emptying the self of all notions of selfhood, achieved not through worldly action but through psychic action (meditation), can certainty of salvation be attained. And the result of such psychic action is the abandonment of any desire for further worldly action. When one achieves that psychic state in which the delusion of selfhood is destroyed, all attachments to the world (arising from the notion of self) therefore extinguished, one may be certain of achieving salvation, since in effect one has then achieved it.

Although, as the above discussion reveals, there is no bridge by which nibbanic Buddhism is connected to the world, there are some few nibbanic Buddhists who *are* concerned with the world, and paradoxically enough they justify their concern by relating it to the quest for nirvana itself. Before continuing with our argument, it is necessary briefly to examine this position. Reasoning that certain social conditions are more conducive than others to attaining detachment, certain Buddhist political rulers (from Asoka to U Nu) have attempted to institute governmental policies which would create such conditions: economic welfare, social justice, impartial administration, and so on. Sarkisyanz (1965), in his discussion of Buddhism and Burmese politics, has labeled this application of nibbanic Buddhism to the world "Asokan Buddhism," after the famous Indian emperor who attempted to found his empire on a Buddhist ethos. The notion is related, of course, to the Buddhist idea of the Universal Emperor (chapter 7) who, by rolling the Wheel of the Law, creates the proper conditions for the practice of Buddhist doctrine.

Although there is no denying that Asokan Buddhism attempts to forge a bridge between Buddhism and the world, there are at least two reasons, empirical and doctrinal, why it does not refute the claim that essentially nibbanic Buddhism does not articulate with the world. Empirically, to begin with the first, the fact is that Asokan Buddhism has had little influence on Buddhist history and society. To be sure, in U Nu not only has contemporary Burma had a remarkable prime minister, but Asokan Buddhism has had a strong advocate and a relentless promoter. Thus, in moving the adoption of the parliamentary act which would make Buddhism the state religion of Burma, U Nu's first argument was in the classic Asokan mode.

> If the Government provides for the welfare of the people in such matters as education, health, and economic prosperity in the short span of life of this existence, it should provide for their welfare in the inestimably long future existences. [*The* (Rangoon) *Nation*, May 24, 1961]

U Nu, however, has not only been a rare exception in the political history of Southeast Asia, but even in his case it is impossible to know which of his political and economic policies followed from his belief that government should be concerned with the welfare of the people in their "inestimably long future existences." We know that he wished to create a welfare state so that, free from worry and insecurity, people could devote their energies to meditation. But there was little if anything in his economic and social programs which distinguished them from those of his political opponents and rivals.[1] Moreover, his own programs changed importantly over the course of his political career.

[1]It should be noted here that Buddhists (like members of other religious groups) deduce quite varied social and political policies from the same normative religious beliefs. Thus, when I inquired into the "Buddhist view" concerning sundry social issues there was much variation even in my blue-ribbon sample. For example:

Economic development. Of the fourteen respondents, eight said Buddhism approves, four said it disapproves, one said it is neutral, and one did not answer. Those who said that Buddhism disapproves argued that economic development leads to an increase in attachment to the world and to greater concern with *saṃsāra.* Nevertheless, all four said that they favored economic development despite the fact that Buddhism opposed it. This disjunction between their personal and the Buddhist point of view was defended on the usual grounds of the *loki-lokuttara* dichotomy; i.e., although, so far as religion and salvation are concerned, economic development is bad, so far as worldly happiness is concerned it is good. They would take their stand, they said, with "worldly happiness"—as indeed one would expect from kammatic Buddhists. All the village monks, incidentally, said that Buddhism is opposed to economic development. For them, the very desire itself is an expression of greed, which in turn leads to suffering, anger, rebirth as a monster, etc. Unlike the laymen, the monks were content to let the "Buddhist view" represent their personal view.

Independence from British rule. Eight said Buddhism approved, five said it was neutral, one did not answer. Of the five who said it was neutral, three personally favored it, and two disapproved. The monks were equally divided, half saying Buddhism was neutral toward the elements involved, and half saying independence would be a good thing, since only thus could Buddhism become the state religion.

War. The entire sample said that the Buddha disapproved of war, even in self-defense, because killing can never be condoned. Nevertheless, most of them admitted that if Burma were attacked, not being saints, they would fight. All the monks, interestingly, said that defense of one's country was a worldly matter and not, therefore, of concern to Buddhism. It was a matter for the government to decide.

On the other issues in my questionnaire, Buddhism, it seems, is on the side of the angels. Either unanimously, or overwhelmingly, the sample agreed that Buddhism favored good hospitals, good schools, racial equality, and democracy (over a monarchy). On the other hand, they agreed (as did the monks) that a classless society cannot be achieved, because class is determined by karma, and most laymen said that the Burmese, being Buddhists, were superior to the hill tribes in Burma.

Apart from empirical objections to the argument that, contrary to Weber and others, nibbanic Buddhism (in its Asokan guise) does in fact articulate with the world, there is an even more important theoretical objection. For Weber, it will be recalled, a religion provides a bridge to the world when —as in Calvinism—worldly action alone constitutes a means to, or a proof for, salvation. This is certainly not the case with Asokan Buddhism, which sustains neither relation to Buddhist soteriology. But even when "religion and the world" are conceived in the very broad terms in which they are conceived in this chapter, it would be impossible to defend the thesis that Asokan Buddhism is a bridge to the world. I know of no political, social, or economic action in any Buddhist society that can be systematically traced to nibbanic Buddhism, even in Asokan guise.

To conclude, then, Weber's interpretation of Buddhism as providing no bridge to the world is unqualifiedly correct—so far as *nibbanic* Buddhism is concerned. But, since, as we have seen, salvation is conceived by most Buddhists in terms of *kammatic* Buddhism, any assessment of the influence of Buddhism on the world must examine the latter—a very different kind of Buddhism—rather than the former.[2]

If Weber exemplifies the fallacies inherent in the first type of argument (p. 426) concerning the effects of Buddhism on Buddhist society, a variety of writers on Burma exemplify the fallacies inherent in the second type (*ibid.*). Cady, for example, has argued that Buddhist monasticism has been important "as a democratic leveling agency" in Burmese society, because "the sons of princes and of fishermen enjoyed the same status at the monastery, for entrance was open to all alike and all were subjected to the same discipline." (Cady 1958:61) This leap from the monastery to society is surely without theoretical justification, nor is there evidence for the empirical attribution. There have been and are dramatic status differences in Burmese society, despite the fact that the monastery was (and is) the temporary domicile of both prince and fisherman.

Ray is also impressed with the democratic effect of Buddhism on Burmese society, though he attributes it not to monasticism but to the general spirit of Buddhism. "Whoever has cared to enter into its spirit and understand the meaning [of Buddhism] knows very well that it [democracy] is one of those remarkable gifts Buddhism has given to Burma." (Ray 1946:265) It is difficult to know what Ray has in mind by Burmese "democracy" (except for a brief, post-Independence interlude, Burma has never been a democracy), and it is equally difficult to know in what respects the Buddhist message is conducive to either the creation or the maintenance of democ-

[2]Hence, whatever may have been the important obstacles to the development of capitalism in ancient India (and in contemporary Southeast Asia), nibbanic Buddhism, contrary to Weber's argument, could not have been one of them. Ironically, however, kammatic Buddhism has had many of the effects (for different reasons) which Weber attributed to nibbanic Buddhism. These will be examined below.

racy, even supposing the latter had been a characteristic feature of Burmese history. The fact is, democracy has never struck roots in any of the Buddhist societies of Southeast Asia.

Again, Bigandet (1912: Vol. 2, p. 33) attributes the high status of women in Burma and other Buddhist countries to Buddhism. "Who could think of looking upon the woman as a somewhat inferior being," he asks rhetorically, "when we see her ranking, according to her degree of spiritual attainments, among the perfect and foremost followers of Buddha?" It is true that women enjoy a high status in Burma—although it must be remarked that it is high in fact rather than principle. "Males are much nobler than females," the Burmese say; so much so that "a male dog is nobler than a female human." It would be difficult to attribute the genuinely high status of Burmese women to Buddhism, since there have been other Buddhist societies where the status of women was low. Conversely, as the Mother of God and the Queen of Heaven, the Virgin occupies a much higher place in the Catholic sacred hierarchy than any female follower of the Buddha has ever held, without this having affected the relatively low status of women in traditional Christendom.

Nash, in a more recent assessment of the role of Buddhism in Burmese society, argues that the doctrine of karma alone has had far-reaching effects on Burmese behavior and social structure. By its "placing of each single nucleus of kan [karma] at the center of its own universe, [Buddhism] permits the Burman wide swings in his reactions to the world." (Nash 1963:293) This explains, he claims, why it is that in Burma there is "no room for guilt, anxiety, remorse, or worry"; that there are no "deep involvements, outside of the family"; that deviant behavior evokes no moral censure from others; that there are no "perdurable associations"; that leadership is "personalistic and charismatic"; and that society is essentially "equalitarian." (*Ibid.*:293-94) Although agreeing that some of these attributes are true of Burmese behavior and Burmese society, I submit that there is neither evidential nor theoretical justification for arguing that they are a consequence of the belief in karma; at least I do not know of any, and Nash produces none. There are far sounder grounds for tracing these attributes—as, indeed, Piker (1968) has convincingly done for some of the same traits found in Thailand—to a constellation of perceptual and motivational sets acquired long before the concept of karma is either learned or understood, in early childhood experience. The absence of "perdurable associations," to give but one example, is more accurately related to the deep lack of trust which, as I noted in chapter 5, characterizes Burmese interpersonal relations, an attitude which is in part realistic and in part projective.

Other commentators on the Burmese scene also argue that the alleged callousness which many Burmese—and other Asian peoples—often display to human suffering derives from their belief in karma. Since suffering is attributed to karma, it is both fruitless and impious (so the argument runs) to alleviate it. Thus Sir George Scott, that superb observer of Burmese behavior, writes:

> This doctrine of kan [karma] also accounts for the equanimity and callousness with which Buddhists view human misery and the taking of human life, notwithstanding the law which forbids the killing of even the smallest insect. They recognise apathetically the working out of inexorable destiny, and watch a man drowning in the river with undisturbed tranquillity, for they are not called upon or even justified in stirring a hand to prevent it. You cannot combat manifest fate. [Shway Yoe 1896:430]

A contemporary Burmese scholar makes a similar point. Each individual

> . . . must go the destined way, and to the best of his ability build the destiny for his next existence. . . . [Hence] people who would give all their savings to a religious festival, toward the building of a pagoda, or covering the images at the temples with gold leaves, go about unmoved when unfortunate children wander in search of homes, or go waste in need of schooling. [Maung Maung 1963:81]

These arguments, like those considered above, have little to support them. If the Burmese are indifferent to certain forms of suffering, it is not because of their belief in karma, but because of a basic lack of concern for other people, a characterological disposition rather than a religiously motivated response. Chinese Taoists, for example, do not believe in karma but are as callous to human suffering as the Chinese Buddhists, who do. Indeed, to return to Burma, few Burmese themselves attribute any seeming instances of indifference to their belief in karma. When, for example, the good people of Yweisu village refrained from helping a certain woman (who had been bitten by a snake) to get to a doctor, it was not because of their belief in karma, but because she was a stranger in the village, and therefore outside the category of people for whom one has responsibility.

If karma is offered as the basis for the Buddhist's indifference to human misery, it is less likely to be a reason than a rationalization. After all, if (as Shway Yoe argues) "you cannot combat manifest fate," this should apply to one's own fate as much as to that of others; yet few Burmese remain indifferent to their own drowning. Similarly, if religious doctrine molds character rather than being used to justify it, we might ask why the Burmese have not been influenced by the behavior of the Buddha Himself, who in numerous *Jātaka* stories (which the Burmese know well) sacrificed life and limb, kith and kin, to assist those in need. The Burmese know, too, that loving-kindness *(mettā)* and compassion *(karuṇā)* are central Buddhist virtues, and that their practice is essential to the attainment of salvation. Why, then, using this Buddhist charter, don't they try to save the drowning man? In short, I would argue that there really is no good *Buddhist* reason why orphans and widows and drowning men should not compel the sympathetic assistance of the Burmese, but there may well be a good *Burmese* reason.

The above discussion reveals, among other things, that often an assumed relationship between a Buddhist doctrine and the behavior of Buddhist actors is flawed by a misunderstanding of the doctrine. Probably the best example, especially prominent in popular works on Buddhist societies, is the putative relationship between the doctrine of karma and the fatalism that allegedly characterizes many Asian populations. In almost all popular—and some scholarly—works on Buddhist Asia, it is held that, given their belief in karma, Buddhists live in a fatalistic universe, their lives being controlled and determined by a force over which they have no control. This allegation contains a half-truth at best, as Burmese Buddhism amply reveals.

Distinguishing, as the Burmese do, between present karma *(bwa: kan)*, which is the effect of past action, and future karma *(nauk-bwa: kan)*, which is created by present action, it is obvious—indeed, true by definition—that so far as the latter is concerned the actor is the master, rather than the servant, of his karma. What determines one's future fortune is not some kind of destiny or fate over which the actor has no control. It is not a Calvinistic sort of predestination, which for no apparent reason assigns some persons to everlasting salvation and others to everlasting damnation. This future karma, of course, is lawful, deterministic, causal; but the causality is the reverse of fatalism. Instead of one's karma determining one's behavior, behavior determines karma. To be sure, since future karma, according to normative Buddhism, consists not only of the merit and demerit acquired in this birth but of all the merit and demerit (for which retribution has not yet been made) acquired in all one's previous births, the proportion of total karma contributed by behavior in any one rebirth may be quite small. The Burmese, however, have managed to minimize this aspect of normative doctrine. Most of them act on the belief that action in this life can significantly, though not exclusively, affect their future karma.

What is at issue, then, so far as the fatalistic argument is concerned, is present karma and since this is the result of past action, it would seem to follow that one can do nothing to affect one's present fortune—this at least has already been determined. The conclusion, however, is erroneous on two counts. In accordance with normative Buddhism the Burmese do not believe that karma is the exclusive determinant of one's destiny. Even if it were, they hold with normative Buddhism that it can be affected and changed by present action. Let us examine these possibilities in turn.

Present action, on either of the two interpretations of karma discussed in chapter 5, produces karmic consequences which take effect not only in a future but also in one's present existence. Thus, according to the interpretation which distinguishes good and bad karma as separate causal forces, an increase in merit cannot avert retribution for demerit, but by improving one's good karma it can improve one's present fortune. As we have seen, a great deal of Burmese Buddhist practice is intended to achieve this very result, viz., to change one's karma. The interpretation of karma which fuses good and bad karma into a single causal force is even more conducive to karmic change and hence to an improvement in one's fortunes. By neutralizing bad karma through the acquisition of merit, it is possible not only to improve good karma but also to avert the misfortunes caused by bad karma. Indeed, much of popular Buddhism discussed in previous chapters (6 and 10) is both motivated by this intention and based on the assumptions that present karma can be changed, and that karmic retribution in one's present existence can be averted.

The second reason why the doctrine of karma, as applied to one's present fortune, is not fatalistic is that neither nibbanic nor kammatic Buddhism teaches that karma is the exclusive determinant of one's life-fate. To be sure, the general character of one's station—as male or female, Burmese or Indian, rich or poor, intelligent or stupid, and so on—is determined by karma; but within the broad limits permitted by this general station, one's destiny is a function not only of karma but of free choice. For according to Buddhism there are, in addition to karma, two other determinants of one's life: wisdom (Pali, *paññā*) and initiative or effort (Pali, *viriya;* Burmese, *wiriya*). A man's destiny is the product of all three working together.

That the Burmese act upon the assumption that effort and wisdom, together with karma, are codeterminants of their fate is obvious from even a cursory examination of their daily economic lives. Although rice production, for example, is certainly influenced by karma—sudden droughts, inadequate irrigation, invasion of pests, and so on—Burmese farmers realize that in the first instance their rice production depends on their own intelligence and effort. The ground must be harrowed and plowed, seedbeds sown, the tender crops transplanted, irrigation controlled, and so on. If, all things being equal, there are nevertheless important differences in yield, they are explained by differences in karma.

But it is not only in daily economic action (where it is obvious that effort and intelligence are required) that the Burmese refuse to rely on karma alone. In stressful situations, in which (if karma were believed to be the crucial determinant) one might expect them to be resigned to whatever outcome their karma had in store for them, they make every effort to influence the outcome. Perhaps one example, among scores which might have been cited, will suffice.

A young man, a relative of some residents of Yeigyi, was indicted for murder and brought to trial. In answer to my query, his relatives said that it was impossible to predict the verdict—"it all depends on his karma." At that very time, however, they were doing everything within their power to influence the verdict. They had not only hired the best lawyer they could afford, but had bribed a doctor to give medical testimony favorable to the accused, and were attempting (with much greater subtlety) to bribe the judge. When I asked why, since "it all depends on his karma," they bothered to do all these things, the senior relative said that effort and intelligence, and not merely karma, would determine the outcome. Typically, he then cited a so-called *Jātaka*—often recounted in this connection—to illustrate the importance given by Buddhism to wisdom and effort.[3]

The Embryo Buddha, in his rebirth as a fish, was hauled into a fishing boat with two other fish. One of these, using initiative but not intelligence, attempted to leap from the boat and was killed by the fisherman. The second thought, "There is nothing I can do; it all depends on my karma." He, too, ended in the fisherman's pot. The third, the Embryo Buddha, using both intelligence and initiative, and refusing to believe that karma alone would determine the outcome, saved his life. Waiting for a storm to blow, he leapt from the boat while the fisherman was busy steering his course, thus gaining his freedom and his life.

The Burmese are also fond of telling the following non-*Jātaka* story to prove that Buddhism places as much emphasis on wisdom and effort as on karma. Three princes, named Kan (karma), Nyan (intelligence), and Wiriya (effort), were traveling together when, becoming tired, they broke their journey at a certain resthouse. Hungry, but without food, they did not know what to do. The Lord Sekka, seeing their plight, dropped a cake near the resthouse. Prince Wiriya found it while he was wandering about searching for food. Eating some of it while he walked back to the resthouse, he gave what remained to Prince Nyan, who in turn ate what he wanted, leaving only a small amount for Prince Kan. When the latter bit into his tiny portion he discovered that it contained a precious gem. "Hence," the storyteller usually concludes, "all three determinants are important."[4]

Having indicated my skepticism concerning these and many similar attempts to discover links between Buddhism and the world, I do not mean to suggest that I am doubtful of the possibility of discovering any links at all. On the contrary, I believe that such links do exist and that they are important. Before examining them, however, it is necessary to clarify our use of the terms "religion" and "the world."

The Intention of the Present Analysis

Following Max Weber, who has provided us with both the expression and the paradigmatic model (cf. Weber 1930; 1946: chs. 11-13; 1963: chs. 13-16), an analysis of the influence of religion on the world is not primarily

[3]This is obviously a corruption of the *Mitacinti Jātaka* (no. 114 in the Cowell edition). Even as a corruption, however, it is so distorted that I call the Burmese version a "so-called" *Jātaka.*

[4]Although recounted to prove the coordinate influence of intelligence, effort, and karma, the above tale (as I read it) suggests that karma is the most important—after all, it was Prince Kan who found the precious gem. And in fact karma *is* taken by the Burmese as the most important of these three determinants of one's present existence. Still, it is not taken to be the exclusive determinant. As already indicated, I know few Burmese who, given the opportunity, will not use their intelligence and initiative to better their lot.

concerned with those obvious but—even when they are important—theoretically uninteresting effects of religion on social and cultural life which constitute the typical interests of religious sociology. Thus, although social control may indeed be affected by religious ethics, and although religious affiliation may importantly contribute to social solidarity, and—again—although religious ritual may promote social integration, such findings are neither very interesting nor are they theoretically illuminating. Since, however, a discussion of these and similar relationships are the stock-in-trade of religious sociology, they will also be touched upon in our discussion, lest it be (falsely) concluded that Buddhism does not have such effects.

But for Weber, it will be recalled, "religion and the world" refers to the extent to which religious conceptions of salvation, though concerned with otherworldly goals, provide a motivational basis for action in the world, such action being viewed as a means either for the attainment of salvation or for providing the desired proof that one has been saved or is destined for salvation *(certitudo salutis).* Where the quest for salvation is man's strongest motive, this otherworldly dimension of religion, he rightly argued, may provide the most powerful instigation—or obstacle—to worldly action. Conversely, where the quest for salvation leads rather to indifference to the world, if not worldly renunciation, no other link between religion and the world is likely to be of much importance. If, then, there is a relation between conceptions of salvation and worldly action, the comparative study of religion and society should be able to show that differences in the one variable change systematically with those in the other.

Although I am in full agreement with Weber's analysis—in fact, much of the following discussion will be devoted to it—I would add an additional dimension. Even when the quest for salvation leads to purely religious rather than worldly action, it may yet have important—albeit unintended—consequences for social institutions, if not for social action. These unintended consequences of Buddhism will also be included in our discussion.

Finally, although less significant than its conceptions of salvation, there is still another class of religious ideas which may have an important bearing on the world, viz., those that constitute its *Weltanschauung.* Conceptions of man and society, nature and history, time and causality—these and many other metaphysical and ontological ideas may seriously affect social behavior and institutions, as some students of culture and personality have demonstrated. (Cf. Hallowell 1955.) Hence, this dimension of Buddhism also is discussed below.

In sum, in the discussion of influence of Buddhism on the world, the Buddhist influence will focus on three variables—affiliation, soteriology, and *Weltanschauung;* and "the world" will refer to Burmese society, taken both as a set of macro-institutions (social, political, and economic) and as a collectivity or social group.

CHAPTER 19

Buddhism and Burmese Society

Buddhist *Weltanschauung* and The Burmese Social System

Introduction

We have noted many times that, although much of the *Weltanschauung* of nibbanic Buddhism is rejected by the Burmese, some of its elements are genuinely internalized. Among the latter one may include the doctrines of karma and merit and the Buddhist conception of time, especially in its relation to that of rebirth. These notions are, of course, also linked with Buddhist soteriology, which will be dealt with below. Here, however, we are interested in their conceptual, not their soteriological, status. As conceptual categories, these doctrines have important effects on the world because they predispose the Burmese to perceive the world and act within it in very special ways. In this connection, I shall explore the social consequences of karma for the Burmese perception of privilege and power, the influence of Buddhist cosmology on their moral action, and the influence of Buddhist time conceptions on their attitude toward ambition.

Karma and the Moral Authority of the Social Order

Since in all societies there is a differential distribution of the goods of this world—power, wealth, prestige, and so on—it may be expected that, in the long run, the persistence of the social order does not depend so much on the equality or inequality of their distribution so much as on the degree to which the distribution is perceived to be equitable or inequitable—i.e., whether people believe that they (and others) are, or are not, receiving their fair share of these goods. This is another way of saying that in the long run the persistence of the social order depends on the moral authority which the distributional *system* can command, or with which the inequalities in *actual distribution* are invested. It may further be expected that those who enjoy less than what they assume to be their *fair* share of these goods will constitute a potential source of either structural or positional change. If they believe the distributional system has no moral authority, they may constitute a potential source of change in the system itself (structural change). If, however, they accept the moral authority of the system but view the actual distribution of power, wealth, and so on as unfair, they may aspire to change the distribution so as to obtain a greater share of these goods for themselves (positional change).

The doctrine of karma, being Janus-faced, provides any social order with a powerful moral authority. On the one hand, it promises a better status in a future life by meritorious action performed in this life; on the other hand, it explains one's status in this life by reference to meritorious and demeritorious action performed in past lives. It is the latter, explanatory aspect of karma that renders it a salient social force. First, it establishes a moral basis for the very notion, hence the *system* differential distribution of worldly goods and values, because differences in power, wealth, prestige, and so on are viewed as the just (karma-determined) consequences of differences in merit. Second, it provides moral justification for the inequalities that obtain in any *actual distribution* of these goods and values because it represents the karmic—and therefore just—recompense for each person's merit and demerit. In short, since (according to the doctrine of karma) everyone reaps what he sows, whatever is, is just, and whatever anyone has, he deserves, in the perspective of the countless rebirths that comprise a person's total life. Not, to be sure, in the perspective of this single lifetime. From that invalid angle, any fool can see the frequent ill-fit between merit and fortune. But in the former light, even the wicked may deserve their good fortune because of merit acquired in previous rebirths, while even the righteous may deserve their bad fortune because of demerit acquired in previous lives. By the same token, for the merit and demerit acquired in their present rebirth, the wicked and the righteous alike will receive their just deserts in a future rebirth; and these differences in turn, provide the moral justification for the inequalities that characterize a future social order.

So far as the social order is concerned, the karmic message, then, is very clear. Inequalities in power, wealth, and privilege are not inequities; rather, they represent the inexorable and just working of a moral law which guarantees that (in the long run) everyone receives and will continue to receive his true deserts. As one Burmese monk put it, if complete equality—a classless society—were desirable or achievable, "then why shouldn't the scorpion share his legs with the snake? There are two-legged, four-legged, and many-legged animals. There is no equality in nature; it all depends on karma. If you want to establish a classless society, you are against karma." In a religiously constituted culture, this explanation for the differential distribution of the goods of the world provides a most powerful support, or religious authority, for the status quo.

Although this relation between karma and the social order seems straightforward, it has some paradoxical and unpredictable consequences. This being so, I should now like to explore the sometimes contradictory consequences of karmic moral authority for the Burmese political and social orders.

Political Instability. In relation to the political system, the belief in karma plays a curiously paradoxical role. Conferring legitimacy on the regime in power, and at the same time providing an incentive for the overthrow of that regime, this doctrine has played an important part in the political instability that has persistently plagued Burmese history. There is no doubt, to begin with the first point, that by guaranteeing the legitimacy of whichever ruler is in power, the belief in karma can be and has been a powerful force for political stability. The holding of political power, far from being an accident of history, is viewed as karmic retribution for merit acquired by the ruler in all his previous lives. It is this presumably which accounts for his being "of the Royal Bone," which, as Lehman (1967:115) points out, was a required qualification for any claimant to the throne. Hence, in an important sense political rebellion constitutes an attempt to abrogate the law of karma—to interfere with the moral law which is not only the foundation of human society but the keystone of Buddhist ideology. This is especially so in the case of a king,[1] who represents the culmination of an incredible storehouse of merit, a staggering concentration of good karma. It is no accident that the traditional attitude toward Buddhist monarchs was—and is—one of overwhelming reverence and awe. This does not mean, it should be emphasized, that he is liked or respected. Indeed, in Burmese tradition all rulers are evil; the ruler—together with floods, fire, thieves, and foes—being one of the traditional Five Enemies. Nevertheless, even when his rule is despotic, oppressive, or unjust, rebellion is unjustified because his status is his karmic reward for behavior not in this but in former existences. Although he will, of course, have to suffer for his present evil behavior in a future existence, he is revered and honored for the merit and attendant karma acquired from his past. Thus, for example, I was told by more than a few Burmese that the many troubles suffered by Burma in the

[1]Buddhism, incidentally, explicitly endorses a monarchical form of government, viewing it as a necessary institution. According to the *Cakkavatti-Sihanāda Suttanta* (*Dialogues of the Buddha*, Pt. III), mankind originally lived in a utopian state, without any government. As people began to develop a notion of self, however, there followed a chain of consequences—the rise of desire, followed by the origin of property, followed by the origin of theft, followed by the origin of lying—which culminated in the necessary institution of the monarchy.

post-Independence period are karmic retribution for having risen up against the British monarch.

To this karma-derived argument is added still another. Just as we say that people get the government they deserve, in a different sense many Burmese say that people get the government their karma requires. I have heard even bitter opponents of the present oppressive military regime in Burma interpret its accession to power as the fruit of karmic seeds which the Burmese people themselves had sown in the past.

But the doctrine of karma plays a dual role in this drama. For while, from a juridical point of view, it is a powerful force for the legitimation of the government in power, it may also serve as an equally powerful force for its overthrow. Unlike Hindu *dharma*, which, by prescribing compliance with one's own caste norms, militates against positional change, Buddhism in no wise adopts such a conservative stance. One's position in the social order —whether in the social, economic, or political systems—is determined not only by the karmic effect of past lives, but by the wisdom and effort one employs in the present—the limits of which, to be sure, are determined by one's past karma. Since, then, one never knows in advance what those limits are, and since moreover it is impossible to know the karma-determined trajectory of anyone's life, for karmic retribution may change more than once in the course even of a lifetime, the doctrine of karma, while proscribing structural change, does not proscribe and may even be said to encourage positional change.

In the political order positional change is frequently disruptive, for it does not merely mean that a person of low rank becomes a person of high rank (as it might in the social or economic orders), but that the low-ranking person replaces the high-ranking person. The ruled becomes a ruler only by replacing the existing ruler. This being so, positional change with respect to the distribution of power can only be achieved through the voluntary relinquishing of power or its usurpation. In the latter case the old ruler is not only replaced but is displaced by the new. To the extent, then, that it is impossible to know the karma-determined trajectory of anyone's life, the doctrine of karma can always be used by the politically ambitious as the basis for his hope, and the justification for his claim, that the ruler's karmic fortune has come to an end and that his own karmic turn has arrived. Such hopes and claims can be—and have been—powerful incentives for the usurpation of power in Buddhist societies. Ascendancy to the Burmese throne has not infrequently been achieved by usurpers acting upon this premise.

To be sure, attempts at usurpation of power must confront a powerful karmic obstacle. For, to the extent that his ambitions really represent an attempt to abrogate the karmic law, and to the extent that his efforts entail deceit and murder, the usurper must expect the inevitable karmic retributions for his flagrant violation of Buddhist precepts. For some men, of course, insensitive to these Buddhist claims, such expectations hold no fears. For those sensitive to these claims, however, one accepted interpretation of karma provides them with a way out. As we have seen, the most popular Burmese interpretation of karmic retribution holds that the consequences of demerit may be avoided by an equal or slightly greater amount of merit. And since, as the Burmese view it, the most powerful instruments of merit are the construction of monasteries, the building of pagodas, and the provisioning of monks, the apprehensive usurper, having the entire wealth of the country at his disposal, can accumulate a fantastic store of merit by these forms of *dāna.* This is one of the important reasons for the large number of royally sponsored pagodas found throughout the country, whose history has known an extraordinary incidence of usurpation of royal power.

Granting, then, that the doctrine of karma may be used by the politically ambitious as an incentive for the usurpation of power, how can the new regime, in the face of the karmic legitimacy invested in the old one, ever acquire legitimacy? The answer is found in this very same doctrine. For the same karmic logic that militates against the usurpation of power justifies the loss of it; and the same karmic logic that invested the old regime with legitimacy will confer it on the new. Specifically, a successful seizure of power must mean that the karmic fruit of the former ruler's merit has dried up and the karmic seeds of the usurper have come into fruition. To the extent that the usurper has lied, cheated, and killed in order to acquire power, he is of course a bad Buddhist, and no doubt will suffer inexorable karmic retribution in a future existence. But this in no way affects the karmic legitimacy of his rule, for his accession to power is viewed as recompense for merit acquired in a past existence. In short, just as the diplomatic recognition of a foreign government does not imply political approval of its policies, so the karmic legitimacy of the new regime is not affected by the methods it has employed in seizing power. *Sub specie karma*, nothing succeeds—it may truly be said—so well as success, and nothing fails like failure.

Unlike most scholars, then, who interpret the doctrine of karma as providing powerful support for the status quo—as being an agent of political conservatism and a force for political stability—it is my contention that, by ignoring the paradoxes inherent in the doctrine, these interpretations are only half-true. To be sure, the doctrine of karma is a profoundly conservative force in that, converting the social order into a moral order, it militates against any structural change. In this sense it is, indeed, a powerful force for systemic or structural stability. But at the same time it can be—and in the political domain has been—a powerful force for positional change and therefore of political instability.

To recapitulate, the doctrine of karma plays a uniquely paradoxical role in its relation to politics. On the one hand, by interpreting the political order as a moral order, the doctrine not only invests the political system with moral authority but confers legitimacy on the political regime. In that sense it is a force for positional, as well as structural, stability. But precisely because it confers legitimacy on the political regime, this doctrine is also a powerful force for positional change. For by the paradox inherent in its logic, it confers legitimacy on *any* political regime—not only on the regime in authority, but on the regime that usurps its authority; not only on the present distribution of power, but on any change in the distribution of power. Since, from a karmic point of view, the usurper of power has as much moral authority as the person deposed from power, there can be no illegitimate regime. When legitimacy is based on karma, all regimes are equally legitimate.

It is for this reason that, *in certain cultural contexts*, the doctrine of karma can be such a powerful source of political instability. The qualification, however, is crucial. So long as the rule of political succession is rigidly patterned, so long as political power is not a prized value, so long as the drive for political power is not strong (so that there is no strong motivation for positional change), the doctrine of karma, by opposing any change in the political system and conferring legitimacy on the political regime, all but guarantees political stability. It is only when the rule of succession is loose, and the value of power and the drive for it are strong that the doctrine of karma is a source of political instability. At the same time in such a context the usurper need not be deterred by the expectation of popular opposition, for since the doctrine of karma legitimizes any change in political regime, he can anticipate that his ascendancy, too, will receive almost instant legitimation.

Burmese culture provides such a context. Profoundly concerned with questions of power, both respecting and resenting political authority, fulsome to their superiors and arrogant to their inferiors, aspiring to power even when claiming to disdain it—the Burmese provide a context which incites to the pursuit of power, the overthrow of power, and the acceptance of changes in power. Conjoined to this cultural context of profound ambivalence about power, the doctrine of karma, I submit, has importantly contributed to the persistent instability of Burmese political history.

Social Stability. In the socioeconomic system, as in the political, the doctrine of karma serves as a conservative force. By converting the socioeconomic order into a moral one—differences in rank representing just retribution for past merit and demerit—the doctrine of karma justifies the differential distribution of wealth and prestige in society, thereby militating against any structural change. To resent the good fortune of the rich, let alone to overthrow them, is to deny the very essence of Buddhism, the efficacy and justice of the karmic law. Thus, in Yeigyi poor villagers would almost always attribute the success of the wealthy to their good karma. By the same token to blame one's poverty on the putative oppressions of the rich or the evils of the social system is equally impious. The poverty of the poor man is determined by his karma no less than the wealth of the rich is determined by his.

The significance of the conservative implications of the doctrine of karma can best be gauged by the extent to which the underprivileged themselves invoke it. Thus, for example, without a single exception, all the poor in Yeigyi explained their poverty as karmic retribution for insufficient *dāna* in their past existence. (And they are all attempting, by means of *dāna,* to alter their economic status in their next existence.) To be sure, attributing to karma both the economic success of the rich and their own lack of economic success, the poor are also spared the negative self-image occasioned by attributing wealth to intelligence and initiative, while attributing poverty to failure—poor planning, low intelligence, indigence, etc. —as happens in so many other cultures. This inference is strengthened by the observation that even when, objectively viewed, lack of success is indeed due to personal failure, the doctrine of karma is used in Yeigyi to rationalize failure by interpreting it as bad fortune *(kan-makaung:bu).*[2] Nevertheless, even if the motivation for invoking karma is ego-defensive, the conservative consequence of the belief in this doctrine is still apparent. The attribution of one's own bad fortune or failure to karma means that they are not attributed to alleged evils of the social order which must be changed or overthrown.

By emphasizing the socially conservative implications of this use of the doctrine of karma as a culturally constituted defense against failure, I do not wish to minimize its ego-defensive function, i.e., its importance in maintaining ego integration. On the contrary, this is a most important *psychological* function of the belief in karma, and the only reason for slighting it is that this chapter is concerned with the *social* functions of Buddhism. Indeed, it might be pointed out in passing that this psychological function of karma is as important in the moral as in the economic domain. Karma is used to maintain a positive self-image by justifying moral as well as economic, failure. Thus when I asked Burmese males why, if monasticism (as they claimed) is such an important Buddhist institution, they had not beome monks, I almost invariably received the same response: "I don't have the *pāramitā.*" (These it will be recalled, are the qualities of mind and character necessary for monkhood, arahantship, Buddhahood, etc., and they are determined by karma.) In short, their practice of the lesser good while knowing the greater is excused by karma. Almost always, however, they would go on to say that, with the merit acquired in this existence, they hoped to

[2]Indeed, the doctrine of karma is used to rationalize not only past failure, but as an emotional cushion against possible future failure as well. Aspiring to some worldly ambition, the Burmese temper their hopes with a healthy dose of possible karmic obstacles. Thus for example, a Buddhist monk with a strong desire to become an abbot said he could not be sure whether he would achieve this goal. "If my karma is good, I shall one day achieve it [abbothood]; if it is not good, I will remain an ordinary monk."

acquire the karma conducive to monkhood in a future rebirth.

To cite another example, a wealthy and pious village woman said (during a discussion of monasticism) that monks are much happier than wealthy laymen because happiness is derived from spiritual, not from physical, possessions. When I asked her the obvious question—if material possessions do not bring happiness, why does she live in an expensive house, wear silk skirts, and so on?—she said this was not her choice; in her style of life she was only carrying out the karmic retribution determined by the merit acquired in her previous lives. Again we see the ego-defensive function of karma. Here it is used to rationalize noncompliance with a cultural value, thereby resolving intrapersonal conflict between cultural norm and personal desire.

Important as these psychological functions are, we must return to the subject of this chapter—the social functions of belief in karma. Although this belief militates against structural change in the socioeconomic as in the political order, it does not constrain positional change in the former any more than it does in the latter. There is nothing about the doctrine of karma which implies that the poor must be content with their poverty. From a karmic point of view, any one's momentary station in life may be only temporary. Poverty may be suddenly converted into wealth, either by a stroke of good luck—which, of course, is determined by one's karma—or by the exercise of wisdom and initiative, which within the limits set by one's karma may produce a dramatic change in wordly possessions.

Unlike the case in the political order positional change in the socioeconomic order is, of course, neither disruptive nor a force for instability, for social and economic mobility may be achieved without displacing those of higher rank. One can become rich by the accumulation of wealth rather than by dispossessing others; one may enter the ranks of the wealthy without displacing those already there.

To be sure, one might become rich by dispossessing the rich (through theft, for example); and as in the usurpation of power, one might find karmic justification for one's action. But there are many more constraints in the case of economic usurpation than operate in the political variety. To kill or steal in order to acquire wealth not only leads to karmic punishment (as it does in the acquisition of political power) but also to legal punishment. This the successful usurper avoids because, once in office, he controls the means of power. The successful thief, however, has still to face the police and the courts. Economic dispossession could avoid legal retribution only if it were part of a political revolution—i.e., if positional change were a function of structural change—but this is precisely what is constrained by the doctrine of karma. A few isolated individuals might be willing to face karmic retribution by political rebellion—i.e., by usurping power for themselves—but a whole population would rarely be willing to face this hazard in order to support political revolution.

In short, in the socioeconomic order the doctrine of karma is truly a conservative force, lending powerful support to the status quo. It not only provides a moral justification for unequal distribution of wealth—in Yeigyi, it will be recalled, the poor unanimously attributed the fortune of the rich to their meritorious deeds performed in earlier lives—but confers moral as well as social prestige on the rich. They enjoy prestige both because of their wealth, and because of their obvious merit. To be wealthy is to be virtuous. It is no accident that the prestige accruing to the rich is called *goung:*, a term which in its original meaning denoted virtue. To be sure, this is *lo:ki goung*: (worldly prestige) by contrast to the *lo:kouktara goung*: (otherwordly prestige) of monks and those laymen who are experts in Buddhism or practice meditation, but it is *goung:* nevertheless. Moreover, this prestige = virtue equivalence is strengthened by its future as well as its past referent. On the one hand, a rich man has prestige because of his wealth, the latter both symbolizing and deriving from past merit (morality and giving). On the other hand, by means of his present wealth he can contribute even more *dāna* than in the past, thereby acquiring even more prestige in the present and more merit for the future.

To summarize, it would be difficult to invent a more convincing moral justification for, and therefore a more stabilizing influence on, the economic status quo. The poor (at least in Burma) say that the rich have achieved their wealth because they have been openhanded in earlier lives; they themselves, on the other hand, must have been closefisted. For the poor, then, their misery is not caused by the exploitation of the rich, nor by the injustice of the social system, but by their own neglect to offer charity in their former lives, for which they alone are to blame. Hence there is no point—and it is impious—to rage against the system or those who possess wealth. Rather, it is both pious and more effective to remedy the situation in a future existence through one's own efforts in this one—by offering more *dāna*. What better ideology and attitude could one have to assure the stability of the socioeconomic order?

This karmic justification for the economic status quo, when combined with other Buddhist notions, can form the basis for any opposition to change in the distribution of wealth. Thus, for example, the great majority of the people in Yeigyi said that, as Buddhists, they were opposed to the land nationalization and redistribution program initiated by the government shortly before the beginning of this study. Their opposition stemmed from their belief not only that the program was a repudiation of karmic punishment and reward, but also that it was an act of theft. Involuntary expropriation of land, said one villager (quoting a monk), is one of the twenty-five kinds of stealing prohibited by Buddhism. Indeed, it is precisely because of this expropriation that the peasants, he said, are much poorer today than before the land redistribution.[3] Such arguments, I hasten to add, are ad-

[3]It is important to note, however, that at least two members of the sample said that, nevertheless, they still favored the land redistribution. Although it violated Buddhist doctrine and was therefore evil from the point of view of religion *(lokuttara)*, it did in fact benefit the

duced not merely by the dispossessed landowners, but by poor peasants who, as a result of nationalization, have acquired land for the first time in their lives.[4]

Although the doctrine of karma provides a powerful moral justification for the differential distribution of wealth, it must be emphasized that (in Burma at least) it is not so much exploited by the rich (as suggested by various species of vulgar Marxism) to justify their wealth, as it is used by the poor to justify their poverty. Indeed, rich and poor alike are much more concerned about their "subjective" *amour propre* than about an "objective" class struggle, and this explains the dramatic difference in their use of the doctrine of karma. We have already seen that the poor and the unsuccessful in Yeigyi use this doctrine primarily as a mechanism of defense, i.e., to exonerate themselves from responsibility for their condition and from the immediate onus of it.

The rich, by contrast, only rarely attribute their affluence to good karma. In the villages, at least, I never heard a wealthy man explain his good fortune by reference to karma. Almost always the rich would attribute their success to their own efforts (for which, as we have seen, there is partial Buddhist justification). They were wealthy, they claimed, because of hard work, diligence, frugality, and so on. Conversely, they usually attributed the poverty of the poor not to their bad karma, but to their indigence, extravagance, laziness, etc.

In short, the rich achieve a positive self-image by attributing the misfortune of others to their personal deficiencies, while attributing their own good fortune to their personal abilities. The poor, on the other hand, achieve a positive self-image by the opposite maneuver. Almost always poor villagers would attribute the success of the wealthy to good karma (not to their intelligence or effort), while attributing their own misfortune to bad karma (and not to any deficiency in their own intelligence or effort). We may conclude, then, that although karma is not used as a weapon of class exploitation, its differential "exploitation" as an explanatory principle depends on the actors' position in the class structure.

Cosmology and Social Control

Much of the Western literature of an older period, most of it reflecting a missionary or Christian bias, argued that a religion like Buddhism, which does not provide for divine reward and punishment in an afterlife, offers no

---

peasants and was therefore good from the point of view of secular values *(loki).* We have encountered this distinction before.

[4]Since the land nationalization and redistribution act was instigated by U Nu, the pious Buddhist prime minister, it is of interest to understand his Buddhist justification for a law which other Buddhists viewed as a violation of doctrine and precept. "Property," he said, "is meant not to be saved, not for gains, nor for comfort. It is to be used by men to meet their needs in respect of clothing, food, habitation, in their journey toward nirvana or heaven." (Maung Maung, 1963:4)

motivation for complying with a moral code. The following comments on the role of Buddhism in Ceylon are typical of this genre.

> In confiding all to the mere strength of the human intellect and the enthusiastic self-reliance and determination of the human heart, it makes no provision for defence against those powerful temptations before which ordinary resolution must give way; and affords no consoling support under those overwhelming afflictions by which the spirit is prostrated and subdued, when unaided by the influence of a purer faith and unsustained by its confidence in a diviner power. From the contemplation of the Buddhist all the awful and un-ending realities of a future life are withdrawn—his hopes and his fears are at once mean and circumscribed; the rewards held in prospect by his creed are insufficient to incite him to virtue; and its punishments too remote to deter him from vice. Thus, insufficient for time, and rejecting eternity, the utmost triumph of his religion is to live without fear and to die without hope. [Tennent 1860, Vol. 1, 537–38]

Actually, nothing could be farther from the truth. The level of "virtue" in the Buddhist society of Burma is as high as in any other society, and its level of "vice" as low. Moreover, the motivation for moral behavior and the deterrent to immoral behavior, regardless of contrary arguments, is primarily derived from Buddhism.

In the first place, in my Burmese study the entire sample of Buddhist laymen (with only two exceptions) held that if the Buddha had not instituted the moral precepts there would be no moral code—ordinary people would not have decided, independently of His insights, that lying, killing, and so on, are wrong. Moreover, so they held, even if these moral rules had been discovered independently of Him, they would be violated more often than not if He had not sanctioned their observance. It is only because they carry, as it were, the imprimatur of the Buddha, that people comply with the precepts. In a Hobbesian state of nature—i.e., in a world without a Buddha—life would be nasty and brutish (if not solitary, poor, and short).

But the imprimatur of the Buddha is not the only Buddhist variable which accounts for compliance with the precepts; even more important is the doctrine of karma. Indeed, the belief in karmic retribution for one's actions is undoubtedly the most important determinant of moral behavior in Burma. If the Burmese perform acts of merit to assure a better rebirth, they similarly avoid acts of demerit which lead to an unpleasant rebirth. The violation of the Buddhist moral code is the most likely way of achieving an unpleasant rebirth—in one of the evil abodes, especially in hell—and this sanction constitutes the strongest motive for compliance with the code. Rebirth in hell is not only their most dreaded punishment, but Burmese villagers are very much concerned about the possibility; the more apprehensive among them say that, since they have no hopes of a happy rebirth (because of their many sins), their only hope is to avoid rebirth in hell (by means of their meritorious acts).

The fear of hell as a deterrent to immoral and criminal acts—or, if you will, as an instrument of social control—may be seen in a number of ways. Thus, when my sample of monks were asked which of the following four reasons, or any other, most accounts for compliance with the precepts,[5] the first and fourth, respectively, were always given as the most important. The reasons were: (1) they are ordained by the Buddha, (2) shame, (3) fear of legal punishment, and (4) fear of hell. If the first was listed as most important, the fourth was second, and vice versa. When a lay sample was asked an almost identical question,[6] the results were even more dramatic. With only three exceptions the entire sample ranked the fear of hell as the most important of the four deterrents. Although, when asked to rank in order the other three, hell was followed by fear of legal punishment, shame, and "to violate them is wrong" (in that order), many of the respondents said that the fear of hell was so much more important than the others that it was silly to compare them.

Although Buddhism exerts a strong influence on Burmese morality, it is possible to overestimate it, not because of any weakness in Burmese belief but because of yet another paradox consequent upon the doctrine of karma, by which the fear of hell, for example, rather than serving as a deterrent to immoral behavior may sometimes have the opposite effect. Thus, many men in the village say they have no incentive for observing the precepts because, for the sins they have already committed, they know they will be reborn in hell anyway.

For others, there are other reasons for violating the precepts. Thus, despite their belief in karmic retribution for these acts, most villagers who encounter a poisonous snake will kill it, many men commit adultery, many —as many as one-third of the adult males in the village—have consumed alcoholic beverages (usually country spirit), and many have told lies. In explaining these deviations from Buddhist morality various kinds of rationalization are used, in addition to the generic appeals to weakness of the flesh, insufficient moral strength, and so on. Thus, when two villagers went on trial for having joined a group of Communist insurgents, two other villagers, otherwise pious Buddhists, testified that the former had joined the insurgents because they had been compelled to do so. This, they admitted to me, was a lie. Still, they argued, it was not really a violation of the precept enjoining lying "because it is a political case." (The subsequent discussion did not help to illuminate why this made it exempt from the generic injunction.)

[5]These were the four which, informally, I heard repeated again and again during my first eight months in Burma. Hence these were the ones I proposed to the monks.

[6]"Because to violate them is wrong" was substituted for "because they are ordained by the Buddha." On the basis of the monks' interviews I thought that "ordained by the Buddha" and "fear of hell" might be mutually contaminating questions, since it was the Buddha who ordained the precepts, taught the cosmology (of which hell is a part), and taught about karmic retribution.

Or, take another example. In a divorce case that was heard by the headman and village elders, the husband told (what I knew to be) some outrageous lies in defense of his complaints against his wife. In a discussion of this case with one of my village friends, the latter said that the husband's lies were morally justified because his wife had no right to leave him; in short, they were necessitated by self-protection. When I remonstrated with him, saying that nevertheless the husband had violated a Buddhist precept, my friend expressed considerable annoyance. "This is a case," he said, "of practical life *(lo:ki),* not of ultimate truth *(lo:kouktara),* and in the practical world you must do anything you can [to protect your interests]." When I persisted in my queries, he said (with acerbity), "If you are so pious that you would never tell a lie, you should put on the yellow robe and retire from the world. If you want to remain in the world, you must be prepared to tell a lie, despite the precept."

This distinction between what is good from the ultimate perspective of religion *(lokuttara),* and what is necessary from the relative perspective of worldly existence *(loki),* permeates (as we have seen) Burmese attitudes. To give but one more example, another village friend, exasperated with the economic policies of the government, argued that the latter should lift its ban on the slaughter of cattle and sell tinned meat to the people. When I asked if this would not violate the very precept he had defended so strongly only a few minutes before—against killing—he said, "the people are poor; and when people are poor, they cannot bother with religion. Not to kill animals is fine in *lokuttara,* but in *loki* it must be done."

Despite these qualifications, the fear of karmic retribution for violation of the Buddhist moral code is undoubtedly the most important agent of social control in Burma. In a more subtle form, another dimension of Buddhist cosmology, the doctrine of rebirth, is probably important as well. Although by no means conclusive, there is some evidence for the thesis that the Burmese sometimes use the belief in rebirth as a fantasy solution for inner conflicts and as a fantasy satisfaction for frustrated needs. To the extent that this is true it serves to reduce, if not to stay, certain forms of hostility which might otherwise seek overt expression. Since my data here are meager, one or two examples must suffice.

I would suggest, in the first place, that the doctrine of rebirth is frequently used to resolve important Oedipal tensions, which in turn serve to contain intrafamily conflict. According to the Burmese interpretation of rebirth every living individual is the successor to his own past self and the predecessor of his own future self. Every individual, if you will, is simultaneously his own father and his own son. Although, in one sense, parental intercourse is the cause of his conception, in another sense his conception takes place when, following his last death, his soul or "butterfly spirit" enters his mother's womb. In a very general sense, then, one might speculate that for many people the belief in rebirth may be used to resolve part of the

Oedipus problem. By believing that I am my own father, I am in effect denying my biological father; and by believing that my conception was caused by the entry of my soul into my mother's womb, I am in effect denying that it was caused by parental intercourse. If so, much of the Oedipal-induced hostility is muted.

Although these speculations are intriguing, without data they can be carried no further. Instead we might examine an actual case for insight into how the rebirth doctrine might be manipulated. Take for example the young boy in Yeigyi who believed that in his previous existence he was the wife of his present father. This suggests an attempt to resolve his Oedipal conflicts in a fashion not uncommon elsewhere, viz., a simultaneous rejection of and identification with the mother and submission to the father.

But the belief in rebirth serves many non-Oedipal needs as well. Thus, from my personal knowledge of some of the other cases alluded to in chapter 5, it is obvious that the man who believes he was a headman in his previous birth is using the doctrine of rebirth to satisfy his frustrated need for prestige. The woman who believes that her son was the incarnation of a deceased (and her favorite) monk—his soul, she claimed, had entered her womb—may perhaps have resolved her grief for the loved object by incorporation. The woman who believes that the three-year-old son of a neighbor is the reincarnation of her own dead son is probably satisfying her wish that the latter might still live. The woman who claims to have been the mother of her sister's husband in a previous rebirth is probably satisfying simultaneously a number of needs. Since her sister is her superior in almost every way, she may be expressing her wish for superiority and authority over her sister. As the putative mother of her sister's husband, she becomes the mother-in-law of her sister; moreover, both statuses make her senior to her sister in a society in which age is a crucial variable in the prestige hierarchy.

These cases merely illustrate the kinds of psychological functions which might be served by belief in rebirth. Although extensive and systematic study demanded by these speculations is still to be undertaken, I would suggest that they all indicate how the belief in rebirth can serve as an important source of social control. By providing fantasied satisfactions to frustrated needs and ambitions, it reduces the probability of overt aggression and rage.

Temporal Orientation and Ambition

Like Hinduism, Buddhism deals with time dimensions of incredible duration. Not only is the universe incomparably older than the age attributed to it by modern geology, and not only will it continue long beyond the sun-death predicted by modern astronomy, but the life of any one individual, taken as the sum of his rebirths, can also span all those vast reaches of time.

As a means of comprehending the Buddhist time perspective, we might consider the following. For Buddhism, cosmic time is divided into *kalpas* or world epochs. To grasp the duration of such an epoch, Buddhism compares it to a mountain a million feet in height, length, and breadth. Consider, then, how much time it would take for that mountain to disappear if, once every hundred years, it should be stroked with a fine silk cloth—but even that amount of time would be less than the duration of a world epoch; consider, further, that at least one Buddha appears in every half-*kalpa*; consider, finally, that from the time the Buddha Gautama vowed to become a Buddha until, after many rebirths, he actually attained Buddhahood, a million other Buddhas had become manifest; consider all this, and then perhaps one may comprehend the fantastic time scale within which Buddhism operates.

This is not to say, of course, that the typical Buddhist operates within this time scale—though it was a Burmese peasant who first referred me to the simile of the mountain—nor is it to say that he, any more than we, can even begin to comprehend its meaning. Still, part of this notion of time scale inevitably rubs off on him. He knows that he has many, many rebirths ahead of him, in which he can not only continue to work for salvation, but in which things left undone in this birth may still be done in another. More important, he not only "knows" it, but he believes it and acts upon it. Unlike the dictum of Hillel—"If not now, when?"—the dictum of the Burmese might be said to be, "If not now, then next time." Thus, on countless occasions and in many different circumstances, one hears such statements as: "I don't meditate in this, but I will in my next rebirth"; "I'm not suited to be a monk in this rebirth, but I will be in my next"; "I'm poor now, but never mind, in my next rebirth I'll be rich"; "I failed to become a District Officer, but it's all right, I'll have another chance next time." And so on.

That these sentiments should have an important effect on secular behavior and motivation is inevitable. It is well known that the Burmese respond to trouble and failure with at least partial resignation, that they can laugh in the face of adversity. Part of this configuration no doubt is characterological and part defensive. But even when it is both the one and the other, there is no denying that these grounds are reinforced by the Buddhist conviction that after all, all is not lost, this is not the end, there'll be another chance. As the Burmese say, *keiksa. mashi. bu:*, it doesn't matter.

From one perspective, then, this temporal orientation (when related to the doctrine of rebirth) leads to an irrepressible optimism. From another, however (especially when related to the doctrine of karma), it may lead to the dulling of ambition and a rather defeatist attitude. If you don't succeed at first, try, try again—this kind of resolution is utterly foreign to the Burmese. Rather, their outlook is: if you don't succeed at first, forget it, stop trying. Since my failure is a result of karma, there's nothing I can do about it except to hope for something better in my next rebirth. Part of this, as

I have noted, is characterological, rooted as it is in early childhood experience; but part of it is a reflection of the Buddhist time scale and its relation to the doctrines of rebirth and karma.

This attitude, it should be added, as well as its cognitive basis is not restricted to peasants. Thus, to cite but one example, a Burmese friend, an instructor at Mandalay University, was forever expressing the same thing. Why, he would ask me, should he (like me) struggle to make sense out of a foreign culture? Why should he live in discomfort in a Burmese village in order to further a scientific career or to satisfy intellectual curiosity? Why should he feel upset about remaining an instructor? Why should he try to increase his income, to achieve higher status, to write a better book? "What's the difference? It's all due to karma. In the long run I'll be reborn again, and, depending on my present karma, I either will or will not have these things anyway. So *keiksa. mashi. bu:.*"

Buddhist Soteriology and the Burmese Economy

Introduction

We have already seen that the soteriology of nibbanic Buddhism provides no bridge of any kind to the world. Far from being a means to salvation, worldly activity in nibbanic Buddhism is its irreducible obstacle; rather than a proof, worldly activity constitutes a disproof for one's chances of being saved. But this is not true of the soteriology of kammatic Buddhism, i.e., that of most practicing Buddhists. It, on the contrary, provides profound incentives to worldly (economic) behavior, for economic success is a necessary means for soteriological action, which in turn has important worldly consequences, social and economic alike.

Kammatic Salvation and Economic Motivation

Contrary to the teachings of nibbanic Buddhism, the Burmese believe (it will be recalled) that it is the satisfaction of craving rather than its extinction that brings about release from suffering. Their goal is not the cessation of the cycle of rebirth, but rather its perpetuation—in a form which will enhance their pleasures and satisfy their desires. But since a pleasant rebirth requires excellent karma, and karma is created by merit, they are (as we have seen) enormously concerned with increasing their store of merit. It is in its central doctrines of merit and karma that kammatic Buddhism articulates with the world.

Unlike nibbanic Buddhism, in which worldly action is both an obstacle to and a disproof of one's chances of salvation—and unlike Calvinism, for which success in certain kinds of worldly action is proof that one has been elected for salvation—kammatic Buddhism views worldly action as soteriologically neutral. Since salvation is attained through merit, and merit is not acquired through worldly (economic, political, and so on) action, the latter is neither a means to nor a sign of salvation. But neither, on the other hand, is it an impediment, for one can acquire all the merit one wants while at the same time being completely implicated in the world. In short, in itself, the soteriology of kammatic Buddhism neither encourages nor discourages worldly action.

Nevertheless, although itself soteriologically neutral, worldly (and especially economic) action is indirectly an indispensable condition for salvation, for it is only through economic action that one can hope to acquire the most soteriologically valuable merit, the merit acquired through giving *(dāna)*. To be sure, merit is also acquired through morality *(sīla);* but giving is the royal road, and (short of inheriting it) the wealth required for giving must be accumulated by economic action. The salience of the belief in *dāna*-acquired merit as a primary means to salvation provides a powerful motive for economic action.

But wealth is not only a primary (albeit indirect) means to salvation; it also provides a proof of it. In the first place wealth itself, as we have seen, is a proof of past merit. Inherited or achieved, it represents karmic reward for merit piled up in previous existences, especially that acquired through giving. The wealthy man has both virtue and merit, the merit from the virtue of his past rebirths being converted into the prestige of wealth in his present rebirth. And the very wealth which, on the one hand, is proof of a large store of past merit also augurs well for his chances of an even better rebirth (salvation); the wealthier he can become, the greater the proof that his store of past merit will continue to ensure pleasurable rebirths in the future. This quest for wealth as a criterion of salvation provides a powerful motivation for work which is not entirely dissimilar from the Calvinist drive.

But wealth provides a proof of salvation in yet another and more significant way. Since giving is the most important means for acquiring merit, and hence for achieving salvation, the conversion of wealth into *dāna* is not only a means for but a proof of one's future well-being: the more one gives, the more merit one acquires and the greater one's chances of salvation. This is the reason, of course, that so many Burmans (as we have seen) keep merit account-books; they constitute an objective means for evaluating their chances. And since the merit acquired through giving is the means par excellence for salvation, the merit quest is a most powerful motive for the accumulation of wealth, and hence for economic action.[7] The intensity of this motive can best be gauged by the staggering amounts of money spent on *dāna*.

Before examining this quantitative dimension of *dāna*, which serves to identify yet another point of articulation between Buddhism and the world, it must be noted (lest the soteriological motive be unduly exaggerated) that

[7] For a further discussion of this point, in its relation to Burmese economic rationality, see Spiro (1966 and 1968).

other factors as well contribute to this seemingly disproportionate concern of the Burmese.

Dāna is not only the most important means for acquiring merit, but is equally important for prestige. To sponsor an initiation, to provision a monastery, to build a pagoda—these not only assure one of pleasure in a future existence but provide immediate gratification in present life. There is no greater prestige than that derived, for example, from the titles of "pagoda builder," "monastery builder." These are formal titles, remaining with a person his entire life, and used in all documents and on all formal occasions.

And there is even more to this pattern of prestige-through-religious-giving. The feasting of monks, the sponsorship of an initiation ceremony, and the construction of a monastery are never performed in private. These are public events, involving conspicuous display, consumption, and sharing of wealth. The more people invited, the more goods shared, in the form of food, gifts, and so on; and the more wealth "wasted," in the form of gaudy tinsel, *pandals* (symbolic of palaces), orchestras, masters of ceremony, etc., the more prestige accrues to the sponsor. Thus, for example, a friend in Mandalay, a widow with three children, commemorated the anniversary of her husband's death with a food-offering ceremony costing K99 (her monthly wages were K100). She offered a special meal to three monks and simultaneously fed thirty laymen. The former, she said was for merit *(ku. thou)*, the latter for prestige *(goung:)*.

Indeed, prestige is a sufficiently important motive so that certain opportunities for *dāna* will be relinquished in favor of others which confer both merit and prestige. It is well known, for example, that few Burmans will contribute funds for the repair of a pagoda or monastery unless they themselves have constructed it. Thus, one often sees a pagoda or monastery in the process of construction while adjacent to it an old and beautiful pagoda or monastery is allowed to decay. This is frequently explained by the (alleged) fact that the merit for repairing these religious structures accrues to the original builder rather than to the repairer. (This belief is found in Thailand as well. Cf. Rajadhon 1961:66.) Actually, there is little doctrinal basis for this rationale, and every monk I queried denied its truth. It *is* the case, however, that the prestige derived from the repair of a monastery or pagoda is negligible. First, it continues to be known by the name of the original building, and second, the coveted title "pagoda builder" or "monastery builder" is conferred only on the builder, not the repairer, of these structures.

The fact that merit and prestige are combined in one act is more than a happy happenstance. Since Buddhism is the most important cultural system in Burma, and prestige is one of the salient motives in Burmese personality, this motivational overdetermination of *dāna* is entirely understandable. In any event, whether motivated by merit and prestige or by merit alone, the fact remains that *dāna* requires money, and this provides a powerful motive for work and for saving.

Dāna *and Economic Development*

On one hand, the quest for salvation by means of *dāna* yields a strong motive for economic action (work and saving). On the other hand, this drive generates important economic consequences. Bearing in mind that the average annual family income in Yeigyi is K1,000 (about $200), the incredible percentage of their income invested in *dāna* is not only a measure of the Burmese concern for salvation but entails important, albeit unintended, consequences for the Burmese economy and society. We shall examine these as they relate to economic growth and the development of social services in Burma.

Economic Growth. The most important Buddhist ceremony, which confers the greatest amount of merit, is the initiation ceremony. A special ceremony, it also entails the greatest amount of *dāna.* In Yeigyi, the cost ranges from K200 in very poor families to K5,000 in rich families.[8] In other villages surveyed, the cost has been as high as K10,000, and in the cities it can go even higher. In one case—a very exceptional case, to be sure—a merchant in Monywa (a town in Upper Burma) is reputed to have spent K100,000 on his son's initiation. The funds required to cover these expenses are acquired through accumulated savings, the sale of property, and loans. Part of these expenses, of course, are recovered by financial contributions made by the invited guests; thus the sponsor of one ceremony I attended recovered K1,000 of his K5,000 expenses in this manner. From a Buddhist point of view, of course, these contributors are not merely offering assistance to a friend or a fellow villager; rather—and this is an important element in their motivation—their contribution, too, represents *dāna,* for which they will receive their share of merit. (So far as the effects on the economy are concerned, it makes no difference, of course, whether the expenditures are born by one person or shared by a group.)

A second special occasion for the offering of *dāna* is the *kahteing,* the collective offering of robes to the monks. These offerings occur only in one month of the year, but the average family may participate in five or six. In one ceremony honoring a monk in a forest hermitage and sponsored by all the villages in the area, as well as by many faithful from Mandalay, eleven monks were invited to participate. Each monk was presented with offerings whose value was K150. In addition, the miniature "wishing tree" *(padei-tha bin)* hung with gifts and cash, which is offered to only one monk by the drawing of lots, was worth K350. The total value of the gifts alone was K4,200, and the total cost of the ceremony—including the feasting of the

[8]Two initiations in a village in Lower Burma have been described as costing K5000 and K2200 respectively (Pfanner 1962:352).

monks and the feeding of the laymen—even higher. The most expensive *kahteing* I attended cost K10,000.[9]

A third, albeit infrequent special ceremony by which merit is acquired is the monk's funeral *(hpoung:ji: byan).* I attended a simple funeral in a relatively remote and small (thirty-family) village which cost K2,000. Each family was assessed, depending on its wealth, from K40 to K75 to cover the cost of feeding thirty monks two meals each, and the offerings (of soap, robes, and so on), which cost K10 each. The cost for elaborate funerals may be astronomical. In the year before my study began, the funeral of a certain monk in Mandalay cost K100,000, and the villagers continued to speak of a funeral held a few years earlier in Mogok, the gem center of Burma, which —so they claimed—cost K800,000!

Monks not only receive offerings at a colleague's funeral, but also at a layman's. A typical, simple village funeral costs about K250—this at least was the approximate cost of three such, which I attended—and almost all these funds, except for feeding the laymen who sit up all night in the house of the deceased, are spent on food and offerings for monks. In the case of one village death, the family claimed it could not afford the K15 required to call in a doctor to attend to their sick relative, but ironically, managed to raise K250 in order to bury him. Many of these expenses, to be sure, are defrayed by contributions from the participants, who of course share in the merit of the sponsor and, in turn, share their merit with the deceased.

Funerals of wealthy villagers inevitably entail much more: the monks are offered more costly gifts and food, and more laymen are fed. Thus the funeral for my landlord's mother cost K750. He defrayed his expenses by selling an ox for K200, by receiving donations of K30 each from his brother and brother-in-law, by a loan of K300 from his sister, and by a donation of K96 from the village mutual aid association.

In addition to these special offerings, the monks also receive special meals and offerings at the completion of the harvest season, the opening of the Ecclesiastical Courts, the anniversary of a dead relative, a recovery from an illness, before a wedding, at every *paritta* ceremony, and on any other occasion when one wishes to acquire merit. Almost always, of course, laymen are also invited to participate in these feeding ceremonies—not only for the prestige of the sponsor, but to allow them to share his merit.

The construction and repair of pagodas and monasteries is an even more important source of merit. Especially during the three-month Buddhist Lent, emissaries from other villages and towns arrive in the village at least two or three times a month to collect funds for some monastery or another. Thus, in a two-month period for which I tried to obtain full information, emissaries arrived in Yeigyi from Mandalay to collect funds for the repair

[9]Two village *kahteings* in Lower Burma have been described as costing K1500 and K1700 respectively (Pfanner 1962:355).

of a monastery in that city (they raised K60), from Monywa (a town about forty miles distant) to raise funds for the repair of a monastery in that city (they raised K96), again from Mandalay, to construct a new monastery (they raised K60), and still again from Mandalay, to repair both a monastery and a pagoda (they raised K74).

Although everyone can (and does) contribute to the construction or repair of a pagoda or monastery, only the special few can afford to construct one themselves. Those who can, make every effort to do so, since (as we have seen) this yields merit (and prestige) beyond all other things. In Yeigyi, only one villager is sufficiently wealthy to have constructed a monastery—at a cost of K10,000. This was a relatively inexpensive enterprise compared to even modest ones in the city.

Merit is also acquired by offerings to the Buddha and to His symbol, the pagoda. It is especially important to make offerings at famous pagodas—those that have annual festivals, or serve as pilgrimage centers. The total expenses are considerably increased by the additional cost of travel and the offerings made to monks.

Thus far I have only discussed the expense of offerings for special occasions, occurring at infrequent intervals. In addition, there is the regular expense entailed by the daily feeding of monks—the ordinary alms food offered daily and the special meals on Sabbath days—and their normal upkeep. This alone consumes about 10 per cent of the income of the average family in Yeigyi.

It should be obvious by now that in addition to the great output of time and energy, the economic investment in *dāna* is staggering. Even excluding special meals to the monks, construction and repair of pagodas and monasteries, contributions to emissaries from other towns and villages, and individual pilgrimages, the remaining investment in *dāna* in one village in Upper Burma for the year 1961 was K42,000, or about $9,000. (See Table 16.)

TABLE 16
ANNUAL NORMAL EXPENDITURE ON BUDDHISM IN ONE VILLAGE IN UPPER BURMA IN 1961

Item	Amount
Eight initiation ceremonies	K24,000
One *kahtein*	1,200
Daily feeding of monks (exclusive of special meals)	4,600
Pilgrimage to Arakan pagoda in Mandalay (exclusive of other pilgrimages undertaken separately)	12,000
Total	K41,800

Wealthy villagers, as we have abundantly seen, spend more on religious giving, both absolutely and relatively, than do their less fortunate brethren.[10] Thus the richest person in Yeigyi spent K2,210 in 1961—K400 for the daily feeding of monks, K210 for a *kahteing*, and K1600 for the repair of the monastery she had constructed a few years earlier. The latter, incidentally, originally cost K10,000, while the resthouse adjacent to it had cost K1,000. For a more extended period, her wealthy son-in-law incurred the following expenses. He spent K5,000 (more than $1,000) on his son's initiation, and this does not include the costs of the orchestra, the *pandal* (a collapsible gold and silver tinsel structure representing a palace, in which such ceremonies take place), and the master of ceremony, which were defrayed by his relatives. Five years earlier he had spent another K5,000 for the ordination of twelve novices, and had offered the following gifts (whose cost I did not determine) to each of twenty monks: a bag of rice, a tin of cooking oil, a tin of kerosene, an umbrella, a pair of sandals, and a pair of robes. The following year, he repaired the floor of the Buddhist resthouse at a cost of K1,000. Two years later he entered the monastery for seven days, the ceremony costing K1,600. The following year, he repaired the resthouse in the cemetery at a cost of K200. The year before our study, he arranged for the transportation of villagers making a pilgrimage to the Sagaing hills, and also defrayed the costs of feeding the monks whom they visited. The expense was K360. In addition to these special occasions, it has been his custom three times a year (at the Buddhist holydays) to feed the monks and villagers of Yeigyi at a total cost of K240. Excluding his daily food offerings to the monks, U Lum Byei's average annual expenditure on Buddhism, for the eight-year period prior to our study, was approximately K2,000.

Keeping all these figures in mind, it seems not entirely incredible that the typical Upper Burmese village is reported to spend from 30 to 40 per cent of its net disposable cash income on *dāna* and related activities. These, at any rate, are the minimum and maximum figures obtained from village headmen and elders in fifteen villages in the Patheingyi township. They are only slightly higher than my own estimate, based on a detailed house-to-house survey, of 25 per cent for Yeigyi.[11] If this is so, it is no exaggeration to say that the economy of rural Burma is geared to the overriding goal of the accumulation of wealth as a means to acquiring merit. Which leads us

[10]Pfanner (1962:423) and Nash (1965:160) found this to be true in other villages—in both Upper and Lower Burma—as well.

[11]The difference between my estimate and those of the village headmen can easily be explained by various expenses which, being newly arrived in Burma, I did not know to inquire about. It is much more difficult, however, to explain the much wider discrepancy between my estimates (and the estimates of my informants) and those of Nash (1965:160) and Pfanner (1962:421). Even for the *wealthy* families in his Upper Burma village, Nash's estimate is 14 per cent. (It drops to 4 and 2 per cent, respectively, for his middle-and lower-income villagers.) Pfanner's estimate for the average family in his Lower Burma village is 6 to 8 per cent.

back to the Weberian problem of the relation between the quest for salvation and worldly—especially economic—action.

For the Buddhist—i.e., the *kammatic* Buddhist—no less than for the Puritan, the pursuit of salvation provides a powerful motive for economic action. If, then, Buddhism and Puritanism have had opposite consequences for economic development and growth, it is not because the soteriology of the one (as Weber has argued) provides a motive for wordly action while that of the other provides no such motivation. It is rather—so far as the role of religion (rather than social structure, culture, or character) is concerned—that their soteriologies lead to different motivations with respect to savings. For the Puritan, who has already been predestined for salvation or damnation, successful economic action—if Weber (1930:ch. 5) is correct—provides him with proof that he is one of the elect, and savings are to be reinvested to create further wealth—for the greater glory of God. For the Buddhist, whose salvation is problematic, successful economic action is a prerequisite to enhancing his chances of salvation, and savings are to be spent on *dāna*—for the greater increase of his own store of merit. For the Buddhist, the proof of salvation is to be found, not in accumulating and creating new wealth, but in giving it away in the form of *dāna*.

In addition to its (negative) consequences for the development of capitalism, the Buddhist soteriological theme of merit-through-*dāna* (as both a means to and a proof of salvation) has important consequences, of course, for the problem of economic growth in contemporary Burma (and other Buddhist societies); and these consequences, given the Burmese motivational structure, are ironic. Unlike the Puritan, who (if we can believe Weber) disdained wordly pleasures as sinful and was interested in wealth only as a means of glorifying God, the Burmese Buddhist views worldly pleasures as a boon to be enjoyed; indeed, his very notion of salvation consists in being reborn as a wealthy male, with the means to satisfy his desire for worldly pleasures, or even better as a *deva*, for whom these pleasures are both greater and of longer duration. It is in order to be reborn to these very worldly future pleasures that he invests such a large percentage of his savings in religious giving, thereby deferring present joys. But notice: by channeling such a large percentage of his savings into activities that will assure him of a pleasurable rebirth, he is left with very little, if any, capital for the one activity that will provide him with the chance of greater enjoyment in this birth, viz., economic investment. Rather than invest his savings in economic enterprise, he puts them into *dāna*.

That this merit-through-*dāna* pattern has had important consequences for the Burmese economy, especially for economic development and growth, should be obvious. It takes little imagination to realize that, if even part of the economic surplus that for so long has been devoted to *dāna* had been available instead for economic investment, Burmese economic history might have been significantly different. For the picture painted above, in which almost every product the economy is capable of producing (or, indeed, acquiring in international trade) is lavishly offered to religion, has characterized Burmese Buddhism from its inception in ancient Pagan. Thus, except for the inclusion of slaves and livestock,[12] the sumptuous offerings made to both monasteries and pagodas and described in early Burmese inscriptions differ little from the rich abundance of contemporary gifts. Today automobiles (offered to very famous monks) take the place of the elephants and horses mentioned in the following catalogue found in those inscriptions.

> Dedicated objects included lands and houses, gardens, wells, tanks, cattle-like goats, buffaloes, horses, and elephants, rice and paddy, boats, gold, silver, ruby, iron, lead, copper, robes, cloth and garment, libraries with manuscripts, fans and umbrellas, betel and betelnuts, betel-boxes, oil lights, flowers, pots and utensils including bowls, spitoons, bells, trays, basins, lamp-stands, chains, etc., and the most important of all, slaves. All the pious foundations, remains of which we see even to this day in Pagan and hundreds of which were brought to being by anybody who could afford to do so, had to be maintained by thousands of slaves that were dedicates along with lands, fields and other necessities of an active monastic life. Literally, hundreds of names of these slaves—quite as many women as men amongst them—are mentioned in the inscriptions. [Ray 1946: 160][13]

In sum, the aspiration of the Burmese for worldly pleasures in a future rebirth, and their consequent concern for merit and *dāna,* has been a serious obstacle to a better standard of living in their present life. This, of course, is the very reverse of the effect of Puritanism. The opposition of the early Puritans to worldly pleasures, combined with economic investment, made possible for later generations increased worldly enjoyment.

Having indicated the dysfunctional consequence of the merit-through-*dāna* pattern for the economic history of Burma (and ultimately, for the standard of living of succeeding generations of Burmese), I must observe

[12]Slaves were used to wash the hands and feet of the monks, as well as to draw their water, cook their food, and clean the monastic compound. For a detailed description of monastic slavery in the Pagan period, see Than Tun (1955).

[13]Although Burmese monasteries may receive land as donations if it is held by a lay steward, they are in no sense the large property-holding corporations they were in medieval Burma, or Buddhist monasteries have been in such Mahayanist societies as medieval Japan (cf. Sansom 1946:chs. 10–11) and contemporary Mongolia and Tibet (cf. Miller 1961), or, for that matter, present-day Theravadist Ceylon (cf. Bareau 1961; Ames 1964:42–46). In medieval Burma the lands contributed to monasteries were so vast that the twelfth-century King Klawa found it necessary to confiscate them. (Than Tun 1955:174) Today, however, according to the Ministry of Religious Affairs (personal interview), only 300,000 acres of paddy land are owned by monasteries. For the township in which I worked the figure is 300 acres. Even this is much larger than it would have been prior to Independence, for at the time of the passage of the Land Nationalization Act (in 1953) many landowners, rather than permitting their lands to be nationalized, preferred to offer them to their favorite monasteries (thereby acquiring much merit).

that for the *individual* Burman this pattern is entirely rational, because for him its consequence is not dysfunctional. For the peasant, at least, the difference in objective economic consequences of investing his savings or spending them on Buddhism is negligible, while the subjective difference—i.e., as he sees it—is enormous. Indeed, given his soteriological beliefs, as well as the objective conditions of Burmese society, his choice is not between investing his savings or spending them on religion, but rather between two types of investment, one yielding slight returns and the other enormous ones. Let us see.

The returns from *dāna* are not only immensely profitable (leading to much greater wealth and pleasure in a future rebirth than any economic investment could yield in this life), but since the law of karma is immutable they entail no risk. Moreover, in addition to its future returns, *dāna* produces an immediate harvest in the form of both prestige and material pleasure. Affording an opportunity to dress in fine silk, to partake of sumptuous meals, to be entertained by excellent orchestras and talented masters of ceremony, merit-making ceremonies are one of the few occasions on which ordinary peasants can satisfy their desires for material enjoyment.

Economic investments, on the other hand, are neither very profitable nor very sound. For although the investment potential of the total economy could, in the aggregate, have a crucial influence on Burmese economic growth which in the long run would raise the standard of living of the individual Burman, the savings of the average peasant are too small for his investment returns to increase appreciably his present standard of living. In addition, he would be deferring known present pleasures for a very risky future pleasure. Like most other Asian societies, Burma has had—and continues to have—an almost continuous history of unrest, dacoity, insurgency, and warfare; except for some brief interludes in Burmese history—most especially *pax Britannica*—few Burmese governments have been able to guarantee the internal security, political stability, or social control necessary to protect savings and investments. Worse, government itself has been one of the important predators. From the traditional Burmese monarchy to the present military dictatorship, confiscation of private wealth has been a consistent policy of almost all Burmese governments, a policy which has discouraged either conspicuous saving or conspicuous consumption. In addition detailed sumptuary laws have precluded the enhancement of one's life style in one's present status. Considerations of salvation aside, these factors alone have served throughout Burmese history to channel savings into religion. In this connection, the following description of eighteenth-century Burma holds for most of Burmese history, including the present.

> With very few exceptions, there exist no substantial structures in the country, except those which are dedicated to religious purposes. The insecurity of property forbids that the matter should be otherwise. If a Burman becomes possessed

> of wealth, temple-building is the only luxury in which he can safely expend it. Hence the prosperity of a place, which is never more than temporary, is to be judged of in this country, not by the comforts or luxuries of the inhabitants, or the reputable appearance of their habitations, but by the number, magnitude, splendour, and actual condition of its temples and monasteries. On these are wasted [sic] substantial materials, labour, and even ingenuity, equal to the construction of respectable towns and villages, calculated to last for generations. [Crawfurd 1834:79–80.]

To return, however, to the strictly cognitive variables, we may conclude that, given his acceptance of Buddhist soteriology and the more general world view from which it is derived, the preference of the *individual* Burman for religious over secular investments represents the more rational choice. This observation, of course, in no wise blunts the thrust of my argument concerning the relationship between *dāna* and Burmese economic history. For, even granting the unpropitious conditions alluded to above, it can hardly be doubted that over a period of successive generations, the channeling of Burmese savings into economic investments rather than religion would have made a significant difference in the development and growth of the Burmese economy. By the same token, it is probably safe to predict that, all things being equal, the continuation of this soteriological pattern of merit-through-*dāna* will continue to pose a serious obstacle to the future economic growth of Burma.[14]

Social services. The soteriological importance of giving has had significant consequences not only for economic growth, but equally seriously for the development of social services in Buddhist societies. These social consequences, which have affected the quality of life in Burma as much as its standard of living, flow from a rather narrow conception of *dāna.*

Although giving creates merit for the giver, regardless of the beneficiary of the gift, the Burmese, it will be recalled, believe that the merit is proportional to the sanctity of the recipient. Thus, as we have seen, contributions to religious structures confer more merit on the donor than contributions to secular structures, just as contributions to monks confer more merit than those made to laymen. The Burmese are lavish in their support of monks, monasteries, and pagodas, while at the same time tightfisted in their charity to the poor or for secular institutions. Why waste money on causes from which little or no merit is to be gained?

There are, of course, some exceptions to this generalization. A village

[14] Pfanner (1962:423) has pointed to other important consequences of this emphasis on *dāna* which, for lack of detailed data of my own, I can only state without developing. Since the wealthy offer much more *dāna,* both relatively and absolutely, than the poor, this has an important leveling effect on the differences in the Burmese standards of living. Moreover, since the rich villagers tend to be the moneylenders, and since a great many merit-making ceremonies are accompanied by feasting and entertainment, this merit-through-*dāna* pattern results in the redistribution of income.

elder said that *dāna* most certainly includes assistance to the poor and the unfortunate. Another elder, contrary to most of the villagers, insisted that public works for the common good—for example, the repair of roads— was also *dāna*, which would confer merit on the volunteer worker. Indeed, he argued, the prolonged British presence in Burma could be explained by the great merit they acquired by the construction of roads, irrigation canals, and so on. For him, the construction of such facilities conferred as much merit as the construction of a monastery. A village headman went even further, in describing a recently completed dispensary constructed by means of private donations: he asserted that such merit is greater than that derived from building a pagoda. "There are," he said, "too many pagodas already in Burma. The rain falls into the river; of what use is it to the river? Of what use is another pagoda in this country? Instead of religious buildings, we should have more clinics and hospitals."

These, however, are minor voices. Overwhelmingly it is believed that assistance, physical or financial, to secular objects or lay persons provides the donor with very little merit. In describing the conception of merit held by the Pa-O, a hill tribe of eastern Burma, Hackett (1953:592) observes that projects which do not affect their family or community are unsupported unless they can be assured that they will acquire merit. If anything, this sentiment is even stronger among the Burmese, for whom projects even within the community will receive no support unless they are believed to confer merit. Hence, however laudable they may be, secular activities such as road building, social welfare, education, public health, and so on receive only negligible support, either material or financial, from the Burmese. "Let the government provide such things" is their attitude. Why build a school, which has but ephemeral value, they argue, when for the same funds one can build a monastery and appreciably augment one's store of merit?

The belief that nonreligious giving confers little or no merit on the donor has deep historical roots in Burma, and as we shall see, is found throughout Buddhist Southeast Asia. Here, however, I am concerned neither with the historical nor the psychological bases for the belief, but with its consequences for Burmese society. Thus, to concretize the examples alluded to above, although for years many people in Yeigyi have talked about the desirability of a new school or (even more important) a dispensary, the necessary funds for the former have never been raised, and the latter project has never developed beyond the talking stage. On the other hand, contributions are always available for the many emissaries who come to the village from as far away as Mandalay or Monywa to collect money for the construction of a monastery or a pagoda, buildings which they may never visit or even see. Indeed, during the same two-month period in which emissaries from these distant towns were successful in raising K290 in Yeigyi for the repair of their monasteries and pagodas, the village schoolmaster was unable to raise K60 to repair the roof of the dilapidated village school. The government had already contributed the materials, and the village was merely asked to contribute the funds for the labor. Nevertheless only K15 were contributed by the villagers for the repair of the school.

This attitude to giving applies as much to people as to buildings and institutions. Thus, oxcarts are always available—and sometimes a wealthy villager will even rent a truck—to transport pilgrims to a pagoda festival. But when a sick baby, or a boy with an infected leg, or a woman suffering from a snake bite has to be taken to the district clinic, these same carts are usually unavailable.

This lack of support for nonreligious charity is as characteristic of the cities as of the village. We have already seen that, when a small group of monks organized a training school for orphans, they received only negligible financial support for this endeavor. Their activities were sustained, instead, with a grant from the Asia Foundation. In general, and almost without exception, the few good private schools and hospitals in Burma are the creations of foreign (Christian) missionaries, rather than Burmese Buddhists.

Nor is this a particularly recent attitude. The following anecdote, first recorded in 1901, even then had occurred "many years ago." The Burmese British Government, planning to build a small hospital in Kyaikto, asked the Assistant Commissioner to attempt to raise funds for this project. Convening the headmen and elders of the surrounding area, he explained the purpose of the hospital. "After much explanation of the benefits, and many inquiries as to whether contributions would have to be made monthly, annually, or once for all, the list was opened by one of the most influential men present saying that he would give sixpence (four annas)." (Nisbet 1901: Vol. 2, 224) Nisbet explains that, "apart from money spent on works of religious merit . . . generosity is wanting." *(Ibid.)*

The same attitude, it is important to observe, obtains in other *Theravāda* countries as well. In Thailand, despite a concerted effort by the government and ranking members of the Bangkok monastic hierarchy to associate social services and community development projects with merit, its traditional association with religious giving is undiminished. (Mulder 1969: 1–13). To offer but one example, a district abbot acting at the government's request attempted to raise funds in his own village in northern Thailand for the construction of a local school. Although he preached a sermon saying that the people could acquire as much merit for building a school as for the construction of a temple, he had little success. The villagers, according to Moerman (1966:166), insisted that nothing confers as much merit as the construction of a temple, and since they had one under construction at that time, they could not divert their efforts for the benefit of a school. It is not accidental that when Wells characterizes the "emphasis on giving" as one of the "assets" of Thai Buddhism, the only illustrations he offers are alms food for monks and offerings to temples (Wells 1960:11).

It should be added, lest an invidious distinction be drawn between *Theravāda* and *Mahāyāna* Buddhism, that the identical situation obtained, for example, in traditional China. In a case study in 1948 of a village (near Canton) it was discovered that although the villagers spent $500 for only one temple festival (celebrating the birthday of the earth god), they could not raise a similar amount for an irrigation reservoir, nor could they gather even one-third of the amount for a literacy class for underprivileged children. (Yang 1967:16) This attitude, according to the same authority, was found throughout China, where it characterized official religious organizations as strongly as the individual layman. Although government officials and business leaders established and maintained institutions for the care of the aged, orphans, and the ill, Buddhist and Taoist religious organizations "... showed a singular lack of participation in charitable work" *(ibid.*:335).

It should be obvious, then, that the belief in the soteriological importance of merit, combined with the belief that religious giving (but not secular giving) is a most effective means for acquiring it, has had important consequences for the quality of life in Buddhist societies. Equally obvious, in modernizing societies it can have even more important consequences for the implementation of programs of social and economic change. In Burma the present military government, painfully aware of the fact, has attempted, albeit with little success, to alter this attitude. Thus, in order to construct a hospital for the employees of the Rangoon municipality, funds were raised from the proceeds of the annual Independence Day carnival. Speaking at the laying of the cornerstone, a member of the Revolutionary Council, after expressing his dismay that Burmese generosity was channeled almost exclusively toward religious ends, went on to argue that donations for social service were equally meritorious. His exhortations fell on deaf ears. In order to channel more capital into nonreligious ends, the government finally placed a ceiling on the amount of funds that would be permitted for any one religious enterprise.

It should be evident, then, that just as Burma might have achieved more rapid economic development if such a large percentage of its wealth had not been spent on *dāna,* so too its standard of education, the level of its social services, the quality of its medical facilities, etc., might have been markedly improved if the Burmese were not so deeply absorbed in acquiring merit through *dāna,* or if contributions to secular institutions were also interpreted as *dāna.* Indeed, if the funds spent only on superfluous gifts for monks —the second monastery which remains unoccupied, the fourth grandfather clock, the extra food which is eaten by the pi-dogs, etc.—were allocated to education, the effects on Burmese society would not be inconsiderable. This is all too well recognized by some of the Burmese themselves, although they are too few to change the system. Thus, the headman of one village said to me that

> the entire township spends about 10 per cent of its income on provisioning monks, but far less than 1 per cent on education. If we spent, say, 9 per cent on monks and 1 per cent on education, surely that would not harm Buddhism, and how much better off our children would be.

Lest it be objected that perhaps the lack of support in Burma for hospitals, schools, and so on more validly reflects an attitude of indifference to such services, it should be emphasized that, on the contrary, the Burmese are extremely interested in these and in many others. They not only want them but feel that they can and should have them. However, from the villagers' point of view at any rate, the responsibility for providing them is not their own but the government's. In the eyes of the average peasant, the government is viewed in some magical way as the possessor of huge amounts of largess which it acquires almost independently of its powers of taxation. Indeed, the villagers see little relationship between taxation, government expenditures, and economic development. For them the government is an enormously wealthy institution which can easily build all the roads, schools and hospitals required or desired. That they are not built is not due to lack of funds, but to the greed, corruption, and inefficiency of government officials. If the latter did not keep the wealth for themselves, all these services—and more—would have already existed.

In short, from the villagers' point of view, the products of economic development can and must be achieved by government, independent of the people—i.e., themselves—who are governed. Their own action with respect to such ends is both irrelevant and unnecessary. The ends to which *their* efforts are more properly devoted are religious—religious development, if you will—and few of them appreciate the fact that the more they invest in religion, the fewer are the resources available to the government for developmental projects and goals. It must be admitted, however, that even if this fact were appreciated, it would probably have little effect on their behavior. As between hospitals and monasteries, their savings will go to monasteries.

Lest the thrust of this argument be misunderstood, I must emphasize again that the mere existence of Buddhism as an official religion does not, in itself would not, have the consequences I have outlined here. Just as nibbanic Buddhism does not have the consequences usually ascribed to it because its basic doctrines are not internalized by most Buddhists, so kammatic Buddhism has the consequences outlined above only because *its* basic doctrines *are* internalized. If the belief in rebirth were weak and the belief in karma only loosely held, if *dāna* were to lose its salience as a means for acquiring merit—if the belief in any one of these doctrines were weakened, let alone rejected, the entire motivational structure described above would collapse, and with it the social and economic consequences I have pointed out. Moreover, even if this doctrinal set remains strongly internalized, a modernizing government which has not cathected these doctrines can obviate most of these consequences by fiscal and tax policies.

In contemporary Burma there are certainly some Buddhists for whom the doctrinal set and its motivational consequence are weak; these form the small group of entrepreneurs in Burmese society (or at least they did, before the present government abolished private property). In contemporary Thailand, which is undergoing rapid economic development, one has the impression that Buddhism in any of its soteriological guises is worn more loosely, at least by the modernizers. For the latter, and for their counterparts in Burma, Buddhism remains an important, perhaps an essential element in their lives, but more as an apotropaic than as a salvation religion. Indeed, it is at least arguable that in a *realistic* confrontation between the expectations held out by modern technology and industry in this existence and those held out by Buddhism for a future existence, Buddhism would inevitably lose so far as the modern elite is concerned. Traditional societies, and peasants in modernizing societies, who do not face this realistic confrontation remain wedded to the promises held out by Buddhist soteriology. The modern elite, however, still intoxicated with the prospects of industrialization, may be expected instead to choose immediate satisfactions over satisfactions deferred.[15]

Nevertheless, once the first flush of industrial success is passed—say in a few hundred years—it is not improbable that some nominal Buddhists, like nominal Christians before them, disillusioned with the fruits of "progress," will then return to some form of neo-Buddhism. Indeed, if one may generalize from the experience of many contemporary Western intellectuals, we might predict that this neo-Buddhism will be nibbanic rather than kammatic in its orientation, i.e., will stress detachment rather than merit as the way to salvation. If this were so, then, to the extent that only one of the Buddhist ideologies discussed in the first section of this book is dominant in any given historical epoch or sociological setting, we might conclude that nibbanic Buddhism is the religion of a world-weary elite (whether pre- or postindustrial), that kammatic Buddhism is the religion of a preindustrial peasantry, and that apotropaic Buddhism is the religion of a rising and prosperous bourgeoisie.

Buddhist Affiliation and Burmese Social Integration

Buddhist Action and Social Cooperation

Just as the large capital investment in *dāna* has had unintended but important consequences for Burmese economic growth and the development of its social services, so other facets of Buddhist action have had

[15]Indeed, this is already happening even on the village level in Thailand, where, because of increasing economic development, "... the value placed on making merit ... has been tacitly challenged by a major alternative: satisfaction through material satisfaction." (Pfanner and Ingersoll, 1962:359)

important consequences for social integration in Burma. In the first place, Buddhist ritual, including the quest for merit, is typically performed in consort with other people through collective ceremonies (offerings to monks and pagodas, recitation of the precepts on the Sabbath, etc.). These ceremonies, from observance of the Sabbath in the village monastery to participation in a district-wide monastic funeral, serve literally to integrate their participants into a physical unit. And this integration occurs at almost every structural level of Burmese society: an entire family may observe the Sabbath together in one monastery, a whole village may collectively celebrate a Buddhist festival in the village resthouse, or a monastic funeral or robe-offering ceremony may bring together scores of villages comprising a large district.

In addition to bringing people together physically, Buddhist ceremonies demand and create the transformation of the resulting physical group into a social group, characterized by cooperation and reciprocity. Guests invited to a Buddhist initiation help defray its expenses by making a contribution to its sponsor, and in turn eat a festive meal cooked for the sponsor of the initiation by members of the village "bachelors' association."

These activities are not only conducive to cooperation, but seem to create, if only temporarily, a strong feeling of unity within the group. Significantly, this unity transcends the divisiveness which, at least in some villages, is brought about by almost continuous factionalism. (Cf. Spiro 1968.) To be sure, Buddhism is also implicated in the factionalism. Conflicts among monks, as we have seen, find important reverberations among villagers; sometimes, too, factional feelings may be so intense that some villagers boycott Buddhist ceremonies sponsored by factional rivals. In general, however, factional rivalry is suspended at Buddhist ceremonies, and instead unity (or at least the façade of unity) prevails. Thus, despite their rivalry, the leaders of the two opposing factions in Yeigyi attended a pagoda festival together, their conflict being temporarily displaced by outward marks of good will and fellowship as throughout the day they engaged, together with other villagers, in discussion of Buddhist doctrine. Similarly, to prepare for a robe-offering ceremony, members of the two factions worked together on various planning committees, and during the ceremony sat and ate together in a spirit of at least outward amity. Again, when U Htein, a leader of one of the factions, held an initiation for his son, it was his bitter factional and political opponent Kou Lwin who was given the honor of leading the horse ridden by the initiate.

Cooperation for acquiring merit extends beyond the boundaries of the village. Thus, members of village *A* raise funds for a robe-offering ceremony to be held in village *B*. The Buddhist sodality in village *C* raises funds in villages *D* and *E* for the repair of a monastery in village *C*. Villages *D* and *E* not only contribute their quota but provide the sodality with food and lodging. And so on. Sometimes this cooperation is extensive. Thus, annually the entire village of Pounagoun comes to Yeigyi, about five miles away, to worship the remains of a former Yeigyi abbot, buried under a small pagoda, who was once the master of their own abbot. Each year, each villager contributes one *kyat* to feed their guests, and a meal is prepared for them by the village "bachelors' association." Moreover, they decorate the pagoda on behalf of their guests and construct a special *pandal* for their use. On their part, the villagers from Pounagoun entertain their hosts with a professional orchestra and dance troupe, after which they stay up all night worshiping at the pagoda.

The extensiveness of intervillage interaction and cooperation instigated by the requirements of Buddhist action cannot be exaggerated. Throughout the entire three-month Buddhist Lent, village sodalities *(ayoung:do)* are constantly moving from one village to the next for the collection of *dāna.* During the agricultural slack period—from the end of the harvest to the beginning of the planting season—villagers are forever attending Buddhist ceremonies (ordinations, initiations, monastic offerings, and so on) in other villages. And throughout the year, emissaries from other villages and towns come to the village to raise funds for the repair of a monastery, the construction of a pagoda, the preparation of a monastic funeral, and similar meritorious activities.

To fully appreciate the significance of Buddhism, and especially the quest for merit, as an agent of integration (on both intra- and intervillage levels) it must be emphasized that, except for the cooperation exhibited in such ceremonies, the Burmese village is marked by an almost total absence of collective activities, other than those which are either motivated by external pressure or based on a cash nexus. Of course, collective road repairs may be undertaken—at the army's command. Of course, collective agricultural activities are undertaken—when the participants are payed either in cash or in kind. But Buddhist activities almost alone are occasions for *voluntary* collective and cooperative participation. The only voluntary mutual aid organization in Yeigyi is the *tha-hmu. na-hmu.* (literally, pleasant-unpleasant) society, which contributes financial assistance to poor families for Buddhist expenses, especially those connected with initiation and funeral ceremonies.

Buddhism is the primary source not only of intravillage cooperation, but also of intervillage integration. This interaction, although motivated by the desire for merit and other Buddhist goals, often leads to intervillage marriages, and the consequent family alliances contribute to much intervillage interaction for non-Buddhist ends. Similarly pilgrimages and pagoda festivals, which lead to the exchange of contacts and information on a district- and even nationwide basis, are one of the most important instruments for the promotion of social and cultural integration beyond the village level. Since an important pagoda festival draws participants from all parts of the district, sometimes from all parts of the country; it provides an important opportunity for the dissemination and diffusion of knowledge, ideas, and customs from widely separated areas. It gives the villager an opportunity to hear politicians, read newspapers, and discuss political and other current events. Finally (like *nat* festivals) pagoda festivals serve as markets where itinerant merchants bring their wares and display them in temporary stalls, set up as a bazaar. These merchants—peddlers is probably the more accurate designation—travel up and down the country from one festival to the next, on an annual circuit. And not only merchants of physical wares; itinerant shamans, healers, magicians, astrologers, and other specialists in the occult have their stalls in the bazaar. All, of course, are very important agents of social and cultural diffusion.

In the absence of Buddhism, then, Burmese society might well have consisted of atomized and fragmented villages, with little relation to each other, while within the village each family might well constitute a more or less self-contained entity sufficient unto itself. If this has not happened, Buddhism has certainly been a primary instrument for preventing it.

The Buddhist Heritage and Social Solidarity

We have seen earlier (chapter 1) that Buddhism constitutes the most important component in the set of elements that comprise the Burmese ethnic identity—to be Burmese is to be a Buddhist. This being so, Buddhism is the most important symbol of, and primary basis for, their feeling of mutual identification. To the extent, that is, that the Burmese identify with each other, this identification—except, of course, in times of external threat when the need for common defense becomes the salient factor—is based on their common allegiance to and membership in the Buddhist church. If, then, group solidarity derives from a feeling of mutual identification, it may be said that Burmese solidarity is fashioned from a common religious identity.[16]

[16]Buddhism not only contributes to the solidarity of the ethnic Burmese, but is one of their few bases of affinity with the tribal peoples of Burma, some of whom are Buddhists either in part or in whole. (And from the point of view of the Buddhist tribal peoples, Buddhism is one of the few grounds for their membership in a common political union with the ethnic Burmese.) We have already noted in chapter 1 that the Burmese, for the most part, hold the tribal peoples in low esteem and that their attitude is countered by hostility and resentment. This mutual suspicion and ill will has been in part responsible for the perduring conflict between the Burmese and the tribal peoples in the country, a conflict which continues to this very day, taking the form of ethnic insurgency against the central government. In the light of this ill will, the role of Buddhism in providing a basis for any feeling of political unity among these diverse ethnic groups is even more important. Ray does not exaggerate when he writes:

> Buddhism has also been a great unifying factor in Burma. Racial jealousies and rivalries did indeed exist even within the Saṃgha, but it was Buddhism that eventually brought the Talaings and the Pyus, the Burmans and the Shans, the Thais and the Karens and numerous other smaller ethnic groups under one banner in the name of one common religion, and unified them as one whole, though racially they had hardly anything in common and were even hostile to one another. Buddha was their common teacher, Dharma was their one common goal and Saṃgha was their one common meeting ground. [Ray 1946:264]

Any identity, of course, can be associated with either a positive or a negative feeling tone. Some people like, while others despise, what they are. Hence it should be noted in passing that the shared identity which is the basis for Burmese solidarity is highly positive and suffused with pride. This derives not only from the Burmese conviction of the greatness of Buddhism, but from its implication in the (real or putative) glories of the Burmese past. To many, Buddhism is associated with the trappings of historical royalty, the pageantry of a historical court, and the greatness of a still-remembered Burmese empire. The Burmese throne, it will be recalled, was not merely a secular throne; it was also a Buddhist throne, the king being the Defender of the Faith and a potential claimant to the title of Universal Emperor or of Future Buddha. To this very day most important Buddhist ceremonies, especially the initiation *(shin-byu)* and robe-offering *(kahteing)* ceremonies, take place in tinsel and gold replicas of a terrestrial and celestial palace. Dressed in their best silk, partaking of the finest food, and listening to court music, the Burmese participate in these Buddhist ceremonies with all the panoply appropriate to nobility. In short, even for a lowly peasant, to be a Buddhist is to be identified with the pomp and circumstance of nobility.

But if the Burmese insist that they are Buddhists and that Buddhism is the core of any definition of "Burmese," it is because they value whatever it is that Buddhism teaches or stands for. To be affiliated with the Buddhist church means to accept (or at least value) a set of beliefs and values which are "Buddhist." Although the worldly consequences of this dimension of Buddhism have already been discussed in relation to Buddhism as *Weltanschauung* and as soteriology, they must now be discussed in relation to Buddhism as a church, i.e., in relation to the meaning of Buddhist affiliation.

The Buddhist Monk and Group Identification

No one who has lived in Burma or in any other traditionally Buddhist country can doubt that the status of the Buddhist monk, taken as an ideal type, is the pivotal status in Buddhist society, or that the role of the Buddhist monk (taken again as an ideal type) is the central role in Buddhist thought and behavior. So far as the latter thesis is concerned, almost the entire Buddhist cultus, as I have emphasized over and over again, is centered on the monk not so much as its officiant as in the role of its focus and beneficiary. Whatever motives enter into ceremonies comprising the merit quest, the primary goal of these ceremonies is the feeding of monks, the offering of robes to monks, the provisioning of monasteries, and so on. Indeed, when one includes the daily feeding of monks as an element in the cultus, one might argue that the *raison d'être* of the Burmese village is the maintenance and sustenance of the monk and the monastery—that this is the primary goal to which all its activities, including its economic activities, are directed.

Obversely, this is the overriding purpose which, it might be argued, is primarily responsible for keeping the village together as a cohesive entity and a cooperating group, and which provides it with whatever integration and unity it may possess.

But one is tempted to go even further and to say that Burmese society as a whole—peasant society at any rate—is one collective enterprise whose primary function is the care and provision of monks. This almost obsessive concern with the monks is not, of course, a response to their intrinsic importance. Rather it is in part a response to their instrumental, and in part to their expressive value (chapter 17). The latter dimension is the relevant one for our present thesis concerning the relation between Buddhist affiliation and group solidarity.

Monks, of course, symbolize to each Buddhist many and different things, both conscious and unconscious. As beggars, as recipients, as celibates, as ascetics, as social isolates, as contemplatives—one might add many other attributes to the list—monks can and no doubt do evoke a variety of cognitive and affective responses, each associated with a wide set of conscious and unconscious symbolic meanings. Unfortunately, our present data are insufficient to discuss the personal and essentially unconscious symbolism associated with the monks. With respect, however, to their conscious and cultural symbolism, I think it is fair to say that (whatever else they may symbolize) the monks represent renunciation, i.e., the rejection of the worldly and profane for the otherworldly and the sacred.

If, then, the monk is a symbol of worldly renunciation, and if (as we have seen) he is venerated above all else in Burmese society, it must be because renunciation is a paramount value for Burmese laymen—despite the fact that they themselves are incapable of abandoning the world. To say, on the one hand, that they are hypocritical for not practicing what they preach is to confuse a people's values (what they think they ought to do, and indeed even wish to do) with their drives (what they are immediately motivated to do). To say, on the other hand, that this is a paradox is to misunderstand the social function of utopian values.[17] Representing what ideally people would like to be, but cannot and never will be, they nevertheless are of the greatest symbolic importance in human society.

If renunciation is a paramount value for the Burmese, the world-renouncing monk is for them the symbol of the ideal personality—one detached from all worldly interests *(loki)* in his exclusive devotion to otherworldly concerns *(lokuttara).* It is important to understand this symbol for

[17]In a provocative paper on Sinhalese Buddhism, Ames observes:

> There is no question that the ascetic, otherworldly salvation ideal is highly venerated by the Sinhalese. In this respect they are devoutly Buddhist. But on the other hand, and here is the paradox again, there is also no doubt that very few Sinhalese actually practice the ideal they venerate. [Ames 1964:27]

its contribution, not to our knowledge of the semantics of Burmese religious symbolism, but to our understanding of Burmese society, although the thesis to be developed—like almost all functional theses—is easier argued than proved. As a symbol of renunciation, the monk is a living example—a model—of what, though he cannot attain it himself, the Burmese values most. Although the monk may not be emulated, he is a model nevertheless, for he is not only a constant reminder of the Buddhist ideal, but demonstrates in his own life that this ideal can be approximated (if not attained). The monk, in short, is a vindication, a proof, of both the viability of the ideal and—to the extent that he appears to have achieved sanctity—its desirability.

But one may say even more. Ideals are difficult to sustain without models who embody them; without exemplary models the idea itself can die. A villager expressed this very well when he said that it is important that monks comply with the *Vinaya* rules because "otherwise, Buddhism will be destroyed." This is why he is "very unhappy," he continued, when he sees a monk in the theater or walking with a woman, for, "if the monks do not obey the *Vinaya,* there will be no *sāsana* [Buddhist church]." Translated into our concepts, I believe he was saying what I have tried to say, i.e., that without the exemplary monk, the layman would have no otherworldly model to emulate; and without a model of renunciation this central Buddhist ideal, and hence Buddhism itself, could well come to an end.[18]

As a symbol of worldly renunciation, the monk is important, not only for the preservation of the Buddhist ideal, but—what is more significant for the present argument—for the Burmese conception of themselves. Although holding to this otherworldly ideal, the Burmese, as we have seen, are not an excessively otherworldly people; indeed, their very brand of Buddhism represents an attempt to transform an otherworldly religion (nibbanic Buddhism) into a worldly one (kammatic Buddhism). Moreover, religion aside, the ethos of *secular* Burmese culture is worldly to the core. Although it is hazardous to summarize a cultural ethos by means of a few catchwords, we shall not go far astray if we say that the Burmese ethos can be highlighted by means of three terms: prestige *(goung:),* especially the prestige derived from wealth; charismatic power *(hpoung:);* and authority *(o-za),* in the sense of command over others.[19] These terms not only designate the three core concepts of the secular ethos of Burma, but as values

[18]This analysis is reminiscent of Durkheim's more general interpretation of the function of asceticism. Asceticism, he argues, is the "necessary school where men . . . acquire the qualities of disinterestness and endurance without which there would be no religion." (Durkheim 1954:316) The great ascetics, then, serve as a symbol of the sacrifice which every member of society must make if social life is to be maintained. A Burmese villager went even further than Durkheim in his analysis of the exemplary function of the Buddhist monkhood: "If there were no *Saṅgha,* people would behave like animals. Therefore they must be fed even if no merit were acquired from feeding them."

[19]For a brief discussion of these terms, see Nash (1965:76-79).

they represent the goals for whose attainment the Burmese strive and which (when possessed by others) they admire and respect.

This trinity, it will be noted, is not only exceedingly worldly—its three terms sum up almost everything which Buddhism designates as *lo:ki*—but subsists in constant tension with a parallel trinity of concepts which leads Buddhism to reject *lo:ki* in favor of *lo:kouktara,* the otherworldly. Thus the Buddhist doctrine of suffering *(dukkha)* derogates the Burmese value of prestige (acquired through wealth) by insisting—as it does with respect to any other secular value—that its attainment in no sense reduces suffering and that to aspire to it increases suffering. The Buddhist doctrine of impermanence *(anicca)* ridicules the Burmese value of power by pointing to its evanescent character. The Buddhist doctrine of nonself *(anattā)* impugns the Burmese value of the enjoyment of authority by indicating that the belief in a self that enjoys its exercise is a delusion. In the most general sense, the Buddhist truth that desire *(taṇhā)* must be subdued and overcome is the direct opposite of the Burmese wish that desire should (and may) be satisfied.

In order, then, to understand my argument concerning the crucial contribution of the monk to social integration in Burma, it is necessary to understand the tension that obtains between the worldly values of the Burmese—those that (in psychoanalytic terms) comprise the desires of their id and ego—and their otherworldly values, those that characterize their ego-ideal (again in the psychoanalytic sense). The former represent what the Burmese are; the latter what they think they ought and would like to be—but aren't. The former values are important to them; they aspire to their attainment and respect and admire those who exemplify them. And yet, their veneration is reserved not for the worldly successful but for the monk, the one who has rejected the values of the world. Thus, the Burmese admire and aspire to political power, but they literally worship the monk because (ideal-typically) he disdains it. They respect and aspire to great wealth, but they worship the monk precisely because he has renounced all wealth. They aspire to rebirth in *saṃsāra,* but they worship the monk because his aim is to achieve nirvana. In short, the Burmese worship the monk as a cultural symbol of their personal ego ideal, an ideal which they value but which (given their worldly desires and ambitions) they cannot live up to.[20]

Yet it is precisely because they cannot themselves live up to this ego ideal that it is all the more important for them that others in their society

[20]King points to another, symbolic meaning. The monkhood, he writes,

> is conceived to be the nearest possible approximation to the ideal society possible in time and space, which all men ought to approximate as nearly as possible in their social relations to each other. [King 1964:186]

However important this may be in Buddhist political thought, it finds little resonance among the Burmese—the villagers at any rate.

—the monks—should do so, for in venerating the monks they are, as it were, venerating what they most value in themselves.[21] In short, it is precisely because of the wide discrepancy between what they are and what they value, between their spiritual attainment and their spiritual goal, between (to use the jargon) their level of moral achievement and their level of moral aspiration, that the Burmese revere those who represent the value, the goal, the aspiration. For the Burmese the monk's renunciation is the vicarious expression of their own otherworldly ideal. In venerating the monk, they are venerating the symbol of their own ego ideal.[22]

Which brings us to the importance of this symbol for the integration of Burmese society. For it is through their reverence for this common symbol of a shared ego ideal that the Burmese, I believe, come to identify with each other; as Freud (1960:61) puts it, they "... have put one and the same object in the place of their ego ideal and have consequently identified themselves with one another in their ego." And this is how Burmese society achieves its highest degree of integration. To the extent that the members of a social group identify with each other, to that extent is the group characterized by

[21]Dutt's comments on the role of the ascetic in ancient—and contemporary—India is just as relevant for the Burmese as for the Indian context. Indian civilization, he writes,

> has clung to a fixed standard of values in which moral and spiritual values have preference over the material. It is because the *Bhiksu* or the *Sannyasin* embodies this standard in his own person in the most extreme and striking form, forsaking the world and all its goods for the spiritual quest, *Brahmacarya,* that the Indian mind perceives in him a symbolic relation to the hoary culture it is heir to. To the notion of those who suppose that it presents a phase of ancient Indian mentality that is now outgrown or outmoded, a corrective is supplied by the observation of what is a well-known phenomenon of Indian life even today. One who has need to sway the group-mind—whether a religious preacher, a social reformer or even a political leader—finds it to his purpose to appear in a *Sannyasin's* likeness in this country, for in that semblance he is able to command the highest respect and the readiest following. [Dutt 1962:43-44]

This comment on modern India describes the Burmese scene as well. For the Burmese it was the otherworldly U Nu, rather than his worldly political rivals, who was the true charismatic leader. It was his devotion to the ascetic ideal rather than his political programs that accounted for his extraordinary popular appeal.

[22]To say all this is to say little more than what a century ago Bishop Bigandet said:

> There is in man a natural disposition and inclination to admire individuals who, actuated by religious feelings, are induced to leave the world and separate from society in order to devote themselves more freely to the practice of religious duties. The more society is corrupted, the more its members value those persons who have the moral courage to estrange themselves from the centre of vice, that they may preserve themselves from contamination. In fact, religious are esteemed in proportion to the extent of the contempt they have for this world. The Phongyies occupy precisely this position in the eyes of their co-religionists. Their order stands in bold relief over the society they belong to. Their dress, their mode of life, their voluntary denial of all gratification of sensual appetites, centre upon them the admiring eyes of all. They are looked upon as the imitators and followers of Buddha; they hold ostensibly before ordinary believers the pattern of that perfection they have been taught so fondly to revere. The Phongyies are as living mementoes, reminding the people of all that is most sacred and perfect in practical religion. (Bigandet 1912:303-304).

social integration. This, of course, is the main reason that monastic worldliness poses a serious threat to Burmese society. Tainted by implication with the profane, monks who engage in political action and other forms of worldly behavior are no longer revered. If, then, the common veneration for the symbolic ego ideal is weakened, one of the few bases for mutual identification is similarly weakened, and with it the primary basis for social integration in Burma.

Appendix

On the Burmese Romanization by F. K. Lehman

In order that scholars who are interested may be able to make the connection between the Burmese words as used in this work and standard Burmese-language texts and dictionaries, I have employed a transcription that is based upon recent linguistic analysis of modern Burmese phonology. The transcription is not of the written but of the modern spoken form, but anyone who knows any Burmese can easily work back to the written forms from it. Two recent works provide the basis for this transcription: Maran La Raw, *Tone in Jinghpo and Burmese*, doctoral thesis, University of Illinois, 1970 and F. K. Lehman, "Some Diachronic Rules of Burmese Phonology," forthcoming in *Occasional Papers of the Wolfenden Society on Tibeto-Burman Linguistics,* II, 1970).

The principles on the transcription are simple. First, every syllable has one of several "tones," viz., the First or Short tone, marked by a subscript dot (.); the Second or Middle tone, marked except on a word final syllable by the hyphen (-), and in word final position unmarked; and the Heavy Long Breathy, or Third tone, marked by a postposed colon (:). If a syllable other than word final is not separated from the following syllable by any mark or space, it is to be read as toneless or proclitic, the vowel being the short, neutral vowel, as in first syllable of English p*a*rade. First tone is high in pitch, short, and the vowel ends in a weak or creaky-sounding glottal closure; Second tone is middle in pitch; Heavy tone is high in pitch, long, and the vowel before the pause ends in a breathy drop in pitch.

Burmese syllables are either open or closed. In open syllables the vowel qualities are:

i with the approximate sound of English	*ee* in *sleep*
u	*oo* in *stoop*
ei	*a* in *tame*
ou	*o* in *row*
e	*e* in *pen*
o	*aw* in *law*
a	*ah* in *bah!*

In closed syllables the vowels are:

i with the approximate sound of English	*i* in *sit*
u	*u* in *put*
ei and *ou* as above for open syllables	
e as above for open syllables	
ai with the approximate sound of English	*i* in *kite*
au with the approximate sound of English	*ou* in *out*
a with approximately the sound of English	*u* in *cup*

As seen above, some vowels are simple, others are diphthongs, and in modern Burmese there is a very simple rule, viz., in closed syllables a diphthong is followed by a velar (*k* or *ng*), but a simple vowel is followed by a dental (*t* or *n*). These finals are very weakly articulated, especially in the dialect of Rangoon, but instrumental studies in phonetics show that they are clearly present, even though what one hears most prominently in syllables closed with stops is a strong glottal stop, and in syllables closed with a nasal, nasalisation of the vowel as in French nasalised vowels, say the vowel of *mon* (my). However, for at least many speakers, if a syllable final velar *k* or *ng* is followed within a word by a syllable with a dental or labial initial (*t,d, n,* or *p,b,m*) the final is pronounced at the point of articulation of the following initial, i.e., either as a dental or a labial. I have not shown this in the transcription. I have, however, indicated the voicing of initial consonants that generally takes place when a syllable with an otherwise unvoiced initial consonant follows, within the word, a syllable on First, Second, or Third tone, either open or closed with a nasal. Thus, verb-ending *-te* (non-future), as in hket*te* (is difficult), but na-*de* (is painful), with assimilative voicing. Where, less regularly, this assimilative voicing occurs after a toneless proclitic syllable, I have also shown it. Syllables closed with stop consonants are uniformly pronounced with high pitch and a somewhat short, checked vowel, and so have no contrasting tones.

In a number of places I have used the standard, nontechnical English spellings of Burmese words, especially in place names, such as Rangoon or Yeigyi. In these cases syllable-initial clusters *ky* and *gy* and *hky* represent, as in the Burmese writing system, what is now pronounced as *c, j,* and *ch,* respectively.

Burmese initials are also easily explained. No syllable can begin with a vowel, and any syllable written without anything before the vowel is to be pronounced with an initial glottal stop. Nasal and unvoiced stop consonant initials are distinguished as either aspirated or unaspirated, and this contrasts with English, where there are no aspirated nasals and where word-initial unvoiced consonants are *invariably* accompanied by a puff or air (aspiration). In this transcription, then, the initials are:

k with approximately the value of English final *k* in *back*
hk initial *k* in *kill*
g *g* in *good*
ng *ng* in *sing*
c final of *catch*
hc initial *ch* of *church*
j initial of *judge*
sh has about the sound of English *sh* of *shoe,* and
th has about the sound of English *th* in *thing* (note that the aspirated dental consonant is written *ht,* so that there is no ambiguity thus, *thi,* "to know," vs. *hti:,* "umbrella."
ny initial sound of *new*
hny which is the foregoing with the addition of strong aspiration, and so on for dental and labial initial consonants and nasals, and for the contrast in aspiration between *s* (unaspirated, as in *sa:de,* "eats") and *hs* (aspirated, as in *hsaya,* "teacher").
When *th* undergoes assimilative voicing, it is transcribed here as *d.*

NOTE: Many words listed in the text as "Burmese" are in fact simply Burmese *pronunciations* of *Pali* words. In many of these cases, where the word has no currency except in purely Pali contexts, it will not appear in standard Burmese dictionaries, but where it has achieved some currency in Burmese prose contexts, written or spoken, it is likely to be found in the dictionaries. There is no rule or consistency about this matter.

References Cited

Pali Texts (Translations)

The Book of the Discipline. Translated by I. B. HORNER. London, Oxford University Press, 1938, 1940, 1942.

The Book of the Gradual Sayings. Translated by F. L. WOODWARD. London, Luzac, Co., 1960.

The Book of the Kindred Sayings. Translated by C. A. F. RHYS DAVIDS. London, Oxford University Press, 1917.

Buddhist Suttas. Translated by T. W. RHYS DAVIDS. Oxford, Clarendon Press, 1881.

Dhammapada. Translated by C. A. F. RHYS DAVIDS. London, Oxford University Press, 1931.

Dialogues of the Buddha. Translated by T. W. and C. A. F. RHYS DAVIDS. London, Oxford University Press, 1921.

The History of the Buddha's Religion. Translated by BIMALA CHURN LAW. London, Luzac & Co., 1952.

The Jātaka. E. B. COWELL, ed. London, Luzac & Co., 1957.

The Mahāvastu. Translated by J. J. JONES. 3 vols London, Luzac & Co., 1949-56.

The Middle Length Sayings. Translated by I. B. HORNER. London, Luzac & Co., 1957.

The Minor Readings. Translated by BHIKKHU ÑĀṂAMOLI. London, Luzac & Co., 1960.

The Path of Purity. translated by PE MAUNG TIN. London, Oxford University Press, 1956.

The Pāṭimokkha. Bangkok, The Social Science Association Press of Thailand, 1966.

The Questions of King Milinda. Translated by T. W. RHYS DAVIDS. Oxford, Clarendon Press, 1890.

Sutta-Nipāta. Translated by V. FAUSBOLL. Oxford, Clarendon Press, 1881.

The Vinaya. Translated by T. W. RHYS DAVIDS and HERMANN OLDENBERG. Oxford, Clarendon Press, 1885.

Woven Cadences of Early Buddhists. Translated by E. M. HARE. London, Oxford University Press, 1947.

Other Works

ALABASTER, HENRY
1871 *The Wheel of the Law.* London, Trübner.
ALEXANDER, FRANZ
1931 "Buddhistic Training as an Artificial Catatonia." *Psychoanalytic Review,* 18:129-45.
AMES, MICHAEL
1964 "Magical-animism and Buddhism: A Structural Analysis of the Sinhalese Religious System." *Journal of Asian Studies,* 23:21-52.
1966 "Ritual Prestations and the Structure of the Sinhalese Pantheon." In *Anthropological Studies in Theravada Buddhism,* Southeast Asia Studies No. 13, Yale University.
ANESAKI, M., and J. TAKAKUSU
1911 "Dhyana." In the *Encyclopedia of Religion and Ethics,* Edinburgh, T. & T. Clark.
BA U
1959 *My Burma, the Autobiography of a President.* New York, Taplinger Publishing Co.
BAREAU, ANDRE
1961 "Indian and Ancient Chinese Buddhism: Institutions Analogous to the Jisa." *Comparative Studies in Society and History,* 3:443-51.
BASHAM, A. L.
1961 *The Wonder That Was India.* London, Sidgwick & Jackson.
BATESON, J. H.
1911 "Creed (Buddhist)." In the *Encyclopedia of Religion and Ethics,* Edinburgh, T. & T. Clark.
BIGANDET, PAUL AMBROSE
1912 *The Life or Legend of Gaudama, the Buddha of the Burmese.* 2 vols. London, Trübner.
BLANCHARD, WENDELL (in collaboration with HENRY C. AHALT, *et. al.*)
1958 *Thailand: Its People, Its Society, Its Culture.* New Haven, HRAF Press.
BODE, MABEL H.
1897 Introduction to *Sasanavamsa.* London, H. Frowde.
1909 *Pali Literature of Burma.* London, Prize Publication Fund.
BROWN, R. GRANT
1914 "Thieves' Night at Mandalay." *Journal of the Burma Research Society,* 4:229-30
1917 "The Dragon of Tagaung." *Journal of the Royal Asiatic Society,* 13:741-51.
BURLAND, C. A.
1967 *The Arts of the Alchemists.* London, Weidenfeld & Nicolson.
BUTLER, C.
1962 *Benedictine Monachism.* London, Allen & Unwin.
BYLES, MARIE BEUZEVILLE
1965 *Paths to Inner Calm.* London, Allen & Unwin.
CADY, JOHN
1958 *A History of Modern Burma.* Ithaca, N.Y., Cornell University Press.

CARSTAIRS, G. MORRIS
1957 *The Twice Born.* London, Hogarth Press.
CHARLES, G. P.
1955 *Buddhism in Burma.* Rangoon, Commission on Buddhism of the Burma Christian Council.
COCHRANE, HENRY PARK
1904 *Among the Burmans.* New York, Fleming H. Revell.
COEDÈS, G.
1968 *The Indianized States of Southeast Asia.* Honolulu, East-West Center Press.
COHN, NORMAN
1961 *The Pursuit of the Millennium.* New York, Harper Torchbooks.
1962 "Medieval Millenarism: Its Bearing on the Comparative Study of Millenarian Movements." In *Millennial Dreams in Action,* SYLVIA L. THRUPP, ed. (Comparative Studies in Society and History, Supplement II). The Hague, Mouton & Co.
COLQUHOUN, ARCHIBALD ROSS
1885 *Amongst the Shans.* New York, Scribner & Welford.
CONZE, EDWARD
1953 *Buddhism: Its Essence and Development.* Oxford, Bruno Cassirer.
COOMARASWAMY, ANANDA K.
1935 *Elements of Buddhist Iconography.* Cambridge, Mass., Harvard University Press.
COPLESTON, REGINALD S.
1908 *Buddhism, Primitive and Present in Magadha and in Ceylon.* London, Longmans, Green & Co.
COX, HIRAM
1821 *Journal of a Residence in the Burmhan Empire and More Particularly at the Court of Amarapoorah.* London, J. Warren [etc.]
CRAWFURD, J.
1834 *Journal of an Embassy from the Governor General of India to the Court of Ava in the Year 1827.* 2 vols. London, Henry Colburn.
CROSTHWAITE, SIR CHARLES
1912 *The Pacification of Burma.* London, E. Arnold & Co.
DAVID-NEEL, ALEXANDRA
1932 *Magic and Mystery in Tibet.* New York, University Books.
DAVIDS, C. A. F. RHYS
1921 Introduction to "Ātānātiya Suttanta," in *Dialogues of the Buddha,* Vol. 3. London Oxford, University Press.
DAVIDS, T. W. RHYS
1908 *Early Buddhism.* London, A. Constable & Co.
1912 "Expiation and Atonement." In the *Encyclopedia of Religion and Ethics.* Edinburgh, T. & T. Clark.
DUCKETT, ELEANOR SHIPLEY
1961 *The Gateway to the Middle Ages: Monasticism.* Ann Arbor, University of Michigan Press, Ann Arbor Paperbacks.
DURKHEIM, EMILE
1954 *The Elementary Forms of the Religious Life.* Glencoe, Ill., The Free Press.
DUROISELLE, CHARLES
1921-22 "Wathundaye, the Earth Goddess of Burma." *Annual Report, Archaeological Survey of India* :144-46.

DUTT, SUKUMAR
1924 *Early Buddhist Monachism.* London, Trübner.
1962 *Buddhist Monks and Monasteries of India.* London, George Allen & Unwin.
EDGERTON, FRANKLIN
1942 "Dominant Ideas in the Formation of Indian Culture." *Journal of the American Oriental Society,* 62:151-56.
ELIADE, MIRCEA
1958 *Yoga: Immortality and Freedom.* New York, Pantheon Books.
1962 *The Forge and the Crucible.* New York, Harper & Row.
ELIOT, CHARLES NORTON E.
1921 *Hinduism and Buddhism, an Historical Sketch.* 3 vols. London, E. Arnold & Co.
EVERS, HANS-DIETER
1968 "Buddha and the Seven Gods." *Journal of Asian Studies,* 27:541-50.
FERENCZI, SANDOR
1952 *First Contributions to Psychoanalysis.* London, Hogarth Press.
Final Report of the Riot Inquiry Committee
1939 Rangoon, Government Printing.
FRAZER, SIR JAMES GEORGE
1920 *The Golden Bough.* London, Macmillan & Co.
FREUD, SIGMUND
1956 *Collected Papers.* London, Hogarth Press.
1960 *Group Psychology and the Analysis of the Ego.* New York, Bantam Books.
GARD, RICHARD A.
1965 "Buddhism." In *A Reader's Guide to the Great Religions.* CHARLES J. ADAMS, ed. New York, The Free Press.
GOGERLY, D. J.
1908 *Ceylon Buddhism.* Colombo, The Wesleyan Methodist Book Room; [etc., etc.]
GOMBRICH, RICHARD
1966 "The Consecration of a Buddhist Image." *Journal of Asian Studies,* 26:23-36.
GOONERATNE, DANDRIS DE SILVA
1866 "On Demonology and Witchcraft in Ceylon." *Journal of the Royal Asiatic Society, Ceylon Branch,* 4:1-117.
GORER, GEOFFREY
1943 "Burmese Personality." New York, Institute for Intercultural Relations. (Mimeograph)
GOULLART, PETER
1941 *The Monastery of Jade Mountain.* London, John Murray.
GOVERNMENT OF INDIA
1902 *Census of India.* 1901, Vol. XII, Part I (Burma Report). Rangoon, Government Printing.
GRIMM, GEORGE
1958 *The Doctrine of the Buddha.* Berlin, Akademie-Verlag.
HACKETT, WILLIAM DUNN
1953 "The Pa-O People of the Shan State, Union of Burma." Unpublished Ph.D. thesis, Cornell University.

HACKMANN, H. F.
1910 *Buddhism as a Religion: Its Historical Development and its Present Condition.* London, Probsthain & Co.
HAGEN, EVERETT
1962 *On the Theory of Social Change.* Homewood, Ill., Dorsey Press.
HALL, FIELDING
1903 *The Soul of a People.* London, Macmillan & Co.
HALLOWELL, A. IRVING
1955 *Culture and Experience.* Philadelphia, University of Pennsylvania Press.
HALPERN, JOEL MARTIN
1958 *Aspects of Village Life and Culture Change in Laos.* New York, Council on Economic and Cultural Affairs.
HAMILTON, ALEXANDER
1930 *A New Account of the East Indies.* 2 vols. London, Argonaut Press.
HANKS, L. M., Jr.
1949 "The Quest for Individual Autonomy in Burmese Personality." *Psychiatry,* XII, 285 ff.
HARDY, R. SPENCE
1850 *Eastern Monachism.* London, Partridge & Oakey.
HARVEY, G. E.
1925 *History of Burma from the Earliest Times to 10 March 1824, the Beginning of the English Conquest.* London, Longmans, Green & Co.
1946 *British Rule in Burma, 1824-1942.* London, Faber & Faber.
HITSON, HAZEL MARIE
1959 "Family Patterns and Paranoidal Personality Structure in Boston and Burma." Unpublished Ph.D. thesis, Radcliffe College.
HLA MAUNG
n.d. "My Early Monastic Education." Rangoon, International Institute of Advanced Buddhistic Studies. (Mimeograph)
HORNER, ISALINE BLEW
1938 Introduction to *The Book of the Discipline.* London, Oxford University Press.
HPE AUNG
1954 "Clarification and Critical Analysis of the Various Processes Involved in the Attainment of Lokiya Samadhi through Samatha." *Journal of the Burma Research Society,* 37:17-23.
HTIN AUNG
1948 *Burmese Folk Tales.* London, Oxford University Press.
1962 *Folk Elements in Burmese Buddhism.* London, Oxford University Press.
1966 *Burmese Monk's Tales.* New York, Columbia University Press.
HUBER, JACK
1967 *Through an Eastern Window.* Boston, Houghton Mifflin Co.
INGERSOLL, JASPER C.
1963 "The Priest and the Path." Unpublished Ph.D. thesis, Cornell University.
JOHNSON, O. S.
1928 *A Study of Chinese Alchemy.* Shanghai, The Commercial Press.

JUNG, C. G.
1953 *Psychology and Alchemy.* New York, Pantheon Books.
KAPLEAU, PHILIP
1967 *The Three Pillars of Zen.* Boston, Beacon Press, Beacon Paperback.
KARDINER, ABRAM
1945 *The Psychological Frontiers of Society.* New York, Columbia University Press.
KING, WINSTON L.
1964 *A Thousand Lives Away.* Cambridge, Mass., Harvard University Press.
KLAUSNER, WILLIAM J.
1964 "Popular Buddhism in Northeast Thailand." In *Cross-Cultural Understanding,* F. S. C. NORTHROP and HELEN H. LIVINGSTON, eds. New York, Harper & Row.
KNOX, ROBERT
1911 *An Historical Relation of Ceylon.* Glasgow, James MacLehose & Sons.
LA VALLÉE POUSSIN, LOUIS
1911 "Cosmogony and Cosmology, Buddhist." In the *Encyclopedia of Religion and Ethics.* Edinburgh, T. & T. Clark.
1917 *The Way to Nirvana.* Cambridge, Eng., The University Press.
1918 "Religious Orders: Indian." In the *Encyclopedia of Religion and Ethics.* Edinburgh, T. & T. Clark.
1921 "Tantrism." In the *Encyclopedia of Religion and Ethics.* Edinburgh, T. & T. Clark.
LEHMAN, F. K.
1967 "Ethnic Categories in Burma and the Theory of Social Systems." In *Southeast Asian Tribes, Minorities and Nations,* Peter Kunstadter (ed.), Princeton, Princeton University Press.
LEUBA, JAMES HENRY
1925 *The Psychology of Religious Mysticism.* New York, Harcourt, Brace & Co.
LÉVY, PAUL
1957 *Buddhism: A 'Mystery Religion'?* London, University of London Press.
LOUNSBERY, G. CONSTANT
1935 *Buddhist Meditation in the Southern School.* London, Kegan Paul, Trench, Trübner & Co.
LU PE WIN
1966 "The Jātakas in Burma." In *Essays Offered to G. H. Luce,* BA SHIN, JEAN BOISSELIER, and A. B. GRISWOLD, eds. Ascona, Switzerland, Artibus Asiae.
LUCE, G. H.
1940 "Economic Life of the Early Burman." *Journal of the Burma Research Society,* Vol. XXX, Part I (April 1940), p. 326.
1956 "The 550 Jatakas in Old Burma." *Artibus Asiae,* 19:291-307.
MALALASEKERA, GEORGE PEIRIS (ed.)
1960 *Dictionary of Pali Proper Names.* London, Luzac & Co.
MALCOM, HOWARD
1839 *Travels in Southeastern Asia.* 2 vols. Boston, Gould, Kendall & Lincoln.
MAUNG MAUNG
1959 *Burma's Constitution.* The Hague, Martinus Nijhoff.

1963 *Law and Custom in Burma and the Burmese Family.* The Hague, Martinus Nijhoff.

MAUSS, MARCEL
1967 *The Gift.* New York, W. W. Norton & Co.

MENDELSON, E. MICHAEL
1960 "Religion and Authority in Modern Burma." *The World Today,* 16:110-18.
1961*a* "A Messianic Buddhist Association in Upper Burma." *Bulletin of the School of Oriental and African Studies, University of London,* 24:560-80.
1961*b* "The King of the Weaving Mountain." *Royal Central Asian Journal,* 48:229-37.
1963*a* "Observations on a Tour in the Region of Mount Popa, Central Burma." *France-Asie,* 179:786-807.
1963*b* "The Uses of Religious Skepticism in Burma." *Diogenes,* 41:94-116.
1964 "Buddhism and the Burmese Establishment." *Archives de Sociologie des Religions,* 17:85-95.
1965 "Initiation and the Paradox of Power: A Sociological Approach." In *Initiation,* C. J. BLEEKER, ed. Leiden, E. J. Brill.

MILLER, ROBERT J.
1961 "Buddhist Monastic Economy and the Jisa Mechanism." *Comparative Studies in Society and History,* 3:427-38.

MILNE, MARY and WILBERT WILLIS COCHRANE,
1910 *Shans at Home.* London, John Murray.

MOERMAN, MICHAEL
1966 "Ban Ping's Temple: The Center of a 'Loosely Structured' Society." In *Anthropological Studies in Theravada Buddhism,* Cultural Report Series No. 13, Southeast Asia Studies, Yale University.

MORGAN, KENNETH W. (ed.)
1956 *The Path of the Buddha.* New York, Ronald Press.

MULDER, J. A. NIELS
1969 *Monks, Merit and Motivation.* Special Report Series No. 1, Center for Southeast Asian Studies, Northern Illinois University.

NASH, JUNE and MANNING
1963 "Marriage, Family and Population Growth in Upper Burma." *Southwestern Journal of Anthropology,* 19:251-66.

NASH, MANNING
1965 *The Golden Road to Modernity.* New York, John Wiley & Sons.

NISBET, JOHN
1901 *Burma Under British Rule—and Before.* 2 vols. London, A. Constable & Co.

NYANAPONIKA, THERA
1962 *The Heart of Buddhist Meditation.* London, Rider & Co.

OBEYESEKERE, GANANATH
1968 "Theodicy, Sin and Salvation in a Sociology of Buddhism." In *Dialectic in Practical Religion,* E. R. LEACH, ed. Cambridge, Eng., The University Press.

The Pali Text Society's Pali-English Dictionary. London, Luzac & Co., 1959.

PERTOLD, O.
1929 "The Conception of the Soul in the Sinhalese Demon Worship." *Archiv Orientalni*, 1:316-22.

PFANNER, DAVID E.
1962 "Rice and Religion in a Burmese Village." Unpublished Ph. D. thesis, Cornell University.
1966 "The Buddhist Monk in Rural Burmese Society." In *Anthropological Studies in Theravada Buddhism*, Cultural Report Series No. 13, Southeast Asia Studies, Yale University.

PFANNER, DAVID E., and JASPER INGERSOLL
1962 "Theravada Buddhism and Village Economic Behavior." *Journal of Asian Studies*, 21:341-61.

PIKER, STEVEN
1968 "The Relationship of Belief Systems to Behavior in Rural Thai Society." *Asian Survey*, 8:384-99.

PRATT, JAMES BISSETT
1915 *India and its Faiths, a Travelor's Record.* Boston and New York, Houghton Mifflin Co.
1928 *The Pilgrimage of Buddhism.* New York, The Macmillan Co.

PURSER, W. C. B., and K. J. SAUNDERS
1914 *Modern Buddhism in Burma.* Rangoon, Christian Literature Society.

PYE, LUCIAN W.
1962 *Politics, Personality and Nation Building: Burma's Search for Identity.* New Haven, Yale University Press.

RADHAKRISHNAN, S. (ed. and trans.)
1950 *The Dhammapada.* London, Oxford University Press.

RAHULA, WALPOLA
1956 *History of Buddhism in Ceylon.* Colombo, M. D. Gunasena.

RAJADHON, PHYA ANUMAN
1961 *Life and Ritual in Old Siam.* New Haven, HRAF Press.

RAY, NIHAR-RANJAN
1946 *An Introduction to the Study of Theravada Buddhism in Burma.* Calcutta, Calcutta University Press.

REDFIELD, ROBERT
1956 *Peasant Society and Culture.* Chicago, University of Chicago Press.

Report on the Rebellion in Burma up to 3rd May, 1931.
1931 *House of Commons, London. Sessional Papers: Vol. XII for 1930-31 (Cmd. 3900)*, pp. 1-15.

RHYS DAVIDS. See DAVIDS.

RYAN, BRYCE (in collaboration with L. D. JAYASENA and D. C. R. WICKREMESINGHE)
1958 *Sinhalese Village.* Coral Gables, University of Miami Press.

SANGERMANO, VICENTIUS
1893 *The Burmese Empire a Hundred Years Ago.* Westminster, A. Constable & Co.

SANSOM, GEORGE
1946 *Japan: A Short Cultural History.* London, Cresset Press.

SARATHCHANDRA, E. R.
1953 *The Sinhalese Folk Play.* Colombo, Ceylon University Press Board.

SARKISYANZ, E.
1965 *Buddhist Backgrounds of the Burmese Revolution.* The Hague, Martinus Nijhoff.

SCOTT, SIR JAMES GEORGE. See SHWAY YOE.

SCOTT, SIR JAMES GEORGE, and J. P. HARDIMAN

1900 *Gazeteer of Upper Burma and the Shan States.* Vol. 1, Rangoon, Government Printing.

SEIN TU, U.

1964 "The Psychodynamics of Burmese Personality." *Journal of the Burma Research Society,* 47:263-286.

SHATTOCK, E. H.

1958 *An Experiment in Mindfulness.* London, Rider & Co.

SHWAY YOE (JAMES GEORGE SCOTT)

1896 *The Burman: His Life and Notions.* London, Macmillan & Co.

SLATER, ROBERT HENRY LAWSON

1951 *Paradox and Nirvana.* Chicago, University of Chicago Press.

SMITH, DONALD EUGENE

1965 *Religion and Politics in Burma.* Princeton, N.J., Princeton University Press.

SOBHANA PHRA SĀSANA

1966 Introduction to *The Patimokkha.* Bangkok, The Social Science Association Press of Thailand.

SPIRO, MELFORD E.

1955 *Kibbutz: Venture in Utopia.* Cambridge, Mass., Harvard University Press.

1958 *Children of the Kibbutz.* Cambridge, Mass., Harvard University Press.

1965 "Religious Systems as Culturally Constituted Defense Mechanisms." In *Context and Meaning in Cultural Anthropology,* MELFORD E. SPIRO, (ed). New York, The Free Press.

1966 "Buddhism and Economic Saving in Burma." *American Anthropologist,* 68:1163-73.

1967 *Burmese Supernaturalism.* Englewood Cliffs, N.J., Prentice-Hall.

1968 "Religion, Personality, and Behavior in Burma." *American Anthropologist,* 70:359-63.

1969 "The Psychological Functions of Witchcraft Belief: The Burmese Case." In *Mental Health Research in Asia and the Pacific,* WILLIAM CAUDILL and TSUNG-YI LIN (eds.). Honolulu, East-West Center Press.

SPIRO, MELFORD E. and D'ANDRADE, ROY

1958 "A Cross-Cultural Study of Some Supernatural Beliefs." *American Anthropologist,* 60:456-66.

STEELE, JAMES

n.d. "A Preliminary Analysis of the Burmese Rorshachs."

STERN, THEODORE

1968 "Ariya and the Golden Book." *Journal of Asian Studies,* 27:297-328.

STEVENSON, MRS. [MARGARET] SINCLAIR

1915 *The Heart of Jainism.* London, Oxford University Press.

SUZUKI, D. T.

1963 *Outlines of Mahayana Buddhism.* New York, Schocken Books.

SYMES, MICHAEL

1800 *An Account of an Embassy to the Kingdom of Ava.* London, Printed for J. Debrett.

TACHIBANA, S.
1926 *The Ethics of Buddhism.* London, Oxford University Press.
TAMBIAH, S. J.
1968 "The Ideology of Merit and the Social Correlates of Buddhism in a Thai Village." In *Dialectic in Practical Religion,* E. R. LEACH, ed. Cambridge, Eng., The University Press.
TAYLOR, F. SHERWOOD
1962 *The Alchemists.* New York, Collier Books.
TENNENT, JAMES EMERSON
1860 *Ceylon, An Account of the Island.* London, Longman, Green, Longman, & Roberts.
THAN MAUNG
1915 "A Note on the Burmese Thieves' Night." *Journal of the Burmese Research Society,* 5:33-34.
THAN TUN
1955 "The Buddhist Church in Burma During the Pagan Period 1044-1287." Unpublished Ph.D. thesis, University of London.
THITTILA, U. See MORGAN (ed.).
THOMAS, E. J.
1960 *The Life of Buddha as Legend and History.* New York, Barnes & Noble.
THOULESS, ROBERT H.
1940 *Conventionalization and Assimilation in Religious Movements as Problems in Social Psychology.* London, Oxford University Press.
THRUPP, SYLVIA (ed.)
1962 *Millennial Dreams in Action.* (Comparative Studies in Society and History, Supplement II.) the Hague, Mouton & Co.
TIN, PE MAUNG
1936 "Buddhism in the Inscriptions of Pagan." *Journal of the Burmese Research Society,* 26:52.
1964 *Buddhist Devotion and Meditation.* London, S.P.C.K.
TIN, PE MAUNG and LUCE, G. H. (trans.)
1923 *The Glass Chronicle of the Kings of Burma.* London, Oxford University Press.
TIN SWE
1965 "Sixteen Days in the Sasana Yeiktha." *The* [Rangoon] *Guardian,* 12:40-43.
TINKER, HUGH
1959 *The Union of Burma, a Study of the First Years of Independence.* London and New York, Oxford University Press.
TRANT, T. A.
1827 *Two Years in Ava from May 1824 to May 1826.* London, John Murray.
TROELTSCH, ERNST
1931 *The Social Teaching of the Christian Churches.* London, George Allen & Unwin.
TUVESON, ERNST LEE
1964 *Millennium and Utopia.* New York, Harper Torchbooks.
VON DER MEHDEN, FRED R.
1963 *Religion and Nationalism in Southeast Asia.* Madison, Wis., University of Wisconsin Press.

WADDELL, L. AUSTINE

1911 "Demons and Spirits (Buddhist)." In the *Encyclopedia of Religion and Ethics*, Edinburgh, T. & T. Clark.

1926 "Jewel (Buddhist)." In the *Encyclopedia of Religion and Ethics*, Edinburgh, T. & T. Clark.

1967 *The Buddhism of Tibet.* Cambridge, Eng., W. Heffer & Sons.

WEBER, MAX

1930 *The Protestant Ethic and the Spirit of Capitalism.* New York, Charles Scribner's Sons.

1946 *From Max Weber: Essays in Sociology.* H. H. GERTH and C. WRIGHT MILLS, eds. New York, Oxford University Press.

1958 *The Religion of India.* Glencoe, Ill., The Free Press.

1963 *The Sociology of Religion.* Boston, Beacon Press.

WELBON, GUY RICHARD

1967 *The Buddhist Nirvana and its Western Interpreters.* Chicago, University of Chicago Press.

WELLS, KENNETH E.

1960 *Thai Buddhism: Its Rites and Activities.* Bangkok, The Christian Book Store.

WHITE, SIR HERBERT THIRKELL

1913 *A Civil Servant in Burma.* London, E. Arnold & Co.

WIJESEKERA, N. D.

1949 *The People of Ceylon.* Colombo, M. D. Gunasena.

WILSON, DAVID A.

1962 *Politics in Thailand.* Ithaca, N.Y., Cornell University Press.

WINTER, CHRISTOPHER TATCHELL

1858 *Six Months in British Burmah; or, India Beyond the Ganges in 1857.* London, Richard Bentley.

YALMAN, NUR

1962 "The Ascetic Buddhist Monks of Ceylon." *Ethnology,* 3:315-28.

1963 "On the Purity and Sexuality of Women in the Castes of Malabar and Ceylon." *Journal of the Royal Anthropological Institute,* 93:25-58.

YANG, C. K.

1967 *Religion in Chinese Society.* Berkeley and Los Angeles, University of California Press.

ZIMMER, HEINRICH

1962 *Myths and Symbols in Indian Art and Civilization.* New York, Harper Torchbooks.

Index

72 73 74 12 11 10 9 8 7 6 5 4 3 2 1

Vol. II: Renaissance, Enlightenment, Modern TB/39

LUDWIG WITTGENSTEIN: The Blue and Brown Books ° TB/1211

LUDWIG WITTGENSTEIN: Notebooks, 1914-1916 TB/1441

Political Science & Government

C. E. BLACK: The Dynamics of Modernization: *A Study in Comparative History* TB/1321

DENIS W. BROGAN: Politics in America. *New Introduction by the Author* TB/1469

ROBERT CONQUEST: Power and Policy in the USSR: *The Study of Soviet Dynastics* ° TB/1307

JOHN B. MORRALL: Political Thought in Medieval Times TB/1076

KARL R. POPPER: The Open Society and Its Enemies *Vol. I: The Spell of Plato* TB/1101 *Vol. II: The High Tide of Prophecy: Hegel, Marx, and the Aftermath* TB/1102

HENRI DE SAINT-SIMON: Social Organization, The Science of Man, and Other Writings. || *Edited and Translated with an Introduction by Felix Markham* TB/1152

CHARLES SCHOTTLAND, Ed.: The Welfare State ** TB/1323

JOSEPH A. SCHUMPETER: Capitalism, Socialism and Democracy TB/3008

Psychology

LUDWIG BINSWANGER: Being-in-the-World: *Selected Papers.* || *Trans. with Intro. by Jacob Needleman* TB/1365

MIRCEA ELIADE: Cosmos and History: *The Myth of the Eternal Return* § TB/2050

MIRCEA ELIADE: Myth and Reality TB/1369

SIGMUND FREUD: On Creativity and the Unconscious: *Papers on the Psychology of Art, Literature, Love, Religion.* § *Intro. by Benjamin Nelson* TB/45

J. GLENN GRAY: The Warriors: *Reflections on Men in Battle. Introduction by Hannah Arendt* TB/1294

WILLIAM JAMES: Psychology: *The Briefer Course. Edited with an Intro. by Gordon Allport* TB/1034

Religion: Ancient and Classical, Biblical and Judaic Traditions

MARTIN BUBER: Eclipse of God: *Studies in the Relation Between Religion and Philosophy* TB/12

MARTIN BUBER: Hasidism and Modern Man. *Edited and Translated by Maurice Friedman* TB/839

MARTIN BUBER: The Knowledge of Man. *Edited with an Introduction by Maurice Friedman. Translated by Maurice Friedman and Ronald Gregor Smith* TB/135

MARTIN BUBER: Moses. *The Revelation and the Covenant* TB/837

MARTIN BUBER: The Origin and Meaning of Hasidism. *Edited and Translated by Maurice Friedman* TB/835

MARTIN BUBER: The Prophetic Faith TB/73

MARTIN BUBER: Two Types of Faith: *Interpenetration of Judaism and Christianity* ° TB/75

M. S. ENSLIN: Christian Beginnings TB/5

M. S. ENSLIN: The Literature of the Christian Movement TB/6

HENRI FRANKFORT: Ancient Egyptian Religion: *An Interpretation* TB/77

Religion: Early Christianity Through Reformation

ANSELM OF CANTERBURY: Truth, Freedom, and Evil: *Three Philosophical Dialogues. Edited and Translated by Jasper Hopkins and Herbert Richardson* TB/317

EDGAR J. GOODSPEED: A Life of Jesus TB/1

ROBERT M. GRANT: Gnosticism and Early Christianity TB/136

Religion: Oriental Religions

TOR ANDRAE: Mohammed: *The Man and His Faith* § TB/62

EDWARD CONZE: Buddhism: *Its Essence and Development.* ° *Foreword by Arthur Waley* TB/58

H. G. CREEL: Confucius and the Chinese Way TB/63

FRANKLIN EDGERTON, Trans. & Ed.: The Bhagavad Gita TB/115

SWAMI NIKHILANANDA, Trans. & Ed.: The Upanishads TB/114

D. T. SUZUKI: On Indian Mahayana Buddhism. ° *Ed. with Intro. by Edward Conze.* TB/1403

Science and Mathematics

W. E. LE GROS CLARK: The Antecedents of Man: *An Introduction to the Evolution of the Primates.* ° *Illus.* TB/559

ROBERT E. COKER: Streams, Lakes, Ponds. *Illus.* TB/586

ROBERT E. COKER: This Great and Wide Sea: *An Introduction to Oceanography and Marine Biology. Illus.* TB/551

WILLARD VAN ORMAN QUINE: Mathematical Logic TB/558

Sociology and Anthropology

REINHARD BENDIX: Work and Authority in Industry: *Ideologies of Management in the Course of Industrialization* TB/3035

KENNETH B. CLARK: Dark Ghetto: *Dilemmas of Social Power. Foreword by Gunnar Myrdal* TB/1317

KENNETH CLARK & JEANNETTE HOPKINS: A Relevant War Against Poverty: *A Study of Community Action Programs and Observable Social Change* TB/1480

LEWIS COSER, Ed.: Political Sociology TB/1293

GARY T. MARX: Protest and Prejudice: *A Study of Belief in the Black Community* TB/1435

ROBERT K. MERTON, LEONARD BROOM, LEONARD S. COTTRELL, JR., Editors: Sociology Today: *Problems and Prospects* || Vol. I TB/1173; Vol. II TB/1174

GILBERT OSOFSKY, Ed.: The Burden of Race: A Documentary History of Negro-White Relations in America TB/1405

GILBERT OSOFSKY: Harlem: The Making of a Ghetto: *Negro New York 1890-1930* TB/1381

PHILIP RIEFF: The Triumph of the Therapeutic: *Uses of Faith After Freud* TB/1360

ARNOLD ROSE: The Negro in America: *The Condensed Version of Gunnar Myrdal's* An American Dilemma. *Second Edition* TB/3048

GEORGE ROSEN: Madness in Society: *Chapters in the Historical Sociology of Mental Illness.* || *Preface by Benjamin Nelson* TB/1337

PITIRIM A. SOROKIN: Contemporary Sociological Theories: *Through the First Quarter of the Twentieth Century* TB/3046

FLORIAN ZNANIECKI: The Social Role of the Man of Knowledge. *Introduction by Lewis A. Coser* TB/1372

A. H. M. JONES, Ed.: A History of Rome through the Fifth Century # *Vol. I: The Republic* HR/1364
Vol. II The Empire: HR/1460

SAMUEL NOAH KRAMER: Sumerian Mythology TB/1055

NAPHTALI LEWIS & MEYER REINHOLD, Eds.: Roman Civilization *Vol. I: The Republic* TB/1231
Vol. II: The Empire TB/1232

History: Medieval

NORMAN COHN: The Pursuit of the Millennium: *Revolutionary Messianism in Medieval and Reformation Europe* TB/1037

F. L. GANSHOF: Feudalism TB/1058

F. L. GANSHOF: The Middle Ages: *A History of International Relations. Translated by Rêmy Hall* TB/1411

HENRY CHARLES LEA: The Inquisition of the Middle Ages. || *Introduction by Walter Ullmann* TB/1456

History: Renaissance & Reformation

JACOB BURCKHARDT: The Civilization of the Renaissance in Italy. *Introduction by Benjamin Nelson and Charles Trinkaus. Illus.* Vol. I TB/40; Vol. II TB/41

JOHN CALVIN & JACOPO SADOLETO: A Reformation Debate. *Edited by John C. Olin* TB/1239

J. H. ELLIOTT: Europe Divided, 1559-1598 α ° TB/1414

G. R. ELTON: Reformation Europe, 1517-1559 ° α TB/1270

HANS J. HILLERBRAND, Ed., The Protestant Reformation # HR/1342

JOHAN HUIZINGA: Erasmus and the Age of Reformation. *Illus.* TB/19

JOEL HURSTFIELD: The Elizabethan Nation TB/1312

JOEL HURSTFIELD, Ed.: The Reformation Crisis TB/1267

PAUL OSKAR KRISTELLER: Renaissance Thought: *The Classic, Scholastic, and Humanist Strains* TB/1048

DAVID LITTLE: Religion, Order and Law: *A Study in Pre-Revolutionary England. § Preface by R. Bellah* TB/1418

PAOLO ROSSI: Philosophy, Technology, and the Arts, in the Early Modern Era 1400-1700. || *Edited by Benjamin Nelson. Translated by Salvator Attanasio* TB/1458

H. R. TREVOR-ROPER: The European Witch-craze of the Sixteenth and Seventeenth Centuries and Other Essays ° TB/1416

History: Modern European

ALAN BULLOCK: Hitler, A Study in Tyranny. ° *Revised Edition. Illus.* TB/1123

JOHANN GOTTLIEB FICHTE: Addresses to the German Nation. *Ed. with Intro. by George A. Kelly* ¶ TB/1366

ALBERT GOODWIN: The French Revolution TB/1064

STANLEY HOFFMANN et al.: In Search of France: *The Economy, Society and Political System In the Twentieth Century* TB/1219

H. STUART HUGHES: The Obstructed Path: *French Social Thought in the Years of Desperation* TB/1451

JOHAN HUIZINGA: Dutch Civilisation in the 17th Century and Other Essays TB/1453

JOHN MCMANNERS: European History, 1789-1914: *Men, Machines and Freedom* TB/1419

HUGH SETON-WATSON: Eastern Europe Between the Wars, 1918-1941 TB/1330

ALBERT SOREL: Europe Under the Old Regime. *Translated by Francis H. Herrick* TB/1121

A. J. P. TAYLOR: From Napoleon to Lenin: *Historical Essays* ° TB/1268

A. J. P. TAYLOR: The Habsburg Monarchy, 1809-1918: *A History of the Austrian Empire and Austria-Hungary* ° TB/1187

J. M. THOMPSON: European History, 1494-1789 TB/1431

H. R. TREVOR-ROPER: Historical Essays TB/1269

Literature & Literary Criticism

W. J. BATE: From Classic to Romantic: *Premises of Taste in Eighteenth Century England* TB/1036

VAN WYCK BROOKS: Van Wyck Brooks: The Early Years: *A Selection from his Works, 1908-1921 Ed. with Intro. by Claire Sprague* TB/3082

RICHMOND LATTIMORE, Translator: The Odyssey of Homer TB/1389

ROBERT PREYER, Ed.: Victorian Literature ** TB/1302

Philosophy

HENRI BERGSON: Time and Free Will: *An Essay on the Immediate Data of Consciousness* ° TB/1021

H. J. BLACKHAM: Six Existentialist Thinkers: *Kierkegaard, Nietzsche, Jaspers, Marcel, Heidegger, Sartre* ° TB/1002

J. M. BOCHENSKI: The Methods of Contemporary Thought. *Trans. by Peter Caws* TB/1377

ERNST CASSIRER: Rousseau, Kant and Goethe. *Intro. by Peter Gay* TB/1092

MICHAEL GELVEN: A Commentary on Heidegger's "Being and Time" TB/1464

J. GLENN GRAY: Hegel and Greek Thought TB/1409

W. K. C. GUTHRIE: The Greek Philosophers: *From Thales to Aristotle* ° TB/1008

G. W. F. HEGEL: Phenomenology of Mind. ° || *Introduction by George Lichtheim* TB/1303

MARTIN HEIDEGGER: Discourse on Thinking. *Translated with a Preface by John M. Anderson and E. Hans Freund. Introduction by John M. Anderson* TB/1459

F. H. HEINEMANN: Existentialism and the Modern Predicament TB/28

WERER HEISENBERG: Physics and Philosophy: *The Revolution in Modern Science. Intro. by F. S. C. Northrop* TB/549

EDMUND HUSSERL: Phenomenology and the Crisis of Philosophy. § *Translated with an Introduction by Quentin Lauer* TB/1170

IMMANUEL KANT: Groundwork of the Metaphysic of Morals. *Translated and Analyzed by H. J. Paton* TB/1159

WALTER KAUFMANN, Ed.: Religion From Tolstoy to Camus: *Basic Writings on Religious Truth and Morals* TB/123

QUENTIN LAUER: Phenomenology: *Its Genesis and Prospect. Preface by Aron Gurwitsch* TB/1169

MICHAEL POLANYI: Personal Knowledge: *Towards a Post-Critical Philosophy* TB/1158

WILLARD VAN ORMAN QUINE: Elementary Logic *Revised Edition* TB/577

WILHELM WINDELBAND: A History of Philosophy *Vol. I: Greek, Roman, Medieval* TB/38

LOUIS B. WRIGHT: Culture on the Moving Frontier TB/1053

American Studies: The Civil War to 1900

T. C. COCHRAN & WILLIAM MILLER: The Age of Enterprise: *A Social History of Industrial America* TB/1054
W. A. DUNNING: Reconstruction, Political and Economic: 1865-1877 TB/1073
HAROLD U. FAULKNER: Politics, Reform and Expansion: 1890-1900. † *Illus.* TB/3020
GEORGE M. FREDRICKSON: The Inner Civil War: *Northern Intellectuals and the Crisis of the Union* TB/1358
JOHN A. GARRATY: The New Commonwealth, 1877-1890 † TB/1410
HELEN HUNT JACKSON: A Century of Dishonor: *The Early Crusade for Indian Reform. † Edited by Andrew F. Rolle* TB/3063
WILLIAM G. MCLOUGHLIN, Ed.: The American Evangelicals, 1800-1900: An Anthology ‡ TB/1382
JAMES S. PIKE: The Prostrate State: *South Carolina under Negro Government. ‡ Intro. by Robert F. Durden* TB/3085
VERNON LANE WHARTON: The Negro in Mississippi, 1865-1890 TB/1178

American Studies: The Twentieth Century

RAY STANNARD BAKER: Following the Color Line: *American Negro Citizenship in Progressive Era. ‡ Edited by Dewey W. Grantham, Jr. Illus.* TB/3053
RANDOLPH S. BOURNE: War and the Intellectuals: *Collected Essays, 1915-1919. ‡ Edited by Carl Resek* TB/3043
A. RUSSELL BUCHANAN: The United States and World War II. † *Illus.* Vol. I TB/3044; Vol. II TB/3045
THOMAS C. COCHRAN: The American Business System: *A Historical Perspective, 1900-1955* TB/1080
FOSTER RHEA DULLES: America's Rise to World Power: 1898-1954. † *Illus.* TB/3021
HAROLD U. FAULKNER: The Decline of Laissez Faire, 1897-1917 TB/1397
JOHN D. HICKS: Republican Ascendancy: 1921-1933. † *Illus.* TB/3041
WILLIAM E. LEUCHTENBURG: Franklin D. Roosevelt and the New Deal: 1932-1940. † *Illus.* TB/3025
WILLIAM E. LEUCHTENBURG, Ed.: The New Deal: *A Documentary History* + HR/1354
ARTHUR S. LINK: Woodrow Wilson and the Progressive Era: 1910-1917. † *Illus.* TB/3023
BROADUS MITCHELL: Depression Decade: *From New Era through New Deal, 1929-1941* ^ TB/1439
GEORGE E. MOWRY: The Era of Theodore Roosevelt and the Birth of Modern America: 1900-1912. † *Illus.* TB/3022
WILLIAM PRESTON, JR.: Aliens and Dissenters:
TWELVE SOUTHERNERS: I'll Take My Stand: *The South and the Agrarian Tradition. Intro. by Louis D. Rubin, Jr.; Biographical Essays by Virginia Rock* TB/1072

Art, Art History, Aesthetics

ERWIN PANOFSKY: Renaissance and Renascences in Western Art. *Illus.* TB/1447
ERWIN PANOFSKY: Studies in Iconology: *Humanistic Themes in the Art of the Renaissance. 180 illus.* TB/1077
HEINRICH ZIMMER: Myths and Symbols in Indian Art and Civilization. *70 illus.* TB/2005

Asian Studies

WOLFGANG FRANKE: China and the West: *The Cultural Encounter, 13th to 20th Centuries. Trans. by R. A. Wilson* TB/1326
L. CARRINGTON GOODRICH: A Short History of the Chinese People. *Illus.* TB/3015

Economics & Economic History

C. E. BLACK: The Dynamics of Modernization: *A Study in Comparative History* TB/1321
GILBERT BURCK & EDITORS OF *Fortune:* The Computer Age: *And its Potential for Management* TB/1179
ROBERT L. HEILBRONER: The Future as History: *The Historic Currents of Our Time and the Direction in Which They Are Taking America* TB/1386
ROBERT L. HEILBRONER: The Great Ascent: *The Struggle for Economic Development in Our Time* TB/3030
FRANK H. KNIGHT: The Economic Organization TB/1214
DAVID S. LANDES: Bankers and Pashas: *International Finance and Economic Imperialism in Egypt. New Preface by the Author* TB/1412
ROBERT LATOUCHE: The Birth of Western Economy: *Economic Aspects of the Dark Ages* TB/1290
W. ARTHUR LEWIS: The Principles of Economic Planning. *New Introduction by the Author°* TB/1436
WILLIAM MILLER, Ed.: Men in Business: *Essays on the Historical Role of the Entrepreneur* TB/1081
HERBERT A. SIMON: The Shape of Automation: *For Men and Management* TB/1245

Historiography and History of Ideas

J. BRONOWSKI & BRUCE MAZLISH: The Western Intellectual Tradition: *From Leonardo to Hegel* TB/3001
WILHELM DILTHEY: Pattern and Meaning in History: *Thoughts on History and Society.° Edited with an Intro. by H. P. Rickman* TB/1075
J. H. HEXTER: More's Utopia: *The Biography of an Idea. Epilogue by the Author* TB/1195
H. STUART HUGHES: History as Art and as Science: *Twin Vistas on the Past* TB/1207
ARTHUR O. LOVEJOY: The Great Chain of Being: *A Study of the History of an Idea* TB/1009
RICHARD H. POPKIN: The History of Scepticism from Erasmus to Descartes. *Revised Edition* TB/1391
BRUNO SNELL: The Discovery of the Mind: *The Greek Origins of European Thought* TB/1018

History: General

HANS KOHN: The Age of Nationalism: *The First Era of Global History* TB/1380
BERNARD LEWIS: The Arabs in History TB/1029
BERNARD LEWIS: The Middle East and the West ° TB/1274

History: Ancient

A. ANDREWS: The Greek Tyrants TB/1103
THEODOR H. GASTER: Thespis: *Ritual Myth and Drama in the Ancient Near East* TB/1281

Revised January, 1970

harper torchbooks

American Studies: General

HENRY STEELE COMMAGER, Ed.: The Struggle for Racial Equality TB/1300
CARL N. DEGLER: Out of Our Past: *The Forces that Shaped Modern America* CN/2
CARL N. DEGLER, Ed.: Pivotal Interpretations of American History Vol. I TB/1240; Vol. II TB/1241
A. S. EISENSTADT, Ed.: The Craft of American History: *Selected Essays* Vol. I TB/1255; Vol. II TB/1256
ROBERT L. HEILBRONER: The Limits of American Capitalism TB/1305
JOHN HIGHAM, Ed.: The Reconstruction of American History TB/1068
ROBERT H. JACKSON: The Supreme Court in the American System of Government TB/1106
JOHN F. KENNEDY: A Nation of Immigrants. *Illus. Revised and Enlarged. Introduction by Robert F. Kennedy* TB/1118
RICHARD B. MORRIS: Fair Trial: *Fourteen Who Stood Accused, from Anne Hutchinson to Alger Hiss* TB/1335
GUNNAR MYRDAL: An American Dilemma: *The Negro Problem and Modern Democracy. Introduction by the Author.* Vol. I TB/1443; Vol. II TB/1444
GILBERT OSOFSKY, Ed.: The Burden of Race: *A Documentary History of Negro-White Relations in America* TB/1405
ARNOLD ROSE: The Negro in America: *The Condensed Version of Gunnar Myrdal's* An American Dilemma. *Second Edition* TB/3048
JOHN E. SMITH: Themes in American Philosophy: *Purpose, Experience and Community* TB/1466
WILLIAM R. TAYLOR: Cavalier and Yankee: *The Old South and American National Character* TB/1474

American Studies: Colonial

BERNARD BAILYN: The New England Merchants in the Seventeenth Century TB/1149
ROBERT E. BROWN: Middle-Class Democracy and Revolution in Massachusetts, 1691–1780. *New Introduction by Author* TB/1413
JOSEPH CHARLES: The Origins of the American Party System TB/1049
WESLEY FRANK CRAVEN: The Colonies in Transition: 1660-1712† TB/3084
CHARLES GIBSON: Spain in America † TB/3077
CHARLES GIBSON, Ed.: The Spanish Tradition in America + HR/1351
LAWRENCE HENRY GIPSON: The Coming of the Revolution: 1763-1775. † *Illus.* TB/3007
PERRY MILLER: Errand Into the Wilderness TB/1139
PERRY MILLER & T. H. JOHNSON, Eds.: The Puritans: *A Sourcebook of Their Writings* Vol. I TB/1093; Vol. II TB/1094
EDMUND S. MORGAN: The Puritan Family: *Religion and Domestic Relations in Seventeenth Century New England* TB/1227
WALLACE NOTESTEIN: The English People on the Eve of Colonization: 1603-1630. † *Illus.* TB/3006
LOUIS B. WRIGHT: The Cultural Life of the American Colonies: 1607-1763. † *Illus.* TB/3005

American Studies: The Revolution to 1860

JOHN R. ALDEN: The American Revolution: 1775-1783. † *Illus.* TB/3011
RAY A. BILLINGTON: The Far Western Frontier: 1830-1860. † *Illus.* TB/3012
GEORGE DANGERFIELD: The Awakening of American Nationalism, 1815-1828. † *Illus.* TB/3061
CLEMENT EATON: The Growth of Southern Civilization, 1790-1860. † *Illus.* TB/3040
LOUIS FILLER: The Crusade against Slavery: 1830-1860. † *Illus.* TB/3029
WILLIM W. FREEHLING: Prelude to Civil War: *The Nullification Controversy in South Carolina, 1816-1836* TB/1359
THOMAS JEFFERSON: Notes on the State of Virginia. ‡ *Edited by Thomas P. Abernethy* TB/3052
JOHN C. MILLER: The Federalist Era: 1789-1801. † *Illus.* TB/3027
RICHARD B. MORRIS: The American Revolution Reconsidered TB/1363
GILBERT OSOFSKY, Ed.: Puttin' On Ole Massa: *The Slave Narratives of Henry Bibb, William Wells Brown, and Solomon Northup* ‡ TB/1432
FRANCIS S. PHILBRICK: The Rise of the West, 1754-1830. † *Illus.* TB/3067
MARSHALL SMELSER: The Democratic Republic, 1801-1815 † TB/1406

† The New American Nation Series, edited by Henry Steele Commager and Richard B. Morris.
‡ American Perspectives series, edited by Bernard Wishy and William E. Leuchtenburg.
α History of Europe series, edited by J. H. Plumb.
§ The Library of Religion and Culture, edited by Benjamin Nelson.
‖ Researches in the Social, Cultural, and Behavioral Sciences, edited by Benjamin Nelson.
Σ Harper Modern Science Series, edited by James A. Newman.
° Not for sale in Canada.
+ Documentary History of the United States series, edited by Richard B. Morris.
# Documentary History of Western Civilization series, edited by Eugene C. Black and Leonard W. Levy.
^ The Economic History of the United States series, edited by Henry David et al.
¶ European Perspectives series, edited by Eugene C. Black.
** Contemporary Essays series, edited by Leonard W. Levy.
* The Stratum Series, edited by John Hale.